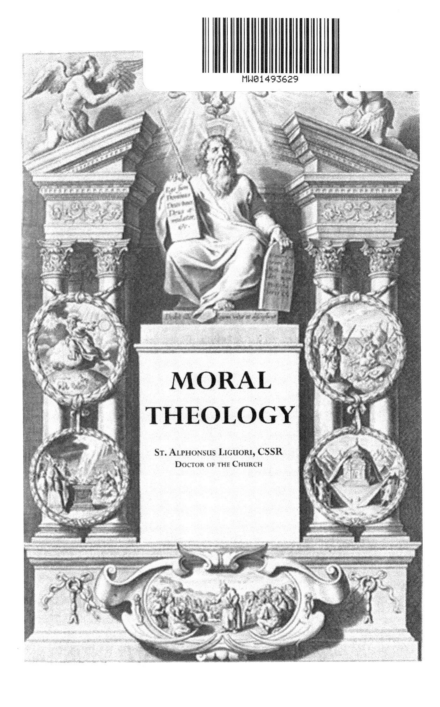

MORAL
THEOLOGY

St. Alphonsus Liguori, CSSR
Doctor of the Church

MORAL THEOLOGY
VOLUME I

BOOKS I - III
ON CONSCIENCE, LAW, SIN AND THE
THEOLOGICAL VIRTUES

BY

ST. ALPHONSUS LIGUORI, C.S.S.R.
DOCTOR OF THE CHURCH

TRANSLATED BY
RYAN GRANT

First English Edition

MMXVI
MEDIATRIX PRESS
www.mediatrixpress.com

Moral Theology, vol. 1
Translated from:
Theologia Moralis, vol. 1-2
Mechlin, 1852

ISBN-13: 978-0692864579
ISBN-10: 0692864571

Cover art: © Ryan Grant.

Published by:
Mediatrix Press
607 E. 6th St.
Post Falls, ID 83854
http://www.mediatrixpress.com

TABLE OF CONTENTS

TREATISE ON SINS

CHAPTER I

On Sin in General

ARTICLE I

ARTICLE II

DUBIUM III

On the distinction of Sins

ARTICLE I

ARTICLE II

CHAPTER III
ON THE CAPITAL SINS IN PARTICULAR

DUBIUM V
    On Gluttony

ARTICLE I

BOOK III

ON THE PRECEPTS OF THE THEOLOGICAL VIRTUES

TREATISE I
On the precept of Faith

CHAPTER I
Which mysteries of faith must necessarily be believed?

CHAPTER II

CHAPTER III

DUBIUM I

DUBIUM III

TREATISE II

ARTICLE III

SACERDOTIBUS SANCTAE ECCLESIAE CATHOLICAE
UT OPERE S. ALPHONSI UTANTUR
DIRIGANTQUE ANIMAS AD JESUM PER MARIAM

T is a curious thing that the Church's moral Doctor, St. Alphonsus, has hitherto not been translated into English. At first glance this seems like a drastic oversight in the history of Theology. On the other hand, with a consideration of the strength of Latin scholarship until the 20th century, we can understand a bit better how this came to be.

The study of Latin had to "become a science" following the Enlightenment program, and the living nature of the language was replaced with an ossified grammatical approach that held the ancients as the only pure exponents of Latin prose and all else to be barbarism.

Instead of being trained to know Latin as a living language, at least in terms of reading, they learned by mere grammatical formulas and translation exercises based around an interpretation of the Classics that left the student unable to grasp the higher principles of syntax and also cut off from the vocabulary and style or writers in the Renaissance or from the 16th and 17th centuries. The result left Latin studies searching for meaning, which found place in appeals to better knowledge of vocabulary, legal terms, medical terms or the terminology of botany. This was all fine and good for its own purposes, yet insufficient for approaching Theological Latin or the very notion of acquiring a classical education at all. Catholic Seminaries were not immune from this train of thought and Latinity began to diminish even in the early 20th century.[1]

The result was that the next generations of priests were cut off from the Latin tradition. Whereas, in the past, one could always be expected to know enough Latin to read St. Alphonsus, as well as any of the other classical theologians,

---

[1] Pius XI, "On Education", *Acta Apostolicae Sedis*, 22, 80.

in the new situation seminarians and priests would have summaries and notes, while only the more exceptional could read the texts in Latin. As the currents in Theology were in flux, more dramatically so from the 1960s onward, the study of older texts in Latin seemed less and less relevant, even of a doctor of the Church highly recommended by numerous Popes. To remedy that situation would take more than the contribution that any humble Latinist could offer; instead, I have made my work over the last several years to translate works into English so as to make them available to readers today, not when Latinity restores at some future date. Thus, I am pleased to present the first translation of St. Alphonsus' *Moral Theology* to English speaking readers.

In the first place, we must make some notes on the translation and the principles we have followed in producing it. In the first place, St. Alphonsus originally created this as a commentary on another work of Moral Theology, that of Herman Busembaum, S.J. St. Alphonsus held Busembaum's treatise to be the best of the treatises in his day, and followed what was for him the golden mean between laxism and rigorism, both being courses that in his words, "pave the way to hell." As time and revisions went on, the saint transformed his modest commentary into a full work, which in some places still bears the resemblance of the original commentary on Busembaum, yet shows the expansion made into other areas with numerous other treatises to address new problems that he saw through praxis and refinement. Thus, we have made use of the following editorial device to differentiate the two: Busembaum's text, where it appears, is indented in quotation marks, while St. Alphonsus' meets the full width of the margin with a first line indent. This will be evident where Busembaum's text first appears, in the treatise on *Laws*.

Next, we have followed the order of the 1852 Mechlin edition, edited by Heilig, while we have also used the critical apparatus of the edition of Fr. Gaude. In the case of any discrepancy in the Latin text, we have followed the version of Gaude. Thus in this edition, St. Alphonsus' treatise on sins comes as book 2, the treatise on the Theological Virtues constitutes book 3, and the treatise on the Ten Commandments will constitute book 4 (in the next volume), rather than book 3 as it is in the edition of Gaude. This is because the treatise on sin seemed to us more properly placed in the Heilig edition than that of Gaude.

Furthermore, St. Alphonsus compiled the opinions of seemingly every source of his day, and quotes them frequently. Following the advice of several experts in this field, as well as dealing with the formatting problems, we have rendered all sources in the text, parenthetically when possible, and intra text when the grammar will allow for an easy in-sentence citation. As a result, the references are at times paralyzing; but this should not intimidate the reader. They are necessary both for showing the breadth of St. Alphonsus' scholarship and for seeing clearly the authority of the discussion. Alphonsus is careful to distinguish where he thinks certain authors erred and what position must be held, and where the discussion is open but he follows one or another view, and for what reasons. We have taken great care to maintain the character of these opinions in the text.

As regards technical vocabulary, there are certain terms in use not only in St. Alphonsus' time, but today as well in moral theology that do not translate well out of Latin. Consequently, we have left these in Latin with an explanation of the terms in a footnote.

Next, St. Alphonsus begins the work with a list of condemned propositions, *i.e.* propositions that various Popes had to condemn as contrary to the Church's moral teaching. These are important as a grounding to the work and should be used as a reference. Papal condemnations are infallible by ordinary Magisterial infallibility, as numerous Theologians note, and are not mere guidelines and suggestions from

Popes of yesteryear. This is especially relevant for St. Alphonsus, as they constitute objective criteria by which to judge propositions affecting moral problems.

Out of fear of mistranslating or losing the force of St. Alphonsus' teaching, we have attempted to stay as true to the Latin as possible without any gloss or florid language, while at the same time striking the balance to avoid the paralysis that would be effected by too literal a rendering into modern English.

Lastly, we would like to thank all of those who assisted in the editing and suggested corrections to this work, especially those that appeared at the eleventh hour when others had fizzled out from the daunting task of editing this very small portion of St. Alphonsus' Moral Theology. Above all, I would like to thank my wife, whose patient support has made it possible to see this to completion.

It is our supreme hope that this translation will be a boon to the study of Moral Theology from the Church's great moral doctor who maintained the spirit as well as the letter of the moral law written on our hearts.

Post Falls, ID
February 2017

APOSTOLIC LETTER
ON HONORING ST. ALPHONSUS MARIA DE LIGUORI
WITH THE TITLE OF DOCTOR OF THE CHURCH

PIUS PP. IX
AD PERPETUAM REI MEMORIAM.

HRIST the Lord, who promised his Church that it was never going to fail, since he especially has regard for the welfare of his immaculate Spouse, raises up men conspicuous for their piety and doctrine, who, "filled with the spirit of understanding, he sends like the eloquent rain of his wisdom." For it happened not without the most provident counsel of God almighty, that since the doctrine of the Jansenist innovators turned all eyes to themselves, and enticed many to the sight of their error and led them over to it, it was then that Alphonsus Maria Liguori stood up, the founder of the Congregation of the Most Holy Redeemer and the Bishop of St. Agatha of the Goths, who, "fighting the good fight, opened his mouth in the midst of the Church"; and by his learned writings and labors eradicated this plague, roused from hell, and saw to it to tear it out and so exterminate it from the field of the Lord. Not only did Alphonsus appoint these shares for himself, but focusing his mind on the glory of God and the spiritual salvation of men, he wrote many books, filled with holy erudition and piety, whose opinions were between those embraced by both more lax and rigid theologians, to fortify the safe path by which the confessors of Christ's faithful could advance without dashing their foot upon a stone; whether to train and establish the clergy, or to confirm the truth of the Catholic faith and to defend against the heretics of every kind or name; or to assert the laws of this Apostolic See; or to rouse the souls of the faithful to piety. Moreover, this can most truly be preached, that there is no error of our times which, for the most part, was not refuted by St. Alphonsus. For are not these, such as both the Immaculate Conception of the Holy Mother of God, and the infallibility of the Roman Pontiff teaching *ex cathedra*, with the approval of the Christian people, and the constant consent and approval of all the Bishops of the Catholic world, ratified by Us, to be found in the works of Alphonsus, and outstandingly explained and proven by the strongest arguments?

For this reason, that most noble declaration of divine Wisdom beautifully falls to this purpose: "His memory will be held in honor, and his name will be pined for from generation to generation, the nations will proclaim his wisdom, and the Church will make known his praises."[2] And Pius VII, Our predecessor of blessed memory, marveled at the supreme wisdom of Alphonsus and advanced this very important testimony about him: "By word and writings, in the middle of the century he showed the way of justice to those wandering at night, whereby they could pass from the power of darkness into the light and kingdom of God." Likewise, Our predecessor of celebrated memory, Gregory XVI, spoke of the *incredible power* of Alphonsus, *the copious and variety* of his doctrine, and continuing with the greatest praise, enrolled him on the heavenly catalogue of the Saints. At length, in these very times, many cardinals of the Holy Roman Church, all bishops of the whole world, the supreme governors of religious orders, the distinguished bodies of associations of theologians, the illustrious colleges of canonists, and learned men from every body have humbly offered prayers to Us, that we might add to St. Alphonsus Maria Liguori the title and honors of DOCTOR OF THE CHURCH. Therefore, we, willing to comply with these pious

---

[2] Sirach 39:13.

prayers with a cheerful mind, consigned this business, as is customary, to the Sacred Congregation of Rites of the Church, to be weighed by the expositors. Already, when the aforesaid Congregation in ordinary committees at the Vatican held on 11 March of this year, heard the relation of our Venerable Brother Constantine Cardinal Patritius of the aforementioned congregation, the Bishop of Ostia and Veliterenena, prefect of the same Congregation, as well as the Reporting judge of the causes; after all matters were observed by our beloved son Fr. Peter Minetti, Promotor of the Faith, likewise, with the responses of the patron of the cause, and also for the truth in the opinions of theologians, and at length, all matters of importance for the reasons earnestly and attentively weighed, it censed to reply with a unanimous consent: "To counsel Your Holiness for the concession, or the declaration and extension to the universal Church of the title of Doctor in honor of St. Alphonsus Maria Liguori, with the Office and Mass already conceded, with the addition of a *Credo*, of the antiphons for the *Magnificat* of both first and Second Vespers, "*O Doctor*," and readings for the first Nocturn *Sapientiam*, and the eighth Responsory *In medio Ecclesiae;* — we have determined to approve and confirm that response, published on the 23rd day of this same month and year in a general decree *Urbis et Orbis*,

Furthermore, our beloved son, Fr. Nicholas Mauron, Superior General and *rector Major* of the Congregation of the Most Holy Redeemer, added the plea to the aforesaid Cardinals of the Congregation for the Rites of the Church, that in the Feast of the same St. Alphonsus, by the decree already mentioned, that among the Doctors of the Church enrolled in the Roman Martyrology, after the words: "*Sanctorum fastis adscripsit*," the following should be added: "*Et Pius IX, Pontifex Maximus, ex Sacrorum Rituum Congregationis consulto, universalis Ecclesiae Doctorem declaravit*;" likewise, in the Sixth Reading, after the word:

"*accensuit,* these other words be added: "*Tandem Pius IX, Pontifex Maximus, ex Sacrorum Rituum Congregationis Consulto, universalis Ecclesiae Doctorem declaravit;*" and that all the concessions made on this matter should be confirmed by our Apostolic letter. Such Congregation of Cardinals, when in a meeting on 23 April of this year, replied: "*pro gratia;*" We on the 27th of the same month ratified that response and commanded an Apostolic Letter to be made ready in the form of a Brief. Since these are so, yielding to the pleas of our Beloved son Nicholas Mauron, and by the counsel of the Cardinals of the Congregation of Rites, by Our Apostolic Authority, with the tenor of the present, we confirm the title of DOCTOR in honor of St. Alphonsus Maria Liguori, the founder of the Congregation Most Holy Redeemer and Bishop of St. Agatha of the Goths, and insofar as it is necessary, again attribute and bestow upon him; so that in the universal Catholic Church he shall always be held as a Doctor, and also on his anniversary a feast will be celebrated both by regulars and by secular clergy, both in the Office and Mass according to the decree and response of the Sacred Congregation of Rites, which we commemorated. Additionally, the books, commentaries, *opuscula,* works and at length everything of this doctor, as of the other Doctors of the Church, we will and decree to be cited, advanced and when the matter will demand, applied not only privately but publicly in gymnasiums, academies, schools, colleges, readings, disputations, interpretations, sermons, homilies, and all other ecclesiastical studies and Christian exercises.

At length, that the piety of the Christian faithful be enkindled to rightly venerate the feast day of this Doctor, and piously implore his aid, by the mercy of Almighty God and of Blessed Peter and Paul, his Apostles, trusting the authority, to each and every member of the Christian faithful of both sexes, who on the feast of the same Doctor, or on any day of the week immediately following, and who, of their own accord, truly penitent and having already made a sacramental confession, if they receive the Most Holy Eucharist and will have devoutly visited any of the churches of the Congregation of the Most Holy Redeemer, and there will have poured fourth pious prayers to God for the peace of Christian princes, the extirpation of heresy and the exaltation of Holy Mother the Church, on the day that they will have done the aforesaid we concede a plenary Indulgence and remission of all their sins mercifully in the Lord in perpetuity, which can be applied by the mode of suffrage even to the souls of Christ's faithful, that have passed from this life to God to whom we are joined in charity.

Wherefore, we entrust to all the venerable Patriarchs, Primates, Archbishops, Bishops and beloved sons and Prelates of other Churches, constituted throughout the world for the present, that what has been ratified above be solemnly published in their provinces, cities, churches and dioceses, and see to it that they be inviolably and perpetually observed in all Orders of regulars, of every place and nation. This we command and entrust to synodal councils, general or particular Constitutions and Ordinances, all things to the contrary not withstanding. Moreover, we will that the same integrity of the present Letter be altogether employed in all copies whether printed or written out by the hand of some notary public, and fortified with the seal of a person constituted in ecclesiastical dignity, which is employed in the present letter, if it will be shown or displayed.

Given at Rome, at St. Peters under the ring of the Fisherman, 7 July 1871, in the twenty-sixth year of Our Pontificate.

Pro Domino Card. PARACCIANI CLARELLI,
FELIX PROFILI, *Substitutus.*

Loco + Annuli Piscatoris.

WHO IS ASKED TO READ THIS PREFACE FOR THE
UNDERSTANDING OF THE WHOLE WORK

 INCE the particular intent of our very small Congregation of the Most Holy Redeemer is to have time for missions, and since the exercise of the missions is necessarily connected with the duty to direct consciences of men by instructions and confessions: therefore, a great many years ago I devised a book for the young men of our order to hand down a treatise on moral matters, which would hold the mean between some of the more rigid books, or the exceedingly lax. I finished the work, but because I had worked at an exceedingly hasty pace to meet the demands of printers, as well as to satisfy others, I did not satisfy myself. Also, a great many things that were laid down there did not fall out well, or were explained in a confused order. For that reason, when I noticed that it needed a more diligent examination, and also a clearer method, I applied my mind to the second edition, in which I took care to render all things to better order, and give a more copious book with very useful doctrines. Also, recognizing several opinions (in the course of the time matters that I recalled to a more assiduous treatise), I reformed them. And I am not ashamed of this, since St. Augustine was not ashamed to retract himself in a great many matters, and even St. Thomas did this, as Cajetan, Catharinus, and Capreolus witness, not to mention the Angelic Doctor himself (3, q. 8, art. 4) so affirmed it: "Although I wrote otherwise in another place." So did Cicero when he said: "It is the mark of a wise man to change counsel." And in another place, "Endurance in one opinion has never been praised."

Moreover, nobody will find it superfluous, after so many books treating the moral science, that I took up this labor, as if to accomplish the act; since a great many authors that I also discovered, who indulging those more than what is just, who (as Isaiah says, in chapter 30): "Do not look to us for those things that are right, say pleasing things to us," they stitch together little pillows under their head, that they might rest miserably in sins. It can hardly be doubted that it is a great detriment to the Church of God to think with the followers of these authors, since a greater part of the men of more lax life agree with them. On the other hand, others are found who, to rebuke whatever does not favor extreme rigidity, confound counsels with precepts, and aggravate consciences with new commands, and having no thought of human frailty, remember nothing of the sacred canon (*cap. ult. de Transact.*) which advises: "But in these matters, in which an express law is not discovered, you shall proceed *aequitate servata*, always by diverging to the more humane side, according to what persons and causes, places and times seem to demand." And in this mode the yoke of Christ the Lord, which is sweet, they render intolerable, and they close off the way *of salvation* to many, according to what St. Ambrose says: "There are even among us those that have the fear of God, but not according to knowledge, establishing harder precepts which the human condition could not possibly support." (In Psal. 118, serm. 5). Both extremes are very dangerous, for the first opens a spacious road by relaxation to perdition; the other (as the very learned Cabassutius says, *in Theor. jur. Praef. ad Lect.*), by a twofold path urge souls into ruin, viz. by an erroneous conscience and desperation; since a great many, after hearing this more rigid doctrine, fall into mortal sins, or believing a lethal sin is present where it is not, are also discouraged by the difficulty, thinking it is impossible for them to be saved in any manner, and they altogether abandon the care of their salvation.

For that reason, I pondered publishing this new work, which would not only hold the mean between exceedingly severe opinions, but at the same time would neither be so expansive that it would not easily be read nor so brief that it would be deficient in many matters. You will find in this work all questions addressed on moral matters, which are of more service to praxis. Yet, that I would select opinions more in conformity with the truth in each question, I expended no small labor; for many years I have opened the volumes of as many classical authors as you like, both of rigid and lax opinion, which in the latter case (I think), they advanced public. Furthermore, I have done my best especially in annotating the doctrines of St. Thomas, which I have taken care to observe in the sources. Moreover, in more intricate controversies I have also consulted more recent doctors.

Besides, here you will discover citations in their own proper places with diligent zeal, texts both canonical and civil pertaining to these matters. Likewise, condemned propositions, and (what is more useful) more recent decrees of the Supreme Pontiffs and especially the bulls and sanctions published more recently by our Most Holy Lord Pope Benedict XIV. Still, here I have given expositions of a great many things which I have learned more from the exercise of missions and Confessions than in reading books. To preserve a just method, I thought to make preface the work with the *Medulla* of Herman Busembaum, not because I follow every opinion of that author, but only that I would follow the same method, which, among the methods of other authors, seemed to me to be more accommodated to explain moral matters; next, that for the novices of our Congregation, according to the purpose that I have principally proposed, I brought out my Appendixes that I labored to dig up to take to an easier mode. For in this I have greatly kept a zealous watch to abound more in clarity than in elegant discourse.

But in the selection of opinions my vast care has always been to put reason before authority; and before I would impose judgment on it (unless I am mistaken), I was entirely of a mind that in individual questions I should be indifferent, and that I would be free from every burning ember of passion. That is enough, benevolent reader, you could know from that that I do not hold to a few opinions which I had in earlier editions of this work, and I did not hesitate to change them in this last. Moreover, I have been hard-pressed to explain my opinion a great deal, by attributing a just weight to the greater, or equal or lesser probability for each opinion, exactly as it appeared to my weakness, lest I should leave behind two types of readers, after the fashion of some, who by only relating the opinions of others, thereby show no little hatred to readers. But where I did not find a convincing reason for one side, I did not dare condemn the opposite, after the fashion of others, who too easily rebuke opinions that a great many serious authors uphold, whose doctrines our celebrated Most Holy Lord Benedict XIV (by far different from those, who slight these doctrines more freely), calls to mind and not without esteem in his elaborate works, you will find with all erudition, and he often uses them; moreover, he not only relates their opinions in no small measure, he also rests upon them when instructing the Christian faithful in many things, as is seen in his *Bullarium*.

Moreover, generous reader, I want to admonish you lest you would think I approve opinions to the extent that I do not rebuke them; in these, when I faithfully explain them along with their reasons and patrons, it is so that others might make a judgment of what their weight may be. Lastly, you will notice that when I call some opinion truer, then I do not hold the contrary as probable, even if I do not expressly condemn it as improbable. In addition, when I appeal to one of several opinions as more probable, without having given judgment on the probability of the other, or I use this phrase, "I do not dare to condemn," I do not, for that reason, mean to say it is probable, but remit it to the judgment of the more prudent. Lastly, if you wish to see what System is going to be held in this work, I myself opine in regard to the choice of moral opinions, see cap. 3, *in Tract. altero de Conscientia probabili*, pag. 7, n. 53, *et seq.*[3] Vale.

---

[3] *In this edition, the moral System that St. Alphonsus is referring to is in the Treatise on Conscience, n. 55 et seqq., page 63.*

Thursday, 24 September, 1665

1. A man is not bound at any time at all in his life to elicit an act of faith, hope, and charity by the force of the divine precepts pertaining to these virtues.

2. A man belonging to the orders of Knights when challenged to a duel can accept this to not incur the mark of cowardice among others.

3. That opinion which asserts that the Bull "*Coenae*" only prohibits absolution of heresy and other crimes when they are public and that this does not diminish the power of Trent, in which there is a discussion of secret crimes, in the year 1629, July 18th, in the Consistory of the Sacred Congregation of the Most Eminent Cardinals, was seen and sustained.

4. Regular prelates can, in the forum of conscience, absolve any seculars at all of hidden heresy and of excommunication incurred by it.

5. Although it is evidently established by you that Peter is a heretic, you are not bound to denounce [him], if you cannot prove it.

6. A confessor who, in sacramental confession, gives the penitent a paper to be read afterwards wherein he incites him to venereal lust, is not considered to have solicited in the confessional, and therefore is not to be denounced.

7. A way to avoid the obligation of denouncing solicitation exists if the one solicited confesses with the solicitor; the latter can absolve that one without the burden of denouncing.

8. A priest can lawfully accept a twofold stipend for the same Mass by applying to the petitioner even the most

special part of the proceeds appropriated to the celebrant himself, and this after the decree of Urban VIII.

9. After the decree of Urban, a priest to whom Masses are given to be celebrated, can give satisfaction through another, by paying a smaller stipend to him and retaining the other part of the stipend for himself.

10. It is not contrary to justice to accept a stipend for several sacrifices and to offer one sacrifice. Nor is it contrary to fidelity if I promise, with a promise confirmed also by an oath, to the one that gives a stipend, what I offer for no one else.

11. We are not bound to express in a subsequent confession sins omitted in confession or forgotten because of the imminent danger of death or for some other reason.

12. Mendicants can absolve from cases reserved for bishops, when the faculty of the bishop was not obtained for this.

13. He satisfies the precept of an annual confession, who confesses to a regular, presented to a bishop, but unjustly reproved by him.

14. He who voluntarily makes a null confession, satisfies the precept of the Church.

15. A penitent by his own authority can substitute another for himself, to fulfill the penance in his place.

16. Those who have provided a benefice can select as confessor for themselves a simple priest not approved by the ordinary.

17. It is permitted a religious or a cleric to kill a calumniator who threatens to spread grave crimes about him or his order, when no other means of defense is at hand; as it seems not to be, if a calumniator be ready to spread the aforesaid about the religious himself or his order publicly or among people of importance, unless he be killed.

18. It is permitted to kill a false accuser, false witnesses, and even a judge, from whom an unjust sentence threatens with

certainty, if the innocent can avoid harm in no other way.

19. A husband does not sin by killing a wife caught in adultery on his own authority.

20. The restitution imposed by Pius V upon beneficed clerics that do not recite [the Divine Office] is not due in conscience before the sentence of a judge, to the extent that it is a penalty.

21. He who has a collective chaplaincy, or any other ecclesiastical benefice, if he is busy with the study of letters, satisfies his obligation if he recites the office through another.

22. It is not contrary to justice not to confer ecclesiastical benefices gratuitously, because the contributor who confers those ecclesiastical benefices with the intervention of money does not exact that money for the contribution of the benefice, but for a temporal profit, which he was not bound to confer upon you.

23. He who breaks a fast of the Church to which he is bound, does not sin mortally unless he does this out of contempt and disobedience, *e.g.*, because he does not wish to subject himself to the precept.

24. Masturbation, sodomy, and bestiality are sins of the same ultimate species, and so it is enough to say in confession that one has procured a pollution.

25. He who has had intercourse with an unmarried woman satisfies the precept of confession by saying: "I committed a grievous sin against chastity with an unmarried woman," without mentioning the intercourse.

26. When litigants have equally probable opinions in their defense, the judge can accept money to impose a sentence in favor of one over the other.

27. If a book is published by a younger or modern person, its opinion should be considered as probable, since it is not established that it has been rejected by the Holy See as improbable.

28. The people do not sin, even if without any cause they do not accept a law promulgated by the ruler.

Seeing that these are completed, while care and study are devoted to similar propositions, meanwhile our same Most Holy Lord, after mature consideration, has stated and decreed that the aforesaid propositions, each one of them, must be condemned and forbidden as scandalous, just as he condemns and forbids them; so that whoever will have taught, defended or published these separately or together, or treated on them in a manner of disputation whether in public or in private, except perhaps to impugn them, *ipso facto* incurs excommunication, from which he cannot (except at the point of death) be absolved by another no matter how great their dignity, unless by the present Roman Pontiff for the time being.

Moreover, he strictly forbids by the virtue of holy obedience under the threat of divine judgment, all of Christ's faithful of whatever condition, dignity and state, even worthy by a most special mark, lest they would introduce the aforesaid opinions or some one of them into practice.

On Thursday, 18th March, 1666

29. On a day of fasting, he who eats a moderate amount frequently, even if in the end he has eaten a considerable quantity, does not break the fast.

30. All officials who labor physically in the state are excused from the obligation of fasting, and need not make certain whether the labor is compatible with fasting.

31. All those who make a journey by riding, under whatever circumstances they make the journey, even if it is not necessary and even if they make a journey of a single day, are altogether excused from fasting.

32. It is not evident that the custom of not eating eggs and dairy products in Lent is binding.

33. Restitution of income because of the omission of stipends can be supplied through any alms that a beneficiary has previously made from the income of his service.

34. By reciting the paschal office on the day of Palms one satisfies the precept.

35. By a single office anyone can satisfy a twofold precept, for the present day and tomorrow.

36. Regulars can in the forum of conscience use their privileges which were expressly revoked by the Council of Trent.

37. Indulgences conceded to regulars and revoked by Paul V are today revalidated.

38. The mandate of the Council of Trent, made for the priest who of necessity offers Holy Mass while in mortal sin, to confess as soon as possible, is a recommendation, not a precept.

39. The expression "*quam primum*" is understood to be when the priest will confess in his own time.

40. It is a probable opinion which states that a kiss is only venial when performed for the sake of the carnal and sensible delight which arises from the kiss, if danger of further consent and pollution is excluded.

41. One living in concubinage is not bound to dismiss the concubine, if she is very useful for the pleasure of him so living (in the vernacular, *"regalo"*) provided that if she were missing, he would carry on life with very great difficulty, and other food would affect him living in concubinage with great loathing, and another maid servant would be found with very great difficulty.

42. Someone that borrows money is permitted to exact something beyond the principal, if he obligates himself not to seek the principal until a certain time.

43. An annual legacy left for the soul does not bind for more than ten years.

44. So far as the forum of conscience is concerned, when the guilty has been corrected and the contumacy ceases, the censures cease.

45. Books prohibited "until they are expurgated" can be retained until they are corrected by the application of diligence.

PROPOSITIONS CONDEMNED BY
INNOCENT XI

On Thursday, 4 March 1679

1. It is not illicit in conferring sacraments to follow a probable opinion regarding the value of the sacrament, the safer opinion being abandoned, unless the law forbids it, convention or the danger of incurring grave harm. Therefore, one should not make use of probable opinions only in conferring baptism, sacerdotal, or episcopal orders.

2. I think that probably a judge can pass judgment according to opinion, even the less probable.

3. In general, when we do something confidently according to probability whether intrinsic or extrinsic, however slight, provided there is no departure from the bounds of probability, we always act prudently.

4. An infidel who does not believe will be excused of infidelity, since he is guided by a less probable opinion.

5. Even though one sins mortally, we dare not condemn him who uttered an act of love of God only once in his life.

6. It is probable that the precept of love for God is of itself not of grave obligation even once every five years.

7. Then only is it obligatory when we are bound to be justified, and we have no other way by which we can be justified.

8. Eating and drinking even to satiety for pleasure only, are not sinful, provided this does not stand in the way of health, since any natural appetite can licitly enjoy its own actions.

9. The act of marriage exercised for pleasure only is entirely free of all fault and venial defect.

10. We are not bound to love our neighbor by an internal and formal act.

11. We can satisfy the precept of loving neighbor by external acts only.

12. Scarcely will you find among seculars, even among kings, a superfluity for [his] state of life. And so, scarcely anyone is bound to give alms from what is superfluous to [his] state of life.

13. If you act with due moderation, you can without mortal sin be sad about the moral life of someone and rejoice about his natural death, seek it with ineffectual desire and long for it, not indeed from dissatisfaction with the person but because of some temporal benefit.

14. It is licit with an absolute desire to wish for the death of a father, not indeed as an evil to the father, but as a good to him who desires it, for a rich inheritance will surely come his way.

15. It is licit for a son to take joy from his murder of his parent carried out while drunk, on account of the vast fortune that he then obtained from his inheritance.

16. Faith is not considered to fall under a special precept and by itself.

17. It is enough to utter an act of faith once during life.

18. If anyone is questioned by a public power, I advise him to confess his faith to a noble person as to God and (to be)

proud of his faith; I do not condemn silence as sinful of itself.

19. The will cannot effect that assent to faith in itself be stronger than the weight of reasons impelling toward assent.

20. Hence, anyone can prudently repudiate the supernatural assent which he had.

21. Assent to faith is supernatural and useful to salvation with only the probable knowledge of revelation, even with the fear by which one fears lest God has not spoken.

22. Only faith in one God seems necessary by a necessity of means, not, however, but not explicit (faith) in a remunerator.

23. Faith widely so called according to the testimony of a creature or by a similar reason suffices for justification.

24. To call upon God as a witness to a slight lie is not a great irreverence, because of which God wishes or can condemn man.

25. With cause it is licit to swear without the intention of swearing, whether the matter be light or serious.

26. If anyone swears, either alone or in the presence of others, whether questioned or of his own will, whether for sake of recreation or for some other purpose, that he did not do something, which in fact he did, understanding within himself something else which he did not do, or another way than that by which he did it, or some other added truth, in fact does not lie and is no perjurer.

27. A just reason for using these ambiguous words exists, as often as it is necessary or useful to guard the well-being of the body, honor, property, or for any other act of virtue, so that the concealing of the truth is then regarded as expedient and zealous.

28. He who has been promoted to a magistracy or a public office by means of a recommendation or a gift can utter with mental reservation the oath which is customarily exacted of similar persons by order of the king, without regard for the intent of the one exacting it, because he is not bound to confess a concealed crime.

29. A grave, pressing fear is a just cause for pretending the administration of sacraments.

30. It is right for an honorable man to kill an attacker who tries to indict calumny upon him, if this ignominy cannot be avoided otherwise; the same also must be said if anyone slaps him with his hand or strikes with a club and runs away after the slap of the hand or the blow of the club.

31. I can properly kill a thief to save a single gold piece.

32. It is not only permitted to defend, with a fatal defense, these things we possess actually, but also those things to which we have a partial right, and which we hope to possess.

33. It is permitted an heir as well as a legatee to defend himself against one who unjustly prevents either an inheritance being assumed, or legacies being paid, just as it

is permitted him who has a right to a chair or a benefice against one who unjustly impedes his possession of them.

34. It is permitted to bring about an abortion before the animation of the foetus, lest the girl found pregnant be killed or defamed.

35. It seems probable that every foetus (as long as it is in the womb) lacks a rational soul and begins to have the same at the time that it is born; and consequently it will have to be said that no homicide is committed in any abortion.

36. It is permitted to steal not only in extreme, but in grave necessity.

37. Male and female domestic servants can secretly steal from their masters to gain compensation for their work which they judge of greater worth than the salary which they receive.

38. No one is bound under the pain of mortal sin to restore what has been taken away by small thefts, however great the sum total may be.

39. Whoever moves or induces another to bring a serious loss upon a third party is not bound to a restitution of that loss incurred.

40. A usurious contract is permitted even with respect to the same person, and with a contract to sell back previously entered upon with the intention of gain.

41. Since ready cash is more valuable than that to be paid, and since there is no one who does not consider ready cash

of greater worth than future cash, a creditor can demand something beyond the principal from the borrower, and for this reason be excused from usury.

42. There is no usury when something is exacted beyond the principal as due because of a kindness and by way of gratitude, but only if it is exacted as due according to justice.

43. What is it but venial sin if one detract authority by a false charge to prevent great harm to himself?

44. It is probable that he does not sin mortally who imposes a false charge on someone, that he may defend his own justice and honor. And if this is not probable, there is scarcely any probable opinion in theology.

45. To give a temporal thing for a spiritual one is not simony, when the temporal is not given for a price, but merely as a motive to confer or effect a spiritual thing; or even when a temporal thing would be only a gratuitous compensation for a spiritual thing, or vice versa.

46. And it is also admissible, even if the temporal thing were the principle motive to give a spiritual thing, nay more, even if it were the end of the spiritual thing itself, so that it would be esteemed more than a spiritual thing.

47. When the Council of Trent says that they sin mortally by sharing the sins of others who do not promote to the churches those whom they themselves judge to be more worthy and more useful for the Church, the Council either first seems to mean to signify by "more worthy" nothing else than the worthiness of being selected, using the comparative rather than the positive; or secondly, in a less proper

expression takes "more worthy" to exclude the unworthy, but not the worthy, or finally, and thirdly, it is speaking of what occurs during an assembly.

48. Thus it seems clear that fornication by its nature involves no malice, and that it is evil only because it is forbidden, so that the contrary seems entirely in disagreement with reason.

49. Voluptuousness is not prohibited by the law of nature. Therefore, if God had not forbidden it, it would be good, and sometimes obligatory under pain of mortal sin.

50. Intercourse with a married woman, with the consent of her husband, is not adultery, and so it is enough to say in confession that one had committed fornication.

51. A male servant who knowingly by offering his shoulders assists his master to ascend through windows to ravage a virgin, and many times serves the same by carrying a ladder, by opening a door, or by cooperating in something similar, does not commit a mortal sin, if he does this through fear of considerable damage, for example, lest he be treated wickedly by his master, lest he be looked upon with savage eyes, or, lest he be expelled from the house.

52. The precept of keeping feast days is not obligatory under pain of mortal sin, aside from scandal, if contempt be absent.

53. He satisfies the precept of the Church of hearing the Holy Sacrifice, who hears two of its parts, even four simultaneously by different celebrants.

54. He who cannot recite Matins and Lauds, but can the

remaining hours, is held to nothing, since the great part brings the lesser to it.

55. He satisfies the precept of annual communion by the sacrilegious eating of the Lord.

56. Frequent confession and communion, even in those who live like pagans, is a mark of predestination.

57. It is probable that natural but honest imperfect sorrow for sins suffices.

58. We are not bound to confess to a confessor who asks us about the habit of some sin.

59. It is permitted to absolve sacramentally those who confess only half, by reason of a great crowd of penitents, such as for example can happen on a day of great festivity or indulgence.

60. The penitent who has the habit of sinning against the law of God, of nature, or of the Church, even if there appears no hope of amendment, is not to be denied absolution or to be put off, provided he professes orally that he is sorry and proposes amendment.

61. He can sometimes be absolved, who remains in a proximate occasion of sinning, which he can and does not wish to omit, but rather directly and professedly seeks or enters into.

62. The proximate occasion for sinning is not to be shunned when some useful and honorable cause for not shunning it occurs.

63. It is permitted to seek directly the proximate occasion for sinning for a spiritual or temporal good of our own or of a neighbor.

64. A person is fit for absolution, however much he labors under an ignorance of the mysteries of the faith, and even if through negligence, even culpable, he does not know the mystery of the most blessed Trinity, and of the incarnation of our Lord Jesus Christ.

65. It is enough to have believed the mysteries once.

PROPOSITIONS CONDEMNED BY
ALEXANDER VIII

When on Thursday, 24 August 1690, in the General Congregation of the Holy Roman and Universal Inquisition the two following propositions were brought into examination, namely:

1. Objective goodness consists in the agreement of an object with rational nature; but formal goodness consists in the conformity of an act with the rule of morals. For this it is sufficient that the moral act tend toward its ultimate end interpretatively. Man is not obliged to love this end, neither in the beginning nor in the course of his moral life.

2. Philosophic or moral sin is a human act not in conformity with rational nature and right reason; but theological and mortal sin is a free transgression of the divine law. A philosophic sin, however grave, in a man who either is ignorant of God or does not think about God during the act, is a grave sin, but is not an offense against God, neither a mortal sin dissolving the friendship of God, nor one worthy of eternal punishment.

The Supreme Pontiff declared the first proposition to be heretical; the second as rash, scandalous, etc.

Next, on Thursday, 7 December, the same Pope, Alexander VIII, condemned the following 31 propositions:

1. In the state of fallen nature, for mortal sin and for demerit that liberty is sufficient by which the mortal sin or

demerit was voluntary and free in its cause, namely, in original sin and in the will of Adam sinning.

2. Although there is such a thing as invincible ignorance of the law of nature, this, in the state of fallen nature, does not excuse from formal sin anyone acting out of ignorance.

3. It is not permitted to follow a (probable) opinion or among the probables the most probable.

4. Christ gave Himself for us as an oblation to God, not for the elect only, but for all the faithful only.

5. Pagans, Jews, heretics, and others of this kind do not receive in any way any influence from Jesus Christ, and so you will rightly infer from this that in them there is a bare and weak will without any sufficient grace.

6. Grace sufficient for our state is not so much useful as pernicious, so that we can justly pray: From sufficient grace deliver us, O Lord.

7. Every human act is a deliberate choice of God or of the world; if of God, it is love of the Father; if of the world, it is concupiscence of the flesh, that is, it is evil.

8. Of necessity, an infidel sins in every act.

9. In truth he sins who hates sin merely because of its vileness and its inconsistency with nature, without any reference to the offense to God.

10. The intention with which anyone detests evil and follows

after good, merely that he may obtain heavenly glory, is not right nor pleasing to God.

11. Everything which is not in accordance with supernatural Christian faith, which works through charity, is a sin.

12. When in great sinners all love is lacking, faith also is lacking; and even if they seem to believe, their faith is not divine but human.

13. Whoever serves God even in view of an eternal reward, if he lacks charity, is not free from fault, as often as he acts even in view of his eternal reward.

14. Fear of hell is not supernatural.

15. Attrition, which is conceived through a fear of hell and punishments, with a love of benevolence for God in Himself, is not a good and supernatural motive.

16. Neither the policy nor institution of the Church has introduced the order of placing satisfaction before absolution, but the law and prescription of Christ, since the nature of the thing in a way demands that very order.

17. By that practice of absolving first the order of penance is inverted.

18. The modern custom as regards the administration of the sacrament of penance, even if the authority of many men sustains it and long duration confirms it, is nevertheless not considered by the Church as a usage but as an abuse.

19 Man ought to do penance during his whole life for original sin.

20. Confessions made to religious are generally either sacrilegious or invalid.

21. The parish priest can suspect mendicants who live on common alms, of imposing too light and unsuitable a penance or satisfaction because of the advantage or gain of some temporal aid.

22. They are to be judged sacrilegious who claim the right to receive Communion before they have done worthy penance for their sins.

23. Similarly, they must be prevented from Holy Communion, who have not yet a pure love of God, without any admixture.

24. The oblation in the Temple, which was made by the Blessed Virgin Mary on the day of her purification by means of two turtle doves, one for a holocaust and the other for sins, sufficiently testifies that she was in need of purification, and that her Son (who was being offered) was also stained with the stain of His mother, according to the words of the law.

25. It is unlawful to place in a Christian church an image of God the Father seated.

26. Praise which is offered to Mary, as Mary, is vain.

27. Sometimes baptism is valid when conferred under this

form: "In the name of the Father, etc. . . . ," omitting these words: "I baptize thee."

28. Baptism is valid when conferred by a minister who observes all the external rite and form of baptizing, but within his heart resolves, I do not intend what the Church does.

29. Futile and many times refuted is the assertion about the authority of the Roman Pontiff being superior to that of an ecumenical Council and about his infallibility in deciding questions of faith.

30. When anyone finds a doctrine clearly established in Augustine, he can absolutely hold and teach it, disregarding any bull of the pope.

31. The Bull of Urban VIII, "*In Eminenti*," is false.

Here it is related to add five Propositions in regard to Dueling, proscribed by Benedict XIV in the bull *Detestabilem*, published 10 November, 1752.

1. A military man who would be considered fearful, timid, abject, and unfit for military offices unless he offers or accepts a duel, and hence would be deprived of an office by which he supports himself and his family, or who would be perpetually deprived of the hope of promotion otherwise due him and merited by him, is free from guilt and penalty, whether he offers a duel or accepts one.

2. Those who accept a duel, or even provoke a duel for the sake of protecting their honor, or of avoiding the disrepute of men, can be excused when they know for certain that the

combat will not take place, inasmuch as it will be prevented by others.

3. A leader or military officer who accepts a duel through grave fear of losing his reputation or his office, does not incur the ecclesiastical penalties brought by the Church against duelists.

4. It is permitted in the natural state of man to accept and to offer a duel to preserve one's fortunes with honor, when their loss cannot be prevented by any other means.

5. This permission, claimed for the natural state, can also be applied to the state of the commonwealth which is badly regulated, that is to say, in which justice is openly denied, either because of the negligence or the wickedness of the magistracy.

THEOLOGIA MORALIS
BOOK I

Monitum of the Author

OTICE, kind reader, that this first Treatise on conscience, where, being added to the universal Moral Theology, it is made clear how I have burnt the midnight oil to apply it for the easier instruction of those of my own order. I say this because next you will find all the other marks of a Treatise drawn from the lines of another author, albeit, joined with my notes. Moreover, I have chosen to insert those Treatises of another author to follow the order of affairs preserved in it, insofar as such an order, on account of the distinction and connection of matters, has universally been reputed the best by most theologians.

CHAPTER I
What is Conscience, how manifold is it, and what must be followed?

1. *On the remote rule and proximate rule of human acts.*

2. *On conscience and synderesis.*

3. *On a right and erroneous conscience.*

4. *On someone who follows a vincibly erroneous conscience.*

5. *On someone who follows an invincibly erroneous conscience.*

6. Whether working in such a way one acquires merit by a work?

7. Response is made to the objection of our opponents.

8. Whether an invincibly erroneous conscience would be granted in natural precepts? (Remissive ad Tractat. II., de legib. n. 169).

9. On someone who erroneously thinks an evil desire is not a sin.

10. On a confused conscience.

11. On a scrupulous conscience. Signs of scruples.

12. Remedies and especially acts of obedience.

13. On the danger to the scrupulous man who does not obey.

14. Assigning general rules.

15. How a confessor ought to conduct himself with the scrupulous who dread to admit any wicked thought.

16. How to deal with those who always doubt their past confessions.

17. How to deal with those who fear to sin in every action.

18. What about those who labor with actual fear?

19. The scrupulous do not sin by overcoming scruples, provided that they lay them aside first.

1.—There is a twofold rule of human acts, one is called remote and the second, proximate. *The Remote* or material is the divine law, while the *proximate*, or formal, is conscience. Although conscience ought to conform to the divine law in all things, nevertheless, the goodness or malice of human actions are known to us, inasmuch as it is apprehended by the conscience itself, as St. Thomas teaches: "human reason is the rule of human will which measures its goodness. (1. 2. q. 19, art. 4.) And more clearly in another place: "A human act is judged virtuous or vicious according to the good perception, in which the will is imposed, and not according to the material object of the act." (*Quodlib.* 3. art. 27). First we will treat on the proximate rule, namely on conscience, then on the remote rule, namely on laws.

2.—Conscience is so defined: "It is a judgment, or practical command of reason, in which we judge something must be done here and now as a good, or something must be avoided as an evil." Moreover, conscience is called a *practical command*, in distinction from *synderesis*, which is the speculative knowledge of universal principles to live well, certainly: "That God must be worshiped, you do not do to another what you would not wish for yourself, etc.," as St. Thomas holds, p. 1, qu. 79, art. 12.

3.—Furthermore, conscience is divided into right, erroneous, confused, scrupulous, doubtful and probable. A *right* conscience is that which dictates the truth; therefore one sins if they work against it, since the Apostle says: "Everything which is not of faith (namely from the dictate of conscience, as Estius and others explain), is sin. (Romans 14:23). Innocent III confirms this in *cap. Litteras, de rest. spol.* "Whatever is against conscience, paves the way to hell." But an *erroneous* conscience is that which dictates what is false as though it were true. Moreover, some erroneous consciences are vincible, and some are invincible. A conscience is *vincible*, when it may and must be conquered by the operation, or because it notices an error, or at least hesitates about an error, and at the same time notices the obligation to conquer it, but does nothing to conquer it, as many teach (S. Anton. 2. p. tit. 5, c. 1 §5; Navarr. *praelud.* 9. n. 9; *Salm.* tr. 20. c. 14. punct. 2. n. 9; Suarez in 5. p. d. 4. sect. 8. n. 18 with Sylvius, Cajetan, communissime aliisque ex S. Thoma *de Veritate*, q. 15. art. 4. ad 10). Furthermore, the Salamancans (*loc. cit.*) and Alphonse de Castro (tr. 2, *de pecc.* d. 1. p. 15. n. 6, with Azor, Suarez, Vasquez, Bonac. etc. and Wigandt *de consc. ex 1. q. 5, n. 7*), teach that it is not necessary to apply oneself to the utmost so as to conquer error, rather it is sufficient to do what is common and ordinary. On the other hand, an *invincible* conscience is such that cannot be morally conquered, since no thought or doubt comes into the mind of the one who acts, nor even confusion while he acts, or when he considers the cause of the action, as it is explained in greater length in the Treatise *On sins* (book 2) where it is argued on the knowledge that is required for sin.

4.—From that we say: 1. Someone has a vincibly erroneous conscience that always sins when he acts either according to it or even against it. He sins in an act against it by choosing an evil that he judges to be evil; but he sins according to it in an act because, although it ought to be an error and can be conquered, he carries out the work rashly by not laying it aside.

5.—We say: 2. Someone that has an invincibly erroneous conscience, not only does not sin by acting according to it, but even that he is held to follow it at any time. The reasoning of each is that he does not sin, because although the action may not be right in itself, nevertheless, it is right according to the conscience of the one who does the act; at anytime one is held to act according to it, if his conscience, which is the proximate rule, so suggests it must be done.

6.—Not only does one that performs an act with an invincibly erroneous conscience not sin, but even more probably he acquires merit, as Fr. Fulgentius Cuniliati rightly supposes (*de consc.* c. 1, n. 6, in common with others). The reason is, because to say some act is good, or at least neutral, suffices that one is directed by the dictate of reason and prudence. Therefore, since the one doing the work acts prudently, there ought to be little doubt about the good end for which it is worked, namely the glory of God or charity towards one's neighbor, just as, on the other hand, someone that performs a good work, yet supposed it to be evil on account of an evil end for which he carries out the work, would lose merit.

7.—Franzoja objects (*Theol. Mor.* lib. 1. c. 1. art. 1.) that an evil action can never be the cause of merit, and asserts St. Thomas on his behalf (1. 2. q. 19. art. 6), "A good is caused from the whole cause, but an evil from one single defect." And so, for this purpose, that it is said to be evil, in which the will is carried, it suffices either according to its nature that it is evil, or because it is taken up as an evil. But for this purpose, that it be good, it is required for it to be good in each mode. Yet, we respond that the Angelic Doctor speaks here about a good taken up absolutely and simply, but not about a good respectively and *per accidens*, insofar as by conscience, which is the proximate rule of action, it is taken invincibly, according to that which he also teaches (as we related above) saying: "A human act is judged to be virtuous or vicious according to which the will is imposed and not according to the material object of the act." (*Quodlibet.* 3. art. 27). According to Fr. Concina (*Theol. Christ.* tom. 2, l. 2, *de consc.* diss. 1. cap. 5), although in the argument he says a work from an erroneous conscience, even if it is invincible, is not provided with any goodness or merit, nevertheless, later he thinks the same thing as we do, which can be seen in the same work, n. 36: "Someone can, when he exercises a work that is materially bad, have a great many good acts, namely a good intention to please God. We say these are good and meritorious, although the acts which he exercises then may be *per se* materially bad, the fault is not imputable to him ... because the work is materially bad, although it is not voluntary, it does not pour malice into those acts." St. Bernard gives a stronger confirmation when he teaches (*de Praecept. et Dispenstione*, c. 12 et 17), that a subject obeying a prelate with a right intention acts meritoriously, although materially he errs against the law. He so writes in chapter 14, n. 55, "I will also say even a mere pious intention is worthy of praise; clearly, the good will itself will not be defrauded of worthy reward in a work that is also not good."

8.—*Quaeritur:* 1) whether an invincibly erroneous conscience can be posited in regard to the precepts of the natural law? We respond briefly, that it can be posited in regard to the mediate and remote conclusions from first principles, but not in regard to immediate and proximate conclusions, that one would be able to take someone else's thing away from its owner against his will, to kill an innocent man, etc. This is the common opinion, which we prove below, especially on the authority of St. Thomas, in *Tr. II on laws, n. 169.*

9.—*Quaeritur:* 2) Whether an invincibly erroneous conscience can be posited in one who desires to accomplish some evil, say fornication, judging erroneously that only the desire to fornicate is not mortal, if fornication does not follow in fact? Sanchez and Cardenas affirm this as more probable, because although he would will an evil object, nevertheless, he invincibly believes his desire does not inflict an injury on God. Still, I could never reckon this opinion to be probable, because I have never availed to understand how someone would deliberately exercise an action in which he knows God is offended and could inculpably believe that he does not offend God while he efficaciously desires to carry it out, whereby he certainly recognizes he turns away from God. But someone will say: How will he formally sin in his desire, if he does not know of its malice? We respond: Although it is posited that he is unaware of the malice of the internal act, still he knows for certain the malice of the external act; therefore, if he wishes to carry it out, and it is already known to him as an evil, how can he be excused from sin? Certainly, everyone discerns from the light of nature that he is held in obedience to his creator; so when someone deliberately means to do something which he knows God has forbidden him, at the same time he necessarily knows that he acts wickedly, and although reflectively he would not sin only by thinking the external act is a sin, nevertheless by exercising it in fact he then sins, wishing to refuse due obedience to God in the time in which he plans to accomplish the sin. Now, one might insist: many unlearned men will not confess these wicked desires because they believe they only sin when they accomplish the sin externally. We respond: They are rather more deceived in a false belief that they are not held to confess the sins which they do not accomplish; but a prudent confessor ought to judge that when they thought about accomplishing the sin, truly they also sinned formally from a wicked will turning themselves from God. From all of this I regard the contrary opinion scarcely probable, along with more recent doctors.

10.—Let us proceed to argue the other species of conscience. A *perplexed* conscience is one in which someone that has been placed in the middle of two precepts believes he sins no matter which side he chooses, *e.g.* if someone could save the life of the defendant in a trial by perjury, and on the one hand he is distressed by the precept of religion to not commit perjury, while on the other (deduced from an error) by the precept of charity towards his neighbor, and he cannot resolve himself to do one or the other. Thus it is a question of what he ought to do in this case. We respond: If he can suspend an action, he is bound to postpone it until he consults a learned man: but if he cannot suspend it, he is held to choose a lesser evil by avoiding a greater transgression of natural law than of human or divine positive law. Moreover, if he cannot discern what is the lesser evil, and he were to choose either part, he would not sin because in a case of this sort he would lack the freedom necessary for formal sin.

11.—Let us treat in this last place on a *scrupulous* conscience, on which it is necessary to have a longer discussion. A scrupulous conscience is that which, on account of a light motive without any rational foundation (for a scruple is an empty perception), he often is afraid of

sin where there none is really present. The signs of a
scrupulous conscience are these: 1) Pertinacity of judgment,
whereby the scrupulous man refused to obey the advice of
wise men, and no matter how many he consulted, took up
the judgment of none; 2) Frequent change of judgment from
weak motives; from that inconstancy in action arises, and
disturbance of the mind, especially in external operations,
for example in the celebration of Mass, in the recitation of
the Breviary, or the administration of the Sacraments, or in
perception; 3) Reflecting impertinently on a great many
circumstances that were present in an action, or could have
been present; 4) To fear sin in all things or to adhere in mind
against the judgment of wise men, even one's own
judgment, and so he is never content with one assertion of
a confessor, but more often seeks out the same thing in the
same act, whether or not his conscience could be free from
fault in an act according to the given counsel.

12.—Moreover, the remedy that must be applied for
scruples of this sort are these. After the confessor will have
perceived from the signs advanced above that the penitent
is scrupulous, let him prescribe: 1) That he should cultivate
true humility, for often scruples have their origin in the vice
of pride; 2) That he should avoid reading books that excite
scruples, and turn away from the conversation of scrupulous
men; 3) That he should not put off making an examination
of conscience, especially in regard to those things in which
he is more disturbed; 4) That he should put to flight idleness,
whereby the mind is often filled with empty perceptions; 5)
That he should urgently commend himself to God to obtain
the assistance to obey the precepts of his director. For this
above all precepts, can truly be said to be the only remedy
for feeble souls of this sort, to altogether acquiesce to the
judgment of their superior or confessor, as all the fathers,
theologians and spiritual masters teach. Hence, it is
exceedingly beneficial, so as to put consciences agitated by

scruples to rest, that the confessor explain to the penitent the outstanding authorities of the learned, which I add here. Nöel Alexander (*Theol. Dogm. Mor.* l. 3, c. 4, r. 1) says: "Moreover, they ought to spurn scruples, approaching the judgment of the prudent, pious and learned director, and he must act against them, as is certain from *cap. Inquisitioni, e sent. exc.* where it is said, 'What if someone has a conscience from light credulity ... he can licitly act on the counsel of his pastor'." St. Antoninus confirms this from John Gerson, who so writes (*Tract. de praepar. ad miss.*), "One who refuses to believe the counsel of superiors and prudent men to lay aside such scruples, as well as argue against them, errs in many ways. Many simple men are deceived in this, not knowing how to distinguish between that which is the superior part of the soul, and that which the inferior suffers without the assent of a superior." Next, he cites what St. Bernard said to a certain scrupulous disciple: "Go and boast in my trust." But someone will say, "would that St. Bernard were here for me! But now, while I consider the wisdom of my superior to be mediocre, I do not dare to commit my conscience to him." St. Antoninus responds from the same Gerson: "Whoever would so speak, errs; for you have not consigned yourself into the hands of a man because he is literate, pious, etc., but because he has been placed over you. This is why you obey him, not as a man, but as God ... Beware of the extreme, lest while you seek security you would rush headlong into a pit." St. Philip Neri used to speak this way to his penitents: "Those who desire to progress in the way of God, let them submit themselves to a learned confessor, whom they will obey as God. One who so does this becomes secure by giving an account of all their actions." Likewise, he said: "Trust must be placed in a confessor because the Lord will not permit him to err. Nothing is more secure than to obey the will of a director in every work; and nothing is more perilous than to follow one's own judgment." St. Francis de Sales (*Introduction to the*

Devout Life, ch. 4), speaking on the direction of a spiritual father, writes about Fr. John of Avila: "In no better way do we become certain about the will of God than through humble obedience to his commands." The Gloss confirms this, in cap. *Ad aures, de temp. ord. lit. f. in fine,* where it is said: "But if a precept were doubtful, on account of the good of obedience one is excused from sin, although in truth it might be evil." The same thing is said in cap. *Quid culpatur, caus.* 23, q. 1. St. Bernard, (*de Praecept. et Dispensat.,* c. 12), says: "Whatever a man in the place of God commands, which is not certain to displease God, can scarcely be taken up in another fashion than if God himself were to command it." St. Ignatius of Loyola (*in Constit. Soc. Jesu.*), says: "One must obey in all things where he finds no sin, *i.e.* (*ut in declar.*) in which there is no manifest sin." St. Humbert (*in l. de Erud. rel. c. 1*) says: "Unless what is commanded is clearly evil, it must be taken up as though it were commanded by God." Denis the Carthusian, (in 2 dis. 39, q. 3), says: "In doubtful matters, or even were it against the command of God, it must stand by the precept of the prelate, because even if it were against God, nevertheless due to the good of obedience the subject would not sin." St. Bonaventure teaches the same thing (*in Spec. disc.* c. 4.)

13.—For this reason, a confessor should take strenuous care to persuade penitents disturbed by scruples, that he will walk altogether secure if he will acquiesce to the counsels of his director and obey in all things wherein an obvious sin does not appear; then he does not obey man, but the same God that said, "He who hears you, hears me, and he who spurns you, spurns me." (Luke 10:16). On the other hand, he should drive the point home with the great distinction that one who refuses to furnish obedience to the commands of his confessor entrusts himself with his eternal salvation; then he exposes himself to the danger of losing not only peace of heart, devotion and progress in virtue but even reason (for how many scrupulous men fell into madness by not giving obedience!), and at length he not only throws away the strength of the body; nay more, what is worse, even the soul, for scruples can reach such an extent in a man that they reduce him to such desperation whereby he will either kill himself, as happens to many, or that so despairing of their eternal salvation, they relax the reigns to embrace every vice.

14.—Besides, the prudent confessor is bound to prescribe rules for penitents of this sort that are rather more general than particular; for by particular rules the scrupulous almost never avail to resolve themselves to work; because they always hesitate whether the rule that was prescribed can avail for that occasion, which often will seem different to him than a past case that he had conferred with his confessor about. Hence, Concina rightly says (*Compendium theol.*, l. 1, dissert. 1. c. 6. n. 7): "After they [the penitents] have received the rules of direction, they ought not importunely approach the director and disturb him with aggravating questions, rather they ought to expel scruples by the benefit of the guidelines which they received."

15.—There are three ways that the scrupulous are greatly disturbed by scruples. Some are tormented by wicked thoughts, to which they are often afraid to assent; others, on account of past confessions, in which they doubt they did enough; others still, on account of the fear of sinning in any work that they are about to do. Hence, I. For the penitent who is terrified of every wicked thought (for example, against faith, chastity or charity) that he gave assent to, the confessor should impose upon him the requirement to affirm that bad thoughts are not sins, rather it is only a sin to consent to them, so that he should altogether despise scruples of this sort. And in this matter he should not omit to use that rule which has been wisely handed down by doctors, namely those who are of a God-fearing conscience, unless they morally know for certain that they consented to a grave sin, must be judged to be free from sin; for, as Fr. Alvarez says, it is impossible for sin to enter a soul that abhors it, since the soul will clearly recognize it for what it is. This is why it is often expedient to expressly impose upon the scrupulous to abstain from confessing thoughts of this sort unless they are so certain that they consented to them that they could swear to the fact.

16.—II. For the penitent that is always anxious about past confessions, because he is terrified that he lacked integrity or sorrow, if he will have already satisfied the others with a general confession or carefully continued his confessions for some notable period of time, let the confessor impose upon him that he not think any longer on past faults, nor mention anything about them in confession, unless he could swear for certain that those sins he committed were mortal, and moreover, that he never confessed them. Nay more, Azor., Bonacina, Becanus, Coninck, Laymann, and others teach that at some point one can be so tormented by scruples, that although it may seem to him that he certainly did not mention them, still he is not held to confess these things. Wigandt suitably writes on this, "The scrupulous man, who means to repeat confessions, must not be heard since after it has been posited that he did not confess some sins, on account of the grave damage and the danger of perpetually continuing in such anxiety, he is excused from the sincerity of confession." But in this let the confessor oblige the penitent to obey him; still, if he refuses to obey, let him reproach him, deprive him of communion and, as much as he can, blunt his insensibility. With the scrupulous that are obedient one must proceed in a winning manner, but with those who are wanting in obedience, the greatest exercise is rigor and austerity, since by this anchor of obedience they can never be without hope of healing.

17.—Lastly, with those scrupulous men that dread sin in every action, let him impose that they act freely, and despise their scruples, and work against them where a clear sin does not appear; because ordinarily they fear sin is present where there is none due to disturbed reason from an excessive fear. Therefore, he must enjoin a command upon them to conquer their scruples, lest they would go out mad or altogether useless, and after would keep themselves from accusing themselves of such actions in confession. Although they might stray from so doing at some time, still it would not be a sin by reason of the obedience which they should furnish to their confessor. Nay more, Sanchez (*in decal.* l. 1. c. 10, n. 81) along with St. Antoninus, Gerson, Valent., Corduba, etc. wisely teach this. Likewise, the Salamancans (tr. 20, cap. 7, punct. 2, n. 10.) along with Cajetan, Navarre, Castropalous, Bonacina, Filliucci, etc., say a scrupulous man is held at some point by the grave obligation to work against scruples, since he can fear grave damage in spiritual progress from the anxiety of scruples, either in the health of the body or the mind.

18.—It is not proposed that he should work with a scrupulous conscience or with actual fear of sinning; for from the common and true opinion, which Concina (tom. 2., l. 2, *de consc. diss.* 1, c. 8, n. 15.), Roncaglia (*eod. tit.* c. 4, q. 2.), Anacletus (*eod. tit.* qu. 5. n. 72.), St. Antoninus (1. p. tit. 3, c. 10. §10.), the Salamancans (tr. 20, c. 7, n. 10), along with Navarre, Cajetan, Bonacina and a great many others teach, that the scrupulous man so doing hardly sins. The reason is because a scrupulous conscience or the dictate of the mind rising from scruples, cannot take away the assent from the integrity of an action previously formed from the judgment of a confessor, or by another mode; for as Father Concina says, "A doubt suspends assent, and a scruple vice versa, insofar as it is distinct from doubt. Therefore, scruples are certain troubles which can somewhat obscure the judgment

of the intellect, still in no way do they avail to suffocate it."
That is also especially valid if the obedience to be made to a
confessor presses one against scruples, where clearly a fault
is not perceived, as it is contained in *cap. Inquisitioni* 44, *de
sent. excom.,* where the Pope declares that a man is secure
that abandons scruples while following the advice of his
pastor; thus it is said: "By the counsel of his pastor (a
conscience of light and reckless credulity rejected) one can
licitly act." The text advanced by some, *in cap. Per tuas* 35. *de
simon.,* where the Pope prescribed to a certain man with an
excessively scrupulous conscience to not advance to higher
orders unless he had first laid aside that conscience, would
not impede us here. For, in that text a mere scruple is not
treated, rather an error whereby the ordinand is held, as the
Gloss explains: "were he to have an erroneous conscience."
It is also expressed this way in the text, "Unless he would lay
aside the error."

19.—Hence, in regard to practice it must be concluded,
that the scrupulous man must always be constrained to
obey, that bravely expelling the fear of his scruples he might
act freely. It is not necessary that he should form a judgment
on any particular act, without a doubt he ought to scorn
scruples by the precept of a confessor; for it is enough that
he act from an earlier judgment formed against a scruple,
because on account of an old experience in his conscience
that judgment either virtually or habitually exists, although
obscured by darkness. So much the more, when a scrupulous
man works in that confusion, he does not act certainly with
a formed and deliberative conscience, which is certainly
required to constitute a sin, as John Gerson (*Tract. de consc.
et scrup.*) properly writes in these words: "A conscience has
been formed when after discussion and deliberation,
concludes from a definitive judgment of reason that
something must be done or avoided and to act against it is a
sin. But fear or a scruple of conscience is when the mind

vacillates between doubts, not knowing what it is held more to do; still it ought not omit what it knows is pleasing to the divine will; and to act against this fear or scruple is not always a sin, although it might be very perilous," (understand unless the fear is condemned as vain, especially if the counsel of directors should agree), therefore, Gerson adds, "as much as it can be done, it must be cut off and extinguished." Next, the same Gerson (*Cons.* 6), writes: "The scrupulous must act against scruples, and with a firm foot fight against them. We cannot constrain scruples better than through contempt, and regularly but not without the counsel of another and especially of a superior. Otherwise, immoderate fear or thoughtless presumption casts him down." Next, Nöel Alexander says for the scrupulous that the rule of St. Albert the Great must be preserved, as well as that handed down by St. Antoninus: "Between a hard and favorable opinion about precepts, a favorable interpretation must be made in other proportionate matters." It remains to speak about a doubtful and probable conscience. We will treat these separately in the following two chapters.

CHAPTER II
On a doubtful Conscience

20. *What is a doubtful conscience? What is a positive or negative doubt?*

21. *What is a speculative and practical doubt?*

22. *It is never lawful to act with a practically doubtful conscience.*

23. *In a matter where someone knows something is evil, but doubts whether it is grave or light.*

24. *What should one do who is practically doubtful?*

25. *Whether it is lawful to act with a speculatively doubtful conscience?*

26. *On the many reflexive principles, from which a practically certain conscience can be formed.*

27. *On a doubtful law, or one doubtfully promulgated and on a certain law doubtfully abrogated.*

28. *On uttering a doubtful vow; and on a certain vow, as well as fulfilling a doubtful vow.*

29. *What about someone who judges that he probably fulfilled a vow?*

30. *What if someone already fulfilled the burden of the vow, but does not remember it?*

31. *Whether a subject is held to obey a superior in a matter which is doubtfully bad?*

32. *Doubt about different matters.*

33. *What about doubt on the validity of matrimony? Refer to book 6, n. 903 and 904.*

34. *What about a doubt on the payment, if the debt is certain?*

35. *What about a doubt on what is owed if someone possesses a thing in good faith?*

36. *What if probable reason should urge against the possessor and he has nothing in his favor?*

37. *What if the possessor, when a doubt arises, should have failed to find the truth?*

38. *Whether one can receive the Eucharist who is uncertain whether he swallowed any food or drink?*

39. *What if someone is uncertain whether he ate before or after midnight?*

20.—A doubtful conscience is that which suspends the assent for each part of the doubt, and remains doubtful and hesitant. Moreover, a doubtful conscience is divided into practical and speculative doubt. Furthermore, doubt is divided into negative and positive. *A negative* doubt is when probable reasons do not come to mind favoring either side, rather only light ones. *A positive* doubt is when a grave motive is present favoring each side, or at least one, sufficing to form a probable conscience, although with fear of the opposite side; therefore a positive doubt always coincides with a probable opinion, which we will speak of in the *following chapter.*

21.—Next, doubt is divided into speculative and practical. A *speculative* doubt is when someone is uncertain about the truth of a matter, *e.g.* whether some war is just or unjust; whether to paint on a feast day would be servile labor or free: whether baptism with trickling water is valid or not, and similar things. A *practical* doubt is when there is uncertainty about the integrity of a matter, *e.g.* whether it is lawful for me to fight in a war that is dubiously just: whether to paint on this feast day; whether this boy was baptized with trickling water. Therefore, the fact must be distinguished from what is licit; for a speculative doubt although in an oblique mode, and consequently regards more the liceity, but in a direct matter, a speculative doubt principally regards a true thing, while a practical regards a licit one.

22.—Since these have been positive, we say: I. It is never licit to act with a practically doubtful conscience; and in a case where someone acts he sins and certainly it is a sin of the same species and gravity for which he doubts, because someone who exposes himself to the danger of sinning, now sins according to what is said in the Scripture, "He who loves danger will perish in it." (Eccli. 3:27.) For this reason, if he doubts whether it is mortal, he sins mortally.

23.—What if someone knows something is evil, but doubts whether it is mortal or venial, and acts with such a doubt? Some think this man would sin gravely or lightly insofar as the object of the sin *in specie* is grave or light, as Vasquez and Sanchez, etc. But others, Azor, Bonacina, Castropalaus, etc., think he would always sin gravely. At length, many others along with Navarre, Valentia, Granado, hold he probably only sins venially, if that man did not notice either in a confused state the danger of sinning gravely or the obligation of examining the matter and provided the object is certainly not a grave sin in itself. I would add, also provided that the man is of a fearful conscience.

24.—Therefore, whoever is practically uncertain concerning some action, ought to first lay aside doubt through a certain principle, or reflect on the sincerity of that action according to what we will express in the dissertation on the use of probable opinion; it would suffice for the man to form for himself a practically certain conscience, and then he can act. But if it is insufficient for the man (for example because he is unlearned), then he is held to consult a parish priest, or a confessor or another pious and learned man, and act according to their counsel. Were someone uncertain, but after weighing all things noticed that the doubt is inane, he can rightly lay aside his doubt without any other reflection and thus carry out the action (as Collet, the continuator of Tournely, correctly writes, *de act. hum.* c. 7, art. 4, *de consc. dubia*). Then, if the malice of it is unknown to him, that ignorance is altogether involuntary, insofar as it cannot be conquered with study, as the Angelic Doctor teaches.

25.—We say: II. It is licit to perform an act with a speculatively doubtful conscience while always both acting by other reasons or reflexive principles, he judges practically that his action is certainly morally good. Yet, there are other reasons (as Bishop Abelly wisely argues), whereby we judge about the truth of a matter, namely on the probability or on the dubiousness of some opinion, *e.g.* that this war might be probably or dubiously just; others in which we judge on the integrity of an action, clearly that in this war, with the prince in command, it would be lawful for a subject to fight in, according to the doctrine of St. Augustine related above in *cit. can. Quid culpatur.* Moreover, that a morally certain conscience can be well formed about the integrity of an action from reflexive principles will be clearly obvious below in the dissertation on probable opinion, which we will present at the end of this treatise.[4]

26.—Of these principles the most principal is that *A doubtful law cannot induce a certain obligation.* The truth of this principle (which is affirmed even by those favoring a more rigid opinion) will be evidently proved in the dissertation we recently mentioned. See what will be said there. From this first principle the second is formed: *The condition of the possessor is better.* For as often as a doubtful law hardly binds a man, indeed a man remains free, and free from the obligation of the law, and in that case can licitly use his freedom which he may truly follow since the law is doubtful; for St. Thomas says, "It is said to be licit which no law forbids." (4 Sent. dist. 15, q. 2, art. 4. ad 2). Furthermore, this second principle, although some try to weaken it, saying that it is only valid for commerce or in a matter of justice, still I do not know how it can be denied to apply in all things. The question can only be whether *lex possidet*[5] in every moral doubt, or freedom. The Antiprobablists say *libertas possidet* always, but we say *lex possidet* sometimes, and *libertas possidet* sometimes, namely when the law has still not been promulgated. This (I say) is the question, but nobody can deny the principle that the condition of the possessor is better. Therefore, when in some case *lex*

---

[4] See below, n. 55 and 69.

[5] Translator's note: *Throughout, where the phrases, lex possidet; libertas possidet occur, we leave the Latin in place because they are technical terms in both law and moral theology. Essentially, lex possidet* means "The law has mastery", and thus, one must follow the law; whereas, *libertas possidet,* means freedom has mastery, and thus one is free to follow his will. This meaning should be transposed as often as the terms arise.

possidet, possession favors the law; but if *libertas possidet,* it must favor freedom. But to distinguish for which side possession would favor in doubtful matters, it must be seen which side the presumption favors. But the presumption favors that side which is not held to prove the fact, rather the burden of proof transfers to the other, since *Factum enim non praesumitur, nisi probetur,*[6] which is another approved principle. (l. 2 *de Probatione*). Moreover, a fact is not presumed in doubt, but must be proven. Yet, if the fact is certain, say if a marriage was certainly entered into, and a doubt arises whether it was entered into with due observance, another principle ought to be preserved: *In dubio praesumitur factum, quod de jure faciendum erat.* Or, *Standum pro valore actus.*

27.—It is inferred from the aforesaid, 1) that if a law is doubtfully made or doubtfully promulgated, it does not oblige, because possession does not favor the law, but freedom. The same thing must be said if it is uncertain in a law that was promulgated whether some burden is also included; for then we are not held to fulfill something, because on that side in which the law is doubtful, it is not the case that *lex possidet.* On the other hand, if a law is certainly made and certainly promulgated, and after that a doubt arises as to whether it was abrogated, revoked or dispensed, it must be observed since then *lex possidet.* So, even in doubt as to whether a law in itself was justly received, it ought also to be observed because it must be presumed that it was received by that other principle: *In dubio praesumitur factum quod de jure faciendum erat.*[7]

---

[6] A fact is not presumed unless it is proven.

[7] In doubt a thing is presumed to have been done which must be done lawfully.

28.—It is inferred from the aforesaid, 2) what has been said about a law must also be said about a vow. A vow is, by its nature, a particular law which a man imposes on himself. Hence, if someone doubts whether he uttered a vow he is not held to fulfill it, as is commonly taught (Cabassutius, *Theor. jur.* l. 1, c. 8, n. 19; Suarez in 3. p. disp. 40, sect. 5, n. 15; Sanchez *in dec.*, l. 1, c. 10, n. 36; Anacletus *de voto*, q. 2. concl. 3; the Salamancans *eod. tit.* tr. 17, c. 1, punct. 6 §2 n. 143; along with innumerable others). So equally, someone doubts *whether something is embraced by a vow he made or not*, is not held to the vow in regard to the part on which he is uncertain since *votum, non possidet* for that part, as is held from *cap. Ex parte* 18, *de censibus*, where, although some men pronounced specific vows, and later were uncertain about whether they would be held to the greater or lesser part of the promise that was made, it is confirmed that they are held only to the lesser part, and therefore, the Gloss notes, "In doubtful matters, he is free to follow what is more pleasing." On the other hand, if someone is certain about a vow and is uncertain on the satisfaction, he is certainly held to the vow because then *votum possidet.*

29.—Nevertheless, many authors ask, what if someone judges he has probably already satisfied a vow, is he held to fulfill it, this not withstanding? Many authors deny this, namely Roncaglia (*de praec. dec.,* c. 2, *de voto* q. 4), the Salamancans (*eod. tit.* tr. 17, c. 1, punct. 6 §2, n. 145), with Leander, de Lugo (*de peonit.* disp. 16, n. 60) and others, because (as they say), when the obligation of law is doubtful in that case, it is also in doubt whether *lex possidet.* I once thought this opinion was probable, being led more by the extrinsic probability than the intrinsic; but considering the matter better, now I think it is hardly probable. Hence, I say the opposite must be held, with Concina (tom. 3, diss. 2, *de voto,* c. 4, n. 10) Antoine (*de relig.* c. 3 *de voto* q. 5), Filliucci, Leander and others. The reason is that when a vow that was pronounced is doubtful, it is rightly said that the obligation to fulfill it is not present, for then *libertas possidet*; but when the vow is certain, this freedom remains bound by the obligation of the vow, as long as the vow has not been fulfilled for certain. Then, only the first opinion can be admitted, since the probability would be such to presume he would act with moral certitude since he has already satisfied the vow. Furthermore, what we have said about a vow must also be understood on the satisfaction of sacramental penance.

30.—If someone were to make a vow and later furnish the work he already promised, but forgot that the contracted obligation was from a vow, it is very probable that he is not held to furnish that work again, as the authors commonly teach (Suarez, *de rel.* l. 4, c. 26 n. 8; Laymann, l. 4. t. 4. c. 4. n. 7; Sanchez, *dec.* lib. 1, c. 13, n. 10; Bonacina, *de leg.* q. 1, p. 10 n. 15, with Azor, Lessius and others). Nevertheless, it is always apparent (and the one making the vow can certainly judge), that if he would have remembered the vow he would have applied the work for its satisfaction; at any rate, the fact must commonly be presumed that everyone has a general will to satisfy the burden prior to due obligation, so the work adds over and above what is asked.

31.—It is inferred 3) that a subject, although he might not be held to render obedience to a superior that commands him in those matters that are certainly illicit, he is, on the other hand, held to do so in those matters which are doubtful, whether they are licit or not; because in doubtful matters, the power to command favors the possession of the superior, which cannot be despoiled in doubt, as is commonly taught by the authors (Cajetan, q. 169, art. 2 ad 4; the Continuator of Tournely, *de praecip. statuum oblig.* part. 2, cap. 2 art. 3 quaer. 5 r. 2, and many others along with St. Antoninus, St. Bonaventure, Cabassutius, de Soto, etc.).

But, de Soto, Lessius, Sanchez, the Salamancans, etc., most commonly place the limit that, as often as a matter that has been commanded is exceedingly difficult and troublesome, namely, if a subject ought to expose himself or another to the danger of great spiritual or temporal damage by obedience. We will explain these things more fully when we treat on particular precepts (lib. 5, cap. 1, n. 47).

32.—It is inferred, 4) That a young man that is uncertain as to whether he has attained his 21st year is not held to fast. Yet, a man that is uncertain whether he has attained to his 60th year, after that has been completed, the man is probably obliged to fast, as we will say in book 4, n. 1036, he is held to fast because then *lex possidet* in regard to the precept of fasting. The same must be said about a man who doubts that he is of the requisite age for Holy Orders, or to receive a benefice; for then possession favors the precept. The same must also be said about a man who, on Saturday, doubts whether it is past midnight; for then he cannot eat meat since in regard to the precept of abstinence *lex possidet.* Otherwise, if someone is uncertain about this on Thursday because then after attentiveness has been applied he can licitly eat meat, since sill *libertas possidet.* (Laymann l. 1, c. 4, n. 35; Sanchez, *de matr.* disp. 40 et 41; Busembaum and many others).

33.—It is inferred, 5) If after a marriage has been contracted in good faith a doubt about its validity comes up, before the inquiry of truth the one doubting cannot ask for the debt, but is held to render it from *cap. Dominus, de sec. nutp.*, because the spouse that is unaware of the doubt still possess the right of petition. But after the inquiry, the one doubting can also petition; as de Soto, Habert, Wigandt, Roncaglia, Sanchez, the Salamancans etc. hold is more probable. (See what is going to be said in book 6, n. 903 and 904).

34.—It is inferred 6) A man that is certain about a debt and doubtful about the payment is held to pay, as Suarez, Vasquez, de Lugo and others commonly teach with Sanchez (*in dec.* l. 1, c. 10, n. 12). Yet, in some case where even the creditor may be uncertain about the law, Laymann (l. 1, tr. 1, c. 2), Diana (p. 4. tr. 3, r. 35) and Sporer (*de consc.* cap. 1, n. 83) with Tamburinius believe that a debtor is only held to the part proportionate to the doubt. Still, Laymann adds that he would not dare to condemn the creditor if he demands the whole thing.

35.—*Quaeritur:* I. Whether a possessor in good faith, when a doubt arises, is held to restore something proportionate to the doubt? If the doubt is equal for and against, the common opinion (with Sanchez *in dec.* l. 1, c. 10, n. 9, against a few writers), is that the possessor is held to nothing, from *reg. 65 de reg. jur. in 6* where it is read: "*In pari casu melior est conditio possidentis,*"[8] and *reg. 128,* "In pari causa possessor potior haberi debet."[9] But what if the reasons against the possessor were to be valid?

The first opinion says that although he might have a probable reason on his behalf, still he is held in that case to the restitution proportionate to the greater inclination, because the condition of the possessor is certainly better when all parties are equal, but not in an unequal doubt. Thus Sanchez (*de matr.* l. 2, disp. 41, n. 19) with Coninck., Valent., and Ledesma with the Salamancans (tr. 15, *de rest.* c. 1, punct. 3 §3 n. 67).

Nevertheless, *the second opinion* is more probable and common, and teaches he is held to nothing unless it is morally certain that the thing is someone else's. Thus Palaus, tr. 1 d. 3 p. 2, n. 11; de Lugo d. 17, n. 93, Roncaglia *de rest.* c.

---

[8] In the same position, the condition of the possessor is better.

[9] In an equal case the possessor is in a better position.

2, qu. 3. r. 2 with Laymann, Cardenas, Dicastillus, Tamb., Diana, Burg., and others with Croix, l. 3, p. 2, n. 563, Mazzot., *de consc.* c. 3, Sporer *de consc.,* c. 1 sect. 4, n. 66, with Molina and St. Augustine, lib. *de fide* et op. c. 7, related in *can. Si Virgo,* caus. 34 q. 1, which says, "He is rightly said to be the Possessor as long as he is unaware that he possesses someone else's thing." However, while it is not established for certain (Sporer says), the thing is another's as long as the possessor is unaware that he possesses another's. The particular reasoning of this opinion is that through possession in good faith a true right is acquired; for possession is so defined by the jurists: "*Jus insistendi in re non prohibita possideri.*"[10] This is the reason why ownership of a thing, until there is a doubt, the possessor retains the right of insistence; nevertheless so that before diligence has been applied to ascertain the truth, he is held to preserve the thing; but after diligence, and the truth has not been ascertained, he can consume it and even sell it, after the buyer has been made aware of the doubt concerning the thing. And on account of this principal reasoning Sanchez (*in dec.* dict. n. 9.) changed an opinion that he had defended elsewhere and followed the second opinion. Even Cardinal Sfondratus, *in reg. sac.* 1. § 20., n. 11, says that one may not proceed against the possessor except from certitude. Hence it seems hardly probable what Roncaglia adds (*de restit.* c. 2, q. 3, r. 2), namely that if the reasons favoring the possessor are only tenuously probable, then he is held to restore a thing, at least in regard to the greater part; on the other hand, if the most probable reasons were against the possessor in this way, then they would lay the foundation of moral certitude against him so that he is held to restore the whole thing; but if it is otherwise, he is held to restore nothing.

---

[10] The right of insistence on ownership of a thing not forbidden.

36.—*Quaeritur:* II. What if there is a probable reason against the possessor, and nothing on his own behalf?

The first opinion holds that if the probable reason generates a unique supposed assent that the thing is someone else's, so that the possessor could not assent that the thing is his own, then he is held to restore it. If it is otherwise, he may still probably reckon the thing to be his own. So the authors teach (Sanchez, *dec.* l. 1, c. 10, n. 9, citing Vasquez; Paulaus, tom. 1, tr. 1, disp. 5, p. 2; Renzi, *de 7 praec.*, 3 sect., 2. q. 15; Tamb., dec. lib. 1, c. 5, 5, 7 *verb. Restitutio*, n. 7), Viva *opusc. de consc.* dub. q. 2, art. 1, n. 8, in fin., where he says that when the possessor has a probable reason against him, and nothing on his own behalf, then he has moral certitude that it is someone else's thing.

The second opinion, which Salas holds, (1. 2. q. 21, tr. 8, disp. *unic.* sect. 23, n. 231), says that still, when reasons for the opposed party generate assent; they do not convict nor is the assent certain morally, rather it is merely supposed, including the terror which is necessarily included in opinion, then the possessor can retain the thing because the possession outweighs all other reasons that do not convict.

It seems that the aforesaid opinions can be reconciled. It is certain that a legitimate position attributes to someone a certain right of retention of the matter, so long as the right of the other party is not certain, as Palaus, Laymann, Sporer, and others commonly say that were cited above with what Croix said (n. 563). And Viva himself (*loc. cit.*) concedes it, saying that, "possession in good faith produces a certain right which ought to prevail over a probable right and thus, the right of the other is not morally certain." The reason is that legitimate possession is founded on the certain presumption on the justice of the possessor, as Wigandt (*exam.*, 3, *de Consc.*) and de Lugo (*de just.*, d. 17, n. 94) argue. Therefore, even if a probable judgment is present against the possessor, and no probability assists him, nevertheless the presumption arising from that possession is present, which attributes to him a certain right that cannot be overcome, unless they convict it by the certain right of another with certain reasons.

For that reason, the first opinion saying that the possessor is held to make restitution when he has a contrary supposed assent and nothing on his own behalf, is rightly understood when the possession would be weak in some part, inasmuch as it was begun with a doubt, or with doubtful faith, so that no legitimate presumption would seem to arise for the possessor; for then, truly, no probability would assist him and then the unique supposed judgment itself would hold the thing to be someone else's. Otherwise, if he had certain and legitimate possession in good faith, then that possession alone, even if no other reason were to support him, would offer him a certain right that cannot be overcome except by certain opposed reasons, but not by probable opinion, which necessarily includes fear. And in this, Cardinal de Lugo clearly agrees (*loc. cit.*), when he says possession of itself begets the prevailing presumption for the possessor, lest he would be deprived, unless it should not be established on the right of the other party through proof overcoming the presumption of possession. Wherefore, Croix rightly concludes (lib. 1, n. 501), that although there might not be a probable argument for the possessor, still, if there is no other argument for the claimant but a probable one, the possessor still licitly retains it, because possession is a certain right of retention, against which nothing prevails but certitude. This same thing will be equally said on a probably null marriage. (See book 6, n. 904).

37.—*Quaeritur:* III. What if a possessor in good faith, when a doubt comes up, were to culpably neglect to apply diligence, but later could no longer be found to be the owner? La Croix, lib. 3, p. 2, n. 564; Roncaglia, loc. cit., et the Salamancans tr. 13 *de restit.*, c. 1, punct. 3 § 3, n. 64, with

Sanchez, Lessius, etc., say that in that case, the possessor is held to restore the matter proportionate to the doubt. But on the other hand, Palaus, tom.1 tr. 1 d. 3 p. 2, n. 9, Bonacina, *de contr*. d. 1 . q. 2. p. 2 n. 8, Tamburinius *de consc*. c. 3, v. *Restitutio*, n. 9, cum Diana et Rebellus, think it is probable that the possessor, although he would sin mortally by omitting diligence, nevertheless is held to nothing since on one side the loss inflicted is uncertain, and on the other he should still retain the right of possession of what was acquired in good faith.

But I believe it must be more truly said, that such a possessor would be held to restore something (either to its owner or to the poor if the owner is uncertain). The reason is that when he culpably deprived the owner in regard to the hope which the owner could have for a thing, and that hope was certainly of an estimable price, now the damage inflicted on the owner is certain, who also certainly possessed that hope. Still, I think restitution must not be made for a quantity of the doubt, so that, if the reasons of either party were equal, the thing must not be restored for half of its price, but less and perhaps much less; because that hope of the owner could not be reckoned for half of the value of the thing, but much less when the probability of reasoning on the one hand favors one party, and certainly on the other side favored the possessor and still favors him: for possession of the thing is reckoned to be greater than possession of a hope.

Moreover, Tamburinius (*l. c.* n. 7), with Villal. and others notes: I. that if a possessor should begin to doubt from probable reasons, he is certainly held to discover the truth, but he may act otherwise if he were uncertain for only tenuous reasons.

Moreover, Croix (l. 3 p. 2 n. 562 along with Vasq., Laymann, Palaus, Sanch., Mol. etc. and Roncaglia dict. q. 3 r. 1), notes: II. It is not improbable that when the possessor (even one who began possession with a doubt) were to have a thing from a possessor in good faith, if later due diligence were impossible, he is held to restore nothing; for then he legitimately succeeds to every right of it.

38.—At length, what must be said in a doubt on a case where, if one should consume some food or drink, whether he could then receive the Eucharist? Sanchez (lib. 2 *de matr.* disp. 41 n. 40), Roncaglia (*de Euchar.* c. 5 qu. 6) and the Salamancans (*eod. tit.* tr. 4. c. 7, punct. 4 n. 69) with others say he cannot; besides, (as they say) because he does not, by means of a dubious satisfaction, satisfy a certain law to not communicate without fasting; and because it seems it is not without grave irreverence. But others say, that in such a doubt he can rightly communicate (de Lugo, *de Eucharistia*, disp. 15, n. 43; Castropalaus, disp. 5 punct. 8 n. 9; Laymann. l. 1, tract. 1, c. 5, n. 36; Diana tom. 2, tr. 4 *de sacrament.* resol. 29; La Croix, l. 6. part 1 n. 576; Sporer, *de sacrificio missae*, cap. 6. n. 274, with Sa., Carden, Med., Gobat., Boss.). The reason for this is because the law of fasting is not positive, so that one were commanded to fast absolutely as a necessary requisite to communicate; rather it is prohibitive, whereby each man is forbidden to accede to communion if he has taken some food or drink, lest he would join earthly food with divine food. For that, as de Lugo says (*loc. cit.*) is established from the Council of Braga; II, can. 10, where it is forbidden "lest someone after having taken any food, would consecrate the oblation on the altar." Likewise, in the seventh Council of Toledo, can. 2, it is contained: "No one can presume to say Mass after having taken up the least food and drink." Likewise, in the Ecumenical Council of Constance, sess. 13 § *In nomine Sanctae*, etc., it is said: "The authority of the holy canons and the approved custom of the Church has preserved and preserves that a sacrament of this sort ought not be confected after dinner, nor received by the faithful who do not fast except in the case of weakness or of another necessity by a law, that has either been conceded or admitted by the Church." It is likewise cited by de Lugo, (loc. cit., n. 18 and 19). So, now that we have posited that the law of fasting is prohibitive, namely, lest someone were to communicate after taking up food, the fact that one broke the fast must be proved, so that he should be forbidden to communicate. In a doubt it is the case that something was done which law in force forbids, he is not held to abstain from communion while still *libertas ejus possidet*, for, as de Lugo says, someone who, after an examination has been made, does not know that he ate something, is not opposed to the precept of the Church to not communicate after eating food. Therefore, he communicates licitly in doubt about the breaking of the fast, and, as a matter of fact, since in that case communion would only be forbidden to the one that broke the fast, rightly *libertas possidet* in regard to communicating, until it is not certain about the breaking of the fast. This reason does not seem to be condemned as futile, at least in the case the law forbidding communion does not seem certain, and as much as doubt does not oblige, according to what must be said in n. 55, *et seq.* But to the second reason of irreverence I make the opposite response. It is not considered irreverent when someone uses the right of his freedom; especially if he approaches communion out of devotion.

39.—Whether the same must be said, that one can communicate, who doubts whether he consumed food or drink after midnight? De Lugo says no, because (as he says) when someone knows that he ate and is uncertain whether he ate after midnight, it seems the burden of proof is incumbent upon him to show he did not eat after midnight. On the other hand, for the sake of the peace of such a man, we say that the reason which was adduced above, that the law is prohibitive, not positive, if it avails for the first case, also avails for the second. The prohibition is for men to not communicate if they ate something after midnight; therefore, if they are not able to communicate, it must be proven that they ate something, so the fact that they ate something after midnight must also be proved. Moreover, other learned doctors hold the affirmative opinion cited above, to which the learned Father Eusebius Amort is added (*Theol.* tom. 2, disp. 5, qu. 4). He asks if a man that eats in doubt as to whether the bell tolled midnight, could communicate on the following day? He responds that: "He can communicate because the condition of the possessor is better, so long as presumptions are not given to the contrary that are so strong that the one acting would more probably believe that the bell tolled midnight.

CHAPTER III

On a Probable Conscience

40. *What a probable conscience is. How many different species of probabilities are enumerated?*

41. *What is probability of fact, and what is law?*

42. *It is never permitted to use probability of fact with the danger of harm to another.*

43. *What opinion are we held to follow in a matter of faith?*

44. *What opinion ought a doctor to follow?*

45. *Whether one can use a remedy that is less safe?*

46. *What if he despairs of the health of a sick man?*

47. *What opinion is a judge held to follow?*

48. *What opinion is a minister held to follow when he confers the sacraments?*

49. *What if necessity is present?*

50. *Whether it might be permitted to use probable opinion in regard to contracting a marriage as well as in regard to the jurisdiction of the confessor in a case where it is presumed the Church supplies? (On this see what must be said in book 6, n. 573, and on common Error, n. 572).*

51. *Whether what is said about the administration of the sacraments regarding the use of a safe opinion, the same must be said on the reception of the sacraments?*

52. *What if a hunter doubts whether he is about to slay a wild animal or a man?*

53. *Whether it is permitted to use probable probability of law? On an opinion tenuously probable.*

54. *On a very probable opinion.*

55. *Dissertation on the regulated use of probable opinion, even to n. 89.*

40.—A probable conscience is when someone, supported by some probable opinion, forms for himself a dictate of reason from certain reflexive or concomitant principles to act licitly. Nevertheless, here we must notice a different species of probability is given: one opinion is tenuously probable, another is probable, another is more probable, and another still is the most probable; one is certain morally, another safe and another safer. A tenuously probable opinion is that which rests upon some foundation but not on such that it would avail to bring the prudent man to assent to it; however, we cannot licitly use this opinion according to *Proposition 3* condemned by Pope Innocent XI, which says, "In general, when we do something confidently according to probability whether intrinsic or extrinsic, however slight, provided there is no departure from the bounds of probability, we always act prudently."[11] It is probable, which rests upon a serious foundation, whether inwardly on reason or outwardly on authority, which avails to bring the prudent man to assent, even if with fear of the opposite. A more probable opinion, is that which rests upon a more serious foundation, but also with a prudent fear of the opposite, so that the contrary will also seem probable. The most probable opinion is that which rests upon the most serious foundation, for which reason the opposite is either thought to be tenuous or doubtfully probable. We always licitly use this opinion and it is certain from a proposition condemned by Pope Alexander VIII, which says: "It is not lawful to follow a (probable) opinion, even the most probable among the probables." The opinion, or a morally certain judgment, is that which excludes every prudent fear of falsity, so that the opposite is altogether considered improbable. At length, an opinion is safe which recedes from every fear of sin. But

---

[11] Denzinger 1153.

a safer opinion is that which recedes more from danger, even if it does not rest upon firmer reasoning.

41.—Next, it must be noticed that on the one hand there is probability of fact, and on the other, of law. Probability *of fact* is that which is in the truth of a matter, or the substance of the matter, without a doubt whether a sacrament conferred with such a matter would be valid, or not; whether a contract resting upon such an agreement would be usurious or not. Moreover, probability *of law* is in regard to the integrity of the action, *i.e.* whether it would be permitted to confer a sacrament with such a matter, or whether to enter into a contract with such an agreement.

42.—Now that we have posited these, we say it is never lawful to use a probable opinion in a probability *of fact* with danger of harm to another or to himself; because a probability of this sort hardly removes the danger of harm; for, if that opinion is false, it will not avoid harm to one's neighbor or the one carrying out the work. For example, baptism conferred with saliva is really null, so that the infant would remain without baptism; the probability for the opposite cannot even effect that it would be valid.

43.—Hence, it is inferred, 1) It is not licit in a matter of faith, and in all things looking to eternal salvation by the necessity of means, to follow an opinion that is less probable (as Proposition 4 condemned by Innocent XI ineptly said), nor more probable; rather we are held to follow the safer opinion, and by the consequent, we ought to embrace a religion more safe, such a kind that is far from doubt as our Catholic religion; for when any religion you like is false, even if something would seem more probable to someone, nevertheless embracing it, while leaving behind what is safer, by no means escapes the loss of his eternal salvation.

44.—It is inferred, 2) That a doctor is held to apply safer medication that is going to be beneficial for the sick, but he cannot use remedies that are less probable, after abandoning the more probable or safer: for in medication what is safer for the health of the sick man is more probable.

45.—But there is a doubt as to: 1) Whether, when a medication does not appear certain, a doctor can use a remedy that is less probable, after the more probable has been abandoned? Azor, Aragon, Montesinus, Salas, etc. cited by the Salamancans (*de V. Praec. decal. tr. 25, cap. 1, punct. 6, §2., n. 143*) affirm it. But Sanchez (*dec.* l. 1 cap. 9, n. 41), and the Salamancans themselves (loc. cit., n. 144) along with de Soto, Suarez and Bonacina more probably reject it, because a doctor, by reason of his office, is held to provide better for the health of the infirm not only from charity but also from charity and of a tacit contract, and for this reason receives his wage.

46.—There is a doubt, 2) Whether a doctor that despairs of the health of the sick man could apply remedies to him when he is uncertain whether they would help or hurt him? It is certain and common that, *a*) if it were probable that the remedy were going to be beneficial then he can, nay more he is held, to apply it when he does not have one that is more certain. (See *Salamant.* loc. cit., n. 150, in fine.) It is certain, *b*) that he is not permitted to apply a remedy to a sick man, when he has despaired of the latter's health, when he is unfamiliar with whether it is healthy or harmful, simply to experiment upon the him. Commonly the Salamancans (n. 148.), with Navarre, Azor, Castropalaus, Salas, Perez, etc. hold this. The reasoning is that it is illicit is to try out an experiment that brings danger of death to the sick man or would accelerate it. It is certain, *c*) with Sanchez (*loc. cit.*, n. 42, et Salm. n. 152, in fine), that if a remedy is doubtfully beneficial and certainly not going to do harm, it must altogether be applied to the sick man. In regard to the question, however, there is a two-fold opinion.

The *first opinion* denies that (as we said above), it is never lawful to expose the sick man to danger of death, nor to accelerate it, as the Salamancans say (*loc. cit.*, c. 1, n. 150), along with Azor, Castropalaus, Sylvestrus, Villalobos, etc.

But the *second opinion*, which is probable, is perhaps more probable, and Sanchez holds it (*dec.* l. 1, c. 9, n. 39), along with Valencia, likewise Busembaum, (l. 5, infra n. 291 ad IV), and Bonancina, Filliucci, Reginaldus, Bardi (cited by the Salamancans n. 149); this affirms it is licit because if he despairs of the health of the sick man, it is more in conformity with prudence and the will of the sick man (especially if he expressly consents to this) to apply a dubious remedy to him when to omit that would mean certain death. Antoine (*Tract. de Oblig.* c. 7, treating on the duty of a doctor) holds it for certain. Additionally, Sanchez (n. 42) with Navarre note that even if the doctor cannot lend his authority to a remedy against his opinion, still, if it is approved by other doctors, and the sick man consents, he can licitly use it.

47.—It is inferred 3) That a judge is held to make judgement according to a more probable opinion; for he is held by divine and human precept to bestow his justice upon someone for the greater weight of reasons which favor him. For this reason, the second proposition condemned by Pope Innocent XI said: "I think probably a judge can make a judgement according to a less probable opinion." Yet, Cardenas and others rightly notice that if a guilty man is in legitimate possession of a controversial thing, and has for himself probable reason, a judge cannot rob him of it, even if the actor brings more probable reasons for his behalf; for legitimate possession (as we said in n. 35) gives to the possessor a certain right to retain a thing, until the right of the other man is established. (See what will be said in book 5, n. 212, Qu. II, where it is profusely proved.)

48.—It is inferred 4) That in the conferring of the Sacraments the minister cannot use an opinion that is neither probable nor more probable in regard to their validity, but is held to follow a safe opinion, that which is either safer or morally certain. It is clear from the 1st proposition condemned by Innocent XI, which said: "When conferring the sacraments it is not illicit to follow a probable opinion on the validity of a sacrament while the safer is forsaken, unless the law, convention or danger of incurring grave injury would forbid it. For that reason one must not use a probable opinion only in the conferral of Baptism, priestly or episcopal Orders."

49.—I said, unless *necessity were present*; and indeed in extreme necessity we can well use any opinion, not only a probable one, but even a tenuously probable one for the validity of the Sacrament, as Holzmann, (*de Bapt.* a. 2, n. 97.), Antoine, (*de bapt.* q. 1.), Cuniliat., (*de Sacr.* in gen., c. 1, §3. n. 3) and others commonly say. However, this is so provided that the sacrament is conferred *sub conditione*, since the condition sufficiently repairs the injury to the sacrament that would result if, perhaps, it were conferred invalidly, and vice versa; sufficient necessity is a just cause to confer the sacrament conditionally. (See what will be said in book 6, c. 1, *de bapt.* n. 103, v. *Uncertain matter*, and *de poen.* n. 482, in fine).

50.—A great many authors say that we can licitly use probable opinion where it is presumed that the Church supplies; that can come about in the sacrament of matrimony to convalidate a contract only probably valid, if perhaps the contract is null on account of an impediment which the Church removes by supplying, and in the sacrament of Penance to supply jurisdiction to a confessor if by chance he lacks it. They call this the most common opinion (*Viva in prop. 1, damn. ab Innocent. XI*, n. 20; La Croix, l. 6 n. 117, with Suarez, Lessius, Coninck, Regin., etc.). On the other hand, Sporer (de consc. c. 1, n. 56) with Dicastillus, calls it morally certain; and the practice of the whole Church attests to this. (De Lugo, disp. 19, n. 31, with

Ariaga, Suarez, and Diana quoted by Cardenas, *in prop. 1, damn. ab Innocent. XI, diss.* 11, n. 166 et *seqq.*) Yet, see book 6, n. 573, where a great many things are said about the jurisdiction of a confessor, and how and when it is presumed that the Church supplies. Moreover, whether the Church always supplies jurisdiction in the Sacrament of Penance while common error remains, see *ibid.*, n. 572.

51.—Besides, it is asked whether what has been said about the administration of the sacraments must also be said on the reception, so that no one could receive the sacrament with probable opinion?

The first opinion affirms this, and Cardenas (*in prop. 1 damn. ab Innocen. XI,* diss., 2, c. 3., n. 18), Viva (sup. *ead. prop.* 1), and La Croix (l. 6, n. 103) hold this. Their reason is that the special reverence due to the sacraments demands that they not be exposed to the danger of deceit. Hence, these authors say, from the aforementioned proposition 1 that was condemned in regard to the ministration, that it is also virtually condemned in regard to the reception, since the same danger is present in both.

But *the second opinion* denies this, which Pontius (*de matr.* l. 4, c. 25, n. 9), Sanchez (*dec.* l. 1, cap. 9, n. 33), along with Vasquez, Salon., Syr. Perez and others quoted by Cardenas (n. 17) hold. Likewise, Sporer (*de cons.* c. 1, n. 57), and Viva (in his *Th. Mor. de poenit.*, q. 3, art. 3, n. 9), where it seems he revoked himself, at least in regard to his opinions which are deduced on the side of those receiving are everywhere deduced by the faithful in praxis. The reason is that no injury is thought to be inflicted on the sacrament when someone uses probable opinion; nor does it seem the sacraments demand a greater reverence than probable, which other divine precepts demand. And this opinion, says professor Hozes (in the same propos., 1 quoted by Cardenas, n. 27) has not lost its probability from the condemnation of the Pope, because it is not certain the proposition was not condemned more in respect to the reverence toward the sacraments than in respect to charity towards those receiving them. Nevertheless, these not withstanding, I think we must not recede from the first opinion, at least because the second can almost never be deduced in practice by those receiving the sacraments without their own detriment to the soul.

52.—Lastly, it is inferred, 5) that if someone is uncertain whether what he saw in the forest was a wild animal or a man, he cannot slay it even if he thinks it is probable or more probable that it is a wild animal; for if that animal really were a man, that probability, or greater probability, would not free the man from death. Therefore, it must be said in respect to the whole, it is never lawful to use a probable opinion in a probability of fact, where there is danger of loss or injury to one's neighbor.

53.—Nevertheless, it must be said otherwise about an opinion which is probable in a probability of law; for then someone can licitly use that opinion, forming a morally certain conscience for himself about the integrity of his action. Because then, although the law might be doubtful, and not proposed manifestly enough, a law of this sort is no law, or at least not one that obliges, as we will see below in the dissertation on the use of probable opinion, n. 57 et *seqq.*

54. Now it remains to be seen, what probability an opinion ought to gain so that we might avail to use it licitly? There are two things for certain from no. 40. The first is, it is illicit to use a tenuously probable opinion, as is clear from propos. 3 condemned by Innocent XI. Moreover, this proposition was duly condemned; for a tenuous probability cannot be called true probability, just as tenuous strength or tenuous expertise cannot be called true strength or true expertise, but must rather be called feebleness and ignorance. We also say the same thing about the opinion which is certainly less probable; and indeed, while an

opinion for a law, *e.g.*, is by far of greater weight (as we will explain more distinctly below, n. 56), it evades moral certainty, and effects that the opposite would be rendered in favor of freedom, so it is either improbable, or dubiously probable, and therefore we cannot use it. On the other hand, it is certainly permitted to use the most probable opinion, as is certain from propos. 3 condemned by Alexander VIII, which was related in the aforesaid n. 40.

Now two questions remain to be argued, which it is fitting to address in particular in the following dissertation.

DISSERTATION
On the Regulated Use of Probable Opinion
or
The Moral System
For the Selection of Opinions which we can Licitly Follow

55.—We propose to discuss two questions in the present dissertation. The first is whether it would be licit to follow an opinion that is less probable, after forsaking the more probable, which favors the law. The second, whether it would be lawful to embrace something that is less safe when there are two concurrent contrary opinions, equally or as it were, equally more probable. It is said, *equally or, as it were equally more probable*, because (just as all probablists and antiprobablists agree) when among each opinion there is a restrained preponderance, so that it would go beyond very tenuous and dubious, then both opinions are reckoned equally probable according to that common axiom: *parum pro nihilo reputatur*.

56.—In regard to the first question I shall answer far more expediently; for the resolution is clear.

I say: I. That if an opinion, which favors the law, should seem *certainly* more probable, we are altogether held to follow it, but we cannot embrace the opposite, which favors freedom. The reason is because we ought to licitly act in doubtful matters to seek the truth and follow it; but where the truth cannot be clearly discovered, we are held to embrace at least that opinion which is nearer to the truth; such is a more probable opinion.

I said certainly more probable, because when an opinion favoring the law is certainly, and without any hesitation, more probable, then that opinion cannot be anything but notably more probable. In that case the safer opinion will not now be dubious, rather it is morally or almost morally certain. At least, it cannot be strictly said to be more dubious, since it should have a certain foundation for itself that it is true. For that reason, it then happens that an opinion being less safe, which lacks a certain foundation, shall remain of either tenuous or at least dubious probability in respect to the one that is safer; and therefore, it is not prudent, but imprudent to will to embrace it. For as often as it appears certain to the intellect, a truth favors the law much more than freedom, then the will cannot prudently and without fault on its part, adhere to what is less safe. Accordingly, in that case where a man does not act resting upon his own judgment or credulity, but rather by some attempt where he inserts into his intellect by his own will to remove that side which appears to have the greater appearance of truth and bends toward that side which does not appear true to him, nay more, which seems to have no certain foundation whereby it could be true. And thus the Apostle says, "For all that is not from faith is sin." (Romans 14:23).

57.—Now in regard to the other question, which we will flesh out here more broadly, I say that when a less safe opinion is equally or nearly equally probable, someone can licitly follow it, and this must be proved.

Before all things, we ought to suppose two as certain: first, that to act licitly we must necessarily have a moral certitude about the honesty of the action. Second, that this certitude can be held not only from a direct principle, but also from a reflexive one, in which that moral certitude is communicated to the action. So, with these prefaced:

58.—I say: II. That if an opinion which favors freedom is only probable or equally probable and there is another which favors the law, someone cannot follow it insofar as it might be probable, since to act licitly, probability alone does not suffice, rather a moral certitude on the honesty of the action is required, according to what St. Paul says in Romans

14:23, "Everything that is not from faith is sin." It is said, *from faith*, namely from the certain dictate of conscience, so that were a man to persuade himself in his conscience that by acting he does rightly, exactly as St. John Chrysostom, St. Ambrose and others with St. Thomas (qu. 17 *de verit.* art. 3) explain the phrase *from faith*. For that reason, I think the saying of the Probabilists, "He who acts probably acts prudently," is false.

59.—I say: III. When two equally probable opinions coincide, although a less safe opinion cannot be held, since (as we said), probability alone (note: probability alone), scarcely offers a firm foundation to act licitly, nevertheless, that opinion which favors freedom, since it is with equal probability as the opposite which favors the law, certainly introduces a serious doubt whether the law exists as well as what action it might forbid, and hence it can be said it was not sufficiently promulgated. Consequently, provided that in this case it was not promulgated, it cannot oblige, so much the more because an uncertain law cannot induce a certain obligation. This is also the opinion of St. Thomas Aquinas, which I follow, and which appears certain to me, both on account of the authority of theologians (as we will see), the Fathers (whose doctrines can be observed in this dissertation, n. 70. See also, Christianus Lupus (tom. xi Dissert. *de usu senten. probabl.*, where he amasses many authorities of the Fathers), and on account of intrinsic reasons which have not yet been clearly presented, but are certain and evident, as will be shown.

60.—The prince of theologians, St. Thomas (1. 2. qu. 90, art. 1), so teaches: "A law is a type of rule and the measure of actions, according to which someone is induced to act, or is restrained from acting; for a law is so called from binding (*ligando*), because it obliges one to do something." Hence it follows that the Angelic doctor teaches that this rule is the measure as it is applied to all men, and that they are held to keep it, so it ought to be manifest to them in promulgation. He says in the same place, "A law is imposed upon others through the manner of a rule and measure; but a rule and measure is imposed through this, which is applied to these that are ruled and measured. For this reason, for the purpose that a law obtains the power to oblige (which is proper for law), it is necessary that it be applied to men, who ought to be ruled according to it. For such an application happens through this, that in notice of these matters it is deduced from the promulgation itself. This is the reason that promulgation is necessary, that the law would have its force."

61.—Moreover, that a law cannot oblige subjects unless it has been promulgated to them is an axiom ascertained as a fact by all, "Laws are established when they are promulgated," as Gratian writes in the canon *In istis*, dist. 4. The reason is clear, because a law remaining only in the mind of the legislator is nothing but a mere thought, or an intention to constitute a law, but in fact no law has been constituted which obliges subjects. Hence, St. Thomas defines a law as, "A certain ordination of reason to the common good promulgated by someone that has care of the community." (1.2. qu. 90, art. 4.) No one has any doubt, as Francis Henno writes (*tr. de leg.*), that the promulgation should be the very essence of a law; for as Louis Habert rightly said (t. 3 *de leg.*, c. 6 q. 4), promulgation pertains to the reasoning of the law, and the force to oblige." Cardinal Gotti adds (*Theol.* tom. 2, tr. 5, *de leg.*, q. 1 dub. 5 §5 num. 18), that promulgation is an indispensable requisite to oblige subjects, "On this point, that a law would oblige in the second act, it is indispensably required that it be proposed to those subject to it by promulgation." Domingo de Soto hands down the same thing (*de Justitia et Jure*, lib. 1, q. 1 art. 4), saying: "No law has any force of law before promulgation, but then they are established when they are promulgated."

He adds right after, "Therefore, this conclusion permits no exception." The French doctor Duvalius writes the same thing in 1. 2. S. Th. *de leg.*, q. 2, saying that an eternal law could not oblige men from eternity, "because," as he says, "the reasoning of the law is that it is promulgated to subjects; but no one was subject from eternity." Fr. Gonet writes the same thing (*de leg., d.* 2, art. 2), "an eternal law could not oblige creatures from eternity by a defect of promulgation." Lorichius Thesaur. writes the same thing (ver. Lex, n. 6), "[The eternal law] was promulgated to men when it became known to them." My bitter adversary, Fr. Patutius says the same thing in his *Theologia Moralis* (*de leg.*, c. 5, n. 7), "Certainly all agree that promulgation is altogether necessary for a law to obtain the power to oblige." Someone will wonder why I have amassed so many authorities here to prove this doctrine since no one calls it into doubt; but he should know that I have done this because the strength of my opinion depends upon the fact that a doubtful law does not oblige, as we will see below.

62.—Next, St. Thomas, holding the same thing as certain, objects to himself with this opposition, "Natural Law has especially the reasoning of a law; but natural law does not need promulgation, therefore it is not from the reasoning of the law that it be promulgated." And he responds thus: "It must be said that the promulgation of the law of nature is from itself, that God inserted it into the minds of men to know naturally."(1.2. q. 90, ar. 4 ad 1.) So Sylvius speaks with a clearer explanation (1. 2. qu. 90, art. 4, in fine): "Actually, then (the law) is promulgated to each man, when he receives the cognition from God dictating what he must embrace according to right reason, and from what he must flee." John Gerson teaches the same thing, "Law is a certain declaration made to a rational creature by which it recognizes what God determines about certain things to which he obliges the creature to perform or omit." (*de vita spir.*, etc., lect. 2, col.

176). Finally, Petrus de Lorca adds that, "In the same way, promulgation is intrinsic and essential for human laws, just as the judgment of reason and the intrinsic understanding is to the law of nature." (1.2, disp. 6, *de leg.*) This is why, without the judgment of reason and understanding, the promulgation of law is in no way sufficient to oblige.

63.—For a law to oblige, it not only must be promulgated but also must be promulgated as certain. And here, this point must be firmly established and so when assessing this for a long time it will not be recalled in vain, since it is necessary to repeat here many times what I have already written elsewhere and, moreover, from a foundation of this sort our opinion draws strength, namely that an uncertain law does not impose a certain obligation. Therefore, we say that no man can be held to keep some law unless it is manifested to someone as certain. With that posited, as we said, that a law necessarily must be promulgated that it would oblige, if a doubtful law were promulgated, it will merely promulgate a doubt, an opinion or a question, as to whether there is a law forbidding an action, but a law will not be promulgated. Hence, all agree in the assertion that a law, to oblige someone, ought to be certain and manifest and it ought to be manifested as certain or be made known to the man to whom it is promulgated. Let us hear that which the doctors commonly say on this opinion, or on this principle which we hand down as the greatest of all others. St. Thomas proves it. St. Isidore says that among the conditions for a law to oblige is that the law must be manifest. It is also held in the canon *Erit autem*, dist. 4, "A law will be manifest, etc." And that is also certain in civil law, as is clear from *Authent. Quibus modis nat.* ff. §. *Natura*, where it is said, "In doubt no one is presumed to be obligated.

64.—St. Thomas, speaking on the eternal and natural law, teaches that to this end, that it could be a measure to us, it ought to be very certain and made known to us. Let us attend to the words of the Holy Doctor. He objects to himself, "A measure ought to be very certain (nota); but the eternal law is unknown to us; therefore, it cannot be the measure of our will that the goodness of our will would depend on it." And he so responds, "Although the eternal law is unknown to us according to what is in the divine mind, nevertheless it is made known to us in some way through natural reason, which is derived from it as its own image, or is added from above through some revelation." (1. 2. qu. 19, art. 4, ad 3). The reason is obvious why law ought to be certain; since law, according to the Holy Doctor, is a measure and a rule whereby a man is measured and ruled concerning certain actions; he can in no way be rightly measured and ruled unless the measure and rule were certain that it would oblige, that it would also be made known to a man. "For law," writes the most learned Pierre Collet, "to oblige, ought to be given as a rule and hence be made known; and yet a law is not known except through promulgation, since through that alone it shall be made known in that manner which induces the necessity to obey." (Collet, *Theologia moralis, de leg.*, cap. 1, art. 2, concl. 2.) John Gerson hands down the same thing, saying that a law, to oblige, necessarily ought to be made manifest to a man, otherwise God cannot oblige him to keep it: "It is necessary (the words of Gerson are rather notable), for a manifestation of the ordination and will of God to be given, for through ordination alone, or through his will alone, God cannot absolutely impose an obligation on the creature; rather it is necessary for this end, that he would communicate notice equally to one and the other." (Gerson, *de vita spir.*, etc., lect. 2).

Gonet hands down the same thing, saying: "A man is not held to conform to the divine will ... except when the divine will is manifested to us in a command or a prohibition. (Gonet, *Clyp.* t. 3, d. 6, art. 2, n. 37 *in fin*). And in the same place he offers the reasoning for this, writing that the sin of man depends upon the will to transgress the law; but if sin (he says) would depend upon the existence or non existence of the law, then sin would be of fate, or of the case, no longer of the will, which would be a great absurdity: "Moreover," he writes, "it would be of fate, not of the will, that men sin or do not sin, insofar as that which they do is in conformity or not with the natural law unknown to them, which is most absurd since the true and only cause of sin is the created will, as acting out of conformity with the rules of morals. (Gonet *in Clypeo* theol., tom. 3, disp. 1, art. 4, §1, n. 48).

Sylvius teaches the same thing, saying, "Actually, then (the law) is promulgated to each man, when he receives the cognition from God dictating what must be embraced according to right reason, and from what he must flee." (in 1. 2. qu. 90, art. 4, in fine). Therefore, someone is not held to the law unless he understands that he must necessarily embrace it according to right reason. Fulgentius Cuniliati hands down the same thing, advancing absolutely: "The violators of the law are not those to whom the law has not yet been made known. (Tract. 1 *de reg. mor.* c. 3, §1 n 5.) Jodochus Lorichius hands down the same thing: "But the law is promulgated to men when it is made known to them." (*Thesaur. theol.*, verb: Lex, n. 6).

65.—From all the aforesaid the moral certitude of our opinion evidently appears, or rather the opinion of St. Thomas, who teaches this in many places. He expressly and absolutely advances this moral principle: "No one is bound by this precept except through the medium of knowledge of that precept."(Opusc. *de verit.* qu. 17, art. 3). The distinction between opinion and knowledge is taught by all philosophers along with St. Thomas: *Opinion* denotes a dubious or probable understanding of some truth; *knowledge*, on the other hand, signifies a certain and clear understanding. But let us hear the Angelic Doctor himself; that St. Thomas precisely understands by the term *knowledge* a certain understanding is clear because he proposes this question, "Whether conscience binds?" in the passage we just cited: "Yes, ... in respect to a command of some guide to bind in voluntary matters by the mode binding, which can happen to the will, just as a corporal action is in respect to binding some corporal matters by the necessity of coercion. Moreover, the corporal action of the agent never induces necessity in some matter except through contact of compression itself to the matter in which it acts. For that reason, someone is not bound by the command of some lord unless the command itself touches upon the man that is commanded. Moreover, it touches upon him through knowledge; for that reason, no one is bound by some precept except through the medium of knowledge of that precept. ... Just as the corporal agent does not act in corporal things except through contact; so in spiritual things it does not bind except through knowledge." The similitude that St. Thomas gives cannot be more clear and convincing to prove our opinion, or principle, namely that an uncertain law cannot induce a certain obligation. The Angelic Doctor says that knowledge of the precept is the nature of the bond which binds the will; for that reason, just as it is necessary to use rope to tie something, so to bind the will of a man so that he would exercise some action or be held to omit it, it is necessary that he have knowledge of the precept, otherwise that man remains free. On account of which, while he is in doubt as to whether there is or is not a precept forbidding or commanding (just as it happens when there are two coinciding opinions of the same weight that are equally probable), then he does not have knowledge of the precept, and therefore is not held to keep the precept.

To this end, the Angelic Doctor adds this in the same passage to explain the matter further: "Moreover, to see when (conscience) binds, it must be known that the binding taken morally from corporal things to spiritual ones conveys necessity; for he that is bound has the necessity of stopping in the place where he has been bound, and the power to divert to another is taken from him." Therefore, vice versa, just as someone who has not actually been bound by some bond has the power to divert when he wills, so he who has not been bound through knowledge of the precept is free from the obligation of the precept. Thus, the Holy Doctor writes that *law* is so called from binding,[12] "For a law [*lex*] is so called from binding [*ligando*], because it obliges one to act." (1. 2. qu. 90, art. 1).

St. Thomas vigorously confirms his opinion in another place, namely in 1.2. q. 19., art. 10, where he asks, "Whether it is necessary for the human will to conform to the divine will in the thing wanted, for the purpose that it is good?" And he responds in the affirmative, but a little later, in the same place, (art. 10, ad 1), the Holy Doctor objects to himself: "It seems that the will of man ought not always be conformed to the divine will in the thing wanted; for we cannot will what we do not know ... But we do not know what God wills in many things, therefore the human will cannot be conformed to the divine in the thing willed." He also responds: "*Ad Primum*, it must be said that what is willed by the divine is such according to common reason that we can know it; for we know when God wills anything, he wills under the reason of the good. And therefore whoever wills something for any reason of the good, he has the will in conformity to the divine will in so far as for the reason of the thing willed. But, (*note the following words*) we do not know in particular what God may will and to that extent we are not held to conform our will to the divine will." Therefore, St. Thomas teaches that when a man always

---

[12]   *Dicitur lex a ligando.*

wishes something for the sake of the good, he is already conformed to the divine will: but he is not in any way held to conform himself to the divine will in particular things that are unknown to him, and especially in precepts where this divine will has not been manifested. Moreover, Fr. Gonet clarifies it more distinctly, saying: "A man is not held to conform to the divine will in a material thing that is desired except when the divine will is manifested to us by a precept or prohibition." (*Clypeus* tom. 3, d. 6, art. 2, n. 57, in fin). Consequently, in doubt where we do not know whether God has imposed or forbidden something to us in a particular matter by some precept, we are not held to conform to the divine will in regard to such a precept unless the precept is manifested to us; as a matter of fact, as John Gerson hands down, where God does not manifest his will to us he can not (he says) oblige us to follow it. Let us repeat here his words that we related above: "It is necessary (the words of Gerson are rather notable), for a manifestation of the ordination and will of God to be given, since, through ordination alone or through his will alone, God cannot absolutely impose an obligation on the creature; rather, it is necessary for this end, that he would communicate knowledge equally to one and the other." (Gerson, *de vita spir.*, etc., lect. 2)

St. Thomas more boldly confirms the same opinion in another place (2, 2, q. 104, art. 4) where he expressly speaks on the obedience that is due to divine precepts. He so asks: "Whether God must be obeyed in all things?" The Holy Doctor affirms this, but objects to himself (ad 3): "Whoever obeys God conforms his will to the divine will even in the thing desired; but not insofar as we are held to conform our will to the divine in all things, as was held above (1.2. q. 19, art. 10, the text of which we already related above), therefore a man is not held to obey God in all things." He responds in this way (here let us pay attention to how the Holy Doctor was always firm and uniform in this his opinion): "Ad tertium, it must be said that even if a man is not always held to will what God wills, nevertheless he is always held to will what God wills him to will. And this is especially made known to a man through the divine precept." Therefore, a man is held to obey God and to be conformed to his will in regard to precepts, not now in all the ones which God wills, but only in those which God wills us to want (*Quod Deus vult nos velle*). But how will we know that which God himself does not only will, but also wills us to want? We will know, St. Thomas says, when it is made manifest to us by his divine precepts. "And this is especially made known to a man through the divine precept." Therefore, a doubtful acquaintance of a precept does not oblige one to keep it as if it were divine will, rather, a certain and manifest understanding of the precept, which certainly the word *innotescit* (it is made known) signifies. Therefore, where there are two opinions of equal weight, then in that case the promulgation of the law lacks sufficient promulgation, and it does not have the power to oblige, as it was established under the beginning of this *Monitum*. Moreover, a law which does not oblige is not a law, since "a law is so called from the word binding", as St. Thomas says; therefore a law that does not bind cannot be called a law.

Furthermore, both ancient and recent authors have followed this opinion that, when a precept is truly and strictly dubious, the obligation to keep it is not present. Raymundus wrote, (lib. 3 *de poenit.,* § 21), "You should not be inclined to judge mortal sins where it is not established for certain for you by a certain Scripture." Lactantius wrote (lib. 3, *Instit.,* c. 21): "It is for a very stupid man to obey their precepts, whether true or false, if he is uncertain." The text is contained in c. 31, *Cum in jure, de offic. et pot. jud. deleg.* where it is said: "Unless you will have been certain about a command, you are not compelled to carry out what is commanded." John Nyder wrote the same thing (*in Consol., An.*, par. 3, c.20), citing Bernard of Claremont: "From some matter where there are opinions among great men, and the Church has not determined another side, one ought to hold what he wills." St. Antoninus wrote the same thing: "According to Cancellarius, it harms a man no more to err in an article of faith which has still not been declared by the Church, when such an article must be believed from necessity, than for an act perpetrated against something doable to not be able to be moral, when it is not said to be certain from Scripture or a determination of the Church that such an act would be illicit. But it is certain that in a matter of faith it is licit before a determination of the Church to hold one side or the other without danger of sin; therefore, by comparison, it is lawful to hold one opinion in morals according to the limits noted above, where at least those knowing more do not think the contrary. (St. Antoninus, *part. 1 titl.* 3, c. 10 §10, *verb. Revertendo*). Therefore, according to St. Antoninus and Cancellarius (and especially Gerson), we are not held to follow a safer opinion where the safer does not seem to be more probable. Gabriel Biel wrote (in 4 sent. d. 16, qu. 4, concl. 3); "Nothing should be condemned as a mortal sin when there is no evident reasoning about it or the manifest authority of Scripture." Domingo de Soto writes that a law, since it is a rule of actions, a man must *observe* it, without a doubt, because he should understand it as certain: "It is necessary for one that uses a rule to observe it." (*De just.* l. 1, q. 1, art. 4). For that reason, he wrote later (*ibid.*, l. 6, q 1, art. 6, near the end): "When serious doctors hold probable opinions, if you follow either one, you hold your conscience in safety." So also Cardinal Lambertini (who later was carried to the pontificate under the name of Benedict XIV), wrote in his

Notificationibus (notif. 15): "Bonds ought not be imposed when there is no manifest law to impose them."[13]

66.—The very learned Melchior Cano, writing against Scotus, who obliged sinners to elicit contrition on every feast day, says: "Human or evangelical law would be null were this precept to be asserted; let them discover it, and we will be silent." (Cano, *Praelect.*, 4, de poen., p. 4, q. 2, prop. 3), and he also writes in the same place (*ibid,* n. 5): "Because I do not know for what reason these doctors arrived at this opinion, I can freely reject what has been commanded without sufficiently investigating it." Joseph Rocafull, put in charge of Valentia, wrote: "In some case, if it is not certain after due diligence whether a law was imposed, but the doubtful matter remains, it would not oblige, whether it were a law or a natural precept." (Lib. 1, *de Leg.* in comm, c. 4, num. 65). Suarez writes thus: "As long as a judgment is probable that there is no law forbidding an action, such a law has not been sufficiently proposed to a man; for that reason, when the obligation of law is in itself onerous, it does not force until it is established for certain on it." (*De cons.* disp. 12, sect. 6, et in 3, par. d, 40, n. 45). The Dominican father John Ildephonsus writes the same thing, "If there is a doubt on the very existence of a law, whether such a law exists, or whether it was published, whether this case is included in such a law; if the doubt endures after sufficient diligence has been made then you are not held to conform yourself to such a law or obligation." (In 1. 2, disp. 209, n. 1132). A recent author, Father Eusebius Amort (a very erudite German, and in all respects known for his doctrine and many excellent conventional works), holds the same thing. In his *Theologia Moralis et scholastica*, (absolved from fault at Bononia in the year 1753 and later corrected or at

---

[13] *Non debbono imporsi ligami, quando non vi è una manifesta legge che gl' imponga.*

least revised by Pope Benedict XIV, no doubt as the author himself humbly asked from him), so writes: "Whenever the existence of a law is not rendered more credible, it is morally certain that a law is not given because from the nature of divine providence God is held to render his law more believable, etc." (Tom. 1, d. 2, § 4, qu. 20.) And in another place (d. 2, §4, q. 5), he says that when there are two equally probable opinions present, "a law directly forbidding is not given because in this case a sufficient promulgation of the law is not given, which is the essential character of law." Vasquez (1. 2. disp. 62, c. 9, n. 45) holds the same thing, as does Cardinal de Lugo (*de poenit.* disp. 16, sect. 3), Mastrius (*Theol. mor.* disp. 1, q. 2, art. 3, n. 56), Holzman (*mor.* to. 1, p. 29, ann. 135), Roncaglia (*Theol. mor.* lib. 2, c. 3), Salmant. (tract. 6, de poen. c. 8, punct. 2, n. 23 and tract 11 de leg., c. 2, punct. 5, n. 100), and many others whom we omit for the sake of brevity.

67.— Therefore, with the principle handed down by St. Thomas posited, and sufficiently proved above, namely that *No one is bound by some precept except through the medium of knowledge of that precept*, which is the same as to say an uncertain law cannot induce a certain obligation, necessarily it is elicited to be morally certain, because where two opinions of equal weight coincide, there is no obligation to follow the safer. Yet, if anyone were to request the reasoning on the certitude of this opinion, we will make the response briefly from all that has been proven in this *Monitum*, that a doubtful law does not oblige. And if he were to continue to ask why a doubtful law does not oblige, we will make the response with a succinct argument: A law not sufficiently promulgated does not oblige: a doubtful law has not been sufficiently promulgated (because, while a law is doubtful, a doubt or a question has been sufficiently promulgated, but not a law); therefore, a doubtful law does not oblige. Someone that may wish to deny this argument ought to show, either why a law obliges when it has not been promulgated or why a doubtful law is truly promulgated against that which St. Thomas and others expressly teach in common, as we see, one will never prove one of these propositions. At length this must be the conclusion of this opinion: after considering the equal weight of each opinion, a man remains uncertain and he would not be able to act; but after considering the force of the law when it was not sufficiently promulgated in that case, it does not oblige or bind. And therefore, a man, insofar as he is not bound by a doubtful law of this sort, is rendered certain about his freedom and thus can act licitly.

It is certain, however, from the dictate of natural law itself, it is lawful for us to do everything that is not forbidden by law, just as Heineccius writes (*Elementa jur. nat. et gent.*), saying: "God measures exactly all things for the freedom of man which he does not command or forbid. For example, when God forbade only the tree of knowledge of good and evil to men, God altogether rightly showed to the first man that it was lawful for him to eat the fruits from the rest of the trees. (Genesis 3:2). After the obligation of the law ceases, *libertas viget.*" Next, it is more strongly confirmed from the texts of civil law as well as canon law. *Instit. de jure person.*, §1, says: "One may act at their pleasure unless it is forbidden by law." Likewise, cap. 31 *Cum injure, de offic. et potest. judic. deleg.* so holds: "Unless you know about a law for certain, you cannot compel someone to carry out what is commanded." For that reason, St. Thomas teaches that it must be held as a common and certain axiom in natural law, writing: "What is said to be licit is not forbidden by any law." (In 4 Sent. dist. 15, q. 2, art. 4, ad 2).

Hence, a certain author argues ineptly, saying: "Where there is a doubt as to whether there is a law, doubt also follows as to whether there is freedom." He argues badly (I say), for where there is a doubt as to whether a law is present, it is certain that the law does not oblige. For St. Thomas teaches (as we noted above) that, "No one is bound by some precept except by the medium of knowledge of that precept." Moreover, it is clear that knowledge brings certain understanding about the law, and the reasoning for this is obvious; as long as a law is doubtful, it has not been sufficiently promulgated; still, a law that has not been sufficiently promulgated does not have the power to oblige or bind, as the Angelic doctor says, according to what was said from the beginning of this; further, where a law binding for forbidding does not exist, a man acts licitly as St. Thomas says in the same place we just cited.

I have said from the beginning, because where the opinion favoring the law seems certainly more probable, we are held to follow it; otherwise if it is of the same weight, the fact is the opinion favors freedom. Moreover, the Author of *Ephemeridum Galliarum* objects to me that this proposition is exceedingly proven; for if we are not held to follow an opinion which favors the law, then the opinion favoring freedom is of equal importance, since then the law is doubtful; nor would we be also held to follow the opinion favoring the law, since the opinion favoring freedom would be less probable, because the less probable opinion causes the law to be in doubt and so was not officially promulgated. Yet, I respond that when the safer opinion is certainly more probable, in that case (as we prefaced in the beginning of this Monitum) although the law would not be altogether uncertain, nevertheless on account of the greater probability the opinion favoring the law seems morally truer, and consequently, appears morally and sufficiently to have been promulgated. Therefore, he cannot say then that it is dubious by a strict doubt; it remains only in that case a certain broad doubt which does not permit one to disregard the safer opinion. Since the opinion which favors freedom is of equal importance, then a strict doubt is present on the existence of the law; and for that reason, just as we showed, then the obligation to embrace the stricter opinion or to keep the law on which there is a doubt, whether it exists or not, is not present.

68.—But before I bring an end to this Dissertation, I do not want to fail to respond to two opposing points which I find were objected by Father Flaviano Ricci in *Theologia Moralis*, recently revised by Father Analecti, where he writes: "All divine and human laws are certain and sufficiently promulgated; as a result, the controversy does not fall upon the existence of the law or over its promulgation but over the extension of the same. So in a particular case we ought to apply the general law to it and investigate whether that case is taken up or not by the law." From there he falsely imposes upon us, that in the occasion where two opinions that are of equal weight should coincide, we judge that the law is not extended to that case; but that author supposes two things to happen: *First*, that then our freedom would come into doubt; *second*, then place must be attributed to the rule of the canons which says: "In doubtful matters the safer road must be chosen," next, he adds that Scripture: "He who loves danger will perish in it." (Eccli. 3:27).

I respond to the first. When one is in doubt as to whether a case is taken up by the law or not, by no means do we say then that the law is not extended; rather we say that in the case of two opinions of equal weight, even though the general law (for example, to not steal or not kill), is certain in regard to its existence, and was sufficiently promulgated; nevertheless, in respect to that case there would be both a doubt in regard to existence and in regard to promulgation, and for that reason, because one then doubts whether the law would extend to that case, it is certain that it is not extended in regard to obligation; for as we have broadly shown above, in that case when the law is doubtful, it cannot bind the certain freedom of a man which, until it should be bound by the law, remains unfettered. St. Thomas recognized it when he said the law is the nature of the bond, which, as long as it is applied to someone through contact, "He has the power to turn away when he wills," are the words of the Angelic Doctor (*de verit.* q. 17, art. 3). Hence, he advances that opinion, "No one is bound by some precept except by means of the knowledge of the precept." (*Ibid.*)

Moreover, St. Thomas especially confirms this in another place, where he writes, "Law is a certain rule and measure of acts, according to which someone is induced to act, or is restrained from acting; for a law is so called from "binding", because it obliges one to act." (1. 2. qu. 90, art. 1). Further, "The measure," says Cardinal Gotti, "does not measure unless it is applied to something measurable," and so he adds: "It is indispensably required that the law should be proposed to those subject to it by promulgation." How will someone be able to rightly measure their actions unless that measure were certain and not ambiguous? Nor does it avail to say that where the law is doubtful, so also is a man's freedom doubtful; because freedom always remains certain, so long as he is not bound equally from a certain and manifest law. Therefore, in as much as the general law is certain, certainly it exists, and certainly it was sufficiently promulgated; nevertheless, as long as it is not applied in a particular case, one remains free, inasmuch as he is still not bound.

I respond to the *second*, namely to the rule of the canons that Father Flaviano adduced, and I ask from him: Is it certain that the aforesaid rule embraces all speculative doubts and not only practical or a doubt about a fact? Indeed, it is not certain, for the more common opinion hands down that this rule merely has place in practical doubts , as well as doubts on fact. Look at what St. Antoninus writes: "Moreover, wishing to prove that a contract is illicit, they bring in 'In doubtful matters the safer road must be chosen'. This response is true concerning the honesty and the majority of merit, not on the necessity of salvation in regard to all doubts, otherwise it would be necessary that all enter religion." (Part 2, tit. 1, cap. n. §31). Christian Lupus writes the same thing, (*diss. de op. prob.*) arguing the point from the doctrine of St. Augustine. Navarre, Domingo de Soto, Nyder, Tabiena, Suarez, Angles, S. Bonaventure, Gerson, Isambert, Jo. Ildephonsus, Salas, Cornejo, St. Thomas and others follow the same opinion. Their citations can be observed in another dissertation of mine, which I once published more widely on this material, where I clearly proved that the rule of the canons of this sort only considers practical cases, and those on fact.[14] At least the aforesaid rules or the law of the canons is truly doubtful outside of practical cases, and on fact; therefore, it was not sufficiently promulgated, and for that reason does not have the force of law.

But let us grant for the sake of example that this law proceeds for all doubts; again I ask, what does this law or rule say? *In doubtful matters the safer road must be chosen.* Therefore, when a man is in doubt, he cannot act. But what if he would morally form a certain dictate for himself about the honesty of his action? Then he is not *in doubt*, but is outside of doubt, and outside the case of the rule on account of that principle that has already been more than fully proved, that a doubtful law does not oblige because then the promulgation is wanting which is the very essence of the law.[15]

---

[14]   St. Alphonsus, apart from his Italian works, which he wrote in a great number, also published four very useful Latin works on the moderated use of probabilism which were in the years 1749, 1755, 1763, 1773. -Editor, Mechlin edition, 1852.

[15]   Confer below, n. 79, where the same objection is profusely refuted.

Moreover, the text which he adds, "One who loves danger will perish in it," I do not know how it can favor his opinion. I do not know that a Scripture of this sort is advanced by all those champions of the same rigid opinion, but I do not desire to understand what these teachers could elicit from it (as they boast) for health and purer doctrine. We should look to the context of the Scripture; there it is said, "A hard heart will have it badly in the end, and he who loves danger will perish in it." (Eccli. 3:27). Here is the case of Scripture, in which a man gravely sins, is when he throws himself into true danger of his salvation by prolonging his conversion even to death; just as equally he incurs true danger and gravely sins that voluntarily refuses to remove the near occasion of sin, the case altogether differs from ours, in which, it has been posited that a doubtful law does not oblige, there is no danger of transgressing the law: because when in that case it was not sufficiently promulgated, it has no power to oblige.

Moreover, from this doctrine of St. Thomas, namely that a law has no power to oblige unless it has been promulgated and made known, two corollaries come down in which our aforesaid dissertation is more solid: first, that a doubtful law does not oblige, second, related to it, that an uncertain law can not induce a certain obligation. Hence we add:

FIRST COROLLARY
A doubtful law does not oblige.

69.—From the principle, however, now so firmly and in so many ways proved by St. Thomas, namely that a law that has not been promulgated has no power to oblige, thus the certain aforesaid first conclusion comes down that a doubtful law does not oblige. A conclusion of this sort is proven from the fact that it is certain and explored among all doctors, that a moral certitude of some opinion is not proven from some certain principle *directly,* nevertheless, it is equally certain from some *reflexive* principle, as is proved firstly from canon 4, *Quid culpatur,* caus. 23, q. 1, where St. Augustine writes: "A just man, if perhaps he were to fight a war under a king, even if the man were impious, he can rightly make war at his command if in turn, preserving the order of [civic] peace that is commanded him, if indeed it is not against a certain precept of God, whether it may be certain or not; so that if the iniquity of command would make the king guilty, the order of obedience would reveal the soldier innocent." Therefore, although a subject might be doubtful about the justice of a war, still, can he licitly fight by the command of his prince, and for what reason? It rests upon the reflexive principle that a prince has a certain right to always be obeyed and it is not based upon injustice. It is equally proven from the chapter, *Dominus, de secund. nupt.,* where it is said if a man is uncertain about the death of the first husband of his wife, he cannot ask for the debt, but is held render to his wife, who is not uncertain and asks in good faith; and why? On account of the reflexive principle, that when a wife is in good faith, she has the right to seek the debt in doubt.

Father Jo. Laurentius Berti holds this doctrine as certain in his *De Theologicis disciplinis* (tom. 2, lib. 21, c. 13, prop. 3, vers. Patroni). He says that it is illicit to follow a less safe opinion although it might be equally probable; but how is it proved? It is proved from the falsity of the two principles, whereby the probabilists hold it is lawful; the first is, "He who acts probably, acts prudently." Really and truly Fr. Berti says that this principle is not sufficient to act with an opinion that is only probable; and since the opposed probable opinion equally favors the law, certitude about the integrity of the action, which is necessary to act, is rightly not supplied. The second principle of certain probabilists is this, that: "When each opinion is probable, a man suspends judgment in regard to a safer opinion and acts resting upon the probability of a pleasing opinion." But, the same Father Berti justly condemns such a principle, since it by no means avails to render us certain about the honesty of an action, since the suspension of judgment of this sort is merely voluntary, and for that reason cannot excuse so that the ignorance would be truly vincible, and therefore the doubt cannot be laid aside in that mode. This is why Fr. Berti concludes that, when that has been posited, since another foundation is not present to lay aside the doubt than that probability alone of a pleasing opinion, it will not be lawful for us to use that opinion. Fr. Berti himself writes that it is otherwise, in some case apart from that probability of opinion, another reflexive reasoning offers itself, even a certain principle that renders us morally certain about the honesty of the action in practice: accordingly, then, the certitude of our judgment does not rest upon the reasonings of that probable opinion, but upon a certain supervenient reflexive principle. He asserts the example of a religious that is uncertain whether to break a fast so as to devote himself to study, can indeed break it if the precept of a superior would urge, whereby it would become certain that he could take food short of sin. He asserts another example of a possessor, who possesses an estate in good faith, but when overcome with doubt, he can licitly continue in possession if the doubt were rendered safe by a learned man, because no man is held to be despoiled of a legitimate possession in a doubtful matter. From here, he concludes in this way: "Without any doubt a morally practical judgment can be made by this agreement from the reflection of a previously perplexed mind." Fr. Wigandt of the Order of Preachers writes the same thing, saying: "It is more probable that there is no sin in acting with a speculatively doubtful conscience, while having an attached practical judgment on the integrity of the act." The reasoning is that one who so acts, prudently judges that it is licit for him to do so in these circumstances and to act honestly. (Tract. 2, ex. 1, q. 5, art. 2.)

The lords Ballerini, in their work titled *Moralium actionum regula*, or *Questio de opinione probabili*, although they strenuously defend a rigid opinion, nevertheless willingly subscribe to this certain doctrine when they say, "That which in praxis, is uncertain from certain direct principles, becomes altogether certain from a certain reflexive principle." They equally adduce many examples from this, and especially that which we recently related above on a dubious impediment to contract matrimony, for in such a case they say that although on account of direct principles there may be uncertainty as whether the doubtful spouse could render the debt, just the same, on account of the reflexive principle, which is deduced from canon law and reason, one can safely avail to render [the debt]. For that reason, they conclude: "In all these examples it must be observed, reflexive principles do not answer the particular question, but leave it uncertain; only the practice is certain, inasmuch as reflexive principles establish a certain rule of direction in that doubt." Father Gonet writes the same thing (*Manual*, t. 3, tr. 3, c. 16, circa fin.) At length, Fr. Lector Jo. Vicentius Patutius, who strenuously opposed himself to me in this controversy in a twofold book, admits it favoring exploration, namely that when a reflexive principle is certain, it already renders the action certainly honest; for thus he says in his book, *La causa del probabilismo*, etc., §IV, page 40, and more expressly on page 45, where he writes, "If it were true that in a case of an uncertain law, there were no law, inasmuch as it was not sufficiently promulgated, certainly (as I said), were you to have a certain principle, not direct but rather reflexive, in which you would form a certain prudent dictate that could be undertaken (He speaks here on a type of contract of dubious justice). Therefore, since a forbidding law is not present, by what reasoning could one give place to a prudent fear of violating the law, when no such law exists?" He would have said it better if he had said which *certainly does not oblige*, which otherwise is reduced to the same thing, because a law which does not oblige is just as if there were no law at all.

And it is so understood how a speculatively doubtful or probable judgment on the integrity of the action can, in practice, become morally certain. But someone will object, how can only speculatively probable reasons evade being morally certain in practice? This comes about, as Bishop Abelly and Father Eusebius Amort excellently relate, it is not from the fact that the reasons for some opinion themselves become speculatively probable: but because on the one hand there are reasons for the opinion that are only probable, and on the other there are reasons of the reflexive principle by which in practice a final judgment is formed that is morally certain from that certain principle; and thus an action which is only speculatively and probably moral, in practice certainly avoids being morally upright.

70.—Now let us strengthen our conclusion, namely that a doubtful law does not oblige. We so argue with a certain course: The principle was already proven above from St. Thomas, that a law has no power to oblige unless it has been sufficiently promulgated and made known. Moreover, when in some case two opinions of equal weight coincide, then the law certainly cannot be said to have been sufficiently promulgated, for then a doubt has been promulgated as to whether the law exists, but a law was not promulgated; and for this reason it cannot oblige.

Recently, Eusebius Amort, a German and a learned man, defended this opinion as though it were certain in his *Moralis et scholastica Theologia*, printed at Bononia around 1753, and later it was corrected at Rome by the command of Benedict XIV, whom the author himself begged to see to it that prudent men revise the work as much as they thought to be necessary before its publication in Rome. The Pope agreed to his plea, transmitted some corrections that must be made in the work to him, except for the question on an equally probable opinion, as it is seen in the work itself. The author writes that where an opinion favoring the law does not evidently and notably appear more probable, it is morally certain that a law obliging someone does not exist, saying that God, according to his providence, when he wished his law to oblige, is held to cause it to appear evidently and notably more probable: "Whenever the existence of the law is not rendered more credible by reason, it is morally certain that a law is not given; because by the nature of divine providence, God, just as he is held to render his religion more credible by reason, so also he is held to render his law more credible, or more probable by reason.." (Amort, *Theol.* tom. 1, disp. 2, §4, q. 10).

Next, he adduces in another place, the reason why a law that is strictly doubtful sufficiently lacks promulgation, without which a law is not a law or is not a law that obliges: "In this case (namely when each opinion is equally probable), a direct prohibitive law is not given because in this case sufficient promulgation of the law is not given, which is the inseparable and essential character of law; accordingly the only promulgation of the law is one in which the law becomes more credible." (*Loc. cit.*, disp. 2, quaest. 5, p. 283). And he adds that the Fathers thought the same thing. "The Fathers strictly, in such a doubt where the opinion of the mind is bent to neither side, relinquish to a man the power of following what is more pleasing, therefore, they understood some general principle in which a concomitant prudent judgment can be formed on the non-existence of the law." And St. Gregory Nazianzen (Orat. 39), speaking about a certain Novatian, said, "And will you refuse to grant liberty of marriage to young widows on account of the liability of their age to fall? But Paul did not hesitate to do so, whose teacher you obviously profess to be. But this is not after baptism you say. By what argument do you confirm it? Or is the matter thus proved? If it is not, let you not condemn. What if the matter is doubtful, then let humanity and charity prevail." Likewise, St. Leo the Great said, (Epist. 90 *ad Rustic., Narbonens. in praefat.*) as his words are contained in the canon, *Sictu quaedam,* (fin. dist. 14): "Just as there are certain things which no reasoning can overthrow (as are the precepts of the Decalogue, and the form of the sacraments, as the Gloss explains), so there are many things which it is necessary to refrain from, either for the necessity of times or for the consideration of ages: since that consideration has always been preserved, that in those which are either doubtful or obscure, we know it must be followed because it is neither contrary to Evangelical precepts nor is it found opposed to the decrees of the holy fathers." He says "must be followed," for prelates ought to permit subjects to be able to use less rigid opinions where they are opposed neither to the Gospel nor to the doctrines of the Fathers, according to that document of Chrysostom: "In regard to your life be austere, in regard to the foreigner generous." (Cited in the canon *Alligant,* caus. 26, qu. 7). Likewise, Lactantius (lib. 3, instit. c. 27) writes, "It is for a very stupid man to obey their precepts, whether true or false, if he is uncertain."

Likewise, St. Augustine confirms the whole of what we say in a few words: "For what is clearly shown not to be against faith and good morals (note, *clearly shown*), must be held indifferently." (Serm. 294, c. 11, col. 224, edit. Paris). Therefore, each action is permitted to us in the mode it is proved, or we might not be morally certain that it is against faith or good morals. Likewise, St. Ambrose, writing to Januarius, reproaches those that have excessively cowardly minds, who think nothing is right when in doubt, unless it has the authority of Scripture or a tradition of the Church, or what is recognized to be certainly useful to correct one's life. Look at his words: "For, I have often sorrowfully sensed many disturbances of the weak are made through the contentious obstinacy of certain brothers, or a superstitious cowardice which in matters of this sort, where neither by the authority of Scripture, nor by a tradition of the Church, nor what seems to be useful to correct one's life, can they arrive at a certain end ... as they rouse litigious questions that if they are not in those categories, they will think they must do nothing." (Ambrose, epist. ad inquis. Januar., cap. 11, n. 3.) St. Basil is added to these, speaking on certain men who assume that an oath they advanced was invalid, he so wrote: "Both the species of the oath, and the words and the mind in which they swore must be considered, and in turn what words were added; so much that if there is altogether no reason to mitigate it, such thoughts must be altogether dismissed." (Epist. 188, can. 1, cap. 10). Therefore, he said not only must these merely be dismissed (or not listened to), but even more thoroughly favoring no pleasing reason was their basis. Then comes St. Bernard, who, when speaking generally on disputed matters on each side, so wrote to Hugh of St. Victor: "There, each of us rightly abounds secure where it is thought that something does not meet either certain reason or an authority that cannot be condemned." (1 Vol. Oper. cap. 5, n. 18, edit. Maur., Paris, col. 634). Therefore, the Angelic Doctor says that each man proceeds safely in following those opinions which are not opposed to certain reason, or authority, which may be of such importance, that no man could deviate from it. To these St. Bonaventure must be added, who, treating on vows which the Pope could dispense, brought three opinions to the fore, and then concludes: "I own that I do not know which of these three opinions is more true; and anyone could support any of them. Nevertheless, if anyone would accept this last one, a manifest unsuitability would not oppose him." (In 4, dist. 38, art. 2, quaest. 3). He does not say the safer must be preferred, but that one can support and accept any of them.

Let us hear in addition Melchior Cano; while attacking the opinion of Scotus obliging sinners to make an act of contrition on all feast days, wrote: "Either Human or evangelical law would be null, were this precept to be asserted; let them prove it and we will be silent." (*Praelect.* 4, *de poen.* p. 4, quaest. 2, prop. 3, et n. 5). He adds: "Because I do not know from what reason these doctors arrived at this opinion, I can freely reject what has been commanded without sufficiently investigating it." It seems that Scotus sensed the same thing seemed certain, where he wrote on a certain opinion: "When the negative side might be more probable to many, someone exposes himself to doubt without sin by following an affirmative less probable opinion." (In 4, dist. 11, quest. 6.) Therefore, according to Scotus, one who follows an equally probable opinion does not sin. Likewise, Cardinal Lambertini (later Pope Benedict XIV), equally wrote on this, saying: "Bonds ought not to be imposed when there is no manifest law to impose them." (Notif., 13.)

Yet, now we arrive at the intrinsic reasons for our opinion, a matter favoring such from its own principles, for which we take up the matter, as always, from the lead of the Angelic Doctor. St. Thomas so defines law: "Law is a certain rule and measure of acts, according to which someone is induced to act, or is diverted from acting: for a law is so called from binding, because it obliges one to act." (1. 2., quest. 90, art. 1). Next, St. Thomas teaches the same thing, this rule or measure of law, for this purpose, that subjects are constrained to observe it, ought to be manifest to them through promulgation; for that reason, in article 4 he proposes the question: "Whether promulgation is of the reasoning of the law?" And he responds: "Law is imposed on others by the mode of a rule and measure; moreover, a rule and a measure is imposed by this which it is applied to those things that are ruled and measured. Wherefore, by this reasoning, the law obtains the power to oblige, which is proper for law because it is fitting to be applied to men who ought to be ruled according to it. For, such an application happens through this, that in the notice of these things it is deduced from the very promulgation. For that reason the promulgation itself is necessary for the purpose that the law would have its force." Consequently, law before its promulgation does not have the force to oblige: for laws, as Gratian writes on the canon, *In istis*, dist. 4, then acquires the force of law and then laws begin properly, and are such when they are promulgated: "Then laws begin to be such, since they are promulgated." Hence, St. Thomas defines a law this way in another place: "A certain ordination of reason promulgated for the common good." (1.2. quest. 90, art. 4). The words, "ordination promulgated" should be noted.

So this promulgation is altogether necessary to oblige, not only in human laws, but even divine and natural laws, according to what the same holy Doctor relates: for in this place we cited, article 4 *ad primum*, where he objects this to himself: "Natural law especially has the reasoning of law; but a natural law does not need promulgation, therefore it is not from the reasoning of the law that is promulgated." And he responds this way: "It must be said that the promulgation of the natural law is from this very thing, that God inserted it into the minds of men to know naturally." Therefore, St. Thomas does not deny that natural law lacks promulgation, he merely says that the promulgation of natural law is not made in a human mode, but by the natural life which God thrust upon the minds of men. Hence, the very learned Cardinal Gotti says: "For this purpose, that a law would oblige in the second act, it is indispensably required that it be proposed to those subject to it by promulgation." (Theol.

tom. 2, tract. 5, *de leg.*, quest. 1, dub. 3 § 3, n. 21). He says, "in the second act," because a law that still has not been promulgated has in itself the force of obliging in the first act, namely that the very thing actually then obliges when it will have been promulgated; but that in the second act, namely that it would actually oblige, its promulgation is indispensably required to be made to those subject to it: "Actually," (writes Sylvius), "then law is promulgated to every man, when (man) receives the understanding dictated by God so that he embraces what he must and flees what he must by right reason." (In 1.2., quest. 90, art. 4, in fin). On this necessity of promulgation, that the law would oblige, Domingo de Soto assigns the reasoning, saying, "No law has the strength of a law before promulgation. This conclusion permits no exception. And it is proved from the nature of law itself, for there is a rule of our actions; but the rule, unless it is applied to those acting, is vain. It cannot be applied except through notice; for one who uses a rule, has the necessity to regard it, (*note regard it*). Therefore, the consequent becomes that before the promulgation, which begins with subjects, it does not constrain them from obliging, but then it is perceived when it is promulgated." (de Soto, *de justitia et jure*, lib. 1, quaest. 1, art. 4). For that reason, John Gerson says that not even God can bind a creature to observe a law unless it was commanded already, and God manifests his will to the creature: "It is necessary for a manifestation of the ordination and the will of God be given; for through ordination alone, or through his will alone, God cannot absolutely impose an obligation on the creature, but for this purpose it is necessary that he would communicate notice of one equally with the second." (*De vita spirit.*, etc., lect. 2, col. 176). From this, Father Gonet deduces that invincible ignorance can rightly be posited, even of natural precepts that are remote from first principles and he so argues: "Law does not have the force to oblige, unless it is applied to men by promulgation; but natural law is not promulgated to all men insofar as regarding all precepts, which are very remote from first principles; therefore it does not oblige all in regard to those precepts. Thereupon, invincible ignorance can be posited even excusing from sin." (*Clypeus* theol. tom. 3, disp. 1, art. 3, n. 47).

But now we come to refute the objections laid out by Father Patutius, by which the certitude of this, our principle, is more clearly made known.

71.—The father reader objects: 1) against this principle, to render a law sufficiently promulgated, a merely probable notice is enough, which is already held from a probable opinion favoring law. I say firstly to this objection, that the word *notice* (*notitia*), according to all vocabularies, is the same as *cognition* (*cognitio*). Moreover, cognition of a law, and the probable opinion of law are altogether different. In addition, I respond that if it were to be admitted that under the word *notice* a probable notice were understood, it could only be admitted to the highest degree; in which case, were a probable notice alone present that favors the law, then a certain moral certitude would assist the law, but when on the other side an equally probable opinion favoring freedom is present, then probability on either side cannot conquer, or a fitting probable reason to get the assent to it of the prudent man; for from these equal probabilities some other mere doubt does not result as to whether the law exists or not. St. Thomas clearly teaches this: "Our intellect, in respect to the parts of contradiction stands in diverse-mode; and when it is not inclined more to one than to another, or on account of a defect of movers, just as in those problems on which there are no reasons, or on account of the apparent equality of those things which move to either side, and so is the disposition of those doubting, who fluctuate between two sides of the contradiction." (*De Verit.*, quaest. 14, art. 1). He teaches the same thing more briefly in another place: "Even among an equality of reasons, the place of arguments is for doubt alone."

Besides, Fr. Berti says that just as both scales are in equilibrium when no weight is imposed upon them as well as when equal weights are placed upon them; in the same mode, when two probable opinions coincide, truly suspend judgment and if no probability were to exist on either side, "The pan of the scales remains in equilibrium, either nothing on either side, or an equal weight imposed on both sides." (Theol. tom. 2, lib. 21, c. 14, prop. 3). Fr. Gonet, Vasquez, La-Croix and commonly all the probabilists and probabiliorists say the same thing, and at length the same Fr. Patutius affirms in these words, (*in Instruct. de reg. prox.*, etc.) "The scale remains unmoved when an equal weight is placed on each plate, nor does it bend to one side or the other." He also confirms the same thing in a little book (*La Causa del probabilismo,* etc., pag. 48), where he says: "It is evident that two equally contradictory probable opinions cannot generate a doubt."[16] Therefore, in respect to our controversy, in which it is a question of two opinions that are equally probable, it does not avail to say probable notice of the law suffices to effect its promulgation; for in that case by no means is notice sufficient to promulgate a law, but only to promulgate a doubt or a mere hesitation as to whether there is a law or not: just the same, when two opinions of equal weight coincide, it comes about (as we said) that none of them have weight.

72.—He objects 2) the promulgation of the law is one thing, its publishing is another, or even the private notice which subjects receive about the law. For the law, when it has already been promulgated, without this notice received by those subject to it has the power to constrain them.

---

[16] *Essendo evidente, che duae opinioni contraddittorie equalmente probabili non possono se non generare il dubbio.*

Moreover, he adds that all laws, whether human or divine, have already been sufficiently promulgated. And in the first place, speaking on human laws, he says these, for them to oblige, it would be sufficient for the community if they were promulgated through proclamations or through the posting of some writing in public places.

We concede that for human law to have the force to oblige, it is enough that it would be promulgated to the community, but it is not required that every subject would attain notice of it. Rather, to notice, it avails only in regard to the material object of the law, what is commanded by the law, or forbidden by it, but not in regard to the obligation of conscience to keep the law. I explain myself: if, for example, a certain law were promulgated, in which some contract were declared invalid without resting upon certain solemn rites, then the subject, although he were uncertain about the law, is still held to stand by the prescription of the law bidding the contract to be held as void, or perhaps to pay some penalty because he received notice about it; for in the external forum, when a law has already been promulgated, all are presumed to know it. But in respect to conscience, certainly one does not sin who does not keep a law that was not known to him, if it happens that he did not know only on account of his neglect. In this way, the text adduced by Fr. Patutius from St. Thomas must be understood, "Those, in whose presence the law is not promulgated, are obliged to observe the law insofar as it arrives or can arrive in their notice through others, that it has been promulgated." (1.2. q. 90, a. 4, ad 2.) The "or can arrive" is understood insofar as notice of the law could have arrived to those subject to it, and on that account does not reach their negligence; for otherwise, if their ignorance were inculpable, by not keeping the law they would not sin. This is how Cajetan rightly explains the text that was related (*loc. cit.* S. Thomas), saying they are only guilty of an offense of law who do not know it, "either because they refuse or because they neglected to do what they could to know it. Otherwise those that were absent and do not know that a law was promulgated are not bound. On account of which, to be accused neither by God nor by men can be of ignorance." Fr. Peter Collet (*de legib.* tom. 3, c. 1, art. 2, concl.) and Suarez (*de leg.*, lib. 3, c. 17, n. 3, et seq.) write the same thing. Many authors add the same thing, not only are they thought to be unknowing, who are altogether ignorant of the law, but even those who are uncertain about it after due diligence (Suarez, in another place, tom. 5, in 3, p. disp. 40, sect. 5, n. 45; Aravius, in 1.2. q. 97, disp. 3, sect. 3., diffic. 3; Tapia, lib. 4, q. 15, art. 2; Castr., tom. 1, tract. 1, disp. 3, punct. 7, num. 1; Gregory Martin., q. 96, art. 4, dub. 5., concl. 3 et 4; Sanchez, dec., lib. 1, cap. 10, num. 32, et 33; Villalob., tom. 1, tract. 1, diss. 24; the Salamancans, *de leg.*, c. 2, n. 110). For law (as we said), does not bind unless it is applied to those subject to it for certain, not, however, doubtful notice. And it is handed down by the same St. Thomas, who teaches: "No one is bound by a precept except by the medium of knowledge of that precept." (*De vert.* q. 17, art. 3.) But on this text we will treat more broadly below.

That is enough on human laws; but Fr. Patutius, speaking on divine laws, says that they were promulgated from eternity and have the power to bind from eternity, before any creature heard and acknowledged them. And he says that it proceeds from the fact that an eternal law has eternal promulgation *causal, virtual and eminent*, which thereafter, inserts even a formal promulgation in time. He deduces this from the words of St. Thomas, who says, "It must be said that promulgation is made by word and writing; and in each mode the eternal law had promulgation on the side of God the promulgator, because the divine word is also eternal and the written book of life is eternal; but on the side of the creature hearing and inspecting it the promulgation cannot be eternal." (1.2. q. 91, a. 1, ad 2.) Even so, I assert (and will clearly prove) that the eternal law, in respect to men, is not a proper law; for a proper law in regard to them is the natural law, which, although it participates in the eternal law, still it is that which properly binds men, since the natural law should only be promulgated to men and is applied by the light of reason. At least I say (insofar as other theologians say) that the eternal law, although it has in itself the force to oblige in the first act, still was not a law actually obliging, and in the second act, until it was proposed, and through its understanding was applied to creatures; and thus I say emphatically it is taught by St. Thomas and by other theologians.

Look how Duvallius speaks: "Lastly, you will doubt whether the (eternal) law itself always had, and should have, the true and proper reasoning of a law? I respond, in time, when creatures were produced, to have the reasoning of law *de facto* truly and properly introduced and imposed on all creatures subject to it; still if it is considered from the eternal, it must be said that it is not truly and properly a law, but only something in respect to the resemblance of a law." Next, he assigns the reasoning: "Both, because on the reasoning of the true law is that it is imposed and promulgated to those subject to it; but there were none subject to it from eternity; and because a law is essentially a certain practical rule, this rule could not be imposed upon the Word and upon the Holy Spirit, because they are rule and rectitude itself." (In 1. 2., S. Thom. *de leg.*, q. 2.). Peter de Lorca writes the same thing: "If in some mode the eternal law regarded creatures, it regards them remotely insofar as they are moved by God and governed by him, but not because it is a broad command to creatures, or because it is proposed to them as a rule whereby they could measure and compose their actions. ... The eternal law is not a principle and a reason for someone to act, who is subject to the law, nor is it to him a proximate rule of his actions, rather it is the reason of action for God himself, and the rule of divine actions, whereby he governs the world; therefore, if it were a law to someone, it would be to God." (In 1.2. St. Th., disp. 5, *membr.* 2). And speaking about those words of St. Thomas, "*et verbo et scripto,* he says: "That expression in the divine word was eternal in God by the necessity made from nature, and not related to some creatures because the promulgation of the law is required, for the promulgation of the law is always related to those subject to it." Louis Montesino writes the same thing: "Resp. An eternal law of this sort has been promulgated from eternity by God himself ... God himself is the law, and the rule is for him and so we understand that God promulgated the law for himself." (De leg., disp. 20, q. 4, n. 83). Louis Lorichio writes the same thing, speaking about the eternal law: "By this law God orders all things to himself, and he promulgated it himself from eternity; but he promulgated it to men when he made it known to them." (*Thesaur.*, novus utr., Theol. Verb., lex n. 6). Furthermore, how can it be reconciled by these two doctrines that Fr. Patutius asserts, namely the eternal law completed from eternity has the power to oblige, and sooner than the creature would hear the law, and acknowledge it?

Now, the aforesaid doctrines agree with what St. Thomas himself teaches in another place, saying the eternal law is not a proximate rule of human will, but rather the reasoning of God; look at his words: "But the rule of human will is two-fold. One proximate and homogenous, namely human reason itself; but the other is the first rule, namely the eternal law which is, so to speak, the reason of God." (1.2. q. 71, a. 6.) Now, the words of the same Doctor related above are not opposed: "The eternal law has promulgation on the side of God the promulgator." (1.2. q. 91, a. 1, ad 2). For, in the same place the Holy Doctor already added: "But on the side of the creature hearing and inspecting there cannot be an eternal promulgation." Now, I ask what promulgation of divine law is that, which binds men? Promulgation *on the side of God*, or promulgation *on the side of the creature*? St. Thomas explains the very matter in the place where he said that for a law "to obtain the power to oblige, it is necessary that it be applied to men ... such, however, an application is made through this, that in the notice of these it is deduced from the promulgation itself." (1.2. q. 90, a. 4). And then, objecting to himself, (*ad primum*) that the natural law does not need promulgation, he responds that, "promulgation of the law of nature is from this very thing, that God naturally inserted it to be understood in the minds of men." Now, I argue: If it were true, that St. Thomas thought the eternal law, inasmuch as it has an eternal promulgation, obliges men from eternity, before they would know the law itself, indeed he would respond on account of this reason, the natural law, which is a participation of eternal law, does not lack promulgation: but he responds that promulgation of the law of nature happens when it is recognized by men through the light of natural reason. Nor could he respond otherwise, since before, in the same article, he firmly stated that no law has the power to oblige unless it is deduced from the promulgation into the notice of men.

Add that which St. Thomas hands down in another place, where he asks: "whether there is some natural law in us?" he so responds: "It must be said that a law, since it is a rule and measure, can be in someone in a two-fold mode, in one mode, just as in regulating and measuring, but in the other mode, just as in a thing regulated and measured, because insofar as something participates in a rule, ... it is so ruled ... and such a participation of the eternal law in a rational creature is called the natural law." (1.2. q. 91, a. 2.) Therefore, the Angelic Doctor distinguishes the eternal law from the natural, and teaches that the eternal law regards God the ruler, while the natural law regards man as ruled;

and because the natural law is the participation in the eternal law, therefore "in as much as he participates in something of the rule through the natural law, he is so ruled." Therefore, in such the eternal law binds men, insofar as men participate in it through natural law, it is made known to them by promulgation, according to what Duvallius says: "You ask, how is that eternal law made known to us, which is the same as if one were to ask how shall it be published? I say it, just as it is in creatures subject to it, it is made known to us through other laws, since those laws are a participation in it." (In 1.2., de leg., q. 3, art. 3). Francis of Aravio writes the same thing: "Since the eternal law does not oblige rational creatures except by the medium of natural law or divine positive law or human law, in regard to their promulgation this will also be sufficiently promulgated." (In 1.2., q. 90, disp. 1, sect. 5). Therefore, a law which binds a man, is only a natural law because it can only be a rule for man, and a measure whereby he will be ruled and measured.

Besides, although we may admit that the eternal law is the proper law even in respect to men, and has the force to oblige them in the first act, what of it? Certainly the eternal law does not bind in the second act, so long as it is not promulgated to creatures and applied through recognition of it. Cardinal Gotti wisely relates: "It follows that the eternal law would oblige no one from eternity in the second act, not from a defect of power but on the side of the *terminus* ... So from eternity the law was conceived in the mind of God, although it was not promulgated for eternity nor fulfilled nor obliging in the second act ... still, the law was from eternity because it is enough for the reason of the law, that it would have the force to oblige although, it does not yet bind because it was not yet applied and promulgated. (Theol. tract. 5, q. 2, dub. 1, n. 13). The words will be noted, "*Although it does not yet bind because it has not yet been applied and promulgated.*" The continuator of the Honorable Tournely wrote the same thing (*de legibus,* cap. 2, quaer. 3, in fine): "Still, because the eternal law was not obliging, since there was nothing outside of it that it would obligate, it is clear that the full and complete reasoning of the law then could only coincide with it, since creatures existed to whom it was intimated and promulgated, or at least began to be ordained and moved by the impression of the very thing." P. Cunilaiti said the same thing: "Violators of the law are not those to whom the law has not yet been made known." (Tract. 1, de moral. etc., cap. 2).

Fr. Patutius insists, saying: But if the eternal law was a true law before men would know it, truly, before the law was made known to them it obliged them, since it is the essential property of every law to oblige someone. And he cites Cardinal Gotti for his part, who says that the eternal law was a true law and for that reason had the force to oblige from eternity. I respond and distinguish: There is one property of a promulgated law, and another of an unpromulgated law. The property of a law that has been promulgated is to perfectly and actually oblige even in the second act. But the property of a law that has not been promulgated is to oblige imperfectly only in the first act; for a law that has not been promulgated has, accordingly, an intrinsic force in itself to oblige, but merely in the future, in that time in which it is intimated and will have been applied through notice; but so long as it has not been applied, it does not oblige, nor does it actually have the power to oblige: "For this reason, that a law (as the Angelic Doctor teaches) would obtain the power to oblige, it is necessary that it would be applied to men who ought to be regulated according to it." (1.2., q. 90, art. 2). Moreover, nothing is against what Cardinal Gotti writes, saying that the eternal law, even if it has not yet been promulgated to men, has the force to oblige; for St. Thomas speaks on the actual force to oblige even in the second act, but Gotti speaks on the force to oblige only in the first act: this certainly conveys the obligation in the first act, namely that a law is suited to actually oblige, since it will be promulgated, but not before the promulgation: just as fire has in itself the force to burn, but it does not actually burn unless it will later be applied to a thing to be burned. Look how the same Cardinal Gotti instructs us about the eternal law, saying: "So the law was conceived in the mind of God from eternity, although it was not promulgated nor fulfilled from eternity, nor obliging in the second act ... And in this mode, since the creature did not exist from eternity, which it would oblige, and to whom it would be applied, it did not oblige by an eternal act; still, it was a law from eternity, because it is enough for the reasoning of the law, that it would have the force to oblige, although it does not yet bind, because it has not yet been applied and promulgated." (*Theol.* tract. 5, q. 2, dub. 1, n. 15).

Nor can it be said that the eternal law does not oblige from eternity from a defect of the *terminus*, namely because the creature was not present from eternity; for therefore, the eternal law does not merely not oblige the creature from eternity, because he did not exist from eternity, but also because the law could not actually oblige the creature in the second act, before it would have been applied and promulgated to him. Cardinal Gotti already said in another place that "For a law to oblige in the second act, it is indispensably required that it be proposed to those subject to it by promulgation." (Quaest. 1, dub. 3, §3, n. 31). That is why he later writes, as above, that the eternal law was a law from eternity, "although it did not yet bind, because it was not yet applied and promulgated." And the continuator of Tournely, as we have seen, wrote the same thing, speaking about the eternal law: "It is clear that the reasoning of the law then completed could only be fitting for him since creatures existed, to whom the law was promulgated."

Aeneas Sylvius wrote the same thing: "Actually, (the eternal law) is promulgated to everyone when they receive recognition dictated by God, of what he must embrace by right reason, and from what he must flee." (In 1.2., q. 90, art. 4, in fine).

73.—Fr. Patutius objects 3) Natural law is promulgated in habit, when God created the soul and pours into the body, because then he impresses in it the light of reason. Patutius infers from this that a man is bound by the law even from his conception; for God, when he impresses the law into the soul, then promulgates it. And here he cites for himself the text of St. Thomas: "The promulgation of the law of nature is from this very thing, that God naturally inserted it into the minds of men to understand." (1.2., q. 90, art. 4, ad 1). The response is made: To the mind of St. Thomas it is fitting to observe what must be sought, what the Holy Doctor wrote in the body of the article; there he teaches the law is imposed through the mode of a rule and measure, from which he says that, as the law has the power to oblige, it is necessary that it, "is applied to men who ought to be ruled by it: moreover such an application (he adds), happens through this, that it is deduced into their notice from the promulgation itself." Therefore, law, according to St. Thomas, then binds men when it is applied to them through their notice, or cognition. Moreover, when he says the promulgation of the law is "*from this very thing, that God naturally inserts it to be understood*," it is without a doubt, lest we would mean the Holy Doctor would contradict himself in the same article, it must be understood that the law really is promulgated, and obtains the power to oblige, since it is actually applied and understood. For that reason, the Angelic doctor says the same thing in another place (1.2., qu. 91, art. 1, ad 2): "But on the side of the creature, listening and inspecting the promulgation cannot be eternal." Then, the law is promulgated when the creature *hears* the law through the voice of the Church, or *inspects* it by the light of reason. Hence in art. 2, he says that the law of nature is none other than the "Light (signed over us) of natural reason, in which we discern what is good and what is evil." Moreover, this light, by which we discern good and evil, and in which the natural light consists, St. Antoninus says shows to man good and evil no earlier than a man has the use of reason: "Diligently note that according to St. Thomas, the fact is that light of the natural law does not show to man what might be good until the time when he attains to the use of reason." (Part. 1, tit. 13, c. 12, §3). Therefore, the natural law is not promulgated to man except when he attains the use of reason. For that reason it is concluded, that properly and strictly speaking, in the infusion of the soul the law is not yet inserted, rather a light is inscribed whereby the law will be known by man, when he attains to the use of reason, or the potency, capacity or ability to know the law in the time of the use of reason is inserted. And then, when a man shall know the law, the law will be perfectly and truly promulgated to him; otherwise, until the law is not deduced into the notice of man from promulgation, St. Thomas teaches that the law does not obtain the force of obliging. It is added to what Domingo de Soto writes, that the law, "cannot be applied except through the notice of man, since one who uses a rule, has the necessity of regarding it." (*De Just.*, lib. 1, q. 1, art. 4, et q. 3, art. 2), and what John Gerson said in notable words: "That law is a certain revelation, and properly so called a declaration made to a rational creature, by which he knows those things that God shall judge on certain matters, to which he means to oblige the creature to either furnish or omit, so that he would be made worthy of eternal life." After positing such a definition of divine law, he adds: "It is necessary for a manifestation of the ordination and will of God to be given; for through his ordination alone, or through his will alone God cannot yet absolutely impose an obligation on the creature: but for this it is necessary that he would communicate notice equally of one and the other. From which it is clear that the conclusion is immediately deducible, a rational creature cannot be unworthy of the friendship of God, nor properly guilty of sin unless, while knowing, willing and freely placing the action forbidden to him, or omit a thing commanded of him." (Lib. *de vit. spir., etc.*, lect. 2, col. 176, edit. Paris). Therefore, according to Gerson, not even God can command a man to observe a law which he has not yet manifested to him.

Nor is what St. Thomas says (1. 2. q. 94, art. 1 ad 3), opposed to this, because the natural law is in man even from his childhood, for the Angelic Doctor himself said the same thing, the law is properly an act, not a habit. The reasoning is, that a law consists in an act, in which the law is enunciated by the means of reason while prescribing a dictate, what must be done and what must be avoided; so appositely, Sylvius writes: "Natural law is an act of reason, clearly an actual judgment, and the dictate of practical reason. Because every law is in respect to the mode of enunciation, the enunciation is a certain act." In 1., 2., q. 94, a. 1, concl. 2, et. art. 2, prob. 2 he says: "The force of the obligation is not simply from cognition, insofar as it is such and such a thing. ... Rather, from the dictate of reason prescribing these which according to themselves are goods and must be done, or things forbidden which according to themselves are wicked and must be fled." Cardinal Gotti profusely explains it, saying that from these it is clear that we speak on the natural law, as in the second act giving notice, in which the essence of the law consists, which is contained through the mode of giving notice. What if we were to take the natural law in the first act, so in virtue, and in a certain measure by habit the natural law, even while someone considers its principles in act, since the light of reason would always remain in the intellect, that together with the nature God introduced into each rational creature:

from which, if he were to exert the use of reason, he can form a judgment and a dictate on what must be done or omitted." (*Theol.* tr. 5, *de lege* q. 2, §1, n. 9). Therefore, Cardinal Gotti distinguishes the natural law in the first act and in the second act: and he says that the natural law, considered in the first act, and in habit, consists in that habitual light of reason which is inserted into us with nature: by such a light, then the practical dictate is formed in the time in which a man attains the use of reason. But when the natural law is considered in the second act, it essentially consists in the actual declaration of the law, which is made to man through that practical dictate. Now, I ask, where in the world is the essence of the law properly discovered? Perhaps in the habit of the law inserted when the soul is created, or on the other hand, in that actual declaration of the law? And it certainly renders natural law a properly completed law and obliging only that light inserted in creation, either the actual declaration, or the intimation of the law. Gotti says (and Sylvius and all others, such as St. Thomas, Gerson, de Soto, Gonet, as we have seen, say the same thing as well as others that we will see below), that it is not in habit but in the actual declaration of the law that the essence consists. Let us repeat the words of the Cardinal: "*It is clear we speak about the natural law, as in the second act declaring, in which the essence of the law consists, which is held through the mode of declaration.*" And from the declaration, next the dictate of reason is formed in man, obliging him to the law.

Sylvius does not think otherwise when he says in 1. 2. q. 90, art. 4 that, according to the words of St. Thomas, the natural law is inserted into man at the moment when the soul is infused into him, for he acknowledges the same difficulty, how through that habitual insertion of law can a man be bound since it was not first made manifest to him; and for that reason he adds: "Therefore, it must be added, the natural law, was promulgated, as it were, in habit for the very reason that God impresses it on the minds of men. ... Moreover, then it is promulgated in act to everyone when they receive the cognition of the dictate from God, to embrace what is right according to natural reason and to know what must be avoided." Therefore, Sylvius, when he conceives this first insertion of the law in man, appeals to one *as if promulgated* in habit, but he absolutely calls that promulgation which actually happens when the law is made known to man, whereby he ought to be ruled. Therefore, certainly advancing it he intends to say that the impression made in man before man actually recognizes the law, is not sufficient to oblige him; for that reason, he adds, "Therefore, what must be added, etc." And after he says the promulgation is then made in act when man receives cognition of the law, because this is the sufficient and necessary promulgation whereby a man is bound by a law by which he is measured. Further, that Sylvius so indubitably senses it is certain is clear from the very fact that he writes it in another place: "The eternal law was from eternity only materially a law, but it was not formally so from eternity, or by the reasoning of a law that actually obliges, because then it was not in act and the promulgation not completed." (1.2., q. 91, art. 1 ad 2.) Therefore, Sylvius says the eternal law (and it proceeds from the natural law, which is a certain participation in the eternal law) is not formally a law, and actually obliging except when the actual promulgation is present, which then is effected when a man discerns what to do and what he ought to avoid; according to what Sylvius himself already expressed: "Actually, then (the law) is promulgated to everyone when he receives, from the dictate of God, the knowledge of that which, according to right reason, must be embraced, and what must be avoided. (1.2., q. 90, art. 4, in fin.)

Therefore, natural law is not promulgated to man, nor does it bind him, except when a man attains to the use of reason, whereby the law is made known to him and promulgated. Fr. Louis Montesino says: "Natural law is promulgated in all, when they first attain the use of reason; and although then that law is only promulgated in regard to the most common principles of the law of nature, nevertheless afterwards, little by little, the same law is promulgated through progress in regard to other things." (*De leg.*, disp. 20, q. 4, n. 85.) Duvallius writes the same: "You ask, in what time the law of nature began to oblige each and every man? Resp. It began when it was promulgated. Then, however, it is sufficiently promulgated when each man begins the years of discretion." (In 1.2., *de leg.*, q. 3, art. 3). Peter de Lorca writes the same thing: "To the extent that promulgation is intrinsic, and essential for human laws, so the judgment of reason and the intrinsic cognition is by the law of nature." (1. 2., disp. 6, *de leg.*, p. 386). Now note: *judgment and intrinsic cognition is from the law*; therefore, without judgment and cognition of the law, the law does not bind. Fr. Cuniliati writes the same thing: "Violators of the law are not those to whom the law has not yet been made known. ... The actual promulgation of natural law comes about when someone receives cognition of the dictate from God, of what must either be avoided or embraced." (Tract. 1, *de moral.*, et cap. 2). Fr. Gonet writes the same thing: "Promulgation of the law of nature happens through the dictate of reason intimated to a man, those things which are prescribed by the law of nature or are forbidden by it; therefore, when such a dictate is lacking, the law of nature does not oblige one to its observance." (*In Clypeo, theol.*, t. 3, disp. 1, art. 4, §1, n. 55). The learned Fr. Mastrius writes the same thing: "Moreover, this law (of nature) is intimated to men and begins to oblige them from that time in which they receive the use of reason and by such a law intimated to them they begin to discern between good and evil; by these, the use of reason is like a notification and manifestation of the natural law itself. And Paul focuses on this in his letter to the Romans with these words: 'At some time I saw without the law, but when the command arrived, sin revived.' (Romans 7:9). Jerome so explains these words (*epistle to Aglasia*): '*When the commandment arrived*, this means the time of understanding to desire goods and avoid evils; *then sin revived*, mean that a man is guilty of sin.'" (Mastrius, *Th. mor.* disp. 2, *de leg.*, q. 2, a. 2., n. 34).

74.— Fr. Patutius objects, 4) "It cannot be the case that a law would be doubtful, and that it should be uncertain whether such a law exists or not since laws, both divine and human, which we are held to observe, are all certain and sufficiently promulgated. Therefore, a doubt remains not on the existence of a law but on particular cases, whether or not they are included under a law. For that reason, if the principle which has been proposed, that we might wish, namely, that a doubtful law cannot oblige, we cannot say that a doubtful law is not a law but we should only say, 'Since each side contains a probable opinion that the law extends itself to them or not, law certainly does not extend to them.' But if this is said, the difficulty of the principle returns, for when there is uncertainty whether such an action is licit or not, as in a comprehensive law or one not comprehensive, such a principle cannot stand for certain." To this point, at every turn the good Father adheres to that which Fr. Daniel Concina wrote in his Theology.

But the response is the same one that Fr. Concina himself wrote in the compendium of his Theology (t. 1, *de leg., cap. 2, n. 10*), where he says that, although a law were certain, just the same the different circumstances which happen cause that a law now obliges and now does not oblige: accordingly, the precepts, although they are immutable, nevertheless at some point do not command under this or that circumstance. Hence, we take up again and say: It does not avail to say that the laws are certain: for after the circumstances of the cases have changed, they are rendered not obliging, or at least uncertain, and, as it were, uncertainties do not oblige. Therefore (Fr. Patutius repeats) according to our principle that a doubtful law does not oblige, do you conclude that in a doubt as to whether the law extends itself to that case or not that it certainly is not extended? But we respond by reframing the argument: Therefore, according to our opinion, in doubt as to whether the law extends itself to that case, or not, should we say it certainly is extended? This is, what we deny. Moreover, we do not assert that a doubtful law certainly is not extended to that case; rather we say as often as there are equally probable opinions on both sides, although it is not certain, then the law extends to that case, and in respect to that case, the law is rendered doubtful and as doubtful it does not oblige because then it was not sufficiently promulgated. The matter will become clearer with an example. We have a universal law that forbids usury; but when on both sides the probability is equal that something may be contracted, and it will not be usurious, then it appears for certain that there is no law which forbids it. For that reason, until it will be prudently doubted whether the contract is or is not usurious, although the opinion that the contract is forbidden by law is present, nevertheless no certain law is assigned whereby it is forbidden. In respect to usury, the law forbidding it is certain, but in respect to that contract the law is uncertain. Therefore, to object to something (as our adversary opposes) that here he does not argue whether the law exists or not, while the law forbidding usury is certain, but only scrutinized whether it extends to this case or not, the response is clear: Since to posit that it is truly probable that case is not embraced by the law is the same thing as to say there is a doubt as to whether the law extends itself to that case, and to say the law in respect to that case is doubtful, and hence does not oblige in respect to that case.

Second Corollary

An uncertain law cannot induce a certain obligation, because for man libertas possidet previous to the obligation of law.

75.—"Moreover, the law will be manifest," says St. Isidore (*can. Erit autem,* dist. 4). Hence Panormitanus[17] wrote (in the final chapter *de Const.*), "Where the law is doubtful, one is excused by ignorance of the law." Indeed, the same natural reason dictates that no one who is in doubt in regard to those precepts, as to whether they exist or not, is held to observe them, as is held in *Authentica, Quibus mod. nat. etc.,* § *Natura*, where it is read: "In doubt no one is presumed obligated." St. Thomas teaches this very thing, saying that law (and he speaks about divine and eternal law), that it would oblige, out to be certain. (1.2., qu. 19, art. 4, ad 3). There, the Angelic Doctor objects to himself, "The measure ought to be very certain, but the eternal law is unknown to us; therefore it cannot be the measure of our will that the goodness of our will would depend upon it." And he responds: "Although the eternal law is unknown to us, according to what is in the divine mind, it is nevertheless made known to us in some measure through natural reason, which is derived from it, just as its own image, or through some sort of revelation superadded." Therefore, St. Thomas does not deny that divine law, insofar as it is the measure of our actions, ought to be certain; he merely says that it is not enough that we distinguish those in the same mode by God,

---

[17]   Translator's note: Nicolò de' Tudeschi, a Sicilian Benedictine Canonist, 1386-1445.

but it suffices that it is made known to us by the light of natural reason or some special revelation.

But the Angelic doctor stated this more clearly and more firmly in another place, where he asks: "Whether conscience is binding?" And he so carries the discussion: "It is so in respect to a command of some governor to bind in voluntary matters by that mode of binding, which can happen to the will, just as in regard to a corporal action to bind corporal matters by the necessity of compulsion. But the corporal action of the agent never induces necessity in another matter except by the contact of constraint itself to the matter in which he acts. For that reason, someone is not bound by the command of some master unless the command touches the very one that is commanded. But it touches him by knowledge. For that reason, no one is bound by some precept except by the medium of knowledge of that precept. And therefore, he that does not have the capacity to notice the precept is not bound; nor is someone ignorant of the precept of God, bound to carry out that precept, except insofar as he is held to know the precept. But if he were not held to know, nor knew, in no mode would he be bound by the precept. Moreover, just as in corporal matters the corporal agent does not act except through contact, so in spiritual matters he is not bound except by knowledge." (*De verit.*, q. 17, art. 3). Note that, "*For that reason no one is bound by some precept except by the medium of knowledge of that precept.*" But now let us listen to the objections of Fr. Patutius according to this principle, and distinctly in respect to this text of St. Thomas.

76.—He objects, 1) Under the term *knowledge* (*scientia*) certain cognition is not understood, but only the simple notice of the precept, which (as he says) in our case is probably held on account of the probability of each opinion. I respond and say firstly: The idea that by the term "*scientia*" probable notice is understood, is a new meaning of a new vocabulary, while all philosophers with the same St. Thomas distinguish an opinion by *scientia*, which is received as a certain cognition of some truth. But Patutius insists that St. Thomas understands by the term *scientia* a probable notice, which is already held in our case: for the Angelic Doctor (as he says) adds in the same place, "and therefore, he who does not have the capacity to notice the precept is not bound." But I say equally, in all vocabularies *notice* (*notitia*) and *cognition* (*cognitio*) mean the same thing, and so *notice* of the law is the same as cognition of the law. Moreover, even with that granted, that by the term *notice* probability for the existence of the law could be understood, that probability will be able to be admitted to the highest degree, which only favors the law, without the probability to the contrary; otherwise, when an opinion favoring freedom is equally probable, then it is certain (as we said), that nothing else remains but a pure hesitation of the law, which can be called neither *scientia* or *notitia*; for then, we do not have notice of the law, but only notice of a doubt or a question as to whether the law exists or not. But what St. Thomas intended to speak about, when he said *by the medium of knowledge*, was not a doubt or a dubious opinion, but a true opinion, it is certain from the context of the same article when he said: "Just as in corporal matters the corporal agent does not act except through contact (of compulsion to a matter, as we said above); so in spiritual matters a precept does not bind except through knowledge." And later he adds: "But to be in force, when (conscience) binds, it must be known that binding is taken metaphorically from corporal things to spiritual ones, it conveys the imposition of necessity; for he who is bound, has the necessity of remaining in the place where he has been bound, and the power to leave from there is taken away from him." Therefore, just as one who is not actually bound, has the power to leave when he wishes; so one who still has been bound by a precept, by the medium of knowledge of that precept has the power to do what has been willed. Moreover, how can it be said that someone knows the precept if he would know the precept is doubtful? Then, it altogether must be said that one that is ignorant of that precept, when he is in doubt, whether there is a precept or not.

Besides, Fr. Patutius objects over the same text of St. Thomas on those words: "Nor is someone ignorant of the precept of God bound to do the precept except insofar as he is held to know the precept." Therefore, (Patutius argues), although someone might lack notice of the precept, still if he is held to keep it, now he is bound by the precept, nor excused if he transgresses it. But the Angelic doctor does not understand this at all; there he only teaches he is not excused from sin if he is held to know the precept and is culpably ignorant of it. It is clear from that which he added in the same article (ad 4): "Then an erroneous conscience does not suffice to absolve one when he sins in error." How does *he sin in error*, except when the error itself is a sin on account of voluntary negligence? (According to what St. Thomas declares from St. Augustine in another place). "Ignorance, which is altogether involuntary, is not a sin and this is what Augustine says: 'Fault is not imputed to you if you are ignorant against your will, rather, if you neglect to know.' (lib. 3, *de lib. arbitr.*, cap. 19). What he says through this, 'but if you neglect to know', gives us to understand that ignorance means it is a sin from a preceding negligence, which is nothing other than to not apply the mind to know those things which someone ought to know." (*De verit.*, q. 3, art. 7, ad 7). Therefore, by no means does one sin when he scrutinizes the law with the hesitation of two equally probable opinions, and after applying due diligence, finds it altogether dubious and therefore not obliging.

77.—He objects, 2) The possession of eternal law precedes the possession of our freedom, so he says that an opinion in doubtful matters which favors the law ought to be given preference. I respond: We already saw above that the Theologians say the eternal law in respect to men is not truly and properly a law. But I submit that were it so, by no means can it be said the obligation of the eternal law is prior to the freedom given to man by God. For, even if there was no cognition in God and succession of counsel, since all present things were from the eternal God, just the same by the *priority of reason* or *nature*, man was contemplated in the mind of God before the law; just as the legislator considers a subject according to their nature and state and then considers a suitable law to impose upon them. I say *suitable*, in as much as God established one law for angels and another for man; one for the latter and one for priests; one for laity and one for celibates. But this doctrine is not my own, rather it is of St. Thomas, who poses this question: "Whether some law is eternal?" And he objects to himself (*ad primum*): "it seems that no law is eternal; for every law is imposed upon someone, but it is not an eternal law, but it was not eternal, upon whom some law could be imposed for only God is eternal; therefore there is no eternal law." And he responds: "To the first it must be said that these which are not in themselves exist in God, insofar as they are known by him and preordained, according to what is in Romans 4:17: 'Who calls those things which are not as though they are.' So therefore, the eternal conception of divine law has the reasoning of eternal law, according to what is ordained by God to the governance of those things foreknown by him." Notice, "*of those things foreknown by him.*" Therefore, *by the priority of reason*, a man was considered as free and then a law was considered whereby a man was to be bound. *E.g.*, God forbade murder from eternity, therefore, *by the priority of reason*, he considered men first, who could be killed, and then gave them a precept lest they would kill one another.

Therefore, does Fr. Patutius say a man is born free and independent? By no means, he is born subject to the divine power and consequently is obliged to obey all the precepts which God has imposed upon him; but that a man would be bound by precepts of this sort, it is required that these would be promulgated to him, and made known through the light of reason; but as long as the precept has not been made manifest to a man, he possess the freedom given him by God, which, when it is certain he is only bound by a certain precept and since the law is a rule and measure by which a man ought to regulate and measure his actions, it is necessary that this rule and measure not be uncertain. Moreover, what our adversaries assert is false, namely that a man can do nothing unless he would know for certain that it were permitted by God. For if this were so, the divine law could not lack promulgation, rather it would only be necessary that God should declare everything which he permits us to do. But God did not do this: God constituted man in the beginning, and left him in the hand of his counsel. He laid down his commands and precepts: "If you will keep the commandments, they will preserve you, etc." (Eccli 15:14). Consequently, the Lord first created man free by giving him freedom *ad libitum*, according to that which the Apostle writes: "Having the power of his will." (1 Cor. 5:37). And after the commands which he was held to keep, he laid down and imposed; and thus, the freedom of a man, when it is certain, possesses before the obligation of law, it is only bound by a certain law.

Furthermore, this is what the old authors commonly taught when the law was obscure, and there was no text of Scripture, determination of the Church or evident reason found favoring it, he will not be condemned for a grave sin; they hold for certain that a doubtful law does not oblige. Look at how St. Raymund wrote: "Be not prone to judge mortal sins where it is not constituted for you by a certain

Scripture." (lib. 3, *de poen.*, §21). St. Antoninus writes the same thing, saying: "But if (a confessor) cannot clearly perceive whether it is mortal, it does not seem that the sentence should be laid down, as Guillelmus says, that he would deny absolution on this account, or burden the conscience of the penitent with a mortal sin. And when the right to absolve is more manifest than to bind (c. *Ponderet*, dist. 50), and it is better to render account to the Lord for excessive mercy than for excessive severity, as Chrysostom says (c. *Alligant*, caus. 26, q. 7), it seems better to absolve." (St. Anton. part. 2, tit. 4, cap. 5, § *In quantum*). Gabriel Biel, who lived in 1480, wrote the same thing, saying: "Nothing ought to be condemned as a mortal sin where there is no evident reason or manifest authority of Scripture." (*In 4*, d. 6, qu. 4, conclus. 5). St. Thomas taught the same thing, where he said: "One who assents to an opinion of some teacher against that which is publicly held according to the authority of the Church, cannot be excused from the vice of error." (*Quodlib.*, 3, a. 10). Therefore, St. Thomas merely condemns one who follows some opinion against the manifest testimony of Scripture, or against the common opinion according to the authority of the Church; but not one who follows an opinion which is not opposed to a certain law, as John Nyder records: "These words of St. Thomas cannot be understood but on those things where it is manifestly clear from Scripture or a determination of the Church that it is against the law of God; and not on those where it does not appear, otherwise he would oppose himself in the same book." (*In Consol.*, etc., cap. 11, art. 3). St. Thomas declares the same thing in another place, where he writes: "Every question in which one scrutinizes about mortal sin, unless the truth should expressly be contained, perilously makes a determination; because an error in which something that is mortal is not believed to be a mortal sin does not excuse the conscience from the whole, although perhaps from some part. But an error, in which it is believed that something which is not mortal is a mortal sin, binds from conscience to mortal sin." (Quodlib., 9, art. 15). Notice the words, *unless the truth is expressly contained, he perilously makes a determination*". Therefore, the principle of our adversaries is false, that in doubt, *lex possidet*, and hence in doubt the safer part must be held. But Fr. Patutius will say: If *libteras possidet*, why does St. Thomas write that in doubt one following the more pleasing side "cannot be excused from the whole?" The response will be made that here the Angelic Doctor does not speak on the last practical judgment which can be made certain by some certain reflexive principle, rather he only speaks on direct judgment, which is doubtful, since both opinions are doubtful and therefore he says he cannot be excused who only embraces the gentler side in a direct judgment. Otherwise, it would still be, St. Antoninus says, if anything were embraced by a probable opinion, say when the last certain dictate is formed from a certain reflexive principle. Let us listen to the Holy Archbishop: "It must be known that St. Thomas says, in a certain question from the *Quodlibetus*, that a question, in which it is argued on some act, whether it is a mortal sin or not, unless the express authority of Sacred Scripture or a canon of the Church, or evident reason were present, it is determined only perilously. For, if one would determine that something is mortal and it is not, one acting against it sins mortally because everything which is against conscience paves the way to hell; but if it were determined that it were not mortal, and it is, his error will not excuse him from a mortal sin. But this seems right according to what has been understood, when someone would err from crass ignorance; otherwise, if from probable ignorance, say because he consulted experts in such a matter, and he was told by them that such a thing was not mortal, it would seem then in that case the ignorance would be almost invincible which excuses from the whole. And this in regard to those matters which are not expressly against divine or natural law, or against the articles of faith and the Ten Commandments, in which an ignorant man will be unaware ... And if it were said here it is usury, and usury is against the Decalogue, the response can be made, rather this contract is usurious or it is not clear, since wise men think contrary things amongst themselves." (P. 2, tit. 1, cap. 11, § 28). Therefore, according to St. Thomas, and St. Antoninus, where the truth is not clear, the law, just as in the case of a doubtful law, does not oblige.

78.—Our adversaries object, 3) Nothing is lawful to us unless it conforms to the divine will. I am glad that they advance this objection to me, because what St. Thomas teaches on this point only suffices to strengthen our opinion. The Angelic Doctor asks (1.2., q. 19, art. 10): "Whether it is necessary for human will to be conformed to the divine will in a regard to thing willed for it to be good?" And he says, men are held to conform themselves to the will of God in what is desired *formally*, that is in "regard to a thing willed for the common good (for no one can licitly will something unless it is good), but not in regard to a thing willed *materially*. Next, the Holy Doctor (*ad primum*) poses this objection: "It seems that the will of men ought not always be conformed to the divine will in regard to a thing willed, for we cannot will what we do not know ... But what God wills we are unaware of in a great many things; therefore, human will cannot be conformed to the divine will in regard to a thing willed." And he responds, "*Ad primum*, it must be said that a divine thing willed according to common reason is such that we can know; for we know that whatever God wills, he wills by reasoning of the good. And therefore, whoever wills something under each reasoning of the good, has a will conformed to the divine will, in regard to the reasoning of the thing willed," which is the thing willed *formally*, or commonly. Next, he adds: "But in particular, we do not know what God wills; and in regard to this we are not held to conform our will to the divine will." Therefore, a man is not held to conform to the divine will in particular even in respect to divine precepts, where this will of God still has been made manifest to man, according to what Fr. Gonet declares more distinctly, saying: "A man is not held to be conformed to the divine will in regard to a thing willed materially, except when the divine will is manifested to us by precept or prohibition." (*In Clypeo*, t. 3, d. 6, art. 2, n. 37, in fine).

But Fr. Patutius presses on, and says: "By reason of precept and prohibition (he freely notes this with his own words), it is necessary that we always be conformed to the divine will, even in regard to a thing desired materially, accordingly God gave precepts to us to be observed and these are already made known in the law."[18] Yet, I ask: If some precept is in doubt or obscure, insofar as it happens in a conflict of two equally probable opinions, how can it be said that the precept has been sufficiently made known? For then it is not enough that the precept has been made known, but only a doubt about the precept, according to what we showed above, that where two equally probable opinions coincide, neither of the probable, but only doubt would remain. For that reason, in that case it can merely be said that we have doubt about the precept, but not cognition. And really, how could it ever be said that we have cognition of the law when we truly do not know whether the law exists or not? Then we avail to assert that we do not know the law and therefore are not held, according to St. Thomas, to be conformed to the divine will in regard to the thing desired materially, which is unknown to us; for God does

---

[18]   *Riguardo al precetto, e proibizion, sempre dobbiamo conformarci alla volunta divina, eziandio quanto al volito materiale, mentre Dio ci ha dati i suoi precetti, affinchè gli osserviamo, e questi già sono notificati nelle sue leggi.*

not command us to obey his will, which is still not made plain to us.

And so, St. Thomas confirms our case more expressly in another place (2.2., qu. 104, art. 4, ad 3), where he asks: "Whether God must be obeyed in all things?" He responds in the affirmative, but later, he proposes this objection to himself (*ad tertium*): "Whoever obeys God, conforms his will to the divine will, even in regard to the thing willed. But not insofar as we are held to conform our will to the divine will, as it is held above (1.2., q. 19, art. 10. This is the passage we already related above on the thing willed materially). Therefore a man is not held to obey God in all things." And so he responds: "*Ad tertium*, it must be said that even if a man is not always held to will what God will, nevertheless he is always held to will what God will him to will, and he especially makes that known to man through divine precepts." Look at how well the Angelic doctor explains it, we are not held to keep his precepts unless they have been manifested to us. Therefore, a man is held to obey God and to conform to the divine will, not in all things, "which God wills," but in that only, "which God will us to will." But how will we know that which God will us to will? St. Thomas says we will know particularly "when he makes it known through divine precepts." Consequently, a doubtful notice of the precept does not suffice that we would be held to keep the precept as willed by God, rather, a certain and manifest notice is required in addition: this is certainly what the word "makes known" means.

I seek now to conclude this point: In some case where the divine will has still not been made known to us in regard to the observance of particular precepts, are we held to conform to it? Hardly, says the Angelic Doctor, noting: "But in particular, we do not know what God wills, and so for this reason we are not held to conform our will to the divine will." And Fr. Gone expressly confirms it, as we have seen:

"A man is not held to conform himself to the divine will in regard to a thing desired materially, except when the divine will has been manifested to us by a precept or a prohibition." (*Clyp.*, disp. 6, art. 2, n. 37). Nay more, John Gerson wrote, as we related in another place, that God cannot oblige the creature to keep his will unless he would first manifest it to him: "It is necessary that the manifestation of the ordination and will of God be given, for through his will alone God cannot yet absolutely impose an obligation on the creature." (*De Vita Spir.*, lect. 2).

Hence it is clear that St. Thomas was always uniform, instructing us that certain laws ought to oblige; for in all citations where he treats on the matter he always uses express words which clearly show this is his mind. He said that for a law to oblige it is necessary, "that it be applied by notice of it." (1.2., q. 90, art. 4). He said in the same place, *ad primum*, that promulgation of the law is, "from the very fact that God inserted it into the minds of men to know naturally." He says, "*to know naturally*" therefore, then a man is held to keep the law when he acknowledges the law, but not when he is uncertain about the law: he said the law is a measure whereby a man ought to measure himself and hence said that this *measure ought to be very certain.* (1.2., q. 17, a. 4, ad 3). He said that, just as a rope does not bind unless it is applied to a thing that must be bound by contact, so a precept does not bind except by knowledge of the same. Therefore he adds: "For that reason, no one is bound by a precept except by the medium of knowledge of that precept." (*De verit.*, q. 17, art. 3). He said not only is held to obey God, but even more, his divine will especially *when it is made known to him* through divine precepts. (1.2., q. 19, art. 10). Therefore, according to all these doctrines of St. Thomas, it must be concluded that divine law does not oblige not only when it has *understood*, not only when it is *most certain*, not only when one has *knowledge* about it, but when the very thing *is made known.*

For that reason, since these have been posited, our adversaries object in vain, that when there are two equally probable opinions, the safer opinion, even if it does not induce a certain obligation, at least induces a probable obligation; and therefore it lacks the morally certain dictate on the honesty of an action; without that it is not lawful to act. But the response has been made above to a great many things, namely, that when a twofold equally probable opinion occurs, the opinion which favors the law, does not induce any obligation but to lay aside doubt; but a doubt of this sort, according to all of the probabilists and probabiliorists, and of Fr. Patutius himself, as we saw, can well be laid aside not only from a direct principle, but even from a certain reflexive principle, in which certitude on the honesty of the action is not contained.

79.—They object: 4) That rule of the Sacred Canons: "In doubtful matters the safter way must be chosen," as is contained in cap. *Illud Dominus, de clerico excomm. deposito, etc.*, and the same is said in cap. *Ad audientiam, de homic.*, and in cap. *Petitio tua, eod., tit.*, and likewise in *Clement. Exivi,* (to the words "Likewise because"), *de verb. signif.*, and in cap. *Juvenis, de sponsal.* Our adversaries say: These canons generally speak on all doubts, therefore they must be generally received. I respond and concede as long as they must generally be received in regard to all practical doubts, and facts, such as indeed were these, which occurred in respect to the cases of the aforesaid canons; but not in regard to all speculative doubts, even of law, as St. Antoninus, Christianus Lupus, Joannes Nyder, Domingo de Soto, Suarez, Tabiena, Silvester, Angelus, Henriquez, Angles, St. Bonaventure, Gerson, Pelbartus, and others nearly commonly say, as we shall soon see; for they say the aforesaid rule of the canons is in regard to speculative doubts about counsel, not about precept.

Look at what St. Antoninus said: "They introduce the phrase, 'In doubtful matters the safer road must be chosen.' The response is made that this is true on the honesty and greater part of merit, and not on the necessity of salvation in regard to all doubts; otherwise it would be necessary that everyone enter religion." (Part. 2, tit. 1, cap. 11, §31). The words of St. Antoninus are quite clear, but Fr. Patutius says that the holy Archbishop only speaks on one who holds a mild opinion favoring a unique truth, and infers from those words, "otherwise it would be necessary for all to enter religion," therefore, Fr. Patutius says that St. Antoninus means to speak here on two equally safe and morally certain opinions, and on the other hand he pretends to show that St. Antoninus supposes this by the force of the aforesaid rule that in all doubtful opinions the safer must be held; but to clarify the issue, here he omitted what St. Antoninus prefaced in §28 (*loc. cit.*), speaking on a certain contract in regard to which wise men disputed among themselves as to whether it would or would not be usurious. So the Saint writes: "And if it were to be said that it is usurious, and usury is against the Decalogue, the response can be made that it is not clear if this contract is usurious since even wise men reckon the matter differently among themselves. Moreover, although it is said that ignorance of the natural law does not excuse, it is understood on those matters, which are expressly in themselves or reductively in regard to natural and divine law, as against faith or precepts through evident reasons, either by a determination of the Church or the common teaching of doctors, and not on these matters, which are carried out through many mediums and are not clearly proved to be against precepts and articles."

Next, in §31, he says: "But wishing to prove that the contract is illicit, they argue this: 'In doubtful matters the safer road must be chosen.' The response is made that this is true on the honesty and majority of the merit, but not on the necessity for salvation in regard to all doubtful things; otherwise it would be necessary that all enter religion." Therefore, St. Antoninus by no means thought that a universal law was present, whereby we must follow the safer road in all doubts; for in speculative matters, which occur when two probable opinions coincide, according to the case which he then argued, he thought the aforesaid rule of the canons is not about a precept. The example he poses, although it is absurd, that otherwise it would be fitting for everyone to enter religion, is in no way opposed to our teaching; for there the Saint was not speaking against those who would have presumed to say that everyone was held to enter religion on account of that rule, rather he responds directly to those who say the contract is forbidden by the force of the aforesaid rule obliging one to follow the safer side: "But wishing to prove that the contract is illicit, they argue this: 'In doubtful matters the safer road must be chosen'." Here, therefore, the discussion is precisely on a contract that is speculatively doubtful, and St. Antoninus responds: "The response is made that this is true on the integrity and majority of the merit, but not on the necessity for salvation in regard to all doubtful things." For that reason, it does not avail to say: "St. Antoninus intends to speak on one who, wishing to enter into a contract, does not think it is doubtful but certainly licit; for the holy Archbishop does not intend even to speak on an opinion held uniquely favoring the truth, but on an opinion altogether in doubt; otherwise, why would he respond so ineptly to the objection of some who meant to show the contract is illicit because the canons command that the safer path must be chosen in doubts, that the rule is on the honesty and majority of merit, but not on necessity in regard to all doubts? Rather, he would have needed to respond that the rule proceeds only in doubts but not when the one acting has an opinion favoring its truth; for the Saint said that the rule of the canons is not on the universal precept "in regard to all doubts", for in regard to all he says it is only, "on the honesty and the majority of merit."

Just as St. Antoninus writes, so also do other theologians think. John Nyder says: "That one is to choose the safer path is of counsel, not of precept." (*In Consolat.*, part. 3, cap. 10). Tabiena so thinks: "It odes not avail, that in doubtful matters the safer path must be chosen, because this is not a precept, but a counsel." (*In summa verb.*, Scrupulus). Navarre writes the same thing (*Manual*, cap. 27, n. 181), as do Domingo de Soto (*de Justitia et Jure*, lib. 7, part. 3, art. 2); Abbas (*cap. Significasti*); Sylvester (*verb. Jejunium*, quest. 10, n. 27); Suarez (tom. 5, in 3, p. disp. 40, sect. 6, n. 8); Angles (p. 1, *de jejun.*, q. 9, art. 1, dub. 2, concl. 3); Henriquez (lib. 14, *de irreg.*, cap. 3, n. 4, in fin). Likewise, St. Bonaventure, Gerson, etc. quoted in Terillus (*de probab. quaest.* 26, num. 21).

And really, according to the cases of the canons that were related, that rule was altogether to be preserved because there were practical doubts, as well as doubts of fact; it could not be held as some certain, direct or reflexive principle, in which the obligation to follow the safer side would be excused, on account of scandals and other evils which ought to be avoided in those cases. So that this may be clearly distinguished, here it is fitting for us to discus what cases happened then, and the decisions of the texts that have been presented to us in objection. In regard to the chapter *Illud Dominus de clerico excomm. deposito*, etc., there the case was of a certain Bishop, the public notoriety of the excommunication imposed against him, rashly preferred to celebrate, for which affair we say he was rightly punished with deposition by Innocent III; since he had persistent doubt about the excommunication, he was held to apply due diligence to become more certain about the truth, and meanwhile he ought to have ceased from the celebration [of the Mass]. Therefore, the Pope duly said: "Because in doubtful matters the safer road must be chosen, even if he might be uncertain about what was imposed on him, nevertheless he ought to abstain all the more from celebrating the Sacraments in the Church."

In regard to the chapter *Ad audientiam, de homic.*, the case was about a certain priest that inflicted a wound upon a man, on account of which the man died. Next, he was uncertain whether the man died due to a wound of this sort. Clement III decreed that it was fitting for the priest to abstain from offering Mass and therefore, said: "Since we ought to choose the safer path in doubtful matters, it is fitting for you to enjoin this priest that he should not carry out ministry." Here, it must be noticed firstly that the truth of the matter was not yet sufficiently explored, namely, whether such a wound caused the man's death, which is why the text adds: "If he died from another infirmity, the priest will be able to continue ministry." Therefore, the Pope wisely established that in the meantime, the priest should not celebrate Mass; for he said in such a doubt the safer road must be chosen. Secondly, it must be noticed with Navarre and Suarez, that in such a case it was not a question on the observation of some precept, but only on a certain fittingness, that if later it would be established that the priest was a murderer, the people would not have been scandalized from seeing him celebrate Mass. The same thing was established in a similar case of a doubtful homicide in *cap. Petitio tua, 24, de homic.*, where it was said: "He must be consulted more to abstain in a doubt of this sort rather than to rashly celebrate Mass." Who does not see that in these cases, to necessarily flee scandal it was fitting that the safer way be chosen by abstaining from the celebration of Mass?

We respond to the Clementine law *Exivi*, that there the Friars Minor requested of the Apostolic See, whether they were held *sub grave* to those rules of the order that were conceived by mandatory words? The Pope responds: "In those matters that regard the salvation of the soul, to avoid serious remorse of conscience, the securer side must be held." In the first place, as Fr. Eusebius Amort censed, when the Pope said, "the securer side must be held," he did not mean to speak on material security by embracing the safer part, but on formal security of conscience in an act of moral certitude without a practical doubt; for if he had meant to speak on material security, he certainly would have made it known that all terms in the imperative mood denote a command which would have been materially safer and far from doubt; but the Pope said that only those words must *be understood* as imperative which seem to be so *from the force of the word*, namely on account of the expression of the words, "or at least by reason of the matter." Moreover, he said: "Although the Friars are not held to the observance of all the things which are placed under the words of the imperative mood in the rule just as if were equivalent to precepts, nevertheless it is expedient for the Friars themselves to observe the purity of the rule and the rigor which they know they are obligated to just as equivalent to commands, which here are noted further down." And after this the Pope designates that they must be held just as a precept. So Fr. Eusebius Amort responds to this Clementine law.

But I add a more convincing response. The case was, as is read in the same text: Previously the Friars were in doubt as to whether the rule only obliged to the vows of poverty, chastity and obedience; but Pope Nicholas III already declared it obliges even in regard to those evangelical counsels which are expressed in the rule with the obligatory words of a precept, or equivalent to a precept. Next, the Friars asked Clement V to make plain to them, "What they ought to thinks as equivalent to precepts?" For that reason, Pope Clement, as we saw earlier, explained these things which seemed equivalent to precepts from the force of the words and by reason of the grave matter that was in question; he prefaced those words "to avoid grave remorse of conscience," the securer side must e held. Therefore, in that case it was not a question on two equally probable sides, but only whether there was an obligation to follow a side which, according to the rigor of the rule, as well as what Nicholas III had already declared was not only safer, but the only safe path; since it was already established, the rule, from the force of the words, and the gravity of the matter oblige one to keep just as precepts not only the three principal vows of religion, but also the evangelical counsels, which are explained in the rule and therefore, could not be omitted without grave remorse of conscience. Hence, Clement said to avoid a remorse of this sort, the securer part must be held, which really was the only true and secure one; and no reasons for the other side are sufficient that a transgression of these counsels availed to excuse one from a serious fault.

At length, in regard to cap. *Juvenis*, 3, *de sponsal.*, the case was that a certain young man when seven years old was married to a certain girl, and after the latter's death, contracted nuptials with her cousin. Hence, when a doubt arose as to whether the first marriage was invalid due to the impotence of the seven year old, Eugene III commanded the man to be separated from the aforesaid cousin, on account of the honesty of the Church, adding: "Because in these matters, which are doubtful, we esteem more certainly that we ought to hold, etc." Now that we have posited these we say, 1) The Pope rightly commanded the separation, not because he thought in doubtful opinions the safer road must be held, but because the separation was necessary to avoid scandal, and also to preserve the uprightness of the Church made safe and protected. We say, 2) that the Pope, by proffering the words, "we esteem more certainly that we ought to hold," did not say it in regard to the youth who knew well enough if in the time of the first marriage he was potent or impotent, but in respect to the judgment which in that forum, since the reasons of the different sides were dubious, it was far from doubt what is more certain they are held to follow, and hence he said "*more certain* (not safer), namely that the Pope himself had judged it was more certain, that the separation must be imposed, because still doubt persisted on the validity of the first marriage, for which possession stood stronger. Moreover, what is there between this and our question, where it is a question on the internal forum and not about a doubt of fact, rather on an equally probable opinion? Thus it is clear, that all doubts pertinent to the text of the case were practical doubts, as well as of fact, which could be laid aside by nothing from a reflexive principle.

So much more, what the Popes themselves in speculative doubts did not always use this rule that the safer side must be held. Adrian VI, as Domingo de Soto relates, (in 4, dist. 27, quaest. 1, a. 4) not withstanding that he thought the opposite, dispensed in a certain consummated matrimony, relying only on the testimony of Cajetan. Besides, in *cap. Laudabilem, de frigid., et mal.*, it is held that the Pope, to a certain husband, who was uncertain about the power to carry out marital relations, conceded that he could attempt for three years. If a doubtful law must always be preserved, as our adversaries would have it, then there were any doubt whether that woman would be someone else's, how could the Pope permit that man to go to her for three years and try to enter relations? Add that if that law to follow the safer part were universal in all doubts, even speculative ones, then not even Probibalism could be held as an opinion, which indeed is not safer but remains within the boundaries of probability; but this cannot be said, since the proposition was proscribed by Alexander VIII, which says: "It is not lawful to follow an opinion even if it is the most probable among probable ones." Add, that even if the matter were doubtful, whether the aforesaid rule of the canons must be understood on all doubts and not only on practical doubts, the reasons themselves, whereby it is so clearly proved that a doubtful law, inasmuch as it is not sufficiently promulgated, does not oblige, the same things prove this rule of the canon is not a universal law in regard to all doubts, but only in regard to doubts of fact and practical doubt.

Next, to put an end to the present point, I ask (and for this purpose advance this reason to which I do not believe a response could be made), What do the canons command? They command in doubtful matters a safer road must be chosen. Therefore, it is said *in doubts*, but what if we are not in doubt? Why would that rule stand in the way, if a man rests upon some certain principle? Then he forms his conscience morally certain about the honesty of the action, and goes forth from the boundaries of doubt, nor can he be said to any longer be in doubt. Besides, our adversaries themselves concede that the aforesaid canon to follow the safer side does not hold place in a matter of justice; but if the rule of the canons which is safer, were a universal law for all doubts, even someone that legitimately possesses a thing, in doubt whether it were his or someone else's, would be held to despoil himself of it; but St. Augustine teaches the contrary, (*in can. Si virgo,* caus. 54, q. 1), saying: "In the law of estates, each possessor is said to be of good faith, as long as he does not know he possesses someone else's good.

80.—They object, 5) the decision of a certain concession of the French Bishops, where it was decreed in equally probable opinions the safer part must be held. I particularly revere the authority of such prelates as these, but all teach extrinsic authority of great wise men cannot be of weight where the intrinsic reasoning seems certain and convincing;

so much more, when the sufficient authority of others is not lacking. Moreover, I notice that there exists no less extrinsic authority favoring our opinion than there does for the opposite, nay more even greater. It cannot be denied that our opinion has at least for eighty or even ninety years been the nearly common opinion among the authors of moral science, among whom are a great many Cardinals, Bishops, doctors of universities and characteristically a great many teachers of the Dominican Order, in which great doctrine has always flourished. Here for the sake of brevity I omit all the names and to note the citations of their propositions, which I have already given in another little work of mine, titled *Dell' Uso moderato dell' opinione egualemente probabile.*

Nor does it avail to say the authority of these in this matter must be thought insufficient, even by me, while they are held by me as deceived, since to uphold out opinion they rested upon that principle, which I myself rejected: "One who acts probably, acts prudently." Now I said from the beginning of this dissertation, that such a principle alone, and taken up directly in itself is not sufficient to regard the use of an equally probable opinion. Nevertheless, I advert, now a great many authors (as we saw above) rested upon the same, our principle, in defense of our opinion, namely that a doubtful law cannot oblige. Besides, I say, that not even those authors use only the aforesaid principle, "One who acts probably acts prudently." And I so confer the matter: These authors already affirmed one side, that to act licitly a moral certitude about the honesty of the action is necessary. On the other hand, the same authors established our very same principles in their Words in different places, namely, that a law not sufficiently promulgated does not oblige, and that where *libertas possidet*, an uncertain law cannot induce a certain obligation, from that principle so acclaimed by them, that "In doubt the condition of the possessor is better." Therefore, on principles of this sort, by speaking on the use of probable opinions, if they did not make express mention, or at least they indubitably supposed them. For that reason, it must be rightly determined that they, by that saying, "One who acts probably acts prudently," they use it more as a type of corollary or even a consequent, which is inferred by reflexive principles. To much the more, that this matter of probable opinions was then very confused, for that reason they spoke confusedly on it, after more ancient authors spoke more confusedly on it. Moreover, that saying, "One who acts probably, etc.," can be received twofold: if it is received as a dependence upon reflexive principles, it is truly prudent and certain; but if it is received as a direct principle, excluding the reflection of judgment, it is false. And so on that saying taken up directly, the Gallican prelates rightly showed that they were not content, and took up the decree which they published, namely: "In doubtful matters on the business of salvation, where both sides offer for themselves reasons of equal importance, we ought to follow that which is safer, or which is in that case uniquely safe; not that of counsel but of precept we should hold in that place, by the saying of Scripture: He who loves danger will perish in it." After the last words have been noted, it appears for certain that these prelates spoke on acting with practical doubt, having no principle in which one could lay aside doubt; for if they really mean to speak on one acting, who forms a final judgment, not only from the probability of the opinion but from another certain reflexive principle, otherwise I think that the prelates would have decreed it. But, in regard to a great many edicts of the Bishops proclaimed in France, which Fr. Patutius asserts and transcribed in his work, *La regula prossima delle umane azioni*, and in which he said probabilism was proscribed, he chose those attentively and considered that all these regard precisely a certain book by the title: *Apologia Casuistarum*, which was rightly condemned, inasmuch as it asserts very lax propositions, namely that any opinion can be securely held, not only less probable but even probably probable, according to the authority of four, or three, or even one author. This is why the aforesaid edict opposes nothing, or at least insufficiently our opinion. Moreover, in regard to the intrinsic force of the reasonings (which ought to be principally heeded, for the extrinsic authority does not act on something which advances the presumption of intrinsic force), by that judgment, and a great many others side with me, now holds suitable and evident. Furthermore, what pertains to the extrinsic authority of doctors, I think, as I showed above, holds the most sufficient. So much more, when we notice that our adversaries make no adequate response to our reasons; and on the other side, if their arguments would avail, they would prove, at any rate, the condemned *tutiorism* would necessarily need to be held. But, by speaking about these matters, where they have not yet written on what has been proposed for the rigid system, but only what they approve orally, I venerate all and repute them wiser than me; but I say that then these assert a greater authority to me, if I would know they maturely weighted the moment of each opinion; but on this I exceedingly doubt, and rightly, while I see the same writers of the rigid opinion show from those, or scarcely heed our arguments, or respond to us with equivocations and fallacies, in which each one understanding very easily avails to make a response. I add, those giving approval of this sort, like a great many (as we said above) regard direct motives, but bend the mind insufficiently or not at all to heed reflexive principles, which require great reflection from the others; but I hold for certain that reflection of this sort by those, who today betray themselves as anti-probabilists, and boast, scarcely apply it. But let us progress beyond this because the matter is odious, and in it I hardly avail to explain myself. In a little book on this controversy that I recently published, I wrote the opinions of a great many Bishops, Abbots and other erudite persons at the end of its pages, that do not hesitate to appeal to our system as true and certain.

81.—They object, 6) The text of Ecclesiasticus (Sirach) 3:27: "He who loves danger perishes in it," therefore they say that he who throws himself into transgression of the law, has already sinned. But we must here notice the equivocation, or ambiguity, which intercedes. One that uses an equally probable opinion, resting on a certain principle, is indeed in danger of transgressing the law, but not sinning. But why? Our adversaries repeat, how does he not sin who exposes himself to the danger of transgressing the law? I repeat, he does not sin; it is necessary to distinguish a certain law from an uncertain one. When the law is certain, indeed we cannot be exposed to the danger of transgressing it, like someone that delays his conversion even to death, just as in the aforesaid text, it is said: "A hard heart will have a bad time of it in the end, and he who loves danger will perish in it." The law of charity is certain, which everyone ought to have for one another, to not long remain in sin on account of the danger of dying in mortal sin; but loving this danger, he will perish in it. Equally, here they object with the doctrine of St. Thomas, which coincides in the same thing: "Whoever commits to the peril of mortal sin, sins mortally." (*Quodlib.*, 9 a 15). These words can be explained in two ways: either on placing oneself in the danger of transgressing a certain law according to the case expressed in Scripture, or rather on acting with a practical doubt, according to another text of the same Angelic Doctor, where he said: "One who commits something, or omits it, in which he is uncertain whether it is a mortal sin, commits himself to peril." (In 4, dist. 21, quest. 2, a. 3, ad 3). It must be noted that the Angelic doctor does not say that in a case where one doubts he offends the law, but in which he doubts it is a mortal sin; for speaking in another place about an uncertain precept, he said, as we related above: "No one is bound by precept, except by the medium of knowledge of that precept." (*De Verit., quaest.* 17, a. 3).

82.—Therefore, our adversaries say that when the law is doubtful, one who exposes himself to danger transgresses it, and certainly he sins from the Scripture they produced, "One who loves danger, will perish in it." Therefore, I say again, to avoid this danger it will be necessary to embrace strict *tutiorism*, by not acting except with certain moral certitude, and immune from all fear because the opinion which one wants to follow is true. They respond, it is not sufficient that the opinion is very probable, based on the proscription of Alexander VIII of the opposed proposition, which said: "It is not lawful to follow an opinion even if it is the most probable among probable ones." Therefore, I say firstly, it is deduced from this, that it is not a true opinion because when the law is doubtful, he still sins who exposes himself to the danger of transgressing it, for even with the most probable opinion, acting he incurs danger (although it might be more remote) of transgressing the law. Rather, I add besides, (and here we slightly recall) because he, who believes nothing is licit, exposes himself to danger of offending the law, and on the other hand says the less safe opinion can be held, merely when it is very probable, it is quite difficult, and hardly ever will he be able to be induced to follow it with a secure conscience, unless he finds it strictly certain, and immune from all fear. And I reason in this way: The most probable opinion is that which, even if it occupies the highest degree, nevertheless, does not exceed the confines of probability, according to the limits of the same proposition as the one condemned above, which said: "the most probable among probable," and therefore, according to what the doctors commonly say, the most probable opinion which is also called morally certain (still, broadly in speech), does not exclude every prudent fear that it might be false; in regard to a difference of opinion or feeling strictly certain, which excludes every prudent fear. Therefore, if the most probable opinion does not exclude all prudent fear, then the opinion of the most probable is not indeed opposed to that which is only tenuously probable; for a tenuous probability is not probability, but merely a certain false appearance, or a vain apprehension of probability which can produce no prudent fear, but only some imprudent fear; but imprudent fear is not a fear which would avail to cause any danger of sin. Both the rigid and strict tutiorists commonly say that imprudent fears of this sort ought to be condemned and that there is no reason for them to hold them. It would be really foolish to say that God imposed upon us to also avoid irrational fears. Therefore, by speaking properly the opinion of the most probable is not opposed to that which tenuously, but those which are doubtfully probable: and this, just as the most probable (as we said above) does not lack all prudent fear which is false; so the opposed opinion of the most probable does not lack every prudent motive, which is true. Now I ask, if it is posited that an opinion favoring the law, and the opposite of the most probable favors liberty, it is doubtfully probable how one who regards it is illicit to be sent into the danger of transgressing the law, wishing to follow the most probable, could ever in practice be induced to believe firmly with a peaceful conscience, because the opinion favoring the law may not be truly probable, and so to use the most probable that he would be exposed to the danger of transgressing the law? Where will he discover the scale so exact, that it renders him safe that the opinion favoring the law indeed only lacks the weight of probability, which makes it probable, and so he could act securely and immune from danger? Thus I repeat what I have said from the beginning, that one who believes he cannot be held in practice to some opinion that is less safe unless it is the most probable, could with great difficulty form a certain dictate to act unless he embraced strict tutiorism, because that alone is immune from all danger of transgressing the law, and thus is free.

85.—Our adversaries insist and say: "One who embraces safer opinions advances safer. I respond: It is certainly unlawful to relax the observance of divine laws more than is lawful, but it is no less evil to render the divine yoke harder than it ought to be; for exceeding severity (as Cabassutius writes *in Praefat.* theor. juris, etc.), "while it compels men to exceedingly arduous things, it precludes the path of eternal salvation; it condemns those that must be saved (as St. Bonaventure says), and consigns those conscious of their own weakness to desperation. For it happens that miserable men, after hearing this more rigid doctrine, will believe or be uncertain that mortal fault is present where there is really is not any; nevertheless, conquered by the difficulty of the matter they will sin mortally from an erroneous conscience, and be condemned." Therefore, St. Bonaventure says (*Comp. theol. vert.*, l. 2, c. 23, n. 3): "One must take precautions against a conscience that is too liberal and too strict; for the first generates presumption, the section desperation; likewise, the first often says a mad thing is good, while on the other hand the second that a bad thing is good; often the first saves the damned while the second damns the saved." Hence, John Gerson wisely wrote: "Learned Theologians ought not be to quick to assert something is a mortal sin where they are not very certain on the matter; for through rigid assertions of this sort, and excessively strict ones in all affairs by no means are men lifted from the mud of sinners, rather they are sunk deeper in it because they are more desperate. What benefit is there, nay more, what does it not harm to narrow the command of God more than is just, which is very broad?" (*De vit. spir.*, lect. 4). St. John Chrysostom gives us the best instruction: "Be austere in regard to your life, but of great liberality in regard to someone else's." It is also so in the canon *Alligant*, caus. 26, q. 7. Suarez adds: "Nay more the danger incurred to souls is greater if so many bonds are laid down in doubtful cases." (In 2.2., qu. 89, a. 7). Cardinal Pallavicino explains this more profusely: "That saying 'In doubt the safer part must be chosen,' if it is considered in itself is very true provided it is understood rightly: for it is a question on the practical choice, and this always ought to be the safest, because it ought to always be evidently licit: or on the choice of a speculative opinion, and in regard to it a greater security must be sought for the opinion, not a greater security of action. If an opinion were to be induced that we are always held to do an action which is more secure, even from the material transgression, this opinion ought to be safer, but is especially exposed to the frequent danger of formal transgression; because the safer is the opposite." (In 1.2, disp. 9, c. 4, a. 11, n. 12). Fr. Bancel Dominicanus wrote the same thing: "There are many things that are safer to do, but at the same time it is also safer not to believe one is obligated to do them, unless he were constituted morally certain about such an obligation." (*Brev. univ. theol.*, p. 2, tract. 6, q. 5, a. 5). For that reason the same author concludes: "Since we ought not form a conscience on the obligation to something under a penalty, unless the obligation were morally certain, we ought not impose some burden while it is certain to us morally that the freedom to embrace whatever we will from the opinions of the same remains."

So that I might sincerely affirm the truth, when I began to devote myself to moral theology, because it happened that I studied under a teacher of a more rigid opinion, at that time I contended with others on this point; but after better pleading the reasonings of this controversy, the opposite opinion which favors an equally probable opinion, appeared morally certain to me: and indeed, I have been induced by it to repeat here this principle so many times that a doubtful law does not oblige. Hence, I remain persuaded that it is unlawful to bind consciences to follow the safer when there are equally probable opinions since it brings the danger of falling into a great many formal faults. Besides, I have in our time, the reclamation of a gentler opinion so bitterly opposed, that I have diligently recalled this point to a balance of scales, reading and re-reading all the modern authors I have at hand, who fought for the rigid opinion, I was prompted to abandon my opinion, on the spot and it no longer appeared certain to me; for according to a great many authors, which I at one time held as probable, later I did not blush to reject; so all the more I am not ashamed to retract this opinion, which is of greater moment. But the more diligently I have been pressed to assess the reasoning of our opinion, they seem to me to be all the more certain. Moreover, if anyone were present who could illumine me with clearer points by showing the falsity of the two principles which I have taken care to explain here, I should be extremely thankful for him, and on the spot I promise to revoke my writing in public. Nevertheless, until it is otherwise for me, than I perceive it at the present, I will not be persuaded, I say that without grave remorse of conscience I could not bind others to follow the safer way when there are equally probable opinions, unless the Church were to declare the opposite, to which I would gladly submit my judgment if she will declare it.

Moreover, I protest that I do not approve of those confessors who, adhering to excessive austerity, quickly condemn the use of a great many opinions, which rest upon a serious foundation; so on the other hand I cannot approve those who are quick to acclaim opinions without a certain foundation as though they were probable. The confessor, before he were to embrace some opinion, is held to weigh the intrinsic reasons, and when some convincing reason occurs to him for a safer opinion, that does not seem to supply an adequate response to him, then he cannot embrace the opposite as less safe, even if the authority of a great many doctors would favor it; only the authority would not be of such a weight, that it would seem to have more deference than apparent reason, according to what St. Thomas teaches: "Someone of little knowledge is made more certain about that which he hears from some science than from that which appears to him according to reason." (2.2. q. 9, a. 8, ad 2).

84.—For this theory, rather insofar as it considers in practice choosing opinions, it is usually asked whether it is expedient to give preference to rigid ones or gentle ones? I respond: Where it is a question of removing a penitent from the danger of formal sin, the confessor ought, generally speaking, as far as Christian prudence will suggest, use gentler opinions; but where gentler opinions render the danger of formal sin more proximate, (insofar as there are several opinions of authors, *e.g.*, in regard to avoiding the near occasion of sin and others of this sort), then it is always expedient that the confessor use, nay more I say that as a doctor of souls he is held to sue safer opinions which induce the penitent to preserve himself in a state of grace.

Moreover, I do not know how it could be taught with a good conscience (generically speaking), that absolution could be denied to a penitent, who had already obtained the certain right to absolution due to the confession of his faults, for the reason that the penitent refuses to follow the safer of two opinions of equal weight. This is that rigor which I hold to be immoderate and without any doubt unjust, and I condemn it, since this austerity can be the reason that a great many souls will be damned. While I discover a great many authors, even probabiliorists, both modern and ancient, related by our adversaries favoring the use of rigid opinion who teach the opposite. Look at how the probabiliorist Pontassus speaks: "Still, it must be affirmed that if the confessor were persuaded that the opinion of his penitent is probable (now he speaks on opinion, to which the safer opposite is also probable), then the penitent can demand absolution from him, seeing that then he would not act against his conscience." (*Verb., Confessarius,* cap. 2.) Moreover, if the confessor can absolve the penitent, he is held to when the latter has a right to absolution. The probabiliorist Cabassutius says the same thing: "Each confessor ought to absolve that penitent, who does not wish to abstain from an action that is licit according to the probable authority of pious men and doctors that has not been condemned in the Church, even if it is held as less probable according to the probable authority of others which the confessor himself follows (It must be understood, not notably less), as Navarre, Sylvius and others show." And he gives the reasoning for this, "because the cconfessor acts to be against his own opinion, but not against his own conscience, since he is held to absolve one disposed." (*Theor. jur.* l. 3, c. 13, n. 13). Additionally, Victoria, who wrote before the year 1545, said: "But what will (the confessor) do when there are a pair of probable opinions, and they have their proper asserters? I respond, whether it is the priest's own, or not, he is held to absolve in such a case; so also Paludanus. It is clearly proved, for such is the grace, and a confessor has probability that he is in such a grace because he knows his opinion is probable, therefore he ought not deny him absolution." (*De confess.,* n. 109). Likewise, Adrian writes similarly: "If the contrary is held by a great many doctors of a more serious or even equal authority, the priest ought not presume of his own authority to bind in his opinion which perhaps might be erroneous." (*De confess.,* q. 5, dub. 7). Navarre wrote the same thing: "If there are contrary opinions of doctors, and the confessor entrusts himself to an evident text, or rests upon reasoning, but the penitent on a doubt, he ought not absolve him; but if the penitent uses equal reasoning, or nearly equal, and has for himself some famous doctor, he will be able to absolve him." Moreover, he adds: "When it is uncertain whether the penitent does this, or ought to give, the confessor ought to choose the gentler opinion," and he cites the Angelic Doctor and Sylvestrus (*Manual*, cap. 26, n. 4), favoring this position. St. Antoninus confirms the same thing in a great many places: "Goffredus de Fontibus seems to think the same thing, in these contrary opinions which are tolerated by the Church, as has been said, and because he ought to propose to the man that confesses what would be good for him to labor to be informed on this by prudent men, to the extent that others hold a contrary opinion, especially if the confessor were not his ordinary one and of a contrary opinion, and so absolves him. Ricardus supposes the same thing in a clear manner, but he does not distinguish whether the confessor is his ordinary one or not." (Part. 1, tit. 6, cap. 10, §10). In another place, the holy Archbishop, speaking about that contract (which we discussed above) debated in Florence, said that one that would enter into such a contract must be counseled not to do so; but after he adds: "But if such he refuses to receive such a counsel ... it seems he must be left to his judgment, and neither condemned on that account, nor denied absolution." (Part. 2, tit. 1, cap. 11 § 29). At length, in another place, he said: "But if he (the confessor) cannot clearly perceive whether it is mortal, it does not seem then that a sentence must be anticipated, as Guillelmus says, that he should deny absolution for this reason, or burden the conscience with something mortal; because later, by acting against it, even if it was not mortal, it will be mortal for him because everything, which is against conscience, paves the road to hell. And since the laws are more eager to absolve than to bind, it seems better to be absolved and dismissed to divine judgment." (P. 2, tit. 4, cap. 5, §. *In quantum*). John Gerson says the same thing, as we noted above: "Learned theologians ought not be so quick to assert that some things are mortal where they are not very certain on the matter."

(*De Vit. Spir.*, lect. 4). Note, "Where they are not very certain." Look at how these authors of great name, whom no one will dear to accuse of laxity, speak unanimously. Finally, Domingo de Soto writes: "After the opinion of the penitent is probable, he excuses him from fault and therefore has the right to seek absolution, therefore the priest is held to extend it." (In 4, d. 18, q. 2, a. 5, ad 5). Soto himself already said in another place: "And when there are probable opinions among serious doctors, you may follow whichever you like and have a safe conscience." (Lib. 5, *de Just. et jur.*, q. 1, a. 6, circa fin.) After considering these things, it is fitting that the very listening minds of the confessor do not hesitate to provide absolution to the penitent that refuses embrace the safer opinion after the confession of his crimes while the opposite is less safe, but of equal weight. Last of all that have been listed here, St. Thomas firmly confirms the principle we hand down, which is a law, unless it were sufficiently and certainly promulgated, does not oblige. Thereafter it is concluded, that unless an opinion which favors the law were either certain or at least more probably certain, as we said from the beginning, we are not held to follow it.

MONITUM

In which a Decree of the Sacred Congregation of the General Inquisition held at Rome in 1761 in regard to the use of probable opinions is explained

85.—A certain pastor at Avicii in the diocese of Trent, in the year 1760 published a pamphlet together with eleven theses containing more propositions, which later were publicly promulgated by the same pastor. The pamphlet was this:

Probabilism in a public disputation by a venerable cleric of Avicii for the sake of exercise strictly explained against probabiliorism, inasmuch as *negotium perambulans in tenebris.* For the 10th day of June, 1760, in the canonical houses of Avicii. *Would that we were to observe the Lord's certain commands! What sollicitude is there among us on doubts?* The celebrated P. Const. Roncaglia, lib. 12, cap. 3.

I. Our probablism consists in these three things: It is lawful to follow what is equally probable favoring freedom, leaving behind what is equally probable favoring law. It is lawful to follow the less probable favoring freedom, while leaving behind what is more probable favoring law.

II. The use of probablism is especially safe: the use of probabiliorism is especially dangerous.

III. The use of genuine probablism can scarcely degenerate into laxity: the use of probabiliorism strictly as such ought to sally into rigorism.

IV. The probabiliorists, whereby such who follow what is more probable from counsel, we affirm act in a rather praiseworthy manner.

V. Probabiliorists, strictly in such matters, who on precept, because they clearly prove nothing, thrust themselves and others to what is more probable, and we rightly place upon them the name of rigorists.

VI. One can in no way aim at Christian perfection except by following probabilism.

VII. The abuse of probabiliorism is strictly such, that it is not only a bridle to license, but a stimulus to license, which we prove by the testimony of the French.

VIII. Therefore, our genuine probabilism, which neither induces corruption of morals nor was ever noted badly by the Holy See, is Thomistic in origin, and

Jesuitical in the progress of time, inasmuch as it was refined and emended, and proposed by the Jesuits against the Jansenists.

IX. Therefore, one who dwells in the aid of the firm foundation of probabilism, does so securely under the protection of a great many of the most excellent theologians tarrying here on earth.

From critical history. X. Hence, without any note of laxism we call upon the most gentle, but legitimate, which every caesarian law as well as pontifical persuades; not to mention the Dominican, which the illustrious order of Dominicans for so long embraced from the first times; as well as the pious, which cherishes Christian piety, which St. Thomas held as his special care, who taught two hundred years ago in his book of the Sentences favoring a great many opinions for freedom, but Christian, which was supremely familiar to Christ the Lord.

For the conclusion. Our Probablism favors freedom, and is notably more probable than the probabiliorism favoring law.

*　　*　　*

Moreover, this pamphlet was proscribed in the following year by the Prince of Trent, as well as by the Bishop and then by the Sacred Congregation of the Roman Inquisition on 26 February 1761, and so it is related was condemned: "But since theses and notes of this sort were examined in the general Congregation in the presence of our Most Holy Lord, Pope Clement XIII, his holiness, having heard, etc., the aforesaid pamphlet, and the theses expressed in it, condemns and forbids, as containing propositions of which some are respectively false, temerarious, and offensive to pious ears; but that exert from number X, namely the Probabilism, which he reckoned was supremely familiar to Christ the Lord, is erroneous and proximate to heresy. Therefore, the aforesaid pamphlet, or theses, as copied out above, Our Most Holy Lord forbids as condemned and prohibited, lest someone would dare to publicly defend the status of such, or publish, cause to be published, or to transcribe what has already been published, or to retain what has been published for himself whether to read privately or publicly, etc."

86.—The Rev. Fr. Jo. Vincent Patutius, in his work titled, *La Causa del Probabilismo*, etc., under the name of Adelphus Dositeus, contends that by this decree in the first theses the whole of probabilism was forbidden, so that it would be illicit to follow not only an equally probable opinion, but not even a more probable one favoring liberty. Yet, he contends this unjustly; for that pamphlet contains many distinct things: it contains different theses, and even different propositions, which are members or parts of theses. Moreover, since the aforesaid pamphlet arose, two difficulties were made by the wise over the proscription of this same pamphlet. The first was, whether they were individually condemned, not only all the theses of the pamphlet, but in addition all the propositions contained in the theses. But it seemed commonly, that although that although it stood in regard to truth that all the theses were proscribed, and each of them, nevertheless, hardly every proposition contained in the theses was condemned, rather only those which merited censure. For in the decree it was said: "His Holiness condemns and forbids the aforesaid pamphlet and the theses, just as containing propositions of which some are respectively false, temerarious, etc." Therefore, the pamphlet was not condemned and the theses in regard to all the propositions contained therein, "but as containing propositions of which some are respectively false, etc."

Furthermore, the proscription of these propositions differs from the proscription made by Alexander VII of the propositions, in respect to which it was said: "His Holiness decreed that the aforesaid propositions and every point of them must be condemned, so that whoever will have taught them jointly or separately, etc., happens, etc." And in the same mode were other propositions condemned by Innocent XI and Alexander VIII. Therefore, each of those propositions were condemned in particular, and to teach them whether in combination or separate was forbidden. But the propositions of the aforesaid pamphlet were not individual in particular, but, as it is said, *in globo* and *respectively*, namely only those which merited to be condemned: nor was it forbidden to teach them in combination or separately, but only taken summarily, according to what the Bishop of Trent expressed in his decree: "Forbidding lest the same articles taken up summarily be deduced even to discussion."

Therefore, what pertains to the first theses of the pamphlet, no part of that first proposition was condemned, which said it is licit to follow a more probable opinion favoring liberty, nor the second on an equally probable opinion. The only difficulty that remains is whether the third proposition on a less probable opinion was condemned; and because the proposition speaks generally, so that still a notably less probable opinion may be embraced, and for that reason it is uncertain whether the very thing was at least proscribed. And so it could even be doubted whether the last thesis, which said: "Our probablism favoring liberty is notably more probable, etc." so that this proposition would affirm the opinion, because that one can follow an opinion still less notably probable, is also a more probable opinion favoring law.

With this posited, now it was ascertained that, although all the theses were proscribed, nevertheless, all the proposition of these theses were not. Doubt merely remains a to whether it was *in globo* and in the confused pamphlet and theses, individual theses were condemned in particular, or merely some of them; and indeed, since in the decree it was not said: all theses; the words, "some of which," etc., it is uncertain whether it ought to refer to the theses or to the propositions contained in the theses. Even so, this doubt was mad clear later by the Sacred Congregation; for when the proscription of the aforesaid pamphlet was later, by the command of the same Congregation, inserted into the index of forbidden books, it was not said, "Folium, and the theses expressed in it," according to what had been said in the decree, but simply "The pamphlet of eleven theses, titled: *Probabilismus disputationi*, etc. For that reason, at present the Sacred Congregation has only proscribed the aforesaid *pamphlet*, that is only the paper as a whole, or the pamphlet of eleven theses, but not every and individual thesis. And really, since I have given letters on this doubt, that I should become altogether more certain about the matter, to two consulters of the Sacred Roman Inquisition, namely to the most reverend P. M. Thomas Augustine Ricchini, master of the Sacred Palace, an to the most reverend P. M. Pius Thomas Schiara, secretary of the Sacred Congregation of the Index; both responded to me that probabilism was not altogether forbidden by the decree of the Congregation, not in regard to the first, second or third proposition on a less probable opinion favoring freedom.

Besides, that I might argue more safely, I also sent a letter on this matter to the most eminent Cardinal Galli, the head of the penitentiary, begging him to clarify the fact of the matter by speaking to the reigning Pope, and the most Eminent Cardinal answered the same thing to me, writing these words: "I can make it more certain for you, O illustrious Lord. In the condemnation of the Pamphlet, about which you wrote me, the condemnation is not intended for any of these propositions on which it is argued in a Catholic school, and which are defended by many Catholics, but that Pamphlet was principally inhibited on account of the propositions which you know were worthy of censure."[19] I think that this response alone of this most eminent and wise cardinal suffices to stop up the mouth of all.

MONITUM II

87.—After I handed this to the press, I was quite surprised to read in the new Moral Theology recently published by Fr. Patutius, where Fr. Sidenius of Verona describes the life of the same Patutius, especially where he enumerates his works, and he confidently asserted that in the controversy between myself and Patutius in regard to the use of probable opinion, since Patutius himself responded to me in the second book, titled; *Osservazioni theoligiche sopra l'Apologia dell' Illustriss. e Reverendiss. Mons. D. Alfonso de Liguori*, etc.; I, convicted by the force of the arguments, having nothing further to oppose my adversary with, while I abstained from again making a response; nevertheless, lest I would altogether yield to what he wrote, since it would be disgraceful, I conveyed all the writings against me to the Sacred Congregation of the Index so that they would be condemned.

To the Pope! I lack this shame, the name of the accuser! But the matter is thus. I once published a certain short dissertation favoring the moderate use of equally probable opinion, led in from that principle that an uncertain law cannot demand one submit to a certain obligation, to the

---

[19]   *Posso accertare V.S. Illustriss. che nella condanna dell' accennato foglio, di cui mi scrive, non si è inteso di condannare veruna delle proposizioni, che si controvertono nelle Scuole cattoliche, e da mmolti cattolicamente si difendono, ma si è avuto il motivo di probirlo, perchè le proposizioni, che ella medesimariconosce meritevoli de censura ec.*

extent that a doubtful law lacks sufficient promulgation, which is essentially required "for the purpose that a law would obtain the power to oblige, which is proper for law," these are the words of St. Thomas. (1.2., q. 9, a. 1). For that reason, the same Holy Doctor advanced later that famous sentence: "No one is bound by some precept except by the medium of knowledge of that precept." (*De verit.*, q. 17, a. 3). Fr. Patutius opposed—with a violent style—my little dissertation in his first book, titled: *La causa del Probabilism richiamata all' esame da Mons. D. Alfonso de Liguori*, etc., published in 1764. He advanced these two objections, the first of which that when the Angelic Doctor uses the phrase "knowledge of the precept," by no means is it understood on the certain cognition of the precept, but only probable, even dubious notice of the precept, which (as he said), is now held, where it is a question on two equally probable but opposed opinions. The second was, that the eternal law, from which all other natural laws emanate, has been promulgated from eternity, before man was created, by a *casual, virtual* or *eminent* promulgation, and therefore it has the force to oblige even from eternity.

I copiously responded to this little book in an *Apologia* for my little dissertation, in which, it seemed to me and others, that I altogether refuted the objections of Patutius. But later, against this my *Apologia* Patutius advanced a second book, *Osservazioni theologiche* etc., which I mentioned at the beginning of this *Monitum*, and there my adversary, recognizing his first objections were hardly strong, considered the responses which he gave to my points, added to others: namely one, in which really he did nothing other than repeat the opposition written in the first book, by merely changing the epithet of promulgation; for where he had earlier said *casual* or *virtual*, in the second he affixed *essential*: the other, that natural law is promulgated to man in the very instant of the infusion of the soul into the body, before he acquires actual cognition of the law. Hence I was forced to respond in a larger book, titled: "*Dell' Uso moderato dell' opinione probabile*. There, I did enough convincingly to these and all other objections of Patutius and added may others which particularly confirmed my opinion.

To the first objection, however, that probable notice of the law, even if it is doubtful, suffices for its promulgation, the response is what was already brought in this dissertation. To the second, and third, namely that the divine law was promulgated to men from eternity by a *casual* or *essential* promulgation, I responded and showed from the authority of St. Thomas and all theologians, whom I have searched out with diligent labor, the divine law in no way binds men unless after it was actually promulgated to them it was also manifested to them. Look at the words of St. Thomas, which Patutius altogether professes to follow (but in this matter he either refuses to follow them, or it seems refuses to understand whereas the Holy Doctor is very clear and teaches our opinion in a great many places): "The eternal Law has eternal promulgation on the side of God the promulgator ... but on the side of the creature hearing it, or inspecting it cannot be an eternal promulgation." (1.2., q. 91, a. 1, ad 2). Therefore, no promulgation of the divine law can be said to have been made to a man so long as a man does not hear or inspect the law, certainly until the law is intimated and made known to him. For all other theologians following St. Thomas teach unanimously that although divine law will have had in itself, the virtue of obliging in the first act from eternity, still in the second act it never actually obliged men, unless after it was applied to them through its actual promulgation. Sylvius writes: "The law is then actually promulgated to each, when he receives cognition as a dictate from God, what must be embraced and put to flight according to right reason." (In 1.2., q. 90, a. 4, in fin.) And in another place he says: "The eternal law was materially a law from eternity, or under the reasoning of law actually obliging; because then it was not an actual and perfect promulgation." (In 1.2. q. 91, a. 1ad 2). Cardinal Gotti so speaks: "For this reason, that law would oblige in the second act, it is required indispensably that it be proposed to those subject to it by promulgation." (*Theol.* tom. 2, tract. 5, *de legib.* q. 1, dub. 3, §5 n. 31). And in another place he says: "From eternity [the eternal law] was in the mind of God, even if it did not yet bind from eternity; because it had not yet been applied and promulgated." (Tract 5, q. 2, dub. 1, n. 13). Fr. Gonet writes: "The eternal law could not oblige creatures from eternity by a defect of promulgation." (See also *in Clypeo theol.*, tom. 3, d. 1, a. 3). John Gerson writes: "It is necessary for a manifestation of the will of God to be given, for through his will alone, God cannot yet absolutely impose an obligation on his creature." Fr. Gonet writes in another place: "The promulgation of the natural law happens through a dictate of reason intimating to a man what has been prescribed or forbidden; as a result, when such a dictate is wanting, the law does not oblige." (*Diss. de op. prob.* a. 6 §1, n. 172). A great many others think the same thing, who can be observed in my own work: *Dell' uso*, etc. But let us come to the fourth objection of Patutius, to which the response I already made is here more forcefully confirmed.

The fourth and last particular opposition was this, that natural law is habitually promulgated to man when God creates the soul, and infuses it into the body, because then he imprints reason in man. I responded to this profusely in the aforementioned work of mine *Dell' uso*; here, I think it is enough to refute Patutius to assert the same words of St. Thomas that he uses: "Promulgation of the law of nature is for this very purpose, that God inserted it naturally into human minds to be known." (1.2. q. 90, a. 4, ad 1). Patutius means to use for his position only the word *inserted*, but he ought to use the following words, *naturally to be known*; consequently, not when the soul is infused in the body, but when a man recognizes the law, the law is promulgated to him. The Angelic doctor confirms this in another place, teaching: "Even if a man is not always held to will that which God will, he is always held, nevertheless, to will what God wills him to will, and he especially makes it known to man through divine precepts." (1.2., qu. 19, art. 10, ad tertium). Thus, then a man is only held to follow the divine will when it is manifested to him, *it is made known through divine precepts*. Let us hear what other authors have to say about this. John Gerson, explaining what natural law might be, says: "That law is properly called a declaration made to a rational creature, through which it recognizes those things to which God wishes to oblige his creature." (*Vita spir.* etc., lect 2, col. 176, edit. Paris). Duvallius writes: "You ask, in what time did the law of nature begin to oblige each and every man? Resp. it begins when it is promulgated; moreover, it is sufficiently promulgated when anyone attains the years of discretion." (1.2, *de leg.*, q. 3, a. 3). Cardinal Gotti writes: "Natural law is in the soul through the mode of acts and indeed while it is considered in act ... In the insane it is in habit, while in children it is in potency, since the divine precept cannot yet be intimated to them, in which the law consist." (*de leg.*, q. 2, dub. 2, n. 21).

St. Antoninus: "Diligently note that this light of natural law does not show to man those things which are good, until he should attain to the use of reason." (Par. 1, tit. 13, c. 12, *vide* §3). Fr. Cuniliatus writes: "The promulgation of actual natural law comes about when someone cognition from God dictating what he must avoid or embrace." (Tract. 1, *de reg. mor.*, c. 2, §1, n. 5 et §3 n. 1). Louis Montesinus writes: "Natural law is promulgated in each and everyone, when he first comes to the use of reason; and although then that law is only promulgated in so far as to the most common principles of the law of nature, nevertheless, later little by little through discourse the same law is promulgated in regard to other matters." (*De legib.*, disp. 20, q. 4, n. 85). Yet, after omitting all the other authors that have been related, let us listen to what St. Jerome says; he (*epist. ad Aegasiam*) so writes: "This law (natural) boyhood does not know, and sinning without a command he is not held a sinner by law. He curses his father and mother and beats on his parents, and because he has not yet received the law of wisdom, he is not dead in sin. But when the command will have come, this is the time of understanding (in which we recognize the commands of God) eager for goods, and avoiding evils, then sin begins to live again, and the man is guilty of sin." Let the words be noted, *when the command will have come, this is the time of understanding*; so then the law comes to man, obviously it is promulgated to him, when a man understands it. Likewise St. Basil wrote earlier (*homil. in psalm 1*, n. 5) "After our reason has been completed, and increased, then what has been written comes to pass: 'But I lived without the law for a time, but when the command came, sin revived.'"

88.— I related all of this in my work, *Dell' Uso moderato*, etc., and I took care to send it to nearly all the Bishops of Italy as well as the primary prelates of the orders, and for this reason, when I was informed that Patutius had published a new moral Theology, and in this I reckoned he was going to make a response to what I wrote, but my opinion deceived me, for in those matters which were of greater weight, I found no response. But that I myself brought what was written against me by Patutius to the *Sacred Congregation of the Index*, this is not true in the slightest, nor did it ever come into my mind; nay more, in regard to the abuse Patutius hurled against me, I rather excused it, by saying he had not written to abuse me in his mind with such things, but that by the art of speaking he would imbue upon the minds of his readers the excellence of his case, and so he would win-over their support for his side. Furthermore, a great many times in my works I have asked the erudite that, if they were to write something against me, let them make it clear to me so that, after I have acknowledged the error I would give up my opinion. Still, there was no man who furnished me with anything, apart from a writer of a French Journal, who only objected to me that when I admit equally probable opinion to the extent that in a case of this sort the law is doubtful, I ought to also admit the less probable, because then the law is also doubtful. But I have already answered this opposition in my book, stating that where a more probable opinion is present favoring law, then the law is morally promulgated and consequently obliges, not withstanding the doubt conveyed favoring the milder opinion, for where we do not find certain truth we ought to follow that opinion which approaches more near the truth; but on the other hand, where the opinions are equally probable, the law is truly doubtful by a strict doubt, so that in no mode then can the law be said to have been sufficiently promulgated.

Here, I refuse to pass over that which I recently found in the last edition of Fr. Fulgentius Cuniliati's *Theologia moralis* (Tract. *De conscientia*, c. 1, in fin., ad § 6), advanced specifically in the medium decreed by the Sacred Roman Inquisition, in which certain theses dug up by a certain parish priest in Avicii in the diocese of Trent in 1761 were proscribed. But I showed in a great many works, in the decree that was related, neither all probabilism, nor some opinion, which they defend in Catholic schools, but only some which were exceeding lax were proscribed, just as two consultors of the Holy Office, and the greater penitentiary of a French Cardinal at that time, wrote back to me as I noted above in the dissertation.

89.—Besides, the matter seems worthy of astonishment, that some think there is no safer way to save souls than to lead them through the more bitter paths; but they no less err than others who lead consciences through a laxer road. Not only are we held to give an account to God for excessive indulgence, but also for excessive rigidity whereby the consciences of souls are ensnared, which is properly (according to St. Antoninus), "to pave the road to hell." The very learned Cabassutius argues rather fittingly from the doctrine of St. Bonaventure, that after he detests immoderate mildness, he condemns immoderate rigor, which, as he says, "while he compels men to exceeding arduousness, he closes off the road of eternal salvation (as St. Bonaventure says); he damns those to be saved and consigns those conscious of their own infirmity to desperation. For it happens that miserable men, after they have heard a more rigid doctrine, believe or are uncertain whether they are in mortal sin when the are not, while still conquered by a difficult matter, from an erroneous conscience they sin mortally and are damned." (*Theor. jur.* in praefat.) Next, the same author adds the words of St. Bonaventure, who taught: "We must fear a conscience that is too liberal as well as one that is too strict; for the first generates presumption, the second desperation. Likewise, the first often saves those that are going to be damned, while the second damns those who are going to be saved." (*Comp. theol. verit.*, l. 2, c. 32, n. 5). John Gerson strengthens the same point, saying: "Doctors of theology ought not be too quick to assert some things are mortal sins where they are not certain on the matter; for by rigid and too strict assertion of this sort, by no means will men be lifted from the mud of sinners, but will sink deeper into it because they are more desperate." (*De Vita Spir.*, lect. 4). Hence, St. Raymundus writes: "Do not be prone to judge mortal sins where it is not established by a certain Scripture." (lib. 3, *de poenit.*, §21). Gabriel Biel, who wrote in 1480, said the same thing: "Nothing should be condemned as a mortal sin concerting which one has no evident reasoning or manifest authority of Scripture." (In 4, dist. 16, q. 4, concl. 5). St. Antoninus wrote the same thing, saying: "The question in which it is argued whether something is a mortal sin, unless one has the express authority of Scripture or a canon of the Church, or evident reason, the determination is made perilously. (par. 2, tit. 1, c. 11 §28). And in another place he wrote speaking of the Confessor: "But if he cannot perceive whether it is mortal, it does not seem then that a sentence must be commanded, as Guillelmus says, that he abide on account of this absolution, or that his conscience should be burdened with something mortal. And since rights are more fitting to absolve than to bind ... it seems rather he must be absolved." (Part. 2, tit. 4, c. 5, § *In quantum*).

TREATISE II

ON LAWS

CHAPTER I
On the nature and obligation of Law in General

DUBIUM I
What is a law, or Precept?

90. *What is a law?*

91. *Who is held to it?*

92. *Do unjust laws oblige?*

93. *Whether we are held to a law in doubt about its justice* (See also n. 99).

94. *Whether laws imposed by tyrants oblige?*

95. *Whether a law that was not promulgate obliges?*

96. *What must be known in regard to the promulgation of the law?*

97. *What about a doubtful law? And in a doubt as to whether a law exists? Or whether there is a case that excuses one from it? Whether the law is promulgated? Whether it was received by use?*

98. *What about whether a superior might be legitimate? And whether he exceeds his power?*

99. *What to do in doubt whether a law is just? Or whether a law commands? Or whether you can fulfill it?*

100. *Whether a human law can command internal acts? And whether it can forbid external or secret ones? See the same place, quest. III, whether in a doubt, if a matter is licit, is a subject held to obey?*

90.—"I respond: A law or a precept, insofar as here they "are taken up without distinction, is right reason to do "certain things or to omit others. Nonetheless, when "something is commanded by a superior, not by a "community rather only by some person or persons in "particular, it is not called a law but only a precept. "(Suarez, Laymann, Bonacina, d 1, q1 p1). For that reason "you resolve:

91.—"1. Someone is held to a law or precept, but not to "counsel since the latter only directs whereas the former "obliges. (*Ibid.*)

92.—"2. When a law is unjust and against reason, it does "not oblige because of a defect of rectitude (*Ibid.*).

93.—"3. When there is a doubt about the justice, you are "held by the law; he who is the legislator possesses the "right to command: and the same is ruled by a higher "counsel and can have reasons secret from his subjects. "Suarez adds, that it would even obliges if there are "probable reasons against the law, because subsequently "excessive license will be given by not obeying the law, "since they could hardly be so just that some apparent "reason could move doubt." (Suarez, l. 1, c. 9; Bonacina, "pag 8, n. 11; See n. 99).

94.—"4. Laws and sentences imposed by tyrants oblige if "they possess their kingdoms peacefully and are "tolerated by the commonweal. Nor is it opposed that "the sentence of an illegitimate judge be declared null, "for it is true on the sentence insofar as it is precisely by "a tyrant, but not in so far as it is at least from the "interpretive and implicit will of the common good, "which, while it cannot expel a tyrant or judges "constituted in it, it tacitly confers power to them to "govern, and it ratifies their laws and acts." (Lessius, l. 2, "c. 29, dub. 9; Salas, disp. 10, sect. 3, n. 14; The

"Salamancans say the same thing, c. 2, punt. 1, n. 10, cum
"Palaus etc.).

95.—"5. Noone is held to a law unless it has been
"promulgated, or publicly enacted." (St. Thomas, 1.2. q.
"90; Laymann l. 1, t. 4, c. 3; Molina, Salas, Suarez and
"others in common.)"

96.—In regard to the promulgation of the law, 1) It must
be noted that St. Thomas teaches (1. 2. q. 90, art. 4),
"promulgation is necessary that the law would have its
force." Also, in the canon *In istis*, dist. 4, it is held: "Laws are
constituted when they are promulgated." The reasoning is
that a law cannot oblige unless it were to attain the notice of
the community through promulgation. Hence the law does
not oblige if it will be advertised only to particular persons.
(De Soto, *de just. et jure,* l. 1, q. 1, art. 4; Suarez, *de leg.,* l. 3, c.
17, n. 5; Palaus, tr. 3, disp. 1, punct. 1, n. 6; the Salamancans
c. 1, n. 75, cum Tapia et Diana). Hence, it is inferred that if
anyone would know some law is fashioned, he would not be
held to keep it except after it was promulgated, as Palaus
(loc. cit., punct. 10, n. 2); the Salamancans (n. 76); et Lessius,
(l. 2, c. 21, dub. 5, n. 45) hold. Moreover, it suffices to oblige
that the law is published commonly and solemnly in places
so that it can attain to the notice of a greater part of the
community, even if it is unknown to some individuals. (See
the Salamancans, *ibid.,* n. 77, 78 and 79).

II. It must be noted in regard to the mode of
promulgation that Caesarian laws, or of those princes
subject to the emperor, ought to be promulgated in
individual provinces, or metropolitan cities, and they do not
oblige except after two months from promulgation (Auth, *Ut
factae novae,* coll. 5).

Quaeritur: I. Whether for pontifical laws (and those of
other princes that are not subject) to oblige, should they be
promulgated, not only in Rome, (or in the curia), but even in
individual provinces?

The first opinion affirms this, and a great many serious authors hold it, such as Becanus, (*de leg.,* q. 5, n. 5); Nöel Alex., (*Theol.* lib. 4, art. 3, reg. 25); Cont. of Tournely (*de legib.,* c. 5, sect. 4); Cabassutius, (*Theor. Jur.,* l. 1, c. 4, n. 4), along with Medina, Angel., etc. The following call it probable, namely Sylvius (tom. 2, in 1.2., q. 96, art. 4, *concl.* 3); Anacletus, Roncaglia, and others. Cajetan is cited favoring this opinion, but Cajetan does not say anything but that canon laws do not oblige those ignorant of them. Lessius is also cited, but Lessius (l. 2, c. 22, n. 89) speaks only on laws which invalidate contracts. Domingo de Soto is also cited, but Soto (*de just.* l. 1, q. 1, art. 4) speaks rather on disqualifying laws, or those revoking privileges. Supporters of this first opinion are principally found in *Authenticâ,* and in *Ut factae novae,* as related above, and they say that where there is no special disposition of canon law, the civil must be favored, according to what is inferred from c. 2, *de nov. op. nunc.,* in which it is said: "The statute of the sacred canons aid the constitutions of princes." Besides, they say it is exceedingly difficult to bind the faithful of the whole Christian world to keep only the laws published in Rome. But still, according to this first opinion, Bulls inserted into the *Bullarium* ought to be received, because these are now the body of laws; and in this all agree; as Cardinal Petra gives as evidence (*in Praemial.* c. 4, n. 50, et 54).

But the *Second opinion* is very common and more probably denies the first, holding that pontifical laws oblige the faithful when the promulgation is only carried out in Rome. (Suarez, *de leg.,* l. 3, c. 16, n. 8; Bon., *eod. tit.* d. 1, q. 1, p. 4, n. 16, vers. *Concedo*; Laymann, l. 1, tr. 4, c. 3, n. 4; Azor, p. 1, l. 5, c. 3, vers. *In hac q.*; Castropalaus, *de leg.* tr. 3, d. 1, p. 11, n. 4, Carden. in 1; Crisi, d. 9, c. 20, art. 12; Ferrar., Bibl. tom. 4, verb. Lex, art. 2, n. 5; the Salamancans, tr. 11, *de leg.,* c. 1, punct. 7, §1, ex n. 86, with Valent., Navar., Vasquez, Menoch., Pontio, Diana, et Salas). The reasoning is: There would be no doubt that a law, so as to have the force to oblige, ought to be promulgated, otherwise it cannot attain to the notice of subjects; but what pertains to the mode of promulgation depends upon the will and intention of the legislator. Hence it is observed, (according to what the Salamancans also give evidence for certain), that among all the Doctors still in the opposition, there is not one who would deny it is not necessary from its nature, that it be published in every province to oblige, but that it is enough for it to be promulgated in the court of the legislator, just as it is in fact done in Spain with royal laws (as the same Salamancans write), to the extent that the king there is not held to keep the Cesarean legislation, for they are only promulgated in the Royal register. And so equally, pontifical bulls like a great many received according to use are only promulgated at Rome but there destined for other places, and by the strength of constitution so this sort all ecclesiastical cases are judged. Moreover, on the other hand, the Apostolic See, when it wishes not to oblige some law, except after publication has been made in the provinces, expresses that, just as it expressed it in the interdict from the Church imposed by the Fourth Lateran Council against doctors who proceed to assist the week before they have finished their confession, as it is commanded in *cap. Cum infirmitas de poenit. et remiss.* And so it was also expressed by the Council of Trent in its 24th session, c. 1, in regard to the invalidity of clandestine matrimony.

Since this has been posited, when the Pope decides to publish his bulls only at Rome, it does not have the appearance of truth that he does not mean to oblige other provinces but only Rome itself. When the Pope means to oblige only Romans, he usually publishes peculiar edicts (and these composed in the Italian language), but making statutes for the whole Church, and solemnly promulgating these with little obligatory clauses, it is presumed far from doubt, that he means to oblige all the faithful, immediately from the moment it obtains their notice. Such a notice is easy that it should attain to the provinces from Rome; for nearly all nations come together at Rome, and all prelates have their procurators who ordinarily busy themselves on new bulls which are promulgated, to make themselves more certain. Besides, that pontifical laws oblige immediately and are solemnly promulgated, is clearly deduced from canon 1. *ad haec, de postulat. praelat.*, where it is said: "It is not necessary, when a constitution is solemnly published or publicly promulgated, for notice of the fact to be put into the ears of each man by a special command or letter; rather, it only suffices that it be held for its observation that one knows it was solemnly published or publicly promulgated." It will be noted, "*solemnly published or publicly promulgated.*" Therefore, one that has certain notice on some bull already solemnly promulgated at Rome, is rightly held to keep it. Likewise, it is sufficiently inferred from the chapter *Quia cunctis*, 1) (on the words, *Nec obstaret*) *de concess. praeben. in* 6, where it is held: "A law, or constitution, or mandatum binds no one until after it has obtained the notice of the same, or until after that time within which one could scarcely be ignorant of it." Therefore, everyone is held to observe those laws which have already attained their notice, since these were promulgated in a mode in which the legislator can promulgate them. Nor must it be doubted whether the Pope could bind all the faithful to the observance of his Bulls through a promulgation made only at Rome, just as every prince (in so far as all authors admit, as we saw above) avails to oblige his whole kingdom to his laws through a publication only completed in his court.

There are two clauses that offer force to our opinion, which are usually affixed in those bulls which are promulgated in Rome, and are printed in customary places. The first little clause so says: "That the present letter should come to the notice of all more easily, and no man should be able to allege ignorance of it, we will it to be fastened to the doors and published, and being thus published obligate and affect all and everyone whom it concerns as if it were personally made known to each of them." The second says: "Moreover, we will that observance of this letter should altogether be applied both in and outside court, after it is adopted and printed, written by the hand of some notary public, and fortified by the seal of a person constituted in ecclesiastical dignity, as if it were displayed or shown to everyone." Moreover, these little clauses very clearly show the mind of the Pope is to bind all the faithful to statutes of this sort independently from their publication in individual provinces. Both Sylvius and Roncaglia, although they admit the first opinion as probable, still hold as certain that all bulls, when they are promulgated at Rome with the aforesaid clauses, oblige in themselves without any other promulgation. Moreover, Roncaglia rightly says that from the words of the clauses that we related above, a firm argument can be adduced for the probability of the first opinion in regard to these bulls where the aforesaid clauses are lacking. For no adjective must be supposed to be in a law without purpose, and these clauses would be altogether superfluous if all bulls published in Rome even without such clauses would oblige before another publication in provinces; he only makes the exception that in some place a custom might not be in force to indifferently embrace bulls promulgated in any mode at Rome.

Furthermore, Sylvius asks in the passage cited above, *vers. Petes,* whether Bishops are held to promulgate or busy themselves as others to observe all the pontifical statutes already promulgated at Rome? And he so responds: "They are held to take care that they are observed when the Pope signifies that he means his law to oblige all, even without another promulgation made elsewhere. Still they are not held to see to it that they are promulgated unless they are directed to do so by a command of the Pope, or should reasonably judge that promulgation is necessary in their dioceses. Just the same, someone that has notice of the law seems obliged to it unless it has not been received or its obligation ceases through lack of use. Moreover, if the Pope does not signify that another promulgation is necessary, and does not direct a command to the Ordinaries, it is probable that they are not held to promulgate the law or see to it that it is observed unless they expect a notable fruit from the promulgation of such a law in their dioceses. For, they can then interpret the mind of the Pope in that the law is then observed in different provinces, or the Ordinaries will see to their promulgation when they will have supposed it is expedient and useful for their places." Diana writes the same thing in *Summa*, v. *Lex*, n. 18, along with Wiggers and Maldero, saying: "When the Pope does not signify that another publication is necessary, and does not command the Ordinaries to so act that it (the law) will be kept, they are not held to publish it nor to see to it that it is observed by the people unless they look forward to the fruit for that place; the mind of the Pope prescribing a general law is that where it can be done with fruit, they will take care to observe it."

Besides, Suarez (*de lege*, l. 5, c. 33, n. 8) and Laymann (*eodem tit.*, c. 2, n. 7), with Molina and de Soto say probably that pontifical laws, which weaken some suitable contract that is valid by nature (exactly as St. Pius V did in a bull in regard to census contracts), or which take away jurisdiction, *e.g.*, in the sacrament of penance, we can interpret these mildly, the mind of the Pope is that he does not wish these to have effect until after they will be promulgated in their dioceses; otherwise they would become redundant to the detriment of a great many who would be invincibly ignorant of them; in another way, it is in respect to penalties which are established against clerics badly ordained, and Bishops badly ordaining them, according to what Sixtus V declared (especially in regard to those promoted through simony as well as those promoting them, for in regard to others the bull of Sixtus was reduced to the limits of the Council of Trent by another bull, *Romanum* of Clement VIII). Also, just as he proceeds otherwise in invalidating laws by some act on account of a defect of solemnity, such laws, after they have the force to oblige, also avail in respect to those ignorant of them, as Sanchez (*de matr.* l. 3, d. 17, et l. 9, d. 32, n. 2), Laymann (*loc. cit.*), and Navarre say as well as others.

Quaeritur: II. Whether, for a law to oblige, a space of two months from promulgation is required? There are three opinions.

The first says it obliges immediately. So think Salas, Vasquez, Villal., etc. quoted by the Salamancans (*de leg,* c. 1, punct. 7, §2, n. 89). The reason is that a law, when it is promulgated, is now constituted in its entirety.

The second says it obliges immediately, or, as it were, at least those abiding at the royal court; yet it does not oblige others until after a sufficient time, more or less according to the distance of places. So think Palaus (tract. 3, disp. 1, part. 11, n. 3), Suarez (l. 3, c. 17, n. 7) and likewise Montes, Gran, etc., quoted by the Salamancans, n. 90.

The third opinion more probably says, when in law a time for the obligation is not determined, it obliges no one, not even abiding at the royal court, until two months from promulgation; but after two months have transpired, when the judgment of prudent men has been examined, it obliges everyone. So think Domingo de Soto (*de Justitia et Jure*, lib. 2, q. 1, art. 4), Bonacina (t. 3, c. 6, concl. 2, n. 3) Sa (v. *Lex*, n. 8); Sylvest. (*eod. verb.* q. 6) and the Salamancans (n. 94) along with Valent., Reg. Men., Tab., and others. The reason is that law does not oblige unless it can attain notice morally to all those subject to it, as is elicited from the book *Leges*, c. *de leg.,* where: "Most holy laws out to be understood as universal by everyone, what is prescribed by them more manifestly understood, avoiding what is forbidden." And from *cap. De Concess., praeb.* in 6, v. *Nec obstat,* there it is said: "A law, or custom and command binds no one until after they attain notice of the same, or until after a time within which they could not be uncertain about it." Moreover, the time in which the law can arrive, by a human mode, to the ears of those subject to it must be assessed by the estimation of prudent men, and examined this estimation in the author's work *Ut factae,* etc. as it was said above: therefore, it favors the will where the time has not been established.

97.—Here various questions are added in regard to a dubious law. It is asked whether, if there is a doubt as to whether the law exists, does the law oblige? It is answered that it does not oblige after due diligence has been sufficiently applied to seek the truth, nevertheless, scandal or some other unsuited notable matter, because then *libertas possidet.* So Suarez (t. 5, in 3, p. d. 40, sec. 5, n. 50); Sanchez (Dec. l. 1, c. 10, n. 32 et 33) Palaus (tr. 1, disp. 3, p. 7, n. 1), the Salamancans *de leg.* c. 2, punct. 6, n. 110), along with Tap., Villalobos, Arav. etc. commonly argue. Several expressly confirm it. St. Thomas (*Quodlib.* 14, de verit., a. 3) says: "No one is bound by some precept except by the medium of knowledge of that precept." Scotus (in 4, d. 3, q. 4) says: "No one is held to some divine precept, unless it is promulgated to him by something suitable and authentic." Likewise the Gloss (*in c. Cum sunt, de reg. jur.* in 6) says: "In doubt no one is presumed to be obligated, *ex Authent. Quibus modis.*) The Gloss also says (*ex cap. Ex parte de cens.*) "In doubt one is free to follow what is more pleasing." Likewise our Most Holy Lord, Benedict XIV (Notif. 13), says: "Bonds ought not

be imposed when there is no manifest law to impose them."[20]
It is clearly proved from *cap. Erit.*, dist. 4, where St. Isidore
so says: "Moreover, a law will be manifest." Likewise, from
c. *Cum jure*, 31, *de off. et pot. jud. del.*, which says: "Unless
you will be certain about a command, you are not compelled
to carry out what is commanded." Likewise, from *cap. Ex
parte de transact.*, "In these, where the law is not discovered
to be expressed, you may proceed, while preserving justice,
always taking the side of the more humane." Likewise, St.
Leo (in can. *Sicut quaedam*, dist. 14), so taught: "In these,
which were either doubtful or obscure, we knew to follow
that which was not contrary to evangelical precepts, nor the
decrees of the most Holy Fathers." Likewise, Lactantius, *in
lib. 3, Inst.* c. 21, said: "It is for a very stupid man to obey
their precepts, whether true or false, if he is uncertain." The
reason is, that God duly gave to man the ownership of
freedom, as the Apostle says: "But having power of his will."
(1 Cor. 7:37) And from Ecclesiasticus, (15:14): "God
constituted man from the beginning, and left him in the
hand of his counsel. He gave his commands and precepts. If
you will have kept the commands, he will save you." For this
reason, a man is free to follow his will to do whatever he
wills when it is not certain to be forbidden him by the law,
as St. Thomas says: "What is called licit is forbidden by no
law," from l. *Necnon*, ss. *Ex quib. caus. maj.*, where:
"Everything is permitted by law which is not discovered
forbidden." Hence, Melchior Cano (*in Praelect.* 4, de poen.,
part. 4, q. 2, prop. 3, n. 5), so impugns the opinion of Scotus
and others, who wanted sinners bound to make an act of
contrition on every feast day: "Because (Cano says), I do not
know the opinion of the doctors comes from, I can freely
reject it, because the precept has not been sufficiently

---

[20] *Non si debbono porre legami, quando non v' è una chiara legge che
gli' imponga.*

explored." And on that account, St. Thomas said: "It is dangerous (to determine something is a mortal sin) where the truth is ambiguous, namely, if in a divine law a it has not been found determinately expressed." (Quodl. 9, art. 15). And St. Antoninus says: "One can well excuse ignorance, in as much as it is invincible, in regard to those matters which are not expressly against divine or natural law." (Part. 2, tit. 1, c. 11).

The Salamancans say the same thing (*dicto* n. 110) along with others; if it is uncertain whether is embraced by the law or whether the law is extended to something, and the same thing in doubt whether the obligation of law will have begun or not, or in another way, in a doubt whether come to an end. (The Salamancans, *ibid.*, n. 120, with Laymann, Sanch., Palaus).

What if you are in doubt as to whether a reason you have would be sufficient to excuse you from the law? Whatever Salas might say, it is truer that you are held to the law; because then *lex possidet* prior to your freedom. (The Salamancans, *ibid.*, n. 112, with Sanchez, Palaus, etc.).

What about a doubt as to whether a law might be promulgated? The following hold with Croix (*ib.* n. 590), and the Salamancans *dicto* cap. 2, n. 110) that the law does not oblige. Still, Croix excepts if the law was already received in use.

What about a doubt as to whether a law has been received in use? There are three opinions.

The first opinion holds then that the law does not oblige, at least if it were penal, according to Azor (t. 1, lib. 2, c. 19, q. 12); Salas (*Dian. Tab.* etc., quoted by the Salamancans *de leg.* cap. 2, n. 113), and the following hold this in all cases on every law: Navarre, Rebell., Felin, Dec., etc. quoted in Palaus, *de consc.* disp. 3, punct. 7, n. 4); and they regard it as probable: Palaus himself, Sporer *de cons.*, c. 1, n. 81, and Tamburinius, *de consc.* c. 3, §7, *verb. Legis.* The reason is because then, when there is uncertainty about the reception of the law, it is also uncertain as to whether the law ever obliged; and therefore *libertas possidet.* Moreover, they say this opinion is probable, because they think necessary reception of the law is probable so that it would oblige, according to the opinion related in *n. 158.*

The second opinion, which Croix holds (lib. 1, n. 591), says the law obliges if it is ecclesiastic, but it would be otherwise if it were civil.

But *the third opinion* must be followed, that affirms the law obliges. And Palaus (*loc. cit.* n. 3), Sanchez (*dec.* lib. 1, c. 11) and the Salamancans (loc. cit. n. 114) The reasons are: 1) because when it is certain on a law, possession favors it, for the general rule is that it should be presumed as a fact that it had *de jure* been done, exactly as here it is presumed reception was made. 2) Because a law, when it has already been imposed and promulgated, does not lack reception, as the aforesaid authors reckon it: at least, as Croix says rightly (lib. 1, n. 591), as well as Mazzot. (c. 6, q 6), a law, that presently has not been abrogated for certain, before the reception already had the force to oblige; wherefore, although someone does not sin against the law because it has not yet been received, still he sins because he does not submit to it, as we will say (*dict. n. 138*).

98.—What about a doubt as to whether the legislator is a legitimate superior? Vasquez, Salas, Diana and Arav., with the Salamancans (c. 2, n. 118, in fin), deny it, because then when the right to command is doubtful, so also is the possession. But it must be affirmed with Sanchez (*dec.* lib. 7, c. 3, n. 29), Croix (l. 1, n. 593) with Oviedo and the Salamancans (*loc. cit.,* n. 118) with Tap. and Martin., a superior is always in peaceful possession of his power, for then his condition is better since he already possesses the right to command.

What about a doubt as to whether a superior exceeds his power? Then Adrian., Rodr., Vasquez, the Salamancans, cited by Palaus (*de consc.* d. 3, part 13, n. 1), and others with Croix (lib. 1, n. 594), think the subject is not held to obey. But others rightly contradict this: Navarre (*de rest.* c. 3, d. 12, n. 252); Palaus (n. 2), along with Tol. Mol. Az. Sa, etc. commonly, along with Sanchez (*dec.* lib. 6, c. 3, n. 4), because possession favors the power of the superior. Still, Sanchez (*ibid.,* et n. 23, et 24) along with Sol., Loth., Tap., Sal., etc. limits, if the matter commanded were harmful to the subject, or, either very difficult or troublesome.

99.—Is a subject held to obey in a doubt about the justice of the law? Dicastillus and others with Croix (lib. 1, n. 595) deny this, because then possession is not held in favor of the law of the superior. But Bon. (*de leg.* d. 1, q. 1 part. 7 §3, p. 11) who cites Vasquez, Suarez, and Salas, then the Salamancans *de leg.* c. 1, punct. 6, n. 115) with others in common altogether affirm it. The reason is that really, in a doubt the superior possesses the right of command. Still, the doctors make an exception if the law is excessively arduous, or if it inflicts serious loss on the subject." (See what is going to be said in book 4, n. 617, Quaer. V.)

What if there is a doubt as to whether a law commands or persuades? Or obliges one *sub gravi* or *sub levi*? The response is then the law either does not oblige, or does not oblige *sub gravi*, from the rule of law, (59, ff. *de Regulis jur.*) "The milder must always be preferred in doubt." So also Croix (n. 596), with Navarre, Sanchez, etc. holds against Laymann. On the other hand, what about a doubt as to whether a law was abrogated or dispensed; or whether there is a cause excusing from the law? In the common opinion we are held to it. (See, Spor, n. 82; the Salamancans n. 112; Tamburinius, n. 2, *ll.cc.*; Croix n. 597 et 598). What about a doubt as to whether or not the time of the obligation of the law has passed? Resp. In doubt about the beginning, for example, whether you have finished 21 years, are not held to fast because then possession favors freedom. In other respects, in a doubt of passing over, for example, whether after the completed of Saturday it might be midnight, you cannot eat meat then because *lex possidet*. Thus, even if you doubt whether you are 16 for profession, or 25 for priesthood, you cannot profess or be ordained. Thus the following reckon in common: Laymann, (lib. 1, tr. 1, cap. 5, §4), Sanchez (*de matr.* lib. 2, disp. 41, n. 4, et dec. lib. 1, cap. 10, n. 38); Pal (tract. 1, disp. 3, punt. 8, n. 6), and the Salamancans (c. 2, punct. 6, n. 120, cum Tapia, Diana, et Villalob).

What about a doubt a to whether you have fulfilled the law? In a negative doubt you are held to fulfill it; you do otherwise in a positive doubt. (Carden. et Ills. cum Croix, lib. 1, n. 600).

Concerning the matter of human law note the following questions.

100.—*Quaeritur* 1: Whether a human law can directly command internal acts? The Salamancans (cap. 1, punct. 5, n. 66), with St. Thomas, Cajetan, Suarez, Bon., etc. more probably deny it against others because the human legislator cannot judge concerning what is internal.

Quaeritur 2: Whether human law can command acts that are indirectly internal on account of the connection with external acts? It is distinguished: He can, if the interior act is joined, *per se*, with the exterior act. And it can be joined in a two-fold manner, just as the constituent form, the external act is in the moral of the virtuous act: in this way, an internal consent is required to contract matrimony to enter a contract, etc. Or, just as a cause with the effect: and so one that forbids homicide, forbids even the will to kill. So, cap. *Commissa* § *Caeterum de electione* in 6, a cleric is obliged to resign a benefice if he received it with a mind to not be ordained within the year. (The Salamancans d. c. n. 69, *cum Tapia, Caj., Palaus,* etc.).

But if an interior act *per accidens* is joined with the exterior, then it cannot be commanded from a human law, take, for example, if it were commanded to give alms from true devotion, etc. (The Salamancans *ibid.*, n. 70, cum Suarez, Palaus, Tapia, etc. against Caj. and Soto).

Quaeritur 3: Whether secret exterior acts could for forbidden by human law? Yes, and in this way one is forbidden from heresy by the fear of excommunication, although it is secret; and in this way secret murders under irregularity. For secret acts, although they do not fall before a judge, nevertheless fall under the law, as St. Thomas teaches (*Quolibet.*, 4, art. 12. See also the Salamancans *ibid.*, n. 72 et 73).

Moreover, whether in doubt as to whether a matter is licit, is the subject held to obey? Sylvester, Ang., Hostiens, etc. with Sanchez (*dec.* lib. 6, c. 3, n. 19) deny, and they say then he is neither held to, nor can, obey unless he should first inquire from experts that the matter is at least not certainly illicit. But Sanchez (*loc. cit.*), Navarre, Val, etc. affirm more truly from St. Thomas (*de verit.* q. 17, a. 5, ad 4) who teaches that it does not pertain to subjects but only to superiors to inquire on the honesty of a matter commanded; and therefore the subject is rightly held to obey, and as always, if it is certain the matter put before him is not evil. (See Croix, lib. 1, n. 439). Moreover, apart from that question whether or not the subject is held concerning the honesty of a thing commanded, first one must seek of the truth of the matter from others; the common opinion of all theologians both recent and ancient, who teach in obscure matters one must obey superiors where there is no certain sin." (St. Bonaventure, in 2, d. 59, art. 1, q, 3; Gerson, *de poll. noct.* conse. 3; Nyder *in consol. part* 5, c. 17, where he cites Raymund., Henr. Halensen, part 2, q. 121, and everyone else who taught on this matter). Likewise, the doctors of Mystical Theology teach this. St. Ignatius of Loyola, (*in pist. de vert., Obed.*) where he says: "Therefore, this is the reason to subject oneself to a proper judge, not only by the customary practice to holy men, but also imitating them in zeal of perfect obedience in all things, which, are not joined with manifest sin." Let the reader especially hear St. Bernard (*de praecept. et dispens.*, c. 12): "Whatever in turn a man of God commands, it can hardly be other wise than that one must altogether receive what is not certain to displease God, as if God commands it." Then he objects to himself: But a man can easily be deceived." And he responds: "Yet, why do you relate this? Are you not aware that you ought especially to hold from the Scriptures, that the lips of the priest safeguard knowledge, etc. Hence we ought to listen to the very one whom we hold for God just as God in these matters, which are not clearly against God." Likewise Pope Leo X (as Casarubius, v. *declarare* n. 4, et 5 relates), conceded to the Friars Minor that they could in all doubts favor the determination of their superiors with a clear conscience. Likewise, St. Bernard of Siena, (*Dialogo de Obed.*) says: "Where the subject is reasonably uncertain whether what he is commanded is a sin or not, then certainly he ought to obey." Likewise, Blessed Humbert (in l. *de erud. relig.*, c. 1): Unless what is commanded seems evil, it must be received as if God commanded you." Dennis the Carthusian (in 2, d. 39, q. 3): In doubtful matters, whether it might be against the command of God, favor is given to the precept of the prelate, because even if it is against God, nevertheless, on account of the good of obedience the subject does not sin." The Gloss agrees (*in. c. Ad aures, de temp. Rod. lit. f. in fine*): "But if a command is in doubt, on account of the good of obedience one is excused from sin, even if in truth it were wicked." St. Augustine taught the same thing much earlier, speaking on the obedience due to temporal superiors, (in c. *Quid Culpatur*, 4, caus. 23, q. 1), where we read: "Therefore, the just man, if perhaps he will fight under a sacrilegious king, can rightly make war at his pleasure if it is not certain whether or not what is commanded of him is not against a certain command of God, so that perhaps to command such a thing makes the king iniquitous, but declares the soldier innocent for keeping the command.

Here, I also ask the question, whether you are held to obey a law founded on a false presumption? All deny it (Rebel., ap. Croix, de rest. n. 174). But Molina and others (*ibid*) as well a Mazzota, (*de leg. c. 5, q. 7*) affirm better that one is held to the law, take for example, restoring damage caused by your animal even without your fault: because the purpose of the law is not only to punish fault, but even to make men more careful. Still, this is not before the sentence of a judge. Nevertheless, if your animal did not inflict the damage, but it is juridically proved it did, then you are not held to pay even after sentence, scandal being removed: And you should be able to be compensated if you paid, because then the law would certainly be unjust, false in presumption, and in the internal forum presumption ought to yield to the truth. (C. *Veritatem*, dist. 8). In common, Suarez, (lib. 3, c. 23, et lib. 5, c. 24.); Pal (tr. 3, disp. 1, puct. 4, n. 12), de Soto (*de just.* l. 1, q. 6, art. 4); Ponitus de matr. (l. 5, c. 5, n. 6); Bonacina (disp. 2, q. 1, punct. 7, §3, n. 2 et 6); the Salamancans c. 2. punct. 4, n. 78) all agree, with others. Nor dis it opposed to say that Trent, invalidating void clandestine marriages, rested upon the presumption of the frauds then occurring, and still no man said such matrimony is valid where they never really discovered fraud. Likewise, wills lacking solemn witnesses are invalidated to avoid fraud; and just the same, if the fraud should cease at some time, a will of this sort does not: but in these and similar cases a distinction must be made between the presumption of law, in which a law seeks to avert dangers that usually come about quite easily (for then the law holds place in cases where there is no fraud) from a presumption of fact, which, if it is lacking, the law duly ceases.

DUBIUM II

In how many ways is a Precept Divided?

101. *A precept is divided 1) into affirmative and negative.*

102. *It is divided 2) into natural and positive.*

103. *Moreover, a positive precept is divided into a divine and human precept.*

104. *Who then can impose laws? Can kings and republics? The Pope? A Council? A Bishop, synod and chapter? An Abbot?*

105. *What do canonical and civil law embrace?*

106. *Whether declarations of the Sacred Congregation and decrees of the Rota have the force of law? Whether civil laws oblige in conscience?*

107. *On custom; and what conditions are required to establish a custom?*

108. *On the effect of custom. And what if it is rejected by law?*

109. *What if custom were revoked by law?*

110. *Dissertation on the Power of the Pope, even to n. 135.*

101.—"I respond: A precept is divided 1) universally into "affirmative and negative. The former commands a good "and the latter forbids an evil. They differ among "themselves because the affirmative obliges always, but "not forever or not for all time; *e.g.* that parents must be "honored is not for ever, but in its time. The negative

"obliges both always and forever. (See Becanus in 1.2. t.
"3, c. 1, q. 3).

102.—"It is divided 2) Into natural and positive. A natural
"precept, or law of nature, is a dictate according to the
"judgment of our reason, in which through the light
"impressed upon us by the author of nature we
"determine what must be done and what we must avoid;
"it is such that: Good must be done, evil must be put to
"flight. From such a general precept, particulars are
"derived, *e.g.*, that God must be worshiped, that we must
"injure no man, nay more, all the precepts of the
"Decalogue (with the exception of the circumstances of
"the Sabbath) and many others. A positive precept, or of
"positive law, is what has been placed by the free will of
"God or of men and depends upon the same thing, *e.g.*,
"the precept on baptism, lenten fasting, etc.

"Moreover, for in what way positive precepts can and
"usually are changed or varied, while natural ones
"always remain, see the Scholastics, and Lessius, (l. 2, *de*
"*jure, et just.* c. 2, d. 2).

103.—"Resp. 2: A positive precept is divided into a
"precept of divine law, which was clearly handed down
"by God, and of human law, which is so from man.
"Positive divine law is divided into the precepts of the
"Old and New Law. The Old Law contained moral
"precepts, as well as ceremonial and judicial (concerning
"which see St. Thomas, 1.2. q. 103). The New Law
"contains supernatural precepts of faith and the
"sacraments. Human positive law is divided into a
"precept of ecclesiastical or canonical law, which is
"established by the authority of the Church, namely of
"the Supreme Pontiff or a Council; and civil or political
"law, which is founded on the secular power."

104.—It is certain that the power is given to men to
impose laws; but this power in regard to the civil laws is

fitting to no one by nature, except the community of men, and it is transferred from this into one, or many, by whom the community is ruled. Hence, the Supreme Pontiff cannot impose civil laws except on the people who are subject to him in his temporal domain. Still, he can abrogate or correct civil laws of other princes if they are opposed to justice. Therefore, in *c. Cum haberet, de eo qui duxit in matr.*, a law forbidding nourishment to be given to illegitimate children is abrogated.

Moreover, kings and supreme princes who know no superior can impose civil laws in their dominions and these oblige in conscience. (See what is going to be said on this in n. 106). Moreover, in regard to queen heirs of a kingdom, there is an uncertainty among the Doctors. If they are not married it is certain they can impose laws; but if they are married, even while the marriage endures, the Salamancans (c. 3, punct. 1, n. 10) with Suarez, Palaus, *etc.* think more probably, against others, that truly the power to govern and so impose laws pertains to them.

Republics have the same power. But, other cities cannot advance laws making themselves exempt except from custom, or the concession of the prince. Still, they can fashion some statues, to which citizens are obliged by the force of contract; or establish other temporal (not perpetual) precepts; nevertheless they are revocable by the prince to whom they are held as subjects. (See the Salamancans, *ibid.*, n. 12).

In regard to ecclesiastical laws, it is certain that in the Church there is a power to impose them communicated immediately by Christ the Lord, the institutor of the Church. And this power is held for certain and is found with the Supreme Pontiff, as the head of the universal Church, the vicar of Christ and successor of St. Peter, to whom the whole rule of the Church was consigned by Christ independently of councils, as the Salamancans (*de leg.* c. 3, punct. 2 §1, n. 14), say with Bellarmine, Cajetan, Laymann, Palaus, etc.

General councils can also impose laws for the whole Church, but only if they are gathered from the license of the Supreme Pontiff and assigned for a place and time. Moreover, do laws or definitions published by ecumenical councils have strength before the confirmation of the Pontiff? Some affirm, if the Papal legates would give consent. But it must altogether be said, that it necessarily requires the express confirmation of the Pope, when he is not personally present at the council; for no faculty is given to confirm the statutes of synods which have no greater authority than that which is conceded to them by the Pope, as St. Thomas teaches (*de potentia*, etc., q. 10, art. 4, ad 13) and with him our doctors commonly hold, as Cardinal Torquemada, Suarez, Laymann, Palaus, Tapia, etc. with the Salamancans (*de leg.* c. 3, punct. 2, §2. n. 24), against more recent French authors. And it is confirmed from the example of so many general councils, which sought and obtained necessary confirmation of the Pope for decisions it had drafted; just as was done in the Council of Nicaea and more recently at the Council of Trent, just as it is read in session 25, at the end. Hence, Proposition 29 was duly proscribed by Pope Alexander VIII, which said: "The assertion on the authority of the Roman Pontiff over ecumenical Councils and in determining questions of faith with infallibility is futile and been refuted many times."

This very false proposition, can be plainly and firmly refuted from principles to strengthen the dogma of both faith and morals. All propositions condemned by the Popes, although not all may be heretical, others are temerarious, while others are erroneous, scandalous, *etc.* Nevertheless, attending a definition of a Pope, it must be held as *de fide* that these propositions truly are temerarious, or the matter of whatever other notes they are inflicted with, which the

Pope declares these propositions must suffer; therefore, one would indeed be a heretic who followed the same as if they were true and licit, or defend them, as Viva rightly says (*in qu. prod. ad prop. damn.*, n. 2). For this reason, we censed it is worthwhile to write a dissertation on the aforesaid proposition which you will find at the end of this dubium, n. 110.

It is true that the power to govern the universal Church was conferred to the other Apostles; still in a different mode than what was consigned to St. Peter, who could oblige them and abrogate their laws (the Salamancans d. c. 3, punct. 2, n. 15 et 16, with Bellarmine, Suarez, Cajetan, de Soto, etc.).

Hence, Bishops, who are the successors of the Apostles, can rightly impose laws for their dioceses without the consent of a chapter, according to *c. de Majorit.* and *c. 6 de const.* in 6, with the exception of those matters which chapters and clergy can concede, as in the chapter *Quanto, de his quae fiunt a praelato.* But from who indeed do Bishops receive this great legislative power? Some say they receive it immediately from Christ the Lord, because the dignity is from him, that established the episcopal office, as Vasquez, Victoria, etc. say, quoted in the Salamancans *d.* c. 3, n. 20. Others say they receive it from the Pope, such as St. Thomas, St. Antoninus, Soto, Palaus, etc. with the Salamancans (*ibid.* n. 21). And so it seems to be defined by Gregory in the can. *Decreto,* caus. 2, q. 6, where: "The Roman Church so communicates with other Churches as her vicars that they would be called into a share of her solicitude, but not into the fullness of her power." Moreover, this question is only about the name, for it is certain on one side that the Bishops, although they immediately receive this power from Christ, still always receive it with subordination to the Pope; and on the other side, although the Bishops receive it from the Pope, they still can impose laws without his license, so long as they are not opposed to pontifical laws, and the power over some things has not been reserved to the Pope (the Salamancans d. c. 3, n. 18 and 19). Moreover, Archbishops cannot impose laws on their suffragan dioceses, unless they have the right from custom (See the Salamancans *ibid.*, n. 22).

Provincial councils, or national councils of some nation are either provincial of some metropolis, namely of Bishops with their Archbishop, or synodal wherein a Bishop comes together with his parish priests; they can also impose perpetual laws for their territory (See *the Salamancans*, d. c. 3, §2, n. 25).

Chapters, however, cannot make laws without the consent of the Bishop (except for their own chapter members, as Palaus and Suarez and others think is probable). The Salamancans *d.* c. 3 n. 31, with Sylvester, Tapia, etc. On the other hand, after the death of the Bishop, can the chapter impose a law for the whole diocese until it is revoked by the succeeding Bishop? The Salamancans (*ibid.*, n. 33) with Laymann, Bonacina, Palaus, Suarez, etc. rightly affirm that with the seat being vacant, the chapter succeeds in place of a Bishop.

Abbots can also impose precepts for the right governance of a house, ans still oblige under grave fault, as Sanchez (dec., l. 6, c. 1, n. 17) and Mazzotta (tr. 1, d. 1, quest. 1, c. 2, q. 4) suppose. See also book 5, n. 52.

105.—Moreover, human law is commonly called either *canonical,* or *ecclesiastical,* or *civil. Civil* law is divided into imperial laws, which are called common law, divided into digest, codex and institute; and in particular royal laws of kingdoms which are called municipal law.

Canon law[21] is taken up in five volumes: 1) The first is the *Decretum Gratiani* (which truly does not have the force of law apart from what is contained there which was decreed of itself, as the Salamancans (c. 1, punct. 4, § 5, n. 43) along with Cajetan, de Soto, Suarez, *etc.* say against others). 2) *Decretales.* (The *Decretum* is cited by cases, questions, distinctions and canons; The *Decretales* are cited by chapter and title). 3) *Sextus Decretalium*; this is also cited by chapters, but was added *in Sexto.* 4) *Clementina* and *Extravagantes.* V. *Bullarium.* These books constitute the ratified statutes of Popes and Councils, and without a doubt have the force of law.

106.—*Quaeritur:* I. Do the decretals, or epistles, responses or declarations of Popes that are not inserted into the body of law have the force to oblige? The response is made in the affirmative from *can. Si Romanorum,* 1, *dist.* 19. There, Pope Nicholas V expressly declares it. Still, Suarez noticed that these do not oblige until after promulgation: for although the cited author (l. 4, *de legib.,* cap. 14, n. 3) says: "Ordinary epistles or pontifical responses are not constitutive but declarative, and have the force of law obliging one to hold that interpretation, or to preserve an old law according to that interpretation." Still, he adds this (1. 6, c. 1, n. 3): "For the interpretation to be authentic, it is necessary that it have the conditions of law, that it be just, sufficiently promulgated, etc. This is why consequently it happens that this interpretive law of another was expressed on doubts, so that other interpretations are necessary." Castr. (tr. 3, *de leg.,* disp. 5, punct. 3, §1, n. 2) teaches the same thing, where he says: "Moreover, this declaration ought to be published with that solemnity as a law; otherwise, it will not be authentic,

---

[21] The description St. Alphonus gives is nearly two centuries prior to the gathering of all canons in force into a code, which was first completed and promulgated in 1917. –Translator's note.

which will have the obligation of law, but it will only be a doctrinal declaration." Escobar writes the same thing (tom. 1, l. 5, *de leg.*, c. 3, n. 21), where he says: "From this I gather that pontifical epistles do not have the force of law unless they are published in that mode, in which epistles are usually published." Bonacina writes the same (t. 2, *de legib.* disp. 1, q. 1, punct. 4, n. 11), where he says: "The interpretation of law made authoritatively does not have the force of law unless it were promulgated, because promulgation concerns the very concept of law; so that those who were present in a public decision of law would not be held to it until after promulgation." He also cites for his opinion Salas and others, and adds (n. 12) saying: "From which it is lawful to infer that pontifical epistles do not have the force of law unless they are published in that mode whereby laws are usually made public." It is sufficiently confirmed from the same citation, *can. Si Romanorum,* where the decree of Pope St. Leo is related and confirmed, in which he declared and decreed the following: "Lest there would be a reason that someone perchance would believe that we have omitted all the decretals constituted both by Innocent, of blessed memory, and of all of our predecessors, which were promulgated on ecclesiastical orders from the (note) of the canons, we so command that they be guarded and preserved by your care." But here, Roncaglia (*de leg.,* quest. 1, c. 2, q. 7, resp. 11), wisely notices that not only the constitutions of the Pope, which are solemnly promulgated induce the obligation of law, but even all other things, which are held by the use and consent of the universal Church already for so many centuries as sufficiently promulgated and authentic.

Quaeritur II: Whether declarations of the Sacred Congregation of Cardinals have the force of law? No one is in doubt that for particular cases for which the decrees are made, they oblige as laws according to the common opinion with the Salamancans (*de legib.*, c. 3, punct. 3, §2 n. 30), and Croix (l. 1, n. 574). There is a doubt as to whether they oblige for similar cases. The opinion is twofold, and each is probable as the Salamancans rightly say (n. 28, in fin.).

The first opinion asserts that such declarations, if they are fortified with a seal, and the subscription of the most Eminent Cardinal prefect, they have the force to oblige all because the Cardinal have such a power to declare from the Pope, and it is elicited from Bull 75 of Sixtus V. Nor is it opposed that they are not promulgated, because new laws lack promulgation, not declarations on laws that have already been promulgated. (Garcias, Salas, Rodriguez, cited by the Salamancans n. 28, Fagnan., Barb., etc. with Croix, n. 574). But they say it is necessary that it is expressed in that declaration, either that it was promulgated or at least imposed by the command of the Supreme Pontiff, or at least in consultation with him, for in the bull of Sixtus V, it is said: "We impart the right to interpret (after we have been consulted)." Moreover, just as it has been said with Roncaglia (n. 105, vers. *Quaerit.*, hic 1, in fin *de declarationibus Pontificiis*), so also it can be said about declarations of the Sacred Congregation of a Council, because those declarations, which by the use and consent of the Church are sufficiently promulgated through the whole Christian world for a number of years, they sufficiently oblige all to their observance.

But the *second opinion* says that, although such declarations are of great weight, nevertheless, they do not oblige all universally, until they are not only published with the Pope's consultation and command, but even solemnly promulgated at his special command for the whole Church, so that the Pontiff commands them to be observed by all. For then, he so speaks as head and teacher of the Church; otherwise it seems he speaks only as the prelate of that congregation, which then does not seem to communicate his whole authority and infallibility. (Sanch. *de matr.* l. 8, disp. 2, n. 10; Bonacina *de leg.* disp. 2, q. 1, p. 8, n. 4; Pontius *de matr.* l. 5, c. 13, §2, n. 7; Suarez *de leg.* l. 6, c. 1 n. 3, et 6; Mazzotta tr. 1, d. 2, q. 1, c. 2, q. 3; Croix, l. 1, n. 215, 216, et 217 with Cardenas and Terril., ac. n. 574, cum Loth, et Delbene, Diana, p. 1, tr. 10, r. 29; with Vega, Valer., Serar, etc. *C.f.* Salamancans c. 3, n. 50, with Vasquez, Tapia, Lezana and Villal.). The reasoning of this opinion is that for a law to oblige, a solemn promulgation of the law is altogether required, according to what was said in n. 96. So, declarations of this sort, when they are not promulgated with solemnity, are indeed of great weight, by they cannot have the force of law and only oblige as particular opinions of those cases; they are sought for the decision of those cases, but not for application to similar ones. Nor is it opposed that promulgation is indeed required for laws, but not for declarations of laws already promulgated. For the cited authors respond that such declarations, when they are made on doubtful matters, in which contrary opinions can exist on the understanding of the law, then they are held as new laws. At least in doubt, whether they have or do not have the force of obliging as laws do, Laymann (l. 1, tr. 4, c. 7 §7, in fin.), says they do not oblige: "This question depends upon the mind of the Pope when he handed power to them (the Cardinals). Again, it must not be presumed to have the force of law, especially when they are not promulgated authentically." He also cites Sanchez and Rodriguez for this.

Moreover, decisions of the Rota have lesser authority than declarations of the Sacred Congregations. (Croix, l. 1, n. 576, with Luca, and Fagundez, cited by Tamburinius, Dec., l. 8, *Tract. de praesc.* § 2, n. 16).

On the other hand, do the rules of the Apostolic Chancery oblige everywhere? Lessius (*in Auctar. v. Beneficium*) says they only oblige in the Roman Curia, and Diana and others adhere to that. But, others affirm it does.

(Mazzotta, *l. c.* q. 3; with Azor, Gomez, etc., because it is carried out in practice. See Croix, l. 1, n. 575).

Quaeritur: III. Do civil laws oblige in conscience? On this point, it is very necessary to know that here it is fitting to call to mind some of the more principle ones. Some civil laws are expressly approved by canon law, others are expressly corrected, while others are neither approved nor condemned. Hence, it must be said: I. Laws that have been approved without a doubt oblige in conscience, such as the law of Justinian (*in Novel.* § *per occasionem*), in which three years are given to try the impotence of the spouses; and this was approved by Celestine III in *c. Laudabilem, de frig. et mal.* Equally, Nicholas I (*in resp. ad Bulgaros,* in c. *Ita* 30, q. 4) approved laws invalidating matrimony among adopted children and adoptive parents, and also those descending from them, just as *l. Quin etiam* 55 *ff. de ritu nupt.* does the same among the adopted and the sons of the adoptive parent, from l. *Per adoptionem* 17, ss. by the same title, likewise among the adoptive and the wife of the adopted, and vice versa from *l. Adoptivus,* 14, *ff. eod. tit.*

It must be said: II. Civil laws corrected by canonical law do not oblige in conscience; such a law is *in princ. Instit. de nupt. et in lib. Nuptiae* 2, *ff. de rit. nup.* where marriages entered into between the sons of a house and household servants are invalidated without the consent of the parents: but these laws were corrected in *c. Cum locum, de sponsal. et c. Matr. et c. Licet ac c. Tua, de spons. duor.* and lastly by the Council of Trent in its 24th Session, c. 1 *de Reform. sac. matr.* So also in *c. Cum haberet, de eo qui duxit in matr.* a civil law forbidding nourishment to be given to illegitimate sons was corrected. Equally, in l. 6, § 1. ff. *de Adulteriis,* and *l. 2. C. eod. tit.,* a married man knowing a divorced woman is not held to the judgment of adultery, although a wife admitting a divorced man will be condemned: but in *c. Nemo.* 32, q. 4, both are subjected to judgment, because the faith of the spouse must be applied on both sides. Likewise, in *l. Liberorum*, 81, *ff. de his, qui not. infam.*, a widow marrying within a year of mourning is subjected to many penalties: but Pope Urban III abrogated this in *c.* 3, and Innocent III in *c.* 5 *de secund. nupt.* Likewise, in *l. Marito. ff. ad Legem Jul. de adult. et l. Gracchus. c. eod. tit.* the right is given to kill a man that foully commits adultery with a wife, and in *lib. Quod ait. ff. eod. tit.* the right is conceded to a father to kill his daughter if she is taken in adultery. But these were condemned in *c. Inter haec, caus. 33*, q. 2 and by Pope Alexander VII in *prop. damn.* 19. There was a doubt as to whether *l. Uxorem. de ritu nupt.* which invalidated a marriage between a step-father and the wife of a stepson had been abrogated. But S.C. Consilii, on 28 March, 1721 (under our most Holy Lord Benedict XIV in *Opere de Synodo*), declared such a marriage valid.

It must be said: III. Civil laws that do not seem to be condemned are tacitly approved by canon law; for in *c.* 1 *De Novi oper. nuntiat.* it is said: "Just as laws that do not reject sacred canons are imitated, so also the statutes of sacred canons are assisted by the constitutions of princes." Likewise, in *c. Super Pecula, de privil.* it is so held: "The Holy Church does not reject the obedience of secular laws that imitate the vestiges of equity and justice." Next, *Fagnanus in c. Cum esses, de test.* n. 18, and our Pope Benedict XIV (l. c. p. 420, n. 1, cum Abbate, Menoch. and common opinion), say an ecclesiastical judge, on questions where no conclusion is found in canon law, ought to conform himself to civil law. Lastly, Pope Gelasius (Ep. 4, *ad Anast. Imperat.*) wrote: "Insofar as they pertain to the order of public discipline the Prelates of religion also obey your laws."

ON CUSTOM

107.—Here we must treat *on custom*, about which nothing is contained in the writings of *Busembaum.*

The discussion has been on the written law, not some things must be added on custom, which is called the unwritten law.

That custom would have the force of law, three things are required: I. That it is not introduced by a particular person, but by a community; at least by the greater part of the community, which has the capacity to impose laws, although it cannot impose laws by act: for then custom has the force of law from the tacit consent of the prince (the Salamancans *de leg. c. 6, punct.* 2, ex. n. 6 with St. Thomas). Here it must be noted that women cannot introduce custom against the proper laws of men, or vice versa; just as churchmen cannot against the laws of seculars, or the other way around, unless the matter is common. (Salamancans *ibid.,* n. 8, et punct. 4, § 1, n. 37). Hence, in regard to spiritual matters, the clergy are not obliged to custom made by seculars. (The Salamancans, *ibid.,* n. 58 with Sanchez, Palaus, etc.) Still, merchants, because they constitute a distinct community, can introduce a custom obliging everyone (the Salamancans, punct. 2, n. 8, with Palaus, Suarez, Bon., Tap.).

II. It is required that the custom should be reasonable: this is why no custom against the natural or divine law is valid, but only against human law. Still, it must be added that good faith is not required, for a custom can even be made by sinning (the Salamancans c. 6, punct. 3, §1, n. 11, with Suarez, Palaus, etc.). For, custom has a threefold status. In the beginning, all those introducing a custom against law sin. In its progression, those using what was introduced by their elders do not sin, but can be punished by the prince. In the end, however, they do not sin nor can be punished using what it prescribes (the Salamancans *ibid.,* n. 13 with Palaus, Caj., de Soto, Laymann, etc.).

III. A continuous and long-lasting period of time is required with repeated acts. How much time is sufficient?

The first opinion says that it is left to the judgment of prudent men, according to the repetition of acts, and the nature of affairs. (Vasquez, Tap., Vill, etc. cited by the Salamancans, *de legibus,* c. 6, punct. 3, §2. n. 15).

The second opinion says to suffice, a period of ten years is required, since this is the long time required by law to introduce a custom; unless another were ratified elsewhere, according to *L. ult., c. de praescriptione* (The Salamancans *ibid.,* n. 15, with Laymann, Suarez, Pal, etc., although they do teach the first opinion is very probable).

On the other hand, Lessius, Sa, Azor, Palaus, Navarre, etc., affirm that a ten year period would suffice against canonical laws. Still, the Salamancans (*d.* cap. 6, n. 17) with Laymann, Bonac., Suarez, Regin., etc., from *c. De quarta, et ex c. Ad aures, de praescript.* reject this. (See below in n. 139). For, The Salamancans (*ibid.,* n. 18), Granad., Salas, etc., note the saying of Suarez, as well as of present doctors, asserting a law is abrogated to disoblige us from the law.

Moreover, it is said that a *continuous period* is required. If it is interrupted by a single action of the greater part of the community, or if in the meantime the prince should punish those introducing the custom, the custom is not prescribed (the Salamancans d. cap. 6, n. 19, with Laymann, Suarez, Bon., Palaus, etc.).

Moreover, it is said *by repeated acts.* For a custom it is required: 1) That the acts should be repeated many times according to prudent judgment, as the Salamancans say (*ibid.,* punct. 3, § 3, n. 21), with Palaus, Bonac., Suarez, etc. against Lessius, Reg., Sa, Diana, etc. They also say two or three acts suffice. 2) That the acts must be free; so if a people thought a law exists which really does not. (The Salamancans, d. c. 6, n. 24, et 25) with St. Thomas, Diana, Tap., etc. 3) It is required that the acts be well known, at least by notoriety of fact, as the Salamancans, n. 26, and 27, with Pal, Suarez, Bonac., Diana, Basil. etc. against some who require notoriety even of law that custom be approved by the determination of a judge.

IV. The intention to oblige oneself or to introduce a custom is required to complete a custom. This is why no custom is made if the people, or a great part of it acts from devotion, gratitude and like things; or if it injures the law with an animus only to not satisfy it from fickleness (the Salamancans d.c. 6 § 4, n. 28, with Palaus, Laymann Bonac., etc.). Moreover, this animus is understood from circumstances, namely if a custom is constantly observed, and with no light inconvenience; if the transgressors were punished; if pious men commonly think so (Croix, lib. 1, n. 571, and the Salamancans *ibid.,* n. 30). Moreover, in doubt as to whether a custom is from devotion or obligation; *sub gravi* or *sub levi*; whether it obliges under pain of sin, or only of a penalty; whether the milder part must be held; for no law obliges unless there is certainty about it (the Salamancans d. n. 30, with Palaus, Suarez, Bon., Diana, etc.). Croix (lib. 1, n. 592) also thinks so, and still, he notes there with Carden., that universal customs of the Church oblige of themselves. But this must be understood on customs taken up properly as obliging such, just as on the custom of fasting on the vigil of Pentecost, and other similar things, if they exist. For a great many authors speak differently about the custom of abstaining from dairy products on vigils outside of Lent (on this see book 4, n. 988). And some speak differently even about the custom of nuns reciting the office in private. On this matter, see book 5, n. 122, for what some say is more common and probable.

V. The consent of the prince is required, from *lib. de quibus, ff. de Leg.* Further, it is required that it should have at least the general, tacit consent of the prince, namely to approve each legitimate custom, while the prince is unaware of that special custom (The Salamancans c. 6, punct. 5 § 5, n. 31, with St. Thomas, Palaus, Suarez, Sach., Laymann, Bonac., Tapia, etc.). But when the prince resists, then no custom is made (The Salamancans, *ibid., in fine*). Hence the same authors (The Salamancans n. 32, with Laymann, Bonac., Suarez, Barbos., etc., against other) no custom is granted against ecclesiastical immunity.

108.—What pertains to the effect of custom, it must be noted that custom can not only abolish law, but also its penalty although the fault remains or vice versa (See the Salamancans, *d.c.* 6, punct. 4, §1, ex. n. 53). Custom can also validate a contract invalidated by law (the Salamancans *de matrim.*, cap. 11, punct. 2, n. 50 *et seq.*). It can introduce new impediments invalidating matrimony (The Salamancans *ibid.*, punct. 1, n. 19).

But what if a law forbids a contrary custom? Distinguish: If a clause were applied: *any custom not withstanding*, it would be understood that the past, opposed custom is rejected, not a future one (the Salamancans *de leg.*, c. 6, punct. 4, §2, n. 42; with Suarez, Tapia, Villalobos). But if a clause rejecting any future custom, the authors (the Salamancans *ibid.*, n. 43, *de matr.* d. c. 11, punct. 2, n. 53; with Suarez, Basil., Bonacacina, etc.) say it is more probable that custom still can abrogate the law.

What if all future custom were to be rejected as unreasonable? The response is made that if it were rejected as contrary to natural or divine law, then no custom can be valid. But if it were rejected as unreasonable for the time in which the law is made, then it can be rendered reasonable from a new cause and be valid (the Salamancans *de leg.*, d.c. 6, punct. 4, §2, n. 44, with Suarez, Basil., Tap., Dian.

Lastly, custom can interpret a doubtful law; and this interpretation can either be authentic, so that the interpretation would be a new law; or it can be probable, since custom excels or follows after law; for law is not understood to derogate from a preceding custom, nor custom from law, unless they are expressly opposed. And for this interpreting custom probably less time is required than for a custom opposing the prescription of law. Furthermore, the doctors commonly assert that laws must be interpreted according to the custom of the place, even if the words of the law may be less properly received (The Salamancans *ibid.*, § 3, ex n. 45).

109.—Moreover, custom can be revoked through a contrary law by a superior. Yet:

Quaeritur I: Does a general law derogate from the custom of some particular place? The response is made that it does not, except in a law where mention of that custom is made, or in one where every custom is revoked. It is proved from c. 1 *de Consuetudine* in 6, where it is so held: "It is not reckoned that a custom is abrogated by a special law because it is presumed that the prince is unaware of such a custom." (See the Salamancans, d.c. 6, punct. 5, §1 n. 52). But if the prince were notified about the custom and refused to revoke the law, then it is reckoned that the custom was revoked (The Salamancans *ibid.*, num. 53, cum Palaus, Suarez, Bon., etc.). Still, Bishops abrogate each particular custom by their laws, because they are presumed to have full notice of the customs of their dioceses. (The Salamancans *ibid.*) Moreover, note that the aforesaid doctrine proceeds from a custom that has already been prescribed, not on one begun (The Salamancans, *ibid.*, n. 54, with Mascardo, the Gloss, etc. against Suarez).

Quaeritur II: Whether after a revocatory clause of any custom has been attached, is immemorial custom understood also to be revoked? No, unless it is expressed, because when a superior wills to revoke it, he expresses it (The Salamancans *ibid.,* n. 55, with Abb., Suarez, Bon., Palaus, and Garcia, who cite many declarations of the Sacred Congregations).

Moreover, some custom can be abrogated by another contrary one, which is prescribed in the mode of repeated acts, as above. (The Salamancans, d.c. 6, punct. 5, §2, n. 56 and 57.

DISSERTATIO

Above, proposition 29 was condemned by Pope Alexander VIII, which said: "The assertion on the authority of the Roman Pontiff over ecumenical Councils and in determining questions of faith with infallibility is futile and been refuted many times."

110.—At some time I was prepared to treat this famous question, greatly agitated in our times, but it would certainly take a whole book (which I have not yet published); so now I am urged to devote a good deal of time to it. Thus I ask the reader to spare me, if I seem to recede too much from my charge. Here, two things of great weight occur that must be explained in great detail: First, whether the authority of the Supreme Pontiff outside of a council to determine matters of faith and morals is infallible? Second, whether the authority of the Pope is above that of an ecumenical council.

§. I. On the Infallibility of the Pope.

Concerning this infallibility of the Pope there are a great many opinions.

The first is of Luther and Calvin, who heretically teach that the Pope, even speaking as universal teacher and even together with a council, is fallible.

The second opinion is altogether the opposite, namely that of Albert Pighius, who thinks the Pope cannot err even when speaking privately.

The third is of several that say the Pope is fallible when teaching outside of a council. In regard to this, it must be prefaced for the greater elucidation of the matter, this opinion embraced by the French clergy in 1682, when they published those four famous propositions. Of these, after omitting others that do not pertain to the present matter, they assert the following: "Thus, the spiritual power over spiritual matters present in the Apostolic See, that the decrees on the authority of councils of the Council of Constance would avail at the same time; those who distort the sayings of those decrees only to the period of conciliar schism are not approved by the Gallican Church." Then the fourth: "In questions of faith, especially on the side of the Supreme Pontiff, his decrees pertain to all Churches; nevertheless that judgment is not irreformable without the consent of the Church." And in the same decree it was demanded of the French faculty that no one should receive their doctorate unless he had first publicly defended these propositions, and then bound himself to them with an oath. A little while after in 1690, Pope Alexander VIII, in a bull which began: *Inter multiplices*, declared the aforesaid of the Paris faculty invalid, and commanded it to be held with no regard. But Louis Maimburgus (to whom another later joined himself, Louis Dupinus), after being dismissed from the Society of Jesus, nay more, rightfully expelled from it, offered himself to defend these, and behaved so audaciously that he received the worthy reward of an unforeseen death from the Lord. Nevertheless, around 1693, the same bishops that agreed to emend these four propositions in a congress in 1682, later retracted themselves in a letter sent to Innocent XII. The Most Christian King, Louis XIV, although he had earlier publicly published an edict favoring the observance of the preceding Parisian decree, revoking, in another public edict, another letter of retraction sent to the Pope. (For more on this see Graveson, t. 7, p. 1, 191; Roncaglia *in animadvers. ad Nat. Alexand.* § xi, *sup. Conc. Constant. et Milante loco infra citando*). Thus for the third opinion.

Yet the *fourth opinion* is common, to which we subscribe, that the Roman Pontiff, insofar as he is a particular person and can err, (just as he is fallible in questions of mere fact which especially depend upon the testimony of men); nevertheless, when the Pope speaks as the universal doctor defining *ex cathedra,* namely by the supreme power bestowed upon Peter to teach the Church, then we say that he is infallible in determining controversies of faith and morals. It is upheld by St. Thomas (2. 2. q. 1, art. 10), Torquemada, de Soto, Cajetan, Alexander of Hales, St. Bonaventure, B. August. Triumph., Nic. de lyra, St. Francis de Sales, Spondanus, Thomass., Ludovic., Bail, Duvallius, and innumerable others cited by Thomas Milanter, the Bishop of Stabia (*in suis doctis Exerc.* 19, *sup. proposit. 29*), Alexander VIII and in common with all remaining theologians, as Cardinal Gotti witnesses (*Eccles. Jesu Christi,* tom. 1, c. xi, § 1), along with Milanter (*loc. cit.*) and Toila, in his *Theolog. dogm.* tr. 6, *de Pontif.,* d. 1, §2, n. 14. There are some present among these, who say the Pope is indeed infallible, but only when he maturely defines questions after listening to the judgment of the wise: but others more correctly say this condition is only in regard to what is appropriate, but not necessity. For the promise of infallibility is necessary so that all, who uphold papal infallibility, affirm it was done not by counselors, nor examination, but by the Pope alone. Otherwise, heretics could always object that there was not a sufficient examination, just as *de facto* partisans did in opposition to Trent. Moreover, it pertains to the providence of the Holy Spirit (as Suarez rightly says, 5, *de fide*, sect. 8), that the Pope would not ever act or determine such matters imprudently.

111.—Our conclusion is proven: I. From the Scriptures, and especially from what we read in Matthew 16:18, "You are Peter, and on this rock I will build my Church, and the gates of hell will not prevail against it." Nöel Alexander explains that the rock means the Church; but that interpretation is inept because it would render the sense inept, namely (as he understands it) *upon this Church I will build my Church*. Nevertheless, it is clear from that sense, that the whole discussion is directed to Peter. The holy fathers in common, such as Basil, Cyprian, Chrysostom, Hilary, Tertullian, Epiphanius and Origen (cited by Jos. Baron. against Piccinin., *diss.* 2, cap. 3), say that for the name of *rock* Peter is understood; St. Basil expressly says about Peter (l. 2 contra Eunom.), "Because he excelled in faith, he received the building of the Church in his own person." St. Leo (serm. 94, *de Transfig.*) said: "He so pleased (Christ) with the loftiness of this faith that, being given the happiness of Beatitude, he received the sacred strength of the inviolable rock, upon which the Church was founded that would prevail over the gates of hell and the laws of death." Likewise, St. Cyprian (l. *de unit. Eccles.*), says: "Primacy is given to Peter that it would show the one Church of Christ and one chair." In another place against the followers of Novation, after the words, "You are Peter, and on this rock, etc.," he adds: "Upon him he builds one Church, and commands him to feed his sheep." Likewise, St. Leo (serm. 3, *in Annivers. Assumpt.*), so represents Christ speaking to Peter: "Since I am the inviolable rock ... still, you also are rock, who will become solid by my power, so that those things proper to me in power, shall be common to you by

participation with me." And it is more clear from the
Council of Chalcedon, act. 3, cited by Bellarmine (*De
Controversiis, On the Roman Pontiff*) where it is said: "It (the
Council) calls Peter the rock of the Catholic Church." Hence,
Bellarmine adds: "Catholics teach a metaphor is meant, the
rule of the whole Church was consigned to him, and
particularly in regard to faith; for this is proper to the
fundamental rock to rule and hold up the whole building."
St. Cyril of Alexandria is added, saying: "According to this
promise the Apostolic Church of Peter remains immaculate
from all seduction." Therefore, if a building of this sort is the
Church, against which hell cannot prevail, it will not fall to
ruin, so it is necessary for its base and foundation to also not
be able to be destroyed, lest, after the foundation has been
destroyed, the whole house will come to ruin. So Origen
says on this passage: "If the gates of hell would prevail
against Peter, on whom the Church was founded, they
would also prevail against the Church." It is also proved
from Luke 22:32: "I have prayed for thee, that thy faith
would not fail." Together with that text Maldonato affirms
that the authors gathered that the Popes are perpetually
infallible.

112.— It is proved: II. from ecumenical Councils. 1) From
the Council of Chalcedon where it is held (as St. Thomas
relates *in Opusc. contra errores Graec.*): "Everything defined
by him, (the Pope), is held as defined just as if it were by the
Vicar of the Apostolic throne." In an act of the same Council,
when the epistle of St. Leo was read, anathema was declared
to all those who did not so believe. Then, in the same act, 3,
the Fathers of the Council embraced the doctrine of the Pope
as of St. Peter, and asked that all the doctrines of the Council
be strengthened by the authority of the Apostolic See. 2)
From the 2nd Ecumenical Council of Lyons, it is held: "Also
the very Holy Roman Church obtains supreme rule over the
universal Church, which recognizes it received it with the

fullness of power from the Lord himself in Blessed Peter, whose successor is the Roman Pontiff; so if some questions will have arisen on faith, they ought to be defined by his judgment." 3) From the Council of Florence (*sess. ult.*), we read: "We define that the Roman Pontiff has primacy over the whole world and exists as the successor of Peter, the head of the whole Church, as well as father and doctor of Christians; and that full power to rule the Church was given to him in Blessed Peter by our Lord Jesus Christ, just as it is also contained in the acts of ecumenical councils and sacred canons." Therefore, if it is certain that the Pope is the teacher of the whole Church, it also must be held for certain that he ought to be infallible, lest the Church could at some time be deceived by its teacher. The 15th general council of Vienne can be added, held under Clement V where it was so ratified: "To make a declaration on a doubtful matter of faith, pertains only to the Apostolic See."

113.—It is proved: III. From the Holy Fathers. St. Irenaeus (l. 3, c. 3), writes: It is necessary that for all to depend upon the Roman Church just as upon a font or head." St. Athanasius (*in epist. ad Fel. Pap.*) says: "The Roman Church always preserves the true teaching about God." And in the same epistle, directing his words to the Pope, the Holy Doctor so addresses him: "You are the deposer of profane heretics and emperors, and all that cause disturbance, the prince and teacher as well as head of all orthodox doctrine and the immaculate faith." Theodoret (an Asian Bishop, *in ep. ad Leonem P.*) said: "I await the decree of your Apostolic See, and I beg and beseech your holiness that you would bring me your just help and right judgment to my appeal." St. Cyprian (*epist.* 8, l. 1), writes: "God is one, Christ is one, and the Church is one; there is one chair founded upon Peter by the Lord's voice. Another new priesthood cannot become constituted apart from the one priesthood. Whoever gathers elsewhere, scatters." Cyprian wrote the same thing in *de unitate Eccles.,* "One who deserts the chair of Peter, upon which the Church was founded, does not trust that he is in the Church." St. Jerome writes (*in ep. ad Damasum Papam*), "I speak with the successor of the fisherman ... upon that rock, namely the chair of Peter, I know the Church was built, whoever eats the lamb outside this house, is profane. If anyone was not in the arc of Noah, he will perish when the flood reigns ... Whoever does not gather with you, scatters, this is, he who is not of Christ, is antichrist." St. Basil (*ep.* 52 *ad Athan*) writes: "The Roman Pontiff must be compelled to determine what must be believed, if it will not be given to be defined through a Council." St. Augustine (l. 1, contra Julianum, c. 5), says: "Through a rescript of the Pope the case of the Pelagians came to an end." St. Thomas (*Quodlib.* 10, art. 6), "One must favor more the teaching of the Pope, to whom it pertains to determine matters of faith, than that of any wise man you like." And he says in 2.2. q. 11, art. 2 ad 5: "After some matters were determined by the authority of the Church, anyone that would oppose it would be a heretic; indeed such authority principally resides in the Holy Pontiff." St. Bonaventure (*in Summa Theol.,* q. 1, ar. 3, d. 3) says, "The Pope cannot error provided two things are supposed: The first, to the extent that the Pope determines something; the second that he intends to make a dogma on faith."

114.—It is proved: IV. From the French Schoolmen, for the heretic Hottingerus falsely objects to us, saying: "All France dissents from you." Just the same, Milanter (*Exercit.* 19, dict. prop. 29 Alexand. VIII) says there are few French that contest the infallibility of the Roman Pontiff in respect to the more noble Frenchmen who defend it, especially Peter Mattei Spondanus, giving a dissertation on the Decrees of Constance. Bosvinus (tom. 4, *de Concordia*). At some time Gerson taught the same thing (*de pot. Eccl.* c. 10), saying: "At length, we can say from these things that the plenitude of power was conferred on Peter by Christ, as his vicar, as well as to his successors. This doctor wrote thus in the aforesaid place. Moreover, there is no doubt that Gerson, as Victoria says (*Tract. de auctoritate Papae et concilii*, tr. 5): "Through all things he was very hostile to the authority of the Supreme Pontiffs, and he imbued many others with his venom; for his opinion on the authority of the Pope differed little from his schism." In 1626 they tried to establish the same thing about the ancient French Bishops (art. 137) and in the 2nd general Council of Lyons (where among others French Bishops are numbered who received the confession of the Greeks, namely that the Holy Roman Church obtained rule over the universal Church, etc., as related below). And although the University of the Sorbonne (acknowledged to have arisen from Robert Sorbonne, the confessor to St. Louis, in the year 1253, and erected into a University in the year 1290 by King Charles), were of a contrary opinion, still this happened only in the time of the Council of Constance by the work of Gerson and Almain, who in the same university ascribed to the idea that to settle the schism of the three Popes it was necessary in a case of this sort to defer the case to a council just as to a higher judge. But the more recent men of the Sorbonne, not noticing that their elders spoke about the Pope in doubt, rested upon their authority, when they said the judgment of the Roman Pontiff is not infallible unless it has the consent of the Church or a general council. Moreover, before the Council of Constance and Basel, Raynaldus, a French writer, noticed that all the older theologians unanimously taught that Pontifical definitions, even outside of a council, make the matter *de fide* (*in Opusc. de Rom. Pont.*). Nay more, it is held with Nauclerus (p. 4, lib. 8, c. 6) that the Parisian Faculty in 1320 condemned as heretical the articles of Marsilius of Padua which said: The Roman Pontiff is fallible. And in the year 1554 (as cited by the same Nauclerus), it condemned the same error against John Morandus. Likewise, Duvallius, a French doctor, who wrote around 1712 (*de Sup. Pont.*, p. 1, q. 7), relates that there was a custom of the Parisian Faculty that they would never permit a doctoral defense to contradict the Roman Church. The same author relates that this very Faculty condemned Marcus Antonius de Dominis as a heretic, because he taught the authority of the Pope is fallible. Therefore, the aforementioned Duvallius, although a doctor of the same Sorbonne, did not hesitate to relate (*loc. cit.*), "I opine that what is held at Rome is free from all rashness, since the whole world, with the exception of a handful of doctors, embraces it and besides, it is confirmed by the most valid reasons both from Scripture, Councils, and Fathers, as well as from principles sought from theology." And he also adds (p. 4, q. 7), "There is now nobody in the Church who thinks the contrary apart from Vigorius and Richerius, whose opinion, if true, would mean the whole Christian world would shamelessly err in faith." For that reason he adds that the opinion on the preference for councils to the authority of the Roman Pontiff, "can scarcely excuse one from rash disobedience; for it fosters much disobedience and many quarrels; and it always excited great tumults in the Church." Next it is for us to see with Troila (tr. 6, *de Sum. Pont.*, ar. 6, ex n. 54) and Milanter (*in Exercit. dogm.* 19 *super prop.* 29 *Alexand. VIII*), how many French provincial councils applauded the infallibility of the Pope. A Synod in Paris itself in 1626, in article 137, *Tit. Monita cleri Gallicani ad dominos Archiepiscopos regni*, look at what it thought: "Therefore, we exhort all Bishops that the holy apostolic Roman Church, inasmuch as it is the mother of Churches by the infallible promise of God ..." and further on, speaking about the Roman Pontiff himself: "For he is the successor of Peter, upon which Christ Jesus founded the Church, when he relinquished to him the keys of the kingdom of heaven and the gift of infallibility in cases of faith." For it must be exceedingly noted that what the French Bishops wrote (as Milanter relates, *loc. cit.*) in obedience to a bull which

Innocent X made known in the refutation of the theses of the Jansenists: "Most Blessed Father, that desired Constitution has come to us, in which by the authority of your holiness it is clearly discerned what must be thought on the five controversial propositions excerpted from the books of Cornelius Jansen the bishop of Yprensis... In such a business it comes to pass what is worthy by observation, as to the extent that Innocent I once condemned the Pelagian heresy; thus Innocent X proscribed the opposed heresy in his consultation to the French Bishops by his own authority. Moreover, the Catholic Church of that ancient age, supported by the authority of the chair of Peter alone, which in the decretal letter of Innocent given to the Africans he elucidated; and which thereafter in another subsequent epistle of Zosimus to the Bishops of the whole world, he subscribed to the condemnation of the Pelagian heresy without delay: for he had the observation that not only by the promise of Christ the Lord made to Peter, but even by the acts of Pius Popes and anathemas against Appolinarus and Macedonius when they were not yet condemned by any ecumenical Council, and a little earlier by Damasus, the judgments for the rule of faith ratified by the Supreme Pontiffs were given, above consultation of Bishops (whether they placed their opinion in the acts of relation or not, as it pleased them) resting equally on divine and the supreme authority through the universal Church, to which all Christians of their own accord also are held to furnish obedience of the mind, etc." Later, the aforesaid Bishops promised to promulgate that bull.

115.—It is proved: V. For the following reasons. 1) St. Thomas, (2, p. q. 25, art. 1) who teaches the promise of infallibility in matters of faith was made only to the successors of Peter, and therefore he says the Church cannot err, because the Pope cannot err: "The universal Church (these are the words of St. Thomas), cannot err because he who in all matters was clearly heard for his reverence, said to Peter: 'I have prayed for thee, Peter, that thy faith would not fail'." 2) The same holy Doctor, who in another place (2. 2. q. 1, art. 10), said that in the Church one faith cannot be preserved except through its head, the Pope, questions of faith were to be defined. "And the reasoning is, because one faith ought to be for the whole Church (according to that of 1 Cor. 1), which cannot be preserved unless a question of faith were determined through one man, who is over the whole Church." 3) The longstanding custom of the Church. The very erudite Melchior Cano uses this reason to uphold our opinion (*Opusculum de locis theologicis*, l. 6, c. 7), where he says: "If no one, therefore (so the author argues), is a more eager interpreter of the laws of Christ than the perpetual use of the Church; but in matters of faith, they do not have recourse to Antioch, or Alexandria, or Jerusalem, but the Roman Pontiff in every time, and hold his judgments as irrefragable, why should we hesitate that he gave a successor to Peter in this prerogative? It is fortified in this testimony of matters: for the prophecy of Christ about Peter seems to have been fulfilled in his Successors. Since the other Churches of the Apostles are either occupied by infidels or at some time were possessed by heretics: but this one has availed to never be expunged among so many enemies, either by infidels or heretics. Hence it is usually asked whether it would be heretical to assert that the Roman See can at some time, just as the others, defect from the faith of Christ? They sufficiently show this, Jerome, saying that it is a falsehood that one would not follow the faith of the Holy See; Cyprian, saying: "He who deserts the chair of Peter, upon which the Church was founded, cannot trust that he is in the Church; the Council of Constance, judging one to be a heretic who believes the articles of faith other than what the Holy Roman Church teaches. Lastly, I add that, when it is drawn out from the traditions of the apostles to conquer a certain heretical argument, it is established that the Roman Bishops succeeded Peter in the magisterium of faith, handed on from the Apostles, why we ought not condemn an opposed assertion as heretical? But we refuse to anticipate a judgment of the Church: I assert that, and indeed faithfully do so, that those who either deny the Roman Pontiff succeeds Peter in authority of faith and doctrine, or certainly pile on that the Supreme Pastor of the Church, whoever he might be, can err in faith, bring plague and destruction on the Church. Certainly, heretics do both: but those who refuse them in both, these are held to be in the Catholic Church." To this point, Cano favors what St. Cyprian carefully notices (*Ep.* 3, l. 2) saying: "For heresy is born from no other source than one refuses to obey the priest of God, nor the one priest in the Church, and for a time the judge held in place of Christ." And the reason for this grave opinion of Cyprian is that those who pertinaciously resist decrees of the Roman See, first (as the Bishop of Sabia rightly notes) become schismatics, then heretics.

At length, from all these, the Holy Doctors, such as Suarez (l. 3, *de Fidei defen.*), Bannez, and Bellarmine (*On the Roman Pontiff*, l. 4, c. 2) advance our opinion as at least *proximam fidei*; and the contrary (as Bellarmine says, *loc. cit.*) seems altogether erroneous and *proxima haeresi*.

After I wrote this, other reasons occurred to me very worthy of notice favoring the infallibility of the Supreme Pontiff, which especially bear down against the declaration of the Gallican clergy. It is said in that declaration: "Nor is the judgment (namely of the Pope) irreformable unless it also has the consent of the Church." Now we ask, how should a consensus of this sort be added? Some say, both pontifical definitions go out irreformable when the consent of all the faithful is added. Others, when there is at least the consent of all he Bishops. Some think the consent of only one province is sufficient. Others, at length, require the consent of a greater part of the Bishops abiding in the Christian world; for this opinion is more in conformity with the custom which the ecumenical councils used in determining doubts of faith. With this posited, it is asked what must be said, if an equal part of the Episcopate were added to a pontifical decree? What then, must be thought about the judgment of the Pope? And what if a lesser part were added, as happened in the fourth century, when only 18 orthodox Bishops adhered to the judgment of Pope St. Melchiadis, while on the other hand 400 others rejected it, as Haunoldus relates (*Introd. ad jus. canon.*, p. 162). In a similar case, who stops the quarrel if one supreme judge is not acknowledged? Who has the infallible power to define causes of faith? For, if the consent of the greater part of the Bishops suffices, by all means, all are held to believe the Pope is infallible, immediately when he determines definitively something in regard to faith or morals; for not only the greater part, but nearly the whole Church with the exception of France teaches it, and always taught it. Therefore, either it is necessary to affirm the infallibility of the Pope, or to say that the Catholic Church is merely reduced to the scanty number of the French.

Besides, it is certain that if the opinion of the Gallican clergy were admitted, so that the judgment of the Pope were fallible until the consent of the Church were added, the mode of convicting heretics for their errors would no longer be sufficient, even if general councils were applied: for heretics would never acquiesce to the judgment of a council in which they were not present, to the extent that without the intervention of those who presume they constitute the healthier part of the Church, they would declare any council to be invalid. Hence, the custom arose that the heterodox, when they saw their errors denounced to the Roman See, either were proscribed by it, had custom to immediately appeal to an ecumenical council to avoid condemnation. For this reason St. Cyprian wisely wrote, whose words it will help to repeat here: "Heresy arises from no other source, nor schisms born, than that the priest of God is not obeyed, nor the one in the Church had for a time as judge in place of Christ; to whom if all fraternity would obey according to the divine magisteria, no one would rend the Church." Hence, Fr. Petitidierus, the Abbot of Senonensis, (*praefat. ad Tract. de auctori. et infallibilitat. S. Pontif*), writes that if this rule of St. Cyprian were preserved, the mouths of the Jansenists would have been closed in so long a condemnation of the bull *Unigentius*; but because the Gallican clergy stood upon the related declaration, whereby the infallibility of the Pope is denied before a consensus of the Church, therefore, even still they fight the reception of the bull, and the quarrel still lives and flourishes in France.

Those in favor of the declaration object that the Church is the mystical body of Christ, wherefore they say that just as the body cannot subsist without a head, so the head cannot subsist without the body. To this one can easily respond. There is no doubt that neither the body can be without the head, nor the head without the body, but this presents no obstacle to our case, where it is a question not on the constitution or integrity of the body, but only on the rule of the body of the Church: indeed the constitution of the body is important that it would not be without a head, and the head not without a body; but the rule of the body of the Church is important that just as the human body is governed by the mind of man, so the body of the Church is governed by the Pope as its head. Therefore, the duty of the head that is of the Pope, is to teach and rule the Church; the duty of the body, that is the Church, is to be instructed and obey the Pope.

By all means, the council of Florence eloquently taught us that, by calling the Pope "the head of the whole Church, father and doctor of all Christians," and adding "And to him the full power to rule the Church was handed on." And it rightly took from the words of Christ the Lord, when he said to Peter: "You are Peter, and upon this rock I will build my Church." And subsequently: "And when you have been converted, strengthen your brethren." Moreover, what the Lord said to Peter, certainly he also said to all his successors, and for, as St. Augustine observes, the power of universal pastor was not conferred to Peter on his own account, but for him to rule the Church, and therefore, power in the Church ought to be conferred on Peter that it be transferred to all the successor Popes, and so that the Church will remain ruled rightly even to the consummation of the age. If the decrees of Popes were not infallible, unless the consent of the Church were added, indeed it would have to be said that the Church was not founded upon Peter, but that Peter was founded on the Church. And so equally it would need to be said that the brethren were not confirmed by Peter, but Peter by the brethren.

Moreover, our doctrine, that dogmatic decrees of the Pope are infallible, Bellarmine witnesses (*De Controversiis*, l. 4 *On the Roman Pontiff*), was truly the ancient doctrine of all Catholic theologians and Fathers. Cano (*de loc. theol.*, l. 6, c. 5,), relates Irenaeus, Cyprian, Ambrose, Cyril, Jerome and Bernard favoring this testimony. That authority is held especially by St. Thomas (2.2. q. 1, art. 10) who advances this as a certain doctrine, saying: "Therefore, to his authority (that is, of the Pope) it pertains to finally determine those matters which are of the faith, so that they would be held with unshakeable faith by all. And the reason for this is because one faith ought to be for the whole Church; it cannot be preserved unless a question of faith will be determined through him who is in charge of the whole Church." John of Paris formerly advanced the same reasoning (*Lib. de potest. regis, et Papae*, c. 3), in favor of the infallibility of the Pope, before he began to be hostile to it;

look at his words: "The Church would be divided unless unity were to be preserved through the judgment of one: moreover, Peter is this one having a rule of this sort, along with his successors."

A great many Popes expressly declared it. Anacletus (*Epist.* 1, *de oppress. Episc.*), so wrote: "Let greater cases be referred to the Apostolic See ... upon which Christ constructed the universal Church, saying to the Blessed Prince of the Apostles, 'You are Peter, and upon this rock, etc.'" The same Pope confirms (*in ep.* 3, *de Patriarch.*, as it is contained in *can. Sacrosanctâ*, dist. 22), and there explaining what is understood by the name *of the Apostolic See*, saying: "This most holy Roman and Apostolic Church obtained preeminence of power from Christ the Lord over all Churches." Nicholas I more expressly declared the same thing, as is read in *can. Omnes,* dist. 22, where it is held: "He certainly does violence who acts against it (the Roman Church) which is the mother of faith." And there he prescribes that he must be said to be heretical, who would deny the privilege of the Roman Church was conceded to Peter, namely that the rights of the earthly and heavenly kingdom were consigned to him by Christ the Lord." And the eighth Council confirmed the opinion of Nicholas against Photius and Michael, who had tried to weaken the privilege of this kind of the Roman See.

Innocent III wrote the same thing (Epist. 208, *ad Patriarch. Constantin.*, with Balbut, l. 3), where speaking on the primacy of the Roman Church, and calling to mind those words, "I have prayed for thee, that thy faith would not fail;" he later adds: "Manifestly agreeing with this, that his successors at no time ever deviated from the Catholic faith, but rather more called back some, bestowing on others the power to confirm that he might place the necessity of obedience to others." Pope Gregory VII wrote the same thing, saying: "The Roman Church has never erred, nor may

he be held as a Catholic who is not joined to this Church."
Many other Popes also wrote the same thing, such as
Evaristus, Alexander I, Sixtus I, Pius I, Victor, Zephyrinus,
Marcellus, Eusebius, and others whom Cano relates (lib. 6,
cap. 4).

The eighth Council confirmed the same opinion on the
infallibility of Pontifical definitions, besides the Councils of
Chalcedon, Lyons, and Florence (n. 112 related above),
where in speaking on the authority of the Roman See, the
Fathers so affirmed: "In which there is the true and whole
entirety of the Christian religion; which is why those not
agreeing closely with the Apostolic See, their names must
not be recited among the sacred mysteries. The Ecumenical
Council of Vienne holds the same thing (as is related in
Clem. unic. de Summa Trinit.) where it was said: "To declare
doubts of faith pertains only to the Apostolic See." Melchior
Cano relates many other clear testimonies, l. 6, c. 6, in which
the authority of the Roman Church is proved.

Fr. Petididierus writes (*loc. cit.*, cap. 14), it is sufficiently
ascertained in history, that no, or nearly no heretic ever
acquiesced to the judgment of councils; while on the other
hand a great many have acquiesced to the judgment of the
Pontiff, since he readily meets them. For what remains, in
the first ages of the Church a great many sowers of error
against the faith were always condemned by the Roman
Pontiffs, and it was immediately held by all that they were
heretics with no expectation of the consent of the Church.
It thus happened in the year 150 when Valentinus was
condemned by Hyginus; in 215 when the Montanists were
condemned by Zephyrinus; in 300 when Jovinian was
condemned by Siricius; in 416 when Pelagius was
condemned by Innocent I. For this reason, the Bishops of
France itself, in their letter to Innocent X, after he proscribed
the propositions of the Jansenists, they so wrote: Not only
by the promise of Christ made to Peter, but from the acts of

the early Popes, the judgments for the rule of faith ratified by the Supreme Pontiffs imposed over the consultation of Bishops, resting equally with divine and supreme authority through the universal Church, to which all Christians are held to furnish obedience of the mind and will." Therefore, the faithful are held to furnish obedience to definitions of the Pope, before their consent were added.

So therefore, all the ancients firmly held it, but Bellarmine writes the same thing (*loc. cit.,*) that today this opinion is of whole nations, with the exception of France. Benedict XIV writes that the same opinion is received everywhere. (In a letter given to the Inquisitor general of Spain, 13 Jul. 1748, as Billuart relates, 2.2. t. 1, diss. 4, a. 5). Moreover, Although (Fr. Petitd. says, c. 15, §5), on account of the fog spread about from the sayings of Gerson and Cardinal de Alliacus, certain German and Polish universities felt otherwise, still later all were in agreement on the infallibility of pontifical definitions; so that today no University, and no theologian found outside of France, who does not uphold the infallibility of the Pope and his authority over Councils. Nay more, Augustin Triumphus, a doctor at the Parisian academy, (*Lib. de potest. Ecclesiae*, q. 10, a. 3), the authority of Gerson not withstanding, did not hesitate to assert that it is a heresy to not adhere to the Pope defining something on faith.

116.—Our adversaries object that a great many Popes erred in judgments of faith. But with a little labor we can be freed from this opposition, generally by responding with Cano and Bellarmine, that these Popes that are led in who erred did not do so as universal teachers of the Church, but only spoke privately, as they make clear from history. But, lest, from some deeds which everywhere and arrogantly are advanced by our adversaries though excessively mangled, someone perhaps may be deceived, therefore, we gladly respond to each individually.

117.—They object: I. That Pope Liberius did not hesitate to subscribe to the Arian heresy. Moreover, in this it must be known that when Liberius was reluctant to subscribe to it at the assembly in Milan, he was expelled by the Emperor Constantius, and in his place Felix II was appointed by the Arians. Thenceforth, the Arians produced the new formula of faith in the gathering of Firmiensi, in which they deceitfully said the Son is similar the Father in substance. To this, Liberius, worn out by exile, conquered, imprudently subscribed to it. For this reason, he was recalled from exile and reached Rome, but he was rejected by the hostile Romans on account of the disgrace of this kind, and Felix was called in his place; who after on account of the constancy in rejecting the formula of the Arians he was condemned to be beheaded. But Liberius, after the death of Felix, when he recovered his senses, condemned the same formula and was again acclaimed Pope. Therefore the private lapse of Liberius, since he did not teach *ex cathedra*, does not harm our opinion.

They object: II. Pope Vigilius, in his epistle to Theodora the Empress, said anathema to those who confessed two natures in Christ, in which it seems that Pope adhered to the Monophysite heresy. But this must be noted, as Baronius relates (*Annales*, 547, n. 40), Vigilius professed this error in the time in which, after Sylverius, the legitimate Pope, had been expelled with the aid of the Empress; he was created Pope, or rather more anti-Pope. But a little while after when Silverius died, he legitimately secured the Apostolic See, and he never advanced that error in any mode, nor feigned it.

118.—They object III. Against the same Vigilius, that he approved the three chapters, which the general council of Constantinople later condemned, although they were already confirmed by Vigilius himself. Here, it must be known that the Emperor Justinian, with the work of Theodore of Caesarea, published an edict in which three chapters were contained, namely the condemnation of the memory and writings of Theodore of Mopsuestia, Ibas, the Bishop of Edessa, and Theodoret the bishop of Cyprus, in which the errors of Nestorius were alleged. Yet, because in the council of Chalcedon a praiseworthy mention was made of the aforesaid authors, a great many Bishops condemned the edict. Then at Constantinople, with the consent of the Pope, a council was convoked, according to the edict of Caesar, that confirmed the three chapters; and Vigilius subscribed to the edict secretly at the persuasion of the Emperor. But, when this became public, a great schism arose in the Church. This is why Vigilius decreed that the effect of the edict would be suspended, and the matter recalled to a general council. Later, the same Vigilius, in a certain rescript called *Constitutus Vigilii*, condemned the writings of Theodoret and Ibas, but left their persons immune from censure. We do not deny it to be true that in the following year the Emperor obtained a revocation of *Constitutus* and a confirmation of the Council of Constantinople, but from this revocation what else can our adversaries advance except that which St. Gregory said at the moment, (lib. 3, epist. 3), "For the fault is not the change of opinion, but the inconstancy of the sense." If anyone would have said that Vigilius erred in faith in his *Constitutus*, he ought equally to say that the Council of Chalcedon erred, which declared the same thing as Vigilius in his *Constitutus*. Moreover, it is established for certain that this matter did not pertain to the faith; for that Theodoret and Ibas not only wrote badly, but even with bad faith, and therefore, not only their writings but also their persons ought to have been condemned, was a matter of pure fact. Hence, lest Councils be said to disagree with themselves, it must be said that in Chalcedon there was a treatment on the persons, but in Constantinople, however, on their writings. Hence, St. Gregory advised: "I want you to know that in it (in the Council of Chalcedon), the matter was only carried out in regard to the persons, not, however, on some issue of faith.

119.—IV. Maimburgus and Jueninus object that in the sixth and seventh Council, Pope Honorius was condemned as a heretic due to the epistles he had written to Sergius the leader of the Monotholites. In the 13th action of the sixth Council it is read: "And at the same time we foresee to anathematize even Honorius, who was the Pope of old Rome, to the extent that we discover in the writings which he made to Sergius, that in all things he followed his mind, and conformed himself to his impious doctrines." Moreover, the second Roman Council declared on him: "Honorius was judged after death by the VI Synod because he was accused of heresy." And it is asserted that this was confirmed by Pope St. Leo II, in an epistle to the Emperor Constantine, in which it is read that Leo counted even Honorius among the heretics.

Resp. I. There is no absence of writers who assert the epistles disclosed by the Greeks were fabricated, and Roncaglia (*in Animad. in Natalem*) says more experienced critics assert that the acts of the aforesaid Council arrived to us adulterated. Nor is this adulteration gratuitously asserted, rather St. Gregory witnesses it as certain (l. 5, epist. 14), and it seems also to be clearly proved from the same Council, in which those who were condemned are listed in another place from where they are in the epistle of Pope Agatho to the Emperor, and in that epistle no mention was made about Honorius, in a word it was pronounced that the Roman chair never defected and never could defect. And it is rightly believed that Agatho pronounced to root out all suspicion of error against Honorius, whose innocence had been discussed long before, and defended with strenuous effort by St. Maximus the confessor, and by the clear judgment of Pope John, the predecessor of Agatho. Equally, the acts of the Seventh Council were corrupted, as

Anastasius the librarian witnesses, (*in Praef. hist. ad VI. Synodum*). Moreover, the response is made to the Roman Council, that the fathers of the council were lead from false and corrupted acts of the aforesaid sixth Council, as was shown above. Equally, Baronius proves that the epistle of St. Leo was by far fabricated by the Greeks with many valid arguments (*ad annum Christi* 683, n. 19, *et sequenti*).

But still, what if we were to admit the acts of the aforesaid Council and the epistle of Leo as true: Resp. II, that the epistles of Honorius can easily be explained in a Catholic sense, as Frassen and Tournely (*Prael. theol. de Eccles. quaest.* 3, art. 4, vers. fin), and very worthy men affirm, such as St. Maximus, who, in a disputation against Pyrrhus, in the same time as Honorius, defended him and made him guiltless of the errors of the Monothelites. Anastasius, the secretary of Honorius, wrote the same thing. John IV, (*in Apologia pro Honorio ad Constantinum Imperatorem*), wrote the same thing, asserting that Pyrrhus hastened to drag Honorius onto his side, but Honorius was altogether foreign to their false doctrine. For Honorius affirmed two wills in Christ, and operations, but by prudent counsel forbade the terms of one or two wills, which then were unheard of; for at that time, when the error of the Monothelites rose, and Cyrus of Alexandria preached one operation in Christ, Sophronius the Bishop of Jerusalem preached two wills, so Honorius, to prevent the schism that was threatening, wrote in his first epistle that all should cease to use the term of one operation, lest it would seem that one will were recognized with the Monophysites, and to cease to use the term two operations, lest it would appear one supported two persons in Nestorius. And this is clear from the second epistle of Honorius, where it is so held: "Therefore, relating as we said, the scandal of novel discovery, it is not fitting for us to preach one or two operations, but for one which indeed they say operation, we however confess the operator Christ the Lord is truthfully confessed in both natures." So with Frassen (t. 7, tr. 1, diss. 2, a. 1, sec. 2, q. 3). Nor is it opposed that Honorius also wrote: "We affirm only one will of our Lord Jesus Christ." For there he only spoke on the human will, when he said on Christ the man there were not two opposed wills, one of the flesh and the other of the spirit, but only one of the spirit; for in Christ the flesh did not lust against the spirit: "Because certainly (look at his words), our nature was taken up by the Divinity, not by fault. ... For another law in the members, or different wills was not either contrary to or above the law born to the human condition." Hence, the aforesaid John wrote: "According to this, therefore, the mode that our said predecessor wrote is distinguished, because in our Savior two contrary wills do not consist in his members, because he took no vice from the prevarication of the first man." So with Nat., who did not doubt to confirm it, saying that Honorius, in his Epistles, spoke with a Catholic mind, accordingly, he absolutely did not deny two wills of Christ, but opposed wills."

Resp. III. Even were it granted that Honorius truly erred, Nöel Alexander says that it must be said that he did not deviate from the course of faith, but he did not repudiate Monothelitism with the strength he ought to have. And although Nöel Alexander may believe that the Sixth Council truly condemned Honorius, still he says it did not condemn him as a heretic in regard to teaching and pertinacity, but as one favoring heretics, on account of excessive patronage for them; for proof of this he asserts the epistle of Leo XII to Constantine Pogonatus for confirmation of the Synod, where, Leo wrote, "We anathematize Theodore, Cyrus, Sergius, Pyrrhus, and also Honorius, who by profane betrayal permitted the immaculate (Church) to be stained." And even though in the canon of the Sixth Council Honorius is asserted to have followed the *mind* of Sergius *in all things, and confirmed impious dogmas*; this must be understood, says Nöel, not by consenting, but by turning a blind eye, or counseling silence: for he says heretics aimed in the same impiety, but those by a wicked assertion of dogma, Honorius by feigning Catholic dogma. Hence he infers that although Honorius was not a heretic, still he was properly condemned due to negligence in condemning the heresy of the Monothelites. The anonymous author of the book *Gallia vindicata* also thinks so (*diss.* 5. 5. n. 9) responding to Louis Maimburgus: "Who does not know the epistles of Honorius were private, and not dogmatic, in which Honorius defined nothing, but only disclosed his private opinion?" For, he conceded the Popes could err, as men, when responding in private writings, but not as teachers of the Church by teaching the faithful: "When this privilege of infallibility (is added) for the good of the Church, God refuses that to the person but joins it to the office and then only does he exercise the pontifical office."

120.—V. They object that St. Cyprian bravely resisted the decree of Pope St. Stephen, and appealed to a future council. But this is answered: 1) The Holy Martyr never thought this matter regarded faith, but only discipline, while he himself wrote to Jubajanus (*epist.* 73) in this controversy that each bishop can act according to his will. For Stephen never declared this to be *de fide*, but only wrote to Cyprian himself: "If anyone will have come to us from any heresy, nothing should be innovated unless it was handed down." And because Cyprian thought it was an ancient tradition that those baptized by heretics should again be rebaptized: therefore, he awaited a general council that from the testimony of so many Bishops of the practice of their Churches, the truth of the matter would be made known. Besides, although earlier Cyprian resisted, at length he subjected himself to the decree, as a great many authors witness (Cabassutius, Baronius, Thomass., Lud., Bail, and others with Milanter), and St. Jerome absolutely witnessed

this from the testimony of the fathers, in his Dialogue
against Lucifer. But I refuse here to argue further, since this
first conclusion is confirmed more deeply from what must
soon be said in the second, to which we now come.

§. II. *On the Authority of the Pope over Councils*

121.—It must be prefaced, I. The fact that a Pope is above
a council must not be understood about a doubtful Pope in
a time of schism, when there will be probable uncertainty
about the legitimacy of his election; because then in each
case the doubtful Pope ought to be under a council, just as
the Council of Constance defined (*sess.* 4). For then, a
general Council holds supreme power immediately from
Christ, just as in a time when the See is vacant, as St.
Antoninus rightly adverts (p. 3, tit. 23, c. 2, §26). It must be
prefaced, II. The same thing avails in regard to a manifestly
and externally heretical Pope, but not for a secret or mental
one. Although some rightly say that then the Pope can by no
means be deprived of his authority by a Council as though
by his superior, rather, he is immediately deprived by Christ
after the condition of deposition has been supposed, insofar
as it is requisite to it. It must be prefaced, III. That a general
council can be understood in many ways in respect to the
Pope: 1) When a Council is considered without a Pope, and
then the Council has no authority, except in the aforesaid
cases of schism and heresy: because a Council is a gathering
of Bishops under the Pope as constituted under a head. 2)
When the Pope presides in a Council, as a head not divided
from the body (namely from the body of Bishops), or when
a Council is confirmed by the Pope; then a Council cannot
be understood to be above the Pope, for otherwise a Council
would need no authority of the Pope, or otherwise the Pope
would approve it against himself, which cannot be. 3) When
a Council is gathered by the Pope and the Pope is considered

as the head, and the Bishops as the body distinct from the head, in this sense it is asked whether the Pope is above the Council, or the other way around?

122.—In regard to this last question, the *first opinion* is of the heretics, that a Council is above the Pope, as Calvin and other say. The Bishops at the council of Basel adhered to this opinion, with John Antiochenus: and at the time of the Western Schism, John Gerson, about whom Victoria says: "That doctor was through all things very hostile to the authority of the Supreme Pontiffs, and he imbued many others with his venom." And so also Almainus Aliacensis and a few others of that time held, whose opinion Fagnanus says is to be accounted as nothing, to the extent that he had rose in the council of Basel from ambition, while the anti-Pope Felix V was well disposed toward him, later deposed Eugene IV. But the Gallican clergy declared, as was related above, that the decree of the Council of Constance on the authority of a Council above the Pope must be extended even outside of a schism. Nevertheless, this opinion differs from that of the heretics who say the Pope is not the head of Church, but only of the Roman See; for Catholics say the Pope is the head of the whole Church, but not gathered in a Council and collectively, but in a divided fashion, over individual Churches, as the Superior General is in respect to the monasteries of his order.

The *second opinion* is of the Gloss (*can. Nos, si incompetenter,* caus. 2, qu. 7), saying that the Pope is above a Council; still, that he should subject himself to a council of his own will, that he should be held to obey the opinion of a Council. However, St. Antoninus, Cajetan, Bellarmine, etc. rightly reject this, because, since Pontifical authority is of divine law, the Pope cannot renounce it, as Boniface VIII declared (*in Extrav. Unam Sanctam, de major. et obed.*), saying: "Supreme power is from God alone, he cannot be judged by man." It would be otherwise were it a question only about discretion in judgment (but not a coercive judgment), that some Popes made when they allowed their cases to be discussed in a Council.

The third opinion, to which we subscribe, holds that a Pope that is not doubtful is always above a general council, and above all Churches, even when taken collectively. And this is upheld by St. Thomas, St. Bonaventure, Alexander of Hales, St. Juan Capistrano, St. Bernard, St. Augustine Triumphus, Baronius, Bellarmine, Sfondratus, Pallavicino, Emman. Schelestrate, Lupus, Cabass., Cajetan, Gotti, and other authors in common (See Militant., *loc. cit.*).

123.—It is proved: I. from the Scriptures. 1) Luke 22:31, "Simon, Simon, behold, Satan has asked for you to sift you like wheat; but I have prayed for thee, that thy faith shall not fail, and when thou has been converted, confirm thy brethren." Take note that Christ the Lord prayed for Peter alone, who alone ought to confirm the brethren. Therefore, if the faith of Peter could fail, the brethren would not avail to be confirmed by Peter. The commentary of some of the Parisians is false, who think in this passage that Christ prayed for the universal Church, or for Peter in the figure of the whole Church; for the Lord designated only one person, "Simon, Simon;" and he began to speak in the plural: "Satan has asked for you that he would sift you; next he changed the manner of speech: "But I have prayed for thee." Certainly, if he would have spoken about the whole Church, he would have spoken more correctly if he had said, "I have prayed for you (*vobis*)." Moreover, those words, "Confirm thy brethren," clearly evince that Christ was not addressing the whole Church: for who can imagine the brethren of the universal Church? Nor are they to be heard who teach that Christ prayed in this passage for the perseverance of Peter, for they labor to interpret those later words, "confirm thy brethren," in that sense. Therefore, the exposition of the text must be upheld that Christ procured a privilege for Peter and his successors, so that they could not teach something against the faith. Pope Agatho wrote thus in his letter to the Emperor Constantine, which was read in the sixth Council, and there it was approved by all: "This is the rule of faith (the words of the Epistle), which the Apostolic Church of Christ held, which will be proved to never have erred from the path of apostolic tradition, by the grace of God, because it was said to Peter: 'I have prayed for thee, etc.' Hence, the Lord promised that the faith of Peter was not going to fail, and admonished him to confirm his brethren, which it is known to all the Apostolic Pontiffs, my great predecessors, always confidently did." St. Leo more elegantly teaches the same thing (*serm.* 3, *Assumpt. ad Pontif.*), "Therefore, in Peter the strength of all is diminished so that the strength which is attributed to Peter would be conferred upon the apostles through Peter." 2) It is proven from the Acts of the Apostles, 15:7, where at a Council held among the Apostles, Peter so addressed them: "Men, brethren, you know that in former days God made a choice among us, that by my mouth the Gentiles should hear the word of the gospel, and believe." By such words, Peter eloquently enough signified that God had so handed to him and his successors the power to teach the Gentiles what they ought to believe. 3) It is proven from John 21:16, 17, "Feed my lambs, ... feed my sheep." Hence, St. Cyprian (ep. 9, lib. 3), said: "The Church is the people united to the priest, and the flock adhering to its shepherd." Eusebius Emiss. (in Serm. Nat. S. Jo.) says: "He first consigned his lambs, then the sheep, because he not only constituted a shepherd, but a shepherd of shepherds." St. Bernard (l. 2 *de Consid. ad Eug. III*), adds: They have flocks assigned to them, but all are entrusted to you, one to one." So the fathers speak, but our adversaries try to show where in the Scriptures that the sheep in a council cease to be sheep subject to their pastor, nay more that there the sheep are changed into the shepherd of the Pontiff. On the other hand, in the Scripture it is read that the Pope was placed as pastor, not only of the sheep but of the whole sheepfold, when Christ pronounced (John 10:16), "There will be one sheepfold and one shepherd." Nor is it opposed to say that (Acts 8:14), the Apostles sent Peter together with John in Samaria; for they did not send him by command but only by counsel, the way that a king is said to be sent to war by his ministers.

124.—It is proved, II. From councils. 1) It was ratified at the Council of Nicaea (can. 18), "All Bishops in more serious cases may freely appeal to the Apostolic See, which the ancient authority of the apostles reserved the disposal of all greater cases." Pope Julius I recalled that canon, as did Nicholas I, who said that a Council would not so speak unless it acknowledged the infallible power in the Pope. And again, it is held in canon 29 of the same Nicene Council (as cited in Fagnan, *cap. Nullus de elect.*, n. 49): "It holds the see of Rome, as head of all patriarchs, just as Peter, who was vicar of Christ over every Christian Church." If, therefore, the Pope is over the Church, he will necessarily be over a Council, because he represents the Church, as the Council of Constance expresses it in the decree of its fourth session which we have already related. 2) From the Council of Chalcedon it is held (as is read in St. Thomas, *Opusc. contra Graecos*): "Everything defined by him (namely the Pope) should be held as from the Vicar of the apostolic throne." Bellarmine relates this (t. 2, lib. 2), from Act. 3 of the same Council, where Dioscorus was condemned because he dared to judge and condemn the Roman Pontiff, even though when he did this he was propped up by the authority of the Council of Ephesus which was gathered as a general Council. Therefore, Bellarmine rightly argues that if Dioscorus could not avail to judge the Pope in a general council, certainly it is inferred that a council is not above the Pope. 3) From the fourth Council of Constantinople, where in its fifth session it is so held: "And we do not advance a new opinion on that judgment, but one formerly pronounced by the most holy Pope Nicholas, which we can by no means change." And in canon 2: "Therefore, holding the most Blessed Pope Nicholas as the instrument of the Holy Spirit, etc." Consequently, this council declared the opinion of the Pope to be immutable. 4) From the Council of Constance, where, as Bellarmine relates, the epistle of Martin V was approved, wherein he commanded those suspect of heresy to be asked: "Whether they would believe that the Pope is the successor of Peter, having supreme authority in the Church of God?" But certainly that supreme power is (as Bellarmine rightly argues), such that there is nothing greater than it, and to which there is no equal. Next, it is held, that the same Council of Constance condemned proposition 37 of Wycliffe, which said: "The Pope is not the immediate and proximate vicar of Christ." So if the Pope is the immediate vicar of Christ, it must necessarily be said also that he is superior to a council, otherwise he would not be immediate, but he ought merely to be called the mediate vicar of Christ. The Council of Florence also strongly confirms our teaching, insofar as it was related above in the proof of the first conclusion, where the Pope is called the head of the whole Church, the teacher and the pastor; for the head does not depend upon the members, a teacher is not instructed by his students, a pastor is not ruled by the sheep. Moreover, the Fifth Lateran Council held under Leo X especially urges, in session 11, in which the decree of the assembly at Basel was condemned, that the Constitution of Leo X *Pastor Æternus* be solemnly received, in which it was distinctly declared: "Only the Roman Pontiff, as having authority above all councils, also has the full right and power to call councils, transfer them and dissolve them; it is certain not only from the testimony of Sacred Scripture, the aforesaid Holy Fathers and of other Roman Pontiffs, but from the manifest confession of the councils themselves." Moreover, Bellarmine says that only two objections can be placed to this express definition of the power of the Pope over councils: first, that this council was not general, because not even a hundred Bishops came to it. But Bellarmine responds that this can scarcely be said, when a council has been legitimately convoked, it was clear to all and in it a true Pope presided: and therefore this council is commonly and certainly held as a legitimate ecumenical council, exactly as it is numbered by Cabass., Grav., Baronius, Thomassin, etc. The second, that the council was not received by all, but this is insufficient (Bellarmine adds), for it is certain the decrees of councils do not need the approval of the people, since they do not receive their authority from them. And if the decrees in regard to morals at some time might need to be abrogated by disuse, because the Pope himself is presumed to consent to the abrogation in the progress of time, still, this cannot be in decrees in regard to faith, which after they have been constituted, necessarily are immutable. "Because this council (Bellarmine adds), did not define that matter properly as a decree to be held with Catholic faith, there is a doubt; and therefore, they are not properly heretics who hold the contrary, but they cannot be excused from rash temerity." Louis Bail holds the same thing, and others cited by Milanter (*loc. cit.*).

125.—It is proved: III. From the definitions of Popes (whom our opponents argue are the innovators of ambition and temerity). For, although the definition of that judge, when it is called into doubt whether he is a judge, would not seem to prove the case, nevertheless it cannot be denied that the definitions of so many Popes add great weight to our opinion, especially since they are justly esteemed because they would not so easily make known so many decrees, unless this opinion were sufficiently received universally in the Church. Moreover, Anacletus (can. *Sacrosancta*, dist. 22, can. *Facta, caus.* 9. q. 3), defined the decrees of the Roman Pontiff to be infallible. Gelasius (can. *Cuncta*, caus. 9, qu. 3) and especially Paschal II (cap. *Significasti, de elect.*) who so decreed: "All councils are strengthened by the authority of the Roman Pontiff, and in their statutes it is clear the authority of the Roman Pontiff is received." Boniface VIII (*in Extrav. cap. Unam Sanct., de major. et obed.*) saying: "Moreover, we declare, define and pronounce that it is altogether necessary for salvation that every creature be subject to the Roman Pontiff." Leo IX, writing to Leo Acridanus (cap. 31), said: "Peter and his successors hold judgment free from every Church." Innocent I declares the same thing, in his *Epistle to the Carthaginians*. Pope Dionysius says the same (Ep. 2 *ad Severum*). Gregory the Great (lib. 4, Ep. 52), holds the same. Indeed, these decrees, although published for their own sake, as the French say, still it is certain they must be preferred to Gerson and certain other authors. Furthermore, because the power of the Roman Pontiff is superior to every council is more clear from the invalidation of canon 28 of the Council of Chalcedon, which Pope St. Leo decreed was against the privilege of the first place after the Roman Pontiff bestowed by the council on the Bishop of Constantinople against the Bishop of Alexandria. For, the Holy Pope (Ep. 53), so wrote to the Empress Pulcheria: "We make void the agreement of the Bishops opposed to the rules of the holy canons enacted at Nicaea by the piety of your faith united with ours, and through the authority of Blessed Peter the Apostle we altogether invalidate it by a general definition." If Councils were superior to the Pope, how could St. Leo invalidate a canon of the council? Hence, Nicholas I (*ep.* 8), to show that all the definitions of councils are enacted with no force unless they are strengthened by the Roman Pontiff, wrote about St. Leo, who not only invalidated the aforesaid canon of Chalcedon, but also rescinded the acts of the Council of Ephesus, although all of those fathers approved of it with unanimous consent: "Therefore, do not assert that you do not need, for the sake of the piety of the Roman Church, that it should strengthen councils by its authority. For that reason, some of these, because they did not have the consent of the Roman Pontiff, lost all their authority. How, if each Council does not need the Roman See when in the robber council of Ephesus, when it was approved by all the prelates, except for the great Leo who, divinely roused, shook the whole world and even the emperors themselves, would not the Catholic religion altogether come to ruin?"

126.—At length, it is proved from reason: because monarchic rule is the best of all, as St. Thomas teaches (in 4, *contra Gentes*, c. 76), after he furnished these words: "The best rule of the multitude is that it is ruled by one, for peace and unity of subjects is the end of rule, but for unity it is more fitting that there is one than many, wherefore Christ said: 'And there will be one sheepfold and one shepherd' (John 10:16). Calvin taught that Christ did not establish monarchical governance in the Church, but truly all Catholics teach the opposite with St. Cyprian, and Gerson wrote the same thing: "He is a heretic that teaches the contrary; Christ constituted no other state in the Church apart from a monarchy." Add, if the rule of the Church were not a monarchy, God would not have sufficiently provided for the Church, for if councils should rarely convene and rarely could be convened on account of the unsuitability, expenses, war, then this rule would rarely exist. And so, St. Antoninus (part. 3, tit. 22, c. 2, §3) said Christ the Lord established monarchy in the Church, by constituting the Pope as his vicar. For this reason it happens more often, as Bellarmine notes (*On the Roman Pontiff*, book 4, ch. 3), that Popes absolutely condemned heresies without a council, such as that of the Pelagians, Priscilians, Jovinians, Viliantists, and many others which, because of this very thing, that they were condemned by the Pope, they were held as true heresies by the whole Church of Christ.

Hence, St. Thomas teaches that authority, which the councils advance for themselves, they draw completely from Pontifical authority. And therefore, one can rightly appeal from a council to the Pope, but not from the Pope to a council. St. Thomas (qu. X *de Potentia*, art. 4, ad 13) so speaks: "Just as a later Council has the power to interpret a creed fashioned by a prior council ... so also the Roman Pontiff can now do of his own authority: by whose authority alone a council can be gathered, and by whom the teaching of a council confirmed, and to him one appeals from a council." And he says in another work (*Opusc. contra impugn. relig.*, c. 4), "The most holy fathers gathered in a council can establish nothing without the intervention of the Roman Pontiff." Add what St. Juan Capistrano says about the Pope and a Council: "It is expressly certain that the Pope is above a council, and a council does not obtain full jurisdiction above the Pope in all things. And a council that is ecumenical as you like is subject to the Pope and held to obey him, upon whom the salvation of the faithful depends after Christ." Moreover, St. Antoninus (p. 1, tit. 23, *de appell. Pap.* c. 3, §3) did not hesitate from declaring the contrary opinion is heretical, in these words: "But one cannot appeal from the Pope to a general council, because the Pope is superior to every council; nor does it have the strength to do anything unless it is reinforced and confirmed by the authority of the Roman Pontiff. Therefore, to think that one could appeal from the Pope to a council is heretical."

127.—Our adversaries object: I. So, if the Pope is above a council, then it is useless and in vain that Popes themselves so often summoned councils to determine questions of faith. But the response to this is clear; for the Popes are not said to call councils because they do not avail to define controversies on faith, but they do this to more powerfully convict heretics, after affairs have been called to balance, and to more firmly establish dogmas of faith after they have been examined by the judgment of the whole Church and so they will be more easily received by the faithful. And therefore, (as our adversaries oppose, but without cause), many Popes convoked councils after their definitions: but all, which were defined in councils in regard to matters of faith, they drew their authority from pontifical authority, exactly as the Lateran council declared (sess. XI), where it is so held: "The fathers of the ancient councils were accustomed for the corroboration of those things which were enacted in their councils, subscription from the Roman Pontiffs, and to humbly seek and obtain his approval, exactly is gathered from what had been done at Nicaea, Ephesus, Chalcedon, the sixth at Constantinople, the seventh at Nicaea. (*Porrect. in D. Th.* 2.2. q. 1, a. 10).

128.—They object: II. The text of Matthew 18:15, which says: "If your bother will sin against you, go and correct him ... but if he will not hear you, go to the Church." Therefore, they say; if the correction must be deferred from Peter to the Church, supreme power is shown to be in a council through the Church. And they confirm it from the words of Innocent IV (*cap. Ad apostolicae, de sent. et re judic. in* 6), who wrote to Frederick II that he was prepared to revoke his sentence by the advice of a council. But the response is made that Christ did not direct those words to Peter as his vicar, but to all the disciples and faithful, by imposing the precept of correction. Next, through those very words, "go to the Church," a council was not designated (which is rarely held), that it could correct delinquents, but by the word "Church" superiors having jurisdiction are supposed, as Chrysostom teaches (*Hom. 61, in Matt.*), "Go to the Church, namely to prelates and those presiding in authority." Moreover, Bellarmine responds to the citation from Innocent (*de Conc.*, lib. 2, c. 18), that it can be understood about a discretionary judgment, but not a decisive one. Besides, that there it is not a question of determining a question of faith, but only on moderating a sentence of punishment, if it seemed suitable to reconcile the excommunicate for peace with the Emperor through the Pope. Hence, St. Irenaeus (l. 3 *adv. haer.*, c. 3), speaking on the Roman Church, said: "For, it is necessary for every Church to agree with this Church on account of its mightier principality, (this is, those who are on every side faithful) in which the tradition that is from the apostles has always been preserved in every way."

They object: III. St. Leo, when he condemned the heresy of Eutychis, again permitted that judgment to be discussed in the Council of Chalcedon, from which they infer the Pope himself sensed his definition without a council was fallible. But the response is made, that the Holy Pontiff did not therefore permit the Council to act thus because he thought his sanction was not irreformable, but so that the error would be abolished by a fuller judgment of a council, and so that all the discord that had arisen, could be put to rest in this mode by the desire of the Emperor. It is clear from Epistle 17 of the same St. Leo, and clearly from the decree of the same subsequent Council where it was ratified: "The definition pleases all, Peter has spoken through the mouth of Leo; this is the faith of the fathers, anathema to whoever thinks otherwise."

129.—They object: IV. From the Councils of Constance and Basel. From Constance they oppose two published decrees, one in session 4, in which it was said: "This most holy Council representing the Church holds power immediately from Christ, which every dignity that exists—even papal—is held to obey in those matters which pertain to faith, the extirpation of the aforesaid schism and the general reform of the Church in the head and members." This decree was published in session 4 and later confirmed in session 5. But before we proceed further, it must be known on this decree, as Milanter relates (*loc. cit.*), and Troila (tract. 7, §8, n. 58 from Emmanuel Schelstratis on the sense of the decree of the Council of Constance), that the sacred college of Cardinals that were present with three nations (against the Germans) in the session, and only on account of the fear of the Emperor Sigismund, without any mind of defining the article; and in writings the fathers protested on the nullity of this session. Moreover, the words of protest of the Cardinals and the three nations, made on 29 September 1447 runs thus: "The clergy and people of several kingdoms have not yet adhered clearly and solidly to this sacred Council on account of rumors of discords, which they heard were made in the same council, now trust in the same council is said to stagger, etc." (So it is quoted by Roncaglia *in Animad.*, in Nat., tom. 20). Moreover, Cardinal Turreer (lib. 2 *de Ecclesia*, c. 99 and 100) witnesses that, "Just as it is abundantly clear from the deeds of that congregation, those decrees, if they are to be called such, were only made by some fathers obedient to [antipope] John XXIII." Such fathers were only concerned with the third part; this is why (as Milanter asserts, *loc. cit.*), the council published that definition, since it was not yet ecumenical. And therefore, anyone sees, of what strength that decree was so tumultuously published, at least without the unanimous vote of the fathers, for, as the same John XXIII wrote to the duke of Bordeaux (cited in Troila, n. 59), votes were not given for individuals, as would have been fitting, but it was inconsistently established for each nation to have one vote. Cardinal Alliacensis confirms this was done (*tract. de Eccl. auth.*, p. 1, c. 4), who was present at the Council, and he proposed this doubt in it, lest later its acts would be called into doubt on nullity. Hence, the aforementioned Cardinal Torquemada (*loc. cit.*), who was also present at the Council, and Cajetan (p. 1, *de auth. Papae*, c. 8), absolutely assert that those decrees were of no importance, since the Church intervened, exactly as Eugene IV also affirms (*Apologia contra Basileenses*), affirming: "That there, such an act ought not be ascribed to the universal Church."

130.—Besides, if the aforesaid decrees were admitted, Bellarmine, Torquemada, Spondanus, and others respond that those decrees were for a doubtful Pope, and at that time schism raged, since among the three Popes that had been constituted, each defended their right to the pontifical dignity, but all of these were deposed by the Council and Martin V was legitimately created Pope by the Cardinals. And this is rightly established from the words of that very Council, as related above: "To whom everyone ... is held to obey in those matters which pertain to faith and the extirpation of the aforesaid schism." Nor do the subsequent words impede us, "And the general reformation of the Church of God in the head and members." For firstly, Troila responds (tr. 7, art. 7, §8, n. 54) from the most learned Emmanuel Schelestis (*de sensus decr. conc. Constant.*), that the last words were adulterated by the council of Basel in the second decree, where the same words of the first decree are read, repeated identically, to those added, "and the reformation, etc." Next, the response is made that those decrees were said in the matter subjected to it, obviously in the case of a doubtful Pope, in which (as was noted in the aforesaid), supreme power is in a council both in regard to matters of faith, and in regard to defining who is the true Pope, for then everyone ought to be subject to the definition of the council. Then, however, the question of the day was who really was the true Pope: and although some contended that the legitimate Pope was John XXIII, still this was not established everywhere. For that reason, as it is contained in the histories (cited by Suarez, *de fid.* l. 3, c. 18), John himself resigned the Papacy of his own will to strengthen the peace of the Church. The same thing is confirmed from the declaration of the same Council of Constance (sess. 5), where it was said: "It likewise declares that anyone who would disregard and refuse to obey the commands of this most Holy Synod, and any other general council considering what has been done and what must be done in the aforesaid cases, etc." From such words it is sufficiently obvious, the Council only spoke on councils which will be celebrated in the aforementioned cases. Moreover, what were these aforementioned cases but to deaden schism and depose doubtful Popes? For this was the true reason for celebrating this Council, namely the event of a doubtful Pope. Moreover, in a congregation held on 11 September 1417, it was decided in common that "a Pope rightly and canonically elected by a Council could not be bound." So if it is certain that a Pope cannot be bound by the laws of a council, it is also certain that a council is not above the Pope, nor can one appeal from the Pope to a council.

131.—Nor is what Jeunin objects (*Inst. theol.* diss., 4, q. 3, ar. 16) an obstacle, namely that Martin V (as is read in the final session of the Council) bid this to be proclaimed by the advocate of the Council: "He wishes to hold each individual matter determined in matters of faith by the Council of Constance, and so approves the conciliar acts and not otherwise nor in another mode." Therefore, (they say), even Martin V confirmed the decrees of the fourth and fifth sessions. But the response is: By those words, *in matters of faith*, Martin only meant to include the decrees against Wycliffe and other heretics condemned in the Council, but not the decrees on the superiority of a council; for these decrees do not consider faith, but only reform, as these holy Fathers said, "for the general reformation of the Church of God in head and members." Therefore, Martin V did not mean to confirm these decrees. Resp. II: Not only did the Pope not approve those decrees, but he expressly condemned them, since a little book of published by John Falckemberg against the king and nation of Poland was condemned by the council as heretical, Martin opposed it and declared this is not a case of faith. And from this, since the Poles appealed from Martin to a future Council, the Pope published a constitution, in which he said: "It is lawful for no one to appeal from the supreme Judge, namely the Apostolic See or the Roman Pontiff, the Vicar of Jesus Christ on earth, or to decline either his judgment in cases of faith (just as greater cases must be conveyed to it and the Apostolic See)." John Gerson calls this constitution to mind (*in Dial. apolog. pro conc. Const.*) and published a treatise on the issue: "whether it is lawful to appeal from the Pope?"

132.—Then we come to the Council of Basel, which not only confirmed the decree of Constance, but also defined that a council is above a Pope that is not doubtful; and proposed the following three impious propositions that must be believed with faith:

> I. *The Truth on the power of a general council, representing the universal Church, over that of the Pope, and any other, declared by Constance, and this general council of Basel, is a truth of the Catholic faith.*

> II. *This truth, that the Pope can in nowise dissolve a general council representing the universal Church, legitimately gathered in act in addition to what was declared in the aforesaid truth, or some of others without its consent, nor to prorogue it to another time, nor to transfer it from one place to another, is a truth of the Catholic faith.*

> III. *Anyone opposing the two aforesaid truths is to be accounted as a heretic.*

At length, the recklessness of the bishops of Basel went so far that after Eugene IV transferred the Council to Ferrara, they dared to depose him from the papal See and declare him a heretic, and Amadaeus, the duke of Savoy, appointed Felix in his place; still, after nearly all the bishops protested they left the council, as St. Antoninus witnesses (*Hist.* tit. 22, c. 10 §4) as well as Spondanus (ad ann. 1431), who so wrote about this wicked deposition: "While dissension arose, their number became so diminished that when they threatened judgment against Pope Eugene, there were hardly thirty present, and in his deposition only seven Bishops." Later, Felix so acknowledged the nullity of his election, that he abdicated from every right of the Papacy, and humbly furnished obedience to Nicholas V, the successor of Eugene.

133.—Louis Dupinus, whom some authors from the French follow, was not ashamed to call this little assembly at Basel an ecumenical council, saying that it was legitimately called by Martin V, confirmed as legitimate by Eugene IV, and at length approved in all matters by Nicholas V. To refute the false suppositions of these would require a very long time and a whole dissertation, but lest I recede much from what I have proposed, I briefly respond and say that a gathering of this sort at Basel in no manner merits the name of a general council, and this is sufficiently clear from its deeds, about which there can be no doubt. 1) Because the number of Bishops was in that time so scanty that it could, by no reasoning, ever represent the universal Church. For in session 2 and 3 in which the aforesaid definitions were published, only seven or eight Bishops were present, and it is held from the response of this Council given on 8th November 1440, where it is read: "When in the time of the first dissolution alleged for peace the Prelates present in the council did not exceed the number of fourteen, which were present at the aforesaid acts, etc." And, although they were in an ample number in the eighteenth session when the decrees of the second session were renewed, still Cardinal Torquemada relates (*in resp. ad Basileenses* given in the Council of Florence, and *Summ. de Eccl.*, l. 2, c. 100), that in that session, the eighteenth, not all agreed, rather a great many protested while others furnished consent either as private persons or more violently; at length others refused to intervene since the decrees were published not only by Bishops, as was necessary, but "by the multitude of the people of little value and no authority." That is confirmed from the speech of Cardinal Arelatensis (which is read in Sylvius in *act. Basil.*), who, although he was the particular promoter of the excellence of a council above the Pope, there bravely deplored this dissension of the Prelates, and therefore, the decrees by the votes of the lower clergy, which he ascribed to, saying: "I affirm the work of God was present this time, that inferiors were received to speak." And the aforesaid Aeneas Sylvius (in *Oratione habita ann. 1451 adversus Australes*, as Louis Muratorius relates, tom. 2, *in suis Anecdotis*), speaking on the decrees that were related, said: "Among bishops we see cooks in Basel, and stable hands judging the affairs of the world."

2) He cannot call the Council at Basel ecumenical, because there were no legates of the Pope present, as would be fitting. For how can a council be called ecumenical where the head is lacking, when there certainly is a Pope? St. Thomas (*Opusc. contr. impug. relig.* c. 4), teaches: "The holy fathers gathered in councils can establish nothing without the intervention of the Roman Pontiff. And the Gloss (*in dist. 17 verb. Gener. con.*) says: "A universal (council) is one that is established by the Pope or his legate with all the Bishops." Hence, Nicholas I (Ep. 7) so wrote: "In all synods, how is it ratified, except because the See of Blessed Peter approved it, as you know is held? Just as, on the other hand, what he alone condemns, is certainly held condemned to this point." Therefore, if we speak on session II, as it was held on 16 February 1452, from *Act. miss. l. 2*, that Cardinal Julian, then the legate of the Holy See, already on the 8th day of February, exonerated himself from the presidency of the council. Add the fat that Eugene, after the first session had already revoked the Council, as Didacus Payva relates (*ex Alexandr.* a. 3, n. 1). So equally, in sess. XVIII, the legates of the Pope were lacking; for others were absent, but others, not as Legates, but as private persons, subscribed, as we

related above, and Roncaglia shows (*in Animadvers. ad Nat. Alex. sup. conc. Bas.* §1).

3) Besides, it is known that the vote given in the aforesaid Council was hardly free, as Cardinal Torquemada relates, and as Eugene IV asserted (in his Bull to Archiep. Colon., published 30 January 1431), saying: "And many are compelled to accede, in which neither force nor power of a general council consists, of which those deliberations are hardly free, since they depended upon the will of those who compelled them." This is why St. Antoninus (p. 3 tit. 22, cap. 10 § 4) called this Council of Basel a vain little assembly of force, and the synagogue of satan." St. Juan Capistrano (*de Papae et conc. auct.*, c. 3) called it, "a profane Council, excommunicated, and den of vipers."[22] The Bishop Meldensis, legate of Charles VII to Eugene (*apud Raynald. ad annum 1441*, n. 10), called it, "The throng of demons." Florence, in a session held on 5 September 1439, condemned the declarations of Basel as impious and scandalous. At length the Fifth Lateran Council, as is read in the Bull published by Leo V approving that council, recognized the Council at Basel as a schismatic assembly, as well as seditious and of no authority. Therefore, who will say that it is a legitimate council, which merited the great name of rash, profane and diabolic? Therefore, after Eugene recalled the Council of Basel, indeed it altogether evaded all illegitimacy. Nor is it opposed that Eugene later recalled its dissolution, as our adversaries object; for Cardinal Torquemada relates (*dict.* l. 2, c. 10), this revocation by Eugene arose from fear and the Constitution of this revocation was in a certain measure published without his knowledge. For St. Athanasius (*Ep. ad Solitar.*) wrote: "The sentence of it must not be believed, which threats and

---

[22]   Translator's note: There is a play on words here, as viper is *basiliscus* which is close to the Latin rendering for Basel, *Basileensis.*.

terrors twist out, but those which it advances when it has freedom." But, given that Eugene freely revoked the dissolution of the Council, still he, as is clear from his epistles (l. 15, p. 117, et 123 et l. 17, p. 201), expressly declared that he only confirmed the decisions to extirpate heresy and establish peace among princes, but not against the power pertaining to the Papacy. And in the very Constitution, *Dudum,* recalling the Council, he placed two conditions, one that the Legates be chosen by him, "that they might be admitted to the presence of the Council *cum effectu*;" and second, as he expressed it: "That each and everything done against our authority would be altogether abolished." But the Fathers at Basel did not fulfill either condition; for they neither rescinded the decrees nor admitted the Legates in the XVIII session, unless they would be deprived of all coercive jurisdiction, against the intention of Eugene; nay more, nor did they even take care to obtain the assent of the Legates in the eighteenth session, where the decree on the preeminence of a Council was renewed, as Cardinal Torquemada witnesses, in the preface of *Respons. ad Basileenses in Concilio FLorentino,* that the presidents of the Pope in the aforesaid eighteenth session, "Did not consent, nay more spoke against and protested them. Although some not as presidents, but as private persons, and as if violently, when they would not otherwise be admitted to the presidency, consented to that renewal [of the decree of the 2nd session]." Then, when, later, the Basel fathers insistently sought approval for their decrees from Eugene , Eugene never conceded that, as he declared in the council of Florence, saying: "We certainly approved the progress of the Council, but not its decrees." And when the King of the Romans and the Electors of the Empire urged for the confirmation of the decrees, Eugene, writing to his legates in Germany, affirmed that it was lawful to venerate each council, both at Constance and Basel in his letter, nevertheless, there expressly protested reception of them;

"still, without the precedent of law, dignity and the preeminence of the Holy Apostolic See, and power conceded to themselves and in the same sitting canonically." And in the Council of Florence, to proscribe the propositions of the Council of Basel favoring a council over a Pope, he published the Constitution *Moyses* (which is read in the new edition of the Councils published at Venice, tr. 18, n. 1202), in which it is held: "Such propositions, according to the depraved understanding of Basel, which are sensed contrary to Holy Scripture, the Holy Fathers and the Council of Constance, as impious, scandalous, and still in a manifest fissure in the Church ... yielding to the approved sacred council, we condemn and reprobate." Here, see how useless the ingenious interpretation of these words is made by Nöel Alexander, when he said that Eugene condemned those propositions because he branded anyone who opposed him with the mark of heresy; for it suffices to prove the lack of substance in this commentary the to reread the words of the bull, in which it is obvious that the Pope refused to avert from heresy only those who thought against the Council, but expressly wished to condemn and reprobate, "just as impious, scandalous and still causing into manifest schism in the Church," those propositions, "according to the (note) depraved understanding of those at Basel," who asserted that a council excels the Pope for certain: and an understanding of this sort, which they show was done (when the fathers at Basel advised Eugene, etc.) that the Pope condemned it.

Our adversaries press on, and say the aforesaid Constitution *Moyses* was later abolished by Nicholas V. But really, in the letter of Nicholas (as is seen with Nöel Alexander, art. 4, num. 15) nothing else is found than the confirmation of the possession and conference of benefices, which were made at Basel, but no mention is made of the pretended power of a council over the Pope.

134.—Lastly, Louis Maimburg urges for the superiority of a council, objecting that the same Popes, at some time confessed the superiority of councils over Popes. He opposes us: I. With the deed of Siricius, who was asked by some Bishops on the error of Bonosius, namely, that the Blessed Virgin gave birth to other sons after Jesus; he answered on this controversy that he could not judge since its judgment was consigned to the Council of Capua. But we respond: 1) that this argument proves too much, for in this manner the Pope would not only be inferior to a general council, but also to a provincial one, such as what was held at Capua. We respond: 2) that these words are falsely attributed to Siricius, since they are only found in epistle 79 of Ambrose. We respond: 3) That, even granted that they were of Siricius, there he did not declare that he was inferior to a council, but he showed that he refused to judge the case concerning the declaration of that council with his authority; and it is clear from the words there, "It is not fitting for us to make judgment from the authority of that council." (See Troil., *loc. cit.*) Maimburg opposes: II. The testimony of Sylvester II, that, "If the Bishop of Rome will not hear the Church, he must be held as a heathen." We respond, that the testimony was not of Sylvester, but of the monk, Gerbert, who (as Baronius for the year 992 and Spondanus for the year 991, n. 2, relate) when he was illegitimately taken up to the Archbishopric of Rhemes, after Arnulphus was unjustly deposed, and then he strove for his own confirmation, not withstanding that the Pope was against it, then he wrote those words to Seguinus the Metropolitan. But after the same Gerbert, with the favor of the Emperor Otto took up the Pontificate, he restored Arnulphus in his Church in Rhemes. Maimburg opposes: III. The confession of Pius II, who in his bull of retraction admitted that earlier, in the Council of Basel, he upheld the old opinion on the superiority of a council: therefore Maimburg argues this is the old opinion. But we respond, that it is necessary to read the aforesaid bull (cited by Troila, tract. 7, art. 7, n. 9), and there clearly anyone would understand in what sense Pius asserted that *old* opinion; it was old because earlier, when he was not the Pope (for in that time he was Aeneas Piccolomini), favoring the superiority of a council, but later, though before he took up the Pontificate, he retracted himself, as is clear from a letter he sent to Eugene IV. Hence it is discerned how fraudulently the miserable Maimburg uses his deeds and words.

135.—Our adversaries say their opinion is favored by Cardinal Cusa and Alliacens, likewise, Gerson, Almainus, Adrian VI, Panormitanus, Alphonsus Tostatus, Dennis the Cathusian, and John Dreido. Yet, it is worthwhile to observe with Roncaglia (*Animadvers.* § xi, against Nöel Alexander *de concil. Constant.*), that qualifications are opposed to the aforesaid authors. For, Cardinal Cusa, although he had earlier advanced that a council is above a Pope in *de Concordia*, still, later he showed that he was opposed to that position, and without any ambiguity. He taught (*in Epist. 2 de Usu Calicis ad Bohem.*) the Roman Church is going to continually be the pillar of truth and hence could never defect from the faith, nor does it need correction from any other See; and the truth is found for certain among those that are not separated from the Roman Pontiff. In regard to Alphonsus Tostato, Spondanus relates (ad annum 1447), that he was hostile to the prerogatives of the Pope because some of his theses were not received by Eugene IV, and were rejected by Cardinal Torquemada: hence Spondanus wrote that he: "appeared driven to uphold from his own zeal the authority of the Popes, but when he did not obtain what he asked for, he could not command his genius to argue the matter more sharply against those who opposed it." Still, Tostatus himself, so wrote on Matthew 16: "Christ willed that the confession of faith should be through Peter alone, that he would approve that such faith must be held, that the

Roman See preaches, which is the mother and head of Churches, of which Peter was in charge of." On Panormitanus (in his compendium of the deeds described of the lives of the Popes by Ciaconio), it is read that this doctor was, by the king of Aragon, irritated against Eugene, sent to labor at the Council of Basel to impugn the authority of the Roman Pontiff; according to what Panzaroli (*de Leg. Interpret.*) relates he did, adding the same man, "enflamed a great sin after publishing so many responses, and did a great many unworthy things." Moreover, reading that which he wrote (cap. *Significasti, de Elect.*) concerning the power of Councils, he could never assert that infallibility was given to councils against the power of the Pope.

On the authorities of Alliacens, Gerson, and Almainus, Andrew Duvallius says they do not amount to much since they wrote in a time of schism. Thomassinus (diss. 15, *in Conc.*, n. 24) adds that Gerson wrote when he was exasperated by the relentlessness of pertinacious schism; "and therefore, greatly degenerated from the reverence to the French Bishops, who were present at the Roman Synod with Leo. Therefore, their antiquity, and number ought to be preferred to the novelty and paucity striving to extricate themselves from an intricate schism." They also boast to have Adrian VI for there said. But really, this Pope, when he was a private doctor at Louvain, wrote (*Sum. Theol.* in 4 Sent. de Sacr. Confirm.) nothing other than that the Pope can teach heresy in his Decretal, but it must be understood, insofar as he teaches as a private doctor, but not as a teacher of the Church. For, who will deny the Pope, as man, can be guilty of errors? They also boast Dennis the Carthusian for their part, but such was the opinion of this doctor, that it is exceedingly doubtful, for when assessing the matter (lib. *de auctoritate Papae et conc.*, part. 2, a. 48), says that an intolerably vicious Pope can be subject to a council; but in the same place he speaks otherwise, saying: "The Pope, as supreme pastor of the Church, cannot be judged or deposed, "because as such he is superior, prelate, and judge of the Church." On the authority of Dreido, (as can be observed in *l. 4, c. in fin.*) he thought nothing other than that the Pope should be subject to a council, if he pertinaciously defends a doctrine contrary to the gospel, which no man denies. Look at how all these authors are adduced by adversaries of the Roman See, or are weak, or doubtful.

Lastly, from all these, by gathering in one the sense of the Scriptures, the Popes, the Fathers and of those very councils, everyone can see that our opinion is not merely ours, but the opinion of the whole Church, as well as the rule and sense. And therefore, not it, but rather more the opposite, must duly be considered and rejected as futile, and very often refuted.

DUBIUM III

Whether force, and substance of positive law would depend upon the reception of the community?

136. *Whether a law that has not been received obliges?*

137. What if a law is not received by the greater part of the people? How much time are laws prescribed for?

138. *Whether those that do not receive the law sin? And whether the law depends upon reception by the people? What about pontifical laws? What about civil laws?*

139. *What if a law is hard, or abrogated, or if the greater part do not receive it?*

136.—"It is answered that, albeit the canonists think this "way, and likewise Navarre, Azor, etc. (cited by "Laymann lib. 1, tr. 4, c. 3), to the extent that they posit "laws are imposed by this tacit condition, if they will "have been received by the people, in general they do "not have force or obligation. Nevertheless, the truer "opinion of the Theologians is that laws of the "Magistrate that have been completed do not depend "upon the acceptance by the people, to oblige the people "to receive them, especially in the laws of the Pope, who "does not receive his power from the people, but from "Christ. (Vasquez, Suarez, Molina, etc.) Wherefore, these "cases are "resolved by Laymann, (*loc. cit.*).

"1. It is incumbent upon Bishops, because of their office, "to promulgate new pontifical laws (just as imperial ones "to princes) through their dioceses, and to put them into "use.

137.—"2. If a law were promulgated in a province, but "were not received by a greater part of the people, nor "observed. Then, if the legislator knew it and were silent, "it is consequently reckoned by this very fact that the "law is revoked. But if he knows it and would urge its "observance, it ought to follow that everyone is held to "keep it because the head is more powerful than the rest "of the members.

"3. If the prince did not know the law is not received, nor "is it deduced to use, the obligation of the law endures "until a period of ten years elapses; after that has "elapsed, it is prescribed against the law, whether it is "imperial or pontifical, and then it no longer obliges. Just "as a law of the Church, even if it were once received, is "abolished through prescription, but the period of years "is longer, namely forty. (Navarre, Azor., Suarez; yet, see "what is "going to be said in n. 139, v. *Lim.* 2).

"4. If you would be prepared to receive a law that has "been promulgated, and after the occasion is given also "observe it, but a great many others from the community "do not receive it, nor does it appear that they are going "to receive it, then at least you will be excused from it by "discretion.

"5. Even if the first Bishops would perhaps sin by not
"receiving a law or compelling its use, still their
"successors, if after a long time see that it has not been
"observed, can believe it has been abolished by
"prescription.

"6. In doubt as to whether a law were received or not,
"the presumption must be in favor of the law because the
"fact is presumed in doubt, if it was done *de jure.* (See
"Azor., l. 5, c. 4; Laymann, hic cap. 3; Salas., *de leg.,* disp.
13, sect. 3)."

138.—*Quaeritur:* whether a law obliges of itself
independently from the reception of the people? It is certain
that anyone who does not receive a just law sins, from
proposition 28 condemned by Alexander VII which said:
"The people do not sin if they do not receive a law
promulgated by a prince, even with just cause." The reason
is that, although a law does not oblige of itself unless the
people receive it, still the prince has the right that his
subjects should receive a just law. There may be a doubt,
however; whether the essence of the law would depend
upon the reception of the people, so that it would not bind
until the people receive it? And here a distinction must be
made between ecclesiastical and civil laws. In regard to
ecclesiastical laws, it is certain that the Supreme Pontiff can
obligate the Christian people independently of their
reception of the laws, because it is certain that the Pope does
not receive legislative power from the people, but from
Christ the Lord, who said: "Feed my sheep; whatsoever you
will have bound on earth, etc." And the same is said about
Bishops, who, whether immediately or by a medium (as
above) through the vicar of Christ have power from the
same Lord. (See the Salamancans, c. 1, punct. 7, n. 94).
Moreover, is the same thing the case in regard to *civil* laws?
(See below).

Therefore, there is a question as to whether a law, where it is not expressed, but the prince means to oblige independently from the reception of the people, obliges of itself without the consent of the people? In regard to the laws of Popes, or of other prelates, *the first opinion* rejects it, (ex c. 3 dist. 4 § *Legis*, where it is held from saint Augustine), "Laws are constituted when they are promulgated; they are confirmed when they are applied by the customs of use." The reason is because this is considered in regard to the sweet rule of the Church, that it should avoid the disturbance of the people. So, many pontifical decrees do not oblige *de facto*, because they have not been received. (Cabassutius, *Theor. Jur.* l. 1, c. 4, n. 5; Valentia *Fill. Reg.*; Bonacina *Cov.* and others quoted by the Salamancans c. 1, punct. 7, § 1, n. 98).

The second opinion is the contrary, to which we subscribe, that affirms that ecclesiastical prelates do not have their power from the people, as we prefaced in the beginning. We make the response to the text of St. Augustine, that the laws *de* facto confirmed by their reception, but not *de jure.* So the Salamancans, think (*ibid.,* n. 99 *et seq.*), with Laymann, Suarez, Palaus, etc. Moreover it is noted, that a law is then said to be received, when the greater part of the community receives it in whole or in part. (The Salamancans *ibid.,* n. 97, with Bonacina et Valentia).

The same thing, which they say about pontifical laws, they also say about civil laws. (Busembaum with Palaus, Suarez, Laymann, etc. quoted in the Salamancans *ibid.,* n. 101; although others deny this with Croix, l. 1, n. 591). The reason is that the obligation of law arises not from the reception of the people, but from the power of the prince, which has the power to fashion laws independently of the people.

139.—Some doctors place the limitation (whether a law is civil or ecclesiastical): 1) if a law is difficult to observe or contrary to custom; which is judged by a determination of the prudent: or if a great many appeal against them. (Palaus, Suarez, Salas, quoted by the Salamancans *ibid.,* § 2, n. 104). Still, Tap., and Gordonus (*ib.,* n. 105, the Salamancans), adhere to the first opinion when a law is too hard, and it is judged through *epikea,* that if the legislator notices these circumstances, he would not publish the law.

They place the limitation: 2) If a law would be abrogated by the greater part of the people through disuse. But it is uncertain among the doctors whether prescription for ten years would suffice to abolish laws of the Church. Busembaum (as above, n. 3), the Salamancans (*de leg.,* c. 6, punct. 3, §2, n. 17) with Bonacina, Laymann, Diana, etc. deny it, because to prescribe against the Church forty years are required, as is held in cap. *De quarta,* and cap. *Ad aures, de praescript.* But other authors say ten years probably suffices, whether the laws were received or not; because no greater reason must be held from custom against ecclesiastical law than civil, since no right distinguishes between these laws. (Lessius, l. 2, c. 6, dub. 14, n. 47, and Palaus, Sa, Granadus, Navarre, and Azor, quoted by the Salamancans, *loc. cit.*) Moreover, Lessius responds to the cited texts, that they do not speak about laws, but prescription concerning rights and immovable goods of the Church; but laws of the Church do not come under the phrase of the rights of the Church. When a law was never received, certainly ten years suffices for both civil and ecclesiastical law, as Busembaum (*hic,* n. 3) says. And then, although the first ones to not observe it would sin, still those at the present would not. (The Salamancans cap. 1, punct. 7, § 2 n. 106, with Suarez, Bonacina, Palaus, and in common with Busembaum, *hic.* n. 5).

They place the limitation: 3) If the greater, or healthier part of the people do not receive a law. Although the first ones not receiving it would sin if disuse had not yet prescribed it: still the others are not held to the law; for it the prince is presumed to refuse to oblige them to observance, because it was not received by the greater part. (The Salamancans, *ibid.*, n. 107, with Suarez, Palaus, Tap., etc. with Busembaum *hic*, n. 2; and Lessius, l. 2, c. 22, n. 98).

There is a question as to whether, if the people would ask the prince to revoke a law, would they be held to observe it? Bonacina, Villal., Salas, etc. quoted by the Salamancans (*ibid.*, §3, n. 111) say no. But the Salamancans, with Suarez and Palaus, rightly argue against that. Still, if the prince should hear the supplication of the people, and be silent, and not urge in favor of the observance, it is reckoned he abrogates the law, unless something else were concluded from the circumstances (the Salamancans, *ibid.*, n. 112, with Palaus, Bonacina, Salas, and others).

DUBIUM IV

Whether human precepts also oblige under pain of sin, and what sort?

> 140. *Whether human legislators can command? And how many conditions are required for a law to oblige?*
>
> 141. *Whether a superior can command a light matter under a grave penalty?*
>
> 142. *Whether a light matter becomes grave by circumstances, particularly contempt?*
>
> 143. *Whether a grave matter can be commanded under a light penalty?*
>
> 144. *When is the law presumed to oblige under a grave penalty?*
>
> 145. *Whether a penal law obliges under pain of sin?*
>
> 146. *What about a law under the penalty of suspension, etc.*
>
> 147. *What if a law assigns a penalty and commands at the same time?*

148. *Whether penalty is incurred before the sentence?*

149. *What about a positive penalty and disqualifying penalties?*

150. *Whether a conventional penalty ought to be paid before the sentence?*

151. *Whether a law invalidating an act lacking solemnities obliges in conscience?*

152. *Whether we are held to abolish an impediment impeding the fulfillment of the law? (See also book 4, n. 1045).*

140.—"Resp. Since God is our Lord, and commands us to "also obey our superiors, not only God himself, but also "those that may and must command us not only under a "penalty but even under fault, or sin. And in that, either "*sub gravi* or *sub levi*, exactly as both the necessity and "quantity of the matter commanded aims at the intended "purpose, and their will has of itself, which is usually "gathered from their words, circumstances, or the "estimation of prudent men (St. Thomas, Suarez, Salas, "etc.)."

For a law to oblige, four conditions are required. I. That the law is for the whole community. II. That the legislator has public power. III. That the law is perpetual. IV. That it should be fore the common good: then, it should be honest, just and possible (See the Salamancans, *de leg.,* c. 1, punct. 2, ex. n. 7, *et seqq.*). Hence, a law differs from a precept, or a command; for a precept is imposed for a particular person, and also by a private person. Next, a precept is for a time, and it ceases with the death of the one who commands it; unless the matter would be more integral, or except the precept were favorable to pious cases, or equally favorable. (See Croix, lib. 1, n. 565 and 566; the Salamancans *ibid.,* punct. 1, n. 5).

141.—"For this reason, these cases are resolved: 1) He "gravely sins who deliberately and in a great matter "violates some precept of the Decalogue, or the Church. "2) When the matter is light, someone transgressing does "not sin mortally, even if a superior would command "him under the penalty of mortal sin, because he cannot "do that (Suarez, Laymann, and others in common). *E.g.* "to not break silence, to not eat a grape, to close a door, "etc., because it is a small matter and incapable of such "an obligation. Nor does God himself oblige under the "penalty of mortal sin in a small matter (See Lessius, l. 2, "c. 4, de 9; Salas, d. 10, s. 7."

It is also very common with the Salamancans, *de leg.* c. 2, punct. 2, § 1 n. 18.). Still, the same Salamancans hold in tract. 15, *de statu relig.*, c. 6, punct. 8, ex n. 85 and *seq*, with St. Thomas, avail against Sanchez, Vasquez, etc. or a prelate to be able to command a regular under a grave penalty, because by a rule, he is only commanded *sub levi*, but if he is afraid, that rule is not otherwise observed.

142.—"3) On the other hand, if the matter is otherwise "light, it may become grave by the reason of "circumstances; *e.g.* scorn, scandal, of the common good "or end intended by the legislator. So, abstinence from "the food in paradise, certainly in itself it was a light "matter, nevertheless it was very grave from the "circumstances of the end. (Suarez, l. 3, c. 23)."

Note that in each matter formal contempt for the law or the legislator (which is to scorn a law, or the legislator, or a superior, inasmuch as he is higher) is always a mortal sin. (The Salamancans *de leg.*, c. 2, punct. 2, § 4, n. 38, with St. Thomas, Suarez, and the common opinion). In another way, if one scorned a matter that was commanded, because they thought it was a little matter, or from a particular indignation against the superior. (The Salamancans, *ibid.*, § 3, n. 35, with Sanchez, Cajetan, etc.) Contempt not for a superior, but for an individual person, *e.g.* because he is unlearned, imprudent, etc., is not in itself a mortal sin; unless perhaps the judgment were gravely rash. (So the Salamancans, *ibid.*, § 4, n. 40, with Palaus, Sanch., Less., Bonacina). Hence, they rarely say it touches upon mortal sin by reason of contempt.

143.—"When the matter is grave, a superior can "command under the pain of sin merely *sub levi.* Because "just as he can oblige in no way when he does not "command, so also, he can oblige only under a venial "penalty. (Suarez, Lessius, *loc. cit.*, against Vasquez)"

The Question is, whether the legislator in a grave matter can oblige merely *sub levi*?

The first opinion rejects this, because the gravity of the obligation does not depend upon the will of a superior but upon the gravity of the matter. Bellarmine, Reg., Soto, Vasquez, Becanus

The second opinion, nevertheless, affirms more probably that in laws the obligation is imposed by the legislator according to the end he intends, to which at some time it is expedient to not impose a grave obligation in a grave matter. Lessius (l. 2, c. 41, dub. 9 n. 46), the Salamancans (*ibid.*, §1 n. 20), with Sanchez, Palaus, Bonacina, Val, etc. Just as one who can rightly make a vow in any matter, even the gravest, under only a light penalty. S. Antonininus, Palas, Sanchez, etc., quoted by the Salamancans (*ibid.*, in fin.).

144.—"5. The foremost signs by which it can be gathered "whether a law obliges under a grave penalty are these. "a) If the matter were grave, and it were not constituted "to the contrary from the will of the one commanding. "This is why Cajetan (*in summ. verb. Cler.*), teaches that "clergy only sin venially when they follow the hawks "and dogs to the hunt against the precepts of positive "law. b) If words have great force such as: we command, "we interdict, by the virtue of holy obedience; or by the

"force of a vow or oath, or we command greatly. c) If a
"great punishment is attached, such as
"excommunication, deposition, eternal malediction,
"perpetual exile, death, etc. d) If use and custom are so
"conveyed among the experts and the God-fearing:
"because custom is the best interpreter of law, as is clear
"in the law of ecclesiastical fasting as well as abstinence
"from meat; likewise of annual communion, which Tol.,
"Laymann (c. 14, n. 4) and Bonac. (p. 7. §4) prove obliges
"gravely."

145.—The author of a law teaches it obliges *sub gravi*, if
a great penalty is attached to it. Here, there are a great many
questions that are necessary to know. And before all things,
it must be noted that there is another purely penal law
which gives no precept, *e.g.* "Whoever does this pays a
penalty." And this does not oblige in conscience, even if the
penalty is very grave (the Salamancans c. 2. punct. 3, §1. n.
53, with Navarre, Palas, Tap., Regin., etc.). Hence the laws of
towns forbidding the felling of trees under penalty, or
cutting grass, fishing, hunting do not oblige under sin, for
custom so holds. (The Salamancans *ibid.*, n. 54, with Navarre
Valentia, Montes, etc.). There is another law that is not
purely penal, but mixed, which commands and imposes a
penalty, *e.g.* No man may do this under penalty, etc.

All laws under the penalty of excommunication *latae
sententiae* oblige *sub grave*, and this is the common teaching
(See the Salamancans, *ibid.*, n. 44).

146.—Quaeritur: 1) Whether a law obliges *sub gravi*
which commands under penalty of suspension, interdict or
irregularity? The authors deny it obliges *sub gravi*, since this
can be incurred without grave sin. (Cajet., Valentia, Salon.,
and Azor in regard to suspension; quoted by the
Salamancans, *ibid.*, n. 45. Still, the the Salamancans argue
against it, both in regard to interdict and suspension, if they
are greater penalties, just as suspension from office, or from

a benefice for a long time, and interdict considering every use, which they say cannot be incurred without grave sin. (Salamancans *de cens.* c. 1, punct. 10, n. 126; Suarez, Bonacina, Con., Palaus, etc., *ibid.* n. 124; see also later book 7 *de censur.* n. 313). And they say the same thing about other very grave spiritual penalties *dict.* n. 45 *de leg. ut sup.*

What if such penalties were to impose sentences, would they oblige *sub gravi?* Some affirm this, but others more probably say no. (The Salamancans, *de leg.* c. 2, punct. 3, §1, n. 46, with Cajetan, Palaus, Suarez, Sanch., Vasquez etc.). Unless it were said that the that the censure were incurred without another warning, or if it were not of itself grave matter.

147.—Quaeritur: 2) Whether laws assigning temporal punishment and at the same time commanding something, oblige under pain of sin, or just punishment?

The First opinion says no, unless the law expresses that it means to oblige also under pain of sin. Navarre thinks such (*Man.*, c. 23, n. 55, and 60), where he says: "Human laws that also command, which constitute a temporal punishment, in doubt oblige forever insofar as they are the laws of the one who established the penalty." So also Cajetan (*Summ.* v. *Clericus* § *Verum*). Likewise, Menchata, Gomez, Imola (quoted by the Salamancans, *ibid.*, n. 47), and Valentia, Bonacina, Dian., Tad., and Villalobos, call it a probable position. Furthermore, Mazzota (*de leg. q. 2, c. 1* with Filliuci), thinks it is also probable when he speaks on civil law. The reason is because, although princes can rightly oblige both to punishment and under pain of sin, sill, since they must not impose burdens without necessity, they are not presumed to mean to bind under pain of sin when a penalty to coerce them suffices: and so laws of this kind are said to be interpreted by custom.

Still, *the second opinion* is opposed to it and is more true. The Salamancans (*loc. cit.*, n. 49) absolutely hold it, and

Valentia, Bonacina, Diana, Tapia and Villalobos reckon it more probable. The reason is because there is a difference between a *purely penal* law, which obliges to punishment, and this is when only a penalty is assigned; and a *mixed* law, which obliges even under pain of sin; this is, when a precept is added in addition to punishment; for after it is commanded, then a superior is believed to mean to oblige under penalty of sin, lest he would seem to command in vain. What if the penalty is great? See what must be said *de rest.* l. 4, n. 616.

148.—*Quaeritur:* 3) Whether one incurs punishment before the sentence of a judge? Spiritual punishments, such as excommunication, irregularity, etc., when they are imposed *ipso facto*, do not need a sentence; that is certain among all authors (see the Salamancans *de leg.* c. 2, punct. 3, §2, n. 57). And it is clear from the canon *Non dubium de sent. excomm.*, c. *Significasti de homic.* and others. The same thing is said on depriving penalties; only the guilty can undergo these without infamy, as if privation would be of the active and passive voice. (Suarez, l. 5, c. 9, n. 5, Bonacina, disp. 1, q. 1, punct. 7, n. 10, and the Salamancans *ibid.* n. 58, with Tapia, Vasquez, Montes., etc.) And in the mode of another place, particular custom should not be held otherwise, (the Salamancans n. 60). Add, that unless a punishment would consist in the depravation of some acquired right, say in a benefice, or election, etc., then a juridic declaration is always required either of the punishment, or at least of the crime, even if the punishment that is imposed *was incurred ipso facto which awaits no declaration.* (Lessius, l. 2, c. 29, dub. 8, et c. 34, dub. 54; Mol. *de just.* t. 2, tr. 2, d. 96, n. 8; Soto l. 1, q. 6, a. 6, et. l. 4, qu. 6, a. 6, Sanch. *de matr.* l. 2, disp. 53, n. 5, et l. 7, disp. 89, n. 11, Palaus tr. 3, d. 2, p. 2 n. 8, and the Salamancans *ibid.* n. 59, and 60, with Ledesma, Cajetan, and Granadus). For when a penal law ought to be received in a milder sense, those words, "with no declaration, etc." can be explained, that it does not await the declaration of the penalty; but it does not exclude a declaration of the crime, so that the punishment can be applied to the guilty. It is confirmed from the chapter *Cum secundum, de haeret.* in 6, where heretics, although they are deprived of their goods by the laws themselves, nevertheless are not held to hand those goods over before the sentence, just as is held in the same text.

149.—What has been said about depriving punishments, from the foregoing must be said about positive ones, which consist in a positive action, *e.g.* to restore something, or to suffer, as is taught commonly by St. Thomas (2.2., q. 62, a. 3); Sanchez (*de matr.* l. 6, disp. 53, n. 1), Mol. *loc. cit.*, Soto, (l. 1. q. 6, art. 6, ad 8), and the Salamancans (*ibid.,* n. 61 and 64), with Tapia, Sa, Vasquez etc. And so, therefore, it must be said on laws depriving benefices that have already been obtained by reason of simony, or of alienation of the goods of the benefice, etc., where a declaration of a judge is always required (the Salamancans, d. n. 64, along with the other cited authors). Moreover, the reason for all of these is because that human law is too hard and unobservable; because the guilty himself ought to follow out punishment against his person.

But incapacitating penalties oblige before the sentence of the judge, such as the penalty imposed by the Council of Trent that those who did not reside [in their dioceses] could not enjoy the profits, and similar things. (See the Salamancans *ibid.,* n. 62). Likewise, when conditional punishments, *e.g.* one having care of a benefice, if he were not ordained a priest within a year, he would be *ipso facto* deprived of his benefice, just as in *cap. Licet, de elect. in 6.* So also, a beneficed cleric not wearing a habit, *ipso facto* is deprived of the *privilegium fori.* The Salamancans *ibid.* n. 63, with Sanchez, Palaus, Bonacina, etc.

150.—*Quaeritur* 4) Whether a conventional punishment in contracts ought to be paid before the sentence?

The first opinion affirms, because everyone is held to observe an agreement before a sentence. (So think Bonacina, Suarez, Molina, Sa, with the Salamancans *ibid.*, n. 66).

The second opinion, which the Salamancans (n. 67) call equally probable, and hold along with Navarre, Lessius, Sanchez, Vasquez, Laymann, Palaus, etc., denies it because it must be thought that those contracting do mean to impose a penalty on themselves other than according to the disposition of law in regard to the penal laws, which are only contracted after the sentence. Certainly, the guilty man is held to the penalty after the sentence, but it must be noted, he is not held to pay money unless it is demanded by the party. And if the punishment were too hard, it is required in addition to the sentence the precept of the judge and execution of ministers. (See the Salamancans, *ibid.*, § 3, n. 70).

Next, it must be noted, that laws which are founded on a false presumption, do not oblige of themselves in the forum of conscience, when the presumption is certainly false. So here, he is not held, if a catalogue is lacking, to pay all the debts if the inheritance really must not be paid. (See the Salamancans, *ibid.*, punct. 4, ex n. 78, as well as what was said in n. 100, v. *Quaeres*).

151.—Whether, when a law requires some condition, without which it invalidates an act, such as an invalidating law a will without solemnities, or a law invalidating the alienation of the goods of the Church without the consent of the chapter, obliges in conscience?

The first opinion denies it, as Navarre, Covarruvias, Tapia, Sylvius, Medina, and others quoted by the Salamancans (*ibid.*, punct. 5, § 2, n. 103). The reason is that such laws are founded on the presumption of fraud, which is not present at that time.

The second opinion affirms it, because such laws are not only founded on the presumption of fraud, but also in the danger of it, which is always present (the Salamancans *ibid.*, n. 104, with Sanchez, Palaus). Both are probable, but the second is more probable.

152.—*Quaeritur:* Lastly, when we are held to abolish impediments, or not to set them up which hinder the fulfillment of the law? It first must be prefaced in regard to the answer of the question, that on the one hand someone may not be obliged by the law or may be removed from its obligation; on the other, that he may be excused from a transgression of the law, while he, nevertheless, remains under the obligation. This is why it happens that you can impede yourself from the observation of the law in two ways, namely if you were to leave a place where there is the precept to hear Mass and go to another place where the precept is not in effect; or by carrying out a work which, although it may imped you from the observation of the law, nevertheless it does not excuse you from the observation of the law; namely of on Sunday you were to leave from a place where there is Mass to the forest, where you could not hear Mass, you are still not excused from the obligation. Next, it must be noted that it is never permitted to put impediments against natural laws to be excused from their obligation, but it must be said otherwise about human laws, which do not bind with such rigor. The Salamancan fathers wisely make this distinction (c. 2, punct. 10, n. 158, 159 and 160).

Hence they infer that the excommunicate does not sin if he would not hear Mass and does not procure absolution; for through the impediment of excommunication he has already been excused from the obligation to hear Mass (see what must be said in book 4, n. 325, *v. Excommunicatus,* and l. 7, n. 161). They infer 2) since they do not sin against the precept of fasting or reciting the office, etc. who become sick by their own fault, even if it was foreseen: nor does someone who makes a journey on foot or labors much, from which he shall be excused thence from fasting: even if he took up the journey for a wicked purpose, namely to steel, etc. (the Salamancans *ibid.*, 161, with Sanchez, Medina, Henr., etc.). But we altogether follow the opposite opinion with St. Thomas. See what is going to be said in book 4, n. 1046.

But will someone sin against the law who places an impediment with a mind to excuse himself from the obligation of law? For example, if he were to tire himself out so that he would not fast? Palaus, Salas, Medina, etc. (the Salamancans *ibid.* n. 163), affirm that he sins, because no man ought to benefit from his deceit. Still, Sanchez, Filliuci, Azor, Villalobos, etc. say no, and the Salamancans call it a probable opinion (*ibid.*, n. 164), because then he uses his right whereby he can be excused from the obligation of the law, in which there is no deceit; just as if he would go out from his country, where there is an obligation to fast so as to excuse himself from fasting. But we altogether follow the first opinion, which is near to the opinion we once followed. (See book 4, n. 1045).

Yet he sins against natural or divine precepts that, foreseeing that he is going to kill a man in drunkenness, does not abstain from drunkenness, or who does not procure absolution for an excommunication during Easter time. Then he traverses the radically graver divine precept of communion. So, one also sins that inebriates himself, or gives himself to sleep at the time of hearing Mass or reciting the office, because those precepts then already oblige him, nor is he excused from the precept by these actions. (The Salamancans, *ibid.*, n. 162, *cum communi*).

CHAPTER II
ON THE SUBJECT TO WHOM A PRECEPT IS GIVEN

DUBIUM I
What persons are obligated by precept?

153. *Whether drunkards, infidels, the ignorant, etc. are obliged to the laws?*

154. Whether a legislator is held to the law?

155. When are children obliged to ecclesiastical laws?

153.—"Resp. Only those subjects using reason are so "obliged, that they would sin by transgression of a "precept. I add the fact, on account of drunkards and "those insane for a period, that even if they are truly "obliged by laws, still they do not sin by violating them "due to a defect of awareness of reason as well as "consent. The first part is common teaching and certain "(Fill., t. 21, cap. 11, q. 10, Bonacina, p. 6, etc., Laymann, "l. 1, tr. 4, c. 10). The second part is of the same authors. "The reason is both because a precept, when it is "directive, supposes the use of reason; and because "obedience is only of those who have use of reason and "the will. Nor can the transgression be otherwise "accounted under pain of sin."

For greater clarity it must be noted, that on the one hand he is not held to ecclesiastical laws; just as children, infidels and the insane are not held to ecclesiastical laws. On the other he is excused from the law, just as drunks, the ignorant, and those that are asleep. Hence it is a sin to offer meat on the second day it is forbidden, but not the first. Just as also sin is to incite all of these to something evil by the law of nature.

Wherefore these cases are resolved:

154.—"1. A legislator is not held to his own laws as in "regard to coercive force and punishment, whether "directly or indirectly, nevertheless, both in regard to "directive force, and from a certain justice he is held, just "as the head, to conform to the members. (St. Thomas, q. "96, a. 5, ad 3, Sylv., Suarez, Bonacina, Laymann, book 1, "t. 4, c. 9, against Azor). He is held in contracts with the "rest to use just terms. (See Fill. t. 21, c. 5)."

So it is from common opinion (the Salamancans *de leg.* cap. 3, punct. 3, n. 57). Is a legislator held to his own law *sub gravi* or *sub levi?* Some say *sub gravi*, just as the law obligates others, such as de Soto, Laymann, Vasquez etc. (the Salamancans *ibid.*, n. 58). But it is probable, scandal being removed, that he is only held *sub levi*: because he is only obligated to the law from integrity (the Salamancans *ibid.*, n. 42, with Lessius, Azor, Bonacina, Palas, etc.). Still, the limitation is placed that if the law has been imposed on taxation of money or on the invalidity of a contract; even the prince is held to favor such a law to preserve justice. (See the Salamancans, *ibid.*, n. 43, and 44).

"2. Unbaptized infidels, even catechumens, are not "obliged by the precepts of the Church, still heretics, and "others who are subject to the Church once, they have "been baptized, are subject.

155.—"Even if children with the use of reason were "obliged under pain of sin (as Sanchez and others argue) "to those matters of the Church, whose matter is suitable "to their age (*e.g.* yearly confession, according to Navar, "Henrique, and Azor), likewise, abstinence from meat,

"hearing Mass, etc.; still, not in regard to ordinary
"punishments, unless they are adults, such as men are
"from their 14th year, and girls from their 12th (de Soto,
"Vasquez, *de poenit.* q. 90, a. 2, SA v. *Censura.*"

Quaeritur: Whether children are held to ecclesiastical
laws to hear Mass, abstain from meat, or milk, and confess
as soon as they attain the use of reason? Sanchez (*Dec.*, l. 1,
c. 12, n. 6), Laymann (tr. 4, c. 10, n. 4), the Salamancans (*de
leg.* c. 3, punct. 4, n. 52) with Palaus, Bonacina, Salas, etc.
And they also say parents sin when they neglect the
fulfillment of these. And they regularly say this use of
reason must be judged to come in their seventh year. Still,
they admit that boys before puberty are not obliged under
pain of sin (the Salamancans *ibid.,* n. 50, *in fine*); nor to
communion before their tenth year, unless they are on the
point of death, if there is the use of reason. (Salamancans, *de
Euch.*, c. 7, punct. 1, n. 15). But St. Antoninus, de Soto, Sa,
Henriquez, March., cited by the Salamancans (*de leg.* c. 3,
punct. 4, n. 51) reject this, saying they are not held right
away, but after some time. This time, Sa says, is the time of
puberty: but De Soto and St. Antoninus say at least 10 years,
or 9 ½ with girls. Yet, the common teaching rightly rejects
this opinion, as Croix says (l. 3, p. 1, n. 615). But are children
obliged, who have attained the use of reason in their seventh
year? Diana, Sanchez, Burgh., (quoted by Croix, l. 1, n. 676),
say no; they think it probable that positive laws only attend
to those matters which they commonly touch upon. Yet,
Bosco affirms the same thing more probably. See what is
going to be said in book 4, n. 270, and 1012.

"4. Unbaptized children and the perpetually insane may
"licitly be given meat on forbidden days and have servile
"works imposed on feast days; nevertheless, not for
"drunkards, since they remain subject to the law; just as
"the insane that are aroused to blasphemy, wounding,
"etc., in so far as such an action were attributed to a

"principal agent, who uses the work of another as
"thought it were an instrument (Laymann, l. 1, t. 4, c. 10),
"Bonacina (p. 6), and Sanchez, (l. 1, *moral.* c. 12)."

DUBIUM II

*Whether pilgrims are held to the laws of their place of
domicile while they are away from it.*

> 156. *Whether a pilgrim is held to the laws of the place
> where he resides?*
>
> 157. *Whether he is held to the laws of the country?
> Thereafter the resolutions of many cases are placed.*
>
> 158. *Whether pilgrims can be dispensed in laws and in vows
> by the Bishop of the place?*

156.—"I suppose: I. There is another local precept, which
"only obliges in a certain place, or, *e.g.* a parish; and
"another that is universal or of common law, which
"obliges nearly the whole Church.

"I suppose: II. Pilgrims are properly called those who
"come from some place not with the intention to remain,
"but only to subsist for a few days, or to the last point for
"a lesser part of the year, such as merchants and
"wayfarers, but not the zealous or handmaids who come
"to serve.

"I respond: they are not obliged. (Navarre, Sanchez,
"Lessius, "L. 4, c. 2, dub. 8). The reason is because local
"precepts in themselves also directly regard a territory,
"and they are fastened to it; and so they do not oblige
"those that do not live within its confines. For law is so
"imposed; e.g. A feast is celebrated in such a place, and
"here the saying avails, 'when in Rome, etc.' Laymann (c.
"2), adds that a local precept expires even within the

"proper territory in a place exempt that is equally
"located in the place and outside the territory."

Here, it is of importance to distinguish before all things
a domicile from a quasi-domicile. One acquires a true
domicile if he lives in some place with a mind to remain
there forever, as the authors commonly teach. (Bonacina, *de
leg.*, d. 1, q. 1, p. 7, n. 39; Roncaglia *eod. tit.* c. 1, p. 3, pag. 44;
the Salamancans, tr. 8, c. 4, punct. 3, n. 48; with Palaus,
Trull., Dicastillus, and others everywhere, from l. 2, c. *Ubi
Senatores*, and *l. Heres. absens. §Proinde, ff. de judic. I.*). It is
thought, however, that to have a mind of this sort, one
dwells in a certain place for 10 years, while showing no will
to leave, or to remove a greater part of his goods, or to sell
his house, or build, as is held in the bull *Speculatores*, related
in l. 6, n. 770 *ad n. V*, or who at least, with expressed words
(as the Salamancans add, *ibid.*, n. 49), will have expressly
shown the will of perpetually remaining there. Moreover, he
acquires a quasi-domicile who remains in some place for the
greater part of a year, as Sylvest. says (v. *Domicilium*, n. 2),
and Sanchez (*de matr.* l. 3, d. 18, n. 9), or who tarries there
for some notable time with a mind to remain there for the
greater part of a year, as the authors rightly say (Roncaglia,
loc. cit.; Laymann l. 1, tr. 4, c. 12, n. 1, v. *Quaeres*, with
Navarre, and our Most Holy Lord Pope Benedict XIV, *Notif.*,
33, n. 6, and as it is plucked out from the cited work, *heres.*,
etc.). With these posited, it is doubted: 1) whether it were
required for someone to be held to the laws of a place where
he is, that he would contract a true domicile there. The
Gloss affirms, (c. *Quae contra*, dist. 8, *verb. Aut peregrini*),
and others with Sanchez (*loc. cit.*, n. 8). Because a new arrival
(as they say), until he acquires a true domicile, at least by a
mind to remain there perpetually, is not a subject of that
place.

But the common opinion is held to teach that if suffices
if he will have contracted quasi-domicile there. (Suarez, tom.

1, *de relig.*, c. 14, n. 5 and l. 3, *de leg.*, c. 33, n. 3, and he thinks the opposite is not practically probable; Sanchez, *loc. cit.* n. 9, the Salamancans *de legibus,* c. 3, punct. 5, §1, n. 55; Laymann *dicto* c. 12, n. 1; wtih S. Antoninus, Palud., Sylvest., Rosella, etc. The reason is because such pilgrims are already subjected to the jurisdiction of the superiors of that place, therefore they are also held to the laws, and held from the first day in which they arrive there with a mind for living there for a greater part of the year, as some rightly note (Sanchez, *dicto* n. 9; with Sylvest., Palud, Rosella, etc.).

It is doubted: 2) If someone tarries in some place for a short time, are they held to keep the laws of the place?

The first opinion says yes; and Pontius (*de matr.* l. 5, c. 7, §1 n. 6), Suarez (*de leg.*, l. 3, c. 33, n. 33 and l. 1 *de rel.* c. 14, n. 9), Salas (*de leg.* disp. 16, sect. 4, concl. 4), Tapia (l. 4, q. 16, art. 3, n. 2), and Covarruvias, Gordon, Henriquez, etc. (Salamancans *de leg.* ibid., n. 56) and many others with Sanchez (*de matr.* l. 3, d. 18, n. 6) and in Dec. (l. 1, c. 12, n. 3) hold this and also call it exceedingly probable, just as the Salamancans (*loc. cit.*, n. 58). The prove: a) from c. *Illa*, dist. 20, where that celebrated saying of St. Ambrose is related: "When I come to Rome, I fast on Saturday, but when I am in Milan, I do not; so even you, when you come to each Church, keep its custom; if you do not wish to cause scandal to anyone, they will not to you." They prove it: b) By reason, which is two-fold. Because one who thinks it is advantageous, ought to think it also disadvantageous, just as such an arrival is no longer obligated by the laws of the country from which he is absent, so it is just for him to be obliged by the laws of the place where he is staying, and in this mode the arrival is truly a subject of the superior of the place, although he may be there for a short time. Then, because it is expedient to preserve the public peace and to avoid scandal so that everyone will keep the laws of the place where they are found, as is gathered from the doctrine related by St. Ambrose; and at least by reason of avoiding the aforesaid scandal, as Suarez says, a Bishop of some place has jurisdiction over pilgrims; for the same jurisdiction, which is fitting for him in regards to his sheep so that he can rule them rightly, it also suits him in regard to guests, lest they give scandal to the sheep by not keeping the laws of the place. Suarez adduces a great many other reasons for this teaching.

Still, the cited authors affirm that it is not enough to only be in transit to take on this obligation; as a matter of fact, Emmanuel Sa says (quoted by Sanchez, *Dec.* l. 1, c. 12, n. 37), a pilgrim is bound if he may remain the day in which he arrives. Loenardus, if the whole day; Sayrus, if he comes there for a great space before lunch, and rests there for the whole day. But it seems that Suarez distinguishes better (*de Relig.,* tr. 2, lib. 2, cap. 14, n. 8), saying that if anyone comes to the destined place as the end of the journey, he is held to its laws, although he might be present there only a little while; otherwise if he is there on the road, or through transit to another place, then if the precept is affirmative, say to hear Mass, he is not held because such a precept obliges those living, such as are not on a journey, but he is held, if the precept is negative, namely to abstain from meat, or from servile work, even if he tarries there for an hour, because the precept is negative, since it obliges for always, it has the successive extent for the whole day.

This opinion is sufficiently probable, but *the second* seems more probable, which says that a guest is not held to the laws of the place where he does not tarry, nor intends to tarry for a greater part of the year, and many authors hold it. (Sanchez, *locis cit. de matr.* n. 6, et in *Dec.* n. 38; Bonacina, *de legib.* d. 1, q. 1, p. 6, n. 36, and 43; St. Antoninus, p. 2, tit. 6, c. 2, §2; Azor, tom. 1, dub. 5, c. 11, q. 2; Cardinal Toledo, l. 6, c. 5, n. ult.; Laymann, l. 1, tr. 4, c. 12, n. 4; with Sylvest., Angles and Medina; likewise Sayrus, Diana, Granado and others quoted by the Salamancans, tr. *de leg.* cap. 3, punct. 5, § 1, n. 58). They call this opinion no less probable. The reason is not only because they do not oblige anyone but subjects, such as are not pilgrims, but even more, those that on account of that short stay are hardly subject to the jurisdiction of the superior of the place, as is held from civil law (l. *Haeres absens,* § *Proinde,* ff *de judiciis*), as well as because he is not said to morally linger in some place who neither remains there nor has a mind to remain there for a greater part of the year. To the text of St. Ambrose we respond: 1) proceeds only where scandal must be avoided; 2) The holy Doctor speaks there about the common law to preserve fasting, which was not preserved at Milan in the first four days of Lent; rather the common law must be kept by pilgrims when they are away from their country where that law is not kept, as the common opinion teaches it. (Suarez, *de Relig.,* tr. 2, lib. 2, cap. 14, n. 27; Laymann, *loc. cit.,* n. 5, with Medina and Henriquez). Although Laymann does not reject the opposite view of Sanchez (*de matr., loc. cit.,* n. 7) that says citizens who are soon going to return to their country are held by the pretense of law for the present.

But this second opinion is limited: 1) in laws on common right, or in regard to solemnities of contracts, or in regard to the desirable things of that place, e.g. on not extracting wheat, arms, etc. 2) It is limited if the same laws are in force in the country of the pilgrim, although Sanchez opposes this with Diana. 3) It is limited if the pilgrim should commit some crime there against common law; then he is a subject by reason of the crime, from c. *Finali, de foro compet.* See also the Salamancans, n. 59 and 60, and Sanchez, *in Decal.,* lib. 1, cap. 12, n. 21, 23, 36, 38, 39).

157.—Moreover, those absent are not held to the laws of the country, as is held by common opinion from c. *Ut animarum, de const.* in 6, even if the law concerns common law; when a pilgrim is in a place, where it has been abrogated. (The Salamancans c. 3, punct. 5, § 2, n. 62, with Palaus, Lessius, etc.). And this, even if he leaves his country to excuse himself from the law. (The Salamancans *ibid.,* 63, with Palaus, Bonacina, Sanchez, etc.).[23] And this also avails, if he should remain in his own country, but in a place that is exempt. (The Salamancans *ibid.,* n. 64; Laymann, Bonacina Palaus, Salas, Diana, Tapia).

But are monasteries of regulars also understood as example places? Suarez, Coninck, quoted by the Salamancans (*de cens.* c. 1, punct. 9, n. 113) say no. But they say only towns are understood, and churches within the diocese but subject to foreign jurisdiction. But the Salamancans (*ibid.,* n. 114) with Avila (part 2, cap. 3, disp. 2, dub. 5), Henriquez, Sayro, Candido and Diana affirm it. And the Salamancans confirm it (*de leg.* d. c. 3, n. 64, in fine) because the Council of Trent (sess. 14, c. 5, *de Reform.,* cap. 5 at the end) names both places and persons as exempt, and it is exceedingly probable. (See also book VII, *On Censures,* n. 24).

From those principles you can resolve these cases:

"1) If a Bishop under the penalty of excommunication "would forbid playing with dice, the clergy playing it are "not obliged since they are exempt from the jurisdiction "of the Bishop. (Bonacina, *disp. 1, de legibus,* qu. 1, punct. "6; Laymann, c. 11, n. 5).

---

[23]   Hence, Palaus teaches there with Basil Pontius (*de Matr.,* lib. 5, cap. 9, n. 6), a pilgrim can, who refuses to confess sins reserved to his own pastor, leave from there to be absolves somewhere else; because then he uses his right. But on this see what is going to be said *de Penit.,* l. 6, n. 589.

"2) If anyone on the day of a fast or of a feast would be
"in someplace other than his own territory, he is either
"exempt, where then there is no fast, or it is a feast,
"there, he can eat and carry out servile works. (Laymann
loc. "cit., c. 11; Bonacina).

"3) It also has place in the precepts of common law, if in
"that place they might be abrogated in use, or not
"received, or a privilege held. This is why one can, for
"example, eat meat on the first four days of Lent in"
"Milan, since it is lawful there. Likewise, one can eat
"meat on Saturdays within Christmas and The
"Purification, or, in a place where the Council of Trent
"has not been received, one can validly (although not
"licitly), enter into a clandestine matrimony (Suarez,
"Sanchez, l. 1, c. 12, Less., etc.).

"4. Someone can, while leaving town in the morning
"where there is no fast, eat meat, even if he is going to
"return home around noon where there is fasting; but
"not after he comes home, for he will be held to keep the
"fast on that day, although he already violated it, and
"therefore, could not keep it; still he will be held to
"abstain from meat at home, since he can still keep it
"there, to the extent that it is partial. (See Sanchez, loc.
"cit., Lessius, c. 2, d. 8).

"5. If anyone is going to be away from a place where
"there is a fast, and he knows for certain that he is going
"to arrive at the place in the evening, where there may
"not be a fast, then, even if he could not eat meat in the
"place where he left (since abstinence might be partial),
"still he can eat breakfast there in the morning, as well
"as lunch at midday, as Lessius and Sanchez teach
"against some named above." (And the Salamancans, de
"leg. c. 3, punc. 5, § 2n, . 70 with Suarez, reckon it
"probable).

"6. It is also probable, even in a secure conscience, which
"Sanchez teaches (l. 3, *de matrim.*, disp. 18, n. 21 and l. 1
"*Mor.* c. 12, against Navarre, Suarez), that pilgrims,
"before they leave their own territory, are not held to
"fulfill the precepts which they discover there, e.g. they
"are not held to hear Mass in the morning on the day of
"the feast, who are going to come before lunch to
"another place where there is no feast; because if he
"would remain in the place, where the precept obliges,
"he could take respite at that time; but when he arrives
"in another place, he ceases to be obligated. It does not
"stand in the way that foreseeing the impediment he
"would be required to come beforehand, because then it
"is only true when the force of the precept remains, that
"he must be impeded; moreover, here he is absolved
"from the obligation of the precept."

(So also the Salamancans, *loc. cit.* n. 67, with Palaus,
Tapia, Salas, etc).

"Still, it would be otherwise if one Mass were said there,
"because he would be held to hear it before he could
"leave, but not held to wait for it. Still the contrary
"opinion, can be persuaded as more pious, unless
"something would stand in the way. (Sanch. l. 1, *Moral.*
"c. 12, and l. 3, *de Matrim.*, dub. 8, n. 21)."

158.—Here a great question occurs that must be treated:

*Whether pilgrims could be dispensed by the bishop of the
place where they are, both in common laws* (for example
fasting or abstinence from servile work), *and in vows and
oaths?* There are four opinions.

The first, which several authors hold (Pontius, *de Matr.*,
l. 8, c. 4, n. 7, Joseph de Januar., *de leg.*, to which Tanner
adheres as Croix says, l. 6, p. 3, n. 754, and Palaus rightly
thinks it is probable, *de leg.* tr. 3, d. 6, §2 n. 5). They
universally affirm both for laws and for vows. The reason is
that a pilgrim, by that journey, although it be of one day,

truly becomes the subject of the superior of the place where he is found, as the authors say. (Suarez, Salas, and Pontius, with Palaus *de leg.* d. 1, p. 24, § 3, n. 12). See what was said in n. 156, as well as what is going to be said in book 4, n. 332, *in fin. v. An autem.* For that reason, just as a pilgrim is held to the laws of that place, so it is just that he should also enjoy the privileges.

The Second opinion is altogether the opposite, which Sylvest., Abb., Tab., Ang. hold, cited by Palaus (*de leg.*, d. 6, §2, c. 14), and it says that a pilgrim, until he acquires a true domicile (*i.e.* by the spirit of remaining there forever), is never considered a subject, and therefore he is not held to the laws of the place, nor can he be dispensed in common laws nor in vows or oaths by the Bishop of the place. For confirmation of this opinion, Farinaccius and Garcia (cited by Palaus, n. 7) assert a certain declaration of the S.C. Concilii, approved by Gregory XIII, where it was said that a pilgrim can receive the benefit of absolution from sins in the place where he is, but he cannot be dispensed by the Bishop of that place. But Mazzotta (*de leg.*, d. 4, q. 1, c. 3) says this declaration is not authentically constituted; at least, as we will see below in the fourth opinion, it was not commonly received. So much more because Henriquez (l. 14, *de irreg.*, c. 18 §2) asserts another different declaration of St. Pius V, where the Pope declared that the Bishop of the place can the vows of students remaining at Salamanca. Palaus (n. 5) considers this second opinion to be probable. But yet Suarez (*loc. cit.*) thinks it is improbable, in regard to exempting a pilgrim from the laws of the place, if he would remain there for a greater part of the year.

The third opinion, which Palaus (*dict.* d. 6, n. 5, et 6), Navar., and Menoch., hold, who reference a great many others, think the pilgrim passing through can rightly be dispensed by the Ordinary of the place even in common laws, because he is subject to the jurisdiction of that superior in regard to laws, but not in regard to vows and oaths, because this jurisdiction depends upon custom, and at the nod of the bishops, which are not held for dispensations of this sort, exactly as it is held otherwise for the absolution of sins and the censures connected to them.

The fourth opinion is very common, as Croix says (l. 6, p. 3, n. 721) and is generally received, as the Salamancans assert (*de leg.,* c. 3, punct. 5, § 1, n. 55) to which we subscribe, holds that a pilgrim can be dispensed by the Bishop of a place, not only in laws but even in vows and oaths, but only if he was of a mind of remaining there for a greater part of the year. The reason is because from the lasting habitation, he contracts quasi-domicile as Abbas and Innocent IV prove. For that reason, then the pilgrim is not dispensed by reason of custom and the approval of his superior, but the proper authority of the ordinary of the place to whom the pilgrim is subject by that quasi-domicile (Sanchez, *de matr.* l. 3, d. 23, n. 12 and 13; Henr. Ang. Arag., etc.; Lessius, l. 2, c. 40, n. 122; Croix, *loc. cit.*, with Laymann; the Salamancans, *loc. cit.*; Sporer, *de leg.* c. 1, n. 254; with Suarez and Manuel quoted in Palaus).

And Sanchez (*loc. cit.*) thinks the same with Henriquez and Manuel in regard to the dispensation of faculties conceded to Bishops by the Council of Trent (cap. *Liceat*), and also the same in regard to conferring all the sacraments, apart from Order, as Croix, Laymann, and the Salamancans (*loc. cit.*) also say. But in regard to Matrimony, see book 6, n. 1083.

DUBIUM III

Whether pilgrims and wanderers are held to the precepts of the places in which they tarry.

159.—"Resp. Regularly they are not held to special "precepts of those places. (Laymann, Sanch., Azor, "Coninck Lessius, Reginald., Filliucius, against Navar., "Suarez, Sa, etc.) and even in regard to wanderers." (As "Lessius, Laymann, Sary, etc. hold with Bussembaum, "quoted by the Salamancans, who argue against it in c. "3, punct. 5, § 2, n. 69, in fine) against Bonacina and "Sanchez. The reason is, because no reason can be given "for this obligation since they are not subject to either "the places or the superiors whose laws they are; and "therefore they are outside their jurisdiction. It is not "opposed 1) that they are held to none of the statues of "partial places, but only to common law, because it is not "absurd; 2) Nor that wanderers can be punished due to "crimes they have committed; for this custom is received "lest crimes would remain unpunished.

160.—"I said 1. Regularly, because they are held to "certain laws, the violation of which would especially "result in the damage and injury of the place in which "they tarry; as also for those which concern the "celebration of contracts.

Wherefore, the following cases are resolved:

"1. Such are not held to hear Mass and can exercise "servile works on the day of a feast there; they are not "held to fast nor abstain from meat when there is a fast "there, and they are not at home. Both must be "understood to the exclusion of scandal, on account of

"which the Bishop of the place can punish (Laymann, *loc.*
"*cit.,* t. 4, c. 12, n. 4).

"2. It is not lawful for pilgrims to take grain and sell it
"above the price established there, to bear arms by night,
"etc. if such are forbidden there (Panorm., Regin., Sanch.,
"n. 36).

"I spoke in 2) *about special precepts;* because if the
"custom of your home were set aside by custom for some
"precept of common law, and you were to come into
"another where that law is in force, you will be obliged
"by the same. The reason is, because common law is
"universal and obliges all without the rank of the place.
"(Laymann, c. 12, n. 3).

Wherefore, this case is resolved:

"Some Belgian coming to Cologne, for example, is held
"there on Saturdays between Christmas and the
"Purification to abstain from meat, because his privilege
"to eat meat is not personal but local, and so expires
"outside the place. (Laymann, *loc. cit.*)"

DUBIUM IV

*Whether pilgrims are held by the precepts of common law, if
they are not in use in the place where they tarry?*

161.—"Resp. They are not held. The reason is, because
"then the local privilege avails, which they can all enjoy,
"who tarry in the place. (Sanchez, l. 2, *Mor.* c. 12; Suarez,
"Laymann, etc.)

Thus the following cases are resolved:

"1. If a German passes through Spain, he can eat the
"entrails of animals. He can eat meat if he travels

"through Belgium or Milan, in the former between
"Christmas and the Purification on Saturdays, but in the
"latter on the first four days of Lent. (Sanchez, Suarez,
"Bonacina, p. 6, n. 61).

"2. If anyone from a Catholic diocese, e.g. Hildesheim,
"where the old Calendar is still in use, should he come
"into another place, where the new is received, *e.g.* a
"Monastery, he can, if Lent has passed by in that place,
he may eat meat, as Sanchez teaches, *loc. cit.*, Salas, n. 69;
"Bonacina, n. 49; Lessius, l. 4, c. 2, d. 8, who still
"persuades the contrary opinion practice, although this
"may be safe, as Laymann also teaches.

"I added *from a Catholic diocese*, because if a Catholic
"would come into the lands of heretics, where there are
"no other Catholics, he is held to keep there the new
"Calendar to avoid scandal, and the contempt of the
"Catholic Church. (See Laymann, l. 1, tom. 4, c. 11, n. 8)."

CHAPTER III
On the Mode in which Precepts Must be Observed

DUBIUM I
Whether Precepts ought to be fulfilled from charity?

162.—"Resp. They can be fulfilled without charity, unless
"precepts include this in substance, e.g. the precept to
"love God. The reason is, because only the substance of
"the act that is commanded is included in the precept,
"e.g. that one should honor his parents, but not the end,
"or the mode of the precept, as St. Thomas teaches. (1.2.,
"q. 100, art. 10). Nevertheless, it is certain that charity is
"required in the one that acts for the fulfilling of the
"precept to be meritorious, according to that of 1 Cor.

"13:1, "If I were to speak with the tongues of men," etc.
"(St. Thomas, Suarez, Sanchez).

Thus the following cases are resolved:

"1. If anyone will fast, or be present at Mass on account
"of vain glory, or even to steal, he can just the same
"fulfill the precept, even by an act that is sinful by the
"circumstances, because he fulfills the substance of the
"precept, although he will sin against another one, to
"which that wicked purpose is opposed, as Sanchez
"teaches (l. 1, *Mor.*, c. 14, Laymann, l. 1, t. 4, c. 4, n. 6),
"Cardinal de Lugo (*disp.* 22, sect. 2, n. 23). With the
"Salamancans, *de leg.* cap. 2, punct. 8, n. 147, and 148.

"2. By a similar reasoning a vow, an oath made to God or
"sacramental penance is fulfilled, even if the act itself is
"a sin, *ibid., loc. cit.*" (Still, note here the condemned
"proposition of Alexander VII, n. 14: "He who voluntarily
"makes a null confession, satisfies the precept of the
"Church."

DUBIUM II
*Whether the intention to satisfy precepts is required for their
fulfillment.*

163.—"Resp. No. (Still, the intention of doing what was
"commanded is required, as the Salamancans c. 2, punct.
"8, n. 139 with Busembaum, see below, Dub. IV). Sanch.,
"Vasquez (1.2., q. 100, art. 9), and others agree in
"common. The reason is, because a law only commands
"the free execution of an external work, e.g. to hear
"Mass, but not that one would will to satisfy another
"peculiar act or intend to satisfy the precept, or as other
"say, the precepts do not oblige to formal obedience, *i.e.*

"that it should be done because it is commanded, but
"only to material obedience, or, that what is commanded
"is done. (See below, book 4, tr. 3, c. 1, dub. 3).

Thus the following cases are resolved:

"1. Someone that forgets some precept, but fulfills it, *e.g.*
"he does not know it is a feast day, but still was freely
"present at Mass, he satisfies it. Nor is it necessary, as
"some would have it, that after he learns that it was a
"feast day that he should then will to satisfy it by
"hearing Mass, because he fulfilled the substance of the
"act of the precept. (St. Thomas, Henriquez, Filluccius, t.
"5, c. 7, q. 7).

"2. He truly fulfills an oath and sacramental penance
"who follows through with the promised or enjoined
"works, even if he does not have the intention of
"fulfilling them: still, he may not apply these for another
"matter. The reason is because vows, etc., are quasi-
"particular laws which a man imposes upon himself or
"another, for that reason they only oblige to the
"substance of the act (Suarez, Azor, Lessius, Laymann, n.
"6)."

DUBIUM III

*Whether a man would satisfy a precept who, while doing the
work, expressly intends to not make satisfaction by it?*

164.—"Resp. He satisfies it. So think Suarez, Valentia,
"Vasquez, and Lessius (l. 2, c. 7, dub. 10), against Navarre,
"Azor, etc. The reason is, that the precepts only oblige to
"the substance of the work that was enjoined: therefore,
"with that posited, it is not in the power of the worker to
"not satisfy. Nor is it of importance: 1) That acts are not

"worked beyond the intention of the agent: because it is
"understood, when it is in the power of the worker, e.g.
"to satisfy or not; 2) that one who ought to give one
"hundred, does not satisfy the obligation if he would give
"two-hundred as a free gift; 3) That one who is obligated
"by a vow to recite the Rosary, if he would recite it from
"a spirit to not fulfill it, does not satisfy the vow. The
"reason is because these and similar obligation come into
"being from the will of the one promising, who, just as
"he freely constituted himself from the beginning of the
"debts, so can freely remain in the debt: moreover, the
"obligation to obey the law comes into being from the
"will of the legislator, and therefore, is not extended
"beyond his intention and will, namely beyond the
"substance of the work commanded. (Coninck, n. 509;
"Lessius, *loc. cit*; Laym). And so the very common
"opinion holds with the Continuator of Tournely, *de virt.*
"*relig.*, part 2, cap. 2, art. 8, sect. 6, in med, Pontas,
"Suarez, Vasquez, Valentia, Salmant., etc. See book 5, n.
"176.

Thus the following cases are resolved:

"1. A priest who reads the Breviary not with that
"devotion with which he meant, and therefore proposed
"to repeat it to satisfy the precept, if later he would not
"repeat it, he will still satisfy the precept. (Suarez,
"Coninck, Cardinal de Lugo, etc.).

"2. Hearing Mass on a feast day, because he knows it is
"the last Mass (or, if it is not the last, intending not to
"hear another one), although he may intend not to
"satisfy, still truly he satisfies the precept to hear Mass,
"even if he sins against another precept, in which he is
"held subject to the legislator. (Cardinal de Lugo, *loc.*
"*cit.*)"

DUBIUM IV

Whether an intention to fulfill the precept is required, or the will of doing what has been commanded?

165.—"Resp. It is required. The reason is since law is "given to men, not to brutes, and therefore must be "fulfilled in a human mode, hence the fulfillment of "every precept, whether human or divine ought to be a "human act joined with the freedom and will of the "worker, *i.e.* that he would will or intend to do what has "been commanded, e.g. to hear Mass, to fast, etc. This is "the most common opinion. (See Vasquez, 1.2. q. 100, a. "9; Suarez; Sanchez).

So these cases are resolved:

"1. One who hears Mass on a feast day while drunk, "sleeping, or demented in any way whatsoever, or not "knowing what to undertake, or what he should wish to "do, is held after he has come to his senses to hear "another Mass. (Suarez, Sanchez, Salas, d. 9, n. 32).

"2. He who heard Mass, fasted, etc. while altogether "violently compelled does not satisfy; for it was not a "human act by a defect of the will. (Vasquez, Suarez, "Azor, Fillucci, n. 232).

"I said 'altogether violently'; because if a servant, *e.g.* "from fear of the master, or a boy for fear of a teacher, "should hear Mass (say if he would not hear it, if the "teacher were away), he, even if he would sin by that "perverse will, still satisfies the precept. The reason is, "because fear does not abolish freedom. (Sanch., Salas, "*loc. cit.*, Laymann, l. 2, t. 4, c. 4, n. 12).

"3. Reciting the Breviary with only the intention of
"reading, or of learning does not satisfy the precept; just
"as he who goes to Mass only to let his eyes wander
"when he speaks to another, or waits for a friend does
"not. (Cardinal de Lugo, *loc. cit.*, n. 23).

"4. Nor does he satisfy who merely prays falsely, *e.g.* he
"prays etc., because it is not his fiction, but the work was
"commanded."

DUBIUM V

Whether a two fold precept is satisfied in one act or different
acts at the same time?

166.—"Resp. I. In one act different precepts can be
"fulfilled at the same time, unless another thing is
"gathered from the mind of the one that commands it. It
"is certain from daily practice: someone is obliged to the
"breviary by reason of the Sacrament of Order, and of a
"benefice, satisfies both in one recitation. (Sanch., l. 1, c.
"14; Salas, Bonacina, p. 10).

Thus these cases are resolved:

"1. When a Sunday and a feast day fall on the same day,
"you are not held to hear two Masses.

"2. A vow and penance enjoined in confession and many
"other things are not fulfilled by an act that is otherwise
"due: because these many other matters are not the mind
"of the vow and the confessor. (See Suarez, t. 4, in 3, p.
"Sanch., l. 1, Mor. c. 14).

"I said 'and many other things', because thereupon, the
"confessors enjoin a work otherwise commanded.

"3. One who owes hundred to another for many
"obligations, e.g. does not satisfy if he will give one
"hundred once, because in those things due to justice
"uniformity of the matter is applied to the thing;
"however one hundred is not equal to one hundred due
"for a great many things. For this reason, there is
"another intention in these matters, and the mind of the
"one obligating himself. (Sanchez, Salas, *loc. cit.*).

"Resp. II: Someone can at the same time satisfy a twofold
"precept by different acts, provided that one would not
"impede the other. This is the common opinion. And the
"reason is, because the diversity of a great many times is
"not commanded. (Suarez, Azor, p. 1, l. 7, c. 5; Sanchez,
"lib. 1, c. 14).

Thus it is resolved:

"1. Someone can at the same time hear Mass commanded
"on a feast day and at the same time say the breviary, or
"other prayers due by a vow or another reason.
"(Bonacina, p. 10, n. 8)."

"2. One that is held to hear two Masses can likewise hear
"them at the same time, nay more even three, as some
"teach, when they are celebrated at the same time on
"many altars (Sanch. 1, mor. c, 14, 12, *Major* in 4, dist.
"18)."

DUBIUM VI

Whether someone that violates many precepts in one act commits as many sins?

167.—"Resp. If one violates precepts that are only "materially different, so that, although there may be "many precepts of the legislators, but they have the same "formal motive, and they turn on the same matter in "number with the same circumstances, he commits only "one sin; but if the precepts may be formally different, "on account of the proximate motives distinct in "appearance, or turn upon a matter different in number, "he commits many sins, because they are obligations and "of a different crime. (Sanchez, lib. 9, *de matrim.*, dist. 15; "Vasquez, 1. 2, dist. 9; Salas; Cardinal de Lugo, d. 16, n. "245 (See what is going to be said in book 2, n. 33).

Thus it is resolved:

"1. Someone that did not fast on a vigil day falling in "Lent, or neglected Mass on a feast falling on Sunday, "committed one sin, and it is enough to confess about "the fasting and one Mass; because in these precepts the "formal reason is one, an the motive proximate, *e.g.* in "the first the wearing down of the flesh, in the second "the worship of God. (Laymann, Sanchez, Cardinal de "Lugo, *loc. cit.*).

"2. Someone violates a vow and an oath, or a vow and a "precept of the Church in regard to the same matter, "commits a twofold crime and hence he must explain it "in confession. Since, observance of a vow is "commanded that good faith due to God would be "preserved; moreover in an oath, lest God will be called "upon a false witness; thus these two are formal "reasons; just as they are in missing a Mass which ought "to be heard on account of a feast day and because of a "penance that has been enjoined. (Card. de Lugo, *loc. cit.*)

"3. If one is bound in marriage should commit adultery "with a married woman, he commits a twofold sin, one "against his own wife, and the other against the husband "of the adulteress: just as if anyone would also kill many "in one act, there are many homicides because in these "the matter is different in number. (Laymann, l. 1, t. 2, c. 10, "n. 3; Sanch., Card. de Lugo, *loc. cit.*)."

CHAPTER IV
WHAT THINGS WOULD EXCUSE FROM THE TRANSGRESSION OF A PRECEPT

DUBIUM I
Whether ignorance would excuse?

168. *Whether invincible ignorance would excuse?*

169. *Whether ignorance would excuse from a penalty connected to a law?*

170. *Whether invincible ignorance is granted also in regard to precepts of the law of nature? Even to 174.*

168.—"Resp. If it were invincible, it excuses; because no "man sins except by a voluntary act; moreover, this "presupposes knowledge. But if it were vincible and "culpable, it does not excuse; when you may and must be "held to know, or learn and came to doubt in the mind; "nor labored to understand. (St. Augustine, St. Thomas, "Sanchez, 10, *Mor.*, c. 6 and other in common against "Palaus).

So it is resolved:

"1. If anyone who on the day of a fast, thinking nothing "about the precept were to dine or eat meat, he does not "sin: similarly in other matters, such as if you kill a man "thinking that he is a thief. (Bonacina, *quest.* 8, p. 3).

"2. If in some matter you merely notice a fault of one "kind, you only contract it; *e.g.* if someone knows a "woman whom he does not know is his relation, but "does not know about the kinship, he only commits "fornication, or adultery, but not incest. (Laymann, l. 1, "tr. 4, c. 2; Bonacina, *loc. cit.*).

169.—Thence it is asked whether ignorance would excuse from a penalty connected to the law? The response is made from Laymann (l. 1, tract. 4, cap. 20) that someone that is inculpably ignorant of the law is excused from fault, and from its penalty. On the other hand, one who knows the law, but is ignorant of the penalty connected to it, he is not excused from the penalty. (Laymann, with the common opinion, *ibid.*, n. 6). The exceptions are: 1) If the penalty were very heavy, exceeding what is merited by the crime; 2) If a censure is ecclesiastical, men do not incur it when they are unaware of it, unless the ignorance were crass or culpable, as Laymann teaches with the common opinion (*de cens.*, c. 5, n. 7). And it is established from c. 2 *de Constit.* in 6. Moreover, ignorance effects the same thing, which because of forgetfulness of the law. (Laymann, *ibid.*). The reason is because to incur censure contumacy is required or virtual contempt for the law. (See book 7, n. 47).

Nay more, if a censure were inflicted the presumptuous or the rash or those sinners knowingly; then even crass ignorance excuses, but, however, not pretended (which is present when someone zealously neglects to know something to act more freely); because it is put on the same level as this opinion. Laymann, *d.c.* 5, and others, but see book 7, n. 48.

DISSERTATION

in which it is shown that invincible ignorance is granted in some men in regard to the natural law.

170. Now it is of an explored truth, invincible ignorance cannot be granted in those matters which a man may and must be held to know. Therefore, although he is not held to what he does not know, in turn, ignorance also *can be conquered by zeal*, that I may use the words of St. Thomas (1.2., q. 76, a. 2), by no means can he be freed from fault. We are held to know certain things, and the Angelic doctor upholds this in the same place; these are his words: "All are held to know those things which are commonly of the faith as well as universal precepts of law; but individuals those things that regard their state or office." For that reason, where the discussion is on natural law, it is clear that invincible ignorance cannot be granted in its first principles, by which arrangement are: *God must be worshiped, do not do to another what you do not want for yourself.* So also we say, they are neither *immediate conclusions* plucked out from themselves, or proximately connected and adhering to the aforesaid principles and can be invincibly unknown. Just the same, the precepts of the Decalogue are certain. Moreover, we shall affirm below, that invincible ignorance of such a kind is not even granted in obligations, which pertain to the proper state or office; seeing that one who transfers himself to some state, *e.g.* from an ecclesiastic or a religious, or one who receives some office to be attended on as a judge, doctor, confessor, or another kind of office, is held to become experienced in the obligations of that state or office, or to be instructed in them, and he who is ignorant of those matters, neglecting to be instructed, or on account of fear lest he would be held thereafter to observe them, or on account of voluntary negligence, his ignorance will always

be culpable and all errors which he commits with such an ignorance, all will be culpable, even if in committing them he may not have actual awareness of the crime; supposing for this purpose that they were culpable, virtual notice is enough, whether it were interpretative (as some call it) which he held from the beginning, when he neglected to know his proper obligations, as the authors wisely and commonly teach. (Habert *Theol. dogm.* t. 3, *de act. hum.* cap. 1, §3, quest. 5; Collet, *Comp. mor.* tr. *e peccatis*, c. 2, art. 2, sect. 1, concl. 1; Antoine, *Theol. mor.* c. 4, *de peccat.* q. 7, and others, following St. Thomas, according to what was prefaced above and for that which the same Angelic Doctor teaches more expressly in *De Verit.*, qu. 17 *de Conscient.*, art. 4, ad 3, and ad 5). He says suitably to this matter, where he teaches that the judge cannot be excused who errs in imposing sentence, and for that reason he is ignorant of the laws which he ought to have learned.

I said commonly, because although many other doctors, such as Sylvius, Suarez, Gammachaeus, Isambert, seem to demand actual notice for individual sins, at least when the case of some sin is placed, then all, without any discrepancy, agree, it is enough that the notice which, a man has from the beginning when he assumes whatever state or receives some office, on the obligation of making himself expert, if he would not be an expert in those things which he ought to do, and in which it is necessary to live by reason of the office, it shall make him culpable in future errors, and not withstanding this he is negligent; because then in confusion he will at least foresee the errors which he has not informed himself of and he will be able to take on instruction, and take precautions lest he should not care for them. But if anyone has sufficiently taken care that he were instructed earlier, and just the same erred in whatever matter which regards his office, or state, not on account of negligence, but invincible ignorance, or invincible inadvertence, he will indeed be altogether free from all fault, as we will teach soon.

Moreover, it is certain that in the first principles of natural law, equally and in proximate conclusions as well as certain obligations of the proper state, invincible ignorance is not granted because by that light of nature such things are known to all, except those who close their eyes lest they would see them. And this is precisely what St. Thomas says (1. 2., q. 94, a. 6): "To the law of nature pertains firstly certain very common precepts which are known to all; secondly, certain secondary precepts, more properly, which are like relative conclusions to the principles;" and he upholds that in both cases one cannot be ignorant except from passion or from culpable ignorance, because, as Suarez teaches, "Nature itself, and conscience assail their acts, that they are not permitted to be inculpably ignorant of them."

171.—On the other hand, the unanimous opinion of theologians, both of the probabilists and the anti-probabilists, in mediate conclusions and by obscure or remote principles, invincible ignorance is certainly granted and ought to be admitted: St. Thomas teaches in this way (1. 2. quest. 76, a. 5) when he stated that ignorance is voluntary and culpable in two ways, either, "directly, just as when someone assiduously wants to not know some things so that he might sin more freely; or indirectly, just as when someone on account of labor or on account of other occupations neglects to learn that by which he is drawn back from sin. For such negligence makes the ignorance itself voluntary, and a sin. But if there were such an ignorance that was altogether involuntary, or because it is invincible, or because it is of one that is not held to know, such ignorance altogether excuses from sin." So the Angelic Doctor, affirming this, rightly shows that still the ignorance of those who are held to know some things, with it posited that, were it invincible, excuses from sin. He equally teaches the same thing with more profitable words (*Quodlib.* 8 art. 15): "Moreover, an error of conscience, whereas it has the force to absolve or excuse when it proceeds from ignorance of that which one can not know, or is not held to know; and in such a case, although an act might be mortal in and of itself, still, intending to sin venially, he would sin venially;" and consequently, if he intended to commit no sin, indeed he would commit none. We must note attentively: "Cannot know or is not held to know." Therefore, even in a case in which someone is held to know a precept; if he cannot know it, his ignorance is invincible and excuses him from fault, exactly as it is in its nature. It is wisely noticed with John of St. Thomas, (1. 2., q. 6, disp. 3, *diffic.* 1), those words "can know" are not understood remotely, but proximately, and expediently, so that the omission of due diligence in a truth that is required would properly be volitional: "That axiom, *He who can and is held to, but does not do it sins*, is understood about someone that can proximately and expediently, but not remotely and obstructed, because (as we said above) an omission, were it voluntary, ought to proceed from the will itself."

In like manner, St. Antoninus clearly warns that invincible ignorance is certainly granted in remote conclusions (p. 2, tit. 1, c. 11, §28), saying: "And if it were to be said that it is usurious, and usury is against the Decalogue, the response can be made that it is not clear if this contract is usurious since even wise men reckon the matter differently among themselves. Moreover, although it is said that ignorance of the natural law does not excuse, it is understood on those matters, which are expressly in themselves or reductively in regard to natural and divine law, as against faith or precepts through evident reasons, either by a determination of the Church or the common teaching of doctors: and not on these matters, which are carried out through many mediums and are not clearly proved to be against precepts and articles." Habert defends the same thing, saying (*Theol.* tom. 3, *de act. hum.* c. 1, § 3, around the end): "In regard to certain more remote conclusions of natural law, such are the prohibition of usury, plurality of wives, the indissolubility of matrimony, even while some grave cause intervenes, there can be invincible ignorance because they are not deduced from first principles, but from a more tedious reasoning." And Gerson (*de vita spirit.*) wrote, "The opinion is unanimous that nothing in those matters which are of the law of nature yield invincible ignorance," but he responded to what is said and affirmed in regard to first principles, and primary conclusions, but otherwise in regard to more remote conclusion, nay more at some time he added the very primary conclusions in certain circumstances one could be invincibly ignorant, *e.g.* if anyone deceived by error would persuade himself that he was held to lie to defend his neighbor from death."

John Baptist Du Hamel makes us no less certain (lib. 2, *de act. hum.,* c. 5, in fin. vers. *Ad legem*), thus writing: "Moreover, what indeed is necessarily from that law but not manifestly deduced, as perhaps simple fornication or polygamy and other things of this kind, it seems probable that one can be so invincibly ignorant that it comes to their minds with no light suspicion that it is forbidden; and although these vices arise from sins freely committed, and moreover seem voluntary and by that reason the ignorance would be the penalty of the sin, from there, it still does not follow that these are voluntary when the wicked things that are going to follow from these sins were not foreseen."

Fr. Laurence Berti (*de Theolog. discipl.,* t. 2, lib. 21, c. 10) defends the same opinion in writing: "Still I think the opposite opinion is very true, and in regard to the most remote consequences of the law of nature I think invincible ignorance can be admitted ... Nearly all the Aegidian Gymnasium and the Thomists hold that, as well as Sylvius, l'Herminier, and others in a common consensus; the reasoning of their assertion seems rather clear, that the conclusions of more remote natural law are deduced from more tedious principles, and by a more involved reasoning, which a great many of the unlearned hardly avail to form." Thus St. Thomas proves it when he says (1. 2. q. 100, a. 1): "There are certain things which, by a more subtle consideration of reason are judged by the wise that they must be observed, and these are on the law of nature that, nevertheless, they need discipline, by which the lesser are instructed by the wise." For that reason, Fr. Berti concludes that the unlearned man, if he were not negligent in this, must not be condemned. And not even an expert must be condemned, I add, if he acts from invincible ignorance, because no one is found, no matter how learned he may be, who knows to judge on all obscure matters pertaining to natural law according to an unshaken truth; for the same truth, as St. Thomas says (1. 2. q. 94, a. 4) is not equally known to all: "But insofar as the proper conclusions of practical reason, truth or rectitude is not the same with all, nor even with those whom it is the same is it equally known." Fr. Gonet holds the same (*Clypeo Theolog.*, t. 3, disp. 1, art. 4, § 1, n. 55), where he is speaking on remote precepts from first principles, he says: "Invincible ignorance can be granted on those matters, even excusing from sin." And in *tract. de Probabil. circa finem*, speaking on the same opinion, he says the contrary is singular, and for a few even improbable. Fr. Collet holds the same thing (*Comp. Mor.* tr. *de actibus hum.*, c. 1, a. 1, sect. 2, concl. 4), in these very words: "Invincible ignorance of the natural law is not granted in regard to first principles and conclusions proximate to them, but it is granted in regard to more remote issues." Likewise, Fr. Antoine (*Theolog. mor., de peccat.*, c. 4, q. 6), saying: "Invincible ignorance is granted in some matters in regard to certain precepts of the natural law that are exceedingly abstruse, and remote from principles: it is the common opinion that when some precepts are very abstruse and remote from first principles, whereby some can easily be invincibly ignorant without a tedious and difficult deduction of reasoning." I am profoundly satisfied that at what I have related from these authors, since they are antiprobabilists. Moreover, there are numberless others who defend this opinion as though it were certain, such as Sylvius, de Soto, Gammachaeus, Isambert, Cardinal Aguirre, Wigandt, Cnuliliati, The Salamancans *scholastici* and *morales*, to all of which St. Anselm, Azor, Suarez, Tapia, Prado, Vasquez, La Croix, Duvallius, Medina, Maldonato, and others adhere. And the very learned prelate Julius Torni did not go into another opinion in Estium, where he wrote that he was of the opinion of Cajetan (which he incorrectly says Contensonius favors) when Cajetan wrote with the conception of these very terms: "A man, insofar as he is excused in the crime of the opinions by divine goodness, if not attaining the truth from what is right he were to deviate from the rule of morals, God does not demand more than man." The Archbishop of Paris, Beaumont, in his pastoral catechesis (*Instruct. pastor.*, 28 Octobr. 1763, part. 3, n. 38, v. f, sub 1), whose words were written in the French language and here are rendered into Latin: "Although they could not be ignorant of the principles of the natural law and their proximate conclusions, just the same they could be ignorant of the more obscure and remote consequences, and often are the matter of invincible ignorance. The support of famous theologians gathers this point in all these words."

172.—Moreover, our opinion is proved and strengthened by the second proposition of the Bajanists condemned by Alexander VII: "Even if invincible ignorance of the natural law were granted, this acting in the state of fallen nature does not, of itself, excuse from formal sin." It is profitably inferred from the proscription of such a proposition that the Pope did not, on that account, condemn it because he holds for certain that invincible ignorance can be granted in some difficult and abstruse matters, and which consider the natural law. Nor is a different meaning gathered from other condemned propositions of the Bajanists: "Negative infidelity in those matters, in which Christ has not been preached, is a sin." Additionally, it is clearly confirmed from the thesis condemned by the same Pope: "It is not lawful to follow the most probable among probable opinions." Unless invincible ignorance were granted in regard to the natural law, as our adversaries say, one would not even be excused from sin who followed the most probable opinion, because still the most probable abides in the distinction of error, seeing that this exists not outside of, but within the confines of probability; the reason for our opinion, that I, at length, would make an end to, which St. Thomas adduces (1. 2., qu. 19, art. 6), is first of all evident: "It is manifest that that ignorance, which causes an involuntary act, abolishes the reason of good and evil."

173.—Yet, we arrive at that part of the dissertation, where space is made to hear what two most bitter opponents say against us. The first none other than Fr. Jo. Vincent Patutius, who writes under his *nomme du guerre* Adelphus Dositheus, the other is anonymous who titles his book *Regula Morum*, both of which are written in the Italian language and here are rendered into Latin. Therefore, absolutely denying that invincible ignorance is granted in regard to any matter, let us hear first what Patutius wrote in Italian (as I said), and which we render into Latin: "According to the idea which we have from the Scriptures, from the Supreme Pontiffs, St. Thomas and the common sense of the Fathers, and even from theologians of the first rank, sins of ignorance, when we are held to know the law, are those (speaking rigorously and properly), which are committed and for which we are guilty in the sight of God, by which we do not know we have committed these, because it arises from our own fault, because we do not know and for this reason St. Thomas lays down a very clear axiom on this matter (in c. 1, Epist. ad Rom.), and teaches as certain: 'Ignorance, which is caused by sin, cannot excuse the subsequent fault; and for this reason sin is committed, although it is not held, not to speak of knowledge demanded of one, namely certain understanding, and it is evident (here he speaks to me in regard to the licit use of equally probable opinion, which I defend), but not even uncertain and obscure of sin, which can be held, and which we were held to uphold.' And lastly he concludes: 'These few are enough that we be instructed in the business, the adequate idea of which you do not seem to have fashioned.'" But here, Fr. Patutius errs, thinking that I am as penetrating and sharp a genius as he is, rather although I am a dull and obtuse mind, I affirm this short instruction is not enough for me, because I could never understand how a man would sin when he labors with invincible ignorance of sin, after he has applied due diligence to be informed and lack ignorance.

But the author of the *Regula Morum* strives to prove in nearly his whole book that we can not be without formal sin if we are ignorant in any matter which considers natural law; but let us see, I say, how he proves it, and indeed our opinion will be more clear from the responses which are rendered by his opposition: "Invincible ignorance of the natural and divine law is not granted (he says on page 345), except in children, the mad and insane." Then on page 354, he so concludes: "Ignorance of the natural law never excuses those who act from knowledge and the free use of reason." Such a conclusion duly rejects and condemns the use of any probable opinion, even if it were the most probable; and binds everyone to embrace proscribed *tutiorismum*.

He chiefly proves his intent, affirming we are held to follow the truth, and for that reason, because the truth is the unique norm of morals and so in ch. 1, on account of this matter he stitches together many texts of scripture: "I am the way, the truth and the life," (John 14:6); "Teach the way of God in truth." (Math. 22:16); "All your ways are truth." (Ps. 118, v. 151); If your sons ... would walk in my presence in truth." (3 Kings 2:4); "Walking in the truth, just as a command, we receive from the Father." (2 John 4); "I shall guard the truth of the Gentiles. (Isaiah 26:2); "He who does the truth comes to the light." (John 3:21); He will not stand in the truth." (John 8:44).

On the other hand, the author could have spared such labor, for no man repudiates that we are held to seek the truth in every work and follow it. But it is allowed to seek whether in another arrangement, we can know the truth unless we are led by reason? Therefore, it must be said that we must follow and embrace the truth which is shown to us by reason, and is posited beyond the eyes. Hence, Fr. Collet (tr. *de aetibus hum.*, cap. 6, art. 1, sect. 1, obj. 2, i.f.), rightly distinguishes the objective morality of the act considered in itself from the formal morality of the one acting, and he teaches when someone acts from invincible ignorance, it can happen that someone not only does not sin, but even merits by acting according to reason which seems right, even if it is really opposed to the most heavenly reason. "But because," Collet says, "this opposition is at some point involuntary, as in those who labor with invincible ignorance, consequently it is not always thought to be sinful, but at some time to be meritorious on account of the good faith of the one acting who seems to follow right reason, even while it is wanting." Therefore, St. Thomas (1. 2., q. 19, a. 1, ad 3), confirms the whole thing, teaching that the object of the act is represented to the will by the medium of reason, and insofar as it falls under the order of reason, that object causes the moral goodness in the will. Look at his words (Ad 3), "It must be said that a good is represented to the will as its object by the reason: and in so far as it is in accord with reason, it enters the moral order, and causes moral goodness in the act of the will: because the reason is the principle of human and moral acts, as stated above in q. 18, a. 5." There the Holy Doctor, while teaching the same thing, notes the good and evil acts of the will are so called exactly as they are manifested by reason: "In good and evil acts, moreover, it is said by a comparison to reason: because, as Dionysius says (4 cap. *de divinis nominibus*), 'The good of man exists according to reason, but evil is that which is apart from reason ...'" Furthermore, some acts are called human acts, or morals, according to what they are by reason."

This is why the same Angelic doctor (1. 2. q. 71, a. 6) established human reason as the proximate rule of the will of nature, because the eternal law, although it is the first rule, just the same is still remote and is rather more the reasoning of God than ours: "But the rule of human will is twofold, one near and homogeneous, namely human reason itself; but the other is the first rule, namely the eternal law, which is the reason of God, so to speak."

Nevertheless, by no means does the aforesaid anonymous author of the *Regula bonorum morum* say that when someone acts against the law he always sins, nor that reason suffices to excuse from sin. So he says in ch. xi, p. 168, where we have rendered what he said in Italian faithfully into Latin: "It is not denied that reason ought to be the more proximate rule of our actions ... But this is understood when it is submitted to the eternal law, etc. But it does not always happen that reason is directed by the will of God; this is why it can not only be said that reason is the rule of our morals, and each cannot fall into error following it, but also that truth is received in all the schools, because when reason fails, the will sins if it follows it; Human reason can err, and therefore the will in accord with human reason is not always right; but the will in accord to errant reason is bad. This is the conclusion of St. Thomas, and of all theologians." So the author concludes.

But let us see, I ask, what St. Thomas upholds in that citation, where he proposes this article: "Whether the will in accord with errant reason is good? (1. 2. q. 19, a. 6). There, the Holy Doctor says: "This question depends upon that which was said above (q. 6, a. 8) that ignorance at some time causes involuntary acts, and at other times does not. And because moral good and evil consists in act, insofar as it is voluntary, as is clear from what came before (art. 2 of this question), it is manifest that the ignorance which causes an involuntary act abolishes the reason of the good and bad moral, but not those which do not cause an involuntary act. It was also said above (q. 6, a. 8) that ignorance, which is in some manner volitional, whether directly or indirectly, does not cause an involuntary act, and I say ignorance *directly* voluntary, in which an act of the will is imposed, but *indirectly* on account of negligence, from that which someone does not wish to know but is held to know. Therefore, if reason or conscience errs in a voluntary error, whether directly or on account of negligence, because it is an error in regard to that which someone is held to know, then such an error of reason or conscience is not excused, that the will in accord with reason, or conscience so erring, would be evil." Let the words be noted: "*If, therefore, reason or conscience would err in a voluntary error, either directly or on account of negligence, because it is an error in regard to that which someone is held to know, then such an error does not excuse.*" This is why, when the error is not volitional, neither directly nor indirectly by negligence, it excuses from sin.

Nor is it opposed to say that when some matter is evil, even if reason represents it as good, it is always evil, and as a matter of fact St. Thomas responds in the same article, *ad 1*, that it is true on account of that general axiom: "Good is caused from the whole cause, but even from individual defects," and therefore the Holy Doctor adds, "For this purpose that which is called evil, in which the will is imposed, suffices either that what is following its nature is bad, or what is apprehended as bad." But this wickedness effects actions that are done against the law, and they are formal sins. When a sin is committed against the law invincibly unknown, a sin is committed only materially, but not formally, because a law is not as in itself, but exactly as it is represented by reason, so it becomes a rule and measure of our actions, as John of St. Thomas wisely adverts (1. 2. q. 18, disp. 11, art. 2, n. 33, near the end), where he writes: "And when it is pressed upon, because reason can propose against a law from an invincible error, we say that he cannot propose formally against the law, but materially, that is, against a law as it is in itself, not against a law as it is appears, but by such a condition the law can measure, not according to itself precisely as *in re*, and as not yet manifested." According to that, which the same author wrote earlier, (*loc. cit.*, q. 18, disp. 9, art. 1): "Morality in free acts is none other than a proportion of those things, and ordination according to the rules of reason."

But the author of the *Regula morum* repeats that St. Thomas adds these words in the same article: "If errant reason would say that a man held to his wife happens upon another, the will concordant to this reasoning is wicked, to the extent that the error comes into being from ignorance of the law of God which he is held to know." Therefore, he infers that as often s one acts against the law of God, he is not excused from sin, although reason represents the contrary to him. And he confirms it with another text of the Angelic doctor (*in Quodlib.* 3, art. 27, ad 2): "If conscience would say to someone that he could do that which is against the law of God, if he does it he sins because ignorance of the law does not excuse from sin, unless perhaps the ignorance were invincible, just as in the mad and insane, which altogether excuses." Additionally, he confirms it with a text of Boniface VIII (*de reg. juris* 13, in 6), "Ignorance of fact, but not of law, excuses."

But the responses to all these texts are clear. When St. Thomas says: "Ignorance of the law of God, or ignorance of the law does not excuse," he only speaks on the ignorance of those precepts of God which is the same thing that he expresses in other passages, exactly as we noticed above (1. 2, qu. 76, a. 2; and q. 19, a. 6). It cannot be ignored without the fault of positive negligence, to the extent that they are first principles of the natural law, and their proximate conclusions, that is the precepts of the Decalogue, as the authors we praised above teach in common with St. Thomas. Nor should the authority of Gerson be understood differently from us, which was objected by our opponent, as Habert explains. The authorities of Albert the Great and Pope Adrian must also be explained by the same reasoning since I find those authors, namely St. Albert the Great (in 2, dist. 22, art. 10), and Pope Adrian (in 4, sent. tract. *de clav. Eccl.*, q. 5) cited in the pastoral epistle of Archbishop Beaumont favoring me. Moreover, it is certain, St. Thomas, with the exception of first principles and the conclusions proximate to them, admits invincible ignorance in the remaining abstruse and obscure matters in many places, as we taught. Accordingly he affirms in 1. 2. q. 76, a. 3, that when ignorance is invincible, although it might be on matters which a man is held to know, it excuses from sin: "But if such ignorance were altogether involuntary, or is of something which a man is not held to know, it excuses from sin." It happens that in another passage advanced above (1. 2. q. 19, a. 6) he teaches that then the evil is voluntary, which follows erroneous reasoning, when the reason errs either directly or indirectly on account of voluntary negligence in regard to those things, which a man ought to know:

"Therefore if reason or conscience would err by an involuntary error, whether directly or on account of negligence, because error is in regard to that which someone is held to know, then such an error does not excuse." Therefore, when an error is not voluntary at least by reason of negligence, at any rate it excuses from sin.

To the text of Boniface VIII which is placed against us, namely "Ignorance of fact, but not of law, excuses," Sylvius (in 1. 2. q. 76, a. 3, q. 7, concl. 7) and Antoine (*de peccat.* cap. 4, q. 6), suitably respond that the passage has place in public statutes where vincible ignorance is often presumed after their promulgation has been made in a public place, provided that some special reasoning, whereby the contrary would be presumed to not be present, as is held in c. *Cum in tua*, tit. *qui matrimon. accusare possunt.*

Next, the anonymous author opposed various authorities of Scripture whereby he strives to prove that invincible ignorance is not granted in regard to the law of nature: "But he that did not know, and did things worthy of beatings, shall be suffer a few beatings." (Luke 12:48); "Do not remember the sins of my youth and my ignorance." (Psalm 24:7); "I obtained the mercy of God, because I acted ignorantly in unbelief." (1 Tim. 1:13). But all these texts, according to what Habert teaches (*de act. hum.*, c. 1, § 3) are interpreted by the agreement of all to be on crass ignorance, which otherwise, lessens sin, but does not escape the crime, "Because," as Habert says, "It is at least indirectly volitional, insofar as someone that labors in it voluntarily omits the diligence to learn or receive the office to be responsible for that which he cannot gain the requisite knowledge to fulfill." And therefore, the author describes the same thing in detail, the proposition of Pelagius that was condemned by the council of Diospolitanus, beginning with these very terms: "Ignorance does not come under sin, because it does not happen according to the will, but according to necessity."

Therefore, it was condemned, because crass ignorance is vincible, and very culpable.

But the anonymous author rises up: "The Jews fastened Christ to the cross not knowing him, according to what our Savior made clear when he said: "Father forgive them, for they know not what they do." (Luke 23:34). The infidels believe they give honor to God by handing the apostles to death: "But the hour comes that those who kill you will think they obey God." (John 16:2). Equally the heretics think they uphold the truth when they persecute Catholics. Yet, whatever he objects, the previously celebrated Habert makes clear in a few words: "The Jews could have known Christ as Lord by miracles and prophecies, according to that, 'If you believed Moses, perhaps you should also believe me, for he wrote of me. (John 5:46)' 'If I did not do works among them ... they would not have sin. (John 15:24)' Heretics and other unbelievers, if they would attend to the notes of true religion, would easily recognize it in the Roman Church."

174.—Still, the anonymous author insists, saying: Ignorance of knowing some natural precept arises from us, or because we do not apply due diligence in a truth that must be sought, or because we do not ask it from God, as is just, the graces that we would know the divine law; because (he says) to the extent that our faith ought to be elevated by divine light to the holy mysteries that must be believed, so our reason ought to be elevated by the same light to hold to the paths observed to lead to God. For this reason the Prophet David prayed: "O Lord, show me your law, and teach me to do your will." Hence, on page 253, he concludes at length: "He cannot be without sin because it is effected by this ignorance against the law of God."

Therefore I respond, since we see so many learned and pious men that are also in the number of saints are related to have been opposed to each other in many questions considering the natural law, perhaps we ought to say both of them sinned and underwent damnation? So Fr. Antoine speaks (*loc. cit. de peccat.*, c. 4) in this matter: "If St. Thomas and St. Bonaventure disagree on many things pertaining to natural law, therefore both erred and still, neither retracted their opinion before they died; therefore, if invincible ignorance of the natural law is not granted in some matter, each ended their days in grave sin, since it would be a grave sin to culpably teach error in regard to divine precepts, and so condemned." And really, it does not escape our notice that St. Thomas defended that the judge ought to condemn someone that is proven to be guilty in law, although the judge knows that he is innocent; but St. Bonaventure denies this. On the other hand, St. Bonaventure upheld that a sinner, unless he immediately confessed to the sin he committed, commits a new sin,[24] and St. Thomas denies that. And St. Antoninus says (p. 1, tit. 3, c. 10, § 10), that nearly six hundred examples of this kind of erudite and holy men, who remained in disagreement on natural precepts could be advanced. The very learned Morinus (part. 3, *exercit.* 5, 9, *de Sacram. Ord.*) teaches the same thing, when he says: "Whoever will attend to the annals of the Church will easily see ecclesiastical authors vacillated in disagreement at some time in a variety of many opinions." Additionally, Nöel Alexander (tom. 3, disp. 16, sect. 2), and Fr. Berti (*Theol. l.* 21. c. 12, n. 5) affirm that many authors, even among the Fathers erred in several slips; "We affirm in individual fathers blemishes are to be found, even in a great many errors." Sixtus of Siena relates about St. John Chrysostom (*Biblioth. sanct.*, lib. 5, annot. 89), "It is related thirdly, that in the aforesaid words of Chrysostom, the assertion is contained

---

[24] Editorial note: St. Bonaventure upholds this opinion on the necessity of immediately confessing mortal sins, but not without a certain limitation (*in 4*, dist. 17, part. 2 art. 2 qu. 2). He says namely, the sinner is held to confess when the opportunity presents itself if he would reasonably think a greater opportunity will not be offered.

that Sarah must be praised and imitated that to save her husband she exposed herself to adultery with barbarians, still with the consent of her husband [Abraham] in her adultery, and even with his persuasion." Hence, it must be concluded that these very Saints, or other ecclesiastical authors were cast down to hell, because of the erroneous opinions they wrote, and did not later emend; or at least it must be concluded, that they at least sinned mortally in these writings; but I do not know if anyone might be found who will dare to assert that.

For that reason it does not avail for it to be said that he who, comes together, labors and prays, certainly would obtain knowledge of the truth in all doubts of the law of nature; accordingly, Fr. Collet opportunely responds (*de act. hum.*, cap. 1, art. 1, sect. 2, concl. 4) that the more excellent lights of the Church hardly neglected study and prayer, nor on that account arrived at the notice of the truth that hey would attain it. "And if any ignorance of the natural law you like could convict, especially through prayer, and still a false consequent when the greater lights of the Church consumed their days and nights in prayer and study, yet they did not obtain the knowledge which they desired." Seeing that, as Fr. Collet adverts to the same thing, of many conclusions of the law of nature, but of ones remote from first principles, not even the fathers and doctors of the Church with all the assistance received from nature and grace could attain the truth in a great many things: "Yet still there are many conclusions originating from first principles, the knowledge of which could not even be held with the grate assistance of nature and grace, since the most keen and pious fathers of the Church were divided on these at the same time."

But he might reply, God is faithful, he promised to hear those praying to him: "Ask and you will receive." If we would demand the light from God under due conditions, he would not fail to answer the request; for that reason, if we do not obtain it, he certainly stood by us and we are in fault. But two kinds of light must be distinguished. On the one hand, the light, or knowledge is natural, or rather more acquired by the strength of nature, whereby we know moral truths of the divine law in regard to what has been commanded and forbidden. On the other hand there is the supernatural light of grace whereby we are illumined, that we might know the strength of divine grace, especially the business of eternal salvation, the means to obtain it, the occasions which can drive us to throw ourselves headlong, and other things of this kind. Moreover, when one sins formally against the law from a defect of the light of this grace, when we have not taken care to ask God for it, there is no doubt that by a negligence of this sort sin is imputed to us, then our gaping is voluntary; for if we would have asked for this light, he certainly would not fail us; for God does not cease to bestow grace upon the one asking so that he would embrace what he knows to be good and avoid what he knows is evil; and this is the light which David asked for when he said: "Give me understanding that I would learn your commands; Teach me to do your will." On the other hand, God neither gave nor promised that he is going to give the light to know all truths which can be known by the natural light; and therefore, when someone materially acts against the law, but invincibly, on account of this natural defect of knowledge, then the error is not imputed to him as a formal sin, since God consents that we shall direct ourselves according to the dictate of conscience, because it is shown to us through reason as if it is right. The Apostle says: "All that is not from faith (that is according to conscience, as Ambrose, Chrysostom, Theodoret and others explain in common) is sin." Therefore, when one acts according to the dictate of his own conscience, he does not sin. St. John also upholds: "If our herd would not rebuke us, we have trust in God." (1 John 3:21). That I might say it in one phrase, God does not condemn except in these actions, in which voluntary malice or voluntary negligence is present; for that reason one who thinks invincibly that he acts rightly, God not only does not punish, but at some time will reward his right intention, even if the work is opposed to his law in itself, "but because this opposition (as Fr. Collet says, related above), is at some time involuntary, that in those matters one who labors with invincible ignorance, so it is not always imputed as a sin, but at sometime to the merit on account of the good end of the agent, who seems to follow right reason, while he also fails in that."

The very severe Fr. Daniel Concina (*Theolog. Christ.*, t. 2, l. 2, *de conscientia*, dissert. 1) equally writes, that although in the argument of the fifth chapter he says a work carried out from an error of conscience is still invincible, wickedness can be good and worthy of merit; just the same, in n. 36, he expressly adheres to our opinion, saying: "For someone can, while he materially exercises an evil, have a great many good actions such as the intention to please God, these goods we say are meritorious, although the act which then is exercised in itself might be materially evil, ... this good intention is stained by no deprave circumstance, because the work that is materially evil, since it was not voluntary, does not avail to redound in acts of malice themselves."

But our anonymous author raises his voice like a trumpet against this and devotes a whole chapter against it (which is 13 in his work) where he tries to prove with great force, when an action is contrary to divine law, a man always sins, even if he acts with a right intention. Look at what he says: "Therefore, there is in the Gospel and in the doctrine of the Fathers the constant axiom, intention and the end communicate goodness or malice to our actions, and makes them good or evil." But a little later he speaks otherwise against himself, and says: "Although the intention might be right, if what is done by its very nature is deprave, or is so by some other peculiar circumstance, or if it is forbidden by divine law, then this notwithstanding a sin is committed by one who does that."

So our adversary thinks, but he does so apart from Fr. Concina whom we praised above, and the common opinion of other doctors, St. Thomas, St. Ambrose, St. Bernard and St. John Chrysostom thought the contrary as we will show. First, St. Thomas proposes a question in 1. 2. q. 18, a. 6: "Whether an act might have the species of good or evil from its end?" And he responds: "It must be said that certain actions are called human inasmuch as they are voluntary, as stated above (quaest. 1, art 1). In a voluntary action there is a twofold action, namely an interior act of the will and the external act: and each of these actions has its object. The end is properly the object of the interior act of the will; while the object of the external act is that on which the act is brought to bear. Therefore, just as the external act takes its species from the object on which it bears, so the interior act of the will takes its species from the end, as from its own proper object. Now, that which is on the part of the will is formal in regard to that which is on the part of the external act: because the will uses the limbs to act as instruments; nor have external actions any measure of morality, save insofar as they are voluntary. Consequently, the species of a human act is considered formally with regard to the end, but materially with regard to the object of the external action." These words of St. Thomas are so clear that they do not need any explanation; for in these he most profitably teaches the human act evades good or evil according to what the end is for which it is done, and as a matter of fact, the human act itself has the reasoning of mortality [*rationem mortalitatis*] in such a thing, that is, as it is good or evil, insofar as it is voluntary. The object of the external act is the matter, exactly as it is in itself, but the object of the interior act of the will is the intention, by which someone acts; for that reason, although the act is materially bad in itself, still, formally it is good when good is the end; nevertheless, this must always be understood when the malic of the material act is invincibly unknown to the agent.

But our adversary asserts in his favor an excessively long sentence from St. Bernard (*de praecept. et disp.* cap. 17), and then he says: "A response of this sort of St. Bernard clearly shows that as a simple eye makes the body luminous, it ought to contain two things, namely a good intention and knowledge of the truth." But I read that St. Bernard gives two doctrines opposed to what our adversary affirms. In the same treatise, St. Bernard says that he that obeys a prelate that "acts meritoriously from right intention even if he were to err materially against the law," and in ch. 18 he has these words: "I said a pious intention alone is worthy of praise, nor should a good will be cheated of what is clearly worthy remuneration in an act that is also not good." St. Ambrose writes (l. 1 *Offic.*, c. 30): "Your attitude imparts its name to your deed." St. John Chrysostom (hom. 19 *in op. imperf.*), writes in a similar fashion: "From a good intention what seems bad is good, because a good intention excuses an evil work."

But one who acts against the law, the author insists, always sins by vincible ignorance, because he does not pray; for if he prayed, the grace would not be lacking for him to know the law. To which I so respond: God does not deny sufficient grace to someone in prayer so that he would avoid formal sin, but he does not always bestow grace that he might avoid a material sin. Fr. Collet (*de act. hum.* cap. 1, art. 1, sect. 2, concl. 4, in fin.) writes: "I concede that he does not lack the grace to formally avoid sin; but I also deny it materially. Moreover, a sin which is committed from invincible ignorance is not a sin except materially, nor does it prevent one from obtaining eternal salvation. Nay more, there are those who believe knowledge of these things is taken away from a man because he prefers that he would not sin on account of a defect of knowledge materially, than that he would formally commit some trespass on the occasion of his knowledge."

Nevertheless, nay more, I do not even scarcely understand what proposition would pertain to our position which they bring against us from the condemned proposition of Alexander VII in regard to a philosophical sin, which holds: "A philosophical, or moral sin, as grave as you like in one who either does not know God or does not think about God in an act, is a grave sin, but it is not an offense against God, nor a mortal sin dissolving the friendship of God, nor is it worthy of eternal punishment." I ask, how does this proposition pertain to our position? Anyone that knows it offends nature, necessarily offends the author of nature also, who is God, even if he would not think of God; but anyone who acts from invincible ignorance of the natural law does not offends God, provided it is only material, or (that I might say it better), he offends in nothing; at any rate the material offense does not have the reasoning of the offense but the matter of the offense would be in the highest degree if a man would embrace what is offensive to God or nature.

Nor would it do our adversary any credit to say in that sense, that just as our faith ought to be elevated by supernatural light that we would believe the revealed mysteries, so also our reason ought to be elevated by the same light, that we would know the business of the law of nature. Now, insofar as it attains to the divine mysteries we willingly concede the point, but to act rightly, although a man were constituted in the darkness, in the penalty of the fall of our first parents alone, even bare natural reason would not suffice, but divine revelation of precepts is also required that one would understand what must be done, and what must be avoided. Then, after a man receives this light of divine revelation to live well and to know all moral truths exactly as they are in themselves, another supernatural light is not necessary; at any rate, God did not promise supernatural graces for this end, but wills that man would use natural reason directed by the revelation made of his precepts; merely that, as was said above, he needs that grace whereby he is illuminated and conformed to embrace that which he knows is good and to flee the evil which he knows must be avoided. St. Thomas cautions in the best manner (1. 2. q. 76, art. 2 ad 2), that a man cannot acquire grace by his own acts, but he can acquire knowledge of these things by his own diligence. "A man can acquire some knowledge by his own acts, but grace is not acquired from our own acts." As a result, if the matter so stands, a man ought not necessarily wait for grace to conquer ignorance of natural precepts; because ignorance of this sort must be conquered by his own diligence, and as often as this diligence is not of such strength that it would guide him to knowledge of the more remote and obscure precepts, the ignorance would be invincible and God would not impute it as sin.

Otherwise, the anonymous author pursues another way to render invincible ignorance of this sort of thing culpable in regard to the law of nature. He says that there are two wounds inflicted upon us and still residing from original sin, namely concupiscence, on account of which the will remains inclined to evil, and ignorance, whereby reason remains clouded; and, moreover, he so argues in Italian, which we here render into Latin: "If concupiscence does not excuse a man that follows the disorders of concupiscence, why should ignorance excuse one that follows the disorders of ignorance?" Then he concludes from that line of argument, that just as the one who acts would sin because of concupiscence, so one who acts would sin on account of ignorance.

But the response is obvious. One following the disorders of concupiscence sins because then he adheres to its malice by his own will, thereupon the concupiscence is voluntary. Yet, it happens differently in invincible ignorance, which is not volitional, and does not please him. It is manifest that there is no sin unless it is voluntary; in that it happens that just as we follow voluntary disorders of concupiscence we sin, so equally we sin volitionally following the disorders of vincible ignorance; still, on the other hand, just as to act according to concupiscence but against our will is not a sin, according to what the Apostle said in Romans 7:19, "The evil which I will not, I do," so also no sin is worked on account of invincible ignorance, when it is not volitional.

Furthermore, the author continues and supposes our ignorance to be culpable, at least on account of the sins we committed earlier, and upholds that to the extent that on account of our sins we are constituted in moral impotence to do the good, so even in moral impotence we are constituted to know the good which must be done and the evil which we must avoid. For that reason, just as impotence does not excuse when we do the evil that we know is evil, so impotence does not excuse when we do not know the evil that we do.

But we respond with Duhamel (l. 2, *de act. hum.* c. 5, *in fin.*). First: the punishment of sin is not evil, which is imputed for his fault when he suffers such a penalty, because although such ignorance would be a penalty for other sins which we committed earlier, nevertheless these sins do not make culpable errors which then we commit from invincible ignorance; because such errors are not volitional with us, nor foreseen. Duhamel writes: "And although these vices arise from sins that were freely committed, and moreover seem voluntary, and for this reason ignorance would be the punishment for sin; hence it does not follow that it is voluntary when evils are going to follow that were not foreseen." We answer additionally, that it is altogether foreign to truth that just as our sins constitute us in moral impotence to do good, so equally they constitute in moral impotence to know natural precepts; because, according to what we prefaced above, that we would do good, grace is required, and anyone that places an obstacle to it would sin; but that precepts would simply be known, grace is not necessary, rather natural reason is sufficient; for that reason, it cannot be called wickedness, that sin places man in moral impotency to know precepts.

But perhaps he will say: Sins blind the ones that sin and snatch away knowledge. I freely agree that sins take that knowledge which wins them over to do the good, away from sinners and removes them from carrying out evil; and that this knowledge were so held, grace is required and it behooves one to pray to obtain it. Without a doubt, St. Augustine speaks on that knowledge against Pelagius (*de Naturâ et Gratiâ*, ch. 17): "he prefers disputing all things rather than to pray, and say 'give me understanding and I will learn your commands.'" Bellarmine, while explaining this text of David (*Comm. in Psalm.* 118:73), "Give me understanding does not mean, give me the force to understand ...; but give me the divine light, whereby my mind shall perfectly learn your commands, (viz.), and persuade it that it is the best thing to fulfill it." Therefore, the Prophet asked for grace to be enlightened and persuade himself, so much as what is the good required to carry out the divine precepts. He also asked that when he prayed: "Instruct me in the way of your justification," that is, as Bellarmine explains (*ibid.*, 118:27, 34), "teach me what is the way of your precepts, how I ought to walk in your law;" namely how I ought to walk according to your precepts. In addition, when he prayed: "Give me understanding and I will thoroughly examine your law," Bellarmine says: "He asks that he could thoroughly consider its advantages." Equally, when he says (Ps. 142:10), "Teach me to do your will;" *i.e.*, teach me, O Lord, to act according to your will, as it was said above, the will of God is that we act according to the dictate of conscience. Therefore, sin deprives the sinner of this knowledge of grace; but not the natural knowledge of precepts, which present themselves to us to be known by merely natural reason, as Habert rightly writes (*de act. hum.* c. 1, §3, p. 17, from St. Thomas), "Sin does not altogether corrupt human nature, otherwise a man would cease to be so through sin."

The author, however, opposes many opinions of St. Augustine, and especially the work *On Grace an Free will* (ch. 3): "But even the ignorance, which is not theirs who refuse to know, but theirs who are, as it were, simply ignorant, does not so far excuse any one as to exempt him from the punishment of eternal fire." The author so writes on this opinion: "St. Augustine hardly contends that someone who committed a crime in ignorance is always guilty, to the extent that one who sins with knowledge of his fault is ... still he adds that this ought not open the asylum to the darkness of ignorance where one might find his excuse in it, because it does not so excuse that he would not be condemned to eternal fire." But I do not know what the author means to infer for the chief point of the matter from this passage of Augustine. If from those words, "from those that are simply ignorant," he means to infer that ignorance does not excuse from eternal damnation, although it is invincible, the second proposition proscribed by Alexander VIII would stand against him, which holds that invincible ignorance of the natural law does not excuse from formal sin. Moreover, Duhamel and Fr. Berti correctly answer this text of Augustine; Duhamel says (*de act. hum.* l. 2, disp. 3, c. 6, n. 6), "This must be understood, simple ignorance does not excuse from sin, for which there is no cause, but removes from that of which it is the cause. For this reason, one who does not know the law of God nor could know it will not perish because he violated a law that he did not know, but on account of the sins which he committed against the law of nature." And by the same reason related in the text of Augustine, Fr. Berti responds (l. 21, c. 10), saying that Augustine wrote because infidels that did not believe in Jesus Christ merit eternal fire "not because they did not believe, for it is not imputed to sin provided they did not will to not know; but because they freely transgressed the law of nature written upon their hearts. Therefore, the mind of Augustine proceeds from the notion that ignorance, namely of those who altogether do not know the true religion, although it excuses them from the sin of unbelief still, it does not from those sins which they know are such against the light of nature. Yet, the Holy Doctor speaks on culpable ignorance, and it is certain from the words which he immediately adds in the text that was cited: "For it was not said without reason: 'Pour out Thy wrath upon the heathen that have not known Thee.'" He cannot not know God except by malice or as it happens by voluntary blindness. St. John Chrysostom writes the same thing in Hom. 27 *on the epistle to the Romans*, n. 3: "The Jews did not know, but this ignorance was not worthy of forgiveness. The Greeks were also ignorant, but they do not have a defense. But after, he immediately added: "For when that which he cannot know, you are ignorant, you will not be guilty of fault." To which that famous doctrine of St. Augustine is conformed (1. 3, *de lib. arb.* c. 19, n. 53): "It is not classified as a sin to be ignorant against your will, but to neglect to seek what you do not know."

Moreover, lest I make this long, and lest I wear out the reader any longer, in all other texts of Augustine with which the Anonymous author objects, we respond with one opinion of the same Saint. In *Retractions*, he seems to think at first glance that one not knowing that he sins still sins, when he voluntarily does what is in itself a sin: "Someone not knowing that he sinned, and suitably refusing can be said to have sinned, although even he, because he acted while he was ignorant, still wished to act so that it could not be without sin in the will." But as Duhamel admirably notices (*loc. cit.* n. 5, in fin.), the same holy Doctor opens his mind, and explains what he meant to say: "Because he willed, he acted; because even if he had not willed, he sinned not knowing the sin which he did. So there is no such thing as a sin without the will, but by the will of the fact, and not the will of sin." He denotes that which, although it might be a material sin, still when the will to sin is lacking, it is only a material sin and not a formal or voluntary sin, as Duhamel says so well: "That namely the fact itself is the matter of sin, not formally, and in the very matter, it is a sin."

It is equally what St. Thomas wrote (*Opusc. de malo*, q. 3, art. 8). "If deformity is not known, say when someone does not know that fornication is a sin, he certainly voluntarily fornicates, but he does not voluntarily sin." Yet, we do not deny (to speak sincerely), that the Angelic doctor denies in another place that one can be invincibly ignorant of fornication; and he rightly denies it, because fornication is forbidden by a proximate precept, and immediately from first principles. Still, the Angelic Doctor, in the citation we most recently advanced, stated the matter as certain and explored, because when someone invincibly ignorant acts even against something considering the law of nature, he would only err materially, but by no means would he sin.

Duhamel gives the same response to the text of St. Jerome, *contra Pelag.*, c. 10, 11, 12, objected to us by the anonymous author, where St. Jerome says against the Pelagians that ignorance does not excuse from sin because it is understood on sin committed materially, but it is otherwise in regard to sin committed formally. And indeed, the Saint speaks on a case of homicide carried out, for which in the old law victims also had to be offered, not withstanding that it happened without fault of the will.

Likewise, the author opposes a certain opinion of St. Bernard (*tract. ad Huon., de quaest.* c. 1, et 4), where he says ignorance is one of the causes of sins which we commit, but which God does not excuse. Nevertheless, it must be noticed on which ignorance St. Bernard discussed; look at what ignorance he is talking about: "Many do not know, or to know carelessly, or learn in idleness, or inquire in madness." But this ignorance arises from the negligence to instruct himself about his obligations, or to inquire the truth, how could such a man ever be able to excuse himself from sin? Nor is it opposed what the Holy Doctor says *de praecept. et dipens.,* c. 14, n. 40: "Therefore, whether you think the evil which you do is perhaps good, or the good which you do evil, both are a sin." Because Fr. Berti Vendrochius (l. 21, c. 14, prop. 2, vers. *Praeterea*), incorrectly gathers from this authority that St. Bernard denies invincible ignorance excuses from sin, for he had written in n. 37: "And he who loves good and unknowingly does evil, certainly the eye of this act is good, because he is pious but not unaffected, because he is blind." And Fr. Berti adds: "Therefore, the eye which is not unaffected and still is not wicked, namely of one not knowing in excusable ignorance."

Look, at length, how those opposing us are opposed to the common consensus of saints Thomas, Bonaventure, Antoninus, Anselm and of other theologians, both of the mild and severe opinion, to deny invincible ignorance of all conclusions even of those that are remote and obscure on matters considering natural law, and they would also utterly overturn the most firm and received axioms of theology, and they have no other purpose than to make the use of every probable opinion illicit.

DUBIUM II.
Whether fear excuses?

175.—"Resp. If one does something that is simply evil
"from fear, he certainly sins; still malice is diminished by
"fear because freedom is diminished. At the same time,
"it often happens that certain precepts do not oblige
"since their observation yields in grave inconvenience to
"someone. Then, if from fear of some inconvenience,
"someone omits such a precept, he does not sin because
"the precept does not bind. This is common opinion."

Thus these cases are resolved:

"1. A natural negative precept, forbidding an intrinsically
"evil matter, does not violate not even on account of
fear."

(And if at the same time it seems lawful to violate a negative
precept, *e.g.* to not steel, not kill, say to defend ones own life,
etc., then it is said the precept does not exist. See l. 3, n. 51).

"2. Grave fear, *e.g.* of death, etc., often does not only
"excuse from a positive precept, both divine and human,
"but at some time even an affirmative natural one, and so
"(as Sanchez says, 1. *Mor.* c. 18), someone is not held
"with danger of life to fully confess, to preserve a despot,
"to fulfill a vow, to succor a neighbor in extreme need.
"(Becanus, t. 2, l. 3, c. 6, Azor, 1, p. l. 2, t. , c. 2, d. 1),
"Laymann (l. "1, t. 4, c. 14. Still, except for the case on
"which we will speak below in book 3, n. 26).

"3. If observation of human law is necessary to preserve
"the common good or avert evil, which is greater than
"one's own life, then that law obliges with danger of life,
"as *e.g.*, if a general commands a soldier to not leave his
"station; likewise, if souls are going to be ruined unless

"a pastor would go to the fields in a time of plague.
"Laymann (cum Salmant., *de leg., c. 2,* punct. 7, n. 127).

"4. Otherwise no human precepts, even ecclesiastical,
"oblige in themselves with danger of life or similar
"inconvenience (Sanch. 1, *mor.* c. 18, as if, for example,
"you are compelled by fear of death to contract a
"marriage with someone having consanguinity in a
"degree forbidden by ecclesiastical law, he could
"contract (in appearance) but he could not consummate
"it, because then the matrimony would be void, he would
"commit fornication, which is intrinsically evil. Sanchez,
"*de matr.* l. 7, d. 5, n. 4).

"5. *Per accidens,* it can happen at some time that a human
"law obliges with danger of life, by reason of another
"precept of the natural law, or of divine concurrence, as,
"for example, if someone would compel another to
"transgress a precept of the Church out of hatred of the
"faith or contempt for religion. (Sanchez, *loc. cit.,* con. p.
"3, t. 2, d. 13, dub. 12; the Salamancans, *ibid.,* n. 130)."

DUBIUM III
Whether impotency of the whole or part would excuse?

176.—"Resp. 1. Since no man is held to do the impossible,
"it is certain that impotency excuses even that for which,
"before the cause one gave with sin, provided that he
"would suffer for it, this is why it is especially uncertain
"here whether someone that cannot fulfill the whole,
"would be held to part."

"Resp. 2. If a precept is such that it can suitably or
"customarily be divided, and were the reason of the
"precept preserved in its part or in the end of precept,
"then someone that cannot keep the whole ought to keep
"the part which he can. On the other hand, if the reason

"of precept is not preserved in a part nor can it be
"suitably or customarily done, then someone that cannot
"keep the whole, *i.e.* it is merely in which morally it is
"thought the whole precept is fulfilled, he is not held to
"a part. All of which must be considered: a) From the
"intention of the legislator; b) from the reason, end and
"matter of the law; c) From the judgment of prudent
"men; d) from common use. (Sanchez, 1 *Mor.* c. 9;
"Laymann, l. 1, t. 4, c. 19."

Thus these cases are resolved:

177.—"1. Someone who cannot read all the hours ought
"to read those which he can; because they are divided
"(Laymann, *loc. cit.,* and Bonacina).

"2. One who cannot fast during lent ought to abstain
"from meat if he can; or someone who cannot on all days
"is held on those which he can. (Laymann, *loc. cit.,* and
"Bonacina).

"3. One who can hear a notable part of Mass (*e.g.* even
"after the consecration), or to say the hours, or can
"suitably do so with another, and usually is bound,
"otherwise he is not. (*Ibid.,* v. *Infra de horis*).

"4. If anyone does not have a Breviary but has
"memorized a few things from the hours, he is not held
"to say them. (*Ibid*).

"5. Someone is obliged to make his *ad limina* visit to
"Rome, and knows he cannot make the journey, he is not
"held to do so because neither the end nor the reason of
"the precept is preserved. (*Ibid.,* and Suarez, Azor,
"Bonacina d. 1. q. 8, p. 1)."

DUBIUM IV
Whether a dispensation would excuse?

178. *Whether a dispensation made for a just cause would excuse? What about when there is no just cause?*

179. *Whether a superior is held to dispense when the cause exists?*

180. *Whether the dispensation of an inferior avails?*

181. *Whether a dispensation made by a superior in bad faith avails when a just cause exists?*

182. *Whether a dispensation could be reckoned valid in doubt?*

183. *Whether someone can dispense himself?*

184. *Whether a dispensation could be extorted by force or fear?*

185. *What if the cause that was related were false?*

186. *See other cases.*

187. *Whether a dispensation must be received strictly? And whether a tacit dispensation could be given?*

188. *On those who cannot dispense in regard the ordinary power.*

189. *Whether the Pope can dispense against divine precepts?*

190. *Whether Bishops can dispense and against what?*

191. *Whether an inferior could dispense against laws of a superior, where the dispensation is not reserved?*

192. *What about in a doubt whether the case needs a dispensation?*

193. *What about delegated power? And whether it continues after the death of the one that conceded it?*

194. *When could regular prelates dispense?*

195. *How many ways would a dispensation cease?*

196. *How it would cease: I. through cessation of the cause.*

197. *How II. through revocation of the dispensation.*

198. *How III. through the renunciation of the one dispensed.*

178.—"Resp. In human law, the dispensation of the law "or of one having equal power, made for a just cause "excuses from the transgression of the precept. This is "common. (Sanchez, Azor, 1. p. l. 5, c. 15; Salas d. 20).

"The reasoning is that the author of his own law can "except anyone. I said: "*For a just cause*, because if he "rashly dispenses without cause, the dispensation "certainly holds, but both the one giving the "dispensation and the one asking for it, sin against the "natural law, dictating that the part ought to be "conformed to its whole unless a just cause would excuse "(Sanch., l. 8, d. 18; Suarez, Fill, n. 438), and certainly (as "Suarez means) mortally; venially, as Pontius says, "quoted by Diana (p. 8, t. 3, r. 8, 9 and 10),"

(The Salamancans hold the same thing, *de leg.* c. 5, punct. 6, § 1, n. 66, with Sanchez, Laymann, Palaus, etc. still with scandal removed, etc. Moreover, using such a common dispensation is not to sin gravely and probably not even lightly, as the Salamancans *ibid.*, §3, n. 76 with Suarez, Palaus, Pontius, etc.).

"whom, if he would doubt whether the cause was just, "could dispense, as Sanchez would have it." (With the "Salamancans n. 75, Tapia, Granadus, Diana, because one "would follow the dispensing power. It would be "otherwise if there would be a doubt as to whether the "cause were present). Against this, Bonacina, says he "sins even if there is a just cause, still he is not held to "dispense except when either a right commands him to "be dispensed from that cause, or it is necessary for the "common or spiritual good of the penitent; or to attend "to the grave damage or public scandal that could "happen without a dispensation. (Diana, p. 8, t. 3, r. 27, "and 29, against Suarez, Sanchez, etc.)

179.—*Quaeritur*, if a cause exists, is the superior held to dispense? Distinguish: if the cause were merely sufficient that the dispensation might be permitted, but not due, a superior can licitly concede it and deny it, or conceded it to one and deny it to another; because although the dispensation may be expedient to the good of the subject, to be sure, observance of the law is expedient to the common good (the Salamancans, *ibid.*, n. 80 with Coninck, Palaus, Bonacina, Sanchez, Suarez, etc.). But if the cause were such that it would effect the dispensation to be due, namely to avoid common loss or a private loss of great moment, or for common advantage, or a great particular (for it is expedient sometimes to dispense even for a particular good, which indirectly redounds to the common good. And therefore St. Thomas, 1. 2. qu. 97, art. 4, teaches that it is suitable to dispense when the otherwise greater good would be impeded to the private individual. Likewise, the Salamancans, *de matrim.*, c. 14, punct. 2, n. 20, with Coninck, Sanchez, and Aversa), then a superior is held to dispense, otherwise he would sin gravely, or lightly according to the matter. Nevertheless, when a dispensation is denied (even unjustly), a subject cannot act against the law; even if such a cause would urge that he extract himself from the law, because if a Bishop would unjustly deny a dispensation from the publishing of the bans before matrimony, it can, provided grave cause would urge it, be contracted without them (the Salamancans, *de matrim.*, cap. 8, punct. 7, n. 92, with Coninck, Sanchez, Palaus, de Soto and others).

180.—I said: "Of the legislator," because a dispensation of "an inferior against the law of a superior without a just "case is invalid, and hence does not excuse from the "transgression of a precept. The reason is, because one "who dispenses in the name of another without cause, "destroys. (Suarez, l. 6, c. 19, Sanch., l. 8, *de matr.* d. 17). "Moreover, an inferior validly and licitly dispenses by "ordinary power for a just cause against the law of a "superior. 1. In regard to light matters, this is which do "not oblige under mortal sin, even if recourse to the "superior would be easy. 2. In regard to those things "which frequently occur, *e.g.* in fasting, celebrating "feasts, etc. (See n. 190, near the end). 3. In regard to "those things which are proper to one community, that "others might not be suitable. 4. When recourse to the "superior is difficult or when there is a necessity and in "danger of death. Dian., p. 8, tr. 3, r. 12, from Granadus, "Salas, Gordonus, and Pal, who adds: 5. If custom would "prescribe that an inferior would dispense, as Dian. (*loc.* "*cit.*, r. 95, 6). When there is a negative doubt whether a "case would need a dispensation. In which case, "according to Palaus, a dispensation is not necessary, "since the presumption favors freedom. (Barb., Dian., p. "5, t. 6, r. 28; p. 4 t. 3, r. 46; p. 8, t. 33, r. 72 and 95). So it "is resolved (See n. 192):

"1. The pope without just cause cannot dispense against "the law of God, nor a Bishop against the law of the "Church. (Sanch., d. 17, n. 3, Suarez, Vasquez).

"2. Dispensation against a vow or oath without just "cause, even made by the Pope, is invalid. (Sanchez, "Suarez, *loc. cit.*)

"3. It is valid if a superior were to think there is a just "cause by error (*In bona fide*, Soto, Laymann, Sanchez, "Azor, with the Salamancans *de leg.* c. 5, punct. 6, §2 n. "71. But the opposite must be held. See *de voto,* l. 4, n.

"251): or (even if he did not think there was just cause "and rashly dispensed), the matter would still be so. "Sanchez, *loc. "cit.*, Azor, Sa, Salas, n. 81."

181.—The question is, if a superior dispenses in bad faith, judging that no cause underlies it, and the cause really exists, would the dispensation avail and could the dispensed use it?

The first opinion says it is valid if it were done by the legislator, but not by an inferior, because the faculty to dispense was given to him only with cause. Palaus, Azor, Covarruvias, quoted by the Salamancans *ibid.*, §3, n. 78.

The second opinion is more probable and common, and it says that when the cause exists, the dispensation would avail and being licitly dispensed he uses it from whatever superior carried it out. The reason is because the validity of the dispensation does not depend upon the recognition of the cause, but on its existence, just as election upon the capacity for a benefice, even if the one elected is unaware of the capacity, from c. *Nihil de electione.*, the Salamancans, *ibid.*, n. 79, with Sanchez, Suarez, Tapia, Basil, Diana, Villalobos Otherwise, still, it must be said if an inferior would dispense in good faith, but without cause, against Busembaum and others, as above; (see book 4, n. 251).

182.—"4. In doubt on the validity of the dispensation, it "is thought valid to the extent that it is presumed in "favor of the act, lest he would perish; Sanchez, etc. "thinks it is probable, with Diana (p. 3, t. 6, r. 9; p. 4, t. 3, "r. 45, 64; p. 8, t. 3, r. 62; the Salamancans *ibid.* punct. 8, "§3 n. 88. See book 4, n. 251).

183.—"5. Having the general power to dispense, he can "also dispense differently directly and immediately. "Sanchez, Diana (p. 8, t. 3, r. 16 against Suarez; the "Salamancans c. "5, punct. 5 n. 60 and 61, with St. "Thomas, Cajetan, "Laymann, Palaus, Bonacina, etc. "Because the jurisdiction is purely voluntary, which he

"can even exercise toward himself. Hence, he can duly
"dispense himself in vows, oaths, fasting, etc.).

184.—"6. A dispensation obtained by force or fear is valid
"(only if the cause were just). Likewise, it is given
"without any words, only the mind. (Turrian., Diana, p.
"8, tr. 3, r. 17, 76; p. 4, t. 4, r. 118).

Quaeritur: Whether a dispensation extorted through fear
would be valid? Resp. That when the cause for the
dispensation exists, the dispensation is always valid,
provided it would not constitute for a superior to dispense
without a mind to dispense. Fear does not abolish volition as
force does. Moreover, the obtaining of such a dispensation
is also licit if fear is justly struck in the prelate; namely, if
the subject threatens to complain to the highest superior, or
that he is going to bring an accusation of some crime. But it
would be illicit if the fear were unjust; and therefore the
dispensation then, can be revoked later at the superior's
pleasure (the Salamancans, *d.* c. 5, punct. 7, n. 82, 83, and 84,
with Sanchez, Palaus, Suarez, Bonacina). But when the
superior compelled by fear only concedes the dispensation
in words, but not in intention, then certainly it is null.
Furthermore, unless it is established that he lacked the
intention, this must not be presumed. The Salamancans, *d.*
n. 82, ex c. *Humanae aures*, 22, quest. 5.

185.—"7. One who obtains a dispensation, for example, in
"a diriment impediment to matrimony, and through
"ignorance, or simplicity, expresses a false cause, it is
"said that he validly contracts matrimony. Pontianus, *de*
"*matrim.*, lib. 8, c. 16, ex c. *Cum inter.*. But Palaus (t. 1, t.
"3, d. 6; p. 16, § 5 *ex. cap. Sup. litteris*, holds the contrary.
"See Dian., p. 8, t. 3, r. 69. See *de matr.* l. 6, n. 1131,
"*Notandum* 2).

Quaeritur: Whether a surreptitious petition or one made
with *obreptitia* will vitiate the dispensation? It is called
surreptitious when the truth is left unsaid: *obreptitia* when

a lie is added to it. *Resp.* The rule is that then the dispensation will be null, when the truth is concealed which ought to be necessarily expressed in the style of the Curia, or is alleged to be false, because he should be silent *de jure* (the Salamancans *de matr.* c. 14, punct. 3, n. 33; with Sanchez, Palaus, Coninck, Suarez, etc.). Another rule is, if one keeps silent about the truth or an impulsive case is falsely expressed, the dispensation is valid, but it will be otherwise if the cause were the motive so that the superior would hardly dispense the matter without it. The Salamancans *ibid.*, n. 55.

What if a great many cases were alleged, of which some were false, and some were true? Resp. Because one may always be true, which would be sufficient to dispense, the dispensation will be valid. The Salamancans *de matr. ibid.* num. 36, with Basil, Sanchez, Palaus, Suarez. But what about in a doubt as to whether the cause was falsely alleged were the motive, or impulsive? Then the dispensation must be considered valid, since in doubt the law favors the validity of the act, from l. *Quoties. ff. de rebus dubiis.* So the Salamancans *ibid.*, n. 37, with Dicastillus, Basil., Sanchez, Palaus, etc.

186.—"8. A subject seeking a dispensation in good faith, "after he has brought the reasons to the superior, can be "secure in the obtaining of the dispensation. See "Laymann, l. 1, t. 4, c. 22; (the Salamancans *de leg.* punct. "6, §2, n. 71, and 76 say the same thing, with St. "Thomas, Sanchez and Bonacina).

"9. He sins, who induces someone to dispense without "cause, or by alleging a false cause. Navarre, Sanchez, l. "8, *de matr.* d. 18, n. 8, Fill. t. 10, n. 314; Salas, disp. 20, s. "6, n. 58, who adds that it is true even if the one "dispensing is excused on account of good faith.

"10. A dispensation can be obtained not only for the "ignorant, but even for the unwilling, when necessity

"demands it. Sanch., Beja, contra Suarez. See Diana, p. 8,
"t. 3, r. 86 and 87. Still that does not hold place in those
"which are obtained from the Roman Poenitentiary;
"unless it is obtained for persons joined or having
"kinship within the fourth degree, or at least from a
"confessor. Marcus Leo *in praxi*, p. 1, s. 14 (the
"Salamancans *de matr.* c. 14, punct. 3, n. 38, ex. c. *Si motu*
"*proprio, de praeben.* in. 6, *A principali tamen, opus est ut*
"*dispensatio acceptetur,* as Sanchez, etc.).

"One might ask if the cause of the dispensation ceased
"would the dispensation itself also cease?

"*Resp.* the following rules will serve for this.

"1. If only the impulsive, or less principle cause would
"cease, the dispensation remains.

"2. Even if the part of the motive cause would cease, or
"the principal, the dispensation remains. See Dian. pag.
"8, tom. 3, r. 62.

"3. If something was dispensed earlier by the faculty
"consigned to dispense, and the principal cause would
"altogether cease, there is no dispensation.

"4. If, because a dispensation were rendered to an
"irrevocable act, were the whole cause to cease, therefore
"the dispensation does not cease, nor does it lose force;
"for example, it was dispensed in an impediment of
"consanguinity on account of the poverty of the woman,
"even if, after contracting marriage, she were to obtain
"riches, it is not made void. The same is, if one will have
"obtained a benefice by a dispensation, and later the
"cause would cease on account of which it was
"dispensed.

"5. If, after a dispensation was made, the final cause
"would altogether cease, and the act can easily be
"revoked, *e.g.* it was dispensed against a vow of chastity
"on account of violent temptations, which later ceased,

"would the vow be revived? Or against a precept to
"recite the breviary, to fast, etc., on account of weakness,
"and later he regains strength, would he be held to
"recite the office, fast, etc.? Sanchez, Amicus, Portel,
"Bonacina, etc. affirm it, because otherwise it would not
"be just. Still the negative opinion is probable, and in
"practice Diana thinks it is safe (p. 8, t. 3, r. 24, from
"Salas., Granadus, etc.), if indeed the dispensation were
"absolved, because the obligation of the law once extinct
"does not revive, and was destroyed, it is not reproduced
"except by the one who can produce it. (See Suarez, *de*
"*leg.*, c. 22; Laymann, Praepos., etc. who rightly concedes
"it when it is not on a separate and successive matter;
"otherwise they deny it. For that reason, after supposing
"the probability of the negative opinion, Granadus,
"Diana, etc., resolve the following cases (in which still,
"others think the contrary is better. See n. 196):

"1. When a dispensation is made to eat meat on account
"of illness, he can eat it although he is altogether well.

"2. When on account of weakness someone is dispensed
"against a vow of religion, and later he recovers, he is
"not held to it. Diana, p. 6, t. 7, r. 45.

"3. When in some place on account of the weakness of
"the eyes someone was dispensed from the burden of
"reciting the Breviary, even if he were to recover, he is
"not held to pray it.

187.—Then it must be noted that the dispensation, when
it is odious, must be strictly received, c. 1, § 1, *de filiis presb.,*
in 6. On the other hand, the power to dispense, when it is
favorable, is taken up broadly (Sanchez, Granadus, Martin.,
quoted by the Salamancans *de leg.* c. 5, punct. 4, § 3, n. 10.

Moreover, a tacit dispensation can rightly be given
which is gathered from conjectures, that if the prelate knows
that someone is excommunicated, and were to confer a
benefice on him, then he tacitly dispenses. Presumption of

the present will of the superior is required for this, or of the preceding one for the act. For the presumption is not on the future, *e.g.* if he knew, he would dispense. Only after the license has been presumed is it admitted about the future, but not the dispensation, which is a wound of the law. (See the Salamancans, *de leg. ibid.*, ex. n. 11 with Suarez, Laymann, Palaus, Sanchez).

Quaeritur: Whether the superior, seeing the subject act against the law, and is silent when he could easily correct him, is thought to dispense? The Salamancans (*de leg. ibid.* n. 15), Tapias, Sanchez, Palaus and Suarez uphold that. Because then it must not be presumed that the superior committed a crime, who otherwise from his office, and to avoid damage, is held to speak. It must be said otherwise if a superior could not correct without inconvenience. *The Salamancans, ibid., n. 17.*

On those who can possess.

188.—Some power to dispense is ordinary, while some is delegated. The Supreme Pontiff can, by ordinary power, dispense against any canon laws, even those ratified by the apostles, and by particular prelates of Churches, such as lenten fasting, observation of feasts on Sundays, etc. The Salamancans, *ibid.*, punct. 4, §1, n. 30, with St. Thomas and the common opinion. Still, not against those laws handed down by the apostles which they received from Christ the Lord, as the principal author, such as laws in regard to the form and mater of the sacraments, the offering of the Sacrifice of Mass, etc.

189.—Moreover, can the Pope dispense against some divine precepts?

The first opinion affirms it from power delegated by God, when dispensation is expedient. Sanchez, Cano, and

Bonacina, quoted by the Salamancans *de leg., ibid.*, punct. 3, n. 25, who call this sufficiently probable.

The second, which the Salamancans (*ibid.*, n. 26), St. Thomas, Palaus, Suarez, etc. think is more probable, denies this, because in no place is this concession made to the Pope by God to be found. The opposing side objects, why can the ordinary minister of confirmation dispense so that a simple priest can confer it? Resp. Because by divine law the Bishop is the ordinary minister for it, but not the necessary minister (the Salamancans *ibid.* n. 27). See what is going to be said in book 6, *de matrimonio*, n. 1119, below.

Moreover, it is certain that the Pope and prelates can dispense against vows when these are made toward God. St. Th. 2. 2. q. 88, art. 12. See the Salamancans *de voto*, tract. 17, c. 3, punct. 10, n. 84.

190.—The Bishop can dispense by ordinary power against all statutes whether episcopal or imposed by a diocesan Synod, independently of the chapter and clergy, as we said above.

And the same is true of a chapter while the see is vacant. Still, this cannot be a Vicar General unless it is expressly conceded by the Bishop.[25] The Salamancans *de leg.*, c. 5, punct. 4, § 1, n. 31 and 32. The bishops can also dispense in laws of a provincial council in their dioceses; provided they were not specially reserved to the council. For this is expedient to good rule. The Salamancans, *ibid.* n. 33, with Sanchez, Suarez, Bonacina, Palaus, etc.

It must be noted that the legislator could not dispense against his own law if the law passed over into a contract, that if one were to say: "Let them rejoice, having immunity

---

[25] "Because in a general commission the faculty to dispense is not included, unless it is specially conceded." From *Homo Apostolicus*, tr. 2, c. 6, n. 57. –Editorial note to the Mechlin edition.

in such a place," etc. (See the Salamancans ib., n. 35). Moreover, an inferior can dispense in the law of a superior, if in the law a dispensation is generally permitted, *e.g.* if it were said: "Until it is dispensed." The Salamancans, *ibid.*, § 2, n. 37, with Cajetan, Bonacina, Suarez, Palaus, etc.

Bishops can also dispense in matters which commonly come about in fasting, in the eating of foods, the observation of feasts, the recitation of the office, vows not reserved. The Salamancans, *ibid.*, n. 38, with Palaus, Basil., Bonacina, de Soto, Suarez, etc. with Busembaum.

Likewise, in laws imposed by the Pope for that particular diocese, in which it seems the faculty to dispense has been left to its prelate.

Likewise, a Bishop can dispense against common pontifical laws, for example against impediments of matrimony, in irregularities, in reserved vows, and similar things, when it is not easy to approach the Pope, and there is danger in delay, because this is expedient to the common good. The Salamancans, *loc. cit.*, with Sanchez, Busembaum, Palaus, Tapia, Granadus, Salas, etc. And even if there might be easy recourse to someone holding the faculty to dispense by a privilege of the Pope. The Salamancans *ibid.*, in fin., with Tapia, and Martin. *de cens.* c. 2, punct. 5, n. 65. Parish priests can also dispense with their sheep in fasting, and the observation of feasts where they do not have easy recourse to the Bishop. Suarez, and Tapias. Nay more, from custom, even if recourse to the Bishop might be easy, parish priests can always dispense against these two precepts, as Sanchez, Granadus, and Sylvius witness, quoted by the Salamancans *de leg.*, c. 5, punct. 4, § 2, n. 40. See book 4, n. 288.

And in all these things Bishops are said to dispense by ordinary right, since such a faculty suits them by the power of their own office, to which it is perpetually connected. The Salamancans *loc. cit.*, with Suarez, Palaus, Basil., etc. And therefore, they can rightly delegate it to someone, as is certain. See n. 193 with the Salamancans, *de voto*, c. 3, punct. 10, n. 83.

191.—*Quaeritur* 1) Whether apart from the aforesaid cases a Bishop can dispesne against the laws of a superior, in which dispensation is not reserved?

The first opinion affirms it; because of this very thing, that the superior does not reserve it, it seems he concedes it: otherwise to what would the reservation be subject to? Soto, in 4, d. 27, q. 1, art. 4, §*At quo*, Covarruvias, in c. *Alma mater* 1. §7, n. 8. And Palaus (*de leg.* tr. 3, d. 6, p. 4, n. 7) and Bonacina (in the same tit., d. 1, q. 2, p. 1 n. 27) while they call the opposite opinion more probable; but St. Antoninus expressly teaches it and calls it common (p. 1, tit. 17, c. *und.* §20), saying: "Moreover, Bishops can dispense according to the common opinion of the doctors, in those matters which are not forbidden to them by right." And the Gloss holds the same thing also, in c. *Nuper, de sent. excomm.* from whcih canon the aforesaid authors prove this opinion; since there, what was asked by a certain Bishop was whether he could absolve someone from an excommunication imposed *a jure*? The Pope responded in the affirmative, so saying: "Because the author of the canon did not specially retain the absolution to himself, because of this very thing it seems the faculty was conceded for others to relax it." And there the Gloss adds, in verb. *Retinuit*, "And this is the argument, Bishops can dispense where a dispensation has not been specially restrained, and it seems conceded that it is not a forbidden form *l. Necnon, ff. Ex quib. caus. maj.*, etc."

This first opinion I once thought probable, but after considering the matter better I think the second opposed opinion must altogether be upheld, which Suarez (t. 5, in 3, p. d. 7, sect. 4), Bonacina (*de leg.* d. 1, q. 1, p. 1, n. 17), Castropalaus (*loc. cit.*) n. 8; the Salamancans (*de leg.* c. 5, punct. 5, § 2, n. 45), with Pontius and Salas; likewise Benedict XIV *de Synod.* l. 7, c. 30. St. Thomas also favors this opinion (1. 2. q. 97, art. 4, a 3) where he says: "No one can dispense against a human public law except he by whom the law has its authority, or he to whom it was consigned." The reason is, because an inferior can do nothing against the law of a superior, as expressed in *Clem. 2 de elect.*, where it is said: "Law of a superior through an inferior cannot be abolished." Nor, altogether, does the cited text conclude in cap. *nuper* for the first opinion; for the faculty to absolve from censures differs greatly from the faculty to dispense against canon laws, exactly as Suarez wisely writes. It is true, laws, in which censures are imposed, are also laws, but it is common to all, and certain from received custom, that censures are not reserved, especially excommunications, could well be absolved by the Bishops, and by parish priests, and still even by an approved confessor; as Suarez proves, *loc. cit.*, n. 9, with Soto, Navarre, and others. For this reason, in this reason well urges, conveyed with the text, namely that when a legislator does not reserve for himself absolution from a censure, it seems he offers the faculty to others to absolve it. But in regard to dispensation against pontifical laws, just the same this received custom is commonly present, that they are conceded by the Bishops always and are not expressly reserved to the Pope; but in regard to these a general and certain axiom proceeds, which arises from the nature of the matter itself, because an inferior cannot dispense against the laws of a superior exactly as it is held in the example expressed in another canon, namely in *cap. Dilectus de temp. ord.*, where it is said that in regard to laws of ordinations, a Bishop cannot dispense, therefore, without a doubt, because it was not conceded to the Bishops: "Since a dispensation of this sort is not permitted to him by the canon," are the words of the text. And not that there it is not said, "when it is not forbidden," but "since it is hardly permitted." Nor was some prohibition present upon the bishops to dispense in such a matter, but only that such a dispensation was never permitted to them; from which the Gloss rightly infers the argument: "Because the Bishop cannot dispense, except in cases conceded to them by law." Nor is it valid to say that the Bishops have jurisdiction immediately from God, according to the opinion of Nöel Alexander, the Continuator of Tourternely, de Soto, Vasquez, Victoria, and others; and therefore, they can obtain a dispensation where that has not been especially forbidden. For the response is made that although the aforesaid opinion might be probable, nevertheless, no man denies such jurisdiction is always subordinate to the Pope. Besides, our opponent argues the first opinion, because if the reason of those favoring it would avail, not only Bishops but even parish priests could dispense against laws of the Pope in the same way, while also it would be permitted to parish priests to absolve from censure that are not reserved, as the text says in *cap. Nuper*, related above, saying: "From his Bishop, or from his own priest he could obtain the benefit of absolution." But who will dare to say this? Moreover, in regard to the axiom admitted by many doctors, as is related in book 6, n. 980, vers. *Sed dubitatur*, namely that whatever the Pope can do in the whole Church, a Bishop can do in his whole diocese unless it is specially forbidden to him, as Suarez says (*loc. cit.*, n. 5) must either not be admitted, or must merely be admitted in those matters which consider the common direction of souls and which are morally necessary. To this order, however, by no means does it pertain to dispensation of canonical laws. Still, this does not exclude, as Bonacina writes (*loc. cit.*, above), that Bishops could dispense in those cases which frequently occur and often require dispensation; or (he says) when some grave necessity urges, or grave utility, and then he cannot suitably go to the Apostolic See, according to what will be said in the Appendix on Privileges, num. 40.

192.—*Quaeritur:* 2) what in a doubt, whether the case needs a dispensation? *Resp.* Whether the doubt were positive or negative, a subject can use his freedom. Still, it is more prudent then to go to a prelate who will declare or dispense; since in such a doubt an inferior prelate can rightly dispense, without the concession of the legislator. So Palaus, n. 3, d. 6, p. 5, n. 10. Laymann, c. 2, n. 4 and the Salamancans, *de leg.,* c. 5, punct. 5, §2, n. 45, with Sa and Diana. Suarez and Sanchez say the same thing about a doubt in regard to reserved vows. The same thing in a doubt as to whether a sufficient cause is present to dispense. The Salamancans, *ibid.* n. 46, with Cajetan, Granadus, and Sylv. And Croix asserts (l. 1, n. 804) that which Sanchez, Gob., and Tappia hold, because the power to dispense must be interpreted broadly, namely if it was given, it is not by the mode of commission, but of grace (as will be said below in n. 194); and then the one dispensing is not obliged to examine the sufficiency of the cause more fully. Moreover, the authors note (Palaus, tr. 3, d. 6, p. 7, nu. 12, with Cov., Sanch., Bas., etc.) that the power, which inferior prelates have to dispense against the laws of a superior by reason of office, inasmuch as the cases frequently occur, ought to be rather more called ordinary than delegated.

193.—In regard to delegated power to dispense, it must be noted that anyone having ordinary power can delegate it, and then, if delegation is by that mode of commission for a certain case, it expires by the death of the one conceding it, if the matter were still whole; But if through the mode of grace, then it does not expire; *ex regul. 16 juris* in 6. Equally, any inferior who can lawfully dispense against the laws of a superior (as Bishops against fasting, vows, etc. as we said above in n. 190), he can also delegate the power to dispense; it is not limited in this mode. (See the Salamancans *ibid.,* § 3, n. 51). Moreover, one cannot subdelegate unless he were delegated by the prince, or by the Pope, as it is found in *cap.*

fin. §1 *de offic. et pot. deleg.* Or, unless it were delegated by a lower ordinary to the sum of all causes, from *Leg.* 1 §. *An ab eo ff. quis., et a quo.* Or, unless the faculty to subdelegate were conceded. But on these, carefully observe what will be said on the Sacrament of Penance in book 6, n. 566, vers. *Generaliter.*

194.—Note, that regular prelates could not dispense against a rule unless it were conceded to them *by privilege*, or *by law.* By reason of privilege which of itself is connected to the office of the prelate, prelates can also dispense inferiors: 1. In light matters which are commanded *sub levi*; 2. In frequent matters; 3. In proper statutes, namely those which are proper to that convent (Peyrin., tom. 2, q. 1, p. 5, and Palaus d. p. 7, with others).

Furthermore, by reason of the faculty conceded to them by law, a prelate cannot dispense against essential vows, from *c. Cum ad monast., de stat. monach.* Yet, against other rules there can rightly be a dispensation in a particular case unless it were expressly interdicted (so Peyrin., with Rod., Angel., Sylv., Torquemada, and Miranda think). For prelates have such a faculty by law, as the Gloss says in *c. Monachum, caus.* 20, q. 4. And the reason is that when human law cannot provide for all cases, it is expedient that the rectors provide in particular cases; otherwise the common good would not sufficiently be provided for. And therefore, from St. Thomas, (1. 2. qu. 97, art. 4 *in corp.*) any rector has the power to dispense against human law for a just cause. But notice what was said in n. 191. Is a subject held to obey a prelate commanding something against a rule? *Resp.* No, if it is certain the matter commanded is against the rule and it will be constituted that the prelate cannot dispense against it, or is not lead from a just cause, as Peryin. d. l.; Sanch., in *Dec.* l. 6, c. 3, n. 8; the Salamancans *de stat. rel.* c. 6, punct. 7, n. 72. Yet in the same place, punct. 6, n. 66 and 67, the latter say a prelate commanding something that is probably licit, or which is not certainly unjust, justly commands; otherwise there would be great confusion if prelates could not command, even if it is evidently just. See what was said in n. 31.

Should the delegated faculty to dispense be interpreted broadly or strictly? *Resp*: Broadly, if it were conceded through the mode of grace, as above, but strictly if through the mode of commission for a certain case. Laymann, tr. 4, c. 22, n. 6, Sanch., *de matr. lib.* 8, disp. 2, n. 1 et 6, and the Salamancans, *de leg. cap.* 5, punc.t 4, § 3, n. 53 with Tapia, Basil., etc. That very dispensation, when it is odious, is always to be taken up strictly, unless the dispensation were due: or if it were from the prince *motu proprio*, or were inserted in the body of law either after some time if it were not conceded to the community, or to the common good. In these cases, it must be received broadly. The Salamancans *ibid.*, n. 54, with Tapia.

195.— Moreover, it is asked, how manifold are the ways a dispensation could cease? For this purpose it must be prefaced that if a dispensation already bestowed its effect, or if some substitution of a burden were joined to the dispensation, then also, when the cause ceases, the dispensation would not cease. See the Salamancans, *de leg.*, c. 5, punct. 8, n. 86, and 87.

It must also be noted in regard to the causes of the dispensations, that some causes in themselves would excuse from a precept, *e.g.* fasting, the divine office, etc. And these do not need a dispensation if they are certain or at least probably just. But others suffice for a dispensation but need it; a sufficing cause is the dignity of the one asking or of the superior, that he would show himself to be kind: and indeed the common or private advantage and similar things. See the Salamancans *ibid.*, punct. 6, §3, n. 73, and 74. Moreover, in matrimonial dispensations of impediments it suffices for the cause the payment of money in support of the Church, as is the practice. The Salamancans, *ibid.* §2. n. 72, in fin., with a common consensus.

196.—Dispensation can cease in three modes: I. By *cessation of the cause*; II. by *revocation of the one giving the dispensation*; III. by *renunciation of the one dispensed.*

And I. by *cessation of the cause*, if the motive cause would cease, so does the whole thing. But is it otherwise? If the impulsive cause were to cease, or the motive cause but not totally, for if something of it would endure, the dispensation would still endure. Busembaum, with the Salamancans. But what if there were a doubt as to whether it had ceased totally? It favors the dispensation, which is to be followed. The Salamancans *ibid.*, punct. 8, § 1. n. 88. See book 6, n. 1133.

But the question is, whether when the cause totally ceases for certain, does the dispensation continue?

The first opinion affirms, because the validity of the dispensation depends upon the will of the superior, who is presumed to refuse to dispense except for the duration of the time in which the cause would endure. Sanchez, *de matrim.* l. 8, d. 30, n. 15; Bonacina, *de leg.* d. 1, q. 2, p. 10, §1, n. 5, and Dicastillus, Coninck, Hurt., and Trullenchus, with the Salamancans *ibid.* n. 89.

The second opinion denies it. The reason is because the obligation of law was already taken away by the dispensation, it does not return unless it is again imposed by the legislator. Palaus, *de matr.* l. 8, c. 20, n. 3; Suarez, *de leg.*, l. 6, c. 20, n. 15, and book 8, c. 30; Palaus, *de priv.* d. 4, p. 15, n. 7; Laymann, tr. 4, c. 22, n. 15, and the Salamancans, *ibid.* n. 90, with Perez, Salas, Sa, Ang., Sylv., Tapia, etc. And Sanchez, Dicastillus, and Trull call it more probable. And it is proven from *reg.* 73, *de Reg. jur.* in 6, "The fact ought not be legitimately retracted, although the causes would come about after, from which it could not begin. It must be said otherwise if the dispensation were not conceded absolutely, but under an express or tacit condition, if the cause would endure. Each opinion seems probable enough.

Still, a greater difficulty follows on its heels; is there any time a dispensation were to be thought conceded absolutely, and when under that tacit condition, would the cause would endure? *Resp.* That if the cause is judged to be perpetual, then the dispensation would be thought to be given absolutely, even if later the cause would cease *per accidens*. Hence, the Salamancans (*ibid.*, n. 91) say that if someone would obtain a dispensation from an office, or abstinence from meat or sickness, which is considered perpetual, then even if he should recover his health, he can use the dispensation. But I can scarcely agree with this, because in those cases, I think the dispensation must altogether be thought to have been given under a condition. Moreover, the agreement with the Salamancans, *ibid.*, n. 92, that an irregular who obtained a dispensation on account of the poverty of parents, on account of the poverty of ministers, or on account of uprightness of morals, can rightly use that, even if later in that case these causes would cease. Moreover, it is otherwise if the cause is judged to endure only for a time; hence if someone obtains a dispensation from fasting on account of illness, which is not judged to be going to remain perpetually, when the cause ceases, the dispensation would cease.

But when the dispensation is absolutely conceded, it does not cease by one act; for example, someone obtained a dispensation against a vow of chastity to contract marriage, after the spouse dies the dispensation endures, unless it were conceded for a special case, viz. to marry a virgin that he had violated; and so for similar matters. The Salamancans *ibid.*, ex n. 91, even to 94; Bonacina, Laymann, Sanchez, Basil., and others cited above.

197.—II. A dispensation can cease by a revocation of the one that gave the dispensation. And certainly, when the cause ceases, or another new contrary matter intervenes, the superior can recall the dispensation, nay more he is held to do so if the motive cause ceases altogether. Still, he will sin (but only venially), revoking it without cause, although the revocation shall be valid. Bonacina, d. 1, q. 2, p. 7, § 2, n. 2, and the Salamancans, c. 5, punct. 8, § 2, n. 97 with Tapia.

Even an inferior prelate, who can concede a dispensation or ordinary law, or from the commission of the legislator, can for a just cause revoke the dispensation; still, without cause, the revocation will be null: Bonacina, *loc. cit.*, Sanchez, lib. 8, de *matrimon.*, d. 33, n. 14, and the Salamancans, *ibid.*, n. 99, with Salas, Tapia, etc.

Here it must be noted, that the dispensation, which is conceded absolutely, would not cease with the death of the one that gives the dispensation, whoever he is, whether supreme or inferior; since the dispensation is a grace, and grace does not expire with the death of the one conceding it. Except, if a superior will have dispensed, *as long as it will have pleased him*, or *at his own judgment*; then it would cease with his death, it the matter were still integral; for example, if a confessor had not yet begun to hear a confession. But if a dispensation were conceded, *until it will be revoked*, then it does not expire with the death of the one conceding it; the same if it were conceded with the death of the Pope, or Bishop. See the Salamancans, *ibid.*, n. 96.

198.—A dispensation ceases by the renunciation of the one dispensed; because he can rightly act when the effect of the dispensation has not yet followed, unless the renunciation would redound to the damage of another, or of a community, in whose favor the dispensation would extend; or unless the prelate were to command a subject to use the dispensation conceded for a just cause. The Salamancans, *ibid.*, § 3, n. 100, with Cajetan and Tapia.

Therefore, the dispensed can expressly and even tacitly renounce the dispensation; and after the renunciation has been carried out, he can no longer use it. Moreover, a renunciation is understood to have been carried out, when it is received by a superior, otherwise the dispensation endures. The Salamancans, *ibid.*, n. 101, with Suarez, Tapia, Bonacina, etc.

Moreover, when is a tacit renunciation made? Some say, when the dispensed does not use it for ten years, when he could have used it, as Maritn says. Others, (Sanchez and Bordon), when the dispensed places a contrary act, say if a dispensation had been obtained to contract with one woman, then he seeks to contract with another; but through these signs in no manner is a renunciation thought to have been made, and the Salamancans (d. c. 5, n. 102), with Suarez and Tapia say it still holds. Hence they say, that the one dispensed to contract marriage with one woman, can rightly use that dispensation even to contract with another woman, provided the first died; or after he discharged a vow of chastity, but only obtained the dispensation of the vow later. Next, one who had dispensation for fasting or the divine office can use it, even if he will later keep the office and fasting. The Salamancans, *ibid.*, n. 103. Here, it is suitable to add something I. on the cessation of law; II. on the interpretation of law; III. On *epikeja*.

I. *On the cessation of law*

199.—Note that a law of some particular place is never abrogated through the general law unless it were expressly said: "Not withstanding each particular law." The Salamancans, c. 4, punct. 2, § 1, n. 14, with Sanchez, Palaus, Suarez, Bonacina, etc.

But here it must be noted the question is great among the doctors, whether a law would cease when the adequate end of the law ceases? The adequate end is that which is the total end of the law: for if the law were to have many ends, the adequate end is constituted from all of them. With this posited, it is certain that when the adequate end of the law ceases, or the total of the law in common, the law would cease; just as if you had vowed never to enter such a house on account of the danger of fornication, when the danger ceases, the vow would also cease. The reason is because when a law is useless, it loses the power to oblige. So St. Thomas argues (1. 2., qu. 103, a. 4, ad. 3, *in fine*, and the Salamancans, *de leg.*, c. 4, n. 3, with the common opinion. But then would a declaration of the legislator be expected, or a contrary custom? Some affirm, but all others deny it with the Salamancans, *ibid.*, n. 4. For, it suffices that it be established for me in particular, or at least that it be probable (as the Salamancans, *ibid.*, with Palaus, and Granadus), that the adequate end of the law ceases in common.

The question presses as to whether the law would cease when the adequate end ceases in a particular case?

The first, more probable opinion, says no, if it only ceases privately, viz. if the law then would be rendered useless: for if it would cease in a contrary fashion, when the matter of the law ere rendered in that case harmful, or very difficult, then all assert the law does not oblige. The reasoning of the aforesaid first opinion is that, although the end of damage would cease in a particular case, still the end of danger in common would not; and therefore, then the adequate end would not cease. The Salamancans, *de leg.*, d. c. 4. n. 6, and 7, with St. Thomas, 2. 2. qu. 154, art. 2, and de Soto, Suarez, Palaus and the more common opinion.

But *the second opinion* (which Cajetan, de Soto, *opusc.* t. 1, tr. 12, q. 2, Silvius, verb. *Lex*, q. 8, and 9, Angel., *ibid.*, n. 4, cas. 7, and likewise, Valentia, Tiraq, Hurt., Cardenas, quoted by Croix, lib. 1, n. 867, Granadus, Henriquez, Castr., and Diana, quoted by the Salamancans, who, *loc. cit.*, n. 5, say this opinion cannot be denied to be sufficiently probable, just as Viva (*de leg.*, q. 6, art. 5, n. 5), calls it, with Panormitanus, Ledesma, Sa, etc., holds that when the adequate end ceases, even privately in a particular case, the obligation of the law ceases. Because, as they say, in each case when the end of the law ceases, the law also ceases; and just as when the end of the law ceases in common for one time, the law ceases, although it may not cease for another; so when it ceases for one particular case, the law would cease for that, although it would not cease in common. So they say it happens even in natural laws, for fraternal correction does not oblige where no fruit is hoped for. Tamburinius (in d., lib. 2, c. 1, § 7, n. 38), with Abbat., Navarre, Com., etc. also hold the same thing. Because (as Tamburinius says), just as when the end ceases universally, the law ceases universally, when in each case the law is equally rendered useless, the end of the law ceases. Fornication is always bad by the law of nature, although in some case the danger of bad education of children would cease. The reason is because in fornication the danger of grate hallucination is always present, nay more, in that beyond the danger of bad education, are other damages; viz. the stupefaction of the mind, subjection of reason to the senses, etc. And so, there, the adequate end can never cease, not even in particular. See Viva, *super prop. 48 Innoc. XI.* And therefore, the authority of St. Thomas to the contrary does not stand in the way, adduced by the Salamancans; for the Holy Doctor only speaks there on fornication which is certain among all. Still, these not withstanding, the first opinion pleases me more, to the extent that it is commonly spoken of, the danger of revery nearly never ceases in particular. But if at some time a case would happen, which someone altogether certain and secure would be away from all danger of revery, then I would not dare to disprove the second opinion; but the cases where this could come about are very rare.

Moreover, would it be probable that forbidden books could be read when the danger and scandal ceases? Felin., Abb., Masc., Decian., say yes on account of the same reasoning, and Laymann inclines toward this (l. 2, cap. 14, n. 5). But it must be denied with Palaus, *de fide*, d. 2, who cites Toledo, Suarez, Sanchez, etc. as well as Tamburinius, who say that in this the danger does not altogether cease, or that the end of the prohibition would not altogether cease, nor even in particular, since the end of the prohibition would be not only that the damage to consciences would be avoided from the reading of bad books, but also that obedience to the Church would be preserved in a matter so dangerous; and lest the occasion were given to heretics or bad writers of demanding their works; therefore, Tamburinius says rightly, the door must in no way be opened with impunity to reading books of this sort, even if someone thinks that there is no danger in it for himself.

II. *On the Interpretation of the law.*

200.—One interpretation is authentic, another usual, and another doctrinal. An *authentic* interpretation can be made either by the legislator himself, or his successor, or a superior. *Usual* is that which is so received from use. *Doctrinal*, however, is a certain declaration of the mind of the legislator, which can be made by any doctor.

Here it is uncertain about declarations, which are made by the Pope, or by a prince on some law; would they need promulgation that they would oblige? In this it is necessary to distinguish declarations *purely such* from others which are *not purely such*, but rather are mere interpretations. Declarations that are *purely such*, since some sense is explained by those, who clearly from the beginning were imbued in the law, for example, if there were a doubt as to whether by the word "of the son" only the legitimate were understood, or also the illegitimate, and the legislator declares that even the illegitimate are to be understood, then which sense was clearly conceived in the law becomes true. Moreover, interpretation, or declaration that is *not purely such* is that, whose sense is not clearly conceived in the law, but in regard to it there are various opinions and it is only deduced from arguments. For example, that under the name of "father" even a grandfather may be understood, or that under the name of death even a civil death, just as a perpetual prison is, or a similar thing, by having recourse to a certain improper signification.

With these posited, we say with Suarez, CastroPalaus, Vasquez, Salas, the Salamancans, Holzman, La Croix, Sporer, etc., that a declaration of the sense clearly conceived in the law does not require promulgation, but immediately obliges all those who know it, since such a declaration is not a new law. But an interpretation of some sense that is not clearly, bot only obscurely or improperly conceived in a law, which is a declaration *not purely such* (as we saw), this, because it is held as a new law, to oblige, necessarily requires promulgation, just as all other laws according to what was said in n. 95 and 96. Hence, it is inferred with Suarez, *de leg.*, l. 6, c. 1, n. 3; and Castropalaus, tr. 3, *eod. tit.* d. 5, p. 3, § 1. n. 5 (who cites for himself Bonacina, Salas and Lorea), that a declaration which is made by a legislator, of some sense clearly conceived in the law (according to the example brought of legitimate and illegitimate sons), does not require promulgation to oblige. On the other hand, a declaration of a sense obscurely conceived (according to the example of a grandparent under the name of "father", or of civil death under the name of "death"), certainly needs promulgation; for then it constituted a new obligation, which in itself was not clearly conceived earlier in the law. And Suarez, *loc. cit.*, and Castropalaus, n. 2, say the same thing on these declarations which are made not by the same legislator, but by his successor or superior; because the mind of the legislator cannot be so known to all as it was to the legislator himself; so then, that the sense would be declared (although conceived in the law) of some obligation, it is always necessary to have recourse to arguments and interpretations, which constitute a new law, by rendering certain what was in doubt; and therefore, promulgation is required, otherwise a declaration is never authentic, but only reputed as doctrinal.

Moreover, the doctrinal interpretation, which is a simple declaration of the mind of the legislator, can be made by each doctor, in the mode that should be done according to rules and the sense received by wiser men; for, since doubts often occur, nor is it always easy to obtain resolutions from a legislator, it was necessary that this faculty of interpretation be offered to expert men, as it is elicited from c. 2, *de privil.* in 6. Now, could an interpretation of the law be made, if in it every interpretation were forbidden! The Salamancans, *de leg.* cap. 4, punct. 3, § 1, n. 23 say no, with Regin., Henriquez, etc. But Palaus, tr. 3, disp. 5, § 2, n. 6, Salas, disp. 21, sect. 2, in fin., Sa, *verb. Interpretatio,* n. 5, all say yes. For then they say only frivolous interpretations are excluded, but not prudent ones. And they gather that from the Council of Trent (Sess. 4, *Decret. de usu sacr. libror.,* where the interpretation of Sacred Scripture is forbidden to be made against the sense which the Church holds: this is why they say, what if someone were to interpret Scripture apart from a consensus of the Fathers, but still not contrary to it, then it would not be opposed to such a prohibition, as Azor p. 1, l. 8, c. 2, q. 3, Bañez, p. 1, q. 11, Barlosa *in Rem. concil., loc. cit. Trid.,* and Palaus, *dicto* n. 6 all say. Still, some notice in n. 7 that at some time a doctrinal interpretation is forbidden, but not whatever doctrinal interpretation, rather that which is in print, and made avowedly; for it seems only this was forbidden by Pope Pius IV, in his bull confirming the Council of Trent, where it is forbidden lest someone would dare to publish commentaries against the aforesaid council: but the word *to publish* is taken up from custom to mean appearing in print, as Barb., *in Remiss., Concil.,* sess. 25, c. 2, and the same for Palaus, with Sa, Rodriguez., Salas, Regin ... nay more, Bonacina *de leg.* d. 1, p. 7, n. 3, in fin., and Palaus, *eod.* n. 7 say the same thing, with Suarez and Salas, nor is any interpretation you like that is printed, but only that which is avowedly taken up for that purpose, but not if someone would interpret one or another decree of Trent.

Rules in interpreting laws, are clearly: 1. That the mind or the intrinsic end of the legislator should be applied: hence, if the mind of the legislator is certain, it must be favored more than the words of the law. 2. The reason of the law must be applied. 3. In a doubt of the mind of the legislator the words of the law must be applied according to their own sense, always and they should not follow something absurd. Moreover, the proper sense can be natural, and this must be applied in penalties; it can also be civil, and this also can be applied in favors. 4. That in doubt an interpretation is made for the validity of the act. 5. That law is embraced in favorable things, and restricted in odious ones. But when the laws are favorable, and when they are odious, the primary motive of the law must be applied. See the Salamancans, 4, § 2.

Quaeritur: whether a law ought to be extended from case to case on account of the sameness of the reasoning? If the same does not occur, but only similar reasoning, the doctors commonly teach it must not be extended, unless a case is expressed in law only for the sake of example, say if the law imposes a penalty against those stealing 100 gold coins, certainly it also includes those stealing something of the same value. It becomes doubtful though, whether an extension ought to be made when it occurs for a case not only similar, but where the adequate reason is the same?

The first opinion affirms from that familiar saying: "Where the reason is the same, there the same disposition of law occurs," as the summary is held in l. *Illud ff. ad L, Aquil. and c. Inter de translat. Episcop.* And Laymann holds this, l. 1, tract. 4, c. 18, n. 9, Roncaglia *de legibus*, c. 2, q. 4, r. 2, p. 50, and the Salamancans *eod. tit.* tract. 11, c. 4, punct. 3, §3, n. 34, *et seqq.* with Suarez, Granadus, Tapia, and the common opinion, as they assert. The reason is because the mind of the legislator is gathered from the reasoning of the law, which therefore, is called the soul of the law; wherefore the legislator is thought to rightly have meant embrace all cases, where the same adequate reasoning of the law is found.

But *the second opinion*, which Palaus holds (*de legibus*, l. 1, tract. 3, d. 5, p. 3, §4 n. 2), Bonacina *eod. tit.* d. 1, q. 1, p. 8, n. 28, and Mazzotta tract. 1, d. 2, q. 1 c. 3 q. 5, deny that the extension is made from case to case on account of the same reason even in favorable cases and to much less in odious ones, and the reason is that the reasoning of the law is not the law, and therefore, although it would look to another case, it does not embrace it since the legislator could mean to embrace one case and not another, or because it is not expedient to command all things or forbid all things, or because some higher reason could be present unknown to us moving the prince, just as in one case, it does not dispose in another.

Still, these opinions are easily conciliated; for although those favoring the first opinion (from which we must not recede when it is common, as the same Palaus upholds), taught the law is extended from case to case when the same adequate reason occurs; still, then they add the same adequate reason occurs, at some time (unless the law were extended), the legislator could be charged with injustice or imprudence; for then the case is not expressed, rather it ought to be called comprehended in law than a law extended to it, Suarez *de leg.* l. 6 c. 3. ex n. 4, Ronc., d. r. 2, and

Laymann *d.* n. 9, *v. Caeterum.* And in this the authors agree, even of the second opinion, such as Bonacina *dict.* n. 25, v. *Ad secundum*, Palaus, *loc. cit.*, n. 8, and Mazzotta, *v. Excipe.*

Yet they say it comes about: I. in correlatives, exactly as in a man and wife, for then what was ratified in one, is also thought of the other, if the same reason proceeds for both. For just as a bride can recoil from the betrothal, if the bridegroom were away without permission, from *c. De illis, de Sponsal.*, so also the husband. Likewise, if the wife can communicate with her excommunicated husband, from *c. Quoniam, caus. XI, qu. 3*, so also the husband. II. In equal things, like election, presentation, provision for a benefice. III. In connected matters, as are a deacon and subdeacon. IV. In disputed things, such as are a Vicar of a Bishop, and a Vicar of the Chapter when the See is vacant, and daughter and granddaughter. In these, all agree even if the law were penal or more corrective.

But the rule of law, 49. in 6, *Odia restringi, favores convenit ampliari*, Suarez l. 6, c. 4, and Bonacina, *loc. cit.* n. 27, with Menoch., to proceed when the disposition of law is extended from interpretation of a congenial matter, as they say, but not when it ought to be extended from the interpretation of necessity, which is rather more called the adequate interpretation of the law, than extension.

Still, 1) Sanchez adverts l. 3, *de matrim.* d. 20, n. 3, as well as Mazzotta, *loc. cit.*, p. 98, that if the law would discern something by a case of more frequent use, it embraces the less frequent case. And therefore, the law of St. Pius V permitting nuns to go out of their enclosure on account of fire, leprosy or an epidemic is also extended to the ruin of the house, flood, and invasion by enemies, as the Doctors commonly teach, and Mazzota says (*loc. cit.*). 2) Laymann, n. 11, Palaus, n. 14, advert that judges are held by the similitude of reason to extend the law to other cases because these, insofar as it can be done, ought to conform to the laws, according to l. 12, ff. *de leg.* When in some case the meaning of these (namely laws, as it was expressed above) is manifest, he who has jurisdiction ought to proceed to similar things.

III. *On the Epikeja* of the law.

201. *Epikeija* or *epikia*, is the exception of a case on account of the circumstances, from which, for certain, or at least probably, it is judged that the legislator refused that case to be included under the law. The Salamancans, c. 4, punct. 3, § 4, n. 41 with Palaus, and Martin.

This *epikeja* not only have place in human laws, but even in natural ones, where the action can be uncovered by the circumstances from malice. The Salamancans, *ibid.,* n. 42, and 43.

Still, that place should be given to *epikeja,* the law ought not only to cease in a negative particular case, because without a doubt then the end of the law will fail; but it ought to cease in a contrary fashion, namely that the law would be rendered injurious, or at least onerous: for that reason one can refuse to lay his sword before his master, if the latter would abuse it. The Salamancans, *ibid.* n. 44, with St. Thomas. Moreover, it suffices if the law were otherwise rendered too hard. The Salamancans, *ibid.,* n. 45, with Arav., Cord., etc. Hence, one would be excused from hearing Mass who fears a notable loss of goods. And he would even be excused from the observation of a feast, who otherwise is compelled to lose great profit, as Suarez, and Palaus, quoted by the Salamancans, *ibid.* in fin. For more on this, see what will be said in book 4, n. 301.

APPENDIX OF HENRY BUSEMBAUM
On dispensations of the Sacred Poenitentiary.

202.—"Because from the office of the Sacred Penitentiary "many dispensations can be obtained (and indeed "graces), at least for the forum of conscience, I have "thought it worthwhile to add certain things in regard to "the praxis of this matter to the advantage of penitents, "and confessors.

"Now there are three things chiefly required in regard to "this matter. 1) In regard to the matter and causes in "which namely these dispensations for cases are usually "conceded. 2) In regard to the form of letters of the "Poenitentiary, in which a dispensation is consigned to "a confessor, whose several words which bring forth the "difficulty, must be explained. 3) In regard to this "execution of dispensation, namely what must be "observed in it. ON such questions, from Bonacina, "Diana, p. 4, t. 4, r. 71 and p. 8 t. 1, r. 103, etc. even to r. "111 and the whole volume of Marcus Paulus Leo "published on the matter.

203.—"Resp. 1. In a threefold matter (for the diversity of "which there is also a different form), dispensations, or "these graces are usually conceded.

"*The first* is in vows, e.g. that a vow of religion, on "account of the poverty of parents or the brothers or "from a similar cause it would be lawful for him to put it "aside; that someone would be absolved from a simple "vow of chastity, or even of religion, after he contracted "marriage, to remain in matrimony, and licitly ask for it "as due; that he would be absolved from a vow of "religion (on account of a weakness of strength, by

"which he cannot bear his burdens, or on account of fear
"of incontinence, or defect of talent), in order to contract
"matrimony."

"*Second,* against secret impediments to matrimony,
"whether they only impeded, or even invalidated,
"whether the matrimony was publicly contracted with
"them, or provided that it was a private act, and
"concluded, especially with good faith, or even when
"they overtake the contract. In regard to which, *it must*
"*be noted*: 1) Impediments are called secret, which are
"either nobody knows, or even if they were made known
"to one or another, still they are not deduced to a
"contentious forum. (See book 6, n. 1115). 2. Even if some
"impediments, *e.g.* of spiritual kinship, were public by
"their nature, when they are contracted in the sight of
"the Church; still it can be done *per accidens*, that they
"might be secret, *e.g.*, a) on account of the long duration
"of time, from which they were contracted; b) On
"account of the distance of the place from the place
"where kinship was contracted. c) By the death of those
"who were knowledgeable of it; d) By ignorance of this
"contraction.

"*Third* against the various censures, such as
"excommunications, suspensions, (likewise
"irregularities), especially if they are secret, to absolve
"from them to dispense, to rehabilitate, etc. Likewise, to
"condone the obligation of restitution on account of
"having neglected the breviary, to chose a confessor,
"even for reserved matters; to transfer to another
"religious house or order (in both forums) even after
"apostasy from it.

204.—"Resp. 2. In more frequent formulas the words of
"the Apostolic Brief itself, which contain substantial
"things, and have a difficulty, are these:

"'If it is so', or, 'insofar as it is so'. Of which the sense is,
"if the pleas rest upon the truth, especially in the time
"that the apostolic letter was given. Moreover, the truth
"of the matters related is required, principally in regard
"to essentials of fact, *e.g.* affinity was contracted, incest
"was committed, and the act or it was treated on
"matrimony (understand perfectly; so that on every side
"they would agree on it), and danger of relation and
"scandal threatens. Secondarily, however, it is required
"in regard to accidentals, *e.g.* an act was done with good
"faith, and similar things, which are merely impulsive,
"and without which such dispensations would be
"conceded just the same; for that reason, even if in those
"or in others of little moment there were an error in the
"petition, just the same the grace [*gratia*] is valid. See M.
"Leo, p. 2, f. 226 and p. 3, f. 391." (See here the Bull of
"Benedict XIV, l. 6, n. 1131.)

"2. 'If a danger of revelation would threaten.' For this
"purpose, that a dispensation would cease, it is required
"that there would be a danger, lest the impediment were
"revealed (understand, when it is express in a formula)
"if the matrimony did not follow, as Marcus Leo teaches
"(p. 2, f. 230). Moreover, this danger does not convey a
"necessary detection, but only a probable and moral
"credulity, a future one, that if he would recoil from
"contracting matrimony, and the causes of this case
"could not be assigned, it should be uncovered from
"vehement suspicion and curious inquisition. (See l. c. f.
"233).

"3. 'And scandal.' In which it is understood by the name
"of grave infamy, from which contentions then follow,
"threats, fights, etc. (Leo F. 230, and 217).

"4. 'That there would be more certainty about the
"aforesaid woman concerning the nullity of the earlier
"consent, etc.' This clause is substantial, and without a

"doubt, if there must be a dispensation against a diriment
"impediment, with which a marriage was contracted in
"the face of the Church, the spouse that is unaware that
"an impediment is made regarding certain nullity of the
"prior consent, and freely offers a new and valid (so, still,
"that in they do not come to know of the secret
"impediment). Leo, p. 251, Diana, p. 8, t. 3, r. 110.
"Moreover, it suffices they present that consent among
"themselves secretly, with no one present, through
"words or sufficient signs, *e.g.* joined in the marital
"disposition. Nor ought the executor of the dispensation
"join them again in his presence with witnesses. Leo, p.
"552. (See what is going to be said in book 6, *de matrim.*,
"n. 1115).

"5. 'After, he will make satisfaction to the aforesaid
"priest, if he has not yet done so.' These words are
"usually in the faculty to absolve from excommunication,
"*e.g.* on account of beating a cleric, and the words
"convey the condition of first making satisfaction to the
"wounded, which could be absolved, this is, to
"compensate for the injury, and all damage accounted,
"which he incurs on account of that beating, the
"estimation of which is committed to the executor of the
"dispensation; nor is the one who beat him freed from
"his obligation by the fact that the one beaten remitted
"the injury. See Leo, p. 382, 384. Furthermore, if he could
"not satisfy at the present, it suffices if after having
"sworn, he would promise that he was going to do it as
"soon as he could.

205.—"Resp. 3. In regard to praxis, or execution of this
"dispensation these must be done:

"1. Letters of the Sacred Poenitentiary are directed to
"the petitioner, *i.e.* to the one who asked for the
"dispensation himself or by another, who ought not to
"open these, but chose such a confessor, of the quality

"inscribed, who will open them after they have been
"handed to him by the petitioner, and then he will
"dispense him according to the commission. But,
"although in each case they are opened by another, they
"do not lack effect. Salas, Dian., p. 8, t. 3, r. 103.

"2. This is required in a confessor: a) That he would be
"approved by the Ordinary of the territory in which he
"is going to dispense. b) That he would be a teacher or
"doctor in theology, or canon law; promoted in an
"academy or a religious having the privilege such as
"what Pope Gregory XIII conceded in 1582 to confessors
"of the Society of Jesus, the General of which or another
"superior on its license, will designate to it. c) That he
"would be specially chosen for this purpose by the
"petitioner, *i.e.* by the one with whom the dispensation
"must be mad; still someone once chosen, unless he
"would find him ignorant, cannot change him. Leo f. 22,
"Diana p. 8, t. 3, r. 10. Still, Sanchez and Perez, *de matrim.*
"d. 48, sect. 5, n. 7, teach the contrary.

206.—"3. The Confessor chosen for this: a) ought to
"dispense in confession, or at least immediately after.
"Diana, p. 4, 6. 4, r. 7, Leo p. 1, f. 54, et 28; b) There
"should be knowledge of the cause, when it is judged in
"a Brief, essentially to begin ahead of time through a
"diligent examination of the penitent, unless it should
"have already been considered; because he is not a mere
"executor, but a judge, to whom power to dispense has
"been delegated. c) In that he ought to believe him, even
"without witnesses and under oath, unless he knows
"form another source that it is false; for then he ought
"not to dispense. Leo, Diana, p. 8, t. 3, r. 108. d) A work
"prescribed in the Brief itself, even if it could be
"moderated, still cannot condone. e) Even if certain
"words are not prescribed to dispense, still he ought to
"preserve the form approved by the Roman Ritual, and

"after those words, "I absolve you from your sins," add:
"and by the same authority, I declare that you remain in
"the aforesaid matrimony, and can render the marrital
"debt, and ought to: still with you being dispensed, that
"you may licitly avail to demand the debt. In the name of
"the Father, etc." But if he must be absolved from
"excommunication, see the formula in book 7, n. 116, 6.
"After the absolution hs been dispensed, he ought to
"destroy the letters, especially the seal, so that they
"could not serve to prove, otherwise he incurrs a major
"excommunication. Leo f. 239. Still, this destruction is
"not of the substance, because it is only intended, that
"they would not lend support to the external forum. f) In
"no mode ought the attestation of the dispensation be
"made, nor the Brief itself, or render a diploma, when it
"ought to serve only the forum of conscience. g) Nothing
"ought to receive, not even by way of compensation for
"the dispensation even made in the external forum: for
"therefore it is entitled, *gratis ubique*. Otherwise, he
"incurs by the very fact a major excommunication.
"Gavant, Diana, *loc. cit.*, from what Cardinas declares.

From the aforesaid, the following cases are resolved:

207.—"1. The Confessor for this dispensation cannot be
"chosen if he is only a doctor of an order, or a professor,
"or has only a license in theology, because here it is only
"understood about those matters which are consigned by
"reason of training, not of dignity, so among those
"favorable should come by the name of a doctor. Leo, p.
"1, f. 21, Diana, p. 4, t. 4, r. 41.
"2. From the privilege consigned to the Society of Jesus,
"even some mendicants can be chosen, on account of
"communication. Still, both the former and the latter
"ought to have for this purpose the special faculty from

"their superior: otherwise the dispensation will be null;
"Auct., cit., and it is clear from the aforesaid.

"3. The confessor ought to so examine the penitent, that
"he would recognize and even distinctly, the merits of
"the case and could discern among them; therefore it is
"inscribed *to a discrete man*. He especially ought to
"enquire whether the petitions rest upon the truth,
"because grace is not conceded simply, but *sub*
"*conditione*, and therefore the little clause is usually
"added: "Insofar as it is so:" or, "If you will find it to be
"so". See Auct. cit., and *de Matrim.* book 6, n. 1131.

"4. He who asks for the dispensation, ought to confess to
"the executor chosen for it; nor does it suffice that he
"had confessed to him before. It is clear from the
"aforesaid; Leo f. 28, Diana, p. 4, t.4. r. 71, Reg., Pont,
"against Sanchez, the Salamancans, Perez, Palaus, whose
"opinion they teach is not more probable. Filliuci,
"Escobar, Lezan., Diana, *loc. cit.* and p. 8, t. 3. 4. 105.

208.—"5. The commission of this dispensation does not
"expire with the death of the Poenitentiary that
"conceded it, when the matter is whole, because the
"grace is not going to be made, but was made in the
"favor of the petitioner, for whom the right was asked;
"and the executor is the necessary dispenser, if indeed
"the petitions rest upon the truth. Nor do they expire on
"the death of the Pope, and on account of the reason that
"we already offered, and because the office of the greater
"Poenitentiary does not expire with the death of the
"Pope. Diana, p. 8, t. 3, r. 89, from Suarez, Sanchez, Garc.,
"etc. against Navarre, Bonacina, etc."

END OF THE BOOK ONE

BOOK II
On the manner to know and discern sins.

PREAMBLE OF THE TREATISE
On human acts in general

 HAVE NO MIND, benevolent reader, since I am writing on moral theology (the whole of which is directed to the practice), to show you a treatise on human acts advanced from scholastic questions; rather, desiring to instead offer counsel for your salvation, and that of souls, I have devised to select only those matters which are more useful in this matter, and everything considered necessary to know for praxis. If I were to do otherwise, wouldn't I perish from burning the candle at both ends, and would you not be worn out to no purpose from reading useless matters of this sort? Therefore, I do not ask for you to wait for me to free this treatise from nearly every number of matters which are more useful and still remain sufficiently entangled. Nevertheless, I have applied the greatest diligence to select doctrines so that I would avail not to place obstacles to the advancement of the souls which it benefits. Furthermore, I do not think one should recoil from the sound doctrine of the Angelic Doctor wherever it can be held, for with his guidance one shall walk in theological matters without tripping upon his feet as it were.

ARTICLE I
On the nature and manifold division of human acts.

I. The human act, taken in the strictest sense, can be defined as: "*An act deliberately proceeding from the will of*

358

man. To be sure, only those actions are properly called human," as St. Thomas, in 1, 2, q. 1, art. 1, says. He continues: "a man is the master of those things; but a man is master of his acts through reason and the will. Therefore, these actions are properly called human, which proceed from the deliberate will." For an action to be human, and moral, it is necessary that it be understood and freely done; second, where that is lacking either due to involuntary ignorance or coercion, it must be said to be more mechanical than moral.

II. Moreover, it is inferred that all actions, which do not proceed from the deliberate will of man, are commonly called actions of a man not human actions.

III. Human acts are divided in multiplicity of ways. Some acts are said to be elicited (*eliciti*), some commanded (*imperati*), and certain of these are said to be good, while certain others evil. Some of the goods are natural, others supernatural; but from the supernatural ones, some are meritorious *de condigno*, some *de congruo*. At length, some human acts are interior, while others are exterior. We will treat these individually.

IV. A human act is said to be elicited (*elicitus*) which immediately proceeds from the will. Love and hate are of this sort. An act is said to be commanded (*imperatus*) which sets out mediately from the will itself, such as to walk, speak, write, etc., which proceed from the commanding will. Other powers, namely, motor skills, elicit acts of this sort. These acts are either elicited or commanded, insofar as those things that freely proceeds from the will are called moral acts, whether *good (boni)* or *evil (mali)*. They are called good which are consistent with right reason; but those that are not, are called evil. *Natural* acts are good, which can be done only by the strength of nature; whereas they are called *Supernatural* only if they can be elicited with the help of grace, *e.g.* an act of faith, hope, love, etc. Meritorious acts *de condigno* are those in which reward is due from justice; meritorious acts *de congruo* are those which merit a reward from their propriety. Lastly, interior acts are made plain by no sensible sign, whereas exterior acts are made clear exteriorly.

V. Now that these have been prefaced, we must speak about the intrinsic principles of human acts. There are these three principles, namely intellect (*intellectus*), will (*voluntas*), and freedom (*libertas*). Intellect flows into a moral action by conscience, or knowledge of the action, as well as law. And therefore in the treatise on conscience a great many things were said about understanding. Therefore, now it remains to speak on voluntary and involuntary, then on free acts, which are loftier principles of human acts. Hence:

ARTICLE II
On voluntary and involuntary acts, and their causes.

§ I. *What is a voluntary act and how manifold is it?*

VI. We must preface that this term, *voluntary act*, is sometimes received in the same sense as *spontaneous*,[1] which is without a doubt of one's own will, and from the inclination of the will when it is not compelled by a precept, or fear, or force, or deceit. But really, *voluntary* is one thing, *spontaneous* is another. To be sure, every voluntary act is spontaneous, but on the other hand, not every spontaneous act is voluntary. Sometimes voluntary is received for free; nevertheless not every voluntary act is free, although every

---

[1] Translator's note: Spontaneous, here, is received not by the current English sense of on the spur of the moment, but something that arises from an act of the will.

free act is voluntary. At length, it is received in this other sense, in which we now define and treat.

VII. A voluntary act can be so defined: "An act proceeding from an intrinsic principle, or from the will with knowledge of the end." So St. Thomas thinks (1. 2. q. 6, art. 1), following St. Gregory of Nyssa and St. John Damascene, whom he praises; Gonet (*Man.* tom. 3, tr. 2, c. 1, §1), Sylv., the Salamancans, Concina, the Continuator of Tournely, and others in common. Therefore, two things are necessary to constitute the reasoning of a voluntary act, namely that it is from *an intrinsic principle, and with some knowledge of the end.*

VIII. Moreover, it is inferred: 1) that these actions, which are done only from an extrinsic principle, as are those which are done from force or compulsion, are not said to be voluntary. 2) Similarly all actions that certainly proceed from an intrinsic principle, but without any knowledge of the intellect, cannot be said to be voluntary. 3) For this purpose, that some action would be said to be completely voluntary, it is necessary that they be known according to all their parts and circumstances; if some of them are unknown, the action is not said to be voluntary in regard to that unknown circumstance. So, if a man has relations with a woman that he does not know is married, he does not commit the sin of adultery but the sin of simple fornication, since it was involuntary in regard to the circumstance of matrimony, which he was ignorant of. 4) It is inferred, that where there is no knowledge, there is no voluntary act, and consequently no sin, such as what happens in acts that take place while sleeping, which are simply involuntary. But where there is partial notice, there is a semi-voluntary act, and it is merely a venial sin, such as what comes to pass when one is half-asleep.

IX. A voluntary act is divided in a multiplicity of ways by theologians: 1) Into what is voluntary *simpliciter*, and voluntary *secundum quid.* The former proceeds from the full inclination of the will without any opposition. The latter proceeds from the consent of the will but with opposition. Of this sort is the throwing of merchant's wares into the see from the fear of shipwreck.

It is divided: 2) Into *free*, or contingent, and *necessary.* The first happens from the will, which acts with indifference to willing and refusing. Such is the love toward God by a man journeying in this life. The second from the determinate will to one thing, such as the love of the Blessed in heaven. Gonet (*loc. cit.*) teaches, against Vasquez, that the reasoning of a voluntary act is more perfectly found in necessary acts than free ones. The reason is, that the greater the love, the greater is the voluntary act, *i.e.* the greater propensity of the will, and the greater understanding of the intellect. Such is the necessary love of God toward himself, or the love of the blessed, in which the whole effort is borne toward God.

It is divided: 3) Into voluntary *in itself*, or *expressed*, and *in the cause*, as well as *implicit* or *virtual.* An act is said to be voluntary *in itself* when it has been willed in itself, and immediately; *e.g.* someone that steals something because he has in himself the will to steal. But it is voluntary *in the cause* if it has not been willed in itself, but in another thing, which is apprehended at least confusedly, such as the cause of some effect. In this mode, when a man murders someone when he has become drunk of his own will, it is said to be voluntary, foreseeing the murder of this kind at least *in confuso.*

It is divided: 4) Into a voluntary act that is *direct* and *indirect.* The former directly and immediately proceeds from the will, just as from an efficient cause. But the latter, although it may not proceed from the will immediately, nevertheless depends upon it mediately. Yet, everyone sees that this fourth division of the will can be reduced to the third.

X. Here, one must notice that some effect following its cause, which has already been voluntarily posited, for it to be said that it is voluntary *indirectly in the cause*, as we said above, and at the same time, is imputed to merit or demerit, three things must coincide: 1) That the agent, by placing the cause, at least notices *in confuso*, that the effect of this sort is from the cause of what follows. 2) That he can impede such an effect by abolishing the cause. 3) That he is held to abolish it, or not to place it. St. Thomas thinks this way: "The subsequent event ... if it is preconceived, is manifest, because it adds to the goodness, or malice of the act. For, since someone supposing that from his work many evils could follow, does not desist from them for that reason, for that reason his will appears to be more inordinate." (1. 2. q. 20, art. 5). Sylvius says on this article, that St. Thomas here takes up the term *preconceived*, insofar as it sounds the same as *willed* and *intended*, or *foreseen* and *intended*; just the same the Angelic Doctor himself (qu. 75, art. 8, ad 1) for the word *preconceived* uses the word *foreseen and intended*, when he says: "Just as it was said above, although it was argued on the goodness and malice of exterior acts; the following event, if it was foreseen, and intended (whereas above he had said *preconceived*), adds to the goodness or malice of the act." But then, the subsequent effect, Sylvius adds, he reckons to be willed and intended, not only when it is intended from what has been proposed, but even when it is so foreseen that it will follow, that it could have and ought to have been impeded, still it was not impeded, for then it is interpretatively or indirectly willed. At length, St. Thomas concludes (*Ibid*, art 5): "However, if the subsequent event were not preconceived, ... if *per se* it follows from such an act, and as in a great many things, ... it adds to the goodness or malice of the act. Otherwise, if *per accidens*, even as it occurs in very few things." Here, Sylvius also teaches that *the subsequent event per se and as in a great many things*, so adds to the goodness and malice, because if it were not preconceived in itself, it is certainly foreseen and intended in another thing, viz., in its cause as well as virtually.

XI. It must be said for the same reason, that without a doubt for an omission to be voluntary and culpable, three things are required: 1) That it would be from an *intrinsic principle*; 2) That it would be with cognition of the end, as we said in §1, n. 7, it is necessary that its opposite, namely an involuntary act, would be done either from *an extrinsic principle* against the inclination of the will, as happens to the agent from force or fear, or would be done without cognition of the intellect, which is either abolished, or at least bound; as happens to one acting from ignorance, or passion. So the Doctors commonly teach according to St. Thomas.

XIII. An involuntary act is manifold. One thing is said to be *privately* involuntary, when only the act of willing that which it can will is lacking. Another is said to be involuntary *positively and contrarily*, when viz., something is not only willed, but positively refused and repugnant to its will. Again, a *contrarily* involuntary act is twofold, one *simpliciter*, the other *secundum quid*. The first is that which so displeases the will that he would not will it in any manner or under any reasoning. Still, the second is so called because although under some respect it would displease the will, nevertheless for another reason it pleases it more and is accepted. Such is the casting of wares into the sea done out of fear of shipwreck, which in respect to the merchant is involuntary *secundum quid*; but in respect to the greater evil threatening, it is voluntary *simpliciter*.

XIV. From the aforesaid we gather many things to praxis. 1) Someone becomes drunk at the principle point of the morning on a feast day, not foreseeing that the consequent would be that he would miss Mass, he would not sin on account of missing Mass. We advance the reason §1 n. 10, where we establish that the subsequent event is not imputed unless it was foreseen *in itself*, or in the cause. 2) If the cause which is posited, by its nature would induce such an evil effect, nevertheless, it ought to necessarily be posited, then the evil effect, even if it was foreseen, still is not volitional and intended and it is by no means imputable if the one acting would apply some precaution. So, pollution is not imputed to a surgeon that foresees what would follow from the necessary touch of a woman's private parts, so long as he does not intend it. Nor is it imputed to someone that must study, on account of his own and of others, the matters of the opposite sex if he would not intend an effect of this sort provided that he repels complacency in an act in which pollution follows. The reason is, because then he is not held to abolish the reasoning, or does not place it, and one who uses his right is not said to have done so for the sake of the effect that was not intended and follows *per accidens*, nay more, in such a case it seems he suffers more than he does. *A fortiori*, the subsequent effect is not imputed from the cause that is otherwise morally upright, and licit, that pollution which arises from riding a horse, or from moderate food and drink; for then the effect was not intended *per accidens*, and according to what St. Thomas says (*loc. cit.*) it is not imputable. 3) A confessor should not easily believe a penitent that excuses himself in fact commits perjury and blasphemy if he advances obscene words without notice, since then it is involuntary as if from a habit; for if he has not labored to root out that habit by applying some remedy, then it is voluntary in the case when he perjures, blasphemes, etc., and therefore he is not excused from fault; it is otherwise if, after due diligence has been applied, he inadvertently blasphemes and breaks out in obscene talk and other like things. Now, let us progress to what is necessary for cases which cause an involuntary act, such as force, fear, concupiscence, and ignorance.

§II. *On violence and fear.*

XV. A violent act is defined as that *which is from an extrinsic principle, repugnant to one who suffers force.* The doctors commonly teach this, St. Damascene, St. Gregory, St. Thomas and the author of Ethics, 3, c. 1. Hence it is inferred, that two things are required for the nature of the act to be violent: 1) That it would be from an extrinsic principle. 2) That the one suffering resists as much as his strength allows both positively and contrary wise to the extrinsic agent. For it does not suffice, that he negatively composes himself; otherwise justification of infants would be a violence. It is gathered from St. Thomas (1. 2 q. 6, art. 5, ad 2) where he says: "When an action is inferred from something exterior remaining in him, who suffers it, by the will to suffer, it is not violent *simpliciter*, because even if he who suffers does not confer to the action, still he confers to the will to suffer it."

XVI. There is another violence which is said to be *simplicter* and *absoluta*; the other *secundum quid.* The first is, when someone can resist everything in some matter. The second is when he does not resist with all his strength.

XVII. I say firstly, that the aforesaid violence *absoluta et simpliciter* causes an involuntary act. The reason is, because when the will of the one suffering it should resist the extrinsic agent with all manner of resistance, then the action of the agent will be in no way voluntary on the side of the one suffering it, because it will be against every inclination of his will, and by the consequent is involuntary *simpliciter*. St. Thomas teaches this (*loc. cit.*)

Hence it is deduced that a woman who resists violence in that is inflicted against her virginity in any manner, does not sin, even if she suffers sexual relations against her will. Hence that quote of St. Augustine (*de civitate* book 1, c. 16), where he speaks about Christian women who were taken from Rome by the Goths and were forcefully violated, "Whatever another person does with the body or upon it is not the fault of the person who suffers it, provided he cannot avoid it without sin." We say the same thing in similar circumstances.

XVIII. I say secondly that violence *secundum quid*, and *insufficiens*, does not abolish but merely diminishes the voluntary nature of the act. The reason is, because where the will does not resist as much as it can, there the plan of a voluntary act remains in some part. And according to the greater or lesser resistance which he applies, his action will be more or less voluntary and culpable.

XIX. Here, Theologians ask whether violence can be inferred to the will. We respond briefly by conceding this *in regard to acts that are commanded*, and *by denying this in regard to acts that are elicited*. St. Thomas thinks this way in the cited question, art. 4, when speaking on elicited acts. St. Anselm says, "No man can will something when it is against his will, because he cannot will while at the same time refusing to will it." (*de Lib. Abitrio*, c. 6). Nor can God himself compel the will in regard to elicited acts; then the will would want and not want at the same time. Hypothetically it would wish: but it would refuse, because he would oppose himself to the one that wills, [*quod implicat in terminis*]. Nevertheless, God can change the will and cause one to go from refusing to wishing through efficacious grace. But then it is not to compel, but to supply for the old inclination, whereby he refused, a new inclination, whereby he would will what earlier he had refused. (St. Thomas, q. 22, *de verit.* art 8; Gone, etc.) Now we will address fear.

XX. Fear is defined as that which *is an alarm of the mind because of immediate or future danger*. L. Praetor (ff) says that it will be done for the sake of fear. Here, we speak only on falling on a steadfast man, or on fear of a greater evil, as Labeo says (l. 5, *eodem tit.*).

Fear is divided into *grave*, or *just*, and *light*. A light fear is said to be that which one fears as a light evil, or certainly fears is a grave evil but from a light and improbable cause. On the other hand, a *grave* fear is said to when someone fears a grave evil from an exceedingly probable cause. Grave evils are commonly reckoned as death, mutilation of limbs, terrible beatings, terrible prison, exile, servitude, great infamy, proscription of goods, removal of the tools of his trade, without which one cannot make a living by his labor, etc. In the rest gravity or levity of the fear must be considered especially on account of the different character and quality of persons; for it strikes children and women forcefully when it does not even lightly touch men. Here we speak *about one who acts with concomitant fear*, which certainly does not abolish the voluntary nature of the action.

XXI. I say that fear does not cause an involuntary act *simpliciter*, but only *secundum quid*, which is the same as to say that acts which are done through fear, whether light or grave, are *simply voluntary acts*, but only involuntary *secundum quid*. This conclusion is held commonly from St. Thomas (1.2. q. 6, art. 6). The foremost reason is that it is simply voluntary and involuntary *secundum quid*, which here and now in the present circumstances we truly will; and only do not will when the matter is considered absolutely and abstracted from the present circumstances. But those acts that are done from fear are of this sort. Therefore, those that are done through fear are voluntary simply, but involuntary *secundum quid*. The matter is obvious in the example of the throwing wares on account of an impending shipwreck. For the merchant wills simply the throwing of his goods overboard in consideration of the danger to life in the present circumstances, which is a greater evil that necessarily must be avoided; but he does not will it *secundum quid*, namely outside the case of impending shipwreck, if we were to consider that throwing of the wares overboard as it is in itself and absolutely, insofar as it is displeasing to the will of the merchant. (*Cf.* St. Thomas, *loc. cit.*, Gonet, Sylvius, the Continuator of Tournely and the moral philosophers treating this matter).

XXII. From the aforesaid a great many things are gathered to practice. I. Contracts which are made from grave fear are valid by the natural law because they are voluntary simply. II. Contracts of this sort having been struck unjustly through fear can be rescinded and made void by the one who suffered the injury. So think Alexander III, *c. Abbas tit. de his, quae vi, etc.;* and Innocent III, *c. ad Audientiam.* III. Still from positive law a great many contracts made through grave fear that were struck unjustly are invalid, and invalidated by the Church, or by civil law for just causes. Matrimonial contracts of this sort made through grave fear have been struck unjustly, even strengthened by an oath; *c. Significavit, de eo qui duxit, c. Cum locum, c. Veniens, tit. de sponsalibus.* Likewise, promisses of a dowry and payments similarly extorted. Vows and solemn professions of vows made through fear; absolution of an excommunication, suspension or interdict, extorted through force and fear. *c. Asbolutionis, tit. de his, quae vi in* 6, and similar matters.

§. III *Whether concupiscence would abolish or greatly increase a voluntary act?*

XXIII. By the name of concupiscence, for the present we understand a certain movement of the sensitive appetite rebelling against the spirit, which tends to an enjoyable good. It is twofold, *antecedent* and *consequent* consent of the will. *Antecedent* concupiscence forestalls the consent of the will and drags it, and inclines to what must be done; such as when a man sees a very beautiful woman, he is induced by concupiscence to desire her. *The consequent,* however, follows the consent of the will, nay more it arises from foreseen consent of the will to some matter already supplied, as when, for example, a man ardently longs for something, a violent passion of concupiscence is aroused in him. So thinks St. Thomas in 1. 2. q. 77, art. 6, where he adds, "For the will cannot be intensely moved toward something unless some passion were aroused in the sensitive appetite." He confirms the same thing in q. 73, art. 6 ad 2. Now it is very certain that the consequent concupiscence supposes the voluntary act is more intense and does not diminish it, but increases all the more the voluntary nature of the act, as well as the sin. Let St. Thomas be heard: "Passion ... following, does not diminish the sin, but increases it all the more, or rather more is the sign of its magnitude insofar as it demonstrates the intension of the will to the act of sin." But we state these conclusions in regard to the antecedent:

XXIV. Conclusion 1) Antecedent concupiscence does not abolish the voluntary nature of the act, but rather more makes something voluntary and increases by reason of a greater propensity, so he concludes in the ends (St. Thomas, 1. 2. q. 6, art. 7). The reason which he advances is that a voluntary act imports a certain inclination of the will with some cognition of the end. By concupiscence, however, the will is inclined to will that which it desires: nor is the mind altogether clouded in cognition of the thing. And because the will, when it acts from concupiscence, is impelled by a greater inclination to the object, therefore it not only does not abolish the voluntary nature of the act, but even increases it.

XXV. Another conclusion is, that antecedent concupiscence diminishes the voluntary nature of the act by reason of cognition. Nay more, at sometime it altogether abolishes the voluntary nature of the act, because it altogether removes cognition. The first part is proved: because cognition of the end is essentially requisite to the nature of the voluntary act, as has been said a great many times. But on the other hand, violent concupiscence impairs this cognition; for it impedes lest the mind, being enticed by the sensible object, would consider the foulness of the act and the offense to God. Therefore, by this reasoning it diminishes the voluntary nature of the act for the diminishing of cognition of the end. See St. Thomas, 1.2. q. 6, art. 7, ad 3 and q. 10; art. 3 and q. 73, art. 6 and q. 77, art. 6.

The second part is proven because at some time, antecedent concupiscence altogether abolishes the voluntary nature of the act, since at some time it forestalls all judgment of reason and all consent of the will.

St. Thomas also affirms this (*loc. cit.* q. 6, art. 7 ad 3) when he says: "If concupiscence entirely takes away cognition, just as it touches on those things, which on account of concupiscence the insane do, would follow because concupiscence abolishes the voluntary act." He teaches the same thing in q. 77, art. 7, q. 10, art. 3.

Hence, we gather that the motion of concupiscence, which is called by theologians *primo primi*, naturally forestalls all consent and freedom of the will, and is altogether involuntary and inculpable. But motion *secundo primi*, which at least suppose a semi-full consent of the will, do not altogether abolish the voluntary nature, but still they diminish it.

§. IV. *What level of ignorance would cause an act to be involuntary?*

XXVI. Ignorance is manifold, and is usually divided into ignorance of simple privation, and ignorance of a corrupted disposition. The first is a lack of knowledge, of which someone were to have the capacity for such a time and state, as if an adult were ignorant of these things which he could know. The second is positive deception, and an error contrary to the truth. 2) It is divided into ignorance of the law and of fact. Ignorance of the law is when someone is ignorant of the law, or that something is a precept or forbidden; e.g. if someone does not know that on the vigil of Pentecost there is a precept to fast from custom. Ignorance of fact is, when someone does not know that what was done is something that is forbidden is really not permitted, such as if someone did not know that it was meat which he ate on a day of fast. 3) It is divided in *concomitant, consequent, and antecedent. Concomitant* ignorance is that whereby someone is ignorant that he does something, but would still do it if he were not ignorant. Such is the ignorance of one who not knowing he killed an enemy, thinks he killed a deer, but if he did know he still would have killed him. This ignorance is not a cause of action, not only *per accidens* accompanies the action.

Consequent ignorance is said of those things, which follow the determination of the will, insofar as the ignorance itself is voluntary, and proceeds from free will. This consequent ignorance is subdivided into *directly voluntary,* or *affected,* in *indirectly* voluntary, or *crass* and ignorance of a bad choice. The first is that whereby the will directly wills ignorance itself, such as when someone wills not to know, or to have an excuse for a sin he has already committed, or to not withdraw from committing a sin; according to what we read in Job: "we do not want knowledge of your ways" (Job 21:14), and in the Psalms, "He refused to understand so that he would act rightly." (Psalm 35/36: 3). They labor by this ignorance who, after they have given it attention, neither seek counsel in doubt, nor are present at sermons and catechesis, lest they would fall upon bad faith and be deterred from what they have proposed. Ignorance that is *indirectly voluntary,* or *crass,* is when someone is not affected to be ignorant, but neglects to learn those things which he may and must know. And according to this mode of ignorance of the law of all things, which someone is held to know, is said to be voluntary, as if coming into being from negligence. At length, ignorance *of a bad choice* is that, which one does not consider in act because here and now he can and ought consider, and it comes into being from passion or from habit.

Antecedent ignorance is that which altogether precedes the consent of the will, so that it is in no way voluntary and, nevertheless, is the cause of willing that which he otherwise would not will if he knew. For example, when someone, after he has applied due diligence, kills a man whom he believed to be a wild animal. This ignorance is also called *invincible.* Still, on this invincible ignorance, just as on vincible ignorance we do not address here, because we already gave a discourse on it in the treatise on Law, n. 169.

XXVII. I say: 1) That *antecedent* ignorance causes an involuntary act *simpliciter,* because in no way is it volitional but is truly invincible, because it can be conquered by no moral diligence, and therefore is inculpable. So the Doctors commonly think. Yet, whether ignorance of this sort can be granted to be invincible on precepts of the natural law, at least on mediate conclusions, *see the treatise on Laws.*

XXVIII. I say: 2) Because concomitant ignorance neither makes a *voluntary* nor an *involuntary* act. Because this ignorance neither induces one to act nor to not act, nor is the cause, nor the effect of the will of the one acting, but *per accidens* stands either to an act of the will, or to the work which is done. It can only be said that it does not make it *voluntary,* for it cannot be willed in act because it is unknown. So St. Thomas (1. 2. qu. 6, ar. 8), Sylvius, Gonet, the Continuator of Tournely, and others think in common.

XXIX. I say: 3) That consequent ignorance does not cause *an involuntary act simpliciter.* Because this ignorance is voluntary, and has the will for its cause, therefore it cannot be said to be *involuntary simpliciter*, but at least causes an *involuntary act secundum quid*, as St. Thomas says (*loc. cit.*) For if the one acting would know it is an evil act, to which he is induced from passion, certainly he would not will to do it.

ARTICLE III
On a free act, or freedom of human acts

XXX. We call an act "free" which is either done from no compulsion, or which can be omitted *ad libitum*. For the theologians usually distinguish a two-fold freedom in human acts, namely *freedom from coercion*, or *spontaneity*, and freedom *from intrinsic or natural necessity;* which is also called of choice, indeterminate, and decision. Freedom *from coercion*, is immunity from every violence advanced against the inclination of the will. By this freedom the blessed love God, and we the good in common. Hence, it is that every act of the will is free from coercion.

Yet, freedom *from necessity* is that which excludes all necessity whether interior and of nature, or exterior and of compulsion. In this manner, one is said to be free who can act or not act, choose or not choose. Hence free will is defined as that which is *elective force, or the faculty to choose one apart from the other.*

Freedom from necessity is subdivided into *freedom of contradiction*, whereby someone can act or not act; into freedom *of contrariety*, whereby he can do something or do the opposite, for example to love and hate; and freedom *of disparity*, whereby he can do this, or another thing, but not the opposite, e.g. to write or to walk.

XXXI. Necessity is opposed to freedom, which is manifold. One is called *necessity of coercion*, which is the same as violence. Another is *necessity of nature*, or *of natural inclination,* which consists in a certain propensity placed in the will by nature itself to necessarily carry out something, or to flee from it. Coercion is from an extrinsic principle, it abolishes the voluntary and free nature of the act; but *natural necessity* is from an intrinsic principle, and takes away the free aspect of the act, but not the voluntary.

Again, another is *absolute and antecedent necessity,* which either precedes the use of reason and will, or so expresses consent that the will cannot refuse it. Another is *consequent and hypothetical necessity,* which follows free consent and determination of the will, and scarcely wounds free choice, *e.g.* it is necessary for me to speak, if I already determined myself to speak. There are other divisions of necessity, namely *of specification,* and *of exercise, physical* and *moral,* the subtle inquiry of which we regulate to the scholastic theologians.

XXXII. Formerly there were Stoics, Astrologers, Manicheans, then the followers of Wycliffe, Calvinists and Lutherans, who called free will a *figmentum in rebus,* and *a thing in name only,* at length the Jansenists, who tried to overturn the freedom of man or free will, attribute everything either to fate or some influx [*syderum*] or efficient grace, and concupiscence, not without incredible insanity, and perhaps after they have protested their conscience and intimate sense. However, the Council of Trent struck them with the singular penalty of an anathema in Session 6, can. 5, resting upon Scripture, and the profitable testimonies of the holy Fathers, as well as their daily experience, which is the teacher of things. I avowedly refuse to pile up the arguments to defend the existence of free will in man since it would be vain to attentively advance argumentation that is hardly necessary in a matter that is beyond doubt. It is enough to say that once you have taken free will away from man, laws would be given in vain; and oaths would be applied to no purpose, no one would be worthy of either praise or virtue, nor would rewards be given to the good, nor punishments to the wicked. I.e., it is so evident that anyone who would dare to deny free will must be convinced rather more by beatings than by words, as Scotus, Vega and others say from Aristotle. Hence it was rightly condemned by Innocent X, *In Constit., Cum occasione*, and by Alexander VII when he condemned the third proposition of Jansen, which denied the necessity of free indifference to merit, or demerit, in the state of fallen nature. Moreover, it was condemned by St. Pius V in the 67th proposition of Baius: "A man also sins damnably in that which he necessarily does."

XXXIII. We merely connect three propositions pertaining to the matter of free will, which the Christian religion forbids one to ignore.

The first is that a man, even after the fall of Adam, rejoices in free will, or freedom of indifference and choice. So the Council of Trent taught (Sess. 6, can. 3) against innovators, as well as the Council of Constance (sess. 8), where the 27th proposition of John Wycliffe was condemned: "Everything comes about from absolute necessity." St. Augustine, in his book on Grace, and in Free choice of the will (ch. 1), wrote: "God revealed to us through the Sacred Scriptures that there is free will in man, and whoever would deny it is not Catholic." St. Thomas (q. 24 *de Veritate*, a. 1) argues: "It must be said that without any doubt that one must classify man by free will. The Faith obliges us to this ... the evidence induces it ... even manifest reason compels it."

The second is that it was defined against the Jansenists by Innocent X and Alexander VII, that for merit or the lack thereof in the state of fallen nature, freedom from coercion does not suffice, rather, freedom is required by necessity, or of indifference, as it was said above.

The third proposition is that the essence of freedom in general does not consist in the will alone, rather an undetermined contradiction is required of its essence, or to act or not to act. St. Thomas thinks thus (2, dist. 24, qu. 1, a. 1, ad 2): "This pertains to the freedom of the will that it could do or not do some action." Yet, an undetermined contrariety is not required from the essence of the will, *i.e.* the power to do a good or an evil; so the Theologians teach in common against Gonet (*dissert. 2, n. 218*) and Molina (*de Concordia*, disp. 2, etc.), who define freedom for those in this life by the *power toward a contrary opposite*. St. Augustine favors our teaching when he says: "Choice will be more powerful in a thing in which a man could not sin." (*de Civitate Dei*, l. 23, last chapter), as well as St. Anselm: "If to be able to sin means it is part of free will, then God and the Angels would not have free will, which is absurd." (*De Libero arb.*, ch. 1). St. Thomas says (*loc. cit.*), "It does not pertain to the argument of free will that one should stand indeterminately to the good, or the bad, and therefore where the will is most perfect, there it cannot tend to evil." He says the same thing in the Summa, *Pars Prima*, quest. 62, art. 8 ad 3.

ARTICLE IV

On the moral goodness and malice of human acts, and on the principles of morality.

§I. *In which the malice or goodness of a moral act is posited*

XXXIV. In regard to the nature of the morality of human acts theologians do not agree. Some say it suffices to constitute the morality that the act is voluntary, nor requires undetermined freedom. So think Gabriel, Almaïnus, Ocham, Major, etc. Some opine that the morality of the act formally consists in freedom, and they confound the latter with the former. So think Francis Felix, who praises Scotus on his behalf, and many fathers of his order. Others, such as Suarez, Vasquez, Salas, etc., assert that it is precisely a certain extrinsic denomination taken up from some extrinsic form. At length, the Thomists think it is something accidental that is superadded to essence, and to the freedom of the act, by which reason it has a special relation to a good or a law.

We, after dismissing the obscure formulas of this sort of speech from the scholastics, profitably say with the common opinion of theologians, that the *moral goodness of a human act consists* in *a certain conformity and suitability of a free act with right reason and law,* so that an act would be called good, which conforms to law and reason. This is why St. Augusitne says in *de Utilitate Credendi,* c. 12: "A right act can in no way be what does not set out from right reason." On the other hand, the moral malice of a human act consists in a discrepancy, or a lack of conformity with right reason. An evil act is said to be that which is not according to the dictate of right reason whether it is uncreated (the eternal law) or created (the natural reason of man), or a participation of the eternal law, according to St. Thomas (1.2., qu. 91, art. 2). In each case, this reason is the rule of human acts, from which the measure of the goodness or malice of human acts is taken up. So thinks the Continuator of Tournely (*De Act. Hum.,* cap. 6, art. 1, sect. 1). I say secondly, that even the moral philosophers, such as Genuensis (*de principiis legis naturae,* c. 15, § 9.), Purchot., and Anthony Murator (*Phil. Moral.,* c. 23 *de bono morali, sive honesto*), where he condemns Aristippus, Epicurus, Carneadis, and other ancient philosophers, and even certain recent ones outside of Italy, who constitute the nature of an honest good *only in the usefulness* to man, and the state; according to that of Horace: "Utility of the just itself, the mother almost of right and of equity." (Serm. 1.3, n. 95) That very famous man teaches that the nature of moral good has been placed *in conformity of the action with the laws of order, which God furnished to men for his honor as well as universal happiness.* Therefore, whatever tends to the glory of God, and the true happiness of man, is in conformity to the order established by God, both through an honest and virtuous consequent. On the other hand, we must judge on moral evil.

XXXV. From here it is inferred: 1) That no moral good, and no moral evil, can be understood without respect to at least natural law. Hence the Epicureans, who took up all laws, said that justice is found in fear of physical punishment, and on account of the utility of life, as Lucretius wrote (l. 5). When it is said commonly that a certain thing is forbidden because it is wicked, this is rightly understood to be a certain thing forbidden by positive law, such as what is opposed to natural law. For nothing is intrinsically evil, if it is not compared at least to the law of nature.

2) It is inferred that freedom is a necessary requisite to the morality of the act. For a human and moral act ought to proceed from deliberate reason, and hence ought to be free. (St. Thomas, 1.2. q. 18, art. 9). But they err who constitute the whole morality of a human act in freedom alone. It is true that freedom is furnished beforehand as the foundation of morality, otherwise one would not fear to assert that everything is ruled by faith, consequently they ought to say there is no sin, just as Spinoza, who in *Append. Prioris Eth., partis* attributes the origin of moral sins to human fantasy and superstition. However, it is false to formally constitute freedom alone as the goodness or malice of a human act without relation to suitability or the unsuitability of an act with right reason and law, as we are going to say and as Gonet (t. 3, tr. 3, cap. 9 *de actibus humanis*), and the Continuator of Tournely (*loc. cit.*) as well as many other theologians of great renown prove.

§II. *What are the principles of morality and how many*
are there?

XXXVI. Theologians call the principles of morality those
from which it is determined that some action is good or bad
or indifferent. They reckon that there are three principles of
this sort, namely the *object, the end, and the circumstances.*
That an action would be called good from the integral cause,
it is necessary that it be consistent with law and right
reason, and *on the side of the object,* both *on the side of the*
extrinsic end of the one that acts, and also *on the side of the*
circumstances. The object from which the act receives its
essential and primary morality, is that in regard to which the
moral act turns, and firstly, is attached, *per se,* to the act
itself; thus someone else's good is the object of theft, God is
the object of the act of love. Such an object is not considered
physically and according to its being, according to which it
is always good by the goodness of being, rather it is
considered morally, insofar as it is in conformity or not with
right reason. If the object is intrinsically and by its nature in
conformity with right reason, such as the love of God, it will
be immutably good. If, on the contrary, it is only
extrinsically and by force of positive law in conformity with
reason, such as fasting, then it can be good at some time, but
evil at another depending upon the circumstances.

XXXVII. Therefore, the first principle of morality is the
object, which, if it is morally good or bad, gives goodness to
an act or essential malice, as St. Thomas says (1.2. qu. 18, art.
2). The reasoning of St. Thomas is that, just as in natural
things the first goodness of a thing is applied from its form,
which gives the species to the thing itself, whether essential
or specific, so the first goodness of an act is applied to a
human act from the suitable object, in which it is primarily
conveyed. IF the object were indecent and out of conformity

with rational nature, the essential malice of the act rises from it.

Others, wishing to use a stricter formula of speech, say the human act takes its morality not from the object itself, but from the *modo tendendi* in the object, whether it is consonant or not with reason. So thinks the Continuator of Tournely (c. 6, art. 2, sect. 1, *Unum addam*). And in this mode they explain firstly the hatred for God, which holds the best object and is still morally the worst because the will is advanced against pursuing God with every love in a manner especially dissonant with reason, namely by having hatred.

XXXVIII. Another principle of morality is *the end*, not the intrinsic end of the work, which coincides with the object, but the extrinsic end of the one acting, who insofar as it is in conformity or not with the rules of morals it is said to be morally good or bad. Hence if an object were good, but the end of the worker were bad, the human act is entirely evil by the malice of the end, which destroys every goodness. The reason is, because such an act is simply evil. Right reason rejects that a good be chosen on account of a wicked end. St. Thomas thinks likewise (2. Dist. 38, q. 1, art. 4 ad 4), "When someone wants to give alms on account of vainglory, this is one act of the will, and this whole act is bad, although it does not have malice from everything which is in it." (See Gonet, *Man.*, tract. 3, *de act. Hum.*, c. 12, and St. Thomas, 1.2. qu. 18, art. 4 and 6). Moreover, if the object is good and the end is also good, then the human act has the twofold species of moral goodness, such as to give alms in satisfaction for sins. (St. Thomas, qu. 18, art. 4, 6 and 7, with the common teaching of theologians, apart from the one exception of Vasquez). But if the object were indifferent, then a good end makes the act morally good, such as to walk from obedience; an evil end makes the act evil, such as to walk to show off wealth. An evil end makes an act from evil worse, such as to steal so as to support a concubine; and it makes an act done from good evil, such as to give alms for vainglory.

XXXIX. The *circumstances* are the third principle of morality. They usually give some goodness to the act, or accidental malice, because goodness or malice of this sort comes upon an act that has already been constituted in its essence in a genus of morals. So St. Thomas thinks (*loc. cit.,* a. 5) with the common opinion.

Moreover, the circumstances are either *of a person,* which often adds a new species of malice, such as if a husband or one bound by a vow of chastity were to fornicate; and sometimes it only increases the malice within the same species. This is understood more on the person acting than on the one suffering the act, such as when those doing good are struck. Then there are circumstances *of place,* such as to steal in a sacred place, which changes the species, and thus on other circumstances of time, manner, auxiliaries, or instruments, whereby the act is carried out, which, as we said on other things, can either change or increase the malice whether notably or lightly within the same species. Note that the evil circumstances lightly present in an act do not remove all its goodness, nor do they erase all merit. So the common opinion holds, which is profusely asserted in *Contensione,* lib. 6, *diss.* 2, c. 2.

Hence, it is inferred for the practice which the confessor ought to question the penitent, who accuses himself of theft, on the intended end; for if he intended by this theft that he might have money to commit fornication, then there will be a new malice. Likewise, if he may have detracted from his neighbor, the confessor should ask whether perhaps he intended on this account do impede him from profit, or from attaining some dignity. For from the intended end, as has been said, the species of malice is easily changed.

XL. Here it is asked whether an external act adds some goodness or moral malice to an internal act? St. Thomas (*loc. cit.,* q. 20, a. 4), along with Gonet, Roncaglia, the Continuator of Tournely, teaches that an exterior act does not add an intrinsic moral goodness or malice, and *per se*, over the interior act, but only rejoices in the intrinsic goodness or malice taken up at the command of an act of the will. It is proved on the authority of St. Thomas (2. Dist. 40, q. 1, a. 3) where he says, "Because an exterior act adds nothing to the essential reward consequently to the intrinsic goodness which follows the essential reward). For someone only merits that has a perfect will to do some good, insofar as if he would do it ... equally while preserving a perfect will. Still, it adds some accidental reward." Take the martyrs, who really suffered for Christ, they have an accidental reward, or the laurel crown over those who desired with equal fervor of charity death for Christ. Now, I said that an external act does not add *an intrinsic* moral goodness or malice, and *per se* over the interior, for *per accidens* it adds, in the normal manner of speaking, some accidental goodness or malice. This is why St. Thomas adds: "Unless it were to happen that the will itself through an exterior act is made according to itself better in good things, it is made worse in evil things." For an external act is often the cause and occasion where an internal act becomes worse; either because interior acts are multiplied until the acts are carried out extrinsically; or because an interior act has a greater duration until it should carry out the work, which cannot be immediately carried out; or because it becomes more intense through the extrinsic nature of the act. Besides, through the external act the senses are made weaker, and the exterior powers are rendered more prone to evil; scandals are suffered; sometimes excommunication is incurred or irregularity, or the obligation for restitution, which are not incurred by an interior act. Still, Scotus (*Quodl.* 18, a. 3) and all Scotists, as Mastrius relates, leave no stone unturned so as to attribute,

for different reasons, an external act adds *per se* some
goodness or malice to an act of the will, because it has
intrinsic goodness, or malice over the interior act. See the
Salamancans on this question, as well as Mastrius and other
Scotists. There is, however, not enough space to explore this
any further.

ARTICLE V

*Whether an Indifferent Act is Granted in an Individual
Thing?*

XLI. It behooves us to explain the state of the question by an
explanation of terminology. A human act (which is the only
thing we will speak of here), is said to be indifferent either
in species or *in an individual thing*. An indifferent act *in
specie* is an act considered in general (by abstracting it from
the end and from individual circumstances) *only
comparatively to its object, which is neither good in itself, viz.
consonant with reason, nor evil, that is dissonant with reason,
but indifferent to both,* such as to walk, to lift straw, to gather
flowers, etc. which from their species, or object, are neither
good nor bad, but by reason of their end, and other
circumstances become upright or made evil. But an
indifferent act in *an individual thing is an act considered
exactly as it is on the side of the thing according to its object,
end, and all individual circumstances,* which still may be
neither good nor bad, but indifferent.

XLII. It is certain *de fide* that not every human act is
indifferent according to its species or object. Rather, certain
ones are good of themselves, such as acts of faith, hope and
charity, etc.; certain ones are evil in themselves, such as
fornication, murder of the innocent, etc. For there are certain
objects of themselves consonant with reason, while there are
also others of themselves dissonant with reason.

XLIII. It is also certain that some acts are granted which, according to their species are indifferent, because of themselves they are neither good nor bad. St. Thomas thinks thus (*loc. cit.* art. 8) with the common opinion. Hence, St. Jerome wrote: "Continence is good, lust is bad, to walk between the two is indifferent." (Ep. 89). The point is rendered by the condemnation of article 16 of John Hus, which was made in the Council of Constance, sess. 15, asserting "that no work is indifferent." It cannot be understood to be about indifferent acts in an individual thing, because a great many good Catholics defend this same thing as probable; therefore it must be understood about indifferent things *in specie.*

XLIV. That we would respond to the proposed question, we say that indifferent acts are not granted in an individual thing. So think St. Thomas (1.2. qu. 18, a. 9) and the Thomists, Bellarmine, Suarez, Valentia, Durandus (in 2. Dist. 40, q. 1), Richardus, Major, Gaet., Medina, Becanus and many others against Scotus and the Scotists, Alensis, St. Bonaventure, Almain., Vasquez, etc. The particular reasoning of St. Thomas is: "A moral act only has goodness from its object ..., but also from circumstances. ... It is necessary that each individual act would have some circumstance whereby it is dragged to good or evil, to the lesser on the side of the end of the intention. When reason might ordain that the act proceeding from deliberative reason, if it were not ordered to the due end, because of this very thing it is opposed to reason, and has the reasoning of evil, but if it is ordained to its due end, it is in conformity with the order of reason, for which reason it has the reasoning of good. Furthermore, it is necessary that it will either be ordained or not to the due end. This is why it is necessary that every act of man proceeding from deliberative reasoning considered in an individual is good or evil." Thus the vigorous Angelic Doctor.

Besides, it cannot happen that some singular act proceeding from the deliberative will would be done without circumstances. Further, those circumstances are consistent with right reason, so namely, that an act should be done, when, where, how and on account of what thing would it be fitting to be done, and so it is good; or, the circumstances are not in accord with right reason, not so much all, but something is lacking and thus it is bad. Consequently, no act is in an individual thing, and considered according to all circumstances it can be indifferent.

To this purpose, a man is held to refer all his acts to God when he acts with deliberation and on account of some end. For the Apostle says: "Whether you eat or drink, or do anything at all, do all things for the glory of God" (1 Cor. 10:31). Therefore, if he refers to God at least through virtual intention, it will be a good act, if he does not refer is intention, it will be evil; therefore nothing is indifferent. I know our adversaries say that the words of the apostle contain a counsel and not a precept. But falsely, since the Fathers recognize a precept not a counsel. So thinks Augustine, Coelestinus I, Maximus, St. Thomas (lect. 3, c. 3, Ep. ad Coloss.), cited in the Continuator of Tournely (cap. 6, art. 1, sect. 2, *de actibus humanis*), to which I send anyone who is eager to find this question treated more profusely with the objections of our adversaries.

Hence, we gather for praxis that more often it is fitting in a day, at least in the morning, generally to offer to God all his actions, so that he might fulfill the precept of the Apostle, at least by virtual intention to do all for the glory of God. In this mode, every act that is also indifferent *in specie* is good, and virtual in an individual thing. Indeed, actual relation of all things, whether of words or works in an upright act is not required; because it would be an immovable weight, and the matter having embraced six thousand scruples, but virtual suffices, as we said, wherefore, although someone coming to the table, does not think about preservation of life, but only on the delight of food, as Gonet says, he does not sin for that reason, because such a delight, at least virtually, he wishes on account of the preservation of life, and thus does not inordinately desire it. Thus concludes human acts, and their principles and morality.

TREATISE ON SINS

CHAPTER I
On Sin in General

DUBIUM I

1. *What is a sin?*
2. *What conditions are required to sin?*
3. *What must be noted in regard to the requisite knowledge to sin?*
4. *Whether formal knowledge is required for a mortal sin, or whether virtual knowledge suffices?*
5. *What must be known in regard to requisite consent to sin?*
6. *Whether one would sin gravely, who stands negatively in regard to inordinate motives?*
7. *What if they are carnal motives?*
8. *What remedies are there in that regard?*
9. *Whether we are held to resist them if the reason to do so were not present?*
10. *How, and in what time are sins of omission imputed?*
11. *Whether venial sin is against the divine law?*

1.—"Resp. 1. It is a transgression of the law, or (as "Cardinal Toledo says), it is a voluntary retreat from the "divine law, through which the rule is understood as a "precept both natural and human as well as divine: "*through retreat* an act is understood, or its omission, "which is not only voluntary but also free with some "actual awareness of malice; I add this because, as "Sanchez teaches (1. Mor. c. 16) along with Vasquez, "Bonacina (d. 2, q. 1, p. 3, n. 3 et 12, etc.) etc., freedom "does not suffice for a sinful act, and any virtual

"knowledge you like, whether interpretative, whereby,
"viz., someone could have known and ought to have, not
"each actual, whereby the intellect attends the *rationes*
"*commode* and *incommode* in an object; rather, it is
"required that he know the moral malice of an object, or
"at least a doubt about it, or at least he should adopt
"some scruple. The reason is, both because without this
"knowledge it is not voluntary, since it would not be
"known, and because so long as such a thought does not
"occur to the intellect it is not a sufficient principle for
"deliberating about the malice, and therefore, neither
"freedom and hence neither fault, and that is considered
"natural inadvertence, and invincible forgetfulness.
"Nevertheless, Tann. (d. 4, *de pecc.* d. 5, q. 5, n. 106), adds
"it is not necessary that the consideration should remain
"in the act while the sin endures; it is enough that it
"should remain either in act or in virtue so that with it,
"either the act of sin has begun, or at least after the cause
"is given, such as it is done in drunkenness, one who sins
"does not do so by the force of present, but past
"deliberation. (See Bald., l. 1, d. 36). Still, more recent
"theologians commonly teach that such a man that is,
"say drunk, does not sin formally when he lacks the use
"of reason; but the malice of those things, which then
"happen, were contracted before while foreseeing the
"evil which he was going to commit, he permitted the
"cause: and they say that while someone sins in act,
"there always remains some weak or confused
"knowledge of the malice (See Scol.)

2.—"Resp. 2. For sin three conditions are required, as is
"clear from the first response: 1) That it be voluntary, *i.e.*
"that it is done from the consent of the will; 2) That it be
"free, *i.e.* that it should be in the power of the will to do,
"or not; 3) That the malice should be known.

Wherefore it is resolved:

"1. By defect of the first condition, no act, which is not
"either in or from the will is a sin, unless the will
"accepts it; and therefore, it does not impede
"communion, whether it would be internal, such as
"thoughts against the faith, blasphemies, obscenities,
"movements of the flesh, even to the effusion of seed; or
"external and violent, for example, if a virgin is raped.

"2. By a defect of the second condition, thereupon
"violent movements of anger or concupiscence are
"excused from sin, whereby the use of reason is
"disturbed and freedom abolished.

"3. By a defect of the third one does not sin who, on a
"fast day, thinking nothing of the precept, would eat or
"eat meat, even if he notices these are delightful to him.
"Likewise, one who throws a stone through a window,
"not knowing the danger of breaking, or one who
"celebrates a usurious contract not knowing it is such
"(Sanchez, l. 1, c. 16, n. 21, Reg. l. 15, n. 75).

"4. Damage and the events (although otherwise frequent)
"following a bout of drunkenness, and in no way
"foreseen are inculpable because they were free neither
"in themselves nor in their causes. But they would be
"culpable if they were foreseen, or if sufficient diligence
"from the prescription of prudence were not applied, lest
"he would follow it; but, when it has been applied, even
"after it comes about, he is free from fault, just as even,
"when according to the circumstances of time and place
"the danger of evil does not appear, therefore no caution
"has been applied. Vasquez so thinks (l. 2, d. 124, c. 2),
"with whom Lessius is in agreement (Lessius, lib. 4, c. 3)
"when he teaches that if by negligence, drunkenness or
"the events that usually follow it were guarded against,
"it is only venial. Also the evils, which can be foreseen,

"will only be venial because, when not they are not free "in themselves but only in the cause, they cannot have a "greater fault than the cause itself.

3.—In regard to the *knowledge* and *consent* requisite for sin, we must note some necessary things.

I. In regard to *knowledge of the intellect* it must be noted 1) what mode in which a sin is carried out: firstly, the object represented to the senses, and moves the sensitive appetite by the physical delight, and knows its malice. At length, the will, so knowing, consents to it. It must be noted 2) that the intellect can know in a twofold manner, either *fully*, namely when we discern with an unencumbered mind; or *half-fully*, when we know a matter with a mind not plainly unencumbered, because perhaps we are either half asleep or half drunk, or in another case distracted. For after the intellect is taken by the delectability of the object offered, that it notices no moral malice in it, hence three motions correspond to this threefold knowledge, viz. a) *Motion in the first of the first*, those who anticipate all knowledge of reason, and these are altogether free from fault. b) *Motion in the second of the first*, those acts which are done with half-full knowledge, and these do not exceed venial sin; because when full knowledge did not precede them, the will does not have the perfect freedom that is required to consent to a mortal sin. c) *Deliberate motions*, which are done with full knowledge of the intellect clearly discerning the moral malice, at least confusedly in general, and with the full consent of the will; these are mortal sins, if the objects are forbidden *sub gravi*. (St. Thomas, *de malo*, q. 7, art. 6; Cajetan; Vasquez; Sanchez; Azor; Bonacina; Navarre, etc. with the Salamancans, tr. 20, c. 1, p. 1, n. 2, et seqq.).

4.—With these having been prefaced, the question becomes whether actual and express knowledge of the malice of the act is required for mortal sin, or whether virtual and interpretive knowledge would suffice?

The first opinion, which Cajetan once held (2. 2. Q. 88, a. 1, d. 3), and Medina, Lopez, Serra, Prado, and others with the Salamancans, *idbid.* N. 5, which is assiduously defended by Concina (*Compend. Theol.*, lib. 8, d. 3, c. 2, n. 14), the Continuator of Tournely (*de pecc.*, c. 4, art. 1), Angelus, Franzoja (*in Bus.*, lib. 5, c. 2, *de pecc. Animadv.* I), Antoine and other more recent theologians, says that actual notice is not required, rather it is enough for it to be virtual and interpretive, which in this consists in that a man would comprehend and could know the malice of an action, although actually he does not notice it; otherwise (they say), all the crimes of men would be reputed immune from fault, that blinded men would carry out a great many evils by their passions or bad habits, noticing nothing.

The Second opinion, which is more common, affirms that actual knowledge of the malice is required, or of its danger, or at least of the obligation to know about it. (Sylvius, in 1.2., q. 66, art. 3, q. 3, concl. 2; Suarez, tom. 5, in 4 p.d. 4, sect. 8, ex n. 14; Tapia, lib. 3, q. 9, art. 5, and 11; Sanchez, *dec.* lib. 1, c. 16, n. 21; Sayrus, Thes., lib. 2, c. 9, nu. 11; Palaus, tr. 2, d. 1, p. 15, n. 3; Salas, tr. 13, d. 8, sect. 11, n. 87; Bonacina, *de Cens.* d. 1; the Salamancans, *loc. cit.* n. 6, both the scholastics, tr. 13, d. 13, sect. 11, n. 1 and the moralists, r. 20, cap. 14, n. 8; Gamachaeus, t. 2, p. 194; Isambert., p. 232; Du Val, p. 178; likewise Vasquez, 1.2. q. 123, c. 2, n. 6; along with Lyranus, Tostatus, Adrian VI, Curiel, Vitoria, Gorduba, and others). The same with St. Antoninus, Wigandt, Sainte Beuve, and Cardinal Gotti, whose citations and words will be added below. They say that for every mortal sin some type of knowledge is required, or suspicion of the malice of the act, either in itself or in its cause; at least *in confuso*. Their reasoning is because nothing is willed except what is premeditated; for that reason, ignorance cannot be imputed to sin unless it were held on the malice of the object at least by some confused apprehension; for he that in no way knows the malice of his action, or the obligation to know it, in no way sins against it by acting.

With these things having been posited, I shall advance my sense and say that, by setting up within the boundaries of the just, the aforesaid opinions can be reconciled. For if it were said that actual and express knowledge were demanded for all mortal sins then this would certainly be false; because it can come about in many ways that a great many evils, although actually and expressly not known, nevertheless are rightly imputed as a sin in those carrying them out, if the ignorance of them is voluntary in some manner, either on account of negligence, or passion, or bad habits, or even a voluntary lack of consideration in acting.

Therefore, in the first mode ignorance would be voluntary on account of negligence, as St. Thomas teaches (1.2. q. 76, a. 3), when he prefaces the rule: "Ignorance which is the cause of the act because it causes something involuntary, of itself has what excuses from sin, to the extent that it is voluntary on the reasoning of sin." Then he adds that ignorance can be voluntary in two modes, "either directly, just as when someone studiously wishes to know some things, that he might sin more freely, or indirectly, just as when someone on account of work or other occupations neglects to add that through which would be withdrawn from sin. For such negligence makes the ignorance itself voluntary, and the sin would merely be of those things which someone can know and is held to know. And therefore, such ignorance does not totally excuse from sin. But if there would be such ignorance which would be altogether involuntary, whether because it is invincible, or because it is of a thing which someone is not held to know, such ignorance altogether excuses from sin." Note, "*such negligence makes the ignorance itself voluntary.*" Besides, note here that the Angelic doctor does not doubt in the last words related, that invincible ignorance can well be granted even

of those things which someone is held to know. He writes
the same thing in another place (*de malo*, q. 3, art. 7 ad 7).
"Ignorance which is altogether involuntary, is not a sin. And
this is what St. Augustine says: 'Fault is not imputed to you
if you were unwillingly ignorant, rather than if you
neglected to know,' he grants to understand, which
ignorance has, because it is a sin from the preceding
negligence, which is nothing other than to not apply the
mind to know those things which someone ought to know."
And in the same passage, *ad* 8, St. Thomas says that not only
is ignorance reputed voluntary, but even more in man "On
account of the work of learning, or lest he would be impeded
by the sin which he loves, refuses to know, and thus
ignorance is in a certain measure commanded by the will."
Therefore, in these very citations, the Angelic Doctor
certainly does not reckon it culpable ignorance which does
not know, rather of one who neglects or refuses in a certain
act to apply his mind by a command of the will to learn
those things which he is held to know in regard to a precept
which urges, as he more expressly declares in the body of
the aforesaid article 3, saying: "The cause of ignorance in the
mind does not apply itself to learn and this very thing does
not apply the mind to know that which one ought to know,
is a sin of omission."

In the second mode, ignorance might be voluntary on
account of a passion, which someone deliberately wants to
follow. Someone who acts according to their passion will
rightly be imputed with every bad effect connected to such
a passion, although in particular it is not recognized. This is
because when a man embraces some passion, consequently
he embraces every effect commonly arising from that
passion, which, even if in particular they are not foreseen,
they are at least foreseen in disorder; for wishing to satisfy
some passion, say vengeance, consequently he at least
admits *in confuso* whatever perverse means which are

expedient to satisfy that passion. This is why the effects come into being, although they are not voluntary in themselves, still they are voluntary in their cause, namely in adherence to the passion. St. Thomas also teaches this in 1.2. q. 6, a. 8, where he calls the ignorance of this agent through passion *"ignorantiam malae electionis,"*[2] saying: "In another mode, voluntary ignorance of a thing is said to be when someone can know and ought to know, so it is said that he does not so act and does not will, but acts voluntarily ... Therefore, in this mode it is said to be ignorance either when someone does not consider it in the act, but can and ought consider it, which is ignorance of an evil choice, or arising from passion or a habit." Likewise, he repeats it in his work *de Malo* (q. 3, a. 20), where he says: "The binding of reason through a passion is not imputed to sin except perhaps in regard to the beginning of such a passion, insofar as it was voluntary, for the will could from the beginning set an obstacle lest a passion would proceed in such a thing." Moreover, in another place (1.2. q. 77, a. 7), he says: "Yet whenever passion is not enough, which might altogether interrupt the use of reason, and then reason can exclude a passion by diverting to other thoughts, or to impede lest he might obtain its effect."

In the third mode, ignorance becomes voluntary by reason of a bad habit, as St. Thomas holds in the passage cited above (1. 2. Q. 6, a. 8); then evil acts which have their beginnings in an evil habit, are equally voluntary either in their cause, viz. when in the beginning an evil custom is voluntarily contracted; or more than that, because, as I believe with Antoine and the author of the book *Istruzzione de' novella confessori*, sinners of this sort are badly habituated, although they might have less expedient knowledge than others, still they always have some actual

---

[2] Translator's note: Ignorance of an evil choice.

knowledge of their crimes sufficient to render the acts deliberate and moral; for when they give little weight to sin, a sensible and memorable impression is not made in their souls, which is made in another having knowledge less crooked; and hence it comes about that in their memory an actual vestige of that knowledge does not remain, which they have enough in the sin beforehand, or the vestige is so light that if they were asked they would easily respond that they did not know, but a cautious confessor ought not place any trust in them. And it seems the same thing can be said about those working according to their bad passions, in which they have not yet lacked all knowledge of the malice of their sins, but the knowledge in them is so obscure that it could hardly be discerned.

Lastly, in the fourth mode ignorance becomes voluntary and culpable, as Tanner says (t. 2, dub. 4, q. 5, dub. 5, n. 103), Antoine (*tr. De pecc.* c. 4, qu. 7 in fine) and St. Antoninus, if a man in acting noticeably neglected to apply consideration which is due to the things that must be done, then those who already noticed (as Antoine rightly says) something more must be considered, and still wish to throw themselves headlong into the act, all the errors which he committed are rightly imputed to him.

On the other hand, it seems to me that it must altogether be held that if ignorance in none of the aforesaid modes were voluntary, and a man had no actual notice of malice, or of danger, neither directly nor indirectly, nor in itself nor in its cause, then in no matter would the errors which he does not notice be imputed to him. The reason is, because for the effects of some cause to be imputed to him, he ought necessarily to precede (at least in principle), actual and express notice of the malice of the object; for interpretive notice, as the Salamancans rightly speak of it (tr. 20, c. 13, n. 7), is founded on some express notice, just as an indirect voluntary act is founded on a direct one. Besides, that interpretive notice supposes an obligation, and the power to know, but with a deficiency in all express notice there is no power to know, and therefore, there is no obligation, since no obligation binds unless before hand it were known in some manner.

One might say: All ignorance in one that is held and can know his obligation is vincible and for that reason culpable. Yet, Sylvius and Suarez correctly respond that one who is altogether ignorant of the malice of the object, and still has the obligation to notice indeed has the remote power, or to know the nature, but lacks the proximate and expedient power which is necessary for man to know the deformity of his actions. "Who does not know that it is not in man's power to know?" St. Augustine says (*de Spiritu et Anima*). For that reason, the man could not naturally and by human means conquer his ignorance. Indeed he will know his action, whereby it is an action, but he will not know it in the respect to which it is evil, for cognition of the object alone in its nature is not a sufficient principle to discern, nor to inquire whether the object is in a moral act, which is altogether different from nature. Suarez wisely says, "When no such cognition abides in the mind whereby the will could be roused to seek knowledge, it is not in the power of man to move himself and consequently such ignorance cannot be imputed to a man (3, p. t. 5, d. 4, sect. 8, n. 18). And this is what St. Thomas teaches (1.2. q. 76, a. 2), saying: "For that reason, on account of negligence, the ignorance of those things which someone is held to know, is a sin. Moreover, sin is not imputed to a man for negligence if he does not know those things which he cannot know: this is why ignorance of these things is said to be invincible, because it cannot be conquered by effort." Furthermore, this effort, or due diligence applied to expel ignorance, as Sylvius (in 1.2., qu. 76, art. 3, concl. 1, and then qu. 3, concl. 1), rightly notices with Medina, and Richardus, ought not to be supreme, rather it suffices if it would be moral, and such as prudent men usually apply in a grave matter; for while doubt remains, the unlearned man ought to consult the experienced; but the learned man ought to consult books or confer on the matter with other learned men.

Finally, I observe this opinion is commonly held by the authors, not only by probabilists, (who do no longer hold it as probable, but acknowledge it *as most certain*; just as Suarez writes), but even the antiprobabilists, and even Saint Beuve, the Sorbonne doctor, writes: "If it will be only noticed what is considered materially or physically in the act, and not formally or morally, the act will be merely volitional as it is something physical, and not as something moral; therefore it is not evil; and in this there will be no malice" (*De Pecc.* d. 5, sect. 1, art. 3). Cardinal Gotti writes: "I say secondly, implicit or virtual notice of the malice, or the danger of it, of an action suffices for mortal sin. And indeed, in the very matter in which someone hesitates or suspects the malice of his action, or the danger of malice, and still neglects to seek the truth of the matter, is reckoned to place the action interpretively and wills the malice itself." (T. 2, tr. 4, *de vitiis*, q. 1 dub. 4, § 3, num. 11). Fr. Wigandt says likewise, "I say: 1) Deliberation, or notice, is twofold. One is full and perfect, which is present when a man notices not only for the operation, insofar as its natural being, e.g. to eat meat, but even its malice, or the danger of transgressing the law; while another is imperfect, etc. I say: 2) That something in an individual thing is imputed to mortal sin, full and perfect deliberation ought to be present" (Tr. 4, ex 2, *de peccat.*, n. 50). St. Antoninus agrees with them, and to sin mortally in *delectatio morosa* requires not only deliberation, but even attention to the danger, in these words: "Therefore, such complacency remains after sufficient deliberation, as well as notice of the danger and then it is a mortal sin." (P. 2, tit. 5, c. 5, in fine). In another place, he says: "A defect of right judgment pertains to the vice of consideration, just as when someone fails in right judgment, insofar as he scorns or neglects to attend to those things from which right judgment proceeds." (*Ibid.*, c. 11, *sub init.*). Moreover, the Continuator of Tournely agrees, because he so concludes: "Therefore, that within the boundaries of what is true we stop on a step, let us judge, one who is not so attentive to the malice of sin, that he could not notice either because he is taken up in a natural distraction or for some similar reason, is not held by sin. Thus the penitent will be excused, who does not fulfill the penance that was enjoined upon him because he forgot. Yet, it must be said otherwise about actions, which men absorbed in worldly things elicit or omit, serving their passions, they are accustomed to think nothing, for they do not think." (*De pecc.*, c. 4, art. 1, obj. 4) Now we already admit the same thing. It agrees even with Antoine, who, while arguing on ignorance, says that the lack of notice or the inconsideration is culpable in one who omits due diligence, or who acts recklessly when he already notices a thing needs greater consideration, or one who in a positive act wishes to follow a passion which impedes advertence. "On the other hand," he says, "if [inadvertence] were invincible in a man having due habitual cognition, is altogether inculpable, and it excuses from those things which are done on account of it against the law; because the malice of the act then is by no means, not even interpretatively, voluntary; for without the power to know an act cannot be volitional." (*De pecc.* c. 4, q. 7).

Hence it must be concluded that the opinion of those who say that all the errors which are committed against the law must be imputed to the worker, even if no actual advertence were to intercede, neither direct nor indirect, in itself or in its cause, at least in a confused state of mind, rather, merely interpretive advertence was present, consisting only in this, that he ought and could notice the malice only by a physical and remote power. This opinion can in no way be held. Otherwise it would follow that a great many men would find themselves weighed down by numerous mortal sins if they ever had any thought at all in their regard. They will say, perhaps, that these men in punishment for their faults, say on account of lusts that they did not repress, or obligations of their proper state which they did not fulfill, and other negligences, merit a loss of grace, whereby in general were they to have known well the malice of their actions, and therefore all their errors are imputed to fault. But that this conclusion could prevails, first the supposed propositions would have to be proven, which is scarcely the case; for by reason of the other defects God will deprive someone of his future grace, whereby he would resists temptations and his own passions, unless he would fall into others; therefore that subtraction will effect that such a man will fall into the sins which he knows well enough to be sins, but it will not effect that errors will be imputed to him which in no mode, expressly or in a confused state of mind, he recognizes as sins; because where there is not cognition, there is no freedom; and where there is no freedom, there is no sin. Some will insist on the point, yet St. Thomas (Lectio 7 in c. 1 *epist. Ad Rom.*) says: "If ignorance is caused by sin, it cannot excuse a subsequent fault." But we say this must rightly be understood on voluntary ignorance in something from the modes explained by the Angelic doctor above. Besides, because the Holy Doctor speaks on infidels, who err in faith, certainly on account of culpable ignorance, all the sins which they commit are rightly imputed to them.

Besides, if it were imputed to a man, all the errors thereof without any advertence, although he, after applying due diligence, will judge that he can act rightly, it would follow that it would not suffice to act honestly to follow the opinions (if they might be less safe) whether probable or more probable, or even the most probable, or even morally certain. But this cannot be said, since it was condemned by Alexander VIII as proposition 3, which said: "It is not permitted to follow even the most probable opinion among the most probable."

It remains to satisfy the abundant objections of our adversaries, but we will see to this in short order. They object: 1) with that in *Reg.* 13, *juris* in 6, where it is said: "Ignorance of fact, not of law, excuses." But Sylvius responds to this (1.2. q. 76, art. 3, qu. 1, concl. 7) that it is understood on public statutes, as the Gloss already explains in the same place; for in the judicial forum, after the promulgation of the law, the ignorance of the transgressor is ordinarily presumed to be vincible unless some reason were present that would cause him to presume the contrary, as is held *in c. In tua, tit. Qui matrim. accus., etc.*

They object: 2) That if actual advertence were required for all sins, the Jews would be rendered inculpable for crucifying the Lord, pagans for killing the martyrs, and heretics for perpetrating their innumerable crimes. But they are answered in one line, namely that the ignorance of all these was and is altogether crass. For, Christ the Lord, speaking about the Jews, said: "If I had not done works among them that no one else has done, they would not have sin." (John 15:24). Certainly, the same must be said about infidels and heretics, to whom, on account of their malice and supine negligence, all their errors are justly imputed to sin.

They object: 3) That knowledge requiring some actual advertence does not differ from that which upholds philosophical sin immune from theological fault. But the response is that the aforesaid opinion was forbidden by Alexander VIII because he that works against right reason, as is supposed in a philosophical sin, even if he does not consider it an offense to God, really offended him, since by offending rational nature he offended, at the same time, the author of nature itself. But in such a sin it is always required that a man notices his action is opposed to right reason. What, therefore, is common between philosophical sin and that action, whereby someone in no manner, not even in a confused state of mind, notices it is evil, and perhaps at sometime considers it good? Thus let us pass from advertence to consent.

II. *On the consent of the will.*

5.—It is certain that "a sin is committed by the will," as all teach with St. Augustine and St. Thomas (1.2. q. 74, art. 1). But we must preface: 1) perfect consent is altogether required for mortal sin, or the deliberation of the will. That is common and certain with all the Doctors, even of a more rigid opinion, since the very rigid Contensonius thinks thus in his theology (t. 1, p. 164, *spec.* 3), as well as the Continuator of Tournely (*de pecc.* c. 4, a. 1, in fine), Concina (t. 10, p. 508, n. 7), Wigandt (tr. 4, ex 2, n. 44), Genet. (tr. 1, c. 9, *de peccat.* q. 12 *in fine*), where he says: "When sin proceeds only from the will, if the deliberation were merely imperfect, it will only be a venial sin." For even Navarre (*Sum.* C. 16, n. 8), says: "A whole judgment is required to constitute sin, from *cap. 1 de delict. puerorum.*" the Salamancans say the same thing, (tr. 20, c. 11, p. 1, n. 5) with Cajetan, Vasquez, Sanchez, Palaus, and innumerable others, following what St. Thomas says (1. 2. Q. 88, a. 6): "It can ... what is in general mortal, be venial on account of the imperfection of the act because it did not perfectly reach to the reasoning of the moral act, since it was not deliberate, but immediate." St. Thomas also teaches the same thing in the Commentary on the Sentences (4, d. 9, quaest. 1, art. 4) where he says that the pollution of one that is half-asleep is mortal when it is advertently accepted with deliberate consent. St. Antoninus teaches the same thing (p. 2, tit. 6, c. 5). Furthermore,

Contensonius explains the matter more clearly (*loc. cit.*) saying that perfect deliberation is required for a mortal sin, because our movements are only culpable insofar as they are voluntary; moreover, as much as they are perfectly voluntary, so also they are deliberate. Moreover, for mortal sin, which is a full and consummated sin, a perfectly voluntary act is required.

It must be prefaced: 2) consent can be express, or direct, and implicit, or indirect, when viz. someone wills a cause, from which necessarily an effect arises; for then if he wills the cause directly, he also indirectly wills the effect. It must be prefaced: 3) that after the advertence of the intellect, in a threefold mode the will can impose itself toward an evil object that has been proposed: a) by positively consenting to it; b) by not consenting nor resisting, but only holding himself negatively; c) by positively resisting.

6.—Hence that great question arises among the Doctors, whether one would sin gravely who in the negative and does not positively resist the movement of the sensitive appetite in regard to a forbidden object, under mortal sin? Here we must preface that it is certain *de fide*, against innovators, the movements of sensuality without any consent of the will are not mortal sins, as taught by the Council of Trent (*sess. 5, n. 5, de pecc. orig.*) where it is said: "Concupiscence, which the Apostle sometimes calls sin, this Holy Council declares the Catholic Church has never understood to be called a sin, which truly and properly is a sin among the baptized, but because it is from sin, and inclines to sin; if anyone should think the contrary, *Anathema sit.*" Nay more, (whatever Cajetan and Gonet might say), it seems certain that such movements are not even venial, by the same decree of Trent, where it is said that concupiscence wounds those that do not consent to it, and vigorously by the grace of Christ not to avail of what is incompatible with it (see Wigandt, t. 4, ex. 2, n. 44). Hence, there are three opinions sought for a response.

First, with Val, Lessius, Vasquez, etc. (quoted in the Salamancans, tr. 20, c. 13, p. 2, n. 13), affirm one sins gravely, even when the danger of consent ceases. Their reasoning, is that the will is held not only to not consent, but even to resist the disordered movements of the sensitive appetite.

Second, with Tamburinius And others cited by Croix (l. 5, ex. N. 109), says such a man does not even sin venially without the danger of consent; but the Salamancans assert this opinion (*ibid.*, n. 14) and it is commonly rejected; wherefore they say rightly with Croix in practice it can be defended in no way.

The third and true opinion, of St. Thomas (qu. 15, a. 4, ad 10), Sanchez (*Dec.* l. 1, c. 2, nu. 13), Gerson, Palaus, Rodriguez, Granadus, and the Salamancans (loc. cit., n. 15 and 16), holds that when the danger of consent ceases, it is venial to not positively resist illicit movements, but not mortal. And St. Thomas seems to expressly confirm this in 1. 2. Qu. 74, art. 4, where he says: "Mortal sin cannot be in sensuality, but only in reason." Thus, the reasoning is both because consent to gravely sin does not proceed from the appetite, but from the will, which, when it does not positively consent, a mortal sin is not committed. And therefore it is commonly venial, insofar as a man ought to beware lest the appetite would drag the will after it, but this obligation, when the danger of consent is not proximate, and only light; then because, if we are held *sub gravi* to positively repel all disordered movements, we would be held to the impossible: for it is impossible (as Cajetan says) to positively restrain these motions taken collectively.

7.—From these, nevertheless, it is inferred that when venereal delight arises, we are held *sub gravi* to positively resist, because commotions of this sort, when they are violent, for the most part, if they are not positively repelled (at least through an act of simple displeasure) they drag the consent of the will with it. (Croix, l. 5, ex. n. 109;

Busembaum, *infra* d. 2, a. 2, in fin.; Holzm., to. 1, p. 325; Sylvius, 1.2. q. 74, a. 2, q. 1; the Continuator of Tournely, *de 6, Dec. praec.* Art. 9, concl. 2, and Sporer T. 1, p. 81, n. 14, as well as the Salamancans *ibid.* n. 19, with the common opinion of doctors.)

8.—Here it must be noted: I. That to repel carnal temptations, in regard to the sense, it is very beneficial that the emotions be restrained, to cover the parts excited with garments, and suppress them as a certain modern author adverts. In regard to preserving the mind from consent, it is truly beneficial to think about the passion of Jesus Christ, or on the punishments of hell, or on death, etc., and even on the torture of remorse that the soul suffers after carrying out a sin. Moreover, it will be necessary in concupiscence of this sort to have recourse to prayer; for chastity is only obtained from God, as Solomon observes: "And as I know, because otherwise I could not be continent unless God would grant it, etc." (Wisdom 8:21) And ordinarily God does not give anything except to those asking for it, as we read in St. John: "Ask and you shall receive." (John 16:14) Hence, when one is tempted he should then implore help from the Lord, from the Immaculate Mother of God, from the Saints, lovers of purity, such as St. Aloysius Gonzaga and St. Philip Neri, etc. However, apart from everything else it will suffice and be a more suitable remedy because it is shorter as well as easier confidently to invoke and to venerate multiple times the most powerful names of Jesus and Mary. It will also especially help to elicit a fervent act of love of God, by renewing one's purpose to undergo death rather than sin. It also suffices in an act of emotion to divert the mind to other things, as well as to positively resist, as Sporer (p. 82, n. 16), the Continuator of Tournely (*loc. cit.*, concl. 3), Contens. (tom. 1, p. 164, spec. 3) and Croix (l. 5, num. 111). And, if the movements were light, it will be better to scorn them without positive resistence. (Croix, *ibid.*, with Bonasp.)

9.–It must be noted: II. There is no obligation to positively resist carnal movements if there is a just cause to not resist, namely if someone were experienced in resisting the movements being roused and increased more; or if the movements should arise from a necessary or useful action, *e.g.* hearing confessions, reading foul literature for knowledge of useful things, from a necessary touch so as to heal someone, and similar things. For then, on the side of the cause of the movements, we are not held to relinquish the work, as the doctors commonly teach. (Sporer *De pecc.*, c. 6, n. 13; Contens., *loc. cit.*; Salam. Tr. 20, c. 13, p. 2, n. 20; Croix, lib. 5, n. 111; Suarez and others). On the other side, we are neither held then to positively resist the movements, if it is not an easy matter to repel them. It is enough then to stand negatively with a firm purpose to never consent: for the very purpose to not actually consent suffices to free a man from fault, unless it were mortal, even if not from venial, if the resistance were weak, as Toledo, Cajetan, Laymann etc. say with the Salamancans (tr. 20, c. 13, p. 2 n. 20). But Croix (l. 5, with Azor and Sanchez), suppose it as certain that in the aforesaid case, when the temptation endures for a long time, and it will be very difficult to continually positively repel the movements, they permit no sin if they stand negatively. And so the Continuator of Tournely counsels to do (*loc. cit.* v. *Duplici porro*), with Sylvius, for those who are reverent in conscience.

Here, at length, some remarks must be made in regard to sins of omission; it must be noted: I. with St. Thomas and the Salamancans (tr. cit. c. 10, p. 2, n. 11) that for any sin of omission a positive act of the will is required; the will is not exercised, nor sins, except through act. It must be noted: II. A concomitant act of omission, such as to play, eat, while, *e.g.* Mass is omitted, is not a sin unless it is the cause of the omission, say when play is the cause of omitting Mass. (The Salamancans *Ibid.*, num. 16; Corn., Montes, etc.) Then the acts influencing the same malice of omission, but not a different thing, such as the Continuator of Tournely (*de pecc. part. 2*, cap. 3) holds against Suarez, Granadus, etc. I say secondly, with de Lugo, Becanus, Bonacina, Azor, Filluci, and the Salamancans (ibid., n. 19, with others in common), the reason why it then suffices to only confess the omission, but if the action which is the cause of the omission, were also a mortal sin, namely if someone were to omit Mass on account of stealing, then the stealing can be spoken of in confession apart from the omission of Mass, because then the theft is none other than the aggravating cause, but not a change of species. (Navarre, de Lugo, Diana, Leand., with the Salamancans *Ibid.*, n. 21, against Cornejo).

10.—It must be noted: III. That a sin of omission begins to be imputed from the time in which its cause is advertently placed. Thus, it must be said with the authors (Sanchez, Bonacina, Filliuci, Becanus, etc., cited by the Salamancans, *loc. cit.* p. 3, §1, n. 22, against Sylvius, Palaus, etc. who hold improbably that a sin is not committed unless one were to truly omit Mass). Besides, it must be said that even a voluntary omission is imputed in the cause to sin, even if the will could not act afterward, say, if someone would make himself drunk, foreseeing that he was going to omit Mass due to drunkenness, for then he is held to confess the cause, and its effect, namely drunkenness, and the omission of Mass, as the Salamancans more correctly say (tr. 2, c. 10, p. 3 § 2, num. 28) with de Soto, Sanchez, Palaus, Ledesma, and others in common (against Vasquez, Bonacina, Laymann, etc.), only if the will would not withdraw before the consequent effect, as Sanchez, Azor, Villalobos, and the Salamancans (*ibid.*, n. 29) teach is probable, for then it is probable he is not held to confess the consequent effect. (See what must be said in book 5, num. 149). From this, it is also deduced that if the effect happens after the reluctance, they do not incur the censure imposed against sinners, because that requires contumacy in the act of sin. (See what will be said in book 7, n. 40)

11.—*Quaeritur*, whether it would be a venial sin against divine law? It seems that St. Thomas denies that (1.2. q. 88, a. 1, ad 1), saying, "It is not against the law ..., but ... apart from the law because it does not yet observe the mode of reasoning which the law intends." Estius, Vasquez, de Soto, Med., Azor (cited by the Salamancans, tr. Cit. c. 8, p. 1, n. 4) agree. And their reasoning is especially persuasive, because really, venial sin is forbidden by God, as we see in *Eccli. Cap. 7, v. 14; Noli velle mentiri; Matt.* 5:54, *Non jurare omnino*. Therefore, it is also venial against a divine precept. And this is a true opinion, for as the Salamancans rightly explain (*loc. cit.*, n. 6), St. Thomas distinguishes the substance of the law and the mode of the law, the reason why, although a venial sin is not against the substance of the law, still it is against the mode of observing the law, such a mode certainly also is commanded by divine law, when it disagrees with right reason. Therefore, it is always true, because venial sin is against the law of God, if it is not substantial, at least (as we will say) modal.

Here, some argue about original sin and its effects, but because this matter is not relevant to the present discussion, you can read the treatises of the Scholastics.

Moreover, on censures in regard to the opinion considering the Conception of the Blessed Virgin Mary, see the dissertation in book 7, *de censuris*, from n. 244.

Nevertheless, here we must note that the proposition which said that philosophical sin, namely that sin which is recognized to be against reason but not against divine law, is not mortal nor that it merits eternal punishment, in these words: "Something in a matter where someone either does not know God or does not think about him in the act, would be a grave sin but would not be an offense against God, nor a mortal sin dissolving the friendship of God, nor worthy of eternal punishment." This proposition was condemned by Alexander VIII. And rightly, because someone that knows his work is opposed to a reasonable thing of nature, also knows enough the injury he inflicts on God (at least *in confuso*), who is the author of nature.

DUBIUM II

Whether, and how, desires and delights might be sins?

By desire, the will, intention or an efficacious resolution for a bad thing is understood; but through delight, simple love and complacency for the object thought of, in enjoying its sweetness without a desire for execution, and it is usually called *morosa*; not by the custom of time when it could be carried out in a moment, but that the will, after full advertence of reason, pays attention to it.

ARTICLE I

What kind of sin is a bad desire?

12. *Whether desire takes up the species from the exterior act?*
13. *Whether desire for a bad object is a sin with conditional consent?*
14. *Whether delight for a bad object is illicit, even if the consent were conditioned?*

12.—Resp. 1. "Absolute desire, whether a thought with "the consent of the will to absolutely carry our a sin at "some time, or complacency in carrying it out, has the "same species and the malice of sin, mortal or venial, "which the exterior act has, in which it is borne. This is "the common teaching, and it is certain from Matth. "5:28, 'Whoever will have looked, etc.' The reasoning is,

"because an interior act has the same goodness and
"malice from the external act as the object.

13.—"Resp. 2. Desire with conditional consent in which
"someone desires something under such a condition
"which takes away the malice of the object, it is not a
"sin, at least not a mortal sin; *e.g.* I would rob if God
"would permit it; if I were the judge I would kill this evil-
"doer. (Val., t. 2, d. 6, p. 4 p. 4; Sayr; Salas in t. 2, tr. 13, d.
"10, s. 27; Vasquez, 1.2. d. 116, c. 2). But if the condition
"does not take away the malice, it is a sin: *e.g.* if you
"were to think, if there were no hell I would commit
"adultery; if I were not religious, I would fornicate; were
"it not for my condition, I would take vengeance, I would
"kill you; likewise, if you did something to me in youth,
"or before I will enter religion I shall take vengeance
"(understand this as: if while he says these things, he
"were to have the desire to take vengeance, if he were in
"such a situation). It is otherwise if he would only show
"what he would prepare to do in another situation.
"(Bonacina *de matr.*, qu. 4, p. 8, n. 9). The reasoning of
"the response is that even if a conditional consent
"would place nothing in the nature of things on the side
"of the object willed, nevertheless, it does place the
"desire in the will to commit that sin, apart from a
"condition that does not take away the malice; and
"hence, the sin will be proportionate to how much he
"loves it without the condition. (Cajetan; Sanchez, l. 1,
"mor. c. 2; Vasquez; Laymann, l. 1, tr. 3 c. 6, num. 10.

Therefore these cases are resolved:

"1. In all matters forbidden by positive law alone, a
"desire is licit with this condition (if it were not
"forbidden), *e.g.* I would eat meat on Friday if the Church
"did not forbid it. The reasoning is, because the condition

"takes away all the malice which is only in the
"prohibition. (Azor, l. 4, cap. 6, qu. 10; Sanchez, l. 1, c. 2;
"Vasquez, d. 16, c. 2).

"2. The same thing avails in matters forbidden by natural
"law that are, nevertheless, licit in some case or
"situation, if a favorable condition were placed; *e.g.* I
"would kill Peter if God commanded it; I would hang the
"thief if I were the judge, I would marry if it were
"allowed, or if I were not a priest, if I were free from a
"vow, etc. The reasoning is, because these are licit under
"that condition. Nevertheless, Sa rightly warns (*v.*
"*Peccatum*), that desires of this sort are perilous and must
"be avoided, and also, as Cajetan says (*ibid.*) these are
"idiotic and diabolic temptations. (*ib.* and *Laymann*, l. 1,
"t. 3, c. 6, n. 10).

"3. Although certain men universally affirm the same
"thing about all things that are simply forbidden from
"the law of nature (such as Cajetan, Sal., and Vasquez),
"if an impossible condition were placed that would
"remove the reasoning of the sin from the object, such as
"if one were to say, if it were not a sin, I would fornicate,
"to the extent that then consent would not seem to be
"borne into the malice; nevertheless, it seems more
"probable what Azor, Sanchez and Laymann teach,
"namely that it is a sin, insofar as it is intrinsically evil;
"nor could it be deprived of its malice (which would
"draw consent in regard to such an object unless the law
"of God would not allow it). Therefore, the will is
"imposed on an evil. Nevertheless, understand that if it
"is efficaciously imposed, because if it were only a
"signification of the natural leaning toward that object,
"it is not a sin. (Sanchez, l. 1, c. 2, n. 25; Laymann l. 1, t.
3, c. "6, n. 11; Cardinal de Lugo, d. 16, n. 377)."

Quaeritur: Whether he would sin that conditionally
desires some evil object if it were allowed? We must

distinguish: If the condition were to take away the malice of the object, then he would at least not sin gravely. And this can happen not only in things forbidden by positive law, precisely if one were to say I would eat meat in Lent if the Church would not have forbidden it; but even in things forbidden by natural law, in a case in which the object can be licit, namely by saying that if God would permit it, I would steal that thing which belongs to Titus; if I were not a priest I would marry, and similar things. (Busembaum, as above; Sanchez, Dec. l. 1. c. 2. n. 24; Laymann l. 1, tr. 3, c. 6, n. 10; Sporer t. 1, p. 82, n. 18) and others in common. We have said *at least gravely*, for ordinarily, desires of this sort are not excused from venial sin, since commonly they are perilous, or at least idle. One would sin lethally when the condition would not take away the malice of the object, namely by saying that I would sin if there were no hell; I would kill my enemy if I had a sword; I would fornicate if I were not a religious, etc. This is certain with all, as Sanchez also says (*loc. cit.* n. 23), together with Sporer (n. 20), and Laymann (n. 11), with Adr. and Azor. It is sinful in such conditional desires when the malice cannot be separated from the object; *e.g.* if one were to say that if there were no sin, I would want to blaspheme, commit perjury, adultery, fornicate, take revenge, and like things; because these are intrinsically evil and can never be immune from sin. This is why Laymann reckons that one is not excused from a grave fault who would desire objects of this sort with a deliberative and efficacious will, even if under the condition that it were lawful. Just the same, the doctors think it sufficiently probable (Bonacina, *de matr.* d. 4, p. 8, n. 21; with Valent. and Suarez, Palaus, t. 1, tr. 2 d. 3, p. 10 § 3 n. 4, with Sa, Vasquez, Sayr. and the Salamancans, tr. 20, c. 13, p. 6, n. 62, with Cajetan, Tapia Sales, etc.), that when the will desires some evil object under an impossible condition, namely if it were lawful, and the never efficaciously consented to it since, the object that you desire by saying, if it were lawful, and you know it is not nor can be lawful, then you do not truly desire it, but only show your propensity towards it. It would be another thing altogether if you would desire that evil object were not forbidden, because *per se* it is evil and you would wish to overturn order and the law of nature, as the Salamancans rightly say (*loc. cit.*, with the others). And so the different aforesaid opinions can be reconciled.

> "14.—To rejoice and delight in a bad work, under a
> "condition (if it were lawful), *e.g.* in the aforesaid
> "efficacious illicit desires, when the condition is possible,
> "even if it can be excused from sin according to certain
> "Doctors, if it were only done according to the rational
> "appetite, or the will (while every danger of illicit
> "consent has been excluded, as well as foul movements;
> "which still, because it commonly and naturally follows,
> "it seems hardly safe in practice), still he cannot be
> "excused if the delight of the sensitive appetite were
> "voluntary, which is properly called delight and
> "commonly happens with some alteration of the body.
> "The reason for the distinction is, that the will can be
> "imposed in an object abstracted from malice, since it
> "would follow the intellect whose function is to abstract;
> "but the appetite, because it follows the imagination, is
> "not imposed on an object apprehended under some
> "certain condition of state, or time, but as it is in itself,
> "and therefore such a delight is on an absolutely bad
> "object. (Laymann and Bonacina, *de matr.* q. 4, p. 8).

Nevertheless, it must be said more truly that while delight is absent from the sensitive appetite, each delight from the evil object here and now is intrinsically illicit *per se*, just as the doctors hold (Sanchez, Dec. l. 1, c. 2, n. 5; Azor, t. 1, l. 4, c. 6, q. 1; the Salamancans tr. 20, c. 13, p. 6, n. 61; Roncaglia tr. 2, c. 3, q. 3, and Laymann; Suarez; cited by Croix, l. 5, n. 82). The reason why, as Croix says well, is, although the consent might be conditional in respect to the object still, in respect to the delight it is absolute; when delight returns the present object, here and now such an object, when it is separated from the condition making it upright, is simply evil. Consequently, the will delights in an object here and now that is simply evil, and therefore cannot be excused from sin. (See what is going to be said below, n. 24). We must say otherwise if anyone were to say that I would delight in this if it is not evil, as the Salamancans rightly say (*ibid.* n.61), with Azor, Palaus, and the common opinion.

ARTICLE II

Whether delectatio morosa[3] *is always a sin?*

15. *In what way do desire, joy and delight differ? What if someone delights in his bride, but not because she is his bride?*

16. *When is delight a sin?*

17. *In what way does delight in an evil thing differ from delight in a thought of a bad thing?*

18. *Whether delight in regard to the mode of acting badly is a sin?*

19. *Whether it is lawful to rejoice in a good effect following a bad work?*

20. *What if a work were formally evil, viz. carried out with a sin?*

21. *Whether one may delight in a neighbor's evil directed to a good end?*

22. *Whether one may desire the death of a daughter if she will not marry on account of poverty, etc. And whether*

---

[3] Translator's note: *The term delectatio morosa* is the pleasure taken in a sinful thought or imagination even without desiring it.

15.—We must preface before all things in regard to bad thoughts, *desire* is one thing, *joy* is another, and *delectatio morosa* still another. *Desire* (*desiderium*) is an act of the will regarding a time in the future, in which someone deliberately intends to devise an action, say to carry out fornication. And this desire is said to be *efficacious* (*efficax*), when someone takes up the means to bring it to effect; but *inefficacious* (*inefficax*) if one does not propose to carry it out, but consents that he would carry it out if he could, such as if someone were to say "If I could steal the treasure of the Church, I would steal it." On the other hand, *joy* (*gaudium*) regards the past, and is when someone takes delight in having carried out an evil work. *Delectatio morosa*, therefore, regards the present time, and it is when through the imagination of a fantasy someone renders for himself a present work of sin, namely an act of fornication, and delights from that deliberate consent, just as if he would actually fornicate, still without the desire to carry it out. Moreover, there is an exceedingly probable opinion of several doctors. (De Lugo, *de Poen.* disp. 16, c. 6, n. 347; Bonacina, *de matr.* q. 4, p. 8, n. 3; Sporer t. 1 p. 84, n. 24; Laymann l. 1, tr. 2, c. 6, n. 15; Azor, l. 4, c. 6, q. 3; Tamburinius *Dec.* l. 10, c. 3, n. 3; Palaus, tr. 2, d. 2, p. 10 § 14, n. 2; likewise Vasquez, Sayr., Reg., Diana, cited by the Salamancans, tr. 20, c. 13 p. 4, § 1, n. 30, although they oppose this opinion, *ibid.* n. 31, along with Cajetan, Lessius, Sanchez, Roncaglia, etc.) They hold that if anyone delights in relations with a married woman, not because she is married but because she is beautiful, etc., then he does not contract the malice of adultery, for the circumstances of adultery then do not enter into the delight; on that account, only chastity is wounded, not justice. And Tamburinius says the same thing is probable, if anyone should look at a married woman with venereal passion, without desire. Nevertheless, this not withstanding, I find what Holzmann says (t. 1, p. 316, n. 698) very persuasive, namely, that although one is not obliged to explain the circumstance of adultery by reason of the delight, nevertheless, in practice by explaining the reasoning of the proximate danger of coveting (at least inefficaciously) a married woman, in which he concludes that he delighted in her. Still, there is no doubt that adultery was committed, as often as there was joy or delight in the thought of sexual relations, or a desire to have sexual relations with a married woman, because then the will embraces the whole wicked object with its circumstances, nor can it prescind from those, therefore he wounds chastity and justice. It is the same if someone will delight in homosexual relations. Likewise, if a person that is delighted were bound by a vow of chastity, it is also a sin against the vow. These are certain with Tamburinius, *Dec.* l. 10, c. 3, ex n. 2, and with all others.

16.—"Resp. If one will conclude to devise an evil act "*secundum se*, it is a mortal sin or a venial one, insofar as

"the work is mortal or venial. So the common opinion
"holds with St. Thomas (1.2. q. 74, art. 8, concl.)

17.—"I said *secundum se*, because if the delight were only
"from the thought itself, but not from the work, it is not
"a sin, because just as the thought, *e.g.* from obscene
"things, in order to teach or preach, etc., is good; but the
"thought on the same things from curiosity is venially
"bad, so consequently, delight from such a thought, just
"as the object, is not bad, but at one time good and at
"another time venially bad."

Consequently, on the one hand there is delight from the
wicked act, so that a bad work is the object of delight, which
is always evil; on the other there is delight from the thought
of the bad object, so that it is not the evil work, but the very
thought from the work would be *per se* the object of delight.
And this can either be good if there were a just cause for
thinking about it, *e.g.* for the sake of study, consultation, etc.,
with aversion to the object; or it can be venially bad, if it
would be done from curiosity, etc., or it can be at some time
even gravely evil, if the proximate danger of consent were
present. St. Thomas argues: "So, therefore, someone
thinking about fornication can take delight in two ways. In
one mode from the thought itself, in the other from the
thought of fornication itself, ... the very thought, *secundum
se* is not a mortal sin, indeed, it may be only venial at one
time, say when someone thinks about it to no purpose; at
another time it is altogether without sin, say when someone
thinks about it to a purpose, such as when he wants to
preach or dispute on it, etc." (1.2. quaest. 74, art. 8). Thus he
says it is a mortal sin *when someone, thinking about
fornication, delights from thinking about the act itself.* And St.
Antoninus, Lessius, Sanchez and Bonacina with the
Salamancans (tr. 20, c. 13, p. 3, n. 27) follow the Angelic
Doctor in common.

18.—"Similarly, it will not be a sin if the delight turned
"on the mode of acting badly, not in regard to the evil act
"itself, in which mode, fables, comedies, homicides,
"deceits, thefts, the fall of men cause delight in us
"without sin. For example, if someone steals while on a
"horse, not *secundum se*, but the mode of theft or robbery
"is crafty and industry, or the mode of an unexpected
"fall."

(Laymann l. 1, t. 3, c. 6, n. 3, likewise Sanchez, Bonacina,
Azor, Palaus, and the Salamancans, *ibid.*, p. 4, §1, n. 39 in
common).

Wherefore, the following are resolved:

19.—"1. It is licit to take joy and *delectatio morosa* from a
"good effect following from a bad action, because then
"the delight is not from the bad object.

"2. If such an effect would follow from an act that was
"bad *secundum se*, nevertheless here and now it is
"without fault, *e.g.* because it was done in a dream,
"madness, drunkenness, or inculpable ignorance; then it
"is also permitted to take delight at some time from the
"act itself, certainly not *secundum se*, but as it is the
"cause of such a good effect, as Lessius teaches (l. 4, c. 3,
"n. 105 and 106, from Vasquez, 1.2. d. 115, c. 2), such as
"in a *solutio naturae* made in a dream. The reason is
"because the object of delight itself is not bad. See
"Bonacina, *de matr.* q. 4, p. 8; Sanchez, l. 1, *mor.* c. 2, n.
"18; Cardinal de Lugo *de poen.* dis. 16, n. 389. On the
"contrary, they add that it is lawful at some time to
"desire (from a simple affect and inefficacious desire)
"that such a thing would happen without sin; *e.g.* that a

"*solutio naturae*⁴ would come about in a dream on
"account of a good end; while the desire would not be so
"intense that it would probably cause such a thing. Nor
"would there be danger of consent to such a desire. The
"reason is, they say, because the object of this desire, or
"of the joy, is not evil. (See Lessius and Bonacina, *loc.*
"*cit.*)

20.—*Quaeritur:* I. Whether one may take delight in a bad
work on account of the good effect that follows from it?
Distinguish: If a work will have been formally bad, namely
because it was carried out with sin, one would sin that takes
delight in it, even if the delight from the bad act were not
taken as a sin, but as the cause of the subsequent effect. It
must be so held with de Soto, Tapia, Roncaglia, and the
Salamancans (tr. 20, c. 13, p. 5 § 1. n. 47), against Vasquez,
Lessius, Palaus, Bonacina, *ibid.* But if the bad act was carried
out without sin, Lessius and Vasquez, as well as
Busembaum, think it is licit to take delight from it, not *per
se*, but as the cause of a good effect. On the other hand, more
truly the opposite must be held with Sanchez (*Dec.* l. 1, c. 2,
n. 16), the Continuator of Tournely (*de pec.* part. 1, cap. 4,
art. 2, q. 5) with Azor, Croix (l. 5, n. 91), Roncaglia (tr. 2, c. 3
q. 4, r. 2) and the Salamancans, *ibid.* § 2, n. 49. The reason is
although the action was not sinful, nevertheless it was
objectively bad; and this, as the Salamancans, Roncaglia, and
Croix rightly note, it does not seem to be any longer in
doubt after proposition 15 was condemned by Innocent XI,
which says: "It is licit for a son to take joy from his murder
of his parent carried out while drunk, on account of the vast
fortune that he then obtained from his inheritance." Nor is
the doctrine St. Thomas lays down in 4, dist. 9, q. 1, art. 4, q.
1, ad 5 opposed to us, where the Angelic doctor says: "If,

---

⁴ Translator's note: "A release of nature," or effusion of seed without
the intention to commit the solitary sin.

however, one were pleased (that is from nocturnal pollution, on which he speaks) from the relieving or lightening of nature, it is not believed to be a sin." And Navarre, Lessius, Sa, Sanchez, and the Salamancans themselves (tr. 20, c. 13, p. 5, § 2, n. 52) follow him with the common opinion. For Sanchez (n. 18), the Salamancans (*ibid.*, n. 53), and Roncaglia (*loc. cit.*) rightly say that St. Thomas must be understood to speak about a purely natural pollution, which arises from the release of nature; and therefore, since that is not objectively evil, one may take pleasure in it, certainly not from the delight caused by it, but from the unburdening obtained on that account. On the contrary, one will not be permitted to take delight in a work that is objectively evil, namely from nocturnal pollution which comes about from touch or from a foul dream, because then this was objectively evil. The Salamancans (*ibid.* n. 54) say it is otherwise if it were to come about from moderated food, or from useful study, etc., because then the pollution is also natural and therefore it is lawful for one to take the delight held from it, only without a disturbance of the spirits. But I am not persuaded by this.

Nevertheless, in each case it is lawful, speaking *per se*, to take delight in each, not from the cause, but from the consequent effect, namely from the unburdening caused by the pollution, even voluntary, or from the attainment of an inheritance on account of homicide, provided that the cause will be detested. I said *speaking per se*, for delights of this sort do not lack danger at some point, as Roncaglia (*loc. cit.*, resp. 1 in fin.), and the Salamancans (*loc. cit.*, § 1, n. 46) rightly say.

21.—*Quaeritur:* II. Whether it might be permitted to take delight from an evil to one's neighbor on account of a good end? Here two propositions condemned by Innocent XI must be prefaced. Proposition 13 said, "If you act with due moderation, you can without mortal sin be sad about the moral life of someone and rejoice about his natural death, seek it with ineffectual desire and long for it, not indeed from dissatisfaction with the person but because of some temporal benefit." Proposition 14 said: "It is licit with an absolute desire to wish for the death of a father, not indeed as an evil to the father, but as a good to him who desires it, for a rich inheritance will surely come his way." These propositions were certainly justly proscribed because according to the order of charity, the life of any neighbor we are held to prefer to our temporal benefit. Nevertheless, someone that rejoices from the consequent effect must not be condemned, viz. from the inheritance obtained from the death of the other, if he does not take joy from the cause, that is from the death, although the matter may be dangerous, as we recently said above with the Salamancans and Roncaglia.

Moreover, it is licit to take joy from the evil of a neighbor, on account of his greater good, or innocence, namely if the one taking delight in the infirmity and even death of a neighbor did so that he would stop sinning or causing scandal, etc., as the authors say. (Cont. Tourn. *de char.* sect. 7, punct. 2; Roncaglia, *ibid.*, with Bonacina, Reg., and the Salamancans, tr. 20, c. 13, p. 5, § 1, n. 43, with Navarre, Bonacina Toledo, etc.) St. Thomas (3. Sent. dist. 30, q. 1, art. 1, ad 4) expressly teaches that: "For this reason, because charity has an order, and everyone ought more to love himself than others, and his neighbors rather than foreigners. ... Someone can, save for charity, desire a temporal evil for someone and take joy in it if it happens, not insofar as it is evil for them, but insofar as it is an impediment to the evils of the other, whom he is held more to love, whether of the community or of the Church." St. Gregory writes likewise: A great many things can come about, that, when charity has not been lost and the ruin of our enemies brings us joy, and again his glory without the sin of envy saddens us, in that ruin, we believe certain things have been raised up, in his advancement, we fear a great many are unjustly oppressed." (Mor. 1. 22, c. 22). Nevertheless, this must always be understood with the order of charity being preserved, namely when an evil which is avoided, outweighs or is equal with the evil desired for the neighbor. Some opine likewise, and the Salamancans (*ibid.* n. 44) and Roncaglia adhere that a father can desire the death of a son if he fears that the family will be dishonored by his crimes. Moreover, it is licit to take joy from a temporal evil of a private person on account of a common temporal good, as Lessius (l. 2, c. 47, n. 21), Roncaglia (ibid.), St. Thomas (as above) and the Salamancans (*loc. cit.* n. 44) say with Toledo, etc. Hence, one is also allowed to take joy from the punishment of an evildoer as an example to others. What was said about delight, must equally be said about desire, as the Salamancans show (*ibid.* n. 45, in fine).

22.—May one desire his own death to avoid an exceedingly hard life due to infirmity, the savagery of men, poverty and like things? The Salamancans reject this (*ibid.,* n. 46), along with Navarre, Abul. and Reg. The reason is that one may not wish death to flee some evils of a lesser moment. Yet Palaus (tr. 6, d. 4, p. 1, n. 11), Viva (in prop. 14, Inn. XI, n. 3), Felix Pot. (de 1 praec. n. 208) do not improbably uphold this, as de Soto, Granadus, Sancius, and Trull., cited by Busembaum (l. 3, n. 30, vers. 2. *Licet,* in fine) in a case in which is so troublesome it seems harder than death itself. Is it lawful for a mother to desire the death of her daughter to the extent that the daughter, on account of deformity or poverty, cannot marry, or because on account of it the mother is badly treated by her husband? Azor (1. p. l. 3, c. 12, qu. 2), Palaus (tr. 6, d. 4, p. 1, n. 11) and Bonacina (*de char.* d. 3, q. 4, p. ult. n. 7) uphold this. The reason is that such a desire is not as much for an evil as for a good that will follow. But the Salamancans (tr. 20, c. 13, p. 5, §1, n. 46) and Roncaglia (p. 18, q. 4, r. 1) rightly reject it. The reason is both because it is never lawful on account of a temporal good to desire the death of one's neighbor (and this seems to be beyond doubt to Roncaglia after the condemnations of proposition 13 and 14 by Innocent XI, related above), and because the evil of the mother does not outweigh the desired evil desired of the daughter.

23.—"3. It is not a sin, at least not a mortal sin, if married "persons would take delight by the merely rational "appetite from the conjugal act whether past, future or "possible, in respect to their spouse whether present or "absent. Likewise, if a betrothed man would desire future "marital relations, or take delight from them, or if a "widow would from past ones. The reason is, because "these acts have a licit object.

"I said *by the rational appetite*; because if a betrothed "man or a widow were to voluntarily consent in a "sensitive and carnal delight (which naturally arises from "a past recollection for future relations) they would sin "mortally, as Lessius teaches (*loc. cit.*, t. 2, c. 6, n. 120), "along with Bonacina, Tanner, and Palaus. See Diana, t. "5, *misc.* resp. 2, against Medina, etc. However, because "for the delight of the will added besides, the sensitive "and carnal as a great many, nay more, since the danger "of consent to fornication follows, that delight of the will "in practice cannot have place, at least in a widow and in "the betrothed. Nevertheless, among married persons, in "a mode where the danger of pollution were removed, "even the sensitive and venereal delight is not mortal, as "Filliuci, Bonacina, (*de matr.* q. 4,), Sanchez, Lessius (*loc. "cit.* d. 1), and Diana (t. 3, *misc.* r. 36) teach both because "the state of matrimony excuses these things, such as "even tacit unchastity instituted for the sake of desire "along; and because these tend *per se* to the conjugal act, "although *per accidens* the act is not exercised.

24.—Here, two things are asked that are more necessary to know:

Quaeritur: I. Whether the betrothed and widows may take delight from future or past relations? Busembaum responds that it is lawful for them to take delight in the things themselves provided they take delectation by the rational appetite and not the carnal. (But he rightly adds that in practice this can hardly be admitted since carnal delectation is connected to the rational in a great many things). The authors also hold this (Salamancans, tr. 20, c. 13, p. 6, n. 57 and 58, with Navarre, Cajetan, Valentia, Bonacina, etc.), saying that the betrothed may take joy not from present copulation, but from its coming about in the future. But, even with the danger of the sensitive delectation excluded, it must be said more truly with Holzman (t. 1, p. 318, n. 701), Roncaglia (tr. 2, c. 3 q. 5), Sanchez, Vasquez, Azor, Laymann, Palaus, Diana, etc. (cited by the Salamancans, *ibid.*, n. 56) every delectation of the will in the betrothed as well as widows about future or past copulation is evil. The reason is, because delectation renders itself a present object; and therefore, the present object is always here and now an evil; since here and now the condition providing the grace of matrimony is absent, all the actual delectation from it is also evil. Another thing must be said with Roncaglia about desire, in which the betrothed wishes for future copulation; for this is lawful because when the will is borne to a future object, it can desire it under the condition whereby the object will be licit. But, because in such a desire the danger of delectation is also present, for that very reason the betrothed are exhorted that they might carefully turn themselves away from bad thoughts of this sort.

25.—*Quaeritur:* II. Whether spouses are permitted to take delectation in the conjugal act, even if the other spouse were not present? The Salamancans (*de matr.* c. 15, p. 6, n. 90) with Navarre, Sa, Roncaglia, etc., (cited by Croix, l. 6, p. 3, n. 537) reject this when the delectation takes place with a commotion of the spirits, because they say such a commotion is not licit for spouses unless it were ordered to copulation. But Roncaglia and the Salamancans do not speak congruently, for they themselves admit (*ibid.* n. 84; Roncaglia tr. 12, p. 296, q. 6, r. 11 with St. Antoninus, Conc. Diana, and it is a common opinion, as we will say in book 6, *de matrimonio*, n. 933), that unchaste touches (which certainly cannot be done without a great deal of arousal) among spouses, provided the danger of pollution is absent, are licit, at least they are not gravely illicit, even if they are done only for pleasure and hardly ordered to copulation. I say, therefore, why is it not the same thing to speak about delectation? This is why I regard Busembaum's opinion as probable, which says it is permitted for spouses to take delectation, even carnally, from carnal relations they have had or are going to have, as long as the danger of pollution is always absent. The reason is, because (exactly as the Salamancans say in tr. 9, c. 15, p. 6, n. 84 when speaking about unchaste touches) the very state of matrimony renders all these things licit; otherwise the matrimonial state would be exposed to excessive scruples. Besides, Bonacina, Sanchez, Lessius and Diana hold this opinion, with Busembaum (as above, n. 23, *in fine*), St. Antoninus (p. 1, tit. 5, c. 1 §6.), Cajetan, (1.2. q. 74, art. 8 ad 4), Coninck (d. 34, dub. 11, concl. 1), Croix (l. 6, p. 5, num. 337) with Gerson, Suarez, Laymann and a great many others; likewise Vasquez, Aversa, etc., cited by the Salamancans (*ibid.* n. 89 and 90), who think it is probable. St. Thomas also favors this opinion in question 15 of *de malo*, art. 2, ad 17, where he says that for spouses, just as sexual relations are licit, so also delectation from them.

26.—Lastly, here, we must note with the Salamancans (tr. 20, c. 13, p. 7, n. 65 and 66, and de Lugo, Cajetan, Navarre,

Palaus, Dic., etc.), that if anyone were to boast about a grave sin that he had truly carried out, in confession he ought to explain also the species of the sin, because then great pleasure is commonly added to boasting which takes the same species of the sin. It is otherwise, however, if the boasting were about a sin that he made up.

27.—"4. *Delectatio morosa*, in matters only forbidden by
"positive law, is not illicit, but it should not be done
"under the reasoning of the prohibition; *e.g.* if a
"Carthusian or another on a fast day, would take delight
"in the thought of eating meat, that is not about an evil
"work, because the law only forbids the external eating.
"(Laymann l. 1, t. 3, c. 6, n. 9; Lessius l. 4, c. 3, d. 15, n.
"111 and 113.)

(And so it must be held with the Salamancans, *ibid.*, p. 4, §2. n. 37 and 38; Palaus, Vasquez, Sanchez, Lessius in common, as well as Roncaglia, tr. 2, c. 13, q. 5 r. 11, whatever Croix might say in l. 5, n. 81. However, one may not have delectation from a Mass missed on account due to forgetfulness, and similar things, because the omission is objectively evil, as Roncaglia, *ibid.* q. 5, says with Azor and Sanchez).

28.—"5. Someone that confesses a mortal sin of *delectatio*
"*morosa* ought to add the circumstances of the act, what
"the delectation was about, *e.g.* in a matter of anger,
"whether it was from killing his brother, or another; one,
"or many, while in a matter of the flesh, whether it was
"about a married woman, a nun, or a kinswoman.
"Nevertheless, Azor, Sa (*verb. Luxuria*), Salas (t. 7, tr. 13
"d. 16 s. 6, n. 59, etc.), place the limit that if delectation
"were taken from an object apprehended according to its
"whole malice, but not merely according to a part, *e.g.*
"apprehended from a woman as not his own, but not
"married to another man, or as a nun. Then they say it
"is probable that such delectations are reduced to the

"species of simple fornication. So also Filliuci, Lessius,
"Bonacina, Diana, Palaus, etc. (See de Lugo, d. 16, n. 363).
"On the other hand, there is on the external work itself,
"that it is always borne in the object according to its
"whole malice, or even by the efficacious desire which is
"born in an external work, *secundum se*, and as it is from
"part of the thing, and hence is with that species of the
"same thing; and therefore, its circumstances must
"always be confessed. (See the cited authors, and what
"was said in n. 15).

29.—"Resp. 2. If someone were to exercise an action
"without cause and necessity, from which he
"understands delectation of the flesh naturally is going
"to arise (*e.g.* he reads from curiosity, or hears foul
"things), still, without direct intention and without
"danger of consent, he sins venially; but if he had a just
"cause, it is no sin at all. (See below on the Sixth
"Commandment, book. 4, n. 482, v. 6, *Si pollutio*).

"Someone will ask, whether the will is positively held to
"repress delectation?

"Resp. 1. If the will, clearly noticing it, stands negatively
"and permissively, so that it neither approves nor repels
"it, it would merely not permit it from the pleasure of the
"very delectation, nor would there be a danger of further
"consent, then what Cajetan and Sanchez (1. mor. c. 12)
"teaches is probable, that one does not sin mortally; both
"because he does not consent in the delectation, and
"because it is morally impossible to avoid all those
"movements, and because for a just cause it is lawful to
"permit them, even according to our adversaries.

"Resp. 2. Nevertheless, in practice it seems truer what
"Azor, Vasquez, Lessius and Becan. (1.2. t. 2, q. 5, c. 5)
"teach, that without a just cause to not resist them, it is
"a mortal sin, because the will is nearly always exposed
"to the danger of consent, and to believe the contrary is

"to place too much confidence in himself, as well as
"presumption. Laymann moderately affirms each
"opinion, and says *delectatio* seems mortal, unless one
"would elicit at least an act of simple displeasure in
"regard to it; and if one neglected to divert his mind
"efficaciously to other things when he easily could, and
"hoped he could drive it away in such a way." (See
"Laymann, l. 1, t. 3, c. 6, n. 3, as well as what was said
"profusely on this point above in n. 7).

DUBIUM III
On the distinction of Sins

ARTICLE I
By what species are sins distinguished?

30. *How do sins differ by species insofar as sin is considered materially and insofar as it is considered formally?*
31. *How manifold is the root from which the diversity of species is taken up?*
32. *Whether sins are distinguished by species from the opposition to virtues, or from the diversity of objects?*
33. *Whether sins are distinguished by species from precepts?*
34. *Whether sin can objectively, and more lightly exceed the gravity of the higher species of sin?*

30.—"*Resp.* Sins, in regard to the material or positive
"being, are distinguished by species from formal objects
"and the species from variant circumstances insofar as
"these have the reasoning of the formal object; in regard
"to the formal, however, it is nearly distinguished from
"opposite forms, or the rectitude of the virtue from
"which it is a privation, but remotely and fundamentally
"from the objects. (Trull., d. 4, *de pecc.* d. 1, q. 2). The

"reasoning of the first part is, because all acts are
"distinguished by species from the objects, moreover sins
"in regard to the material, they call the acts themselves.
"The reasoning of the second part is because privations
"are neatly distinguished by species from the forms from
"which they are a privation, but sins are formally
"privations of the opposite rectitudes. The reasoning of
"the third part, is that the rectitude of a virtue is
"specified proximately from the object: therefore, a
"privation of a rectitude is remotely from the same thing.

From this the following are resolved:

31.—"Sins differ in species, not only which by different
"virtues, but even which are vastly opposed to the same,
"such as prodigality and avarice, or by reason of a
"different deformity, *i.e.* which so touches upon it by a
"different reasoning and malice of the same virtue
"inasmuch as it is from the nature of the same sin, it is
"not the same facility, morally speaking, nor propensity
"to commit each sin; such things as homicide, theft,
"adultery, detraction.

The Council of Trent teaches, in its 14th Session, ch. 5,
that those circumstances must be explained in confession
which change the species of the sin. Hence,

Quaeritur. I. How manifold is the root from which the
specific distinction of sins is taken up? Resp. With
Busembaum, and the more common opinion, it is taken from
a twofold root, namely, 1) From opposition to different
virtues; 2) from a different deformity against the same
virtue, insofar as it happens in perjury and violation of a
vow, or blasphemy; for although these sins are against the
same virtue of religion, nevertheless they are different by
species. The doctors agree in regard to this second root.

32.—But in regard to the first, *viz.* the opposition to virtues, there is a great question between St. Thomas and [Bl.] Scotus, whether the specific distinction is proximately taken from different objects of sins, or from different virtues to which the sins are opposed? St. Thomas (1.2. q. 72, art. 1), the Salamancans (tr. 20, c. 12, p. 1, n. 1, and 2) and others hold that they are proximately taken from different objects by species. The reasoning of St. Thomas, as he says in art. 6, ad 2, is "because sin does not have a species on the side of aversion ..., but on the side of conversion, according to certain acts." Scotus, on the other hand, with Busembaum, and Becanus, Valentia, Bonacina, etc., hold the specific distinction is taken from the virtues to which sins are opposed, because sin, taken formally, consists in opposition to a virtue, from which it is a privation. Both opinions are probable, and really both coincide in the same thing, as the Salamancans rightly say (*loc. cit.*, n. 2). But the second, by distinguishing sins through oppositions to the virtues, is clearer and easier, as Tapia and any Thomist you like rightly affirms. Nevertheless, Roncaglia notices (tr. 20, *de pecc.*, c. 2, q. 1) that, although sins of commission are distinguished from the opposite virtues, as he holds himself, on the other hand, sins of omission are altogether distinguished by opposition to their objects, or to the acts from which they are a privation; for example, to omit Mass and fasting are different sins by species against the obedience due to the Church; because Mass and fasting are different objects by species.

33.—*Quaeritur:* II. Whether from different precepts sins are distinguished by species? Navarre, Granadus, Tanner, etc., uphold this. Yet, it must be said with St. Thomas (1.2. qu. 72, art. 6 ad 2), Cajetan, Valentia, Azor, Laymann, Coninck, Palaus, Bonacina, Roncaglia (*loc. cit.*), Croix (l. 4, n. 47), the Salamancans (*ibid.*, p. 2, n. 5 and 6) from the common opinion, that if precepts are distinguished only on the side of the legislator (as it is done in theft, which is forbidden by divine law as well as human), they hardly introduce a specific distinction of sins; because the diversity of the legislator does not effect that a precept is formally different, but only materially. Otherwise, if precepts were distinguished on the side of the motive to forbid, then different virtues are wounded; so if anyone would break the fast imposed by the Church, at the same time as violate that which he will have bound himself with a vow; then he would wound the virtue of temperance, from which the Church commands fasting, and religion, from which God commands vows to be observed.

To know when laws might be fashioned for different ends, the Salamancans say (tr. 20, c. 12, p. 2, n. 9) it must be seen if the human precepts draws the act to another special virtue, or to opposition with another special virtue. Hence it is inferred: I. If anyone kills a priest, he not only sins against justice, but even against religion, from the motive that the Church forbids the wounding of a priest. It is inferred II: a beneficed priest omitting the divine office commits one sin against religion, but not, however, against justice, if he were to wish to restore the fruit of the benefice, because from the same motive of religion the Church commands the recitation of the office by anyone that is a priest and beneficed, who is held by justice merely to carry out its fruits. (Azor, Trull., Diana, etc., with the Salamancans, *ibid.* n. 12 against Suarez, Laymann and Bonacina. See what is going to be said in book 5, n. 145, qu. I.)

34.—*Quaeritur:* 3. Whether a sin from the object can more lightly exceed the gravity of a sin of a higher species by reason of circumstance? Durandus, Vasquez and others reject it, but St. Thomas more probably upholds it in 2.2. qu. 10, art. 3, ad 1, where he says: "Nothing forbids sin which is more grave according to its genus, is less grave according to some circumstances." Father Concina follows the Angelic

Doctor (t. 10, p. 524, n. 6), as do Suarez, Azor, Palaus, etc., with the Salamancans *ibid.* p. 4, n. 22 and others in common; because regularly a graver sin is that which is opposed to a more perfect virtue, as St. Thomas says (1.2. qu. 73, art. 4). However, when the gravity of a higher species of sin is finite, therefore, even if it cannot physically be exceeded by the malice of a lower species of sin, it can morally. Hence, sodomy and bestiality are graver sins than perjury, as St. Thomas shows (2.2. q. 154, art. 3, with the Salamancans, *ibid.* in fine). Therefore, the aforesaid rule of weighing the gravity of a sin from the opposition to a higher virtue only occurs when the sins are the greatest against each and every virtue, but not when a comparison of the greatest sin is made to the least.

Moreover, do the circumstances only make worse the species that must be confessed, namely the degree of incest, the quantity of theft, the time of the sin's duration? (See what is going to be said on the Sacrament of Penance, book 6, from no. 467).

ARTICLE II
Which sins are distinguished by number?

35. *See all the things which are said on this point by Busembaum.*

36. *From what roots is the numeric distinction taken up? On the first root, which is the multiplicity of acts morally dispersed.*

37. *And I. How are the internal acts dispersed* in regard to sins *of the thought?*

38. *How,* in regard to sins *of the word and action?*

39. *Whether the evil proposed were dispersed through a long time?*

40. *What is, still, the will would remain in some effect?*

41. *II. How are they dispersed or united* for the external act*?*

42. *Whether all the means akin to sin must be explained?*

43. *What if someone at the beginning only wanted to touch, but will later fornicate?*

44. *What if someone will [interpolatim] steal a gold coin 100 times when he meant in the beginning to steal 100 gold pieces once? And how many sacrileges does one commit celebrating three masses in mortal sin on Christmas day?*

45. *On the second root which is* diversity of the total objects.

46. *The conclusions of this root.*

47. *Qu. 1. How many sins does one commit that blasphemes the 12 apostles in the same act?*

48. *Qu. 2. How many if someone detracts or hurls abuse by different contumelies?*

49. *Qu. 3. How many if someone detracts against someone in the presence of many people?*

50. *Qu. 4. How many if someone would deny many articles of faith? Qu. 5. How many of someone desires different evils for his enemy? Qu. 6. How many if a confessor would absolve many people while in mortal sin? What if the priest would minister the Eucharist to many people? What if a priest would throw his breviary in the sea, foreseeing that he would be rendered unable to recite it? (On this see what is going to be said in book 5, n. 149).*

35.—"*Resp.* They are distinguished by number in two "ways. 1. From the different total objects in number, not "only materially and physically, but even formally, and "distinct morally. 2. Through the moral break up of the "acts. (Filliuci tr. 21, c. 8)

"I say *moral*, because even if some break-up would "physically suffice for a numeric distinction, "nevertheless, they are not repeated in order in "confession, unless morally there are many that just as "a moral act in confession, so also the repetition and "moral distinction ought to be attended to.

"Hence, acts are morally broken up, so that they might
"be reckoned to remain neither virtually nor
"interpretatively: 1. Through a contrary will and
"intention; 2. Through cessation from a free and
"voluntary act; 3. Through involuntary and natural
"cessation, whether it happens through a dream or a
"distraction to other things. Through a dream, because
"when in it the use of reason would cease, a free and
"moral action is not continued; by distraction because
"through it the earlier thought becomes involuntary, and
"therefore if it were returned to it, it becomes voluntary
"and is morally repeated. So think Vasquez, etc. Such an
"opinion, even if it must be held by external sins, still in
"internal ones it does not hold second place. (Filliuci, tr.
"21, c. 8, n. 317). The reason is, because even if through
"this break-up the acts are physically repeated, still they
"are not morally because in this very thing, because the
"mind is involuntarily distracted, the prior will remains
"interpretatively, since it was not retracted, or otherwise
"broken up. (See also Bald., d. 21, n. 3).

From there, the following are resolved:

"1. Someone commits one sin in number, that hated in
"one act, or imposed detraction on 10 men; one who
"killed two men in one strike; someone wishes to omit
"the office of hours for a month in one act, or fasting
"through Lent. Because, even if these objects are many
"physically, still they are morally and formally one act,
"insofar as they are joined in one act here and now.
"(Navarre, FIlliuci, Bonacina, d. 2, q. 4, p. 1) against Azor
"and Vasquez, etc., who say, probably enough, that the
"sins are distinct. But whether you will say ten sins, *e.g.*
"I hated ten men, or one, is of little difference when this
"one is equivalent to ten, and then the gravity of the

"object in confession must be expressed, indeed what act
"he constituted in his individual act, as Filliuci, Bonacina,
"Suarez (*de poen.* s. 22, s. 4, n. 36)

"2. An internal act of the will is more often broken up
"and repeated, although physically it is manifold, still
"morally it is one sin in number, in order to the
"confession, if it were consummated in some external
"work through it after being intended and caused, or
"even in a great many external acts subordinated to one
"another, to the same end. Hence, for example, someone
"who steals a library during a whole night, even if he
"renews his will to steal very often, it is one theft; and
"someone who continues to kill another man, and often
"renews his will, still commits one homicide. The reason
"is, that there is one external action intended and caused
"by internal things, in which all internal things are
"fulfilled and morally united. (See Bald., d. 21, n. 4.)

"3. External actions, although distinct by number, are
"related to the same end and principal act, only they do
"not have a distinct malice from it, they are not
"distinguished from the end itself or the principal act,
"morally speaking, and in order for confession. Hence,
"kisses, touches, unchaste words, etc., all precede carnal
"relations, nay more, even accompanying and
"subsequent acts, such as compliments, and assistants to
"a work, are one sin by number, as Navarre (c. 6, n. 17),

"Azor (l. 4, qu. 6), and Filliuci, etc. teach. The reason is,
"because they are either beginnings or parts or
"complements, and assistants of a work, of the same
"human act and object, in which all the aforesaid are
"morally united.

"I said *complements*, because if similar acts were not
"begun, or parts of copulation were carried out, or from
"a past act from the nature of the thing they did not
"attain, they are distinguished by number, *e.g.* if

"someone will boast about fornication: and hence they
"are explained separately in confession, but not as prior
"to the other, as Suarez teaches in t. 4, *de poen.* d. 22, s. 5,
"n. 26-27."

36.—For the understanding of this very difficult matter
on numeric distinction of sins, in regard to which the
Doctors place great labor and make many dissertations, so
that all the things which Busembaum said would be
understood more clearly, we must preface that it is certain
from the Council of Trent that in confession not only must
the species of sins be explained, but also the number, since
it taught in its 14th Session, can. 7: "If anyone will have said
that in the sacrament of penance it is not necessary to
confess all things and each individual mortal sin by divine
law, *anathema sit.*" Hence it remains to be seen, from what
roots is the numeric distinction of sins taken up? The
response is taken from the two roots, namely: I. from *the
multiplicity of acts broken up morally*, and in this all agree; II.
from the diversity of the total objects, although on this roots
others have doubts, as we will see in no. 45 below. And I. by
speaking on the first root, there is a great doubt about when
acts of the will are morally broken up? And here for a
clearer explanation interrupted *internal* acts must be
distinguished from *external* acts.

37.—And I. In regard to *internal* acts one must
distinguish sins *of the thought* from sins *of word* and *of a
action.* If they are sins *of the though,* which are carried out
altogether internally, such as hostility, heresy, *delectatio
morosa,* foul desires, etc., these are on the spot both repeated
and interrupted, so that there are as many sins as there are
acts of the will consented to. The reason why in regard to
such acts one does not depend upon another, and therefore
cannot be morally continued. So the authors commonly treat
it (Suarez, Vasquez, Azor, Palaus, Bonacina, etc. with the
Salamancans, tr. 20, c. 12, p. 5, § 1, n. 32;, Roncaglia, tr. 2, *de*

pecc. c. 2, q. 2,; Fr. Concina t. 10, pag. 526, num. 15, the Continuator of Tournely, *de pecc.* part. 1, cap. 3, art. 2, dico 2, against de Lugo, d. 16, sect. 14, ex. num. 566, Cano, Homobon, etc. with Tamburinius Meth. conf. c. 1, § 5 n. 52). They say these acts are not interrupted by a dream, distraction, etc., but only through the contrary will: and it seems Busembaum adheres to this opinion, with Filliuci (*hic vers. Porro,* in fine), and Tamburinius (*loc. cit.*) calls the opinion probable, although he says the time must always be explained, during which the bad will endured. But this opinion, Concina, Vasquez, Suarez, Diana etc. (with the Salamancans, tr. 20, c. 12, p. 5, §1, n. 34) reject it as false, because the opinion of *de Lugo* and *Cano* was at least doubtfully probable and must not be held. And therefore, the penitent ought to explain, if he can, how many times he consented in his will, but if he cannot, because a bad mind lasted for a long time, then it suffices to confess the time in which he persevered with such a mind, as other authors say (Roncaglia, Viva, *de sacr. poenit.* q. 5, art. 7, n. 2, with Vasquez). Moreover, I. Coninck and de Lugo, cited by Tamburinius, n. 53 (although Tamburinius does not agree) rightly note with Viva, n. 5 and Antoine, that it ought to be explained if interruptions were notably rare, or frequent. They note II. Tamburinius (*loc. cit.,* n. 48) with de Lugo and Viva (d. n. 5) that if a great many acts of this sort proceed from the attack of concupiscence, they consent to one mortal sin, even if some brief interval between the acts intervenes.

38.—This happens in regard to internal acts on sins *of thought.* However, in regard to *internal acts* in sins *of word* and *of deed* that is externally consummated such as blasphemies, thefts, etc., these acts are morally interrupted. I. By retraction of the will. II. By free cessation, namely, if someone voluntarily and freely ceases from a bad action he has purposed to do; for then, if he should again return to the bad act, it will morally be a new act different from the first, since it did not proceed from the first, and therefore will be a new sin. So think Busembaum, Roncaglia and Croix, l. 5, n. 170.

39.—Furthermore, whether a bad purpose is interrupted by common interruptions, such as a dream, distraction, feasting, etc.? De Lugo denies it (dict. d. 16, n. 567), and Tamburinius adheres to him (§ n. 35 and 36), even if a great delay would intervene; but this opinion is against what is held in common, and is rightly rejected, as Croix says (l. 5, n. 178). On the other hand, the probable opinion is altogether opposed, with Henno, Vasquez, Nugn., Diana, etc., cited by Viva, all of whom say internal acts are interrupted by any distraction you like, even if they are involuntary. But it seems more probable that it must be said with the Salamancans (tr. 20, c. 12, p. 5, § 1, n. 38), Viva (*de sacr. poen.* q. 5, art. 6, n. 6, in fin.) Roncaglia, q. 2, that if a short time would intervene, the acts are not discontinued, but it is otherwise if a long time would intervene. Moreover, what length would constitute a long time, Viva says a year, the Salamancans a month, Roncaglia two days, Concina however, one; but I think the onset of one act can be prolonged with great difficulty (by the ordinary manner of speaking) for any longer than two or three days to the end. Hence, one who perseveres in a bad act beyond two or three days, ought to explain the time, that the number of the internal acts in regard to the external sins would be morally understood.

40.—Nevertheless, it must be noted that an act of the will, if it proceeds from the first will and morally remains in some effect, which is expedient to consummate the external sin, through whatever sort of time in which the bad will endures, they constitute only one sin. Hence, it is inferred: I. That if someone proposes to kill a man, and consequently prepares weapons, takes hold of him on the road, and kills an enemy, he commits one sin, although he sought it for many days and repeated his will many times. So St. Bonaventure, Vasquez, Cajetan, Navarre, Bonacina, etc. hold in common, with the Salamancans (*ibid.* n. 56) and St. Thomas in 2. dist. 42, q. 1, art. 1. The reason (as St. Thomas teachings) is because all these acts, "do not have the sin of reason, except that through one will ordered to a perverse end." It is inferred II: That if someone decided not to restore someone else's goods, and in the same will always (for at least a year) remained, he commits one sin because in that retention which was never retracted, the first will virtually remained, as Roncaglia probably says (*de peccat.*, q. 2, r. 1), with de Lugo, *de poen.* d. 16, n. 549), with Navarre, Gabr. and Tanner, the Salamancans (tr. 13, cap. 1, p. 14, n. 264, and tr. 20, c. 12, p. 5, § 1, n. 37) with P. Navarre and Trull., likewise Diana, p. 2, tr. 16, r. 27, Madler, Arag. and Sayro (against Suarez, Vasquez, Bonacina, Tapia, etc. cited by the Salamancans, *loc. cit.*, n. 37. Roncaglia holds the will is interrupted by sleep, distraction, etc., and his opinion is probable.) Nay more, de Lugo says the will is not interrupted, even if there is a retraction, but a very brief interval of the will (see what is going to be said in book 4, n. 683). Nevertheless, Diana rightly censes (*loc. cit.*, in fine with A.A., whom he cites) which if a thief is rendered unable to make restitution, and then later becomes able, if the opportunity is given and he did not make restitution, he commits a new sin. The reason is, because in that case for that time of impotency the will to not make restitution would not persevere in effect.

41.—II. In regard to *external* acts of sins, then these are morally interrupted, when they are not subordinated to some principal completed act, say when someone has many touches, without intention of copulation, or if he would strike someone many times without the intention of killing him; or if he would steal many times parts from the aggregate, without the intention of stealing the whole thing; because then each act has its completed malice. So all theologians hold in common with Holzman, t. 1, p. 145, n. 681. On the other hand, the external acts are united in two modes, so that one would constitute a sin. *Firstly,* if they proceed from the same attack, say, when someone would strike many times from the same attack, or touch impurely many times, or blaspheme the same saint or the saint over many days, or would reproach someone in the same matter, or commit detraction, as the Salamancans rightly say (tr. 20, c. 12, p. 5, §2, n. 41), with Navarre, Tappia, Lessius, and Cov., likewise Concina, t. 10, p. 528, num. 21, Viva (*de poen.* q. 5, art. 6, n. 6) with Palaus, Dic., Bonacina, cited by Croix, (l. 5, n. 179). But whether he commits one sin, who blasphemes many saints, or afflicts a great many contumelies on someone in the same attack in different matters; or a confessor, who in mortal sin successively absolves a great many men? See below, n. 47, Quaer. 1, 2, and 6.

In the second mode, the external acts are morally united if they are directed to the consummation of the same sin, just as we said above on internal acts repeated toward the same external sin, which proceed from the first will. Hence, if anyone buys weapons to carry out homicide, takes the road, seeks the enemy and kills him, he commits one sin. So even if anyone would prepare touches, kisses and poetry to carry out copulation, it suffices if he would confess only the copulation obtained. Moreover, should the touches which immediately follow copulation be explained? There are three opinions.

The first absolutely affirms it with Suarez and others.

The second with *Dicastillus* and Croix (l. 5, n. 168), reject this, if acts of this sort are intended as a complement to the prior desire, but otherwise if they are set up in them as in a new delight.

This is certainly probable, but the *third opinion of Busembaum* (with de Lugo, *de poen.* d. 16, n. 553, Palaus, Navarre, Azor, Viva, *loc. cit.* n. 6 and the Salamancans tr. 20,

c. 12 p. 5, § 2, n. 45) is no less probable, which says with the common opinion that these acts, as even the pleasure held from copulation are not a new sin if they happen immediately after copulation, and are hardly intended for a new copulation because it has the appearance of truth that they are applied as a compliment to the copulation obtained.

42.—Still, it must be noted, I. That they are also explained as distinct sins, all the means placed to carry out the sin, if after the sin it is not consummated, as Viva says (*ibid.* n. 6) with the common opinion. And this, not only if the aforesaid means are bad *per se*, such as touches and indecent speech, but also if they are indifferent, such as to take a road, go up to a house to become acquainted with a woman; to prepare arms to homicide, etc. So what Viva says is exceedingly probable. The reason is, then the sin does not only remain internal but is externalized in these actions, which all turn to evil when they are informed by the malice of a bad action.

43.—It must be noted: II. That if someone that kisses, touches, etc., would refuse copulation from the beginning, but afterward, on account of the increase of lust, carry out copulation, it does not suffice if he only confesses copulation; for then all the acts ought to be explained as distinct sins, because when it is checked in those, any act you like has in itself its own consummated malice. So the common opinion holds. (The Continuator of Tournely, *de pecc.* p. 1, c. 3, art. 2; Collig. 7; Lessius, Dic. with Croix, l. 5, n. 169, and the Salamancans cit. n. 45, circa fin., with Navarre, de Lugo, etc.). And the same must be said of someone that had a mind only to wound an enemy, and then, enkindled by anger, kills him; he commits two sins, as the Salamancans teach (*ibid.*).

44.—It also must be noticed with La Croix (l. 5, n. 170) and P. Mazotta (*de consc.* c. 2, q. 4, L). From the end, which if someone from an intention of stealing a hundred gold coins, but steals a hundred times that are morally interrupted in his theft, then he commits a hundred sins; because the individual acts have in themselves the consummated malice. He also commits three sacrileges, who on the day of Christmas celebrates three Masses in a state of mortal sin, because then the acts are completed of themselves. *I said three sacrileges*, still this agrees with the opinion of those (as Sporer, *de poenit.* c. 3, n. 435 and Neotericus hold) that say to celebrate in mortal sin is one sacrilege, because the actions of the celebrant, although they are many, nevertheless they integrate into the one ministry of the sacrifice. But it must be said more truly at least that these are nine sacrileges, since the celebrant in mortal sin more truly commits three sacrileges in each Mass that he celebrates. Furthermore, although he offers one sacrifice, just the same to offer it there are many actions that he does which *per se* are completely sacrilegious, namely to consecrate unworthily, to minister to himself unworthily, and to take the sacrament unworthily; it must be said otherwise, if after the reception he takes up superfluous particles. Croix (*loc. cit.*), with Viva (n. 7) agrees. I said *at least*, for according to our opinion he commits four sacrileges celebrating in mortal sin. (See book 6, n. 35, v. *Hinc.*)

45.—In speaking on the second root of the numeric distinction, viz. whether sins are multiplied from the diversity of the total objects, we must note that it is a famous opinion among the doctors.

The first opinion denies it, and this is held with Busembaum (num. 37), Suarez (in 3, p. d. 22, sect. 5, n. 34), de Lugo (*de poen.* d. 16, n. 135), Laymann (l. 1 tr. 3, c. 3, n. 2), Viva (*de peon.* q. 5, a. 6 n. 9) Anacl. (p. 81, n. 57) with Navarre, March. etc. and Tamburinius, Meth. (conf. l. 2, c. 1, §9, n. 58), likewise Bonacina, Filliuci, Gob., etc. with Croix, l. 5, n. 150; and probably Vasquez, Rodriguez, etc. (cited by De Lugo, *loc. cit.*) agree. Furthermore, the aforesaid A.A.

upholds this opinion for different reasons, for Suarez, Laymann, Villalobos, etc. prove that in the same act, qua being one, there cannot be many different malices by number, since in the same subject there cannot be many accidents distinct in number. De Lugo and Tamburinius use another reason, saying that although in the same act there can be many malices, still, by the precept of the Council of Trent, we are held to explain the number of sins, not, however, the number of malices.

However, *the second opinion* is more common, which we follow, and it is held by the Continuator of Tourtely (*de pecc., part. 1, cap. 3, art. 2 Dico 1*), Conc. (tom. 10, p. 531, n. 29), Croix (l. 5, n. 149-150), Holzman (tom. 1, p. 142, n. 668), and the Salamancans (tr. 20, c. 12, p. 6, n. 61), with Azor, Hurt., Vasquez Diana, Dic., and innumerable others. This opinion teaches the diversity of total objects rightly constitutes different sins by number. The reason is 1) that, just as an act regarding many objects, by a different species, includes a great many different sins in the species that must be explained in confession, so the act regarding many objects, different in number, includes many different sins in number. 2) Which more strongly proves it, is that the same act can not only include many different malices by species, but even in number. It is clear with an example: If a husband has relations with a married woman that is not his wife, no man denies (as de Lugo himself upholds in n. 241) that he commits a double injustice, because he violates the right of his wife, because he laid with another, as he violates the right of the other woman's husband. Therefore, with the same individual act there can rightly be many sins, different in number, against the same virtue. De Lugo objects that then in another mode to hold that the husband wounds justice, when he violates the right of his wife; when he lies with another woman, the other violates the right of her husband, and therefore he commits two sins of injustice. But this response does not oppose us, for the same virtue of justice in the same mode, not in a different one, in which it obliges the man to preserve the trust of his wife, also obliges him that he should not lie with another, lest he would break the trust due to the woman's husband.

Nor does the reasoning of Suarez oppose us, namely that in the same subject there cannot be many accidents distinct in number. For we respond that this avails in physical things, but not in morals, for in these, although the act may be physically one, still, it can be morally manifold when according to the judgment of prudent men that one act is equivalent to many, while holding the reasoning for totally different objects, insofar as it is clear from the example of sexual relations between a married man and another married woman, and St. Thomas teaches this (2.2. d. 42, q. 1, art. 1). Nor does the reason of de Lugo stand in the way, namely that in confession we are held only to explain the number of sins, but not the different malices of sin, for the response is that after it has been posited that there are many malices in that action, there are also many sins, since there cannot be different sins unless there are different malices.

46.—Hence it is inferred that to commit different sins by number, I. When, someone kills many men in one strike, or commits detraction against many people, as the authors say (Cont. Tournely, *de pecc.* part. 1, cap. 3, art. 2, *colliges* 1; Concina tom. 10, p. 530, n. 23; Bonacina *de sac.* d. 5, q. 5, p. 2, §3 diff. 3, n. 16, and the Salamancans tr. 20, c. 12, p. 5, §2, n. 42 and 43, with Vasquez, Azor, Henr., etc., against Anacl., p. 81, n. 57, Tamburinius *loc. cit., n. 61 and 62* with de Lugo, etc.). And the same thing must be said if anyone would intend to kill or disgrace a whole family, as the Salamancans teach (*ibid.* n. 49), Cont. Tourn. *loc. cit.,* Concina n. 28 and Holzman p. 145 n. 671 against Roncaglia, p. 16, q. 2, r. 2 and Anacl. *loc. cit.*) Nor is it opposed to say that a family has its reputation for one individual person, from l. 1, ff. *Si familia,* etc. Although it is a fiction of law to call one person a family, just the same, that murder or detraction, since it wounds the just of both, because the persons of that family have a distinct life or reputation, for that reason it constitutes different sins. But it would have to be said otherwise, as the Salamancans suppose, if someone would injure the goods that some city possesses, a monastery or a chapter in the commons; then the right would not suffice or individuals in particular, but only for the whole community, which is why one justice is wounded. II. One who desires in one act to meet many women, (against Tamburinius n. 62, with de Lugo), or to see the same woman many times (against Lessius, ap. Tamburinius n. 5), so much more one who knows the same woman many times on the same night (the Salamancans *ibid.* n. 55, with others in common against Zanardum), for each fornication has its completed terminus. III. Someone that steals from many people (the Salamancans *ibid.* n. 44 with Azor and Molina against de Lugo and Tapia). IV. One who causes scandal to many people on one occasion (Cont. Tourn. *de praec.*, Dec. cap. 1, sect. 7, punct. 1 § 2, *in fine*, against Tamburinius, *num. 64*, with de Lugo). V. One who in a single act wants through many days to omit the canonical hours or fasting. (Croix, l. 5, num. 164; Holzm. n. 673; the Salamancans tr. 20, c. 12, p. 5, §2 n. 44, contra Busembaum and de Lugo, etc.) VI. Someone that desires evil for three persons in one act. (Croix n. 158, cum Dicastillus)

47.—*Quaeritur:* I. How many sins does one commit that blasphemes the twelve apostles in one act? The continuator of Tournely (*de pecc.*, part 1, cap. 3, art. 2, *colliges* 3), and Concina (tom. 10, p. 529, n. 21), suppose that he commits twelve sins because he wounds the honor of each Apostle, and it is probable, though what Anacletus (p. 82, n. 58) and the Salamancans (*ibid.* n. 40), and others think is not improbable, namely that he would commit one sin, because when all the blasphemies take-up malice against the Saints from one relation to God, morally speaking, one injury is inflicted upon God through the medium of such a blasphemy.

48.—*Quaeritur:* II. whether one commits different sins if he commits detraction against someone in many matters, or when he afflicts them with different contumelies? Some reject this (the Salamancans *ibid.*, n. 41; de Lugo *de poen.* d. 16 n. 265, with Cajetan, Sa, Azor, Reg., and Molina, likewise Bonacina, Dic., Diana, etc., cited by Croix l. 5, n. 161), saying one commits a sin because although such detractions, or contumelies are materially distinguished by species, nevertheless, morally they wound one reputation or honor. But others sense more probably that he commits many sins (Cont. Tourn., *loc. cit.* Colliges 5; Holzman, n. 674; Concina, tom. 10, p. 529, n. 21; Croix *loc. cit.* with Sylvius, Navarre, etc.). The reason is that different laws for reputation or honor are wounded, which are fitting for the other; for by this, were someone defamed in one crime, therefore he is not defamed in the other. It is not opposed to this that someone who takes many different things from someone commits one theft, for then one right is wounded which he had for his goods; but when someone is defamed in many matters, his many rights are wounded, according to a great many aspects that reputation has to different virtues, wherefore, many sins are committed. Nevertheless, the Salamancans rightly advert that when hussies and low class men quarrel together in the same assault, burdening themselves with many contumelies, then they commit one sin. The reason is because according to the common estimation they do not harm reputation and honor, insofar as on the side of the rebukes among persons of this sort they are not taken as grave, and on the other, hearing furnishes no trust in them, thinking that these set out rather more from the onset of anger than from the mind and truth of the matter, and therefore such quarrels are often excused from mortal sin unless perhaps they would reproach an adversary in a particular act.

49.—*Quaeritur:* III. whether a man who commits detraction against someone in the presence of many would commit many sins? Croix (l. 5, n. 162) and Holzman (tom. 1 p. 143, n. 675) uphold this, because (as they say) as many rights are wounded as there are persons who are defamed. Yet they think he commits only one sin. (De Lugo, *de poen.* d. 16, n. 112; Tamburinius; Meth. *conf.* l. 2 c. 9, § 1, num. 2; Azor, l. 13, c. 5, *dub.* 1, and Mol. *de just.* tract. 4, dist. 19, n. 3). The reason is that to commit detraction in the presence of many is only an aggravating circumstance since the right to a good name is one among all, not however manifold; this is why, since it is a sufficiently probable opinion, according to what is going to be said below (*de poen.* book 6, n. 467), that there is no obligation to explain in confession aggravating circumstances, it is also probable that in the proposed case there is no obligation to explain the number of persons in whose presence detraction had been committed, but it would suffice for it to be said "I committed detraction in the presence of many men."

50.—*Quaeritur:* IV. How many sins does a man commit who denies many articles of faith? Borgia (cited by Croix, l. 5, n. 156) thinks many, because (as he says) each article is a distinct object of faith. But Diana and Oviedo more truly reject it. The reason is that the object of faith cannot be said to be manifold since really it is only one thing, namely the veracity of God the revealer; and this is why one who denies an article of faith is no less unfaithful than someone who denies them all; and so on the other hand one who denies many articles is no more unfaithful than one who denies only one.

Quaeritur: V. How many sins one that desires different evils for an enemy would commit, say, infamy, death, poverty, etc.?

The first opinion, which several authorities hold (de Lugo *de poenit.* d. 16, n. 260, with Valentia, Turr., Bonacina, de 1 pr. d. 3, q. 5, p. ult. § 1, n. 10; Diana, 1. p. tr. 7 r. 30 and 3 p. tr. 4, r. 67; likewise Cajetan, Trull., cited by Busembaum, see l. 3, n. 30, v. *In confessione*), says he commits one species of sin and even in number, if evils are desired in the same attack, because the sins of hatred do not take up a different species from a different evil that is desired, when all are desired under the reasoning of the evil, as contrary to the virtue of good-will; there is no doubt that the species of evils must be explained if the desire were efficacious.

The second opinion, which Busembaum holds (*loc. cit.* with Suarez, Palaus and the Salamancans, *de rest.* c. 4, p. 4, n. 29, with Bann., Salon., Prado, Villalobos, de Soto, Filliuci, and Dic.) says to commit many sins, exactly as they are species of desired evils, if they are specifically express; because desire takes the species from a different desired object, as St. Thomas says (2.2. qu. 76, a. 4, ad 2), saying: "If he who lies would will the evil of killing another, the desire does not differ from homicide." It must be said otherwise if the evil is desired in common, exactly if he were to say: "You are cursed, let evil come upon you."

Nevertheless, *the third opinion* is sufficiently probable, which Croix holds (l. 5, n. 159), distinguished and says he commits one sin by species, in such a case those evils are taken up under one kind of evil, namely, as the means of ruin desired for an enemy; otherwise, if the will were imposed to desire those different things specifically things considered evil, as Sylvius, Molina, Bonacina, etc. say.

Quaeritur: VI. Whether a confessor commits many sacrileges who absolves many people successively in mortal sin? Some authors reject this (the Salamancans tr. 20, c. 12, p. 5, § 2, n. 46; Viva, *de poen.* q. 5, a. 6, n. 6; de Lugo, *eod. tit.* d. 16, n. 558, with Rodriguez, likewise Sporer, Gob., Diana, etc. cited by Croix, l. 5, n. 171; saying to commit one sin because he inflicts one irreverence on God; just as someone who steals many sacred vessels commits one sacrilege. But it is more true what others teach, (Concina, tom. 10, p. 531, n. 27; Cont. Tourn. *de pecc.* part. 1 cap. 3, art. 2, Collig. 4; Croix *loc. cit.* with Bonacina; Dicastillius; Escobar; and others) that he commits as many sacrileges as absolutions he imparts because every single absolution is a single sacrament. He says the same about a priest administering the Eucharist successively to many people, (Croix, num. 172, with Con. Vasquez, Palaus, etc.), because individual communions are individual banquets completed in regard to the communicant. But more probably, Viva, Filliuci, Busembaum, Diana, and others (cited by the same Croix, *loc. cit.*, who also thinks it probable) say in this that one sin is committed, since there is one administration and therefore one banquet. (See book 6, n. 35, v. *Hinc.*) Furthermore, whether to minister the Eucharist in mortal sin would be another mortal sin, see what was said in n. 35, under the beginning.

CHAPTER II
On sins in particular, Mortal and Venial.

DUBIUM I.
What is a mortal and venial sin?

51. *What is a mortal sin, and what is a venial sin?*
52. *How many different ways can a sin be mortal? Notable advertence must be made for those who condemn facile things as mortal sins.*

51.—"Resp. 1. It is a mortal sin which, on account of its "gravity it dissolves friendship with God, and merits "eternal punishment. Something is called a mortal sin "because it abolishes the spiritual beginning of life, "namely habitual grace, and brings death to the soul.

"A venial sin is one that on account of its levity, does not "abolish grace and the friendship of God, even though it "diminishes the fervor of charity, and merits temporal "punishment. It is called venial, because, save for the "beginning of the spiritual life, namely grace, it imparts "a feebleness to the soul that is easily curable, and "forgiveness is easily obtained.[5]

52.—"Resp. 2. A mortal sin is twofold, on the one hand it "is deadly by its genus; on the other hand from its "accident. It is deadly by its genus because in itself it "wounds the charity of God, or of our neighbor in regard "to his person, things or rights, or gravely corrupts our "very person (Azor, l. 4, c. 9, Sanchez, l. 1, mor. c 3).

For that reason, the following are resolved:

"1. Sins committed against someone's good, as are "venial by their genus, such as uselessness, vain "concupiscence, vain delight, prodigality, curiosity, and "superfluous worship or clothing, or trifles, laziness, "excess in food, drink, sleep, laughter, marital relations, "fear, sadness, appetite for money, praise, etc.

"2. Sins against the theological virtues are mortal by "their nature, because they harm some internal good of "God, *e.g.* veracity, mercy, charity. Likewise, nearly all "the things which are done against the Decalogue, "because those which are committed against the first

---

[5]   Translator's note: In English the root meanings are lost in translation, for what St. Alphonsus is trying to explain is that the term "venial" comes from the Latin word *venia*, which means pardon, and as such venial means "pardonable".

"three precepts similarly harm the Godhead, knowledge,
"divine omnipotence, and His external or internal honor,
"which are done against some precepts, harm the person,
"good or right of their neighbor.

"3. Those sins against the seven virtues, which are called
"capital sins, are not all mortal sins by their genus,
"because they do not all gravely wound God or neighbor,
"or corrupt our selves.

"Resp. 3. It is called mortal from its accident when some
"act is venial or indifferent, it becomes mortal *per
"accidens*, on which we will treat more below."

Here we must rightly notice what Roncaglia says (*tract.*
2. q. 1, c. 1, reg. 1, in practice) namely, "Where it is clear that
something is not a mortal sin, the confessor would be far
amiss in judging such a transgression to be grave, and to
pronounce his judgment of such a sin on the penitent." Still,
it is very dangerous for confessors to condemn something as
a grave sin, where certitude is not manifest, as St. Thomas
teaches. "Every question in which it is sought on mortal sin,
unless the truth were expressly held, a determination is
dangerous." (*Quodlib.* 9, art. 15). He adduces the reasoning of
this doctrine a little later, namely that "an error, in which
something is believed to be mortal that is not, binds to
mortal sin by conscience." This is why St. Antoninus says:
"Unless one were to have express authority of Sacred
Scripture, or a canon, or a determination of the Church, or
at least evident reason, something will be determined to be
a mortal sin only with very great danger. ... For if something
were determined to be mortal, and it were not mortal, acting
against it he will sin because everything that is against
conscience paves the road to hell." Next, we learn in such a
distinction that those following rigid doctrines insert
themselves, and easily condemn men for mortal sin in those
things in which grave malice does not appear from evident
reason, and so expose them to the danger of eternal

damnation; the same thing must be said about those, who easily impress the mark of laxity on opinions which clearly do not seem improbable. (see what was said in book 1, n. 89).

DUBIUM II

From what causes is a sin that is mortal by its genus become venial per accidens?

53. What things are required for a mortal sin?
54. From what causes can a mortal sin become venial?
   I. from imperfect notice.
55. II. From imperfect consent.
56. III. From the unimportance of the matter.
57. See resolutions.
58. What if someone vowed three times to give a thousand gold coins, and did not pay three?

53.—"Resp. 1: Three things are required for a mortal sin "and if one of these is lacking, it becomes venial, but "otherwise, it is mortal of itself. 1) On the side of the "intellect, full knowledge and deliberation. 2) On the side "of the will, perfect consent. 3) Gravity of the matter at "least as much as possible. The reasoning of the first and "second part is, because when one considers human "frailty, it does not seem fitting to divine goodness to "punish man with eternal punishments without full "consideration and consent. The reasoning of the third "part is, where the matter is of little moment, there a "moderate offense is morally considered as much as "possible.

54.—"Resp. 2: A sin that is mortal by its genus, can "become venial from three causes, as is clear from the "aforesaid. The first is, if on the side of the intellect there "was not perfect knowledge of the malice or perfect "deliberation. The signs of imperfect deliberation are: a) "If one weakly apprehended that it is evil as if half-"asleep. b) If after, where he might better consider, he "would judge that he was not going to do it if he could "have so apprehended it. c) If one labors with vehement "passion, apprehension or distraction, or was "exceedingly disturbed, so that it was almost as if he did "not know what he did." (See what was said in n. 4).

55.—"The second cause is on the side of the will, if there "was not perfect consent (as St. Thomas teaches 1.2. q. "88, art. 6. See the aforesaid on consensus n. 5). "Moreover, the sins of imperfect consent are: a) If one "was so disposed that, although he could easily carry out "the sin, still he would not carry it out. b) If someone "were hesitant whether he should consent, especially if "he is a devout man. c) If someone usually is so affected "that he prefers to die than expressly commit a mortal "sin, because such does nor easily consent. d) If anyone "were extremely fearful and anxious to recall what "appeared. e) If one was half in a dream and not "sufficiently composed, etc., and will judge that he would "not have done it if he were fully awake. (See Sanchez, 1, "*mor.* c. 10, Baldell., l. 10, d. 8)

56.—"The third cause is on the side of the matter, if this "would be of little moment. Moreover, when it is such, it "must be discerned by a moral judgment of the prudent, "for which the following rules will serve: 1) that it will "be judged on the matter, not only itself *secundum se* "must absolutely be considered, but also respectively to "the end intended, for which if he does a little thing, it is

"light, but grave, if he does much, as Vasquez teaches,
"1.2. d. 158."

(The rule is, the smallness of the matter where on account of
the smallness the reasoning of the offense is not excused, as
happens in infidelity, hatred of God, simony, perjury,
venereal matters and blasphemy.)

"2. The circumstances must be attended to, because it
"often happens that a matter that is of itself light, with
"attention given to the circumstances of the common
"good to avoid scandal, etc., it may become grave. 3.
"Whether some part of the matter commanded is grave,
"these must be considered both absolutely and *secundum*
"*se*, and even in order to the whole. 4. In repeated
"transgressions, if a great many small matters, either
"*secundum se* or according to the effects produced by
"themselves, were morally joined the matter becomes
"grave, because then all are morally reputed as one. But
"on the other hand, then grave matter is not censed if the
"small matters, neither *secundum se* nor according to the
"effects left behind were united among themselves.

Thus, the following are resolved:

57.—"1. One sins mortally so that a matter becomes
"grave if he often steals a small thing and does not make
"restitution, according to what is going to be said in
"book 4, number 533; likewise, if while he interrupts a
"few psalms he omits from the same office; if on the
"same day of fasting more often he would eat a little, or
"work a little more often on the same feast day.

"2. He would not sin gravely if he worked a little on
"different feasts; if daily in lent he would eat a little food;
"which is true even if he would have at the same time
"the purpose for so doing: because when those things are

"not morally united among themselves, the individual "things are small. (See Sanchez, *loc. cit.*)

"3. He does not sin mortally who violates a vow on "different days, daily or on individual days that he will "pray for a short time or give a small alms, if the burden "were fastened to the day; because when the obligation "is daily extinguished, these matters are not continued. "But it is true, even if he proposes always to omit them, "because that purpose is not imposed in a grave matter. "Nay more, against Sanchez, they indeed think it is true, "even if someone were to have 100 different species of "vows on very light matters that he must fulfill in one "day, because these matters, when they are independent "from one another, are not united. Nevertheless, if "similar vows were not fastened to a day, but the days "were only put there as a terminus, beyond which the "execution would not differ, there will be a mortal sin "after it will have come to a notable matter.

58.—"4. It is probable that one who vows three or four "times to pay a thousand gold pieces does not sin "mortally if he does not pay three thousand, because, "even if such a part were absolutely considered notable "in itself, still by a comparison of the whole, in a moral "judgment it does not seem to be esteemed as very much. (See Laymann, l. 1, t. 3, c. 5).

DUBIUM III

By what modes does a sin that is venial by its genus, or an indifferent act, crossover per accidens *into a mortal sin?*

59. *How venial sin becomes mortal, I. on account of the end attached to it.*

60. *II. On account of the final end that was intended.*

61. *III. On account of contempt.*

59.—"There are five modes in which a venial sin becomes "a mortal sin, as the doctors in common, and particularly "Sanchez, teach: 1. By reason of the enjoined end. 2. By "reason of the final end. 3. By reason of contempt. 4. By "reason of scandal. 5. By reason of danger. I shall speak "briefly on each of these.

"Resp. 1. A venial sin crosses over into mortal sin by "reason of the enjoined end, that if someone would lie in "a small way, but to extort carnal relations: because "when the end is a mortal sin, it is also mortal. Still, it is "not necessary to explain that lie in confession, but only "the desire for fornication; because without the malice of "mortal sin, it remains venial.

60.—"Resp. 2. It also crosses into mortal sin, by reason of "an excessive affect in some matter: *e.g.* one would "constitute the last end in it. For this purpose it does not "suffice to be imposed very intensely and vehemently in "the object, but it is required that appreciatively one "should virtually so esteem it that he will be prepared for "his sake of transgressing the precept obliging under "mortal sin, that if anyone would be so inordinately "affected to stories, play, person, that he would prefer a "feast and omit mass, etc., than be deprived of them."

(In the case of one who omits Mass for the sake of games, it suffices for him to confess that he had omitted Mass. See what was said in number 10. If someone, however, by the love of games was prepared to commit any mortal sin, it would be a sin of temerity and indeed very serious, but without a species. The Salamancans tr. 20, c. 12, p. 2, n. 12, and 13, with Palaus, Azor, Bonacina, Reg.).

"Moreover, Bonacina notes this affect is not only "habitual, but ought to be actual, so that sin is contracted "because it is not imputed to that fault, to which he was "prepared to commit by habit.

61.—"Resp. 3. Venial sin becomes mortal by reason of "absolute and formal contempt.

"I say, however, *absolute and formal contempt*, namely "when a precept is violated formally and absolutely, "because he refuses to be subject to it or a higher one, "which is a sin of consummate pride: or when he does "not wish to obey a precept because there is a precept, "and it is a sin of formal disobedience, each of which is "gravely opposed to charity due to a superior."

(Therefore, it is one thing to scorn a law, or a legislator, even a human one, not *quâ* such a person, but *quâ* the legislator, which is a mortal sin, and another to scorn a matter commanded, which is venial if the matter is light. The Salamancans *ibid.*, n. 18, and more profusely in tr. 11, c. 2, p. 2, §4 *per totum*. See also what is going to be said in book 5, n. 161, v. *Quarta*.)

From which the following are resolved:

"1. It is not a mortal sin if you indeed meant to obey and "be subject absolutely, but here and now refused in a "modest matter; or if you would admit the authority of "the law or the one that commands, but here and now "pay no heed to the execution. The reason is, because it "is not absolute contempt and *simpliciter*, but only "*secundum quid*.

"2. If a precept were abruptly violated from indignation, "malice, bad custom, or another cause, and not from "contempt of the power of the superior, it is not mortal "because it is not formal contempt, but only "interpretative.

"3. It is a mortal sin to do or omit something from the
"contempt of a just human law. Likewise, from contempt
"of God the lawgiver, or even the counselor (which, for
"that reason, contains a tacit blasphemy, as if God
"commanded useless things, or merely gave advice); and
"then to do something from the contempt of a prelate,
"such a one having authority from God, but not such as
"a man, unlearned, imprudent, imperfect, because this by
"and by is not to scorn absolutely and simply, but only
"*secundum quid.* (See Sanchez, 1. mor. c. 5; Bonacina, *de*
"*peccat.* d. 2, q. 3, p. 5).

62.—"Resp. 4. Venial sin, or an indifferent work having
"a species of evil, crosses over *per accidens* into mortal
"sin, if the ruin through it that were caused to a neighbor
"were mortal. The reason is, because in such a work
"something gravely opposed to charity is superadded."
(*See what is going to be said on scandal,* as well as Filliuci,
t. 21, c. 5, q. 10, n. 212).

63.—"Resp. 5. A venial sin, or an indifferent work,
"crosses over into mortal sin by reason of the danger of
"falling into mortal sin when someone, without
"sufficient caution, does something from necessity
"through which he may come into moral and proximate
"danger of sinning mortally, because he has such
"contempt for his eternal salvation that he would
"expose himself rashly to such probable danger. For this
"reason, in confession the species of the sin must be
"explained, by the danger of which he opposes himself,
"because he sinned in the same genus of sin. Moreover,
"proximate danger is supposed because frequently men
"of a similar condition lead him into mortal sin.

Quaeritur: Whether one sins mortally who exposes
himself to a merely probable danger of sinning mortally?

The first opinion with Sporer (*de poen.* cap. 2, n. 342), and
Gob., Hozes, Lumbier, Murc., etc. all cited by Croix (l. 5, n.

257, etc.), rejects this, because (as they say), when in that case it is also probable that there is no danger of sinning, he does not act rashly who commits a sin on such an occasion; for where the danger is not certain, there cannot be present a certain obligation to avoid it. But the opposite must altogether be held, with Busembaum (as above), whom Croix (*loc. cit.*) follows, with Carden., Eliz., and others. The convincing reason is that if it is illicit to use probable opinion without a just cause with the danger of loss of another's spiritual or temporal goods, it is also certain among all, how much more it will not be lawful where the danger threatens his own soul? Nor is it opposed to say that where the danger is probable, there also it is probable that there is no danger: for the response is made that in that case, although the sin will be uncertain, whether it were or were not committed, still it is certain that there is danger of sinning. We said *without a just cause*, for where a just cause is present, there is no obligation of avoiding such a danger, unless the fall into sin were morally foreseen as a certainty. (See what is going to be said in book 3, n. 26, v. *Pariter*). And so physicians are excused, if they expose themselves to the danger of death to heal women, since several times in the past on account of such an occasion they already fell; so also a parish priest, who, in receiving confessions experienced the same misery, so also are others excused from their own office, say a curate, soldier, a shopkeeper, or a merchant, they cannot desert without grave detriment. (So think the Salamancans, tr. 26, c. 2, p. 2, § 2, n. 47 and *seqq.*, with Navarre, Hurt., Ant. a Sp. Sancto, etc., likewise, Elbel (*de penit.* num. 102,) Ronc, *eod. it.*, c. 4, qu. 3; Sporer, *eod. tit.*, n. 326, and others everywhere.

The reason is because the danger that is proximate of itself both becomes remote by reason of the circumstance of necessity, and at the same time by reason of means to beware of, which the person proposes (as is held) to apply namely, diligently by adverting the mind from foul delectation or from another passion, and moreover by fortifying himself with pious thoughts, prayers and frequent use of the sacraments. Which means, although they do not suffice to excuse, where the just cause is not present, to the extent that God does not help rashly exposing himself to danger, still he furnishes his aid to one who, from a just cause does not forsake, while in that case he did not remain from affect to sin, but from a certain necessity in that occasion. Otherwise, it must be said about simple confessors who fell a great many times in hearing confessions, because they are held to abstain from such exercise if they could without grave detriment to their reputation or faculties, according to what must be said in book 4, n. 438 and 483, v. *Quid*. But indeed, if someone in those occasions had lapsed and did not show off hope of emendation? See what is going to be said in the same place, n. 438, where we will say this must be held with each lost occasion to desert and save his soul. (See also what is going to be said in book 6, n. 453.)

64.—Whether, however, there were in the state of mortal sin, one who proposed to commit all venial sins? See what must be said in book 5, n. 12, *vers. Quaeriutur autem.*

CHAPTER III
ON THE CAPITAL SINS IN PARTICULAR

DUBIUM I.
What might be pride and what sort of sin is it?

65. *What is Pride?*

66. *What are the daughters of Pride?*

67. *How does pusillanimity correspond to pride?*

65.—"Resp. 1. Pride is a disordered appetite for one's own "excellence; it is a mortal sin by its genus if it is "consummated and carried out, *i.e.* if someone so desired "to excel that he refused to be subject to God, superiors, "and their laws. Nevertheless, it is imperfect in a case "where someone that does not refuse to be subject to "those whom he ought, only magnifies himself in his "own emotions, and it is only venial, as Cajetan and "others teach on the verse: *Superbia*: because without "contempt of God and of others, to raise himself more "than the just, it is not a grave disorder: still it would be "grave if it were to be done with notable contempt of "others, by being pleased with the abjection of others.

"66.—"Resp. 2. The daughters of pride are three: 1) "Presumption, which is the appetite for undertaking "something beyond one's strength. It is commonly only "a venial sin; still it becomes mortal if it causes injury to "God or neighbor, *e.g.* if one were to presume "ecclesiastical jurisdiction, the power of Holy Orders; "likewise if one were to presume the office of a doctor, "a defense attorney, a confessor, etc., without due "experience. (Lessius, l. 3, c. 2, d. 3, n. 18, and below, "book 5, c. 3, dub. 9).

"2. Ambition, which is a disordered desire for dignity "and honor that is not due, or due to one greater, such as "if one were to solicit a benefice or office for which he "was not worthy; or illicit in the mode and measure; *e.g.* "by simony. It is a venial sin *per se*, but it becomes mortal "either by reason of the matter, from which, or by reason "of the means, by which an honor is sought, or by reason "of the loss which is inflicted on one's neighbor. And "then, if honor is moderately sought on account of an "honest end, it will be an act of magnanimity, as "Laymann teaches.

"3. Vainglory, viz. desire for inane glory, has its end in
"the disordered manifestation of a proper excellence,
"whether true or false. It is called vain, when it is sought
"for an evil, false or fictitious thing, or something that is
"not worthy of glory, or is no thing at all, such as from
"riches, trifles, etc., or among those who do not judge
"rightly about a matter, or without a due purpose. It is a
"venial sin of itself, but is often a mortal sin *per accidens*,
"as it was said on ambition. On the contrary, as Sylvius
"and Navarre (cap. 17) rightly teach against Angelus, it
"is only venial, even in sacred matters done principally
"for vain glory; *e.g.* to preach. Moreover, through vain
"glory one sins in two ways, according to St. Thomas
"(1.2. qu. 13). I. *Directly*, and that is done either by words,
"which is boasting which is venial of itself; if it were on
"good things, *e.g.* on fasting, prayer, etc. even if *per*
"*accidens* it is often by reason of loss, if it were false it
"becomes a mortal sin, such as in the following ways: 1)
"If someone were to speak against the glory of God, as in
"Ezechiel 28:2, "I am God"; 2) If one were to break out in
"contumelies, *e.g.* "I am not as the rest of men, an
"adulterer, etc., as this man"; 3) For an evil end; 4) if one
"causes notable damage to one's neighbor; 5) If on a
"matter mortally evil; because approbation of a work has
"the same species with it: (hence, which ought to be
"expressed in confession, at least when complacency for
"the same thing was joined with boasting about sin. I add
"that if it were without it, it does not necessarily need to
"be explained. Navarre, Palaus and Diana, t. 2, tr. 4, r.
"116, against Sanchez, Lop., Rodr. etc. See Cardinal De
"Lugo, d. 16, n. 267), or by deeds, which if they are true,
"and have something of admiration, it is called *inventio*
"*novitatum* (invention of novelties); this is usually
"commonly admired, such as wearing pilgrim's
"garments, opinions, etc.; it is a mortal sin if it notably
"corrupts youth or morals; but if what were done were

"false, it is hypocrisy, *e.g.* if someone were to do
"something of good so that it would appear good even if
"it were not; which is venial of itself unless it were done
"with injury or contempt of God and neighbor. II.
"*Indirectly*, insofar as someone does not wish to be less
"than another. That is done in four ways: 1) By the
"intellect, and it is pertinacity, whereby someone
"tenaciously adheres to his opinion, which is a mortal sin
"if a truth of a greater moment were assaulted, or if it
"were joined with the danger of a third, *e.g.* if a doctor
"with danger to the sick man would remain in his
"opinion; 2. Through the will, and that is discord,
"whereby one sins mortally when it is in regard to the
"good of God, or a neighbor, in which there ought to be
"concord; 3) By words, and that is contention, which is
"a mortal sin when in a spirit of contrariety one were to
"quarrel in regard to a truth pertaining to faith, or the
"salvation of the soul or body; 4) through deeds, when
"someone does not wish to carry out what he ought, and
"this is disobedience. (See Bald.)

67.—"Resp. 3. Pusillanimity corresponds to these three
"daughters of pride, whereby someone lacking in
"confidence would detract honors, glory or a duty from
"himself for which he is worthy. It is venial of its nature;
"and it becomes mortal if one were to detract from
"something to which he is held under mortal sin. (See
"Lessius, l. 3, c. 2, n. 28; Laymann l. 3, sect. 5)

Thus, the following are resolved:

"1. Hearing praise for himself or another on a matter that
"is mortally evil, one sins mortally if he would approve
"it, support it or admire it as worthy of praise. (Sanchez,
"Bald. d. 29, n. 3).

"2. Disparaging another on account of vengeance not "taken up, or some other grave evil, or a sin that was "omitted, *e.g.* fornication, he sins mortally because it is "a species of boasting and it is with approbation of sin, "and the occasion to commit it. (*Ibid.*)

"3. Introducing new customs into a city and foreseeing "that by such an example he imposes moral necessity on "others, that they must take them up beyond their "strength and later they cannot nourish whom they "ought, or satisfy their creditors, sins gravely. (Baldell., "*loc. cit.*)

"4. To exonerate oneself too much from a spirit of levity "or vanity, in itself is only a venial sin. *Ibid.*

"5. To feign holiness with a will to not really have it, "Bald. says is a mortal sin. (*loc. cit.*)

"6. To feign wickedness is a sin (because it is a lie and "certainly scandalous; it can also be mortal). Nor do the "saints do something except by doing that which is of "itself indifferent, and by permitting it to be received by "others as a sign of wickedness, since still neither from "its nature nor is it such by their intention."

DUBIUM II

What is Avarice?

68. *What is avarice?*

69. *What are its daughters?*

70. *When and how will those opening and reading someone else's letters sin?*

68.—"Resp. 1. Is Avarice a disordered appetite for "temporal things?

Wherefore from this, and the rule handed down above on mortal sin, the following cases are resolved:

"1. It is of its nature a venial sin.

"2. Yet, when it grows from there so that one would not "doubt that it is the cause of transgressing divine laws, "it becomes a mortal sin.

"3. Prodigality, which is opposed to avarice, and consists "in a defect of preserving and from an excess to expend "is, from its nature venial; it is lighter than avarice "because it is less removed from the virtue of liberality. "At the same time, it becomes mortal if one would cause "his wife and children to live in poverty; if he would "render himself impotent to pay a debt; if one would "squander Ecclesiastical goods for pious causes. (See "Lessius, l. 2, c. 47, d. 8).

"Resp. 2. The daughters of Avarice are the following:

69.—"1. Hardness of heart (against mercy) by not having "compassion toward the poor and needy, by reproaching "those weighing very hard debts when the creditor is not "to be paid, etc. Sometimes it can be a mortal sin, when "the precept of almsgiving and charity urges and still "from such hardness he does not intervene. (Navarre, c. "27; Toledo, l. 8, c. 26. See what is going to be said on "Charity to one's neighbor).

"2. Inquietude of the heart, this is, vehement and "disordered application of the mind to acquire things, or "to preserve riches, with inane and vain fear, lest they "would not be acquired or taken. It is a mortal sin when "it diverts us from spiritual, or other things, to which we "are obliged by a grave precept. (*e.g.* from hearing Mass). "Furthermore, in induces a superfluous fear and from "this, diffidence toward God. It is venial if it would be on "a good thing, but in an undue time or place, *e.g.*

"concerning the family, the harvest, gathering grapes,
"when someone is in Church, or to be idle for God. (St.
"Thomas, 2.2. q. 55, art. 6, reg. l. 23, c. 2, q. 3; Escobar).

"3. Violence, which is mortal when it is unjust and in
"regard to a grave matter.

"4. Fallacies or treachery in words, which can be a mortal
"sin by reason of the end, or means.

"5. Fraud or treachery in deeds, which is a mortal sin by
"its nature, and in many ways happens in contracts, both
"by reason of the matter (*e.g.* if it would be thought to
"have vices or not) and by reason of the price. (Navarre,
"c. 23; Toledo, l. 8, c. 47; Escobar).

"6. Betrayal, which is a deception against a trust that is
"given or due, to the loss of another, is a mortal sin by its
"nature. In general, it happens in three ways: a) in regard
"to persons, in the manner that Judas betrayed Christ
"and Dalila Sampson; b) In regard to things whether
"immovable (as if a soldier would manifest to the enemy
"the manner of taking the citadel), or movable, such as
"if one would show to a robber someone's hidden
"money, clothes, or whatever you like; c) revealing a
"secret consigned to one (which is against fidelity and
"justice if it was promised), because it is a burdensome
"pact, as Cardinal de Lugo teaches (lib. 14, n. 139 and it
"is certainly a mortal sin if one could have foreseen that
"thence notable damage for others was going to follow,
"or discord, otherwise it is venial). Or, by opening up and
"reading someone else's letters. That last, if it were done
"so that one would know another's secrets, is curiosity,
"and if it were in a grave matter, is a mortal sin *per se*,
"because it is not commonly known before the opening
"of the letter, as the authors teach. (Toledo, l. 7, cap. 45;
"Bald. l. 3, d. 11; Navarre c. pen. d. 6, *de poen.* Mol.,
"Laymann lib. 3, t. 5, p. 1, c. 4, who adds when someone
"treacherously opens someone else's letters and reads

"them with injury or loss to another, he commits the "crime of falsity). I said, *it is a mortal sin per se*, because "*per accidens* it can be venial, or nothing if it were done "with legitimate authority, from a just cause.

Thus, the following are resolved:

70.—"1. To open and read someone else's letters is often "not a sin if one probably knows unjust damage was "written there, or an injury befalls him which he intends "to avert, because one can consult himself. Thus, a prince "can open letters not only of his enemies, but even of "others which in a time of war come from the border "places of the enemy. Likewise, public ministers, as often "as they judge it to be necessary for the common good. "Navarre, c. 18; Regin. l. 24, n. 60, Escobar, Cardenas, de "Lugo, d. 14, n. 148. (And this proceeds not only from the "prince and ministers, but even for private persons, as de "Lugo, d. n. 148; Roncaglia, de 7 praec., c. 4, q. 5, r. 2, "with Sanchez, Navarre, and Bonacina. But see what is "going to be said in book 4, n. 970, *in fine*).

"2. It is commonly held that it is not a sin if one's "consent of the one by whom or to whom they are sent "were expressly possessed (nor does a special law forbid, "Cardinal de Lugo, *loc. cit.*), or at least tacit permission: "so that you would do it under a command, reasonably "trusting it was going to be ratified. Thus Escobar thinks, "from Navarre, Regin. etc. (*loc. cit.*)

"3. A religious superior licitly opens and reads the letters "of his subjects (only if it were not sent to a greater "superior or such a man whom the statutes exempt, and "they do not come from him); or from the statute of "religion, or from custom, or even from probable

"suspicion which may contain something of evil. See
"Payrin., *de relig.* t. 1, "q. 2, c. 1, and Diana, p. 3, t. 6, r. 55.

"4. It is not a sin if it would be necessary or expedient to
"avert an injury threatening another: yet one must not
"read more than what is necessary to that end. Cardinal
"de Lugo, *loc. cit.*

"5. One who opens and reads, thinking it does not
"contain matters of a great moment, only sins venially.
"(De Lugo, *loc. cit.*)."

So the doctors hold in common (de Lugo, d. 14, n. 148;
Roncaglia, de 7 praec. c. 4, q. 5, r. 2). Morever, Concina (*de
rest.* q. 2, n. 5), with Molina, Navarre, Sa, etc., hold that even
if the matter of the reading were light, reading can be a
mortal sin if the other party would take it as a grave injury.
We must rightly admit this can be a mortal sin, but not
against justice, as it seems to Bonacina, because the gravity
of the injury taken is from the object itself, whether the
matter were *per se* suitable, according to the common
estimation of men, or causes grave sadness, as Croix says (l.
3, p. 2, n. 2, with the common opinion), but against charity,
by reason of the grave sadness which the other party suffers
from it even if it is a light injury.

"6. If you were to shred letters from another, and if you
"were to gather what has been thrown away by the
"owner in public and read the parts that were joined
"from curiosity alone it is a venial sin: but (*per se*)
"nothing if you were to provide for yourself by that
"knowledge, because what is left for derelict is lawful to
"convert into another use. Bald. from St. Antoninus, and
"Ros., Sylv. v. *Emptio*, q. 17, Laymann, l. 3, sect. 5, t. 3, p.
"1, c. 4, num. 4, Diana, t. 2, tr. 6, r. 55."

(So also de Lugo thinks, d. 14, n. 150, as well as Roncaglia, de
7 *praec.* c. 4, q. 5, r. 11, even if the owner shredded them into
tiny parts because it seemed his right to it ceased. But others
more probably contradict this, such as Croix, l. 3, p. 2, n.

1236, with Reb., and Petsch. The reason is because in this matter that he tore them into tiny parts showed enough that he did not want them to be read, and therefore did not wish to yield his right).

"Still, Laymann rightly notes (*loc. cit.*) such a person is "held by charity not to manifest a secret contained in "them if from it harm of any kind could come about: still, "(he adds), revealing a secret of this sort (knowledge of "which he justly acquired) will sin against justice if he "were to understand that those hearing it were going to "use this knowledge to unjustly inflict injury. See "Laymann, "*loc. cit.*

"I said 1: "*thrown away by the owner*, because if they "were either thrown away by another (without the "knowledge of the owner) or were lost in some case, it is "not lawful to read them.

"I said 2: *in a public place*; because if in they were thrown "in the fire or in the furnace to be burned, one would sin "if he would extricate them and read them. See Cardinal "de Lugo, d. 15, n. 150.

"I said 3: *per se*; because it can happen that things may be "contained of which the reading would be pernicious.

"7. One who stealthily reads another's secrets against his "will would sin. And a) it is a sin from curiosity, even if "he did it with a mind to learn and without suspicion of "loss; b) Of injustice, because everyone has the right of "secrecy in his writings that he does not want to be "common knowledge among others. Navarre, c. 15, "Molina, t. 4, d. 36, n. 2; Reg. l. 24, c. 6, n. 119, and it can "be mortal some of the time, namely if it were done with "notable damage; or the other party would rather desire "it were secret, and it were going to inflict very grave "damage. Bald. d. 11. See also Cardinal de Lugo, *loc. cit.*

"8. Whoever violates a secret without just cause with
"damage to another; or who unjustly opens the letters of
"another, from which harm to another follows, is held to
"make restitution. Bonacina, d. 2, *de rest.* q. 1, p. 1; Trull.
"l. 7, c. 10, d. 32.

DUBIUM III
What is lust?

71.—"*Resp.* Lust is a disordered appetite for venereal
"pleasures, the use of which, since it was established by
"its nature for the preservation of the human race, which
"is a great good for men and an eternal one for God,
"hence someone who abuses it, wounds God and man. It
"is a mortal sin by its nature. See book 2, ch. 1, d. 2, and
"below, book 4, tr. 4, c. 2.

"*Resp.* 2. The daughters of lust, which follow, are a great
"many, they are eight, four from the side of the intellect,
"and four on the side of the will.

"1. Blindness of the mind, when someone is so addicted
"to this foulness, that he will not think of heavenly
"things.

"2. Haste, whereby someone acts from the same cause
"without counsel.

"3. Inconsideration, when someone in a mode fails in a
"duty, acting inconsiderately which detracts from his
"state or person.

"4. Inconstancy, when someone soon falls away from
"pious propositions by the same affect of desires.

"5. Love of self, for such a man, on account of desires,
"directs his actions to his own end, not to God.

"6. Hatred of God, for a wanton man usually shudders at "divine things, nay more at God himself, as the avenger "of sins.

"7. Affected for the present age; for love of carnal desires "so affects the soul that he would even be prepared, "forthwith, to renounce eternal beatitude if he would "always be permitted to enjoy the present.

"8. Horror of the coming age; when one immersed in "desires will fear death in a disordered way, and refusing "to think about it, is zealous to propagate his life by "illicit means, etc.

"The first four are mortal when they place the final end "in creation, or forego some precept of God that gravely "obliges them; the second four, if they have the full "consent of the will, are mortal sins *per se*, if from a lack "of deliberation, or another imperfection of acts, they are "often venial. See Escobar and Bald., *loc. cit.*

DUBIUM IV
What is envy?

72.—"Resp. There is sadness on another good, exactly as "it is diminutive of a proper excellence, so that these "would be directly against charity; for this rejoices in the "good of our neighbor but envy desires the good of our "neighbor to be destroyed, or is sad when it is not.

(When one disputes on this sin, take notice of propositions 13, 14, and 15 among those condemned by Innocent XI).

Thus the following are resolved:

"1. It is mortal by its very nature, and very serious and "also against the Holy Spirit, if it would be over grace

"itself, or the help of God. 2. The daughters, similarly,
"are mortal of their nature and are numbered: a) hatred,
"on which we spoke of above; b) Detraction, on which
"we will speak on the 8th commandment; c) Joy in the
"evils of our neighbor; d) Gossiping, which is speech
"about one's neighbor to destroy his friendship with
"others, which hence one is held to make restitution for
"gossiping, and again to reconcile, not otherwise and the
"detractor of repute not otherwise. See on the 8th
"commandment.

Whether someone could dissolve the friendship of
another short of infamy by telling others, *viz.* about natural
defects, or similar things, that it would follow he be expelled
from the place? Some authors reject that (Azor, Trull.
Filliuci, etc., cited by the Salamancans *de rest.* c. 4, p. 3, n. 22).
But others uphold it (the Salamancans *bid.*, with de Soto,
Bonacina, Arag. Serra, Prado), because although without
force or fraud to procure good gratuity for someone, with
exclusion of another. But the first opinion is more probable,
while Lessius (l. 2, c. 11, dub. 3, n. 14) and the Salamancans
themselves (*ibid.*, p. 5, § 2, n. 45), with Navarre, Bonacina,
Sayr, and Diana, teach in common that publication of
natural defects will be a grave sin, if thence one impeded
another from obtaining some temporal good: since therefore
a publication of this sort will be unjust in itself, otherwise it
fraudulently is procured from the acquired friendship.

"3. If there will be sadness over the good of another,
"insofar as it is for him, or otherwise if one fears harm,
"e.g. his enemy is carried to office so that he could more
"easily harm him, it is not envy but fear, which is not *per*
"*se* a sin unless it were disordered. Laymann, l. 3, tr. 3, c.
"10.

"4. If sadness were for that which a is good lacking in us,
"which another has, so that, nevertheless, we do not
"desire it for another, it is not envy but emulation, or

"zeal, which is in regard to a genuine good, and it is
"praiseworthy; but if in regard to temporal things, it is a
"venial sin, such as if a good were disproportionate to
"the one that was sad, such as if a country bumpkin were
"sad that he were not king. Laymann, l. 3, tr. 3, c. 10, n.
"2.

"5. If the sadness is over the good of another insofar as
"it is unworthy, it is not envy but indignation, which is
"not a sin; still, it will be even a mortal sin if either one
"would take issue with the providence of God (and that
"is a blasphemy), or if it would so affect that it would
"lead men to imitate an evil. Cajetan, Laymann (*loc. cit.*)

"6. If one were sad that another might increase to be
"equal to him, or not much unequal in an excellence, that
"he would become superior to him and the former would
"apprehend the increase of the excellence as bad for him,
"it is envy properly so called; for one is said to be
"envious because he is not seeing, because he cannot see
"the good of another man without sadness.[6] Bald., d. 29,
"l. 3. So they usually sin: a) the ambitious, and those who
"seek glory in some matter which, when they put in it,
"that in that matter they might alone be singular, they
"are grieved and sad when if others accede to it; b) The
"pusillanimous, to whom all things seem great, they
"think each good of another diminishes them, just as
"some women easily apprehend and are sad if someone
"has a higher good than they, *e.g.* beauty; c) Old men in
"respect to the youth, and everyone that difficulty
"obtains something which others easily obtain. Bald., *loc.*
"*cit.*

---

[6] Translator's note: Again, there is something lost in translation due
to the different word roots, namely, the Latin term is *invidia* (not
seeing), so this is the reason a man not seeing is called *invidus*, or
envious.

"7. Someone in his adversity, or on account of the
"prosperity of others, desires that he was never born, or
"that he were made into a brute animal, or curses the day
"he was born, or that he first saw another man, or
"married, if he only intends to curse irrational creatures,
"*e.g.* days (or the day of his birth or marriage), which
"seems to him to have brought on so many evils or
"punishments, it is only venial (sometimes it is also no
"sin at all, such as Job), moreover, if he deliberately
"intends to desire evil for a man, or himself, or another
"on the day that they were born or married, it is a mortal
"sin. Escobar, and Marchant., *man.* c. 3.

DUBIUM V
On Gluttony

ARTICLE I
What is Gluttony?

73.—"Resp. Gluttony is a disordered appetite for food and
"drink, and it is opposed to abstinence and is committed
"in five ways: 1) If one were to eat before it is time; 2) If
"it is exceedingly exquisite. 3. If it is more than just. 4) If
"he eats voraciously. 5) If it is prepared very exquisitely.
"Laymann l. 3, tr. 1, sect. 4, n. 2.

Thus it is resolved:

"1. Gluttony by its nature is only a venial sin, because
"none of these modes is precisely opposed to the love of
"God or neighbor. (Note here proposition 8 condemned
"by Innocent XI, "to each and drink even to satiety only
"on account of desire is not a sin." Nevertheless, one may

"use delectation to take food or drink for health of the
"body, as the Salamancans teach, tr. 25, c. 2, p. 1, n. 4, in
"fine, from St. Augustine).

"2. Hence it is probable what Navarre, Toledo, etc.,
"teach, and what Laymann says is not opposed, that,
"provided scandal and other things are removed, it is
"only a venial sin to fill oneself with food and drink even
"to vomiting; and that also, if anyone would vomit so
"that he could drink again and again, Sa and many
"others, on the verb *comedere*, think it would be a mortal
"sin. See Bald., Escob. t. 2, e. 2, c. 5. (To eat or drink even
"to vomiting is probably only venial of its nature, unless
"scandal were present, or notable harm to health, as the
"authors commonly say; Holzman, t. 1, p. 154, n. 732, and
"the Salamancans, tr. 25, c. 2, p. 1 n. 8, with Cajetan,
"Navarre, Henriquez, and Laymann, l. 3, sect. 4, n. 2.
"Moreover, one who vomits what he has eaten by his
"own will so that he could eat or drink again, would
"hardly be excused froma mortal sin since this seems to
"involve great deformity, so Holzman, and Wigandt, tr.
"5, ex. 3, n. 70, r 2, hold against Busembaum).

"3. There is hardly any doubt that one may eat or drink
"or otherwise create vomit if it were judged healthy.

"4. Meanwhile, intemperance is considered a mortal sin
"by the circumstance and great disorder in these cases:
"a) If anyone for the sake of gluttony would violate a fast
"of the Church; b) If anyone from gluttony became
"noticeably inept for the functions to which he is held
"under pain of mortal sin; c) If someone would gravely
"harm his health, noticing it, otherwise if only lightly,
"*e.g.* if fevering he would increase his illness from a draft
"of water; d) If feastings and drinking parties were
"continually held so that he would have as a God his
"belly; e) If someone drank to perfect drunkenness, on
"which we will speak below; f) If someone would eat

"human flesh or blood from pure gluttony, both because
"it is repugnant to the piety due to the dead and because
"it is against the instinct abhorrent to nature. It will be
"excused if it were done for the sake of medicine, or for
"another just cause, *e.g.* extreme famine from a siege,
"still therein one is not held to so preserve life. Sanchez,
"1. mor. c. 8; Lessius, Laymann, l. 3, sect. 4, Sa, Bonacina,
"Bald., l. 3, c. 29. So also certain men excuse attendants
"who, to better administer their duty, are said to animate
"themselves with a draft of human blood, especially
"when the blood was not animated according to many.
"See *auct. cit.*

74.—"5. The daughters of gluttony are also venial of their
"nature, on the side of the soul. 1. Sluggishness of the
"mind, or stupidity born from intemperance, *e.g.* that one
"could not pray, etc., which becomes a mortal sin when
"someone from voluntarily eating or drinking in a
"disordered fashion became inept to understand or
"furnish those things which are necessary for salvation,
"or which are due from an office, or other things held
"under grave sin. Bald. d. 29, l. 3, n. 15.

"2. Inept joy, through which not every disorder is
"understood which follows the sin, but those which
"move one to obscene songs, foul acts, dances or
"dishonest group dancing, etc. and it becomes mortal
"when it induces another to consent, or mortal
"delectation, or ordered to it. *Ibid.*

"3. Loquaciousness.

"4. Scurrility, which differs from inept joy and
"loquaciousness, because it is in the appetite, the former
"is in words, this is in words and deed; and it is always
"called dishonesty, although *per se*, so long as scandal is
"removed, it is a venial sin, *e.g.* to say scurrilous things,
"or to sing, to break wind, etc. from levity to excite
"laughter; still it will be a mortal sin if it would become

"the cause of venereal delectation. Bald. *loc. cit.*, Escobar,
"t. 2, e. 2, c. 4.

"On the side of the body, uncleanliness, vomit and the
"effusion of seed. The last, if it were voluntary, will be a
"mortal sin. See Laymann, l. 3, sect. 4, Lessius, l. 3, c. 3,
"Bald. l. 3, c. 29.

ARTICLE II
What is Drunkenness?

75. In what does the sin of drunkenness consist? And
when is it mortal?

76. Whether it is a sin to make oneself drunk by the
prescription of a doctor? or from fear of death?

77. Whether it is always a mortal sin to make another
drunk?

78. When is drunkenness excused from mortal sin?
Whether all the evils committed in drunkenness are
sins?

75.—"Resp. The malice of full and perfect drunkenness
"consists in that, because someone without a just and
"grave cause, merely on account of desire or gluttony,
"knowing and even wishing it would deprive him of the
"use of reason, not simply, that which happens in a
"dream established in a natural mode by the author of
"nature to preserve the bodily strength and image of
"God; but violently, and in an unnatural mode, by
"disturbing reason and disfiguring the image of God into
"the manner of a mindless brute, and at the same time,
"by additionally depriving himself of the proximate
"power of the use of reason for every sudden necessity.
"This is what the Doctors teach in common.

Wherefore, the following are resolved.

"1. Perfect drunkenness, whereby in the aforesaid mode "reason is plainly rendered insensible, is by its nature a "mortal sin because it is reckoned an injury to God, "whose image one would so disfigure. It is the common "teaching of the doctors.

It is certain with all, that for this purpose that for drunkenness to be a mortal sin it is required that it would be perfect, namely that it would altogether deprive one of the use of reason, just as St. Thomas teaches (2.2. q. 150, a. 2), and with him all the doctors. The malice of drunkenness consists in this, that *a man, willful and knowing, deprives himself of the use of reason.* St. Antoninus teaches the same thing (p. 2, tit. 6, c. 3, § 1). This is why one would not sin mortally that did not altogether lose the use of reason from drinking wine, even if the mind were disturbed, but not so much that he were not able to discern between good and evil, as the authors commonly say (Toledo, *de pecc. mort.*, c. 51, n. 3; Cajetan in D. Th. *loc. cit.*; the Salamancans t. 25, c. 2, p. 2, n. 21; Elbel, t. 1, p. 225, n. 663; Wigandt, tr. 3, ex. 3, n. 70, Holzman t. 1, p. 154, n. 730 *in fine*; Laymann, lib. 3, sect. 4, n. 5, and others. Croix adds (l. 5, n. 327) along with Angelus, Tanner, Fab., Gob., and others in common, that drunkenness is not a mortal sin if it would deprive one from reason for only a brief period. Moreover, Croix says an hour seems like a long time. Would, however, one who drinks wine even to vomiting to inebriate himself sin mortally? See what was said in n. 73, v. 2.

76.—"2. It is not a sin to make oneself drunk at the order "of doctors, if one cannot otherwise recover health. "Sylvius, Cajetan, Laymann.

Quaeritur: I. Whether one may make himself drunk by the counsel of doctors when it is judged that inebriation is absolutely necessary to expel a sickness. The authors labor very much on this question, although it seems this case could hardly ever happen.

The first opinion upholds it, and there are several authors that hold it. (Busembaum, Lessius, 1. 4, c. 3, n. 13; Toledo, *de pecc. mort.* c. 61, num. 4; Laymann 1. 5, sect. 4, n. 5; Palaus, tr. 30, d. 3, p. 5, num. 2; Roncaglia, tr. 2, q. 2, c. 4; Sporer t. 1, p. 95, n. 69; Tamburinius *de praec. eccl.* c. 1, nu. 31; and the Salamancans tr. 25, c. 2, p. 3, n. 55; with Sylvius, Cajetan, Sylvester, Escobar, etc.). The reason is because food and drink are then sins when they are immoderate; on the other hand, St. Thomas (2.2. q. 150, art. 2 ad 3) teaches that, "food and drink are moderated according to what is suitable to the health of the body, and so whenever it happens ... that someone who is in excellent health may be moderated by infirmity." Therefore, a draft of wine, even inebriating, must not be said to be superfluous in respect to weakness, for which it is necessary to health. And it seems that St. Thomas favors this same opinion in 1.2. quest. 88, art. 5, ad 1, where he says: "That a man without necessity would render himself impotent for the use of reason only from the desire of wine, whereby a man is ordered to God, and he avoids the occurrence of many sins, it is expressly contrary to a virtue." Note "without necessity," therefore, if necessity were present, it would not be contrary to the virtue.

The second opinion rejects this, and is held by the Continuator of Tournely (*de pecc.* part. 2, cap. 4, art. 3, quaer. 4, n. 8; Petrocorens, t. 2, p. 181, quaest. 3; Holz. t. 1, p. 155, n. 756; Felix, *Potesta de vitiis*, n. 3782), etc. The reason is that a voluntary privation of reason by drunkenness is intrinsically evil; for that reason, just as fornication can never be permitted, so neither can this. Just the same, the first opinion is sufficiently probable, actually, it seems to me more

probable that in a case in which a draft of wine were offered
to expel or correct bad humors, then the privation of reason
per accidens and indirectly would come about, and therefore
licitly can be permitted, just as it is licit for a mother to take
pharmaceuticals directly tending to save her life, although
indirectly a miscarriage may come about, as we will say in
book 4, num. 394, v. *Quaer. igitur.* Otherwise, it must be said
if the drink were given directly for the purpose of
drunkenness or to cause a deprivation of reason, this would
always be intrinsically evil. Hence, as Croix duly adverts (l.
5, num. 341), with Tanner, Dicastillus, and Gob., it is never
licit to make oneself drunk to weaken the senses to not feel
physical pain.

"3. Likewise, it is not a sin if someone were compelled to
"drink under threat of force. See Lessius, l. 4, c. 3, d. 4, n.
"37; Azor, Reg., and Bald."

Quaeritur: II. Whether someone may make himself drunk
to avoid death, which would otherwise threaten him if he
were not drunk?

The first opinion affirms it, and Lessius (l. 4, c. 3, n. 37),
Bonacina, *de praec. eccl.* d. ult. q. 1, p. 1, n. 3, Palaus, (tr. 30,
d. 3, p. 5, n. 2) hold it with Busembaum, and Laymann thinks
it is probable (l. 3, sect. 4, n. 5). The reasoning is both
because a man, although he might not have mastery of the
use of reason, nevertheless has it in order to the good of the
whole, and moreover, he can dispose of such a use exactly as
it is necessary for the preservation of the whole; and because
a privation of reason here is not intended, but only
permitted, wherefore a man is not held to impede it with the
throwing away of his life.

But *the second opinion* more probably rejects that this is
licit, and is held by Holzman (t. 1, p. 155, n. 736), Wigandt,
(tr. 5, ex. 3, n. 71), Azor, (p.1 l. 7, c. 3, q. 5, *in fine*), Cont.
Tourn. *loc. cit.*, and the Salamancans, tr. 25, c. 2, p. 3, n. 45,
with Cajetan. The reason is because (as we said) to deprive

oneself directly of the use of reason is intrinsically evil; and then an excusing cause cannot be present just as in the case of the preceding question, for there the wine is the means *per se* ordered to expel an illness, but not here. Besides, in that case there is a danger to one's life from an intrinsic cause, namely from a vexing plague, and consequently, it is lawful to expel it through a drink of wine; but in this case the danger is from an extrinsic cause, for which reason it is illicit to free oneself from it through drunkenness, just as it is lawful for a woman to expel an unanimated fetus to preserve her life, but it is not lawful to expel it to flee death from relative causes, according to what is going to be said in book 4, n. 394.[7] Our opinion is strengthened by the authority

---

[7] Translator's note: On account of the confusion of our times on this question, we are transposing St. Alphonsus teaching from book 4 (3 in the version of Gaude and others) commenting on the 5th Commandment. It is clear that St. Alphonsus seems to have at least accepted, if not held to, the Aristotelian view that the fetus is not animated immediately at conception. Thus, here he is enumerating what is held by the doctors under this reasoning, but an examination of his position on this question in its proper place will reveal that St. Alphonsus in no way supported the expulsion of an unanimated fetus. So, taking up this question in book 4, n. 391, he summarizes two opinions:

"*Is it lawful to give pharmaceuticals to directly expel the fetus?*

"The first opinion upholds this, and very serious authors hold it: Sanchez, Laymann, with Silvester, Navvare, etc.; likewise Petrocorensis, Viva, Mazzotta, Habert and others. The reason is, because when the fetus is part of the womb, the mother is not held to save it with such prejudice to her life ... Still, Sanchez rightly makes the exception (and asserts it as common with all) that if there is a doubt present as to whether the fetus were animated, to that extent it would then be intrinsically evil since you positively do not know whether you expose an innocent person to danger.

"*The second* opinion is more common and teaches that it is indeed lawful for a mother to take medication to directly cure an illness, even if it may indirectly expel the fetus; but not directly to expel the fetus. So think many authors. The reason is, because if it is never licit

of St. Augustine (serm. 232 *de tempore*), where he says: "Even if it would come about for this that it would be said to you: 'you should either drink or die', it would be better that your flesh should be killed sober than that your soul die in drunkenness." Nor would it avail to say with Lessius (n. 38), that this text must be understood when someone is compelled to drink in contempt of virtue, for there the Angelic Doctor says nothing about contempt, rather he only speaks about drunkenness, those who "usually so excuse themselves that they say: 'A powerful person compelled me that I would drink more, and in a royal banquet I could not do otherwise'." One might insist, someone can licitly will his hand to be cut off lest he would kill someone, therefore he can equally and licitly will himself to be drunk to avoid death. But we respond with Holzmann, the reasoning is unequal, for that part of the body is ordered, in itself, to the preservation of the whole body; still, the use of reason is not ordered to the life of the body, but to preserve the integrity of the soul.

---

to expel the seed, even if death is feared by its abundance, how much less will it be lawful to expel a fetus, which is nearer to human life? Nor would it avail to say that the fetus is an unanimated part of the mother, for we respond that the fetus does not pertain to the integrity of the maternal body, but is in its beginning stages and a distinct individual human. ...

"Each opinion is probable, but the *second* I think is safer and must altogether be embraced in this case, and although the first is of no use in practice it seems vain to dissuade certain teachers from it."

Additionally, subsequent to St. Alphonsus' time, the Roman Rota issued a judgment confirming the side that St. Alphonsus deems "safer", answering a dubium about whether a doctor could conduct operations and apply medicines to cause the abortion of an "unanimated fetus", on 24 July 1895, the Rota replied: "Negative, according to what was otherwise decreed on 28 May 1884 and 19 August 1888." Cf. *Theologia Moralis, Tomus Primus*, Rome, 1945, pg. 645-6, editor's note *c*.

And here again, I repeat that which I protested from the beginning, namely that when I call some opinion uniquely more probable, I do not, therefore, understand the contrary to be probable. Just as, equally, when I speak about some opinion that *I do not dare to condemn,* or *say is improbable,* I do not, therefore, admit it as probable, but I have hesitancy on its probability. Likewise, when I call some opinion more true, I understand the opposite to not have strong probability, although I do not altogether condemn it.

77.—"4. It is a mortal sin to cause another man to be "drunk, or to challenge him to a drinking contest with "the intention of getting drunk, or with the knowledge "that drunkenness is going to follow in him or in the "other man. Lessius, *loc. cit.*

"5. If for a just cause, *e.g.* a great evil could be otherwise "impeded if the author of it is drunk, it is lawful to "induce him to drunkenness, which at least is not "voluntary, viz. apart from intention, and therefore he is "inculpably drunk; *e.g.* a very strong wine, or toasting "with a medicated drink, when the other man is "deceived, not knowing its strength. Wherefore, one can "so make others drunk, who otherwise would betray the "city or abduct him. (Lessius, *loc. cit.*, and Sanchez, l. 2, *de* "*matr.* d. 11). But in this case, would it be permitted to "induce someone to drunkenness if it were a voluntary "act? There is a doubt. Lessius (l. 4, c. 3, d. 4, n. 32), "affirms; because, he says, one may persuade and induce "to a lesser evil that prevents a greater one. Laymann, "(lib. 3, sect. 4, n. 6) more rightly denies it, because in no "case may one induce someone to sin."

Quaeritur: Whether it is licit to induce someone to get drunk, to impede him from a more serious evil, say from committing a sacrilege or a homicide? There are three opinions.

The first upholds it, and Lessius (l. 4, c. 3, d. 4, n. 53) holds it as probable, and Medina, Gob., Diana and others cited by Croix (l. 2, n. 224) think it is probable. The reason is because one may be prepared to commit a greater evil to induce someone to carry out a lesser one.

The second opinion, which Laymann (l. 3, sect. 4, n. 6), Bonacina (tom. 2, d. ult. *de praec. eccl.*, q. 1, p. 1, n. 3), Palaus (t. 7, tr. 50, d. 3, p. 5) and the Salamancans (tr. 25, c. 2, p. 4, n. 51) hold it, saying it is licit to induce another to material drunkenness, *i.e.* when he would otherwise make himself drunk without sin, say by placing a very strong wine in front of him, or one that is medicated; because then on his side he would not sin, and on the other the damage of drunkenness is permitted to avoid even graver damage to others. But it is not licit to say one can induce formal drunkenness, namely when it is by his own sin, since this is intrinsically evil and therefore never permitted. Nor is it opposed (as they say) the reason of Lessius, for they respond that this avails when a lesser evil is included in a greater evil, precisely when you lead one that wishes to kill his enemy to only strike him; but not when the evil is disparate.

The third opinion, at length, which the Continuator of Tournely upholds (*loc. cit.*, *Unde* 9), and Holzman (tom. 1 p. 155, 735), along with Arsdek., says it is not permitted to induce anyone to drunkenness whether formal or material, on account of fleeing both evils, because (and in this they speak rightly), an evil, even if it is material, against the natural law is truly an evil, which is why one may never cooperate with it. Still, these not withstanding, the first opinion seems sufficiently probable to me, and other learned men that I have consulted, whether the drunkenness were material or formal, on account of the reasoning that has been provided, because it is licit to induce another to a lesser evil so that he would be impeded from a greater one, according to what we will say in book 3, number 57. Nor is what the Salamancans say (*loc. cit.*, against Lessius) opposed, for, although the evil of drunkenness does not seem included in that greater evil of sacrilege or murder, since they are *per se* disparate evils; nevertheless, really, virtually it is already included in that greater spiritual evil, since every spiritual evil includes, nay more exceeds, every temporal evil, so much that anyone is held more to suffer every temporal evil to avoid even the lest spiritual evil. Nor does it impede us to say that it is not lawful to persuade a lesser evil to be imposed on a third, because then the one persuading would be the direct cause of damage of the third, because it would not happen to him unless he would persuade, for this occurs when an evil is imposed on a third innocent man, who is not held to suffer the damage, to avoid the spiritual evil of another; but not in our case, where he who is induced to drunkenness, is indeed held to tolerate (as we said above) every temporal evil to put to flight a greater spiritual evil.

78.—"6. If someone does not foresee the danger of "drunkenness and is taken by wine, or going out in the "morning is disturbed by the wind, nor did he foresee "this, is free from sin. For this reason, many are excused "who often prudently judge but still can make for "themselves a little draught without guilt; still they will "cease to judge the matter prudently if they have "experience of it to the contrary."

The doctors agree with this in common, with St. Thomas in 2.2. q. 150, art. 2, where he says: "[Drunkenness] happens in three ways, in one so that a man does not know the drink is immoderate, and has the potency to inebriate him, and so drunkenness can be without sin ... In another way, so that someone who perceives the drink is immoderate, still does not think that it has the potency to make him drunk, and so drunkenness can be with venial sin. In the third mode, it can happen that someone knows well the drink is immoderate, and it makes him drunk ... and so the drunkenness is a mortal sin, because according to this a man wishing and knowing to deprive himself of the use of reason." Moreover, he adds in the first response: "because assiduity makes drunkenness a mortal sin, it is not on account of the repetition of the act, but because it cannot be that a man is made assiduously drunk unless knowing and wishing he incurs drunkenness, provided that he has experienced the strength of the wine many times and its ability to make him drunk."

Here, we must note carefully that if someone takes only a draught of wine, which is suitable, and already knows it tends to drunkenness, in no way is he excused from mortal sin, even though before he is destitute of his senses, he commits himself in a dream in which he flees the effect of the wine, because that drink now of itself is intrinsically evil, since of itself it is already suited to deprive a man of the use of reason, and *per accidens*, stands that itself or by a dream, or deprived of his senses by inebriation.

"7. If someone after a drink could still discern between "good and evil, although he might be disturbed by some "phantasms, or vomiting were to follow, or the tongue "stutter, his feet vacillate, or if he sees double or the "house seems to move around, the drunkenness is not "yet full, and therefore it is only a venial sin, although "from more grave things if it were deliberately "committed. See Laymann, *loc. cit.*

"8. Full drunkenness is noted by these signs, which "Lessius (l. 4, c. 3, d. 3, n. 30) and Regina give: 1) If "anyone has no memory of words and deeds, how or "when he was escorted to the house; 2) If he committed "things which otherwise would usually never do when "he was of sound mind, *e.g.* it is against his custom to "use foul language in speech, to disturb the house, beat "his wife, etc.

"9. Evils committed in drunkenness, if they are not "foreseen, or if caution were applied, free one from "fault."

What if the evils were foreseen? The Salamancans (tr. 20, cap. 10, p. 3, § 2. n. 27, and more profusely in tr. 25, c. 2, p. 2, n. 30) with Domingo de Soto, distinguish and say that if the evils were of a work, as killings, fornications, etc., they are imputed to sin; but otherwise if they are sins of speech, such as contumelies, blasphemies and perjuries, because they say those words are advanced by the drunkard are not formal words by a distinctive act, insofar as they were not said by a man in possession of his reason, but they are simple sounds or material words, such as those advanced by a parrot or a magpie. I do not dare say this opinion is improbable, but I adhere more to the opposite opinion with Sanchez (dec. l, 1, c. 16, n. 44), who, with Cajetan and Toledo, teaches blasphemies that are foreseen are true formal sins in their cause, since he freely placed them; for contumelious words in men advanced in a state of drunkenness he says rightly inflict no dishonor upon men; for otherwise, if they profess belief in God, according to what will be said in book 4, n. 124, where we will say that blasphemies, even without affect, or advanced materially, are not excused from sin since their voluntary pronouncement verges on the diminishing of divine honor. And in our case, although the pronouncement were not voluntary in act, still it seems voluntary in the cause.

DUBIUM VI
What is Anger?

79. *When is anger a sin?*
80. *On which sins arise from anger?*
81. *Whether contumelies are sometimes free of sin?*

82. *How manifold is contumely?*

83. *What is required for a curse or imprecation made against men to be a mortal sin?*

79.—"*Resp.* It is a disordered appetite for vengeance. "Such disorder can happen in two ways, according to St. "Thomas: 1) On the side of the mode of becoming angry, "*e.g.* if one were burning interiorly too much or if he "made it too clear by exterior sins; 2) On the side of the "object, that if one desires vengeance it is plainly unjust "on account of the cause, or if it is more than just, *e.g.* by "desiring the death of an enemy which is not due, or to "carry out by the proper authority or at length, if the "vengeance were just, still, one would not desire it as "just, but to satisfy his malevolent attitude.

Thus the following are resolved:

"1. If vengeance is desired in an orderly manner, it is not "the sin of anger, as when superiors are angry with the "sins of subordinates, and punish them, or vindicate "them.

"2. Disordered anger, in the first mode we already said is "of its nature a venial sin, still it can become mortal from "the accident, as if blasphemy, cursing and scandal were "added to it.

80.—"3. Disordered anger, in the second mode, is of its "nature mortal because it is directly against charity. "Bald., l. 3, dist. 21.

"4. On the daughters of anger, which are partly from the "heart, such as indignation, and swelling of the mind; "and partly from speech, such as shouting, blasphemies, "contumelies, cursing; and partly from actions, such as

"quarreling, fights, seditions, wounds, it must be spoken
"of in different modes according to the afore-given rule.
"For 1) Indignation, which is a disordered affection from
"that which someone thinks himself unworthily treated
"by such, in common it is venial; nay more, if it proceeds
"from a just judgment of reason, it is no sin at all. Still, it
"can be a mortal sin if it were to increase even to
"deliberate hatred and grave contempt of a person. 2)
"Swelling of the mind, in which someone morosely
"devises different ways for vengeance, and after these
"are devised swells his mind, is such a sin as is
"determined from the type of vengeance that has been
"devised. (See Toledo, l. 8, c. 58). 3. Shouting, when an
"angry man raises his voice, pouring fourth disorderly
"and confusedly many things, is commonly venial unless
"something is added. 4. Blasphemy is a mortal sin, in
"which we will speak below (book 4, tr. 2, c. 1, n. 5).
"Contumelies, whereby someone throws out some evil to
"his neighbor, with the intention of dishonoring him, is
"of itself a mortal sin.

81.—"I said, *with a mind to dishonor,* because with a spirit
"to correct, to humble, or any other reason, a superior
"can upbraid with some otherwise contumelious word,
"in the same manner that Christ called the Apostles
"fools; and the Apostle calls the Galatians senseless.
"Nevertheless, in that he can sin if he exceeds the mode
"of due correction, or were the subject to be more
"gravely dishonored than he ought to be by the crime.
"See Bald. d. 34, n. 10. Likewise, as Cajetan teaches,
"contumely can be merely a venial sin, if it were only
"small, or if it were only material without the intention
"to dishonor: only a notable wound to the honor of one's
"neighbor would not follow. And so many parents are
"excused, at least from mortal sin, when they call their
"children asses, etc. Likewise, the meanest sort of

"women, children and men burdening themselves with
"noisy importuning, since trust is not given with them,
"their honor is not gravely wounded. See Bonacina, l. 3,
"q. 2, p. 5.

"Lastly, if for the sake of a joke through suitable
"recreation light defects are thrown out, it is urbanity,
"according to St. Thomas (2.2. q. 72, art. 2) provided
"another is not saddened or moved to anger.

82.—"5. Contumely is also made from a deed, both
"indirectly, as if one were to stomp on or burn the image
"or letters of another; both directly, as if one were to
"strike an honest man with a club, that one would place
"horns at his door, or representing something that
"injures another man's honor. From here, mockery,
"illusion, and derision, namely when it is done with
"signs, such as wrinkling a nose, or extending the lips,
"etc., by intending one's neighbor to be downcast which,
"if it were grave, or at least one's neighbor were made
"very sad, they are mortal sins. (Bonacina, Molina, Badl.
"1. 3, d. 3, etc., from St. Thomas). In regard to the marks
"that someone harms another's honor through
"contumely, he is held to make restitution for this, even
"if his reputation is not wounded. This can be done
"either by an honorific and friendly greeting, or an
"invitation to a meal, or begging forgiveness, (even on
"one's knees in the sight of witnesses), according to how
"grave the injury. See Cardinal de Lugo (d. 15, n. 53).
"Add that it may not be necessary to explain the quality
"of a mortal contumely in confession, as Azor, Sa,
"Molina, de Lugo (d. 56, *de poenit.* n. 269) teach against
"Filliuci, etc.

(See what is going to be said in book 4, n. 984).

83.—"6. Cursing, whereby someone desires or calls down
"evil on another, by reason of the evil is a mortal sin of
"its very nature.

St. Thomas teaches this (2.2. q. 76, art. 3) that cursing or imprecation against man, "according to its genus is a mortal sin and it is graver depending upon the person who we curse, whether we are held to love and revere them more. Nevertheless, it happens that a curse brought forward is a venial sin either on account of the smallness of the curse which someone calls down on another with malediction, or even on account of his emotional state, who advances the curses, whether it is from a light movement, or from a game, or due to some surprise for which reason he utters such words; because the sins of words are especially considered by affect." From which doctrine of the Angelic Doctor it is inferred that for cursing to be a mortal sin, three things are required: 1) That the evil advanced is truly desired; 2) that it is desired with perfect deliberation; 3) that the evil desired is grave. So all the theologians teach in common. See The Salamancans *de rest.* c. 4, p. 4, n. 28. Moreover, for whether all maledictions are of the same species, see what was said above, n. 50.

> "7. Quarrels, if they do not exceed the mode, such as "very small fights, are venial; it is otherwise, if they "progress to seditions, wounds, and slaughter. These are "commonly sins on the side of the one beginning the "fight, for the other can defend himself with restrained "self defense without fault."

DUBIUM VII
What is Sloth?

84.—"Resp. Sloth, or sadness of the mind, can be taken up "in two ways, following St. Thomas (2.2. q. 35, art. 2): 1) "Generally, for every remission of the mind in the "exercise of virtues, for the reason that some labor would "be added; 2) Particularly, for sadness and tiredness of

"divine friendship, to the extent that by the laborious
"exercise of virtues one ought to be preserved; and so he
"does not take care of that friendship.

Thus the following are resolved:

"1) Sloth, received in the first mode is not only a mortal
"sin, but even a forbidden work committed under mortal
"sin.

"2) Sloth received in the second mode is of itself a mortal
"sin, because it is opposed to the charity of God.

"From which a judgment can easily be made on the
"daughters of sloth, which are the following:

"1. Malice, whereby someone has in leisure spiritual
"goods, and does not will to have them, or whereby he is
"sorry to have done good or to have fulfilled that which
"he was held to do, or whereby he scorns the benefits of
"God, *e.g.* by the desire to never have been born, or to
"not acknowledge Christ, etc., but it is of its nature a
"mortal sin.

"2. Pusillanimity, and despairing of salvation, which is
"also a mortal sin.

"3. Rancor, in which those who are led to the spiritual
"life in loathing.

"4. Torpor, when good things are done but without due
"fervor.

"5. Wandering of the mind, whereby someone in the
"exercise of spiritual things wanders in regard to illicit
"things, or through a thought, and it is called curiosity;
"or through speech, and it is called verbosity; or through
"restlessness, and it is called inquietude, which are
"commonly held to be venial sins. See St. Thomas, q. 35;
"Laymann, l. 2, tr. 3, c. 9; Toledo, l. 8, c. 70.

"Moreover, culpable wandering will be a mortal sin,
"when it is notable, and attention is required to fulfill a
"precept obliging under mortal sin, *e.g.* in reciting the
"canonical hours, celebrating or hearing Mass. (Reg.,
"Palaus, *de char.* t. 6, dub. 1, p. 3; Trull., l. 1, c. 6, dub. 1,
"against Tamburinius, *de exped. sacrific.*, l. 2, c. 3, where
he "teaches that a voluntary distraction and for a notable
"time during the sacrifice outside the Canon, is only
"venial, although he concedes that during the Canon,
"especially at the consecration, it is mortal, on account
"of the grave irreverence and danger of error).

"I said *to fulfill a precept*; for in prayer or something not
"commanded or under an obligation that is only venial,
"then it is only a venial sin. St. Thomas, Navarre, Suarez,
"Lessius (l. 2, c. 37, dub. 11), on the contrary, hold it is no
"sin at all, if someone did not intend to pray but merely
"busied himself in the pious exercise of reciting the
"words of the prayers; since he does not pray formally
"but only materially; *e.g.* when someone laboring with
"his hands says psalms, or otherwise recites prayers or
"sings not in the spirit of prayer, but to be on guard
"against vain thoughts, or to take recreation. Sanchez,
"*cons.* pars 2, t. 7, c. 2, dist. 13; Trull. l. 1, c. 7, dist. 10.
"See below in book 5, c. 2, dub. 2.

END BOOK II

BOOK III

ON THE PRECEPTS OF THE THEOLOGICAL VIRTUES

TREATISE I
On the precept of Faith

CHAPTER I
Which mysteries of faith must necessarily be believed?

1. *What mysteries must be believed by the necessity of means?*
2. *Must the mystery of the most Holy Trinity and the Incarnation be believed explicitly?*
3. *What must be known by precept? and must it be known by memory?*
4. *What kind of thing is the material object of faith, and what is the formal object of faith?*

1.—"From those, which the faithful are explicitly held to "believe, some must necessarily be believed by the "necessity of means, or of the end, without which, if one "were ignorant even inculpably, he could not obtain his "final end; another consideration is the necessity of "precept, without which, were it omitted without fault, "one could obtain their final end. Sanchez, 2. mor., c. 2, "Azor, Val.

"Resp. 1. By the necessity of means two things are "necessary: 1) to explicitly believe that there is a God "who is the rewarder of good works, according to what "the Apostle says in Hebrews 11:6, "It is necessary to "believe." (Council of Trent, sess. 6, *de Justificatione*, c. 6, "2.) After the Gospel was sufficiently promulgated, one

"must explicitly believe, as Molina would have it, or at
"least implicitly, as some probably teach with Concina
"and Laymann, in Christ and the most Holy Trinity.
"(See Escobar, ex. 2, c. 9, n. 20, where he teaches from
"Vasquez, l. 2, d. 126, c. 3 that culpable ignorance of
"these mysteries, or negligence to learn them is a grave
"sin, distinct from that which is the cause. (See Diana, p.
"3, t. 5, r. 47 and 48)."

Faith is defined thus: *It is a theological virtue, infused by
God, inclining us to firmly assent to divine veracity in all the
things which God has revealed and proposed to us for belief by
his Church.* It is called: 1) *A Theological virtue, i.e.* which
regards God, for faith, just as also hope and charity, consider
God directly to the difference of moral virtues which regard
him indirectly; 2) *infused by God,* because faith is a divine
supernatural gift; 3) *inclining us to firmly believe,* for the
assent of faith cannot be present without fear, according to
what was wrongly said in the 4th proposition proscribed by
Innocent XI, rather, it ought to be altogether firm; 4) *On
account of divine veracity;* for infallible truth (which God
himself is), is the formal object of faith; 5) *Which God
revealed to all,* therefore, everything revealed by God is the
material object of faith; 6) *And proposed for our belief through
his Church,* for divine revelation is not made clear to us
except by the Church, which proposes revelations; since it
is evident from another source due to the signs of credibility
(such as are prophecies, miracles, the constancy of the
martyrs, and other things) that the Church can neither be
deceived nor deceive. Besides, St. Augustine famously
advanced that saying: "I would not believe the Gospel unless
the authority of the Catholic Church caused me to."

2.—*Quaeritur:* whether the mysteries of the Most Holy
Trinity and the Incarnation, after the promulgation of the
Gospel, must be believed with explicit faith by the necessity
of means or precept?

The first opinion, which is held in common, seems more probable, and it teaches that they must be believed by the necessity of means. (Sanchez, *in Dec.* lib. 2, c. 2, n. 8; Valent. 2.2. d. 1 qu. 2, p. 4; Molina, 1. part. qu. 1, a. 1, d. 2; Cont. Tourn. *de praeceptis Decal.* cap. 1, art. 1 §2, concl. 1; Juven. t. 6, diss. 4, a. 3; Antoine *de virt. theol.* cap. 1, qu. 2; Wigandt, tr. 7, ex. 2, *de fide* n. 22; Concina, t. 1, *diss.* 1. *de fide* cap. 8, n. 8; with Ledesma, Serra, Prado, etc. and likewise, the Salamancans tr. 21 c. 2 punct. 2 n. 15; Cuniliat. tr. 4, de. 1; Dec. *praec.* c. , § 2 and Roncaglia, tr. 6, c. 2, qu. 2). But the last three in the list of authorities, hold *per accidens* and that in rare cases someone could be justified only by implicit faith. They prove this from the Scriptures, whereby, (they say) the necessity of means is clearly proven. For, they prove it by the reason that although before the promulgation of the Gospel implicit faith in Christ sufficed, nevertheless, after the promulgation, to the extent that the state of grace is more perfect, a more perfect knowledge is required, namely explicit faith in Christ and the Most Holy Trinity.

Yet, *the second opinion* is also sufficiently probable, and it says that by the necessity of precept all are held to explicitly believe these mysteries, but it suffices by the necessity of means if they are believed implicitly. Domingo de Soto agrees with this (in 4. *Sentent.* t. 1, d. 5, qu. un. art. 2, concl. 2), where he says: "Although the precept of explicit faith (viz. the Most Holy Trinity and the Incarnation), absolutely oblige the whole world, just the same, many can be excused by invincible ignorance of the same." Francis Sylvius (t. 3, in 2. 2. qu. 2, art. 7, and 8, concl. 6), writes: "After the Gospel was sufficiently promulgated, explicit faith in the Incarnation is necessary for all for salvation by the necessity of precept, and also (as is probable) by the necessity of means." And in the following conclusion he also advances this for the mystery of the most Holy Trinity. Cardinal Gotti says: "I say 1) the negative opinion, that explicit faith in Christ and the Trinity is so necessary that without these no man can be justified or saved, is very probable." (Theol. t. 2, tr. 9, qu. 2, d. 4, § 1 n. 2). And he asserts in n. 1 that Scotus holds this opinion. Eusebius Amort, a recent writer and very learned (tom. 1, d. 3, *de fide* quaest. 17), absolutely upholds the same opinion. Elbel., (t. 4, conferent. 1, n. 17) writes that today this opinion is held by famous theologians such as Castropolaus (part. 2, tr. 4, d. 1, p. 9), Viva (in Prop. 64 *damn. ab Innocent. XI*, n. 10), Sporer (tr. 11, cap. 11, sect. 11, §4, n. 9), Laymann (lib. 2, tr. 1, cap. 8 n. 5) who say this is no less probable than the first, with Richardus, Medina, Vega, Sa, and Turrianus. Cardinal de Lugo (*de fide* d. 12, n. 91) calls the first opinion speculatively probable, but upholds this second one absolutely and profusely more probable, with Javell., Zumel, and Suarez (d. 12, sect. 4, n. 10) and de Lugo writes that it seems St. Thomas holds the same opinion (3 part qu. 69, a. 4, ad 2) where the Angelic Doctor says that before baptism, Cornelius and others like him obtained grace and virtues through the faith of Christ and the desire for Baptism, implicitly or explicitly. This is why de Lugo argues, that just as Cornelius obtained grace through implicit faith, because the Gospel had not yet been perfectly promulgated in that region, so likewise one who was ignorant of these mysteries could obtain grace; for the Gospel has not yet been equally promulgated for them. Moreover, they say it is opposed to the goodness and divine providence to damn adults that are invincibly ignorant, who live honestly according to the light of nature, while on the other hand (Acts 10:35) it is held: "In every nation there is one that fears him and does justice, having been received by him." But they respond that all the Scriptures and the testimonies of the Fathers which are opposed, can easily be explained by the necessity of precept, or because ordinarily nearly no one is saved without explicit faith of these mysteries, because after the promulgation of the Gospel nearly no one labors in invincible ignorance, or because, as de Lugo says, they can be explained on implicit or explicit faith in desire. Besides, Laymann says that an adult man, if he were mute and deaf from birth, although baptized, could not receive the other sacraments if he wanted, nay more he would not be able to be saved, because it is unbelievable that a man of this sort could apprehend the concept and explicitly believe the mysteries of the Incarnation and especially of the Most Holy Trinity.

Moreover, Tanner (in 2.2. d. Th. d. 1, qu. 7, dub. 2, n. 49), Sylvius (*ibid.*, qu. 2, art. 8, concl. 8), Azor (t. 1, lib. 8, cap. 2, qu. 6), and Valent., with Guilielmus Paris, cited by Sanchez (*Dec.* lib. 2, cap. 3, n. 18) that if anyone were so unlearned that he could not perceive these mysteries, then he is excused by reason of impotence and is compared with infants and idiots. Just the same, Sanchez (*loc. cit.*) says that it is one thing to believe and another to know the mysteries, namely to render an account of them; this is why he thinks all adults are held by the necessity of means at some time to believe mysteries of this sort, but by the necessity of precept to know them; by which precept of knowledge those blunted in mind are excused; and so what the cited authors say must be understood in this way. He concludes with Gabriel, who says: "It would suffice for them [*viz.* the unlearned] that they would explicitly believe individual articles of faith when they are proposed to them." However, there are two propositions condemned by Innocent XI, number 64 and 65, which said: "A man that has the capacity for absolution, however much he labors in ignorance of the faith and even if through culpable negligence did not know the mystery of the most Holy Trinity and the Incarnation of our Lord Jesus Christ. ... It suffices that he once believed these." Nevertheless, Viva says with March., that it is probably not necessary to repeat confessions made with ignorance of the aforesaid mysteries, since, from the aforesaid opinion it was probable that they were valid if the ignorance was inculpable. For it is certain that such ignorance, if it were vincible, would be a deadly sin. Next, the aforesaid proposition was rightly condemned, because it said they also had the capacity for absolution even those at the time of the confession he labored with ignorance of the aforesaid mysteries. Moreover, the opinion of Fr. Viva does not seem sufficiently probable to me, although the penitent probably satisfied for a valid confession, so that it would appear he had an exemption from repeating the confession, since he had confessed in good faith, nevertheless, in respect to one who certainly sinned gravely, the obligation to satisfy the confession always presses and beforehand was in place, not only probably but certainly valid. This is why, when he notices his confession was probably valid on account of ignorance of the mysteries of the most Holy Trinity or the Incarnation of Jesus Christ, but even probably invalid, he is held later, after being instructed on those mysteries, to repeat the confession.

"Hence, it is said to believe implicitly that one who "believes something explicitly in which another is "implicitly, *e.g.* if one were to believe what the Church "believes. See Schol. and Laymann, lib. 2, tr. 1, c. 8.

"3.—Resp. 2. By the necessity of precept every member "of the faithful is held to believe and know explicitly, "under pain of mortal sin, at least in a simplistic manner "and in regard to the substance, these following:

"1. The Creed; 2. The Lord's prayer and the Hail Mary; 3. "The precepts of the Decalogue and the Church; 4. The "Sacraments, especially those which are the most "necessary, such as Baptism, Eucharist and Penance; "then the rest when he wishes to take them up. Suarez, "Sanchez, Filliuci, n. 39. Impotence or invincible "ignorance will excuse all these things.

Thus the following are resolved:

"1. Not all are held under mortal sin to memorize these
"aforesaid either in order or in the words in which they
"are proposed, yet in regard to the Lord's Prayer, he is
"required to know all the goods sought from God, which
"is its chief point, while in regard to the Creed, the
"precepts and the sacraments, it suffices if someone were
"asked that he would respond correctly on each point.
"Bonacina, Laymann, l. 2, cap. 9, Sanchez, lib. 2, cap. 3.
"(This is in conformity with what St. Charles Borromeo
"hands down in his *Instruct.* for confessors, where he
"taught it was enough that the unlearned faithful would
"know the Creed at least in its substance).

"2. Although it is a precept of the Church to memorize
"the Creed and the Lord's Prayer, as well as the Hail
"Mary, Barb. (p. 3, c. 27) would have it that one must not
"be absolved if he does not take care to learn these due
"to negligence or human respect; nevertheless, the
"custom, as Navarre and Lopez note, explains the
"obligation to not be beyond a venial sin, as it is not
"beyond a venial sin to not know how to make the sign
"of the Cross, as Sanchez teaches against Sylvius, who
"taught it was mortal.

(So also other authors hold, namely Viva, *super prop. I. Alex.
VII.* with Azor, Trull., and Villalobos with the Salamancans
de praec. fidei cap. 2 n. 47, from the council of Rhemensi and
Toledo, 4. See *Praxis Confess.,* n. 22).

"3. Just the same, it is morally necessary that the more
"unlearned memorize the Creed in their language
"because otherwise they cannot have sufficient
"knowledge of the articles.

"4. The opinion of certain Canonists is false, that it is
"enough for the unlearned to believe the articles of faith

"and the other things mentioned implicitly, by believing "whatever the Church believes.

"5. Those are excused who either lack a teacher or for "whom the obligation to learn these things never came "into their mind, or who are so unlearned that they "cannot understand these things or retain them, which "Azor and Becanus teach often happens, against other "writers.

"6. If the confessor judges it probable that the penitent is "ignorant of those things from Christian doctrine that he "is held to know (because on the literate or those "confessing frequently he presumes not to warn them, "Sanch. 2 mor. c. 3), he ought to ask him about the "negligence in learning these things, since very many sin "gravely by it. Ledesma, Azor, t. 1, l. 8, c. 8; Trull. l. 1, c. "1 d. 4.

"7. They can be absolved (against certain things) who are "ignorant of those which I said must be known under "pain of mortal sin. The reason is, because although they "would sin by omitting to learn, still they can be sorry "for this with the purpose to learn them. Sanchez. (With "the Salamancans, *de praec. fidei*, tr. 21, cap. 2, punct. 5, "n. 58, unless he was already warned and still neglected "to learn them). Still, if one were ignorant of those things "which must be known by the necessity of means, they "ought to be instructed before absolution. Bonacina, d. 3, "qu. 2, p. 2, Sanchez, *loc. cit.* cap. 3, n. 21.

"8. A parish priest (just like a father for his children) is "held, under pain of mortal sin, to teach his flock either "himself or by another, those things which they are held "to know under mortal sin. Sanchez, 2. *mor.* c. 3; Filliuci, "Palaus, Trull. l. 2, c. 1, Concina, etc."

4.—It must be noted, that the *material* object of faith (namely, that which we are held to believe), is principally God himself, and then all the things God has revealed, which

St. Thomas teaches in qu. 14 *de veritate*, art. 8, saying: "Faith which enjoins a man to knowledge of the divine through assent, has God himself as the principal object, while other things are consequently joined to it." Moreover, the *formal* object of faith (*i.e.* the motive on account of which we are held to believe what has been revealed), is the veracity of God. It was argued among the Scholastics whether divine revelation was also the *formal* object of faith. On the affirmative side, there are Jeuninus and others, who say the veracity of God is the formal object *quod*, namely the especial reason on account of which we believe, while revelation is the formal object *quo*, this is the medium in which we believe. But the opinion of Habert, Cardinal Gotti, and Holzman with Scotus, etc., is more common and teaches that the formal object of faith is total, the veracity of God and revelation is only the condition, without which we would not believe, or the medium through which knowledge of those things which we believe is applied to us.

CHAPTER II

How the precept of faith obliges

5. *Whom does the precept of faith oblige and when?*

6. *Must condemned propositions be noted in this matter?*

7. *How often are we held in this life to elicit acts of faith and hope?*

8. *How often are we held to elicit acts of charity?*

9. *When is a heretic held to reject his sect?*

10. *Whether in regard to faith one may follow a less probable opinion?*

11. *When are we held to confess the faith outwardly? And who is held by ecclesiastical law to the outward profession of faith?*

5.—"Resp. 1. The precept of internal faith obliges: a)
"children educated among the faithful when they have
"perfectly obtained the use of reason, hear the mysteries
"of faith and understand them, because to believe these
"things is necessary for salvation, and they sin mortally
"by omitting it. Sanchez and Bonacina (t. 2, d. 3, p. 3) add
"that many of them are excused by inadvertence, or
"invincible ignorance. b) Adult infidels, when reason
"begins to dictate that the affairs of faith are sufficiently
"proposed and the contrary sect is false. (Sanchez, lib. 2,
"*mor. cap.* 1; Concina, d. 14, *de fide*; Filliuci, n. 25). c)
"When a temptation against the faith strikes, which
"cannot otherwise be conquered. Still, it is not fitting for
"the scrupulous, as Sanchez rightly advises, because
"then, by averting their minds to other objects, they
"conquer it more easily. And in the first two cases the
"precept obliges *per se*, in the following *per accidens*. d)
"When a temptation against other virtues strikes that
"otherwise cannot be conquered. e) When an outward
"profession of faith must be made, or from an act of
"another virtue must be elicited, *e.g.* of hope, charity,
"repentance, which suppose faith. Bonacina, q. 2, p. 2.
"Hurt. adds to these, against Sanchez: f) At the hour of
"death; g) Once daily. See Diana, p. 5, t. 13, r. 19."

6.—It is certain that a man is held by the natural law to
turn himself to God through faith, hope and charity, and
therefore to elicit the acts of these virtues, since each virtue
lives in his acts. Hence, before all things we must note all the
propositions proscribed on this matter, namely:

Prop. 1 condemned by Alexander VII: "A man is never
held at any time of his life to elicit an act of faith, hope
and charity by the force of divine precepts pertaining to
these virtues."

Prop 16. condemned by Innocent XI: "Faith is not
reckoned to fall under a special precept and *secundum se*."

Prop. 17, condemned by the same Pope: "It is enough to elicit an act of faith once in life."

Prop. 6, condemned by the same Pope: "It is probable that the precept of charity toward God does not even rigorously oblige one every five years."

7.—*Quaeritur:* How often are we held to elicit acts of the theological virtues in this life?

There are many opinions that consider this precept. Scotus thought we are held to elicit acts of faith on all feast days. Nyder as often as the mysteries are celebrated in the Church. But the Salamancans *de praec. fid.* tr. 21, cap. 2, punct. 3, n. 31, and Croix (l. 2, n. 51) do not approve their opinions; on the contrary, Oviedo, with Croix (*ibid.*) asserts that they are everywhere rejected by other theologians. De Lugo, cited by Croix (d. n. 51) rightly says, that the faithful are held to make repeated acts of faith as often as it would suffice to profess the mysteries of our religion. Yet, since this rule is obscure, it is probably enough what the Salamancans think (*dict.* c. 2) with Sanchez, Trull., Bann., Ledesma, and others, that the faithful are held at least once a year to exercise an act of faith, and Concina as well as Franzoja think the same thing with the common view. Still, Prado and Suarez notice the same thing, and Croix says that for this precept it is enough through an exercise of the other virtues, either through reception of the sacraments, or from any other occasion that an act of faith is called for.

Yet, are we held to elicit these acts of faith formally, *viz.* from the motive of God the revealer? Viva affirms this (*d. prop. I. Alex. VII*, n. XI), "Whatever it may be," as he adds, "always since the faith is supernatural, it rests upon this motive at least lightly touched upon." [revise] But note n. 7, in the end, that timid men may be anxious in this regard in no way, since it scarcely happens, that they abundantly do not satisfy this precept. Croix also says, (d. n. 51) there is no reason why someone would scrupulously make trouble on that account, since to this precept it is sufficient enough (as he asserts in n. 27), by hearing Mass, adoring the crucifix or making the sign of the cross, praying, etc., although these are not done reflexively from the motive of faith. For, someone that says he more often places faith as the rule of his actions, by which he means to aim for God, whatever good he does later, he directs, to God by employing the same rule, although he does not notice it. And also, Hurtad., cited by Cardenas (*prop.* 17 *Innocent. XI*), these acts are truly acts of faith because they arise, radically from the motive of faith. Furthermore, de Lugo (*de fid.* diss. 13, n. 45) so teaches: "When the matter of acting honestly and dishonestly frequently occurs, it must not be doubted that a man who once embraced the Christian faith, should more than sufficiently satisfy the precept of faith."

8.—However, we have already noted what pertains to an act toward the precept of charity above when we referenced the condemned proposition that this precept does not oblige *per se* "does not even rigorously oblige one every five years." Palaus (cited by Croix, d. l. 2, n. 141) says it is a grave sin to delay an act of charity for three years. Others, such as Hurtad., Ills. Mendo, etc., with Croix (*loc. cit.*) say it is required to elicit an act of charity toward God at least once a year; the Salamancans follow this (tract. 21, c. 6, n. 12), as well as Trull., Tapia, Lastra. But others, such as Gabr., Almain, Tapia, cited by Croix (n. 133) say this precept obliges on each feast day. Cardenas, at length, in 2. *Crisi* d. 6, n. 8 (to whom Croix adheres in n. 141), thinks one is not excused from mortal sin that delays an act of charity for a month; and this opinion I find altogether persuasive, since a man could preserve the divine commands for a long time only with great difficulty unless he would frequently foster love for God, which is fostered and nourished only through this act of charity. Morever, Cardinas also notes (n. 14) that it suffices to elicit an act of love, even if it is elicited in order to fulfill other precepts, or to exercise another virtue, say to go to confession, to conquer temptation. Croix also says (num. 143) there are true acts of love in which one rightly satisfies this precept, all meritorious works exercised for the purpose of pleasing God, such as alms-giving, fasting and like things. Moreover, such a right end says what is presumed in those, who already know to please God in this way, only they do not act from a bad end. Croix also adds that still by praying it is satisfied, typically with the Lord's prayer, where it is said: "*Sanctificetur*, etc.; *Adveniat*, etc.; *Fiat voluntas tua*, etc. Proposition 10 is adverted here, condemned by Innocent XI, which said: "We are not held to love our neighbor with an internal and formal act." Therefore, Fr. Viva (cit. prop. 10, n. 8 and 9) rightly says that just as we are held to elicit formal acts of charity toward God, so also we are held to do so toward our neighbor from a supernatural motive, namely on account of the love of God, or to obey the precept of Christ, which said: "A new commandment I give you, that you should love each other." (John 13:34) This is why St. Thomas teaches: "In love of neighbor love of God is included, just like a cause in its effect." (*In epist. ad Rom.* 13, sect. 2). Therefore, just as we are held at least once a month to elicit an act of charity toward God, so also at least once a month we are held to exercise an act of charity toward our neighbor. Moreover, Suarez wisely writes (disp. 5, *de charit.* sect. 4) with others from St. Thomas (2.2. qu. 25, art. 8) that sometimes these acts of charity are well exercised by an occasion of avoiding hatred, or bestowing alms. And occasions of this sort frequently occur, hence Fr. Viva says it is morally impossible that faithful Christians could not abundantly satisfy this precept.

Thus the following cases are resolved:

9.—"1. A heretic, as long as he judges his sect more
"believable or equally believable, is not held to believe
"because the faith has not yet been sufficiently proposed
"to him, and he acts imprudently. Sanchez, 2, mor. c. 1;
"Laymann l. 2, t. 1, c. 10, et 12.

"2. When those who are nourished in heresy are
"persuaded from childhood to slight us as idolaters,
"pestilential deceivers and to flee us like the plague and
"pursue the word of God, they cannot, while favoring
"this persuasion, save for conscience, hear us and labor
"in invincible ignorance so long as they do not doubt
"they are on a good path. Laymann, c. 10; Sanchez, l. 2,
"c. 1.

"3. If a doubt arises to such people about their sect, they
"are held to seek further and to seek the light from God;
"but if they refuse, they sin against faith since they did
"not employ the means to fulfill the precept of faith. But
"if then, our faith were sufficiently proposed to them,
"they are held to embrace it. *Ibid.* See Ferdin. de
"Castropalao, t. 4, d. 1, p. 12, and d. 2, p. 2.

10.—Here, proposition 4 condemned by Innocent XI
must be noted: "An infidel is excused from infidelity not
believing he is led by a less probable opinion." Due to this,
some incorrectly infer it is forbidden in every matter to
follow a probable opinion while abandoning one more
probable; for Viva responds, commenting on the aforesaid
proposition, n. 5, as well as others commonly, that even if it
were permitted to follow a less probable opinion, still one
may never, with danger of grave loss; when to avoid it does
not depend upon the probability of the opinion, as it does in
the conferral of the sacraments, in healing, etc., and this is
equally in following a sect less probably true. Therefore,
from the probability of the opinion it happens that formal
sin is avoided in human actions, but it cannot happen that a
false sect becomes a true sect. Besides, with a sect that is

always false, the danger of damnation is never avoided with each probability, since the danger of lacking faith necessary to salvation, the grace of the sacraments, etc. will not be avoided. Add, that an infidel can never have true probability of his sect without sin; for if he would pray, God, without a doubt, would infuse his light into him about the true religion. (Viva)

11.—"Resp. 2. The precept to confess the faith outwardly "obliges by natural law in a twofold case, namely, when "either an honor due to God, or an advantage to our "neighbor, were detracted against in a depriving or "contrary fashion. I said 1) *in a depriving fashion*, as if, a "great honor toward God would cease, or an advantage "flowing to our neighbor. I said 2) *in a contrary fashion*, "that if otherwise God were inflicted with an injury, or "our neighbor with a great evil, *e.g.* if thence conversion "would depend on others, or perversion, contempt of "religion, scandal, etc. The reason of the response is that "an act of virtue then seems a precept, when it is "necessary to the end of the precept, which this touches "upon, because the end of the precept is charity. St. "Thomas, 2.2. qu. 3, art. 2, Suarez, Reg., Filliuci, tr. 22, c. "3, quaest. 1.

So it is resolved:

"If heretics should destroy images, and afflict the faith "with other injuries, a Catholic is held to uphold it in his "confession, if indeed thence he would prudently hope to "profit.

"*Resp.*3. The following persons are held by Ecclesiastical "law to an external profession of faith under pain of "mortal sin, with an oath to obey the Roman Church,

"according to the Council of Trent, as Filliuci teaches (t.
"2, tr. 22, c. 3):

"1. Those provided as beneficed curates, and within two
"months from the day of possession in the presence of a
"Bishop, or his vicar general, or an official. (Council of
"Trent, sess. 24, c. 22, *de Ref.*)

"2. Those provided of a canonry, or a dignity in a
"cathedral Church, and it is not only in the presence of
"a Bishop, or his Vicar, but even in the chapter, *ibid.* with
"a penalty added (for which they do not seem to be held
"before the sentence), as otherwise they would have a
"fruit that they did not merit. See Sanchez, (l. 2, c. 5),
"Barb., *de potestate Episc.*, 3, p. art. 61, n. 29.

"3. Primates, Archbishops, Bishops in the first provincial
"Council, at which they are present. Council of Trent,
"sess. 25, c. 2, *de Reform.*

"4. Pius IV extends this law to all prelates of religion,
"even over armies; Pius V, however, (cited by Rodriguez,
"t. 2, reg. quest. 72) promoted it to all among doctors,
"teachers, rectors, professors, adding excommunication
"*latae sententiae*, and deprivation of all benefices in one
"who promotes others to such a degree without the
"aforesaid profession. See Filliuci, t. 22, c. 3, quest. 11,
"Barb. *in remiss.* sect. 24, n. 12. But, where this decree
"was not received in use, he does not advise that it
"obliges. Sanchez, c. 3, n. 4.

So it is resolved:

"1. They are not held to the aforesaid profession that are
"provided of canonry in merely collegiate Churches, or
"only in simple benefices.

"2. Even if it were probable that this profession could be
"made by a procurator, as Azor, Navarre and Sanchez

"teach, nevertheless it is more probable that he is held to
"do it personally, as Filliuci teaches. The reason is, both
"because otherwise it does not seem the oath is
"sufficiently done, which the Gloss teaches must be
"made personally (cited in Filliuci), and because the Rota
"so decided (Garc. l. 3, *de benef.* c. 3).

CHAPTER III

*Whether at some time it is permitted to deny the true faith
outwardly or profess what is false?*

12. *Whether one may ever positively deny the faith?*
13. *Whether one can use ambiguous words? Can he be silent?*
14. *Whether one can run away? See others, ibid.*
15. *Whether one may use cloths or markings of unbelievers?*
16. *Whether one may hear the sermons of heretics. See others,
    ibid.*

12.—"*Resp.* In no case may one deny the faith, whether
"by words or by another sign, per the saying of Christ:
"whoever will deny me before men, etc." However, it is
"not lawful to lie, or to feign that which is not, still one
"may dissimulate what is, or cover the truth with words
"and other ambiguous signs and indifferent things on
"account of a just cause, and there is not a necessity to
"affirm the faith. This is the common opinion. St.
"Thomas; Concina, dis. 15, dub. 2, n. 9; Laymann, l. 2, t.
"1, c. 11.

Thus it is resolved:

13.—"a) One asked about the faith in hatred of religion,
"or by a public or private authority, can in no way use a
"mental reservation, or ambiguous words to respond,
"that it would appear to those present that he denied the
"faith, much less to say he is a heretic, or a Calvinist, or
"not a Catholic. Azor; Filliuci, c. 3, n. 97.

"b) One that is asked either by a private or public
"authority, either remains silent or responds obscurely,
"or says he refuses to respond, is not asked under oath,
"is not held to wish to say other than what he believes,
"and in a similar manner, to hang back in a similar mode,
"does not seem to deny the faith, but refuses to promote
"it. For that reason, if he can be so freed from a
"troublesome inquisition, he may as Concina holds (*loc.*
"*cit.*). Generally, it is not true that one asked by a public
"authority is held to positively profess the faith, except
"when it is necessary lest it seem to those present he
"denied it. Concina, d. 13, dub. 2; Navarre, Azor, Sanchez,
"Becanus, c. 9, q. c) (On this matter, see proposition 8
"among those condemned by Innocent XI).

14.—"3. One does not deny the faith but betrays it, who
"flees, yet even if it were allowed, still it is not for a
"pastor, then, when the sheep need his work; on the
"other hand, if he is more prudent with them, that he
"might leave for a time, and spare in their good, he is
"held to flee. Reg. l. 17, n. 26; Becanus c. 9, Filliuci, n. 75,
"etc.

"d) If in some case it were to happen that to be silent is
"to deny, then it would not be lawful, *e.g.* if, when asked
"by others, he wished to deny the faith, and by not
"responding to them he would deny the faith. *Ibid.*,
"Bonacina, *loc. cit.*; Laymann, *loc. cit.* tom. 1, c. 11;
"Toledo, lib. 4.

"e) If a prince were to command by a general law that
"the faithful betray themselves by wearing a mark, or by

"standing for themselves, or otherwise, they are not held
"when no man is held to say the truth unless specifically
"asked. Except, unless the circumstances were that in
"this matter, that he not betray himself, it seems he
"denied the faith, *e.g.* certain men before were known
"and then they were thought to have defected because of
"this. Sanchez, n. 19, Becanus, Reg., Filliuci, n. 88, etc.

"f) When one is not asked about the faith, it is not only
"lawful, but often better to the honor of God and the
"advantage of one's neighbor to hide the faith than to
"confess it; as if hiding among heretics one would do
"more good, or if from a confession more evils would
"follow, *e.g.* disturbance, deaths, exacerbation of a tyrant,
"danger of defection, or if one were going to be tortured.
"For this reason, it would be rash to offer oneself
"wantonly. St. Thomas, Sanchez, Laymann, c. 11, n. 2.

"g) To make good with money, lest there would be any
"inquiry about your faith, is licit, and often the great
"virtue of discretion is a life to serve the glory of God,
"and hide the faith by licit means.

15.—"h) Such a mode is not to use the cloths and signs of
"infidels, which do not have any other use than to be
"professive signs of false religion, or cult, as the clothes
"would be that are used in sacrifices: likewise the
"incensing of frankincense, or genuflection made in the
"presence of an idol; likewise taking up the sacrifice in
"dinner, etc. (Sanchez, l. 2, cap. 4; Filliuci 9), and the
"common opinion.

"i) Moreover, the mode is licit when a cause is the basis
"(as, *e.g.* to overturn grave sin, to obtain victory, to elude
"enemies) for using vestments and signs of the infidels,
"which has some other use than to profess religion, such
"as the garments of a certain type of nation (not
"religion), which they use, even if they were converted,
"as are the clothes and signs of the nation of the Turks,

"which is true even if they are the garb of the religious "themselves, provided they do not have a peculiar sign "for professing error, but are merely indicative of the "cult, such as a wise woman of sages in Germany, or of "more eminent life among them, such as the Bonzi in "Japan. The same thing must be said about the signs "which the Jews use, *e.g.* a little yellow ring on the cloak "by those at Frankfurt, etc., because these are merely "political signs and distinctive of one race of men from "another, but not properly professive of faith. Such an "opinion is probable. See Sanchez, 2. mor. c. 4,; Becanus, 2.2. "c. 9, qu. 5, d. 6; Laymann l. 2, t. 1, c. 11; Vocarr., against "Cajetan, Navarre, Toledo.

"j) Likewise, the mode is licit, when a Catholic passes "through heretical territories and grave danger threatens "his life or his goods (but not if there is merely derision "or vexation, as Becanus holds, c. 9), *e.g.* to dissimilate "the faith or to eat meat on a forbidden day, because the "precept of the Church does not oblige under such a "danger. Nor is this to deny the faith, since the eating of "meat was not established to profess religion, and bad "Catholics as well as the gluttonous do it. Nevertheless, "if from the circumstances it were to become a "professive sign, say if dinner guests would establish in "hatred of the faith that if one is an enemy to the popish "faith, let him eat meat, then he would sin against faith "if he were to eat without protestation, though it would "be otherwise if he were to protest. Sanchez, Azor, "Becanus, *etc.* comm. *l.c.*

16.—"k) In Germany, to hear the sermons of heretics, to "attend funeral rites, to assist at a baptism as a god-"parent, are not held as professive signs of faith, or of the "communion with the worship of heretics. Filliuci, Azor, "Sanchez, *loc. cit.* This is why, so long as scandal, danger

"or a forbidden matter were not present, and if for a just
"cause, they become lawful."

(But in the Synod of Naples, it is expressly forbidden to
assist with sermons, catechisms and any rites of heretics
from any pretext. And the case is reserved with an
excommunication *ipso facto*. Moreover, the Salamancans *tr.*
21, c. 2, n. 522 hold it is lawful provided scandal, danger of
perversion and the communication with impiety are absent).

"Nay more, a god-parent of such an infant, it rather more
"seems would be desired, provided other matters are
"secluded, because it is no other than to oblige oneself to
"one that formerly would have been instructed in the
"Catholic faith.

"l) It is not permitted to be so present at the rites of
"infidels and heretics that one is thought to
"communicate with them, otherwise it is permitted, *e.g.*
"that someone would observe as though it were a play,
"or furnish political service to his master, such as
"Naoman Syri, about whose life you will find more with
"Becanus, Filliuci, Sanchez (*loc. cit.*) and Laymann (l. 2, t.,
"c. 11).

"m) If a heretical prince were to command under the
"gravest penalty that all his subjects be present at the
"sermons of heretics, even if by his words he means to
"exact no more than civil obedience in the matter, nor
"wishes to compel them to leave the faith, although it
"would seem he really means the contrary (for he can
"train their obedience otherwise and this matter is
"suitable, of itself, to pervert Catholics little by little and,
"in addition, conciliate the authority of heresy, not to
"mention the disparagement of the true faith), one may
"not obey. And this is how Pius V twice replied to the
"English (cited by Sanchez, l. 2, c. 4, n. 27; Filliuci; and
"Azor, *ll.cc.*)

"n) Catholics living among heretics, if by the precept of
"the magistrate they were to contract matrimony in the
"presence of a heretical minister, they would sin against
"the faith, even if they had contracted before or were
"going to do it after in the presence of a Catholic priest
"(Concina, d. 15, art. 3; Palaus tr. 4, d. 1, p. 17, n. 12, 13,
"14), and the one contracting those ceremonies, which
"are intrinsically evil, witnesses himself to acknowledge
"the minister of the true faith (Madl. 2,2. quest. 2, art. 3),
"because the authority of the minister and consequently
"his doctrine, is increased and it makes the same claim as
"the heretical rites which the minister exercises in this
"act. Still, they lawfully contract in the presence of a civil
"magistrate, or rather more witness themselves to
"contract, provided that before or after they shall
"contract in a Catholic rite: because this action was
"established for a political end, so they will be held as
"husband and wife and that their children will not be
"considered illegitimate."

CHAPTER IV
On infidelity and the vices opposed to faith

DUBIUM I
What, and how manifold is infidelity?

17.—"*Resp.* 1. Infidelity is generally threefold: 'First, it is
"said negatively, viz. of those who never heard the faith.
"This is both not a sin, and not a punishment for sin;
"because, if they were to do what was in them, God
"would not hide the faith from them. *The second* is
"called contrary, *viz.* of those for whom the faith has
"been sufficiently proposed and they either scorn it, or
"pertinaciously oppose it, like heretics. *Third* is said

"privative, which is privatively opposed to faith, and it is
"culpable ignorance or an error in regard to a matter of
"faith. St. Thomas, Sanchez, Vasquez, Laymann, c. 12.

"*Resp.* 2. Contrary infidelity in a threefold manner to
"deny the faith happens in three ways, namely
"Paganism, which is of faith not yet received, Judaism,
"which is a faith received in a type, and Heresy, which is
"incompatible with a truth of received faith. Apostasy
"from the faith is recalled to heresy and by which it only
"differs in that heresy is an error in faith on the side only
"of the more contrary, but apostasy from the whole. St.
"Thomas, Laymann, *loc. cit.*

DUBIUM II
On Judaism

*Here it is asked: what fellowship with Jews is forbidden to
Christians?*

18.—"Resp. 1: In these cases, some are gathered from c.
"*Nullus*, c. *Omnes*, c. *Judaei*; a) It is not lawful to dwell
"under the same roof; b) nor to be present among the
"dinner guests; c) nor to use a common bath; d) Nor to
"employ them as doctors; e) Nor to receive the medicines
"given by them although it will be permitted to by what
"is prescribed; f) To not rear the sons of Jews in their
"houses; g) To not employ them as servants; h) Nor to be
"in service to them; i) they are forbidden to exercise
"public office among Christians; j) It is forbidden to eat
"unleavened bread with them. Azor adds to this that it is
"forbidden to go to their weddings and feasts and
"Synagogues,"

(To enter Synagogues from curiosity is not a grave sin, as the Salamancans say, tr. 21, c. 2, punct. 2, n. 123, in fine, with Bonacina, Concina, Palaus, etc.),

"to play and dance with them, etc. The reason for these "is not only that the dignity of the Christian religion "would be conserved, but also that one would be on "guard for familiarity with Jews and the danger of "perversion. See Laymann, l. 2, t. 1, c. 12, and 17; "Sanchez, l. 2,, c. 3, Filliuci, tr. 22, c. 5, n. 128.

"Resp. 2. In the ten aforesaid cases to communicate with "Jews seems, of its nature, to be a mortal sin. The reason "is, because if a cleric would do it, he incurs danger of "deposition, but a layperson of excommunication (c. "*Constituit*, caus. 17, q. 4), which are not usually imposed "except on account of a mortal sin. I said *of its nature*, "because it is probable, or on account of the smallness of "the mater, or necessity, or another reasonable cause "(still, if there were no danger of faithlessness, or of "familiarity with the Jews), one is often excused from a "mortal sin and sometimes even from all sin, as the "theologians right commonly. See the authors cited "above, and Bonacina, *loc. cit.* and Laymann, l. 2, t. 1, c. "17. (Christian princes can permit the Jews and pagans, "or heretics freedom of conscience only on account of "the good of religion, and on account of the hope of "conversion, but not on account of temporal advantage. "The Salamancans tr. 21, c. 3, punct. 1, n. 5. Moreover, "the Church can rightly, as well as any supreme prince, "compel the Jews and pagan subjects to listen to our "faith. (The Salamancans *ibid.* punct. 2, n. 8, with Suarez, "Azor, Becanus, Bonacina, etc. (against Concina and "Valentia); and it is certain from the practice which is in "use at Rome.

DUBIUM III
What is heresy?

19.—"Resp. Heresy is a free error of the intellect, as well
"as pertinacity against the faith in a man that has
"received the faith. So commonly, Suarez, Becan., c. 14,
"qu. 2). This is why it is clear for both heresy and
"apostasy two things are required: 1) erroneous
"judgment, which is almost like its material cause; 2)
"Pertinacity which is like its formal cause. Moreover,
"pertinacity to err here is not acridly and tenaciously to
"hold or uphold his error, but it is to retain it after the
"contrary is sufficiently proposed: whether, when
"someone knows the contrary is held by the universal
"Church of Christ on earth, to whose judgment he ought
"to prefer; or if it happens from vain glory or the *libido*
"*contradicendi*, or another cause. The reason is, because
"then he thinks the judgment of the Church is not a
"sufficient foundation for belief, which is true
"pertinacity, which (with Coninck) others more easily
"explain it then to be, when, even if the object of faith is
"credibly proposed, so that he could not prudently have
"a doubt, still he will judge the contrary, from which he
"will refuse to be torn away in any case, or at least until
"he is evidently convicted. See Coninck, d. 18.

Thus the following are resolved:

"1) One is not a heretic who only denies the faith
"outwardly, or worships an idol. The reason is, because
"he would not err; nor does he incur such censures in the
"forum of conscience imposed against heretics, even if in
"the external forum an external censure were to proceed.
"Filliuci, t. 22, c. 6, quaest. 4.

"2) One is a heretic who doubts in the affirmative on "some article of faith, that is, he judges it doubtful. I said "*affirmatively*, because only negatively it is doubtful, this "is suspending judgment, *per se*, and he is simply not a "heretic because he does not have a judgment; therefore "it is not erroneous; still one that does not merely "suspend, but will virtually judge, it is not evident on the "certitude of the object. Sa, Azor, l. 8, c. 9, q. 5; Toledo, "against Sanchez and Maldonado. See what is going to be "said in book 7, n. 302).

"3) No man is a heretic so long as he is prepared to "submit his judgment to the Church, or does not know "that he holds something contrary to the true Church of "Christ, even if he tenaciously upholds it from ignorance, "even culpable and crass ignorance. Laymann *loc. cit.* n. "2.

"4) Nor is one a heretic who is so disposed, at least "habitually, that he would depart from his error if he "knew it was contrary to the faith, provided he would "never have had actual pertinacity. *Ibid.*, and *Con.*, *loc.* "*cit.*

"5) Rustic folk, and other simpler men in Germany, who "are considered heretics, and still are not pertinacious, "can be absolved by their parish priests. The reason is, "because they are not formal heretics; and they have "catholic faith received in baptism which is not lost, "except by pertinaciously erring. Laymann, *loc. cit.*

"6) Although heresy and infidelity are mortal sins, they "also sin mortally who expose themselves to danger "whether by conversing or hearing sermons or reading "books which, if they are dangerous, are illicit by the law "of nature; but if the danger is absent, the reading of "heretical books is just as illicit by the positive law of the "Church, just as even formal disputation by a laymen on "faith. Still, by and by in Germany, and similar places, "where Catholics are mixed with heretics, the custom "abrogates. Azor, Filliuci, Becanus, Sanchez, Bonacina, disp. 3, "q. 2, p. 5.

"7) To contract matrimony with a heretic, even if it is "illicit *per se* and is held in Spain and Italy as a mortal "sin, still is probable on account of the authority of "serious doctors (Sanchez, *de matrim.* l. 7, d. 72, n. 5; "Azor, l. 8, d. 3, c. 3; Reg. tr. 2, l. 32, n. 169; Basilius "Pontius, *de matr.* c. 6; see Cardinal de Lugo, *de* "*sacramentis in genere,* disp. 8, sect. 14, n. 120), in "Germany it is permitted from grave cause, save for "natural law, and with the danger removed both for the "one contracting and for the children, which is why from "the beginning it must be constituted that they will be "given a Catholic upbringing. See Becanus, l. 5, c. 19; Dian. p. "3, t. 4, r. 269.

"8) A man that has fallen into heresy is not held to "explain in confession what sort it was, for the reason "that all are of the same species, as Reg., Diana (tr. *de* "*circumst.,* r. 46, citing others), and Escobar (ex. 2, c. 9). "Nevertheless, others hold the contrary, whom Cardinal "de Lugo follows, *de poenit.* d. 16, n. 288, and n. 291. (See "what was said in book 2, n. 50.)

TREATISE II

On the Precept of Hope

20.—"By hope, which is the second theological virtue, "love longing for God is understood, in which we long "for God more than all other desirable things so that we "are prepared to lose all things rather than God, and "divine things. It is often asked on this, when does its "precept oblige?

"*Resp.* 1. It is probable the precept of hope obliges *per se*, "when man first attains the use of reason, God and "beatitude, as an end, to which he ought to tend, has "been sufficiently proposed so that in such a notable "time he would not put it off. So Becan., c. 17, quaest. 7, "n. 2; Turr. and others in common. And the reason is, "because in the act of hope one is neither justified nor "persists in divine justice, nor do we act in a meritorious "matter. Schol.

"*Resp.* 2. The precept of hope *per accidens* obliges 1) "when an act of prayer, penance, charity, etc. are in a "precept, which, without preceding an act of hope "cannot be exercised. So think the cited authorities, and "Filliuci, tr. 22, c. 8, n. 255. 2) When someone is so "tempted that there would be danger of consent, unless "the mind raised itself in hope. See Filliuci, *loc. cit.* 2., "Laymann l. 2, t. 2, c. 2; Bonacina, d. 5, quest. 3.

Thus the following cases are resolved:

"1. It is a mortal sin to hope in or to love (with the love "of desire) earthly things more than heavenly ones, *e.g.* "if anyone were so composed to desire to perpetually

521

"abide in this life and leave heaven to God if he would "stay behind on earth.

"2. It is likewise a mortal sin to despair of attaining God, "or salvation and forgiveness of sins or the necessary "means to obtain them, *e.g.* to despair of the divine "assistance, and emendation of life. Yet it cannot be a "venial sin by reason of the smallness of the matter, "since it would be injurious to the mercy of God. St. "Thomas, q. 20, a. 3, Laymann, l. 2 t. 2. c. 2. n. 3.

"3. It is also a mortal sin to presume upon the mercy of "God, *e.g.* since someone hopes for that which is "impossible according to the ordinary law; that if he "were to hope for the remission of sins and salvation "without penance, or through his own merits and natural "strength, or even if someone were to determine to "persevere in sins as long as he would will, and yet hope "that he was going to do penance before death. St. Th., q. "21, art. 1; Laymann, *loc. cit.*

"4. Lastly, it is a mortal sin to hate God (viz. with a "hatred of abomination or aversion), *e.g.* if God would "displease us, so to speak, as hostile on account of the "vengeance against sinners. See Laymann, *loc. cit.*, Bonacina, "disp. 3, q. 3.

21.—Hope is defined more briefly and fittingly as: "The virtue through which we place certain trust in the coming beatitude and expect the means to attain it through the help of God." The *primary material object* of hope (namely, that which we hope for), is eternal beatitude, which is to enjoy God himself; the *secondary* object, however is divine grace and our good works obtained by the divine assistance. Yet, the *formal* object (or the motive on account of which we are held to hope) some say is the mercy of God, others the divine omnipotence, exactly as the Thomists hold in common; others say the divine promise, just as Jeuninus thinks; others, at length, say it is the divine goodness, inasmuch as he communicates the graces themselves to us to obtain salvation, and according to this understanding goodness is the same thing as divine mercy; if anyone would will the formal object of faith to be the goodness of God, inasmuch as he is the thing hoped for, the Continuator of Tournely rightly sais that he would not speak correctly. (*de praecept. Decal.* cap. 1, art. 2, sect. 2, concl. 2).

Since we have posited these, I think it must be concluded that the first three aforementioned motives would constitute the *formal* object of hope, namely, mercy, divine omnipotence, whereby God bestows assistance upon us to conquer the enemies of our salvation and these two motives are expressly taught by St. Thomas in *Quaestionibus disputatis*, qu. un. *de Spe*, where he says: "So the formal object of hope is the assistance of divine piety and power, on account of which the movements of hope tend in goods hoped for, which are the material object of hope." I think, in addition to these two, a third must be added, namely the divine promise, just as Jeuninus rightly thinks, or divine fidelity in regard to the promise which he showed to save us on account of the merits of Christ; otherwise, without this promise we would not avail to hope for salvation with certain trust.

The vices opposed to hope, however, as we said above, are despair and presumption. In regard to presumption it must be noted that one would sin by presumption who hopes for salvation either merely due to his own merits or due to the merits of Christ without any cooperation of their good works.

Busembaum says here (n. 3) that one sins gravely that wishes to persevere in sin until death, hoping perhaps that he will be sorry before death, and he cites St. Thomas and Laymann, but neither say this; rather St. Thomas merely says in 2.2. q. 21, a. 1, that presumption is, "to hope for forgiveness without repentance, or glory without merits."

Furthermore, he adds in a. 2, ad 3, that "to sin with a purpose to persevere in sin under the hope of forgiveness is presumption and increases the sin. But to sin under the hope of receiving forgiveness at some time with the purpose to stop sinning and do penance for sin would not be presumption and decreases the sin because by this it seems the will is less established in sin." This is why, according to St. Thomas, it is not a sin against hope to persevere in sin under the hope of being sorry at some time. But it is true that one can only with great difficulty be excused from grave sin against charity toward himself, since from the common consent of the Doctors, those who would so purpose would expose themselves to great danger of their damnation.

Hence, Bonacina and Sporer (*de praec. spei* c. 4, n. 17) and Croix (l. 2, n. 126) rightly say that one who delays penance under the hope of forgiveness does not sin against hope while that hope of remission stands only concomitantly in regard to the sin, but not efficaciously to him the motive or reason to sin. The same must be said about one who would sin under the hope of forgiveness. For then someone must be judged to sin against hope, when the readiness of hope for obtaining forgiveness would become his reasoning, or the motive influencing him to sin. Otherwise it must be said, that if he would sin from passion, by hoping concomitantly that sin would later be remitted. So then he would increase the sins under the pretext that God will forgive ten sins as easily as he will forgive five, he sins from presumption, as the Cont. of Tournely says, *loc. cit.* sect. 6, concl. 2, *Raro*.

TREATISE III
ON THE PRECEPT OF CHARITY

CHAPTER I
Whether, when and how the precept of charity for God obliges?

22. *When must God be loved?*
23. *When does the precept of charity oblige?*
24. *Cases are resolved.*

22.—"The charity of God is the love of friendship, in "which we rightly will God and desire all good things for "him, on account of the supreme and infinite perfection "of divine nature.

"*Resp.* 1. The precept of charity of God commands God "to be loved above all things. It is clear from Scripture. "The reason is because the ultimate end must be loved "more than all the means which are referred to him: "certainly not intensively (even if this would also be "fitting, still it is not in the precept), but appreciatively, "so that one would make no creature more than God, "and one would rather will more to lose all things than "to offend God and so wish ill on him. St. Thom. 2.2. "quest. 27, art. 3; Azor, Sanchez, Becanus, 2.2. c. 19.

(See what is going to be said in book 6, n. 442, v. *Id clare.*)

23.—"*Resp.* 2. It is probable that the precept of charity of "God does not oblige: I. When a man obtained sufficient "knowledge of God infinitely good, from whom he has "all goods, to whom he owes all things. The reason is "because although he may be held to serve God all his "life from filial love, it does not seem it can be done

"unless he would elicit an act of love. (On this matter,
"see the opposite proposition condemned by Alexander
"VII, prop. 1). St. Thomas agrees (quest. 89, art. 6) and
"Navarre and Valent. etc. in common (as Concina notes,
"disp. 24, d. 3, n. 50) not immediately after such notice
"does one mortally sin, but only if he notably delayed,
"*e.g.* beyond a year), against Palaus, who says it is
"probable that it does not oblige. If a scruple troubles one
"as to whether he has satisfied the precept, Escobar
"teaches from Peter Hurt. (2.2. d. 172, setc. 1 § 24), that if
"one did not positively remember he omitted it, he can
"hold that he satisfied it. Trull. (l. 1, c. 5, dist. 13, n. 9)
"nevertheless, warns it is expedient that someone will at
"sometime accuse himself in confession under a doubt,
"if perhaps he violated that precept, or other affirmative
"precepts. on which he is not certain whether they oblige
"or were violated. II. When there is a danger of slipping
"into hatred of God, unless one would elicit an act of
"charity. III. When someone is held to expunge , *e.g.* that
"is going to die, or celebrate, whose confessor is away.
"The reason is, because contrition includes an act of
"charity. IV. If anyone thinks he cannot otherwise
"conquer grave temptation, especially at the point of
"death. In which cases some add absolutely the point of
"death, to the extent that then the road they must choose
"is very secure. See Laymann, l. 2, c. 2; Bonacina, l. 3, q.
"4, part. 2; Hurt. 2.2. dist. 174, sect. 6, § 17."

(And it is very probable, as Sporer, num. 45, and March.,
and Cont. Tourn. *de praecept. Decal.*, cap. 1, art. 3, sect. 3,
concl. 1, num. 2, with Antoine, and in common).

24.—"1) It is mortal if someone were to omit the love of
"God when the precept obliges.

"2) He would also sin mortally if anyone were to love
"God with an appretiative or estimative love lesser than
"for created things.

"3) He would likewise sin against the charity of God, if "anyone does not love God principally and because of "what he is, just as the final end of all things; but only on "account of another thing, *e.g.* eternal life or to avoid "hell, which Sylvest. and Navarre, teach is a mortal sin, "because God is not loved appretiatively above all things, "if a thing different than him were loved as the "principal end. I add, *principal*, because (as Toledo says "well, l. 4, c. 9), God can be loved on account of the "reward of eternal life, but less principally, that viz. "eternal life or the other goods of God would only be "loved as a moving cause, that they might be loved more "easily, expediently and fervently.

"4. It is a mortal sin and the gravest of all if someone "were to hate God formally with the hatred of enmity, or "malevolence (which is opposed to friendly love), *e.g.* if "one wants to not desire God to have knowledge and "power, etc. On this, see Laymann, Bonacina, *loc. cit.*; "Sanchez, l. 2, c. 3 et 5; Reg. l. 27.

The material object of charity toward God is primarily God, secondarily us and our neighbor; moreover, indirectly there are all the things which increase divine glory. The formal object is God, insofar as he is infinite goodness, according to the aggregation of all perfections, or infinite perfection, as the Cont. of Tounrely says (*loc. cit.*, sect. 2, concl. 3). But Gonet supposes that the formal object of charity is the goodness of divine nature, exactly as it is the root of all perfections, but virtually distinct from perfections. Bouvin, however says it is each divine perfection, on account of which God is loved. Moreover, from the common sense of the wise the true act of love is to say: "My God, because you are infinite goodness, or because you are infinitely good, I love you above all things."

Here there is a doubt: 1) whether the desire to possess God is the object of charity? And we say it must be affirmed, because charity (as it was said above) aims at God as its final end, and therefore the desire to possess God, who is certainly our final end, is a more proper act of charity, or more perfect than others, for possession of God is consummate charity. Hence a perfect act of charity, the Apostle uttered when he said: "having desire I melt away, and am with Christ." (Philip. 1:23) And St. Augustine expressly teaches this, writing: "I call charity a motion of the soul to enjoy God on account of himself." Nor is it opposed to say that in this mode the object of charity would avoid being the same thing, and the object of hope, which is equally the possession of God that is hoped for. For Habert rightly responds (tom 3, *de Spe*, cap. 2, quaest. 2), saying that hope aims at the possession of God, as our good, but charity desires to possess God on account of the Glory of God himself; while (as St. Bernard says) "When a man possesses God, he forgets himself and loves God with all his strength."

There is a doubt: 2) Whether an act of charity is to love the divine goodness just as something suitable to us, since here the act seems rather more to be of the love of concupiscence than of friendship? Jueninus, Habert and Gotti rightly respond that if in an act of this sort we regarded our own good as the end, such an act really is the love of concupiscence, which only pertains to hope. But if we regard our good act as the terminus of the glory of God, by loving the divine goodness, just as it is fitting for us, to the extent that it helps us to fulfill the will of God and obtain our final end, which is to love God and on account of which God created us, this is a true act of charity, for which reason St. Augustine says: "So you ought to love that so that you will not cease to desire him alone who will satisfy you for your reward." (*In psal.* 134).

Moreover, to love God on account of benefits is not a true act of charity, but of gratitude, as Habert and Croix (lib. 2, n. 147) say, unless, Habert says, the benefits are considered as communications with the divine goodness: for then in those we love not our final end, which we receive, but the goodness of God, who communicates.

Here, note proposition 10 among those condemned by Pope Alexander VIII: "Intention, whereby someone detests an evil and pursues a good, merely that he would obtain heavenly glory, is not right nor pleasing to God." Then, still (Laymann says, *de charitate*, cap. 2), someone would sin against this when in actual intention he refused to love God except it were due to hope or fear.

CHAPTER II

On the precepts of charity toward our neighbor

"Charity for our neighbor commands: 1) order in loving "him; 2) love of enemies; 3) almsgiving; 4) fraternal "correction. Next, it forbids: 1) hatred of our neighbor; 2) "scandal; 3) that injuries, war, and other grave harm and "evil are not imposed upon him. The last is treated on in "the Decalogue, here on the rest.

DUBIUM I

What order must be preserved among persons whom are loved?

25. *What sort is the order of charity toward ourselves and neighbor?*

26. *Whether it is lawful at some time to deprive ourselves of spiritual goods, or to expose ourselves to danger of sinning on account of charity?*

27. *When are we held to come to the aid of our neighbor?*

"25.—Resp. 1. In the order of charity everyone is held
"after the love of God: a) to love himself, according to
"spiritual goods; b) to love our neighbor, in regard to the
"same goods; c) himself in regard to his corporal goods;
"d) Our neighbor, in regard to the same; e) lastly himself
"and thence his neighbor in regard to external goods. So
"think Laymann, l. 2, t. 3, cap. 3, from St. Thomas, in
"common.

Thus these cases are resolved:

"1. A man would sin against charity for himself if he
"neglected his spiritual or corporal health, which is grave
"if it were done without cause and with grave loss, *e.g.* of
"death or a serious plague. Trull. l. 2, c. 6, d. 1.

26.—Note that by speaking *per se* one that could deprive
himself of spiritual goods that are not necessary for
salvation on account of a spiritual or corporal good for our
neighbor, that it would be he omits to enter into religion so
as to take care of his parents or sons. The Salamancans, *de
praecepto charitatis*, tr. 21, cap. 6, punct. 3, § 1, n. 26. But see
what is going to be said in book 5, n. 78.

Equally it is licit on account of the spiritual salvation of
one's neighbor to expose oneself to danger of probably
sinning, because that danger, when a grave cause is present
for undergoing it, then it is not judged to be taken up
voluntarily (the Salamancans *ibid.* n. 27, with Sanchez, from
St. Basil). On the contrary, *ibid.*, n. 28, with Valentia Azor
and the common teaching say for this purpose one is held
who doubts about his danger, while the danger to a neighbor
is on the other hand certain; namely if an infant is going to
die for certain without baptism if you would not come,
although you could not approach without danger of
subversion. See book 2, n. 63, and book 6, n. 453.

"2. It is not lawful to sin for the sake of obtaining any "good, even venially, because such would be a spiritual "evil. Laymann, *ibid.*

27.—"3. Everyone is held to come to the assistance of "their neighbor constituted in extreme spiritual "necessity, even with a certain danger of life; provided it "were equally certain hope of helping him and a graver "evil would not threaten; *e.g.* one were held with danger "of life to baptize or absolve one that is going to die, if "another is not present who would do it. St. Augustine, "*de mendacio*; St. Thomas, qu. 20, art. 5; Regin., cap. 4).

"I said, in extreme necessity, for example, in a case "where someone were supposed to be about to die in "mortal sin, because he who of his office has care of "another, such as a pastor of a parish, is only obligated "so obligated in a serious matter, consequently he is not "permitted to flee in a time of plague unless there is an "equally suitable substitute. Valent. and Laymann, *loc.* "*cit.*

Certainly, everyone is held to come to their neighbor's aid in extreme spiritual necessity, up to the point of throwing away their life, provided that three things are present: a) That the hope to assist were equal, as Busembaum says, with Laymann; b) That our neighbor had no others by whom he might be assisted; c) that our neighbor would certainly be damned unless one were to help him; so that (Malderus adds) it will be certain for one that his neighbor is not otherwise converted by contrition or from the operation of divine grace.

Hence, if one's neighbor were only in grave necessity, one is not held to come to his aid at danger to his life, good name or goods, unless it were his pastor, as he says with Busembaum, Cont. Tourn. *de praecept. decal.* cap. 1, art. 3, sect. 4, punc. 1, conlc. 2. *Dico* 2; or unless your temporal loss were light, such as the Salamancans, tract. 21, cap. 6, punct.

3 § 1, n. 34. Hence the Salamancans say (*ibid.* n. 32) with Suarez, Palaus, Coninck, from St. Thomas (2.2. q. 26 art. 5 ad 3) that one is not held to bring back sinners with such danger, nor to sail to convert Indians when there are others who can do this and the fruit were otherwise uncertain, as Tamb, Bonacina (*de char.* disp. 3, q. 4, p. 4, n. 2); Palaus, (p. 9, n. 9) and Cont. Tourn. *loc. cit.*

On the other hand, they say one is held (the Salamancans d. n. 32) I. If some community were in grave spiritual necessity; because then grave harm that must be guarded against is more than your particular harm. Hence, they infer that one is held with danger of life to minister the sacraments to the people, who otherwise would be in danger of losing the faith; or if in a time of plague the people were destitute of every priest, as Laymann *de char.* c. 3, n. 3.

They say: II. One is held in grave necessity who, of his office ought to come to the assistance that only hopes for the fruit. Hence, pastors, viz. Bishops, and parish priests, are held from justice with the danger of life to administer the necessary sacraments to the sheep; such as baptism and penance, but not others. Nor can the pastor then renounce his office (although he could substitute others with a just license of the Ordinary, as Laymann *ex communi* with Valent., *de char.* c. 3, n. 3; Palaus, p. 9, n. 13). So with Busembaum, the Salamancans tr. 21, c. 6, punct. 3, § 1, n. 33 and 34 with St. Thomas, Palaus, etc. And this is certain, Croix says (l. 2, n. 174). There, Suarez adds that the Pastor is held also at the risk of great temporal loss of his temporal goods to procure the great spiritual utility of his subject. Moreover, what is an extreme spiritual necessity and a grave one? Croix (d. l. n. 175, with Cardenas, Valent., etc.) says it is extreme when a neighbor is in proximate danger of damnation, or of sinning from the vehemence of his passion (but the Salamancans say it better, *ibid.* n. 32, as well as Palaus, d. n. 9 with Bonacina, that nobody is held with danger of life or goods to extract others from sins from which they can free themselves by on their own or through penance), grave but it is when from circumstances it would render eternal salvation difficult for him.

What is the obligation of absolving the moribund with danger of life? It must be affirmed, if someone were habituated in sins, and were so unlearned that he did not know to elicit an act of contrition. So Palaus, p. 9, n. 6; Coninck, d. 13, dub. 7, n. 90; Navarre, c. 24, n. 9; the Salamancans *ibid.* n. 31; Mazz, c. 2; § 3, etc. But in a time of plague I think with Laymann, that above against Palaus, d. n. 6, in fin. priests are held, after others have fallen away, to absolve the moribund with danger to life, because in such a multitude of those dying those ignorant of this sort will fail.

Quaeritur: whether someone is held to kill a man harming someone for the defense of innocent life? Laymann (*de char.* d.c. 3, n. 5), affirms it as it is more probable with Navarre, Molina, etc., unless he could not kill without grave trouble. But it is more truly denied, as below in book 4, on the 5th precept, n. 390.

"4. Ordinarily it is not permitted to disregard his life for "another. I add *ordinarily*, because it is lawful if it is a "public person upon whom much depends, as even in a "republic, for the faith, to defend religion, nay more even "for a beloved friend on account of God. Lessius, l. 2, c. "9, d. 6; Laymann, *loc. cit.*

"Resp. 2: In regard to neighbors, among them this order "must be preserved: 1) Who is better, more loveable, by "that love which joy accompanies in regards to goods "possessed, likewise honor, cult and reverence. So, *e.g.* "one must be more loved that is a holy man than a "wicked parent. The reason is because he is more joined "with the particular object of charity, which is God. "Likewise parents more than sons or a wife, and

"benefactors more than those for whom we do good.
"Laymann, *loc. cit.* and common.

"2) Appretiatively, and by that delight with which we
"desire good for another that they do not yet possess,
"they are to be more loved with kindness, those who are
"more joined to us in regard to these goods, which are
"due to such a connection and on which these are
"founded.

Thus, the following are resolved:

"1. In goods pertaining to nature, and to preserving
"bodily life, one must provide (outside of extreme
"necessity) first of all for his wife, because she is one
"flesh with her husband. Secondly, for the Children (In
"equal necessity firstly one must provide for children as
"for parents. The Salamancans *de IV praec. Decal.* tr. 24,
"c. unic., punct. 1 § 1, n. 21, with St. Thomas and the
"common teaching). Thirdly, for parents, and indeed for
"father and mother; fourthly, for brothers, sisters, then
"those nearest, domestics and household servants. I said
"*outside of extreme necessity*, because in this parents, to
"the extent that they gave them life, must be preferred
"even to one's wife and children. Laymann, *ibid.*, n. 5,
"and 6, so also the Continuator of Tournely, (*de praecept.*
"*Dec.* cap. 1, art. 3, sect. 4, punct. 2, concl. 4, in fin. num.

"2), and more probably against the Salamancans d. n. 21.
"Note here, trhat in extreme necessity parents must be
"preferred to creditors. The Salamancans *ibid.*, n. 25;
"with Cajetan, de Soto, against Navarre, etc.

DUBIUM II

On hatred and goodwill toward enemies

28. *Whether someone is held to show common signs of good will to his enemy?*
29. *Whether someone is held to forgive an injury?*
30. *Whether an abomination could be licit? Whether the harm wished against our neighbor must be explained in confession? And whether sometimes it might be lawful to wish harm on our neighbor?*

28. —"It is certain that enemies must be loved in some "mode since they are our neighbors, which St. Thomas "says in 2.2. qu. 25, art. 1, in common with all. Rather, it "is asked on the mode and whether they could be held "with hatred.

"Resp. 1. Each man, at least a private man, is held to "show common signs of good will and kindness to his "neighbor, even if it is his enemy by precept, but special "things only by council unless the reasoning of an "obligation comes from another source. So the common "opinion holds, with Laymann c. 4, ex. St. Thomas, *loc. "cit.*, q. 25, a. 8 and 9. I said 1) *common signs*, of the sort "according to Cajetan, v. *Odium*, there are things that "ought to be for a Christian from any Christian in "common, to a fellow citizen from a citizen, from kin to "kin. The reason is, however, because these things deny "vengeance for an injury, which is not lawful for a "private man. I said 2) *unless the reasoning of the "obligation were to come from another source,* such would "be, *e.g.* a) fear of scandal from omission; b) hope of "salvation for an enemy; see Azor, lib. 11, cap. 3, c) "Temporal necessity, or spiritual; d) supplication of fault

"and exhibition of special signs of love. The reason is,
"because to neglect these cases of special signs would be
"an outward declaration of hatred. Laymann, *loc. cit.*

Thus, the following cases are resolved:

"1. By speaking *per se* no man is held to positively love
"an enemy, and by a peculiar act, nor to greet him, speak
"to him, visit him when he is sick, console him while sad,
"receive him as a guest, or behave in a familiar fashion
"with him, etc., because these are special signs of love.
"Filliuci, tract. 28, c. 1. I say, *per se,* because if there were
"a scandalous omission, or for some hours one could
"reconcile an enemy to himself and to God without
"inconvenience, and to omit these would be a grave sin,
"so also, if a person of lower rank would customarily
"precede another in greeting, *e.g.* a subject and a prelate.
"Laymann, *loc. cit.*"

(So also, if one were to earlier persuade an enemy to show
peculiar signs, as Cont. Tourn. *de praecept. charit., loc. cit.*
sect. 3, concl. 3. Fifthly, with Suarez, Bonacina, etc. for this
still one is not held with rave inconvenience to himself,
provided he remove scandal).

"2. It is not permitted to exclude an enemy from common
"prayers, *e.g.* from the Lord's prayer, which was
"established for the community, nor from common forms
"of almsgiving, greeting in return, response, in the sale
"of the wares on display, because these are common
"signs of good will, and therefore to act against these,
"*e.g.* to invite all kin, exposed to all in the neighborhood
"or society, to greet from custom, while only having
"excluded the enemy, it is from its nature, and regularly
"a mortal sin. St. Thomas, Navarre, Laymann, *loc. cit.*

"I add 1) *from its nature*, because if the lightness of the
"matter or a reasonable cause would excuse, *e.g.* if a
"father or superior take these things away from an
"inferior or a subordinate on account of correction for a
"time, it will be light or nothing, because he has the right
"to punish. I add, 2) *regularly*; because if a person does
"not greet a much greater inferior in return, *e.g.* a noble
"and a rustic, a father and son, it does not seem to be a
"mortal sin, as the authorities note. Sa, *verb. charitas*,
"Bonacina, d. 3, qu. 4, p. 3; see Azor, 3, p. 1., 12, c. 2, 13."

(Moreover, the Continuator of Tournely, *loc. cit.*, *Tertio,
si quis*, notes that if one refused to converse with an enemy
because he can expect nothing other than evil from it, or
because (as St. Bernadine of Sienna says), probably he fears
from this a worse thing will come about, then he may
abstain from those signs of friendship, only he must love
him interiorly and repair scandals with others).

Quaeritur? Is one held to greet an enemy? Resp. No,
speaking regularly, because *per se* the omission of a greeting
is not a sign of hatred, unless before one always did it, or
unless from circumstances it is gathered that one hates the
other because he did not give a greeting, or that if he were
a superior, or unless it occurs with a great many people
present, among whom he greets the rest with the one
exception. Palaus, (*de char.* p. 6, n. 5, with Valentia et
Concina, Slam. tr. 21, c. 6, punct. 2, n. 21, Mazz, *de char.* c. 21,
§ 2, q. 3, Bonacina, *de char.* d. 2, q. 2; Tamburinius, *de char.*
c. 1, n. 11; Sporer I praec. n. 29). Or even (it must be added)
if without a great inconvenience by greeting an enemy one
could free him from hatred and serious fault, for this
purpose it seems right that charity binds one, as the Cont.
Tourn. rightly says (*ibid.*, Quinto, num. 4). Altogether, one
is held to greet him in return, because otherwise he would
be thought to scorn his enemy and to mean to persevere in
hostility, as the cited authors commonly teach. Except,

unless one were a prelate, parent, or judge, or unless he was to do this not from hatred but from just sorrow for an injury received, as Sporer, Mazz, and Hurt, (cited by Tamb, *loc. cit.*) teach, only (as Roncaglia and Mazz with Tamb advert) from a short time from when one received the injury. Moreover, a religious who would refuse for a notable time, say, after a week, to speak with an enemy, Sporer (n. 34) rightly says must not be absolved.

29.—"3. Whoever you like is held to not only inwardly "forgive an enemy that legitimately asked for it, but even "show outward signs of forgiveness; still Trul. (l. 15, c. 5, "d. 5) from Azor and Filliuci, deny that he is held "immediately after an offense is forgiven to the extent "that it might be a violent matter, and beyond human "frailty.

(So Sporer also thinks is probable, *de 1 praecept.*, cap. 6, n. 44 with Tamburinius, from comm., because it seems beyond human frailty to compel a wounded man to make reconciliation when the disturbance has not yet been quieted. For this reason, an opportune time must be sought, and meanwhile it will suffice that the offended should lay aside hatred.)

"He is not held to remit satisfaction for the injury if he "were wounded by him, nor accept it, if it were offered, "but can also juridically seek compensation, provided "that in each case hatred has been laid aside, as Valent., "Navarre, Laymann, l. 2, t. 3, c. 4 teach. But if still a "punishment were exceedingly grave, *e.g.* the death "penalty, mutilation, nor for the one wounded from it "would an advantage come into being, it does not seem, "after praying for the other, vengeance could be sought "without sin. Likewise, if it would satisfy in as much as "it can, to that which it cannot, it seems to press him "against charity, as Sylvius and Filliuci teach, tom. 28, "cap. 11, qu. 9.

Although anyone you like would be held to forgive an enemy for an injury, still the Salamancans say (tract. 21, c. 5, punct. 2 n. 18) that no man is held to pardon public vengeance, since the punishment results in the good of the state. But there, Bañez upholds, with Busembaum (as above) that it is difficult then to not use the envy for vengeance if the penalty were capital or of mutilation: and this must be said about every grave penalty, because it is difficult for the offended to love the public vengeance on account of the love of the common good separate from the love of his own vengeance, as the authors advert. (Laymann, *de charitate*, c. 4, assert. 3; Sporer *de I. praec.* c. 6, n. 20; Viva, *de char.* art. 5, n. 3; Roncaglia, tr. 6, c. 2, q. 2). Hence, I adhere to Antoin (*de virt. Theol.* cap. 2 qu. 3), because by speaking practically, it is never allowed to seek out the *punishment of an enemy, even if it is going to be done by the just and legitimate authority.* Moreover, the Cont. of Tournely says (*de praecept. charit.* sect. 3, concl. 3, Quaer. 4, *Dixi*, with Habert), someone can rightly pursue satisfaction for injuries in the presence of the judge, if otherwise, his whole family might suffer infamy. Likewise, St. Thomas (2.2. qu. 108, art. 1) says that vengeance can at some time be licit, namely if it is taken up "for the correction of the sinner, or for his governance, and the rest of others." He adds: "And the preservation of justice," but this last (as it was said) is more speculative than practically true, or at least more rare.

30.—"Resp. 2. Even if the hatred of hostility, whether for "a person as he is in himself, and his goods, by wishing "evil for him, like so, or insofar as it is evil for him, "which of its nature would be a mortal sin, nevertheless, "hatred of abomination, whether of the quality in which "not a man but his malice, or at least a person insofar as "he is only evil, or we avoid him as harmful to us, it is "often licit, as Coninck teaches (a 29, dist. 3) with other "sin common.

Thus the following cases are resolved:

"1. In confession it is enough if one were to say he willed
"a grave evil upon his neighbor, he does not need to
"explain the species of the evil, *e.g.* death, infamy, etc., all
"of which are embraced under one reason of malice.
"(Cajetan, Bonacina, Turr., Trull., lib. 1, cap., teach that
"this is probable; but Suarez and Palaus, t. 6, dist. 4, p. 1,
"teach the contrary is more probable. Moreover, the first
"opinion is not probable if someone were to efficaciously
"propose some special evil to inflict on someone; for
"then the species of the evil must be explained, because
"then a deprave proposition takes the species from an
"outward act, or from intended damage. See what was
"said in book 2, n. 5, qu. 5).

"2. Although to wish some evil on one's neighbor, *e.g.*
"temporal (provided it were not more grave than just),
"insofar as it is good for him, *e.g.* a plague or adversity,
"so that he would be free from sins. Bonacina, d. 3, qu. 4,
"part. ult. §1. *Ex multis.* One must beware, nevertheless,
"to not do it from vengeance, from which, if one read
"Psalm 108 over his enemy he would sin mortally. But
"generally, on account of the spiritual good, his own or
"another's, it is permitted to wish evils for an
"inefficacious punishment upon others from affect,
"because when in this affect the spiritual good is
"preferred to the temporal, it is not disordered. See
"Lessius, lib. 2, cap. 47. (See what has been said in book
"2, n. 21).

"So, although, *e.g.* to desire the death of a heresiarch, or
"a disturber of public peace, on account of the common
"good, and of many things, according to what is written
"in Galatians 5: 'Would they would be torn off.'
"Likewise, to be sad about the fact that dignities were

"conferred on those unworthy of them, or on their
"health, who take occasion from that to sin. So also to
"desire death, extreme poverty or illness for someone
"that they would stop sinning and change their life for
"the better. By the same cause, Bonacina, Azor, and
"Palaus (tit. 6, p. 1, n. 11) excuse from sin a mother who
"desires the death of her daughters, insofar as it is on
"account of deformity or poverty she cannot fittingly
"and honestly marry them. (But this must scarcely be
"admitted, as the Salamancans rightly say, *de pecc.* tr. 20,
"c. 13, punct. 5, § 1, n. 46, Roncaglia, tr. 2, c. 3). Yet, even
"if one could desire his own death, Navarre and the rest
"say it is mortal, but to avoid grave evils, *e.g.* internal
"affliction, it is lawful to wish for it. Sanchez, de Soto,
"Granadus Diana, p. 5, tr. 14, res. 29. (So also Viva rightly
"admits, sup. prop. 14 Innoc. XI, n. 3, if anyone were to
"experience a bitter death, from Eccli. 30:17, where:
"'death is the better part than a bitter life,' for Elijah, 3
"Kings 19:4 asked for his life that he would die 'to avoid
"the snares of Jezebel). So also Trull., lib. 1, dist. 2, n. 11,
"excuses a woman who desires her death or that of
"another to avoid grave infirmity, poverty, a bitter life,
"etc. or other similar evils *e.g.* inflicted by her husband.
"Nevertheless, Diana (*loc. cit.*) condemns for mortal sin,
"weak women desiring death on account of the smallest
"aggravations, unless (as it often happens) it were
"excused by a defect of knowledge and deliberation.
"(And it is not improbable, with *Potestat de I. praec.* n.
"298).

"3. A privatus, who turning away from another flees
"him, if he would do it so that he would deprive him of
"his life and solace, and also so that he would suffer
"sadness and it is evil for him, it is the hatred of hostility,
"and a sin; but if nothing evil is desired for him if one
"flees, because his nature were deformed, or it was

"usually aggravating for you, is a hatred of aversion and
"sin if it were without reason, such will not be if the
"person is exceedingly bitter, provided contempt,
"scandal, and the lust for vengeance are absent. See
"Bonacina, *loc. cit.*"

Note here three propositions condemned by Innocent XI:

Prop. 13: "If one were to act with due moderation, he can
without mortal sin be sad for the life of another and rejoice
in their natural death, to desire it by an inefficacious affect
and to desire, not even from dislike of his person but on
account of softening their temporal life."

Prop. 14: "It is licit with the desire for absolution to seek
the death of one's father, not even as a bad father but the
good of the one desiring because without a doubt if he will
obtain his inheritance."

Prop. 15. "It is licit for a son to rejoice in the murder of
his father perpetrated by the son while he was drunk on
account of the vast wealth that he will thence obtain in his
inheritance."

DUBIUM III

On the precept of Alms-giving, or corporal mercy

31. *Whether we are held to give alms from the goods of
    life, or necessary things for their state?*
32. *Whether to aid the poor is a necessity in common?*
33. *Whether we can do almsgiving from someone else's
    goods?*

31.—"I suppose: 1) The obligation of this precept is born
"from a twofold head: a) From the necessity of the

"nearest poor man; b) from the person possessing bold or
"necessary things, or superfluous things.

"I suppose 2: It is a twofold necessity given to our
"neighbor. a) it is called *extreme*, from which danger of
"life or even of a grave and daily disease, threatens the
"poor man, according to Diana (p. 5, tr. 8, r. 1). b) *Grave*
"from which danger of grave evil, such as captivity,
"infamy, grave loss of goods, or status, whence it
"happens that with difficulty can someone sustain
"himself; *e.g.* if he cannot live according to his state, or
"if a noble man is compelled to serve another, or were a
"skilled laborer or an honest man to beg. c) It is called
"*common*, in which beggars labor on trivial things.
"Laymann lib. 2, tract. 3, cap. 6.

"I suppose 3: Necessary goods and superfluous are called,
"either in respect to life or nature, or in respect to status,
"or decent condition of a person, in the way which
"seculars rarely think they are superfluous, as Laymann
"and Navarre (c. 24). For, those things which are
"necessary to feed one's children, domestic servants,
"worthy donations, dinner guests, taking in of guests
"(still such things are not those that are forbidden to
"everyone as well as pomp, everyone requires this of
"himself, even after common events have been
"considered, heirs, future necessity, etc.), are not
"superfluous."

(Note here proposition 12 condemned by Innocent XI,
which said: "You will hardly find in secular matters, even
among kings, superfluous goods. And so, one is hardly held
to give alms when he is held only in regard to what is
considered superfluous.")

"Resp. 1. No man is held to give alms from his goods that
"are necessary for his life, even if the poor man were
"such a person upon which the safety of the state would

"depend. This is the common opinion, and the reason is
"clear from the order of charity.

"Resp. 2. It is probable from what is superfluous by
"nature, and established that someone is held to give
"even in grave necessity, to come to the aid of his
"neighbor if he thinks he probably is not going to assist
"him; and that, as Azor (lib. 12, cap. 7); Sylvius, and
"Fumus would have it, is under mortal sin, against
"Medina, who means it to only be a counsel. The reason
"is, because when in Scripture men are frequently
"condemned on account of the negelct of the works of
"mercy, these are not restrained to an extreme and rare
"necessity. See Laymann, *loc. cit.*"

(And this must be held with Viva in d. prop. 12, n. 8, and
Bonacina, tract. 6, cap. 3, q. 2, with Suarez, Palaus and Azor,
the Salamancans tr. 21, cap. 7, punct. 1 § 2, n. 12, with the
common opinion from St. Thomas, 2.2. u. 32, art. 5 ad 3. And
it seems clearly inferred from the aforesaid proposition 12.
Nevertheless, Viva notes (and the Cont. of Tournely says the
same thing, *de praec. char.* sect. 5, punct. 2, resp. 1 with
Sylvius), that neither in a grave matter nor in extreme
necessity would one be held to expend great sums of wealth
upon the poor, since these means are very difficult and
almost morally impossible. A beneficiary is held unless he
wishes to apply the rest to other works).

"Resp. 3. One is ordinarily held to come to the aid of his
"neighbor in extreme necessity from goods that are also,
"in some manner, necessary for his state. Suarez,
"Laymann ex. comm. Still, one will probably satisfy if he
"would give with the burden of restitution, when he will
"be more wealthy, Vas. etc. against Suarez, Coninck, etc.
"See Diana, p. 5, t. 8, r. 5.

"I add *ordinarily*, because if it were thought a greater
"loss, that one would be deprived of his state, than the
"death of the pauper, one is not held. Azor, *loc. cit.*

"Resp. 4. It is probable that for our neighbor constituted
"in grave necessity each is held to assist him with the
"least detriment to his proper state; because in his
"modest inconvenience he is held to stop a greater
"inconvenience to his neighbor. Laymann, *loc. cit.*, St.
"Thomas, Bonacina, dist. 3, q. 4, p. 6.

From the aforesaid it is gathered:

"1. Private men are not held to seek out the poor,
"Vasquez, etc.; but if they hesitate on the extreme need
"of someone, he is held to discover the truth. Sanchez,
"Diana, p. 5, t. 6, r. 39.

"2. No man is held to give a great resources of money to
"the poor, to improve the most precious medicine
"necessary to preserve life, or to provide a remedy from
"the danger of death. Sa and Coninck, disp. 27, dub. 8, n.
"135. And the reason is clear from the aforesaid.

"3. If one's neighbor would only need the use of the
"thing, it is enough to bestow upon him, *e.g.* if one were
"to bestow a garment from despoiled enemies, or upon
"a wounded night, until he returned home. Laymann,
"Bonacina, *loc. cit.* (with the Continuator of Tournely,
"*loc. cit.*, r. ad 2).

32.—"Resp. 5. In common necessities of the poor at some
"time one is held to give alms, who has the goods of
"nature and superfluous goods to his state. So St.
"Thomas, Suarez, Bellarmine think in common, against
"Navarre and Vasquez, who deny it is held. The
"reasoning is, both because each is held to love his
"neighbor, just as himself, and because otherwise the
"poor would fall into grave necessity. Still, this
"obligation only seems to be under pain of venial sin, as
"Medina rightly says; and it, if there were no just cause

"for denying it, otherwise *sub nullo.* See Laymann, "Bonacina, *loc. cit.*

Quaeritur: Whether in common necessities of the poor there would be a grave obligation to give alms from what is superfluous to one's state?

The first opinion says no, and St. Antoninus holds this (p. 2, tit. 1, c. 24 § ult.) where, while speaking on riches bound for almsgiving, he only speaks merely on that which "from what is superfluous of each necessity, viz. of nature and person, he does not assist those suffering great necessities, albeit they are not extreme;" likewise Laymann, tr. 2, cap. 6, nu. 5, with Alensi, Major, and Gabr., Dian p. 2 tr. 15, r. 32, with Turrianus, Abbat., Fernand., Victorell., Vasquez and Medina, likewise Sotus and Sylvius, wtih Croix, l. 2, n. 202., with Covarruvias, Fr. Navarre and Malder, cited by Bonacina t. 2, d. 3, q. 4, p. 6 n. 7, who, in n. 8, thinks it probable with Cardenas (cited by Croix, n. 203). The reason is, because in common the obligation of almsgiving does not arise from the superfluity of goods, but from the urgent necessity of one's neighbor; otherwise, it would not be lawful for the rich to bestow donations from superfluous goods on others; at least (as Laymann says), since the common misery of the poor is usually light and tolerable, it does not seem a grave sin to refuse to assist them.

But the *second opinion* is more common, to which I adhere, and it upholds it, and many authorities hold it. (Palaus, tr. 6, d. 2, p. 2, n. 15; Holm. tr. 1, § 4, num. 177; Viva, in prop. 12, Innoc. XI, n. 3; Cont. Tourn. *de charit.* sect. 5, punct. 2, v. *Prob.* 3, pars.; Sanchez; Cons., l. 1, cap. 5, dub. 6, n. 37; with Aragon. Ledesma, Bann., Abul., etc., the Salamancans tr. 21, cap. 7, punct. 1, § 2, nu. 17, with Cajetan, Tapia, and Prado), who follow St. Thomas, 2.2. q. 32, art. 5, where he says: "Therefore, to so give alms from what is superfluous is in the precept and to give alms to one that is in extreme necessity." Prob. 1: from Luke 11:41, "Moreover, give alms, and all things will be cleansed for you." Prob. 2: by reason; both because the division of things made by the common consent of nations cannot be in prejudice to the poor, and because if the rich did not have an absolute obligation of assisting the poor in common, they could ignore all in their necessity. And here it must be noted what Navarre says, (c. 24, n. 6) with Cajetan, namely that it pertains to all things that are required to preserve a decent state, not only for children and servants, and maintaining guests, but even for honest gifts, dinners and to shop moderate magnificence; and so it corresponds to the reason of the first opinion; and Navarre ads (*ibid.*, with Cajetan, and Sylvest., from St. Thomas), that it does not necessarily consist in the decency of the states in the individual, but he shall have the latitude and it is greater in one whose status is greater.

Furthermore, Viva (*loc. cit.*, n. 11), Mazzot. (tom. 1, pag. 441, quaest. 1), Roncaglia (*de charit.* cap. 3, reg. in praxa, n. 2), the Salamancans (tr. 21, c. 7, p. 1, §2, n. 18) with Lorca and Tamburinius (*Dec.* lib. 5, c. 1, §1, n. 17) with others, say it is probable that there is no obligation to bestow all superfluous wealth of this sort on the poor; for this precept does not oblige individuals *in solidum*, but all the rich in common, from which, if individuals bestow something, it is enough to assist them with common necessities. This is why Sylvius writes thus: "The rich are held to give not to all the power that come to mind, nor the whole of what is superfluous, but not so modest for the quantity of their substance that if some riches are so made the poor would lack subsidy." Sanchez agrees with this (*loc. cit.* n. 38) with Ledesma, saying that having superfluous wealth to his state does not hold him to bestow everything on the poor, but at some point, and in a moral manner, so that he would satisfy his obligation as a rich man who has care of the poor, sometimes by assisting them, so he concludes, one sins mortally who decides to give no alms in common necessities, or who is notably negligent in this. Laymann (*loc. cit.*) thinks the same thing, where, although he says this obligation does not bind *sub gravi*, nevertheless, he ads that the rich man lives in a bad state of life who so inhumanly repels the poor. But he adds that the confessor ought not to easily refuse absolution to such a rich man, since on this obligation, the doctors do not agree on how serious it is. Moreover, Viva, Tamburinius, Mazzota, and Roncaglia, with a more common opinion, suppose the rich man probably satisfies by bestowing a fiftieth share of his means, or two gold coins from a hundred, but not in the same proportion, if his riches much exceed that. On the other hand, ecclesiastics are held to bestow on the poor from the means of their benefices whatever remains after their sustenance. Still, it suffices for Bishops to give to the poor one fourth, but clergy in more simple benefices a fifth or sixth, as Viva says (n. 11) and Roncaglia, only they should apply others in other pious uses. But see what will be better said in book 4, n. 491, qu. 1.

So, the following cases are resolved:

"1. When the common poor, even if from nudity, plague, "etc., seem to show signs of extreme necessity, someone "is rarely bound by precept to assist, even from "superfluous goods, because generally this necessity is "exaggerated to move spectators, and because they are "presumed to be assisted by others. Mald., Wiggers, "Diana, p. 5, t. 8, r. 17.

"2. If anyone that is rich and abundant for a long time "would deny all almsgiving, with the purpose of giving "better and in a more suitable place and time, to those in "need, or of converting it into another pious use, he "would not sin since he had a just cause for refusing; but "if such a man were to inhumanely repel the poor from "him without a reasonable cause, then Laymann says he "lives in a bad state.

"3. Altogether to no one, as rich as you like, repelling all "the poor without almsgiving, must absolution easily be "refused, both on account of the doubt and disagreement "of the doctors on this obligation, and because it is "hardly found that one does not pretend at least the "apparent cause, if he affirms he has superfluous wealth.

"4. Even if on the aforesaid almsgiving were understood "in respect to all the needy, even sinners, infidels, and "enemies, still the sentencing magistrates must not "exclude poor pilgrims from their citizens, for a just "cause. Laymann, *ibid.*, Trulench, l. 1, c. 5, d 10.

"5. Equally for religious and other poor, almsgiving "ought to be given, because their poverty and necessity "is true and just, albeit voluntary contracted, since the "will and the cause will have been rational, and pleasing "to God. Lorc., Diana, p. 5, t. 8, r. 18. It is another matter "on those, who are culpably poor of their own accord, "such as vagabonds. *Ibid.*, r. 19.

33.—"Resp. 6. Almsgiving must only be done for good "purposes, and from sources which a man has the free "administration thereof. Still, it can be made from "someone else's goods when a neighbor is in extreme "necessity, and cannot be aided from another source; for "then all things are common."

(But, if you bestow your thing on him, and gave him someone else's, it seems that you will be held to restitution, because you could not determine another's goods when your own were at hand. So think Croix, lib. 3, p. 2, n. 431, with Sporer, because in that case the precept of almsgiving binds you to bring aid from your own goods).

"But in common necessity, it is allowed only with the "tacit or express consent of the owner of the goods. St.

"Thomas, 2.2. q. 32, art. 7; Regina, n. 286, Filliuci,
"Laymann, Bonacina, *loc. cit.*, num. 11, Lessius, lib. 2, cap.
"12.

So the following are resolved:

"1. It is not permitted to give alms from goods liable to
"restitution, *e.g.* from stolen goods; nevertheless, it is
"lawful from what was acquired by illicit work (but not
"with injustice), *e.g.* from the profit from the trade of a
"harlot. The reason is, because the latter are one's own,
"the prior were not.

"2. One may not give alms to the children, children of
"servants, servants, maid-servants, or wives, in which
"the will of parents, masters and husbands is resumed.
"But in particular cases, in which the wife can give, see
"in its place precept. 4 and 6, ch. 1, d. 4, see Bonacina,
"disp. 5, quaest. 5, p. 6, Diana p. 5, t. 8, r. 25, where from
"Hurt., he notes if the father would give no alms, his son
"can give for him."

(In regard to wives, see book 4, n. 540).

"3. Tutors and curators, who have the care of someone
"else's goods, can give a modest alms from the goods
"that they administer, such as they ought to do, without
"a doubt, whose things they are. Vasquez, Azor, Concina,
"Diana, p. 5, t. 8, r. 35."

DUBIUM IV

On spiritual mercy, or the precept of fraternal correction

34. *On account of what sin are we held to correct our
neighbor?*

34.—"Fraternal correction is an admonition whereby "someone tries to recall their neighbor from sin. On that "it is certain that the precept is both from natural law, in "which members of one body are held to help each other, "and divine positive law, "If your brother will have "sinned against you ... correct him." (Matth. 18:15, "Becanus, 2, 2, c. 21, Laym. cap. , Filliuci, Bonacina, p. 7). "Moreover, it is asked, what is its matter? And whom "and when does it oblige?

"Resp. 1. Every mortal sin of our neighbor is *per se* "sufficient matter, as this precept obliges under mortal "sin; so the common teaching holds. And the reasoning "is that since it abolishes the spiritual life of our "neighbor, it induces sufficient necessity of correction. I "said *every mortal sin*, because, even if a venial sin were "mater for correction, still it is not a gravely obliging "matter, nor could it easily be done."

35.—Hence, Laymann says that the correction of venial sin is more rarely under the precept; except if one were a prelate of religion who is sometimes held under grave sin to correct the light faults of subjects, from which the vigor of discipline shall begin to lessen with great detriment to religion. So Cont. Tounr. *de charit.* sect. 6, punc. 2, concl. 1,

v. *Haec conclusio*, Laymann *de charitat.* c. 7, num. 3, with Busembaum, below, n. 40, and see book 5, n. 13.

36.—*Quaeritur:* Whether there is an obligation to correct sins committed from invincible ignorance? The response is made by distinguishing if the sins were against the law of nature, correction ought to be made, because then these are intrinsically evil, as is common (Croix, l. 2, n. 214). And Oviedo says the same thing with the common opinion on the ignorance of divine law, still, were the fruit to be despaired of, or it feared that formal evils would be done from material things, as the Salamancans commonly say (tract. 21, cap. 7, punct. 4, § 1, n. 53) and Roncaglia (*de char.* cap. 3, quaest. 4) with others. But if they might be merely against positive law, it is probable that there is no obligation for private individuals, at least not *sub gravi*, to correct them; otherwise, prelates, parents, confessors, teachers, it would be specially incumbent on all of them because they teach subjects. (The Salamancans, d. n. 53, with Bann., Ledesma. Likewise, Bonacina, *de char.* q. 4, p. 7, n. 11; Navarre, c. 24, n. 12; Viva *de 4 praec.* q. 11, art. 6, n. 11; Palaus *de char.* d. 3, p. 4, n. 2). The reason is both because our neighbor is not in sin that failing, the precept of correction does not urge; and because he does nothing intrinsically evil. But what others say (Palaus, n. 3, Coninck, d. 28, q. 4, n. 38; Sanchez, *de matr.* lib. 2, d. 38, n. 5, Mazz., *de char.* cap. 2, § 6; Cont. Tourn. *loc. cit.*, concl. 3, and Croix, lib. 2, n. 214, with Burgh.) is more probable and common, and teaches that all are held to correction because that transgression, although material, and not intrinsically evil, just the same, after the imposition of the law, is evil, and therefore we are held to impede him by correction.

37.—I said 2: *per se*, because if anyone on account of fear, "modesty, pusillanimity, etc. would think he were not so "strictly obliged, or less suitable to correction, it appears

"he would only sin venially. See St. Thomas, 2.2. q. 32,
"art. 2, and the rest cited above."

Note here, the doctrine of St. Thomas (2.2. q. 33, art. 2 ad
3) where he so teaches: "An omission of this sort is a venial
sin when fear and cupidity make a man slower to correct the
faults of his brother, still, not so that if it were certain to him
that he could draw a brother back from sin, but would omit
it on account of fear or cupidity, by which in his mind he
proposes fraternal charity. And it is in this way that holy
men neglect to correct those failing in their duty."

38.—"Resp. 2. This precept obliges under these
"circumstances. I. If the sins of a man's neighbor are
"certain (or the proximate danger of a neighbor sinning,
"Cont. Tourn. *loc. cic.*, concl. 2, Prob. 2 pars), a superior
"alone is held to investigate. Cont. Tourn. *loc. cit.*, punct.
"1, concl. 2, Sequitur 3."

So that, if it were not certain about a neighbor's sin,
namely, if notice of that sin were to arrive to us only
through hearing, or through other doubtful signs, we are not
held to correct him. (The Salamancans tract. 21, cap. 7, p. 4,
§ 1, n. 52, with Sanchez, Diana, etc.) unless the suspicion
were about a homicide, or on common loss, or unless
someone were a prelate who ought to correct in doubt since
he is held to inquire about the sins of his subjects by his very
office. (Salamancans, with others, d. num. 52, in fin. with
Busembaum).

39.—II. If it were probable that he would not emend, nor
"that he is going to or relapse, because alms must be
"given to the needy.

Quaeritur: Whether, when the danger of a relapse is
removed, does the obligation to correct an errant brother
exist?

The first opinion says no, and they hold it with the
Salamancans, *ibid.* n. 49, Sa, Abul., Palaus, Regina, Com.,

Diana, Villal, etc. and Laymann (de *charitate* c. 7, n. 2 vers. Corripe) call it very probable, along with Sylvester, Turrianus, and the Gloss in c. *Si quis* 24, qu. 1. The reason for these is because a sinner is not even held to immediately destroy sin by penance, so much less is another man held to lift him out of sin, when the fruit of emendation is uncertain. Therefore, Laymann says it is commanded in Eccl. 19:14, "Correct your neighbor, lest perhaps he would repeat.

Nevertheless, *the second opinion* is contrary, and authors think it is more probable (Cont. Tourn., the Salamancans, with Suarez, Bonacina, Lessius, etc.). The reason is because a brother constituted in sin already suffers grave necessity, from which we are held to deliver him, if we are able. Therefore, Christ the Lord commanded, "If your brother will have sinned against you, go and correct him." Nor does the opposite reasoning impede us, for *per accidens* at some time the obligation of another can be greater than our own, *e.g.* someone can, on account of love of poverty, not deliver himself from grave poverty, but another rich man is held to assist him if he can.

"III. If another equally suitable were not present who "was thought to be about to correct him. IV. If there "were the hope of fruit, because when the end has been "despaired of, the means should cease."

In equal doubt, whether correction might be profitable or harmful, the authors say it must be omitted, Concina, *de elem.* c. 3, n. 9, and the Cont. Tounr. *loc. cit.* punct. 3, concl. 2. *Quod si*, with Habert and Antoine. Moreover, the Cont. Tourn. rightly limits: a) If the one that must be corrected were in danger of death; b) if he feared from an omission the repudiation of others in faith or morals. And so also, if correction were more certainly beneficial. Cont. Torn. says the same thing. c) The third condition is not an obligation to correct, if it is probable that the guilty party will become reasonable: from what St. Thomas says in quaest. 33, art. 2, where: "He falls under the precept [of correction] which is necessary for that end." Likewise , Cont. Tourn. notes the same thing with Domingo de Soto, Bann., and Malder., that no one is held to correct in grave spiritual necessity with notable danger of loss of honor or of goods, unless he were a pastor or another person to whom by his duty care of another was incumbent.

"V. If the occasion, place and time were opportune and "good, and one could do it without danger of grave harm "to himself. But if he lacks one of these, the precept does "not oblige. This is why his omission is clear in private "matters or none, or a light fault. See Bonacina, loc. cit."

(Yet, I do not like that he speaks so generically).

40.—"Resp. 5. Even if this precept obliges all, even "subjects, still, it obliges prelates more. The reason of the "first part is because all are united and held to furnish "charity in their external duties. The reason for the "second part is because subjects are only bound by "charity, whereas prelates are held by duty and justice. "This is why they can sin, even gravely, by not impeding "venial sins, if the vigor of discipline is diminished by it. "(See book 5, n. 13). And the same reason on a "householder, especially toward children. Laymann, *loc. cit.* "n. 5, Palaus, Trul., lib. 1, cap. 5, d. 13, and 15, etc."

Therefore, bishops, pastors, prelates, parents, confessors, lords, husbands, teachers, tutors, and curators are held more strictly to correction. But it is uncertain whether they are held to also correct at the expense of grave damage to themselves? What pertains to Bishops and pastors must not be doubted, that they, both from their office and from the stipend which they exact, are held to assist their subjects, and on that account to correct them, even at danger to their life, in their necessity, not only extreme but even grave, as is commonly taught, and St. Thomas, in 2.2. quaest. 185, art. 5, says: "And therefore, where the salvation of subjects demands the persons of the person of their pastor, the pastor ought not to personally desert the flock ... nor even on account of some personal danger that threatens him, from that of John 10:11. A good shepherd gives his life for his sheep." Also, Suarez, d. 9, sect. 2, n. 4; Palaus, tr. 6, d. 1, p. 9, n. 12, Bonacina, d. 3, qu. 4, p. 4, n. 5; Viva *de* 4 *praec.* qu. 11, art. 6, n. 12; Mazz., t. 1, pag. 458, and the Salamancans tract. 21, cap. 6, punct. 3, § 1, n. 33, with Coninck, Trull., Tapia, and Villalobos But whether they are held with danger of loss to correct parents, husband, and others, as above, who receive no stipend for this purpose? The Salamancans seem to affirm it (*ibid.* cap. 7, punct. 4, § 2, n. 58) while they say that they are held to correction from duty, and hence (they add) from justice. But I can hardly acquiesce to this addition, or doctrine, for although superiors are more truly held by their office more than from mere charity, as the authors teach (Sanchez, Palaus, Cajetan, Valentia, and Diana, against Suarez, Tapia., and Lorca, all whom the Salamancans cite, *dicto* n. 58), just the same such a duty, since it has its origin from the obligation of piety alone, or charity, does not seem to oblige from justice to such a burden; for otherwise it would be held from justice by reason of a stipend, as pastors are held, another by reason of office. The Salamancans (*ibid.* § 3, n. 67) add that preachers are held to rebuke public sins, even if, therefore, they were to fear private losses. Still, this must be understood, if from rebuke some fruit were to be hoped for, and a greater common loss not feared.

41.—"Resp. 4. The order must be preserved in correct, "which Christ prescribed in the Gospel (Matthew 18:15), "one must first correct privately, then in the presence of "witnesses, finally one defers to a prelate of the Church, "or of a superior. Nevertheless, I. Except he offer to a "superior that is a good man, and prudent, then make it "known to other witnesses, exactly as it is cautioned in "the rule of St. Augustine (See book 5, n. 243, *et seq.*). II.

"Only if the sin is public, then he can be corrected
"publically. III. Unless he verges on grave damage of a
"third person, or the community, if it is not made
"immediately known to the superior, *e.g.* if anyone were
"to plot betrayal, secretly spread heresy, for then it must
"be immediately made known to a superior, because the
"common good must be preferred to a private one
"(Filliuci, t. 28, c. 7, n. 149 and 155). IV. When the one
"that must be corrected has been secured, that he would
"immediately be shown to a superior, as is with certain
"religious who in regard to this renounce their right. See
"Suarez, Becan., Laymann, Sanchez, Filliuci."

The following cases are resolved:

42.—"1. Someone that easily could impede the mortal sin
"of one's neighbor, and on account of temporal fear does
"nothing about it, sins mortally. Laymann, Suarez,
"Sanchez (lib. 6, mor. c, 18). See Palaus.

"2. If it will be certain that a brother has perfectly
"emended a secret sin, and that there is no danger of
"relapse, or of danger to himself or another, it is not
"lawful (even in the Society of Jesus) to denounce him to
"a Father or prelate, unless the brother expressly
"consented to that denunciation. (Sanchez, 2. mor. l. 6, c.
"18, n. 40, and 60; Palaus, *de char.* t. 6, disp. 3, p. 12;
"Filliuci; Trul. l. 1 ,c 5, d. 14; Suarez; Hurt. disp. 163; and
"then Card. de Lugo, resp. mor. l. 4, d. 46, where he
"notes, nevertheless, that in the Society of Jesus the case
"is very rare. See also book 5, n. 245). The reason is,
"because the motive of charity would cease and so the
"reason for denouncing him, and therefore it is a sin and
"indeed (as Cardinal de Lugo notes from Suarez) it is a
"mortal sin by its nature. See Diana, p. 4, t. 4, r. 71.

"3. If an immediate superior could himself correct a
"delinquent, so that there is no danger of damage or
"relapse for him or another, or a threat to the
"community, it would seem that to manifest the crime to
"a mediate superior would be a sin. Palaus, loc. cit.,
"Trull., d. 16, n. 1.

"4. Prelates and magistrates are held sometimes to
"inquire of the sins of subordinates to correct them, but
"they ought not ask much, and curiously about someone
"in particular; unless he would give special sign if it and
"not easily admit spontaneous accusers, because they
"often seek for themselves by a species of the common
"good. Hurt., and Dian., p. 7, tract. 13, r. 10 et 12.

"5. Bishops, prelates of religious, pastors of souls, are
"held also at their inconvenience, nay more, sometimes
"at danger to their life, to apply the diligence which they
"can to impede public and secret sins; because with
"Christ their job is to have care and be solicitous for
"their flock, for which they receive many goods. Hurt.,
"t. 2, d. 162, *sect.* 7, § 6 (cited by Diana, p. 7, t. 3, r. 28),
"and he says this is the doctrine of all the fathers and
"theologians, which Christ had taught by word and
"example: and add the same thing is of magistrates and
"preachers. Although, the latter are not held to that from
"justice (as prelates and magistrates), still they are held
"to correct public sins (but not easily of prelates and
"religious, of whom the authority for the common good
"is necessary) even if there is no hope of emendation.
"Coninck, Hurt., Diana, *loc. cit.*, r. 13.

"6. Correction must be applied not always immediately,
"but when a greater fruit is hoped for. Hence, sometimes
"a repetition of a sin can be permitted, so that one might
"become more fervently recovered. Diana, p. 7, t. 3, r. 29,
"and 30, from Reg., Filliuci, Trull. And it does not suffice
"for correction to be made once, rather it ought to be

"done again and again so long as there is hope of it
"coming to fruition. (*Ibid.*, r. 32)."

DUBIUM V

On Scandal

ARTICLE I

How manifold is it and what sort of sin is it?

43. *What kind of sins are active and passive scandal?*
44. *The resolution of many cases cited by Busembaum.*
45. *When scandal is a special sin?*
46. *Must the circumstances of its entrance necessarily be explained in confession?*
47. *Whether it is lawful to ask at some time from someone that is prepared to sin to furnish something that he cannot without sinning?*

43.—"*Resp.* 1. Scandal is said to be an occasioned sin, and
"it is twofold: active and passive. *Active* is what is said or
"done (under which term omission is also understood)
"that is less right, offering to another an occasion for
"spiritual ruin. From St. Thomas, 2.2. quaest. 43, art. 1,
"Sanchez, Azor, Laymann, c. 13, Bonacina, d. 2, quaest. 4,
"p. 2. I said *less right, i.e.* that it is either evil in itself,
"such as if one were to say foul things in the presence of
"adolescents, or if it should have a species of evil, such as
"if from a just cause, one ate meat on a forbidden day in
"the presence of those unaware of this cause. Active
"scandal is one type of thing *per se*, and it is another *per*
"*accidens*. *Per se* it is said to be when the ruin of another

"is directly intended, *i.e.* if something were done so that
"someone would be led into sin; *e.g.* if an adulterous man
"solicited another woman to adultery. It is said to be *per*
"*accidens* when it is only caused indirectly and
"interpretively, as if one were to do something that came
"into his mind, suited to induce another here and now to
"sin, and just the same he does it, such as if one were to
"sin in the presence of children, or eat meat on a
"forbidden day without saying that he had an exemption:
"likewise if a Cleric were to support a woman at his
"home and the people suspected (God forbid!) every sin,
"as well as the danger of sinning. See Sa, (v. *Clericus,*)
"Laymann, Bonacina (*loc. cit.*). *Passive* scandal is the ruin
"itself, or the sin, in which a neighbor falls from the
"occasion or deed of another. That is divided into *given*
"or *of the petty*, which arises from active scandal: as well
"as into *received,* which does not arise from active
"scandal but from the malice of the one taking scandal,
"which would be the hatred and envy of the Pharisees
"against Christ, on the occasion of his words and deeds:
"this is why it is called *pharisaical.* From these it is clear:

"1) For active scandal it is not required that passive
"scandal follow *de facto*; but it is enough that the
"occasion were given from which it could follow by its
"nature, such as if a man were to induce someone to sin
"who nevertheless would not consent, just as, on the
"other hand, there can be passive scandal without active.
"Laymann, *ibid.*

"2) Passive scandal is not a special sin, and it does not
"add an aggravating circumstance, *e.g.* someone also
"steals after seeing the theft of another, therefore he
"would not commit a graver sin. Laymann, *ibid.*

"3) It is not always scandal if one were to sin in the
"presence of others, but only when, with the attending
"circumstances of both the person doing it, and those in

"whose presence the act is done, it can probably be "feared lest through this act some are drawn to sin that "otherwise were not going to sin. Sanchez, Laymann, l. "2, tr. 3, c. 13.

"4) All active scandal directly intending the ruin of one's "neighbor is a special sin against charity, as the common "opinion holds. But would be the same thing when it is "intended indirectly? The Scholastics reject this, and it "scarcely relates to practice. Sanchez, l. 7, c. 6, and 9; "Azor, 1, part. l. 4, c. 7; Bonacina, *loc. cit.*

Thus the following cases are resolved:

44.—"1) A man sins mortally that gives occasion to "another of mortal ruin, unless lack of deliberation "would excuse it; so an indifferent work or a venial sin "often passes over into a mortal sin by reason of scandal; "*e.g.* if a religious were to advance a bad joke in the "presence of women, or those who then can take the "occasion of mortal sin. Laymann, *l.c.*

"2) A man sins venially by reason of scandal that gives "occasion to another for ruin of a venial nature. But it is "true, even if he intends it directly, and it is certainly "mortal by act. Sanchez, *l.* 1, c. 6, n. 11) from the common "opinion against Suarez. The reason is, however, that the "ruin is small. And clearly from a similar thing, that if "anyone by fornication intended to steal a small thing, "the theft will merely be venial.

"3) A man causing scandal also commits, apart from the "sin of scandal, the sin of its species to which he induces "another; so he ought to confess the species of the "mortal sin by which and to which he induced with the "number of those induced to it, or those that probably "could have been induced. Sanchez, Azor, Laymann,

"Bonacina, *l.c.*, Card. de Lugo (*de poenit.* d. 16, s. 4),
"Diana, *de sacr.* tom. 2, tr. 4, a. 114. Still, Cardinal de
"Lugo makes the exception if one would give scandal
"without the intention. Tamb, *de exped. conf.* l. 2, c. 1, n.
"9, with de Lugo says, in regard to those seduced, it
"suffices if he would say: "I was the occasion of sin for"
"many people by my example." (See book 2, n. 46).

"4) Even if the man who scandalized others is held to
"again give a good example, as Sa says, if anyone still by
"his naked example induced others to steal, and not in
"any peculiar mode, *e.g.* he cooperated by exhortation,
"counsel, command, he is not held to restitution because
"such a seduction is only against charity, not against
"justice."

(So also Sanchez, *Dec.* l. 1, c. 6, n. 5, and the Salamancans,
tr. 13, *de rest.* c. 1, punct. 5, §1 n. 114 with Molina, Bonacina,
Dic. and others in common, with Roncaglia, *de char.* c. 6, qu.
2, who rightly says that although he would also sin against
justice, according to the more probable opinion, which we
follow, (n. 45 *seq.*) he is still not held to restitution because
he is not the cause, only the occasion of the damage. See the
following number, at the end).

"Lessius teaches the same thing, with Cajus, *e.g.* if one
"were to drink from the intention that after he had spent
"all his money he would steal. See Lessius, cap. 9, d. 16,
"n. 110.

"5) One is not considered to give scandal that, although
"he sins publicly, does it only in the presence of those
"who are so vile, or infamous or wicked that none of
"them would be moved to sin; or who are so good, *e.g.* if
"someone were to fornicate in their presence, who are
"prepared to do it, they are not moved by his example, or
"if in the presence of one mourning someone would get
"into a fight and quarrel, or strike another. Sanchez, 1
"*mor.*, c. 6, n. 6.

"6) Therefore, some deed is not scandal because another
"begins to suspect evil of such a man, or to think because
"he does not sin because he shows sufficiency he should
"be suspected. Still, it is otherwise if he would begin to
"think badly of the Catholic faith, of clergy or a religious
"order, or if his piety were to be diminished. Wherefore
"it is clear that scandal is more easily given by those who
"are in great authority or in the estimation of piety than
"by others. Coninck, d. 32, n. 33.

45.—Here it will be worthwhile to recall three questions
in understanding to balance with necessary praxis. Question
I: At what point will scandal be a particular sin? There are
three opinions.

The first asserts then scandal is only a special sin against
charity when the spiritual ruin of one's neighbor is directly
intended. So Sanchez, *Dec.*, l. 1, c. 6, n. 3; Bonacina, tom. 2, d.
2, *de peccatis* qu. 3, punct. 2, § *unic.* n. 13, with Palaus, Azor,
Bann., Trull, etc., cited by the Salamancans tr. 21, c. 8, punct.
5, § 1, n. 51. The reason of these Doctors is that for some sin
would be specially distinct, it is required that it would have
a special end against an opposite virtue. But when the ruin
of one's neighbor is not intended, it does not specially
wound charity, but rather more that virtue to which one's
neighbor is induced to wound; therefore such a scandal is
reduced to that species of sin to which one's neighbor is
induced; either directly, by command or counsel, or
indirectly, by words or example.

The second opinion, which de Lugo holds (*de poenit.* disp.
16, sect. 4, ex. n. 157), with Navarre, and Tamburinius, (*Meth.
exped. conf.* l. 2, c. 1, n. 105), and other more recent authors,
distinguishes and says someone can induce another to sin in
three ways: a) Directly and formally, by intending someone's
spiritual ruin; b) Directly, but not formally, when, *viz.*, he
wishes that another would violate chastity, not that they
would lose their soul, but so that they would satisfy the one

inducing them; c) Indirectly, namely when by his example another would take up the occasion of sin. Thus, they say that if scandal would happen in the first and second mode, the one scandalizing sins, not only against charity but also against the virtue to which he induces his neighbor to injure. But when he sins in the third mode, viz. by foreseeing but not intending the sin of his neighbor, then he only sins against charity, but not against the virtue which is wounded, for which reason he is not held to explain its species. The reason is, because the other virtues do not oblige, at least gravely (as de Lugo says) that we would impede the opposite vices in others, but only lest we would positively intend to induce our neighbor to offend against them.

The third opinion, to which I ascribe, holds that one who directly or indirectly induces his neighbor to sin, sins in two ways, viz. both against charity and against virtue to which he induces his neighbor to wound. It seems to me that it cannot be denied that he sins against charity, and I cannot acquiesce to the first opinion that was set forth. For, if charity obliges one to correct his neighbor and to stop him, when we can, lest he would ruin himself in sin; how much more does that oblige to not impel him to sin by counsel or example? Nor is the reason that was offered opposed, that to wound charity a special purpose to wound it is required; for generally it suffices to place something destructive to any virtue to offend against it, even if this is not intended; exactly as if someone kills an enemy in the Church, even though he did not intend to offend against religion, nevertheless, he not only sins against justice, but even against religion, since *ipso facto* he wounded it. And so de Lugo holds (*loc. cit.*, n. 139), the Continuator of Tournely, *de charit.* sect. 7, punct. 1, § II, v. *Tota*), Roncaglia *de scand.* c. 6, quaest. 2), Tamburinius (*loc. cit.*), the Salamancans (*loc. cit.* n. 53), with de Soto, Valentia, Suarez, Tapia, Prado. And St. Thomas expressly teaches this, (even though Sanchez cites him for his opinion), in 2.2. q. 43, a. 3, and a. 1 ad 4 the Angelic doctor says: "When someone intends by an evil word or deed to induce another to sin, or even if he did not intend this, the very thing happened inducing him to sin; then he gives occasion for ruin, wherefore it is called active scandal." Moreover, that he would sin even against the virtue, to which he induces his neighbor to wound (even if indirectly), is the reason why each virtue not only forbids the contrary acts, but also forbids lest an occasion be given to others inducing them to sin: for then that occasion, be it not the influencing cause of itself, is nevertheless the moral cause that a neighbor would sin; it is said to be the *moral cause*, which in its substance the direct inductive causes would equally influence one to sin, since without it his neighbor would not sin. So think Cajetan (2.2. q. 43, art. 1), Sanchez, Roncaglia, Cont. Tourn., the Salamancans (*ibid.* n. 55) with Laymann (See what is going to be said in quaest. III, n. 47, near the end). The reason why that example is not the direct influencing cause, but only the occasion which does not furnish the positive influence to steal, which is required for the obligation of restitution.

46.—Question II. Whether the circumstances of inducement to fornication must be explained in confession? Some authors say no (de Lugo, *de poen.* d. 16, and Tamburinius *in meth. conf.* c. 3, §4, n. 24, with Jo., Sanchez, and Vasquez, Leandr. with the others, cited by the Salamancans *de poen.* c. 8, n. 107), who say it suffices to confess fornication because the malice of induction or scandal (as they say) is already contained, although it is not so grave when someone does not solicit but merely consents; for still he participates with another in his sin, and it is the cooperating cause to their ruin. That is why this malice only seems to aggravate more within the same species, when someone positively solicits. And de Lugo argues the same thing must be said about foul speech and like things. Still,

Sanchez (*dec.* l. 1, c. 6, n. 14) Palaus, tom. 1, tr. 6, d. 6, p. 3, n. 4), and Sal. with Diana, Coninck, Filliuci, etc. oppose this, saying that the circumstance of the solicitation must altogether be explained, since this would be a sin distinct from the sin to which one's neighbor is induced. Nevertheless, this reason not withstanding, the first opinion of de Lugo seems probable enough, since a sin against charity is also present in cooperation to fornication, that is rightly distinct from the sin of cooperation with fornication, by cooperating for the ruin of the other party, according to what was recently said in the preceding question, and must be said in the following question. This is why de Lugo infers that induction is nothing other than an aggravating circumstance within the same species, and does not necessarily have to be explained, according to the opinion which we will reference in book 6, n. 467.

Moreover, from this opinion of de Lugo and others, viz. that the circumstances of the solicitation are of the same species, as cooperation to fornication, it is inferred that cooperation to fornication (although in itself fornication is necessarily contained) is a distinct sin both against chastity and against charity; wherefore, one who fornicates, according to this opinion, does not commit only one sin, but many against chastity; and (as I argue), as many as the sins one would commit, if, in turn, he commits pollution with another; for then he causes one sin because he commits pollution; second, because he commits pollution with another (and Cont. Tourn. holds this, *de praecept. charit.* sect. 7, punct. 1, § 2 *ex his patet*, where he says that one fornication sins in two ways, on account of his own fornication and on account of another); third, because he would cooperate that the other would pollute him. Besides two other sins which he commits against charity, by cooperating with his pollution, and with his action, that he would commit pollution. All these sins are also enumerated in fornication, and equally in sodomy, adultery and incest. Moreover, these different sins must not certainly be explained in confession by the one who fornicates, for he sufficiently expresses them by confessing the fornication; and as he already confusedly apprehended these things by fornicating, so also the confessor understands these very things *in confuso.*

It could be said with Suarez (cited in the Salamancans tr. 20, c. 12 *de princip. moral.* punct. 6, n. 60) that, when one act regards many evil objects, then they constitute one sin, even if, *per se,* each object is divided separately it would completely have its own malice, exactly as Sporer says (*de poenit.* c. 3, n. 435), on a priest celebrating Mass in mortal sin, who, although he perpetrates many actions evil actions *per se,* namely by consecrating unworthily, by receiving the host, etc., still, as Sporer holds, because all these actions regard one minister of the Sacrifice, he commits one sacrilege. And so it could equally be said in fornication, where, although many wicked actions coincide, all having their own individual malice *per se,* because still they regard one sin of fornication, therefore (removing the question of the sin of induction), they constitute one sin. But the rule which Suarez places above, the Salamancans reject (*loc. cit.* n. 69) and say that just as many wicked objects, specifically distinct in one act (say in the occasion of the priest), from many sins in a different species; so many objects of themselves having their own complete malice, even in one act they constitute many different since by number. Moreover, that Mass celebrated in mortal sin is one sacrilege, we do not deny with Croix, (see what was said in book 2, n. 44). Nevertheless, these not withstanding, I do not condemn the opinion of those who say fornication is one sin; but am more pleased with the opinion of de Lugo, as above, who recognizes many sins in each fornication. Each one abounds in its sense.

47.—Question III. Would it be the sin of scandal to seek something from someone, which he will not furnish without sin if he were already prepared to sin? Here we must distinguish: if the matter which is sought of itself were intrinsically evil, so that it could be furnished in no mode without sin, say to seek fornication from a prostitute that is prepared to do it anyway, there are not lacking doctors who say it is not a sin of scandal, because, when such a woman always has an actual or virtual will to sin, it is not considered gravely or lightly to cooperate, who furnishes an occasion to him to carry out that sin. (So think de Soto, l. 6, *de justitia et jure*, qu. 1, art. 5, likewise Henriquez, Azor, Valent., Medina, Salon., Manuel, Lopez, etc. cited by Sanchez, *Dec.* l. 1, c. 6, n. 13, with Coninck and Sala, ap. Bonacina *de poenit.* quaset. 5, sect. 2, p. 2, § 3, diff. 3, n. 19 and 20). I venerate the authority of such doctors, but I would not dare to recede from the contrary opinion which I think must be followed, and which other doctors hold that call it common and certain. (Sanchez, *loc. cit.*, n. 14, with Cajetan, Navarre, and Filliuci, likewise Bonacina, *de peccat.* d. 2, quaest. 4, p. 2, § un. n. 21, Roncaglia, tract. 6, *de char.* c. 6, qu. 6, Tamburinius, *dec.*, l. 5, c. 1 § 4, n. 65 and Sporer in v. *praec.* c. 1, ex. n. 45). The reason that I rather prefer it, because although a prostitute would have an actual will to sin, still, certainly she imposes greater ruin to him in completing the work it is a particular sin of fornication. Therefore, a man that cooperates with her to consummate the sin, sins gravely in two ways, both against charity and against chastity, as will soon be more clear from what must be said below.

Furthermore, if the matter which is asked were indifferent, and can rightly be furnished without the sin of the other, such as to ask for a loan from a usurer, an oath from one that swears falsely, or a sacrament from a priest that is a sinner, and similar things:

The first opinion holds that it is not a grave sin to seek the aforesaid without a just cause. The reason is, because, as they say, when a usurious man, or a priest, etc. would already have a deliberate will to sin, one would not infer grave loss for himself if he were to propose an occasion in which a sin were carried out apart from his intention; for that anticipation of the his outward work would only accidentally differ. (de Lugo, *de just.* d. 25, ex. n. 234; Cajetan 2.2. q. 78, a. 4, et in *Summa* v. *Usura,* Soto, *loc. cit.,* dub. 1, Navarre, *summa* c. 17, n. 262, Sa, v. *Usura,* n. 5, likewise Arag., Ledesma, and others cited by Sanchez, *Dec.* l. 3, c. 8, n. 23, and Sanchez himself thinks it is probable, along with Pal. and Tamb).

Yet, *the second opinion,* which we embrace, holds it is a mortal sin both against charity and against the very virtue which the occasion is furnished to one's neighbor to wound, by seeking from him a loan, a sacrament, or an oath without a grave cause; for, were grave cause present, seeking it could altogether be excused, as St. Thomas teaches (2.2. quaest. 78, art. 4) with St. Aug. Elbel, *de scand.* n. 365, and other in common, cited by the Salamancans (*de contract.* c. 3, punct. 13, n. 120); because a man can licitly, for the sake of some notable good, permit the sin of another which comes about only from his malice. But seeking it without a just cause a man would sin firstly against charity, because it is the cause of a mortal sin, such as if his neighbor would suffer grave spiritual damage; while prescinding from the question as to whether an outward act would increase the malice of the internal act, as Scotus and his disciples hole (with Dupasq. *Theol.* tom. 4, disp. 2, quast. 5), because (as they say) integrity, or deformity of the outward act is different from the integrity of the internal act, since the outward and internal act are of a different reasoning, or whether, while the full will toward the sin remains, the outward act would add no malice to the internal act, as St. Thomas more probably holds (Gonet, *Clypeus*, to. 3, diss. 7, art. un., Estius, l. 2, dist. 42 § 2 and others) because the whole malice of the outward act consists in the will. But whatever the case is on that, even the Thomists, according to what Estius declares, say that it touches on the perpetration of an evil act the will is more effected to the thing desired, then without a doubt, by the outward work something is added to the malice, because then the malice of the will is increased. For that reason, although by speaking speculatively the opinion of the Thomists would be more probable, practically we still say that commonly from contingent circumstances through an outward act the malice of the will is always increased on accoung of the greater complacency, attempt, duration, etc., as Habert rightly notices (*de act. hum.* c. 8, q. 2). Hence, Estius (*loc. cit.* in fine) so concludes: "Moreover, because the outward act is really a sin, hence it happens that, as it must always be said he does more evil who perpetrates the sin by work than the one who continues it in the will alone." Therefore, when the sinner infers by an outward act a greater notable ruin to himself, he cannot be excused from grave sin against charity who cooperated in it without a grave cause to carry out the work, as Cont. Tourn. also says (*de praec. char.* sect. 7, punct. 1, § 2, in fine, *Ex his*): for charity does not oblige us to avoid grave damage of our neighbor as often as we can do it without notable inconvenience, and therefore we are indeed excused; but it is otherwise if the cause is light, and so much more if it is illicit or vain. (Busembaum, n. 49, Sanchez, *Dec.* l. 3, c. 8, n. 22, and 23, with Valentia, Arag., and Conrad., Sylvest. v. *Usura* 7, q. 1, Molina, tom. 2 *de just.* d. 335, concl. 4, Roncaglia, tr. 6, *de char.* c. 5, q. 6, Tamburinius *Dec.* l. 5, c. 1, § 4, n. 76, the Salamancans *de contract.* c. 3, punct. 13, n. 123, et tract. 21, c. 8, n. 123, with Palaus, Bann., and Trull., Bonacina *de pecc.* d. 2, q. 4, p. 2, n. 21, with Suarez, and Filliuci). Bonacina thinks the reasoning of the first opinion does not seem firm enough. Likewise Sporer (in V. praec. c.

1, n. 46, with St. Antoninus, Vasquez, Pontius Palud., Aug. and others authors cited). And Fr. Elbel follows the same opinion, *de scand.* n. 365, asserting this is common.

Still, Sporer (n. 47) with Lessius, Hurt. and others probably excuse from this sin against charity one seeking without a just cause a loan from one prepared to carry out usury, if the usurer on account of the multitude of those asking equally certainly and easily will furnish money to the other that is for usury; because then the obligation of impeding the sin is not present because he equally and certainly would carry it out otherwise. But we say, that seeking without a gave cause, even in the case just posed, would not excuse one from another grave sin against virtue, to which he induces his neighbor to mortally wound. And this, even if the cases were given, which practically we already said are morally impossible were to come about, that the malice of a neighbor prepared to sin would not be increased by an outward work. The reason is because without a just cause it is never lawful to cooperate to an objective evil, for to morally coincide, even if it is permissively, to an objectively evil act without a just cause, *per se* is always evil, according to how it is certain that to induce a madman to commit perjury or fornicate, etc., even if he does not sin, is a grave sin against the opposite virtues, as the doctors commonly say. (The Salamancans *de leg.* c. 3, punct. 4, n. 49, and Busembaum, n. 155, with Laymann, Bonacina, Palaus, Sanchez, Granadus, etc. Hence in the same way, asking without a grave cause a loan from a usurer, a sacrament from a priest that is a sinner, although prepared, he would sin not only against charity, but even against justice or religion, as the Salamancans say (*de contract.* c. 3, punct. 13, n. 123, et *de sacram. in genere* c. 8 punct. 2. n. 26), Sanchez, Becanus, with Sylvester, Molina, Valent. Palaus, Trull., Villal., Ban., Tap, cited by the Salamancans *loc. cit.,* n. 123, in fine.

However, Sporer (*loc. cit.* n. 75) and Pontius (*de matr.* l. 5, c. 18, n. 51) note with de Soto and Cajetan, that to licitly ask for a loan from a usurer a precise necessity is not required, rather any notable advantage suffices, either for conservation or for decency of state or family, say (as Pontius says with the same doctors) if a nobleman sought a loan to hold a tournament with his friends, and otherwise by abstaining he would incur some note.

ARTICLE II
Whether, and when, passive scandal can be permitted or on account of it avoiding something it ought to be omitted?

48. *When can passive scandal be permitted?*
49. *When does utility alone suffice to seek a loan from a usurer, and sacraments from an excommunicated minister, or a sinner?*
50. *Whether at some time we are held to omit or delay spiritual goods to avoid scandal of another?*
51. *Whether at some time we are held to omit certain precepts?*
52. *Whether we are held to dismiss temporal goods? Whether a woman would sin gravely wearing men's clothes? See ibid., other cases.*
53. *Whether a girl that is decently dressed would be held to avert herself from the sight of a particular man that desired her?*
54. *What if she would cloth herself in superfluous dress?*
55. *What if she thought some men in general were going to be scandalized? And would women sin gravely by showing their breasts?*
56. *How would one sin composing obscene things, either representing them or painting them?*
57. *Whether it is lawful to persuade to a lesser evil to avoid a greater?*

58. *Whether at some time it will be lawful to permit the ruin of one's neighbor?*

48.—"Resp. 1. Passive scandal cannot be permitted "without necessity either one's own advantage or that of "another. The reason is, because we are held by charity "to impede the sins of our neighbor if we can do it easily. "Laymann, c. 23, from the common opinion.

Thus the following cases are resolved:

"Without cause it is not permitted to seek a loan from a "usurer, or an oath from an infidel sworn by false gods, "the administration of the Sacrament from a priest that "has a concubine, or that he should celebrate; for they "cannot do those things without sin and one would "cooperate in their sin. Suarez, Sanchez, Trull., l. 2, c. 6, "dist. 5, n. 15.

49.—"Resp. 2. For the sake of necessity or advantage it "can be permitted. Clearly in the aforesaid case, it can be "done simply without sin; and therefore it is lawful to "seek such things for a reasonable cause, even if the "other would sin from malice. A greater necessity, "however, is required that the scandal of little ones "would be permitted, which is pharisaical. Likewise the "greater, if there are many that are going to be "scandalized, if a graver sin is feared, and therefore, if it "is certainly foreseen than otherwise. Laymann *loc. cit.,* "Bonacina, d. 2, q. 4, p. 2."

(From there it suffices for the cause of utility of some moment alone to seek a loan from a usurer, as Viva says from the common opinion, and the Salamancans, tr. 21, c. 8, punct. 5, § 3, n. 76, with Cajetan, Navarre, Bonacina, etc. and to seek the sacraments from a minister that is a public sinner or a tolerated excommunicate, as Laymann, *de char.* c. 13, n. 8, with Sanchez, and Navarre, from St. Thomas. See what was said in n. 47, and see also below, n. 77, v. 4, *Licitum*).

50.—"Resp. 3. It ought to be permitted if one would "otherwise put his own salvation in danger, or others, "especially if grave harm threatened the community. "This is why spiritual goods necessary to salvation "neither ought nor can ever be dismissed on account of "some scandal. Filliuci, 28, c. 8.

"Resp. 4: One is not held to omit or delay spiritual goods "(and according to Lorca, ap. Diana, p. 5, t. 7, r. 24, even "temporal) that are not necessary to salvation on account "of pharisaical scandal, according to what that verse in "Matthew 15:14, "Permit them, etc." still, except if the "fruit were hoped for from delay: but more easily and "more often to delay such goods or even omit them on "account of the scandal of little ones: *e.g.* entrance into "religious life ought to be delayed on account of scandal "to parents, if the consent for it were hoped for in a short "time. Laymann *loc. cit.*"

St. Thomas teaches (2.2. q. 43, art. 7) that at some time we are held to delay spiritual goods that are not necessary to salvation on account of scandal to little ones, but not on account of pharisaical scandal. Just the same, it must be noted from Laymann (*de char.* c. 13, n. 8) with St. Thomas, that scandal to little ones, after a warning becomes pharisaical. Hence, although someone ought to delay entrance into religion on account of scandal to neighbors, if the consent were hoped for in a short time, as Busembaum says, still, one can rightly enter if they continue to resist, as Laymann says with St. Antoninus, Palud., etc. (l.c. n. 8, in fine). But in regard to this point, see what is going to be said in book 5, n. 68.

And here it must be noted in addition that it is certain, (as the Salamancans say *de IV. precepto Decal.* cap. unic.

punct. 1 § 1, n. 7) that sons can, without the consent of the father, etner religion or take up the clerical state, especially if they know the father is going to impede them from carnal affect, which regularly happens, as Pinamon observes (*De vocatione*, c. 3, near the beginning). Hence, St. Thomas teaches in 2.2. quaest. 189 art. 6, in the article that "they sons can rightly enter religion while foregoing the assent of their parents even against their command." And in art. 10, he says that, "Sons ought not take counsel except from those from whom it is hoped that they will advance and not impede, by that verse 'Do not treat with an irreligious man about holiness and with an unjust man about justice' (Eccli. 37:12)." And in what was said in article 10, ad 2, he asserts St. Cyril, who on the words of the Gospel above: "Permit me to renounce these who are at home, etc." he so speaks: "To communicate with one's neighbors, he induces one still languishing and retrograde, on account of what he heard from the Lord: No man sending a hand to the plow and looking backwards, is suitable for the kingdom of God. He looks backwards, who seeks to delay with his neighbors." See other very useful things, which are said on this point in the cited place, book 5, n. 68. Then it is only not permitted to sons to enter religion when they would leave behind their parents in grave necessity, or brothers *in extrema*, as the Salamancans *de statu relig.* c. 3, punct. 3, § 2, n. 53, etc. with St. Thomas and the common teaching. Still, in doubt whether there is such a necessity the entry is permitted since in doubt, *libertas possidet*, as Sanchez teaches (*Decal.* l. 4, cap. 25, num. 6). See what will be said in book 5, n. 66.

> 51.—"Resp. 5. To avoid grave scandal to little ones
> "certain precepts ought not be fulfilled, unless that
> "omission would be more damaging than omitting. See
> "Laym, l. 2, t. 3, c. 13. The reason for this is, because then
> "a twofold precept coincides, viz. to beware of natural

"scandal as well as positive which is stronger and greater
"than the natural."

The question is, whether to avoid scandal to one's
neighbor must precepts be omitted? It is certain: I. that
precepts which cannot be omitted without sin, these must
never be foregone on account of scandal to another, or it
would be pharisaical from its malice, or to little ones from its
weakness, or ignorant. Of this sort are precepts of faith, and
the sacraments, which are necessary for salvation, as St.
Thomas teaches (2.2. qu. 43, art. 7), likewise, all natural
precepts; and although some doctors say sometimes natural
affirmative precepts can be omitted, namely to correct
sinners, or to punish delinquents, when damage is more
feared than the fruit is hoped for, still, what Palaus says is
better (de charit. t. 6, d. 6, p. 16), then it is truer in those cases
that the very precepts cease and do not oblige. It is certain:
II. That other positive precepts cannot also be omitted if
there is pharisaical scandal to one's neighbor, because then
the occasion is given instead to him to maliciously impede
the goods of others, as Sporer says (de 5 praec. cap. 1, n. 29),
from St. Thomas (d. q. 43, art. 8).

There is a doubt, however, as to whether positive
precepts must be omitted to avoid scandal of the weak?

The first opinion is probable, which several authors hold
(Navarre, *Summ.* c. 24, n. 44; Vasquez qu. 43, art. 7, d. 1;
Palaus, d. p. 16, n. 3; with A. de Leon, and Croix, l. 2, n. 244
as well as Tamburinius, *Dec.* l. 3, c. 2, n. 8 think it is
probable), rejects it, because both positive and human
precepts do not cause the obligation to cease when scandal
is not given, but taken, then the obligation to fulfill the
precepts enjoined upon one bind more than avoiding the
omission of a precept imposed on another.

But the *second opinion* is more probable and upholds this, which many doctors hold (Busembaum, Laymann, *de charit.* c. 3, n. 10, who calls it common; Melchior Cano *in rel. de poen.* p. 5, Suarez, disp. 10, *de scand.* sect. 4, n. 9; Cont. Tourn. *de charit.* sect. 7, punct. 1, § 3, concl. 1, *Dixi*; Roncaglia, *de char.* c. 6, qu. 7; Sporer, *de 5. praec.* c. 1, n. 29; and the Salamancans, tract. 21, c. 8, punct. 5, § 3, n. 87, with Valen., Sylv. Bann. Ledesma, Hurt., Med., Cord., and Lorca). The Salamancans also cite St. Thomas (*in dict.* art. 7). But really the Angelic Doctor does not speak there on precepts, but on spiritual goods, for which counsels must more truly be understood. The reasoning of this opinion is, that the general precept on avoiding scandal to one's neighbor, when it is natural, must be preferred to positive precepts. But because it would be a great inconvenience for a woman if she were held to abstain from Mass for a long time on account of scandal to another, the authors very probably say that she is not held to this, except for one or another in turn. (Laymann, *de charit.* c. 13, n. 10; Cont. Tourn. *loc. it.*, *Hunc tamen*; and Sporer, *dict.* c. 1, n. 29 et 37) On the contrary, Elbel holds (*de scand.*) with Ills. and many others, that she can well omit Mass once or twice, but she is not held to this when it would happen that the scandal were altogether from the malice of another.

Thus the following cases are resolved:

"1. Ecclesiastical prelates are not held (nay more cannot) "to omit those things which are necessary to preserve "the goods of the Church, *e.g.* the bans [*lites*], to avoid "pharisaical scandal, or even scandal to the weak, even "if the reason for their rectitude ought to be first "rendered. Diana, part. 5, t. 7, r. 24, from St. Thomas, "etc.

52.—*Quaeritur:* Whether to avoid scandal temporal goods must be dismissed? St. Thomas makes the distinction and teaches in 2.2. qu. 43, art. 8 that if the goods are one's own, "then they must be totally dismissed, or the scandal must be otherwise pacified, viz. by some advisory," for after mention has been made on the truth of justice, scandal evades the category of pharisaical, on which no more care must be taken, as St. Thomas teaches in the same place. Nay more, Palaus (*de charit.* tom. 6, d. 6, p. 17); Sanchez (*Dec.* lib. 1, c. 7, n. 11) and Sporer (*de V. praec.* c. 1, n. 32) with Suarez, Diana, etc., say there is never a grave obligation to suffer a great loss in one's own goods lest a neighbor would suffer scandal, even from weakness. The reason is because charity toward one's neighbor does not oblige with such an inconvenience. In this way it proceeds more if the goods were consigned to preserve, as the goods of the Church are consigned to prelates, and like things, for the goods cannot also be dismissed on account of scandal to another, as private goods can be. Although, as the authors rightly warn, exaction ought to be delayed for those things until debtors are instructed about their obligation. (Laymann, *de charit.* c. 13, n. 9, with St. Antoninus, Palud, and Sporer *loc. cit.*, d. n. 32). St. Anoninus, Cajetan, and Val, cited by Laymann, say that if still, after a *monitum* to the people, the scandal would not cease and a great loss of spiritual fruit were to threaten, then it is better for the prelate to so conduct himself if he were to procure the assent of the Church, that the debt would be remitted. Nevertheless, Laymann rightly says on this to examine the circumstances both of dismissing the goods and of the scandal that will come about, and lest perhaps from the remission the malice of the debtors would be more increased: for St. Thomas addresses that case (d. art. 8), saying: "On account of pharisaical scandal, temporal goods must not be released, because this would also harm the common good; the occasion of plundering would be given to the wicked, and it would harm those snatching them up because by retaining someone else's goods they would remain in sin."

"2. If a woman wears men's cloths, or vice versa, only
"from levity without a wicked intention or danger of
"scandal and lust, it will only be a venial sin; otherwise
"it is mortal, but not if from necessity. Diana, part. 5, tr.
"7, r. 32, from St. Thomas, Sylvius, etc.

If a woman were to use men's clothes, of itself it is not a
grave sin; but it could be a grave sin from the circumstances
of the danger of lust, or scandal, as Laymann (*de charit.* d.
cap. 13, in fin.), Sylvius, the Cont. Tourn. *de 6. decal.*
praecept. art. 7, sect. 3, *Quaeres* 3, and the Salamancans tract.
21, d. c. 8, punct. 5, § 2, n. 62. And St. Thomas indicates this
in 2.2. q. 169, a. 2, ad 3, where he says: "Of itself, it is vicious
if a woman uses men's clothes or vice versa, and especially
because this is the cause of wantonness and it is specially
forbidden in the law (Deut. c. 22) because the Gentiles use
such a change of garb for the superstition of idolatry.
Nevertheless, at some time this can be done without sin on
account of some necessity, or for the sake of hiding oneself
from enemies, or on account of a defect of another garment,
or something else of this sort." Otherwise, it is only venial,
and sometimes nothing, if there were a just cause, *e.g.* to
conceal themselves, as St. Thomas teaches, as well as
Laymann, with Navarre and Cajetan, who say the precept of
Deut. 22 because the ceremonial law has ceased.

"3. It is a sin from which the confessor in confession
"(still, from weakness) one knows is rarely scandalized,
"one ought to hold off from speaking. Laymann, *loc. cit.,*
"from Navarre, etc.

"4. A wife ought to omit fasting once or again if her
"husband is gravely offended by it and discord will arise.
"*Ibid.*

"5. If, when you go to Mass on a feast day grave quarrels
"or feuding must be aroused, one is not held to go. *Ibid.*

"6. A superior can often ignore the sins of a subject to "avoid tumults and greater evils, which he would "otherwise be held to punish.

53.—"7. A woman that knows in her self, or in her "appearance something in particular that will cause "scandal, she sins mortally if after it were given attention "she offered herself to be gazed upon; and therefore she "may and must abstain not only from public but even "from Mass on a feast day once or again to avoid that "sin. I said: a) *something in particular*, because on "account of the fear of some scandal to abstain from the "community in general or even of a great many would be "too difficult, and full of scruples. I said: b) *once or again*, "because often it would be too grave and hard to do it "often. Bonacina, Sanchez, Laymann *loc. cit.* n. 10 and "others. See Diana, part. 5, tr. 7, r. 21 and 22 where he "cites to the contrary some authors denying the "obligation to forego a thing that is commanded to avoid "the scandal of others.

So if it is a question of omitting commanded things, namely for a girl to miss Mass lest she would offer herself to the sight of a young man that she knows foully lusts after her, according to what was related in n. 51, she ought to once and later again omit Mass, but probably also according to the other first opinion that was advanced, as Tamburinius says (*Dec.* lib. 4, cap. 2, n. 8) one could rightly, nay more is held, not withstanding scandal to him, to go to Church to hear Mass.

But if it is a question on a thing that was not commanded, it is asked whether a girl would sin mortally, offering herself to the be seen in the sight of the man that is going to suffer scandal? St. Antoninus, Sylvius, Navarre, Azor, etc. say yes, with Busembaum, cited by Sanchez, *Dec.* lib. 1, cap. 6, n. 16, who asserts this is less common, when she offers herself, having no other reasonable cause, say, to visit friends, to go to Church, etc. But those who deny that she sins gravely hold a very probable opinion. (Cajetan, 2.2. qu. 154 art. 4, in fin. and qu. 169, a. 2, ad 5; Sanchez, *loc. cit.* n. 17, with Navarre, Medina, and Azor, likewise Sporer, *de 5 praec.* cap. 1, n. 34 and 35, with Armill. and Palaus, Lessius lib. 4, n. 113; the Salamancans tract. 21, cap. 8, punct. 5, § 2, n. 59, and Croix thinks it is probable (lib. 2, n. 247), with Bonacina and Diana). For it suffices, as they say, to excuse her at least from mortal sin, by reason that she should not be deprived of her freedom, since on her side she does not give scandal, rather, it is taken from the malice of the man; and in turn it would be exceedingly inconvenient to the woman, and make her liable to scruples if she ought to always determine whether she has a just reason to go out or not. Moreover, as Palaus (t. 6, d. 6 part. 7 n. 4), Sanchez (d. n. 17), and Sporer (n. 35) rightly say, I could not excuse her from mortal sin if she were lead by vanity even if she did not intend the scandal of that man after he has noticed her were she to offer herself to his sight. Hence, Sporer and Diana rightly say, with Hurt., that a woman is held under grave scandal of the determined man to avoid him if she can conveniently go to another Church, set out on another road, stay away from the window, and other things. Nevertheless, this must not be understood for a long time, but only for one or another time, until the other man could take notice that she avoids him, as we said in n. 51; Sporer (n. 37) asserts, saying all consent on this point. I also could not excuse the woman from mortal sin if she went to some place which she would not go to unless she knew the lover would be there, as Sporer rightly notes (n. 35).

54.—"8. A woman that probably foresees from her dress, "even if it is suited to her state, that someone in "particular is going to fall mortally, she is held to not "wear it for a short time, or to flee the sight of such a

"man. I said *for a short time*, because for a long one, it
"would hardly be grave. See Diana, *loc. cit.*

The Salamancans (tract. 21, cap. 8, n. 59, with Cajetan,
Trull., Palaus, Navarre, etc. assert that in no way does the
woman sin by dressing according to her condition; if this
was done to please her husband or that she might find a
bridegroom, as St. Thomas also teaches (2.2. qu. 169, a. 2), or
only lest she would be deprived of her freedom. (The
Salamancans *ibid.* n. 60). But this must always be understood
for a long time, otherwise she is held to abstain at least once
or twice from the sight of the young man that lusts after her,
according to what was said recently in n. 53.

"9. But if the same were feared in particular from
"superfluous dress, vanity and unsuitability (which to
"assume for the sake of vanity and pleasure that they
"would appear beautiful, and might more easily discover
"a suitor, which is nothing more than venial), would be
"held to altogether dismiss their dress, even under
"mortal sin; because they have no right to that dress and
"on the other hand she is held to avoid the sin of
"another, when it can be done conveniently. See Sylv., v.
"Ornatus."

(Others say the same thing; the Salamancans *loc. cit.* and
Laymann, tr. 3, cap. 13, in fine; Lessius lib. 4, cap. 4, n. 112
only thinks that women are held to abstain from superfluous
dress for a short time. Not, however, here what St. Thomas
teaches in 2.2. qu. 169, art. 2, where he says women desiring
to please men from vanity, only seen venially whenever they
do it. But in his commentary on the first epistle to Timothy,
chapter 2, the Angelic doctor so speaks: "simple dress, with
right intention, custom and condition of state preserved, is
not a sin. But with regard to make-up it is always a sin; for
women are not permitted to be elegantly dressed except on
account of men, and men refuse to be deceived, as a
powdered woman would appear to them.)

"Nevertheless, others, such as Cajetan, Navarre, cap. 23,
"seem to teach that they are only held under venial sin
"(but less probably), when in a particular case a fall is
"foreseen and they must abstain for a short time; they
"also, with Azor, Lessius and Bonacina, excuse them
"from mortal sin who by the custom of the place uncover
"half their breast, or use powder, makeup, or wigs;
"provided that they only intend greater adornment of
"beauty, not wantonness for others, without any other
"end that would be mortal, or something under a
"particular law forbidding it under mortal sin.
"Nevertheless, they add that the custom of uncovering
"their breast or only lightly covering them is a grave
"matter and a mortal sin where it is not introduced.
"Navarre, n. 19, Lessius, 112, Laymann, *loc. cit.*, etc. See
"Bonacina, *de matr.* quaest. 4, p. 9, n. 17.

55.—"If a woman would think, not in a particular case
"but in general, that only some were going to be
"scandalized over her, provided she did not intend their
"lasciviousness and she would not be pleased by it
"(although it would please her that she is praised as
"beautiful), it does not seem she is held to abstain from
"that ornate dress, even if it is superfluous, under pain of
"mortal sin, *e.g.* by powdering her face; nay more, even
"by exposing part of her breast from the common
"custom, unless the uncovering, or ornateness would be
"exceedingly foul *per se*, and directly provoke one to lust.
"The reason is, not only because it is a scandal that is
"rather taken than given, and that dress and beauty only
"remotely provoke to sin, as Laymann and Bonacina
"teach; but even because it would be exceedingly grave
"for that sex, especially if they seek a marriage, or to
"perpetually abstain, since that occasion is universal and
"perpetual, and because more beautiful women would
"never licitly be able to travel outside since natural

"beauty would cause more harm than the artificial. For
"more on this matter, see Diana, t. 1, r. 30 and Bardel.,
"lib. 3, d. 5, n. 13.

"Nevertheless, a woman bearing a naked chest but not
"from a bad intention, even if some would excuse her
"from mortal sin, still 'I would absolve her with
difficulty,' Sa says. And it is certain that it is incumbent
"on the confessor to dissuade and deter her from dress of
"this sort. See Sa, *verb. Ornatus*, etc., ll.cc.

Quaeritur: Whether women would sin gravely showing
their breasts as part of their dress? Nöel Alexander (*dec.* l. 4,
a. 5, reg. 8 *de scandalo*) and Roncaglia (*de charit.* cap. 6, qu.
5, resp. 3) bitterly inveigh against this custom, saying that
this is a mortal sin *per se*, because it gives grave scandal to
others *per se*; and this is proved, they say, from the Holy
Fathers, who rebuke a custom of this sort with great effort.

When I held the office of a preacher, I also tried with
great energy to reproach this pernicious use many times.
Yet, since here I function as a writer on moral science it is
fitting that I say what I think according to the truth, and
what I learned from the doctors. I do not deny: I. That these
women who introduced this custom somewhere would have
sinned gravely. I do not deny: II. That the uncovering of
their breast can be so immoderate, that *per se* it could not be
excused from grave scandal, just as it exceedingly provokes
to wantonness, as Sporer rightly says (*de V. praec.*, cap. 1, n.
39). But I do say: III. That if the uncovering were not so
immoderate, and the custom is present somewhere so that
women have followed it, it should certainly be reproached
but not altogether condemned as a mortal sin. The most
common opinion of the doctors holds this. (Navarre,
Cajetan, Lessius, Laymann, Bonacina, the Salamancans and
many others). Navarre says: "Women do not sin mortally
when showing their naked breasts because they seem more
beautiful, without any evil mortal intention; because it is

forbidden by no natural, divine or human law, at least obliging to mortal sin." (*summ.* cap. 23, n. 19). Cajetan says the same thing in 2.2. qu. 169, art. 2, on the vers. *Secundo*: "Women in some place that bear a nude chest, because according to the custom of the country it is not of itself a mortal sin." Lessius says the same thing in book 4, cap. 4, ex. n. 112, saying: "It can be a deadly sin if shameful things are not sufficiently defended against; otherwise, in uncovering the chest, as Cajetan, Fum., Navarre, for that part neither nature nor shame demands be absolutely covered.

Nevertheless, it would be a grave sin to introduce a custom of this sort. Laymann (lib. 3, tr. 3, c. 13, *in fin.* n. 6) says this opinion is common. Azor thinks the same thing (*de 4. praec.* c. 18), as do other authors. (Sanchez, *dec.* lib. 1, c. 6, n. 7; Bonacina, *de matrim.* quaest. 5, punct. 9, n. 17) and the Salamancans *de vi. praec.* c. 3, punct. 1, n. 16, with Sylvius, Filliuci, etc., against St. Antoninus, Ros., and Eliz). This is because (they say) the chest is not a part vehemently provoking to wantonness. St. Thomas also seems to adhere to this in 2.2. qu. 169, art. 2, where speaking on superfluous dress of women (as is clear from the third objection), he says: "And if indeed they dress themselves by this intention, that they would provoke others to lust, they would sin mortally. But if it is from a certain levity or even from a certain vanity on account of boasting, it is not always a mortal sin, but at some time venial." Then he adds: "Nevertheless, in such a case some could be excused from sin when this is not done from some vanity, but on account of a contrary custom; although such a custom would not be praiseworthy." Moreover, Roncaglia mocks this reason of an excusing custom, saying: "Could each custom give the right to that which for others, by its nature, offers a grave occasion of sin?" But he unduly mocks it, for it is clear that the custom to so follow, would not indeed give a right to that which is against the law of nature, rather it would rightly diminish the force of concupiscence; for where there is not custom, those women will give greater scandal that show their arms or legs than those that show the chest (provided the uncovering were moderate), where such a custom is in force, because the use causes men to be less moved to concupiscence from such a sight, which is certain from experience. Next, the Fathers spoke either by the mode of preaching or on immoderate use, as we said above. At length, the same Roncaglia concedes that a modest uncovering of the breast excuses from grave sin. And the most learned Sylvius teaches the same thing (2.2. q. 169, a. 2). Moreover, I do not doubt that it would be fitting for a prudent confessor to use the opinion related above with great discretion, lest he would grant too much license to women, which involves lust, since those living piously do not so follow this custom. For, what Croix observes (lib. 2, n. 248) with Eliz., that women of this sort by uncovering their breast do not rarely seek to be desired by men, so the latter would be enraptured and captivated by them, and Eliz. rightly thinks for this reason many women suffer damnation. Hence, I do not doubt that an indecent custom of this sort should be zealously restrained and rooted out by preachers and confessors as often as it can be done. Let us hear what St. Antoninus teaches (p. 2, tit. 4, cap. 5) where, although he earnestly detests the use of women showing their breasts, when such a use was very immoderate, exactly as he relates it was present in parts of the Rhine, in these words: "For if, it is from the use of the country that women wear clothing open at the neck even to the showing of the breasts, as in parts of the Rhine, such a use is exceedingly foul and unchaste, and therefore must not be preserved." Still, in the following paragraph, § *In quantum,* he adds: "For, if a woman dresses herself according to the decency of her state and the custom of the country, and there was not much excess, then those looking with lust at her will cause an occasion rather of taking [scandal] than giving it; which is why not to the woman, but to the man lone who falls to ruin, will it be imputed as a mortal sin. However, such an excess will be able to be such which will be an occasion also for giving scandal." At length, he concludes: "So from the aforesaid it seems it must be said that where in dress of this sort the confessor clearly discovers it is without a doubt a mortal sin, he should not absolve such a woman unless she were to purpose to abstain from such a crime. But if he cannot clearly perceive whether it is a mortal sin, then it does not seem a damning sentence should be given (as Guillelm. says on a certain similar species), namely that he should refuse absolution on this account, or belabor their conscience with a mortal sin, because by doing that should the person act against it later, even if it was not mortal, it will be for them because everything which is against conscience paves the way to hell (28 q. 1, § *Et his*). The laws should be more prompt to loose than bind (cap. *Ponderet*, dist. 1) and it is better for a master to render an account for excessive mercy than for excessive severity, as Chrysostom says (cap. *Alligant* 26, qu. 7), so it seems they should rather be absolved and forgiven in the divine tribunal. Still, I declare that both preachers in preaching and confessors in hearing confessions ought to detest such things and persuade them to be laid aside, when they are very excessive; still, not to assert so obscurely that they are mortal sins.

56.—"11. They would also sin gravely who compose, "describe, represent or paint foul things meant to "provoke lust. Bonacina, Sanchez, Filliuci."

It is beyond doubt that composing or putting on plays that are extremely indecent cannot be excused from grave sin. Sanchez (*de matr.* lib. 9, d. 46, n. 42) with St. Antoninus, Ang., Sylvius, etc., Nor on account of any profit, as Tamburinius says (*dec.* cap. 8, § 5, n. 1).

They equally sin that paint or publicly show obscene images, in which abominable things are found, or to be covered by a light veil. The Salamancans tr. 21, c. 8, punct. 5, § 2, n. 64, with Sanchez, Trull. It is otherwise if where other parts are detected, indecency is covered. The Salamancans, *ibid.*, with Turr., Diana, and many others.

57.—Whether it is lawful to persuade or permit a lesser evil to avoid a greater one?

The first opinion rejects this, according to what Laymann (*de char.* c. 12, n. 7) holds, with Azor and others. The reason is, because the comparative does not abolish the positive; for this reason, one who persuades a lesser evil, truly persuades an evil. Laymann and Azor place the limitation, unless the evil would be virtually included in the other greater act. So, if you could persuade a man prepared to kill someone that he should only cut off his hand, nevertheless it is the same thing, but not planned by the other. So also for one wishing to commit adultery if you could persuade him to commit fornication with someone that was free in general, but not in particular. The Salamancans admit this (*loc. cit.* § 1, n. 58) provided he would decide to carry out both evils. (with Navarre, etc.) But Laymann instinctively says (as well as Sanchez with the second opinion, as will soon be said), that he expressly rejects this limitation because (as he says) then a lesser evil is proposed, not that he would perpetrate another, but that he would withdraw from the greater.

The Second opinion is more probable and holds it is licit to persuade a lesser evil if the other is determined to carry out a greater evil. The reason is because the one persuading does not seek an evil, but a good, namely the choice of a lesser evil. (Sanchez, *de matrim.* lib. 7, d. 11, n. 15, with de Soto, Molina, Navarre, Medina, Sylvest. and many others, and the Salamancans *loc. cit.* with Cajetan, Soto, Palaus, Bonacina, etc; Croix thinks it is probable, lib. 2, n. 223, moreover, Sanchez teaches the same thing in n. 19, with

Cajetan, de Soto, Vocar, Valent.). It is licit to persuade a man prepared to kill someone that he should steal from someone instead, or that he should fornicate. And the defenders of this opinion argue it from St. Augustine (in c. *Si quod verius*, caus. 33, q. 2) where he says: "If he is going to do something that is not lawful, now he might commit adultery and not murder, and while his wife is living he marries another, and does not shed human blood." From such words, "now he might commit adultery," Sanchez proves (dict. n. 15), with de Soto, Molina, Navarre, Abb., etc., that the Holy Doctor spoke not only about permitting, but even persuading. And Sanchez adds this (n. 23) with Salon, it is not only lawful for individuals, but even for confessors, parents, and others, to whom the duty is incumbent to impede the sins of subordinates.

58.—"Resp. 6. The ruin of one's neighbor can be "permitted at some point, when he is prepared for an evil "and the other man does not intend to sin but only to "permits one sin by not removing the occasion, lest "many would be committed, so that the permission "would impede a greater evil.

Thus the following cases are resolved.

"1. It is permitted for a proprietor to not remove the "occasion to steal to his sons or servants when, just the "same, they are inclined to steal, and he knows they are "prepared so that being caught they should be punished "and become reasonable again; for then he reasonably "permits one theft to stop many more. Sanchez, "Laymann, Bonacina."

(And this opinion seems sufficiently common with Sanchez, *de matrim.* lib. 10, d. 12, n. 52, who cites for this de Soto, Ledesma, Navarre, Sa, etc. and St. Thomas aggress in

Supp. 3, part. q. 62, art. 3, ad 4, where he says: "At some time a man that has a wife he suspects of adultery should lay a trap for her that he could take her with witnesses to the crime of fornication so he can proceed to the accusation." Cont Tourn. admits the same thing *de charit.* sect. 7, punct. 1, § 3 in fin with Antoine).

"2. It is probable that it is not licit to place such things "further, or object to them because it would positively "coincide with the sin; and not as much to take away the "occasion as to place it (Sa, v. *Pecccatum*), and Sanchez, "who teaches on the same case that it is not lawful for a "husband to give his wife an opportunity for adultery, or "unchastity, as he would tempt is wife. At the same time, "Laymann probably teaches the contrary (lib. 2, t. 3, c. "13). It can be confirmed by the example of Judith, who "scarcely seems to have done otherwise, (c. 9). For, when "she knew the permission of lust in Holofernes would "impede other evils, she placed the occasion before him, "namely her dress, otherwise licit, and still it is "commonly thought she did not sin in this. See Bonacina, "d. 2, q. 4, p. 2, and Palaus."

And Viva (de IV praec. q. XI, art. 5, n. 12, vers. *Infertur IV*), as well as Laymann (*de charit.* c. 13, n. 5, with Fr. Navarre) also think this is probable. Likewise Elbel (*de scand.* n. 377), and Sporer (*de V. praec.* c. 1, n. 65), with Diana and Tamburinius, and he proves it from *l. Si quis servus, et de furtis*; where it is permitted for a master to give to his servant a thing he has always been anxious to steal, "That he would give to the thief that so taken as a thief with the furtive thing, and punished, he would no longer be anxious for it." Sporer says such a text has place even in the forum of conscience, with Fr. Navarre, Palaus, Tamburinius Still, Sanchez (*de matrim.* lib. 10, d. 12, n. 53, with Sa, Bonacina (*de scand. d.* 2. q. 4, p. 2, n. 34), and Sporer speak against this, calling the former more probable because (as they say) this seems positive induction, or cooperation with sin, which is intrinsically evil. Yet, this not withstanding, the first opinion seems sufficiently probable, because when a husband, or a proprietor offers the occasion to commit adultery or theft, they do not truly induce someone to sin but offer the occasion, and permit the sin of another for a just cause, viz. to preserve unharmed from the danger of meeting loss. For it is one thing to induce, but another to offer the occasion. The former is intrinsically evil, but not the latter; otherwise it would never be licit, even for a just cause, to seek a loan from a usurer, an oath from an infidel, etc., which is against the common opinion of the doctors (whatever someone might say) and against St. Thomas (following St. Augustine, in 2.2. q. 78, a. 4). Wherefore, St. Thomas there gives this rule: "To induce a man to sin is in no way permitted; still, to use the sin of another for a good is licit." Nay more, the Angelic Doctor seems to also adhere to the opinion recently advanced, by the example of ten men who said to Ismael (Jerem. 41:8) "Do not kill us, because we have treasure in the field." And the holy doctor asserted they did not sin.

ARTICLE III

Whether it would be lawful to materially cooperate in the sin of another.

59. *When might it be licit to materially cooperate in the sin of one's neighbor?*

60. *Whether it might be lawful to contract marriage with a spouse that remains in mortal sin, or obliged by a vow of chastity?*

61. *Whether one may render the debt to the same?*

62. *Whether it is permitted to give communion to an occult sinner?*

63. *What is lawful for servants? And what might be material and formal cooperation?*

64. *Would it be lawful to accompany a master to a brothel, etc., and a concubine to his master?*

65. *Is it lawful to convey the gifts to a courtesan?*

66. *Is it lawful to open the door for a harlot? Is it lawful to bring a ladder so that one's master might ascend to a woman?*

67. *Would it be lawful to write love letters?*

68. *Is it lawful to supply meat on a forbidden day?*

69. *Would it be lawful for inn keepers to give wine to drunkards, or meat on a forbidden day? See other matters cited in Busembaum.*

70. *Whether it is lawful to arrange a house for a harlot and a usurer?*

71. *Whether it would be lawful to sell dice, swords, poisons, etc.?*

72. *Is it lawful to sell a lamb to a Jew?*

73. *Would it be lawful for Christian captives to return, etc.*

74. *Would it be lawful to help a tyrant?*

75. *Would it be lawful to carry provisions to heretics? Or for coach drivers to transport a harlot?*

76. *Would it be lawful to receive gifs from a lover? To return a sword to a murderer?*

77. *Would it be lawful to seek an oath from a perjurer? And a loan from a usurer without grave cause?*

78. *Would it be lawful to help a usurer? Or give a loan to a squanderer?*

79. *Would it be lawful to seek sacraments from an excommunicated priest, or a public sinner, and from those prepared to sin?*

80. *Would it be lawful to give forbidden foods?*

59.—"*Resp.* To cooperate only materially by furnishing "only the material and faculty to sin, or by showing the "object, it is permitted if the following conditions are "present: I. If your work, or cooperation were good "*secundum se,* or at least indifferent; II. If it is done from "a good intention and a reasonable cause, and not that "you would help another sin; III. If you cannot impede "the sin of the other, or at least you are not held to for a "reasonable cause. In regard to which Sanchez and "Laymann note, even if its gravity cannot be defined by "a certain rule, but must be measured by a judgment of "the prudent, nevertheless, it is required so much graver: "1) how much graver the sin is whose occasion is given; "2) how much more probable it is that you are not going "to sin by cooperation with the other, or how much "more certain is the affect for the sin; 3) how much more "near your cooperation touches upon the sin; 4) how "much less of a right you have to such a sin; 5) at length, "how much more the sin is opposed with justice, and on "account of the damage of the third: Laymann, l. 2, tr. "3, c. 13.

St. Antoninus, Gabr., Sylvest. etc., cited by Sanchez, in *Decal.* l. 1, c. 7, n. 4, seem to think that in no case is it licit to cooperate with the sin of another: but the doctors commonly permit this if the due conditions are present. See Tamb, *Dec.* l. 5, c. 1, § 4. Also, Sanchez thinks the cited authors spoke about a case in which there was no just cause excusing one; or when the cooperation is intrinsically evil. Further, that action is always intrinsically evil, which is determined of itself to sin, as it would be to seek a concubine for one's master, to fabricate idols, and something similar. Otherwise, if an action can be done without sin, say, to supply at table, to open a door, etc. So, to licitly cooperate with the evil of another, *see the requisite conditions* cited with Busembaum, as above.

Thus the following cases are resolved:

60.—"1. In this mode a bride materially cooperates "contracting with a bridegroom whom she knows "receives the sacrament in mortal sin: but knowing him "to have a vow of chastity she sins by contracting with "him because it is illicit to agree to the contract. "Laymann, *l. c.* from Sanchez, l. 7, *de matr.* d. 11, n. 11.

61.—"2. A wife also licitly materially cooperates after "matrimony has been contracted, if she renders the debt "to her husband bound by a vow of chastity; nay more, "she is held to if from justice, she could not dissuade him "from his purpose of exacting it. *Ibid.*

(And this is the most common and more probable opinion with Suarez, de Lugo, Laymann, Bonacina, Palaus, Sanchez, Concina, Holzmann, Boss., etc., although the opposed with Pontius, Croix, Comit., Sylvius, etc. is also probable, see what will be said in book 6, n.944).

62.—"3. Similarly, a parish priest licitly may and must "administer the Eucharist to a sinner, an excommunicate, "and a secret heretic if he were to ask publicly; nay "more, a confessor ought to offer it to such a one seeking "it, even privately, if he knows of his sin from confession "alone. *Ibid.* (And so it must be held from the very "common opinion with Sporer, *de Sacr. poen.* n. 869, etc. "against Petrocor. See what is going to be said in book 6, "n. 658).

63.—"4. Servants are excused from sin if, by reason of "their servitude, they furnish certain services which they "could not refuse without grave inconvenience; *e.g.* to "clothe their master, to prepare the horse, to accompany "him to the brothel, to a courtesan, to convey gifts to the "courtesan or open the door for her when she comes, "because these stand remotely to the sin and can be done

"by them without sin. Nevertheless, it does not follow
"that it is licit for anyone else to furnish these things.
"Bonacina, p. 11, cap. 26, Azor, t. 2, l. 12, c. ult., q. 8;
"Laymann l. 2, tr. 3, c. 13; Sanchez, l. 1, *mor.* c. 7, n. 21."
(But see what follows in n. 64).

Moreover, to distinguish when the cooperation is
material, and when it is formal, some say (such as Cardenas,
and M. Milante in *prop. 51* Innoc. XI) that the cooperation is
material when it *per accidens* and remotely conduces the sin
of another. On the other hand, it is formal when, *per se* or on
account of some attached circumstance, it proximately
conduces to the execution of a sin, although in itself it would
be indifferent. Rather, it must be said better with others that
it is formal which agrees with the evil will of another, and
cannot be without sin; but the material that which agrees
only to the bad action of another, apart from the intention of
cooperation. Moreover, this is licit when, *per se* the action is
good or indifferent and when there is a just and
proportionate cause present to the gravity of the sin of
another, and to the proximate agreement which is furnished
for the execution of the sin. The reason is, because when you
furnish an indifferent action without a wicked intention, if
another means to abuse it to carry out his sin, you are not
held to impede it except from charity; and because charity
does not oblige with grave inconvenience, therefore placing
your cooperation with a just cause, you do not sin; for then
the sin of another does not come into being from your
cooperation, but from the malice of the one who abuses your
cation. Nor can it be said that your action, even if it is
indifferent, but joined with the circumstances of an evil
intention of another, would evade evils, for really your
action is not *per se* joined with the evil will of another, but
he joins his evil will with your action; wherefore your action
will not then be the cause *per se* leading to sin, but only the

occasion which he abused to sin. See what is going to be said in book 4, n. 571.

64.—*Quaeritur* I. Could a servant, by reason of his servitude, accompany his master to a brothel or prepare the horse? Busembaum affirms, with Navarre, Man., etc. (cited by Sanchez, *Dec.* l. 1 cap. 7, n. 22). But more probably the reason of servitude does not suffice, even if without the help of the servant the master would go there; at least grave fear of loss would be required. So think Sanchez, *l.c.*, Viva (in prop. 51 Inn. XI, n. 5), the Salamancans (tract. 21 c. 8, n. 72) who rightly notice that it is never lawful, if the master would be rendered more furious from the accompaniment. Would it be lawful for a servant to lead a concubine to the house of his master? Sanchez (*l.c.* n. 25, with Navarre and Man.) says that if there had already been sexual relations between the master and the concubine then he would be excused by reason of his servitude when the master already committed the sin equally without the servant (otherwise he would not be excused except by reason of fear of grave loss, as Sanchez says in n.22). And he says he same in n. 23, on a servant leading a concubine in a coach or carrying chair. But Cardenas and Milante, as well as Concina (t. 2, pag. 284 and 285) rightly do not admit it. And it must so much the more not be admitted for a servant calling a concubine to the house of his master, against Azor. And I say the same thing about the coachmen and sailors conveying the harlot to her lover, who can only be excused on account of grave fear of loss; see n. 75.

65.—*Quaretur:* II. Would it be lawful for a servant to convey gifts from a courtesan by reason of his service? The doctors affirm it, by speaking only about food and other small presents. (Busembaum and Sanchez, lib. 1, cap. 7, n. 29; Sporer *de 5 praec.* cap. 1 n. 99 and Palaus *de char.* p. 11 n. 4 with Navarre and Azor. But Fr. Concina reckons more truly

(t. 2 p. 284) that this is intrinsically evil, because really the gifts *per se* foster indecent love.

66.—*Quaeritur* III. Whether it were permitted for a servant to open the door for a courtesan? Croix rejects this (lib. 2, n. 253) but the more common opinion affirms it (the Salamancans d. cap. 8, n. 74; Laymann, *de charit.* c. 13 resp. 5; Tamburinius with Sanchez, Diana, Azor, Sa, Rodriguez, etc.). Nor is this opinion impeded by Innocent XI's condemnation of the 51 proposition, which says: "A servant who, after lowering his shoulders to knowingly help his master ascend through the window to deflower a virgin, and as many times as he would assist him by carrying the latter, opening the door or some similar cooperation, he does not sin mortally if he does it from fear of notable detriment, say, lest he would be treated badly by his master, should be looked upon with fierce eyes, or lest he should be expelled from the house." For the "by opening the door" is, from the very context, understood about opening accomplished by force, as the authors rightly say, for without him opening it, another would be present to do so. (Roncaglia, *de char.* tract. 6, *in reg. pro praxi* n. 4, post cap. 6; the Salamancans *ibid.* n. 74.

Quaeritur: IV. Whether it would be lawful for a servant, out of fear of death or great loss, to lower his shoulders or to carry a ladder to his master ascending to fornicate, or to open the door by force and similar things? Several reject this, because, as they say, such actions are never permitted inasmuch as they are intrinsically evil. (Viva, Milante *in dict. prop. 51*; Concina; t. 2, pag. 280; the Salamancans *ibid.* n. 75; Croix lib. 2, n. 244; and others). Yet, other theologians oppose this, whose opinion after considering reason, seems more probable to me. (Busembaum, *infra* n. 68; Sanchez, *dict.* c. 7, n. 22 and Lessius, l. 2 cap. 16, n. 59). The reason is because, as we recently said above, when you furnish an action that is indifferent *per se*, viz., which can be good and evil, you are not held except by charity to abstain from it lest another would abuse it to sin; when, however, you fear otherwise grave harm, you can licitly permit the sin of another; for on the one hand charity does not oblige you to avert his sin with grave harm, and on the other the malice of the other man cannot change the nature of your action so that from an indifferent act it intrinsically goes into evil. And the learned author of the Continuation of Tournely agrees with me (*de furto et restit. item de charit.* sect. 7, punct. 1, § 3, Quaer. 1), saying: "I am not held to suffer grave detriment to avert the sin of another, for rightly the other man imputes his malice to himself." Nor can it be said that the aforesaid actions are evil in themselves because they cooperate with sinful sexual relations; and it is proved from the very condemned proposition, where it is said "or some similar cooperation." For the response is, "by cooperation" it is not understood on formal cooperation, but material, since the authors only spoke on formal cooperation, and in such a sense the proposition was certainly proscribed. But not by the words, "if he would do it from fear of notable detriment," is fear of death understood, there it is declared that such fear as "to be treated badly by his master, or to receive angry glances, to be expelled from the house," such evils certainly do not embrace the injury of death. Still, because the aforesaid cooperation truly coincides with the sin of sexual relations, although they only materially coincide with the sin of the fornicator, I think no other fear excuses the one cooperating than that of death, for otherwise, only on account of fear of the opportunity of loss or infamy, it is not permitted to assist with the dishonor of deflowering a virgin. See what is going to be said in book 4, n. 571, where we will say that it is equally not lawful for you to give the ladder, or keys to a thief except on account of fear of death or infamy, with the Continuator of Tounrely. Moreover, one may never give a sword to a murderer because it is not lawful to kill an innocent man, and you should avoid the death as Concina (tom. 7, p. 168) and the Continuator of Tournely teach. See book 4, n. 697.

67.—*Quaeritur:* V. Whether it would be lawful for a servant, on account of grave fear, to write or bring love letters to his master's concubine? Whatever others say, I think along the lines of several authors, that it is never lawful to do this because they formally assist in the sin of the master, by fostering his sexual lover. (The Salamancans, tr. 21, c. 8, p. 5, § 2, n. 68; Sanchez, n. 26, Viva, n. 5, Laymann, Bonacina, Tamburinius, etc. with Croix, lib. 2, n. 273). I also think it must be said with Sanchez and the Salamancans (*loc. cit.* n. 67, against Palaus and Reb., ap. Tamburinius, n. 18), even in doubt whether the letters might contain amorous material, because when he is certain about the sexual love, it is morally believed they contain indecent things. But if they only contain signs of urbanity, a just cause is also required to excuse the servant, beyond the obedience of servitude, as the Salamancans, Sanchez and Tamburinius (*ll. cc.*) say.

68.—*Quaeritur* VI. Is it lawful for a servant to supply meat on a forbidden day? The Salamancans say no (*ibid.* § 3, n. 81) with Palaus, Vasquez, Diana, etc. Still, they advert that in doubt it may be presumed the master is excused for a just cause. Yet, see what follows in n. 69, Qu. VII.

> "5. In regard to those works that stand closer to the sin
> "or assist it, *e.g.* to lower one's shoulders or to bring up
> "a ladder for one's master to ascend through the window
> "to a concubine, to bring love letters to a courtesan, to
> "accompany him to a duel, etc., the common reason of
> "the servant does not suffice, but demands a greater
> "necessity and cause to be done licitly, *e.g.* danger of
> "grave or at least notable damage, if they would commit
> "detraction against him. *Ibid.* (But, see what was just said
> "in n. 66).

69.—"6. So shopkeepers are excused for selling meat to "be consumed on a fast day and wine to drunkards, if "others are equally doing so. Sanchez, Bonacina, etc.

Quaeritur: VII. Would it be licit for shopkeepers to sell wine to those whom they foresee will become drunk? Fr. Concina excuses them (n. 29) from fear of death or mutilation (as he says) "both selling and drink are indifferent actions and the drunkenness comes about from the malice of those drinking intemperately," so for that reason, he infers a shopkeeper is not even held by charity to impede their drunkenness. Nevertheless, it seems more probable to me what must be said with other authors is sufficiently common, (Busembaum, *hic* n. 6; Bonacina and Sanchez, Elb. n. 383; Sporer *de 5 praec.* c. 1, n. 82; Cont. Tourn. *de charit.* sect. 7, punct. 1, §3 Quaer. 3, *Si dicas*; Tamb, n. 36 and others cited by Croix, n. 261). This holds that shopkeepers are excused enough on account of fear of any sort of grave loss, say, if they would be otherwise notably wounded from a loss of sales. The reason is, because since there is no grave temporal loss in that case would come upon him that is going to be drunk, charity does not oblige with grave inconvenience to avoid his sin. And I say the same with Busembaum, as above, n. 6, and Sanchez, *ibid.* and Mazzota, on offering meat to those who are going to eat it on a forbidden day. Moreover, what Tamburinius says (n. 37), with Sanchez, and Palaus, *viz.* it is licit to sell wine to those who will resell it mixed with water, if he equally and suitably could not sell it to others, we do not admit it except on account of fear of death or infamy.

"7. These which proximately assist in the sin, or induce "it, or are opposed to justice, even if of their genus they "are indifferent, *e.g.* to give a sword to one's master for "a murder, to show him the one he seeks to kill, to strike "the bell (still, without scandal) for a heretical sermon, a "harlot, even if conducted and provided for, to call he

"from the house to lead her to his master, to steal a
"ladder to apply it, to give loan money to one waging an
"unjust war, to sell a pagan to a heretical master, require
"the gravest cause, *i.e.* fear of such an evil that according
"to the laws of charity no man is held to undergo it to
"stop the other's evil, *e.g.* if he would be killed otherwise.
"Laymann, cap. 13, n. 4.

70.—"8. In cities, in which it is permitted for the sake of
"avoiding a greater evil, it is lawful to provide a house
"for a usurer (the law, nevertheless, excepts foreigners),
"and for harlots, especially if other conductors are
"lacking; nevertheless, harlots gravely harm honest
"neighbors, or on account of the opportunity placed in
"the area they would give greater sin. Sanchez, lib. 1,
"*mor.* cap. 7, Bonacina, *loc. cit.*"

(So also the Salamancans, tract. 21, cap. 8, punct. 5, §2, num.
65, with Trull., Vasquez, Prado, Ledesma, and Viva with
Suarez, Lessius, Azor and others in common.

71.—"9. Craftsmen, and those who make or sell
"indifferent things which someone could rightly use (even if
"a great many abuse them), are excused from mortal sin, and
"even venial sin, if a cause were present; *e.g.* dice, cosmetics
"and swords. The reason is, because they are only remotely
"ordered to a sin, and cannot simply be impeded.
"Nevertheless, if one would abuse against justice, it would
"not be lawful, *e.g.* if you were to give a sword to a murderer
"on account of the great price which he offers. Likewise, if
"someone knew this innocent man was not going to be
"ruined except through these wares, because a little profit
"must be postponed for the certain safety of another.
"Sanchez, *loc. cit.* Evil must not be presumed, wherefore they
"can licitly sell dice, cosmetics, swords poisons (viz. only
"those which can also serve as a medicine), to anyone for
"whom it is certain they will not abuse them. (So think the

"Salamancans, *de contract.* cap. 2, punct 3, num. 32, with St.
"Thomas and the common opinion)."

There is a doubt, however, that turns on when it is
believed with the appearance of truth that the buyer is going
to abuse it? Busembaum, *hic* with Sanchez says that it is not
lawful to sell them on account of profit. But Tamburinius
(lib. 5, cap. 1, § 4, n. 33) and the Salamancans (ibid. n. 33)
with Bonacina, Rebell., Tapia, and Sylvester, say that it is
lawful if the seller could not withdraw from the sale without
loss, or, as Tamburinius says, if he would suffer loss by not
selling his things.

In the same way, it would be licit to sell ornate dress to
young women that are going to abuse them, if they are
equally sold by others, as the authors say, since by then
denying the sale, he would not impede the sin. (Croix, lib. 2,
n. 263, with Navarre, Azor, Sanchez, Bonacina and Diana).
But this must not be admitted, according to what was said in
n. 47, *vers. Secunda*, unless the seller would otherwise suffer
a notable inconvenience.

72.—"10. They are also excused who, on account of a just
"cause, sell a lamb to a Jew or an infidel that is going to
"be used for a sacrifice. Likewise, those who build Jewish
"synagogues or the churches of heretics, with the
"permission of the magistrate, or restore them, especially
"if it would be done equally without others. Navarre, l.
"5, cons. 1, *de Judaeis*, Laymann l. 2, t. 3, cap. 13, n. 4.
"Moreover, to sell poisons except to those who the seller
"thinks will use them rightly, *e.g.* for the creation of
"colors, or medicine, is not lawful. See Sanchez, 1 *mor.* c.
"7. For that reason, the sale of poison that serves no
"other purpose but killing a man is simply evil.

73.—"11. Christian captives, from grave fear, on the
"galleys of the Turks or heretics, licitly row against
"Catholics, or carry Muslim equipment and weapons
"necessary for war, build siege equipment, etc. So

"Lessius, Sanchez, Suarez, Laymann (lib. 2, t. 3, c. 13)
"against Toledo, and others, who teach they sin
"mortally. Nevertheless, if in that place the opportunity
"were present wherein, refusing these they would rescue
"a Christian fleet or confer victory, they are only held to
"prefer the good of their life. Suarez, Sanchez, Lessius,
"*loc. cit.*

74.—"12. The inhabitants of a city or a province, which
"a tyrant occupied, licitly remain among wicked
"possessors and compelled by command to help them in
"watches, digging ditches, and payment, and from the
"presumed consent of the legitimate prince; which even
"from such obedience they licitly promise with an oath
"to their greater evils, and turn aside the legitimate
"prince. Laymann, *loc. cit.*, n. 5.

75.—"13. Catholic sailors and coachmen in Holland, even
"without grave fear, provided it is without a wicked
"intention, licitly convey supplies to the camp of heretics
"if others were present that would do it if they ceased,
"because, unless they did it, they would be excluded
"from all profit as those that hate the public good. See
"Lessius, lib. 2, c. 19; Sanchez, lib. 1, c. 7; Filliuci, t. 22,
"cap. 5.

Would it be lawful for coachmen or sailors to convey a
harlot to her lover only for making a profit? Some authors
affirm this, because (as they say) these are only the remote
cooperating cause. (Sporer *de V praec.* c. 1, n. 94; the
Salamancans tr. 21, cap. 8, punct. 5, § 2, n. 72 with Meroll.
and Diana, cited by Tamburinius d. cap. 1, § 4 n. 30 from
Croix, l. 2 n. 274 with Navarre). But others rightly reject this,
who say the contrary opinion is not solidly probable; all
these say they are only excused on account of avoiding
grave damage; nay more, Angles (cited by Sanchez) thinks
it is never lawful, and even intrinsically evil. (Sanchez, *Dec.*
lib, 1, cap. 7, n. 25; Bonacina, *de matr.* p. 14, n. 6; Roncaglia

de char. cap. 6; Reg., *in praxi* n. 2, and Viva in prop. 51 Inn. XI, n. 5).

76.—Other cases are added: 1. A girl sins receiving gifts from a lover who disgracefully lusts after her, because she fosters the lust. (Croix, lib. 2, n. 264, with Sporer)

2. One sins giving a sword to a murderer, unless grave fear of harm would excuse him. (Croix, n. 265, with Sanchez, Bonacina, etc.) But see book 4, n. 571, *v. Secus* near the end.

77.— 3. Is it lawful to seek an oath from a perjurer? Several authors say no. The reason is (as St. Thomas says in 2.2. q. 98, art. 4 ad 4, "In the oath of a man who swears what is false by the true God, it does not seem to be something good which would be lawful to use." (Vasquez and de Soto, cited by Croix, l. 2, n. 268; likewise Pontius *de matrim.* lib. 5, c. 18, n. 62 from St. Augustine and St. Thomas). But the Salamancans and others more probably affirm it, so long as a just cause were present; namely, if a judge sought an oath by reason of office (St. Thomas admits the same thing in the body of the article cited); or if your concern is great to use a perjurer to manifest another's deceit, that you would obtain your right; and so it would not lack a good use for the one seeking it which suffices for a just cause. (The Salamancans, tract. 21, cap. 8, punct. 5 § 3, n. 78; Cont. Tourn. *de char.* sect. 7, punct. 1, § 3 Quaer. 3, *secund pars* and Roncaglia *de 2 praec.* d. 4, p. 11, n. 1, with Cajetan, Salon., Suarez, Reg., Filliuci, Tamburinius, and Diana, cited by Croix, *loc. cit.*) And St. Thomas must be so understood from the context of his words. Moreover, the common opinion is that it is permitted to seek it on account of a good oath from one swearing by false gods. (St. Thomas, *ibid.*, and Sanchez, *dec.* lib. 3, cap. 8, n. 21, with Gabr. Suarez, Sayr. etc. against Abulens). But if the matter were true and the other did not know it, or if it were false and the other believed it true, it would not be lawful to induce him to swear, as the Salamancans rightly say. (c. 8, n. 28 and 80).

4. It is licit to seek a loan from a usurer on account of some good? It is the common opinion with St. Thomas, who so teaches in 2.2. q. 78, a. 4: "It is lawful receive a loan from a man that practices usury and under the conditions of usury on account of some good which is an assistance to his necessity or that of another." In another place, *de Malo* quaest. 13, art. 4, ad 17, he says: "If someone on account of some good uses the malice of a usurer, receiving from him a loan at usury, he does not sin. But if he would persuade that he should loan it to him at usury, who was not prepared to loan him at usury, without a doubt it would be a sin in every case." Therefore, it is lawful, if a just cause or necessity were present, or a notable advantage, as was said in n. 49, and as the authors say (the Salamancans *loc. cit.* n. 76 and 77, with Cajetan, Navarre, Sanchez, Bonacina, Palaus). Furthermore, de Lugo (d. 25, n. 235) asserts it is common among the Doctors that any advantage, even small, suffices to excuse the one seeking a loan from a usurer from grave sin. But I do not acquiesce to this, according to what was said in n. 47, *v. Secunda*. The reason is, because to excuse grave sin cause is required. Otherwise, therefore, it would have to be said that if a notable advantage were present, as Croix (lib. 2, n. 272) and Sporer (*de V. praec.* cap. 1 n. 75) say, and then it would be lawful also to offer him usury by saying conditionally: "If you want a usurious loan I will give it," as Molina, Sanchez, Hurt., Tamb, say, cited by Croix, lib. 2, n. 267. Nay more, it is also absolutely licit to offer, by saying: "Give me a loan and I will pay you at usury," as Molina, Sanchez, Hurt., Tamburinius cited by Croix, lib. 2, n. 267. Nay more, it is also absolutely licit to offer by saying: "Give me a loan and I will pay you at usury, as the authors say (de Lugo, disp. 25, num. 227; Sanchez, *dec.* cap. 8 num. 26, with Trull., Banner, Diana, Sporer, num. 77, and others cited by the Salamancans *de contr.* cap. 3, punct. 13, num. 121). And although the Salamancans (*ibid.*) with St. Thomas and Bonacina, etc. think the opposite is more true,

nevertheless, they rightly call the first opinion probable, because that offering is really always conditional, viz. if you refuse it for free, I offer it at usury. But I would by no means admit this, if the other, who would entice him to loan, would directly induce him to sin. The Salamancans note, however, that a greater cause is required to seek a loan from one who is known not to give it except under condition of usury; at least a great advantage is required, as above (*loc. cit.* n. 122).

78.—5. One who encourages usury only by counting money, writing accounts or in conveying collateral, can be excused from sin only by reason of servitude; otherwise, if he exacts usurious loans, because the exaction is more proximate cooperation with the sin of the usurer, even if he amicably exacts it. But if he were to exact it through force or threats, not only does he not sin, but he would not be held to make restitution. See what is going to be said in book 4, n. 789.

6. It is licit to give a loan to one that will abuse it if a cause is present, namely if he could otherwise do much harm to someone. So think Croix, n. 269, Azor, and Lessius, who nevertheless say, that the cause of profit, even if it is just, does not excuse.

79.—7. It is more probably lawful to seek the sacraments from a priest that is an excommunicated *tolerandus*, because then he hardly sins by that administration. Tamb, lib. 5, cap. 1, § 4 n. 40, with Sanchez, and Hurt., against Suarez. See what is going to be said in book 7, n. 139.

The doctors also agree that it is licit to seek the sacraments from a priest who is in mortal sin, if the necessity were present, or a notable advantage. But there is a doubt, if the utility were not great, would it then be lawful? Azor, Hurt., and Diana cited by Croix (lib. 2 n. 272) affirm it. But it must be denied with Croix, according to what was said in n. 47, even if the priest were prepared to administer sacrilegiously.

80.—It is lawful for someone to offer to a man that wishes to break the fast whenever he will discover food, by saying conditionally: "If you want to eat now, dine with me," as some authors say. (Sporer, *de V. praec.* n. 48, and Lessius l. 4, cap. 2 n. 24, with Navarre, Cajetan, cited by Viva *de praec. Dec.* qu. 10, art. 4, num 6). The reason is, because then the sin has already been carried out internally, nor can it be impeded as is supposed. But I cannot acquiesce to this opinion and I follow the Salamancans (tract. 21, cap. 8, punt. 5 § 3, num. 81) and Roncaglia (*de charit.* tr. 6, c. 6, q. 6), who with Palaus, Vasquez, Diana, etc. think the opposite, because it is objectively evil in these circumstances, for which it is not lawful to cooperate unless it is only permissively, provided a grave cause were present, according to the principle we posited in n. 47, *vers. Secunda,* and has been repeated so many times, namely that to permit the grave sin of another, which he commits from the occasion furnished by us, it does not suffice that the other man was prepared to sin, rather a grave cause of necessity is additionally required, at least of utility, which disobliges us from the precept of charity: otherwise we sin gravely both against charity and against the virtue which is assaulted by our neighbor.

END BOOK III

CPSIA information can be obtained
at www.ICGtesting.com
Printed in the USA
LVHW111330170520
655859LV00001B/4